*A Centennial History
of the American
Administrative State*

A Centennial History
of the American
Administrative State

Edited by

RALPH CLARK CHANDLER

WESTERN MICHIGAN UNIVERSITY

FP

THE FREE PRESS

A Division of Macmillan, Inc.

NEW YORK

Collier Macmillan Publishers

LONDON

The Free Press
A Division of Macmillan, Inc.
866 Third Avenue, New York, N.Y. 10022

Collier Macmillan Canada, Inc.

PRINTED IN THE UNITED STATES OF AMERICA

Printing number
1   2   3   4   5   6   7   8   9   10

Library of Congress Cataloging-in-Publication Data

A Centennial history of the American administrative
    state.

    Includes index.
    1. Administrative agencies—United States—History.
2. Public administration—United States—History.
I. Chandler, Ralph C.,
JK411.C46   1987   350'.000973   86–23829
ISBN 0–02–905301–3

Contents

INTRODUCTION   xi
RALPH CLARK CHANDLER   *Western Michigan University*

PART I

Historical Development

CHAPTER 1 *The American Administrative State: Wilson and
the Founders*   3
PAUL P. VAN RIPER   *Texas A&M University*

CHAPTER 2 *The Emergence of Public Administration as
a Field of Study*   37
NICHOLAS HENRY   *Arizona State University*

PART II

Theoretical Considerations

CHAPTER 3 *Politics and Administration: On Thinking
about a Complex Relationship*   89
DWIGHT WALDO   *Syracuse University*

CHAPTER 4 *The Administrative State and*
Constitutional Principle   113
JOHN A. ROHR   *The Virginia Polytechnic Institute and State*
University

CHAPTER 5 *The Pluralist Legacy in American Public*
Administration   161
WILLIAM L. MORROW   *The College of William and Mary*

CHAPTER 6 *Toward an Ethical Convergence of Democratic*
Theory and Administrative Politics   189
LOUIS C. GAWTHROP   *Indiana University*

PART III

The Interfaces of Government and
Public Administration

CHAPTER 7 *A Century of the Intergovernmental Administrative*
State: Wilson's Federalism, New Deal Intergovernmental
Relations, and Contemporary Intergovernmental
Management   219
DEIL S. WRIGHT   *The University of North Carolina at Chapel*
Hill

CHAPTER 8 *Congress as Public Administrator*   261
JAMES L. SUNDQUIST   *The Brookings Institution*

CHAPTER 9 *The Public Administration and the Governance*
Process: Refocusing the American Dialogue   291
GARY L. WAMSLEY, CHARLES T. GOODSELL, JOHN A. ROHR,
CAMILLA M. STIVERS, ORION F. WHITE, AND JAMES F. WOLF
The Virginia Polytechnic Institute and State University

PART IV

Public Administration in Practice

CHAPTER 10 *Managing Human Resources*   321
N. JOSEPH CAYER   *Arizona State University*

CHAPTER 11 *The Development of Public Budgeting in*
the United States   345
JERRY L. McCAFFERY   *The Naval Postgraduate School*

CHAPTER 12 *On the Balance of Budgetary Cultures*   379
AARON WILDAVSKY   *The University of California (Berkeley)*

PART V

Public Administration in Theory

CHAPTER 13 *Changing Public Bureaucracy: Values and
Organization–Management Theories*   417
FRED A. KRAMER   *The University of Massachusetts*

CHAPTER 14 *Public Sector Organization: Why Theory and
Practice Should Emphasize Purpose, and
How to Do So*   433
ROBERT T. GOLEMBIEWSKI   *The University of Georgia*

PART VI

Comparative Public Administration

CHAPTER 15 *Comparative Public Administration in
the United States*   477
FERREL HEADY   *The University of New Mexico*

CHAPTER 16 *The Higher Public Service in Western Europe*   509
JAMES W. FESLER   *Yale University*

PART VII

Administration in Fiction

CHAPTER 17 *How Novelists View Public Administration*   543
HOWARD E. McCURDY   *The American University*

EPILOGUE   575
RALPH CLARK CHANDLER   *Western Michigan University*

INDEX   595

Introduction

Ralph Clark Chandler
WESTERN MICHIGAN UNIVERSITY

The year 1987 marks both the centennial and the bicentennial of the American administrative state. We use the term *administrative state* to refer to the organizational arrangements put in place to run the American Constitution. This description means the date is not precise because the framers merely wrote the Constitution in 1787; they did not implement it for another 19 months. And in 1887 Woodrow Wilson merely focused the attention of scholars on the study of administrative practice; he did not "found" the American administrative state. If anyone deserves the title of founder, it is Alexander Hamilton.

Still, single and singular historical events often epitomize eras, and it is in this sense that we commemorate in this volume the end of the first and the second centuries of the implementation of our social contract. Martin Luther King, Jr., once described the contract—the constitutional order—as a promissory note to which every American was to fall heir. For our purposes, the note was signed in Philadelphia in 1787 and given compelling practical direction in 1887 with the publication of Wilson's "The Study of Administration." Hopefully, we will bear in mind as we read the following essays that the framers and then Wilson provide us with no more than stop-action photographs of a moving and developing historical panorama.

As we commemorate, we must necessarily demythologize. In the first essay, for example, Paul P. Van Riper brings historical fact to the Wilson legend by pointing out that Wilson's so-called founding essay "had no influence whatever on the evolution of either the theory or practice of public administration in the United States until well after 1950." In Chapter 4, John A. Rohr illustrates the extent to which there was fundamental disagreement in the founding era about the constitutional

principles that later became holy writ. The Constitution was barely ratified, and its defects continue to this day. Facts do get in the way of
belief sometimes, although they affect it less than one might hope.

We do not wish to overcorrect, however, for myths carry their own
truth. Rather, we wish to describe in the best Aristotelian sense. The
Macmillan Publishing Company wishes to use the occasion of the centen-
nial/bicentennial to reconnoiter the field of public administration and
present a fair assessment of its historical development. To do so, it has
asked seventeen primary authors and an editor to prepare the essays
that appear here. Each essay addresses a different subfield or interest
area of public administration, and each has been prepared by a contributor exceptionally well qualified to write on the subject assigned.

Five of the contributors, Professors Fesler, Heady, Sundquist, Van
Riper, and Waldo, have retired from distinguished teaching and/or administrative careers. They are in a unique position to draw upon their
knowledge and experience to reflect upon the purposes of this volume.
The other contributors range in fame from Aaron Wildavsky, who wrote
the most widely referenced book in American public administration,
The Politics of the Budgetary Process, to the editor, who has sometimes
been blinded by the luminaries of the table of contents.

The essays presented here are not administrative history in the way
that Leonard D. White wrote administrative history. The updating of
White's work is a task waiting to be done. Yet these chapters are full
of administrative history, beginning with the work of one of White's
most able pupils and ending with that of one of his most distinguished
grandpupils. Our collective efforts summarize how American public administration has evolved, using 1887 as a pivot point from which to
look backward and forward, to analyze where the field has been and
where it might be going. The abstract before each chapter constitutes
a summary of the chapter, and together the abstracts form a summary
of the book.

Ralph Clark Chandler
January 1, 1987

PART I

Historical Development

CHAPTER 1

The American Administrative State: Wilson and the Founders

Paul P. Van Riper
TEXAS A & M UNIVERSITY

PAUL P. VAN RIPER is Professor Emeritus of Political Science at Texas A&M University. Previously he taught at Cornell University for eighteen years. He has authored or co-authored three influential books: A Handbook of Practical Politics, A History of the United States Civil Service, *and* The American Federal Executive. *He has also written six special studies and over 50 articles published in a variety of scholarly and professional journals. Professor Van Riper has lectured widely and served as a practicing administrator in both civil and military settings. In 1981 he received the Dimock Award of the American Society for Public Administration for an earlier version of this chapter. Currently he is collecting and editing the work of Luther Gulick.*

Paul P. Van Riper begins the volume with what he calls a report mainly from the administrative engine room of the American ship of state. There are, however, some log entries from the political quarterdeck, especially at the end.

Down in the engine room, or in the stacks of the library, Van Riper discovered that Woodrow Wilson had his sources. In a study published in 1879, New York attorney Dorman B. Eaton referred to a science of administration practiced in Great Britain that he said should also be practiced in the United States. In 1882 Eaton elaborated his views in the first volume of J. J. Lalor's *Cyclopedia of Political Science.* John Hopkins University

3

economist Richard T. Ely was also a source for Wilson, who attended Ely's lectures on administration in 1884–85.

A more serious question about Wilson's role as the founder of self-conscious American public administration is raised by Van Riper's further discovery that no major political or social science work between 1890 and World War I cited Wilson's essay. Of the four public administration textbooks written prior to World War II, only one referred to it. Historian Van Riper concludes that Wilson's essay had minimal effect until the 1950s. Neither was Max Weber's work influential until that time, inasmuch as it was not translated from the German until 1946 and 1947.

Van Riper argues that if anyone deserves the title of founder of the American administrative state, it is not Wilson, Eaton, or Ely, but Alexander Hamilton (1757–1804). He was the chief administrative officer during the first period of American history in which, it can be demonstrated, the criteria of an administrative state were met. What Hamilton was to the first administrative state, Theodore Roosevelt was to the second: intellectual father and driving force. There was an interlude between the administrative states of Hamilton and Roosevelt: the Jacksonian–Radical Republican era, in which the pursuit of individual power and wealth subsumed any serious administrative interest in the public good. The Compromise of 1876 signaled the beginning of the end of that period of unrestrained and corrupt political party activity.

In the 1930s the nation entered into an extended, fully self-conscious, and highly inventive state of improvement and refinement of its administrative mechanisms, culminating in the creation of the Executive Office of the President in 1939. Van Riper delineates what those mechanisms were, both in the Federalist and the scientific management periods.

The second administrative state shaded into a time of dysfunctional effects after World War II, so that by the middle 1980s its disabilities were as discernible as its accomplishments. The symptoms were those of bureaupathology caused by the lesson of proceduralism learned too well, and governmental systems overload occasioned by the high expectation levels of a citizenry that had come to believe that government could and should manage everything. The twin financial problems of more and more grants-in-aid to state and local governments and a rapidly expanding system of transfer payments to individual citizens pushed the deficit to alarming proportions.

In such an environment classical principles of management will no longer suffice. Whether Presidents and Congresses can apply Ashby's Law of Requisite Variety out of cybernetic steersmanship and translate the politically popular retrenchment temperament into new national purposes remains to be seen. Moral rectitude is not enough.

Anniversaries prompt speculation about the past and its meaning.* This review of the administrative evolution of our national government derives from such a stimulus, the forthcoming centennial of (Thomas) Woodrow Wilson's celebrated essay of 1887, "The Study of Administration."[1] The focus is on the system transformations of our administrative state, with an emphasis on founders and the theories and goals that have helped guide them. At the end there are some contentious suggestions for the future in light of the past.

The Idea of an Administrative State

The phrase "administrative state" has been floating around for some time. What do we really mean by it? The recent literature of political science contains two major works bearing the title of *The Administrative State*, one by Dwight Waldo in 1948 and the other by Fritz Morstein Marx in 1957.[2] Waldo defines by indirection, equating his title with the growth of modern public administration as a subject of study. This definition is too narrow for our purposes here. Morstein Marx is interested in administrative action as well as theory, but his definition of the administrative state occurs almost as an afterthought in an early footnote: "The 'administrative state' should be thought of not as a state devoid of legislative and judicial organs but as a state in which administrative organization and operations are particularly prominent, at least in their quantitative aspects." Although Morstein Marx never explains the last clause in this quotation, "quantitative" is a critically important qualifier in any full definition of modern administration.[3] An administrative state without an adequate census, for example, is embryonic at best.

Morstein Marx's neutral and commonsense approach offers the foundation of a definition of the administrative state. Can one do any better? The current explosion of work on bureaucracy suggests the usefulness of several additional concepts. A majority of them derive from Max Weber.[4]

Let me hasten to say that I do not equate the administrative state with "the bureaucratic state," even though they have much in common. I view the latter as another stage of development, when an administrative system begins to take on the attributes graphically portrayed by Ralph P. Hummel in *The Bureaucratic Experience*.[5]

Nevertheless, the literature on bureaucracy does suggest a number

---

* This article first appeared in the *Public Administration Review* 43:477 (November/December) 1983 and is used by permission of the American Society for Public Administration.

of important qualifiers or amplifiers for our definition. Without an extensive exegesis of Weber, most social scientists would recognize the relevance of the six criteria below in characterizing almost any administrative state, ancient or modern:

1. a workable organization in the classical hierarchic sense,
2. the recruitment of expertise by merit,
3. rational decision making,
4. the rule of law, with an emphasis on equality before the law,
5. written procedures and records,
6. and not only a money economy but sufficient public funds to support a complex administrative apparatus.

From here one must go beyond Weber and add four more criteria only implicit in his works:

7. at least a modest base in quantitative data and technique,
8. adequate supporting technology, especially pertaining to records, communications, and numeracy,
9. the enforcement of responsibility and ethical standards, and
10. all of the above in a moderately developed and mutually supporting arrangement.

To deserve the name, an administrative state must typify a working system in the modern sense of the word "system." Such a state is not necessarily good or bad, and I do not see its direction as determined. Direction and quality are consequences of the highly variable factors of culture and purpose. More will be said about these factors in a moment.

Has public administration in the United States met these criteria? Yes, it clearly has, at least *twice,* with each period followed by a decline in administrative effectiveness.

Under the Federalists and Jeffersonians between 1789 and 1829 the United States evolved what I will argue here was the first modern form of the American administrative state, meeting all of the criteria just listed.[6] From 1829 through the Civil War and Reconstruction the highly politicized Jacksonian–Radical Republican interlude followed, with the Compromise of 1876 precipitating the removal of federal troops from the South and signaling the beginning of the end of the period. The nation soon entered into a fully self-conscious and highly inventive state of improvement and refinement of its administrative mechanisms. This development culminated in the creation of the Executive Office of the

President and its wartime administrative machinery. The years since World War II make up a fourth period, during which the dysfunctional effects of the second American administrative state are as discernible as its many accomplishments. The ten criteria already outlined provide guidelines for further discussion.

Bear in mind several limitations. This is an all too brief overview directed almost entirely at the national government. Even there helpful secondary literature is scarce, and I am undoubtedly guilty of sins of omission. Modern administrative development has been so complex or so much in the shadows as to be essentially anonymous. The following discussion is therefore more a report from the perspective of the administrative engine room than a view from the political quarterdeck of the American ship of state. Further prefatory notes follow in the next two sections.

Culture and Purpose

Let us examine the two central factors of culture and purpose. They are less indicators of the existence than governors of the direction and eventual quality of an administrative state.

In its rich combination of resources and an enterprising people, bound together in a democratic, pragmatically experimental, technologically inclined, and mobile society, driven by the Protestant Ethic and inspired by a sense of progress, the cultural milieu of the United States has provided a fertile soil for the growth of an advanced administrative system, both public and private. Moreover, our culture has seldom been very divisive. Except for the great quarrels over slavery and the role of black people, we have had, as many foreign commentators have noted, an exceptionally homogeneous web of attitudes and values supporting our social system. There have been other conflicts, of course. The spoils system has been dying hard for a long time, and we are impatient with "bureaucracy" today. But the gulf between ideals and administrative action has been more narrow than in most nations.

Even Weber saw the administrative state as especially consonant with the growth of modern democracy's mass participation not only in governance but in the fruits of economic development as well. Such divergent ideas as equality under the law and a merit system of public employment are basic to the prospect of individual development and opportunity in a mass democracy. Moreover, the centralization of the administrative state constitutes the first essential step toward any effective decentralization in carrying out such policies as civil rights enforcement. The development of the administrative state in the United States has more often than not been perceived as in accord not only with efficiency and societal improvement in general but also with the securing of personal rights. Such was particularly the thrust of the Progressive and other reform movements in the late nineteenth century.

Despite the current criticism of our administrative systems, a larger proportion of college students than ever before studies public or business administration. The subject is deeply embedded in the American ethos. This fact is responsible for some of our problems because we tend to see difficulties as problems of structure and process rather than of basic purposes and goals. Although few ends can be accomplished in the modern world without the support of competent administration, administration remains only a means. Without firm guidance from clearly articulated ends, administration can hold the fort only temporarily. If administration does not understand its reason for being, it can even cause the fort to self-destruct.

On Founders and Founding

I have already been unorthodox in ascribing the initial version of our administrative state to the Founding Fathers, thus pushing the date back exactly a century farther than conventional wisdom dictates and relieving Woodrow Wilson and his essay of any responsibility. The situation is not even that simple.

Wilson is widely assumed to be the founder of the academic study of public administration in the United States, something to which none of the Founding Fathers can lay claim. Wilson's essay has also been seen as a kind of guiding light for the discipline ever since the essay was published. Recent research makes it clear that both attributions are incorrect, the first by a small and arguable margin, the latter off the mark wildly. Let me summarize my findings.[7]

The story begins with the publication in 1879 of Dorman B. Eaton's well-received study of the *Civil Service in Great Britain*. The study was made at the request of President Hayes. Eaton (1823–1899) was then a well-known New York lawyer and a founder of the National Civil Service Reform League. Later he helped draft the Pendleton Act of 1883 and became the first head of the United States Civil Service Commission. Thirty-five years ago Waldo reported that Eaton's work had referred in passing to the development of a science of administration in Great Britain, which Eaton suggested we should take up in this country.[8] But the impact of a few sentences does not match that of a 10,000-word essay, and Wilson was held to be the real founder. Two years ago I discovered that Eaton had greatly amplified his 1879 asides in the concluding section of a 2,500-word essay published in 1882 in the first volume of Lalor's three-volume *Cyclopedia of Political Science.*[9] We know also that Wilson attended lectures in administration by economist Richard T. Ely (1854–1943) at Johns Hopkins University during the second semester of 1884–85. In his autobiography Ely says, "When I talked about the importance of administration, I felt that I had struck a spark and kindled a fire in Wilson."[10] Who is the founder?

What of the presumed influence of Wilson's essay on the course of public administration after 1887? In reality, any connection between the essay and the later development of the discipline is pure fantasy! An examination of major political and social science works of the period between 1890 and World War I shows no citation whatever of the essay in any of these volumes. In the four public administration textbooks written prior to World War II by Leonard D. White, W. F. Willoughby, John Pfiffner, and Harvey Walker, only White cites Wilson's essay. In the middle of the 1930s others began to refer to the essay, but not until the 1950s did it come into any real prominence. The 1887 work had no influence whatever on the evolution of either the theory or practice of public administration in the United States until well after 1950.[11]

The First American Administrative State

The founding of the first administrative state, between 1789 and 1829, was as forthright as the creation of the Constitution that bounded it. In 1787 there was no useful literature on administration in the United States, but there was a great fund of practical experience. The Federalist administrative state began with a classic pyramidal *organization design* of two major components,[12] a chief executive and a departmental system.

The American Presidency was a significant invention. The word *president* is old, its ancestry going back to the fourteenth century in England. The immediate models available in 1787 were those of the Continental Congress and the colonial governors, some of whom had earlier been designated as "president in council." But these legislatively dependent executives were seen by many as much too weak to handle the demands being placed on the new nation. After the legislative article had been outlined at the Constitutional Convention, James Wilson of Pennsylvania moved on Friday, June 1, that "a National executive to consist of a single person be instituted."[13] Many delegates were startled by so bold a proposal, but the motion was approved on Monday, June 4, and confirmed on July 17. The design of the executive article involved an exceedingly complicated process and can only be termed a group product, which was not completed until September 6, only twelve days before the convention disbanded. To George Washington, Thomas Jefferson, and Alexander Hamilton we owe much of the Presidency's development into the energetic institution envisioned in *The Federalist*. The keystone of an organization design was in place.

A simple hierarchical departmental mechanism was quickly erected under the President by the first Congress, which also explicitly gave the President the power of removal, only implied in the Constitution. American and English precedents favored the kind of committee management typical under the Articles of Confederation, an arrangement that did not commend itself during the Revolution. So the Americans produced a departmental system almost a century before the British did.[14] It was retained with few deviations until the 1930s. By contrast, in American state and local governments, the colonial tradition of committee management and a fragmented executive flourished until well past 1900.

Thus American national government came early and easily to an organizational design appropriate to an administrative state and to a degree of executive centralization comparable to the most modern of contemporary governments. With the President and department heads possessing well-defined powers of appointment and removal, there was almost a military unity of command and control. There were, however, no clearly designated staff agencies for decades, although there was some early central purchasing through Alexander Hamilton's organization of the treasury.

George Washington inaugurated, and the other Presidents of the period maintained, essentially a *merit system* of employment through which the best expertise was usually sought and tenure assured. Of further assistance was the Library of Congress, founded in 1800.

Rational decision making was not a topic of conversation anywhere in the Federalist period. But the Founding Fathers were products of the Enlightenment, and their rationality is evident in the constitutional debates and for years thereafter. Hamilton's state papers on finance and the economy comprise an impressive intellectual effort to provide a rational basis for planning and legislation. There was considerable consultation among the officers of the government, and Washington tried to bring both the Supreme Court and the Senate into a personal consultative relationship with him. The correspondence among the principal political figures of the period was extensive. That of Thomas Jefferson was voluminous beyond belief.

A concern for *law and equality* was demonstrated by the acceptance of the Constitution and the Bill of Rights. The best evidence of continuing concern lies in the quashing of the infamous Sedition Act by the Jeffersonians.

Systematic *procedures and record keeping* were most obvious in the Treasury under Hamilton, where they were most needed. As Leonard D. White records, Oliver Wolcott, an accountant and Hamilton's chief auditor and later Secretary of the Treasury himself, brought order out of "a chaos of old records."[15] Hamilton assured the country a source of revenue by vigorously collecting customs from an astonished set of importers who had not been treated that way in years. Expenditures were closely audited. The First and Second United States Banks represented an early use of the model of the corporation, preceded only by a few approximations in the states and by the examples of the great semipublic trading and colonizing companies of the seventeenth and eighteenth centuries.

A *quantitative data base* arrived with the census. Accounting methodology was satisfactory for the times, and Hamilton insisted on a decimal monetary system. Mathematics and science were developing, precision was being sought in naval charts, and the level of economic and social analysis seen in state papers is surprising in its use of comparatively sophisticated numeracy.[16]

The *technology* of the period was not very helpful to administration, although the steamboat (1807) and the canals, especially the Erie Canal (1825), helped communications. It is symbolic of the end of this administrative era that on July 4, 1828, the first spadeful of earth for laying the track of the Baltimore and Ohio Railroad was turned by Charles Carroll, the last surviving signer of the Declaration of Independence.

The institution of proper audits was one measure of the nation's early sense of *accountability and responsibility*. A firm civil control of the military was another. The first conflict-of-interest legislation was in the surprisingly complete provisions of the act that established the Treasury Department in 1789.[17] Hamilton's hand is again apparent. About the Federalists and ethics, White says in summary that "never has the standard of integrity of the federal civil service been at a higher level."[18]

As a kind of summation to the jury, I offer White's synopsis of the administrative contributions of the Federalists. Within five years "they spelled out the scanty provisions of the Constitution and created from almost nothing an administrative system."[19] "Their handiwork included," he continues:

1. The establishment of an independent chief executive vested with substantially all administrative authority and responsible for the conduct of the official business of the new government.
2. The working out of relations between the executive branch and Congress which left substantial freedom of action to high officials and kept Congress out of most administrative details, but which

recognized the responsibility of the executive to the legislative branch.

3. The effective delegation of authority by the President to heads of departments and by them to their immediate subordinates and representatives in the field, while at the same time retaining controls over performance.

4. The creation of an administrative organization separate from and independent of the states, complete in itself, but with acceptance of state agencies for federal business in certain cases; and the beginning of cooperation between the two sets of officials.

5. Orderly and stable relationships among officials, based on law, instructions, and precedents.

6. The formation of a fiscal system that ensured the proper use of and accounting for funds.

7. The maintenance of good standards, especially canons of integrity and levels of competence.

8. The acceptance of responsibility by the dominant party to determine the policy of the government and to conduct the administration of its affairs.

9. The approval of the right of public criticism of policy and administration, marred by the passage of the Sedition Act.

10. The recognition of the claims of locality in the sense of preference for local and state residents for federal offices with local and state jurisdiction.

11. The recognition of the moral authority of the general government, a victory won by the character of Washington, the integrity of the public services, and the decisiveness with which the challenge to federal authority in western Pennsylvania was met.[20]

The Jeffersonians inherited this system, had sense enough to leave most of it alone, and saw that it continued to function almost as well as it did under the Federalists. Especially effective Jeffersonian administrators were Albert Gallatin, John C. Calhoun (one of the ablest Secretaries of War in early American history), Postmaster General John McLean, and Attorney General William Wirt.

The primary administrative innovations were by the Federalists, however. Washington's firm and practiced hand and his unusual sense of the importance of precedent kept the ship of state afloat, but it was Hamilton's guiding genius that set it rapidly on course. Leonard D. White and Lynton K. Caldwell, the principal administrative historians of the period, concur in their judgment of Hamilton.[21] If anyone deserves the title of founder of the American administrative state, in terms of both theory and practice, it is not Wilson, Eaton, or Ely, but Alexander Hamilton (1757–1804).

The Jacksonian and Radical Interlude

The Jacksonians and Radical Republicans have not often been joined together for analysis, but the regimes had much in common. Politically, the result was what many of the Founding Fathers had feared, the dominance of a demagogic majoritarianism that, driven by an intense concern for power, pandered to the nation's worst instincts through the spoils system and an unbridled exploitation of natural resources. The culmination came with the forcible occupation of the South for a decade, the attempted impeachment of Andrew Johnson, and the incredible corruption of the Gilded Age. The lengths to which both centralized and decentralized government could be manipulated by an unrestrained and corrupt party system were clearly demonstrated during this period. The backlash brought about a major reorientation of government, both politically and administratively.

The half century between the American administrative states was not without administrative accomplishments, however. Several innovations came out of the Civil War. There was a renewed understanding of the importance of organization, line and staff relationships, and orderly procedure, for example. Precedents were set for the creation of a general staff. To Major General Montgomery C. Meigs, President Lincoln's quartermaster general, we owe the nation's first unified logistical organization in wartime. It contributed greatly to Northern success. Lincoln himself played a major role in the founding of the National Academy of Sciences. While the Radicals meddled in everything in the name of congressional government, they, Lincoln, and Grant managed to win the first great modern war and maintain the Union.

An initial dent in the spoils system was made in 1860 through the establishment of the first central service agency. After years of treating printing contracts as partisan spoils involving millions in kickbacks to the party in power, Congress finally created the Government Printing Office with a mandate to receive competitive bidding. Some costs were thereby reduced by up to 90 per cent.

Moreover, we find the beginnings of civil service reform scattered throughout this period.[22] Largely because of the inspiration of Senator Robert M. T. Hunter of Virginia, later the Confederate Secretary of State, Congress in 1853 made pass-examinations a requirement for entrance into most clerical offices in Washington. Lincoln flatly refused to redistribute the offices again in 1864. In 1867–68 Representative Thomas A. Jenckes of Rhode Island, through a serious committee study of foreign personnel practices, spearheaded an initial thrust aimed at personnel reform in the federal government.

The most important action came in 1871 when, almost single-handedly, Senator Lyman Trumbull of Illinois succeeded in getting a reform rider attached to the sundry civil appropriation bill. The rider authorized the President to regulate personnel procedures through a delegation of power that is still a source of presidential authority. Under this law President Grant created the little-known First Civil Service Commission in 1871. It died in 1875 from lack of appropriations and presidential interest. Nevertheless, under the direction first of George William Curtis and then of Dorman B. Eaton, much of the groundwork was laid for the lasting reforms of the Pendleton Act in 1883. In 1873 Attorney General A. T. Akerman opined that some limitation (through an examination requirement) on the President's power of appointment was constitutional.

The ratification of the Thirteenth, Fourteenth, and Fifteenth Amendments with their due process and equal protection clauses, followed by the first civil rights acts in a century, provided a firm legal basis for civil rights movements.

The powerful party mechanisms of the Jacksonians and early Republicans had an administrative component rarely made explicit. To Martin Van Buren goes credit for the first well organized campaign system, as he masterminded the formation of the Democratic party and the election of Andrew Jackson in 1828. Even the spoils system was very much a system. Patronage provided the workers and assessments, and kickbacks provided the funds. The Radicals were thoroughly organized, and they centralized congressional authority very well indeed. But their aim was far from the rational management objective seen as a principal function of the administrative state.

By the time Grant was elected, the combined Jacksonian and Radical system had generated its own depressing symptoms of corruption at all levels of government. It is ironic to note that the next wave of vigorous reform attacked the evils of the centralization of power at the national level, only to supply new versions of centralization to end the corruption and administrative chaos in state and local government.

The Second Administrative State

By 1876 the basic question was becoming: Can the nation simultaneously renovate a run-down administrative system and regain the idealism that fueled the first version of the administrative state?

Unlike the first, the second administrative state was guided by conscious theory, but only in its middle years. Before World War I there were few works that might have assisted, say, Theodore Roosevelt in managing the construction of the Panama Canal, the greatest engineering project in the world up to that time. The second administrative state was set in motion by men like the Federalists, men of affairs and practical experience, many of whom had played important military roles in the Civil War. Size and complexity began generating scientific observation and experimentation. By 1910 literate administrative theory was beginning to proliferate. This has been reviewed for public administration by Dwight Waldo, already cited. The main thrust was provided by the doctrines of classical management, specifically those emphasizing line and staff relationships, functionalism, and the old principles of administration, all to the ends of economy and efficiency. From 1914, Congress forbade the use of Frederick W. Taylor's time and motion studies in the federal government for the next forty years. The budding human relations movement of Mary Parker Follett had little impact either.

While this period saw the beginnings of public administration education around 1890 and its rapid curricular expansion after World War I, academic writing was largely legalistic or descriptive. Between the world wars the working guidelines for public administration were expounded by a small group of practical administrators-turned-theorists on a part-time basis. Harrington Emerson, Luther Gulick, Lyndall Urwick, Henri Fayol, and Mooney and Reily were among the principals in this cast. Gulick and Urwick's *Papers on the Science of Administration* in 1937 provided the first anthology directed at the idea of administration as a universal process. Originally these papers were put together for use by the research staff of the President's Committee on Administrative Management, whose report was the last recommendation that the executive branch be organized along purist classical lines.

In 1876 the simple Federalist *organization structure* was largely intact. From the twin pressures of growing complexity and a nascent desire to exclude partisanship and spoils as much as possible, a few early precedents were set that opened the door to fragmentation of the executive branch. But in two arenas, one civil and the other military, centralization prospered.

Under Presidents Grover Cleveland, Theodore Roosevelt, and Woodrow Wilson the Presidency regained its former prestige and moral authority. Under President Franklin Roosevelt the central proposal of the President's Committee on Administrative Management was authorized by the Reorganization Act of 1939 and put in place September 11, during the invasion of Poland. The Executive Office of the President, staffed by a small corps of administrative assistants, provided the headquarters for an effective superstructure to manage the war effort on the home front. The Federalist administrative keystone was back in place. The balance between the two major branches had shifted again.

On the military front a general staff presided over the army. The staff concept had been evolving rapidly since the time of Napoleon. But this device for executive support and planning did not become a reality in the United States until Theodore Roosevelt and his Secretary of War, Elihu Root, together pushed the General Staff Act of 1903 through a reluctant Congress and over the head of a stubborn Commanding General of the United States Army. Root's case for the reform, spelled out in his report of 1902, has been described as "one of the monumental works of American staff literature."[23] The system was tested in World War I and remained in place thereafter, being applied to the entire military establishment after World War II. The line and staff personnel arrangement, already a model for a few businesses by 1900, became increasingly important in all civil affairs.

Nevertheless, although the Executive Office of the President was greatly strengthened by the end of World War II, the system over which the President presided was undergoing slow fission. After a long period of stability, the departmental system slowly began to expand as the Attorney General was elevated to head a new Department of Justice in 1870. By 1913 Agriculture, Commerce, and Labor had been created for a total of ten executive departments. There the number rested for forty years. But the growth of other hierarchic single-headed agencies continued. During World War I the words *administration* and *authority* were used to describe some of the temporary war agencies. The words stuck, if most of the agencies did not. The largest residual agency was the United States Veterans Bureau, which combined with a treasury bureau in 1930 to become the current Veterans Administration, the first important permanent agency to be named an administration. During the Depression years another dozen or so administrations were added, the Works Progress Administration being a major example.

As for central staff agencies, the treasury's old but modest central purchasing function was expanded in June 1933 to include all civilian purchasing via a Treasury Procurement Division. After World War II this and several related functions were consolidated in the new General Services Administration.

The first well organized staff agency served a personnel function. It was the Civil Service Commission, re-established in 1883. The Pendleton Act set the precedent of a bipartisan commission and gave it the novel role of controlling the executive branch, even top management, by policing the patronage. The first departmental personnel office was that of agriculture, established in 1928 under the supervision of W. W. Stockberger. There was no general requirement for personnel offices in federal agencies until Franklin D. Roosevelt's executive order of 1938 mandated them. It came barely in time to prepare the government for the personnel expansion of World War II. The federal government's civilian work force rose from over 900,000 employees in 1939 to more than 3,800,000 regular employees, plus 330,000 WOC (without compensation) and dollar-a-year personnel, by 1945.

The beginnings of a management analysis function came with the addition to the Civil Service Commission of a Division of Efficiency in 1912. The division had the unusual purpose of investigating the executive branch on behalf of Congress. The juxtaposition was messy, and the division became an independent bureau in 1916. The impact of this first in-house study group was limited because of its great immersion in detail. President Roosevelt abolished the agency in 1933 as a retrenchment move, and the function disappeared until the late 1940s. It reappeared as a responsibility of the Bureau of the Budget and agency staff sections.[24]

Through the reports of the Taft Commission on Economy and Efficiency in Government in 1912–13, plus some state and local experimentation, a foundation was laid for the initiation of an executive budget and a financial staff agency. In most nations executive financial controls preceded controls on other resources, but in the United States they came last. Finance was a jealously guarded legislative function, and the separation of powers did not make cooperation easy. By World War I the budgeting and appropriation processes had become chaotic, and reform finally came in the Budget and Accounting Act of 1921. Through the new Bureau of the Budget, the President proposed and Congress disposed. Control of accounting procedures, post-audit and, before long, pre-audit, was taken from the executive and placed in a new congressional agency, the General Accounting Office, headed by the Comptroller General. Both new agencies were given management study and research authority, but probably because of the Bureau of Efficiency, neither exercised this power very much until after World War II.

Little innovation came from the Comptroller General for another forty years. But the new Bureau of the Budget, renamed the Office of Management and Budget in 1970, got off to a flying start under the direction of General Charles G. Dawes. Dawes was a Chicago banker who had directed the American army's supply service in Europe during World War I and later became Vice President of the United States. An executive budget became a reality, and Congress prepared to examine it as a total entity for the first time since the days of Alexander Hamilton. Central clearance of agency legislative proposals was begun, allotments and budget ceilings for agencies were introduced, and an effort at regional coordination was made.

Planning got a brief and promising trial between 1935 and 1943 through the National Resources Planning Board, only to have a jealous Congress jettison the process when it was most needed.

The creation of central staff agencies enhanced presidential control, but the rise of independent regulatory commissions and government corporations did not. The former moved from the state to the national level in 1887 through the creation of the Interstate Commerce Commission. The Federal Trade Commission was formed in 1914, the Federal Reserve Board in 1915, and other regulatory bodies in the twenties and thirties. A few regulatory officials, such as the Commissioner of Food and Drugs, were placed within executive departments. But most regulatory functions were multiheaded and independent, the appointments were bipartisan and for long and staggered terms, and the appointees were protected against removal for causes other than inefficiency or malfeasance in office. Such provisions made the regulatory agencies independent of all but the most powerful and persuasive of Presidents. By World War II the Supreme Court had upheld these novel arrangements, and the President's removal power was for the first time severely limited.

Generally considered to be the first modern publicly owned and managed agency of a corporate type brought into the federal government was the Panama Railroad Company, purchased from the French government in 1904. Thus began a long line of government corporations, differentiated from other government agencies by having a board of directors, a general manager, and the corporation's own income and resources separate from those provided through the regular federal budget. The protections given to regulatory commissioners were often applied to corporation board members as well. They had the added independence of self-generated revenues and of many exemptions from standard departmental controls. At least twelve federal corporations, some with private sector participation, were listed in the *Official Register* of 1939. A few more were created during World War II and a number afterward.[25]

Expertise and selection by merit via the Civil Service Commission have been noted. If anyone deserves the title of founder of our modern system of public employment, it is Dorman B. Eaton. Yet his and other civil service reformers' views on two important aspects of the merit system have been widely misunderstood.

First, they posed only a limited dichotomy between politics and administration. Basing their understanding of neutrality on the British model, they advocated the partisan but not the total political neutrality of the public service. Career civil servants were forbidden to play an active party role and were protected from partisan removal and assessments, but they were expected to further the lawful policies of the party in power. The Hatch Acts of the 1930s did little but put into law and expand the coverage of traditional rules against partisan political activity by careerists.

Second, the reforms of 1883 closed only what has been called "the front door" to the service. The reformers strongly opposed all protections against removal except that forbidding removal for partisan reasons. The doctrine of public employment as a privilege, enunciated so forcefully by Justice Oliver Wendell Holmes from the Massachusetts bench in 1892 by his dictum that a policeman "has no constitutional right to be a policeman," was in force throughout the period of the second administrative state. It has only gradually expired in recent decades. By 1900 a few reformers, notably Carl Schurz, began to have second thoughts about the ease of removal, and the Lloyd-LaFollette Act of 1912 required removing officers to give reasons in writing and permit those removed a chance to reply, with files kept for inspection. No hearing or court procedure was mandated, however, and there the matter sat for many years. The Lloyd-LaFollette Act also authorized postal employees to join their own unions.

The Pendleton Act did not seriously damage the patronage for decades. The law first applied to only 12 per cent of the service. Expansion was permitted by presidential order. Inclusions grew to about 50 per cent under Theodore Roosevelt, increasing gradually to 80 per cent by 1930. There was some backsliding under Franklin Roosevelt, but in another major fulfillment of the Brownlow Committee's recommendations he signed the Ramspeck Act of 1940. This brought about 95 per cent of the civil service under the jurisdiction of the Civil Service Commission, with 85 per cent career positions, where the figures rest today. The provision of civil pensions in 1920 and the start of position classification in 1923 aided the development of the service greatly.

By World War II modern personnel management was becoming a reality for most of the civil service. During the early days of the war, Civil Service Commissioner Arthur S. Flemming, later Secretary of Health, Education, and Welfare, designed a new management approach to personnel whereby the commission delegated most of its powers to the new agency personnel offices, subject to postaudit control. This important innovation toward decentralization fostered the rapid expansion of the service so essential for fighting the war without upsetting the intent of the merit system. From then on, personnel management was to be primarily an agency function guided by general standards.

By the 1870s sizable numbers of *intellectuals* began to be interested in government for the first time in fifty years. Most of the prominent civil service reformers deserve such a designation: Curtis and Eaton, E. L. Godkin, Moorfield Storey, Richard Henry Dana, and of course Theodore Roosevelt and Woodrow Wilson. Eaton chaired the personnel agency, Roosevelt soon followed as a commissioner, and Thomas M. Cooley, a former Michigan law professor and judge of the Michigan Supreme Court, chaired the new Interstate Commerce Commission. Andrew D. White, first president of Cornell and a noted historian, became ambassador to Prussia and Russia. Roosevelt personally sought to bring bright young men into the government, among them Gifford Pinchot, Felix Frankfurter, William Allen White, and Henry L. Stimson. Roosevelt created a number of unpaid commissions of experts to assist him in diagnosing and prescribing for a wide range of ills. Congress objected to gratuitous advice and sought to prevent such endeavors. Roosevelt replied that he would take advice from wherever he wanted. From this time on the volunteer in public service, soon officially designated as the "dollar-a-year" man, was a frequently observed phenomenon. The six members of the Taft Commission included Frederick A. Cleveland as chairman, plus W. F. Willoughby and Frank J. Goodnow. Between 1905 and 1907 Cleveland and others organized the New York Bureau of Municipal Research, later headed by Charles A. Beard and Luther Gulick. Since 1921 the Bureau has been known as the Institute of Public Administration.

At the same time LaFollette and Van Hise developed the university-state cooperation known widely as the Wisconsin Plan, private consulting commenced on a professional basis, and "the survey" was born. A curriculum for training students in public administration was initiated in 1911 by the Training School for Public Service in association with and later as part of the Institute of Public Administration. This school was the forerunner of today's Maxwell School at Syracuse University. The military already had a long history of technical training, but in 1901 Elihu Root, in another first, founded what has become the United States Army Command and General Staff College at Fort Leavenworth, Kansas. The beginnings of the Army War College also date from this time.

Wilson was ambivalent about intellectuals, but many entered public life during his Presidency. Some 150, known as the Inquiry Scholars, were organized by Colonel House in 1919 to help with peace treaty negotiations.[26] Formal training for the public service received its first major impetus during the Great Depression, when bright young men and women of all classes flocked to the universities and from thence into the government. Discouraged by the inability of politicians and businessmen to solve the problems of the day, Franklin Roosevelt often turned to the universities. The story of his "brain trust" and his reliance on a steady stream of intellectual, often professorial, talent is well known. The President's Committee on Administrative Management consisted of Louis Brownlow, Charles Merriam, and Luther Gulick. This period signified the growing importance of research in modern political decision making, the decline of traditional sources of political innovation, and the rise of intellectuals to a permanent role in public life.

The organizational and expertise base for *rational decision making* and its application was in place by 1940. Meanwhile, the army had adopted its famous "estimate of the situation" format for decision making in the field, a guide that still dominates much of the decision literature.

The new executive budget greatly assisted in civil affairs. There was optimism throughout about the potential for a science of administration, developed more precisely later under the rubric of administrative science.

By 1900 formal *equality before the law* was being given limited assistance from Supreme Court interpretations of the post–Civil War amendments. Of symbolic importance was Theodore Roosevelt's public reception of Booker T. Washington at lunch in the White House. Of more practical influence was Roosevelt's frequent appointment of blacks to public office, even in the South. But perhaps the greatest support for equality of opportunity and upward mobility came with civil service reform. It is not widely realized that Congress modified Eaton's draft of the Pendleton Act in two critical respects. It eliminated the phrase "entrance only at the bottom," and it added a requirement that examinations should be as practical as possible. This changed our nascent personnel concept from that of a closed system on the British model to an open, program-oriented one that anyone with competitively established credentials could aspire to enter. Moreover, from the beginning the Civil Service Commission equated experience with education so that, unlike most foreign systems, the American system has never been limited to formal degree holders. Congress apparently made its changes from deep cultural predispositions. The new system permitted large numbers of blacks and women to enter into and prosper within the national public service long before equivalent opportunity was available in private enterprise.

Theodore Roosevelt's decision in the Miller case in 1903, to reinstate a Government Printing Office foreman who had been fired by the public printer because the man's union had expelled him, declared the civil service to be an open shop. The policy is still in force. Admired at the time but controversial later were the affirmations by Presidents Calvin Coolidge and Franklin D. Roosevelt that there was no right to strike in government, a prohibition made statutory at the federal level by the Taft-Hartley Act of 1947. By 1917 inflation and a threat to increase hours of work sparked the formation of the National Federation of Federal Employees, the first general union of white-collar workers in the federal service.[27]

The recognition of *administrative law* as a legitimate segment of public law in the United States is usually attributed to the influence of Goodnow's two-volume *Comparative Administrative Law*, appearing in 1893. The Stones have described this work as "the first American treatise on public administration."[28] In many ways Frank J. Goodnow was the effective founder of academic public administration in the United States. The formation of special courts for particular administrative purposes commenced in 1855 with the United States Court of Claims. Others followed every decade or two until a total of six was reached in 1971. These courts and the regulatory agencies represented two thrusts at solving the same problem: how to deal with increasing complexity. Under the notion that it takes one to know one, the intent was to use experts to control expertise under the guidance of laws giving considerable leeway to all parties and endeavoring to rule out partisan preference in the manner of civil service reform. Establishment of the *Federal Register* in 1935 finally gave access, if not order, to the burgeoning mass of administrative regulations coming from these and other agencies. Administration even entered directly into the regular judicial system through the creation in 1939 of the Administrative Office of the United States Courts.

From the 1880s *paperwork and record keeping* were becoming real burdens, and precise *procedural analysis* was necessarily more commonplace. These were promoted by growing size and legal requirements but were boosted by new technology as well. A Committee on Department Methods, known as the Keep Committee, was appointed by President Roosevelt in 1905. Between then and 1909 it reported periodically on records, lighting, leave, position classification, and other management concerns. The Bureau of Efficiency, early consulting firms, and the bureaus of government research added their recommendations. By 1913, the Commission on Economy and Efficiency had made more than eighty-five studies of such diverse topics as budgeting, distribution of government publications, travel expenditures, methods of filing, and superannuation. The Brownlow Committee of 1937 followed in its footsteps but examined topics in less detail. Most of these efforts originated in the executive branch, but they were paralleled by congressional committees working in the same vineyard.

The nation had a money economy, of course, but the insurance of *adequate funds* for almost any emergency was gained with approval in 1913 of the Sixteenth Amendment authorizing an income tax. The first truly conditional and managed grant-in-aid program to the states came at about this time also, when the Weeks Act of 1911 addressed the problem of forest preservation. The Supreme Court put its stamp of approval on these measures, which were rapidly completing the transformation of the old competitive federalism into a more cooperative arrangement. In time this would radically alter the fiscal and administrative systems related to state and local government. By 1938 Jane Perry Clark was delineating the *Rise of a New Federalism*, a quarter century before Morton Grodzins' more complete and sophisticated marble-cake analysis.

From the 1870s *technology and numeracy* became inseparable. The census continued, but procedures for compiling analyses were primitive and the data forbidding. This prompted one inventive civil servant, Herman Hollerith, to concentrate on automating the census of 1890. By the middle 1880s he had devised the first punched-card system of electrical accounting. It proved workable, and his later Tabulating Machine Company developed into the International Business Machines Corporation.

The Burroughs adding-machine patent of 1886 was also commercially successful during this period. The quantitative approach to data manipulation continued to flower as did automation, with the first large-scale digital computer, the Mark I, conceived by Howard Aiken of Harvard in 1937 and built by IBM in 1944. The digital computer brought a true tidal wave of innovation to information processing and data management. Meanwhile, the precursor of a Bureau of Labor Statistics was established in 1884 with Carroll B. Wright named as the bureau's first commissioner. He had headed a similar bureau set up in Massachusetts in 1869. The National Bureau of Standards was formed in 1901.

Communications were in flux, too. The telegraph had been a fixture since the 1830s, and the transatlantic cable since 1866. The telephone arrived in 1876, and the radio shortly thereafter. New York and Boston were linked by telephone in 1884. Marconi's first transatlantic radio message was sent in 1901. In 1915, the first transatlantic telephone call was made, and the first transatlantic radio-telephone message sent. Endless refinements followed, greatly speeding up the transaction of business but simultaneously increasing the pressure on organizational systems.

New forms of record keeping appeared, and old ones multiplied. The typewriter, commercially feasible after 1873, was in wide use by the early 1890s. Monotype and linotype machines came into use in 1885 and 1886 respectively. David Gestetner's twin-cylinder stencil duplicating machine was patented in 1900. The inundation of paper prompted still more innovations. Melvil Dewey worked out the first decimal system for the classification of library books in the 1870s. The War Department later prepared a similar system for filing. Vertical file cabinets did not arrive until about 1890, with widespread prophecies that the silly idea of standing papers on edge would never catch on! Electronic data banks were contemplated by the middle 1940s.

The major engineering challenge of the period, also creating significant medical and administrative problems, was met by Theodore Roosevelt and the army when the Panama Canal was constructed between 1904 and 1914 after the French had failed and an initial civilian U. S. management had found itself in difficulty.[29] This accomplishment was overshadowed only by the logistical miracles associated with the two world wars. Even without mention of the impact of the automobile, airplane, battleship, and diesel engine, the pressure of technology on administration was enormous. Henry Adams was not alone in bemoaning the accelerating pace of modern life.

Fortunately, the late nineteenth century also brought with it a renewed sense of *morality and ethical responsibility*. The civil service reformers were the first to challenge successfully, in the name of morality, the widespread corruption of the political system. President Cleveland proclaimed that "public office is a public trust." The attack on corruption broadened with Progressivism and began to embrace a range of moves against privilege and partisanship. The practical idealism of Theodore Roosevelt summed up the movement, and his vigorous and inventive personality made it real. By this time Lord Bryce had said that he had "never in any country seen a more eager, high-minded and efficient set of public servants, men more useful and creditable to their country, than the men doing the work of the American Government in Washington and in the Field."[30] Except for Teapot Dome and other scandals under Warren Harding, and considerable patronage manipulation in the early years of Franklin Roosevelt's administration, the moral tone of the public service remained high, and its prestige was clearly on the rise among all classes of people.

The second administrative state was even more of an *integrated working system* than the first, of which it was still a distant mirror image. There were three main achievements. The extension and refinement of administration, guided loosely by the conscious theories of classical management, comprised the first. More important and as self-conscious was the permeation of the system with a renewed sense of purpose. Not only was the American dream still highly visible as a guiding beacon but during this period the United States won three righteous wars, brought the American coasts together by spanning an isthmus in Panama, fought to a standstill the worst depression of the nation's history, and still managed to have the highest living standard in the world. Such achievement is heady brew!

As a result, an heretical and explosive idea was planted in the body politic. It was that the modern administrative state, properly directed, could accomplish almost anything it might envision and at a reasonable cost. The next quarter century of governmental success only confirmed this belief. By 1945, for the first time in American history, government was perceived as a positive good by a large proportion of the voting public.

The presidential leadership as a whole throughout these years was exceptional. Nevertheless, for his administrative capacity and his energetic revitalization and modernization of American government, Theodore Roosevelt stands out. He was like Washington in his deep commitment to principle, and both sought to set an example in practice. He was like Hamilton in that both were intellectuals and astonishingly eclectic in their wide-ranging interests, experienced in civil and military affairs, and driven to see that things went right. Roosevelt's political capacity was more complete and effective, and he managed to turn the entire politico-administrative mechanism around. Yet Hamilton's state papers show that he reached a level of achievement far beyond that of the first Roosevelt. Hamilton's theoretical and practical capacity in finance and political economy was vast and unique for his time. Theodore Roosevelt's extraordinary ability in almost all other aspects of public affairs made him unique a century later.

Wilson, Hoover, and Franklin D. Roosevelt were also able to reformulate and refuel the national sense of mission in accordance with the needs of the times. Theirs was high leadership, too. However, although frequently innovative and certainly energetic, these Presidents only refined, readjusted, and added to the administrative machinery of state. Most of the administrative model had already been designed, the precedents set, and the foundations put in place by the time each came into office.

The Bureaucratic State

The end of World War II marks the fourth major milestone in the evolution of the American administrative system. The undefined label of *bureacratic* is applied to the current period. The word's ambiguity perfectly corresponds to the nation's very mixed feelings about the administrative state of today.

Social systems carry within themselves the seeds of their own destruction. The Achilles heel of the first administrative state was the widespread perception of its elitism. The fatal flaw of the Jacksonian-Radical era was the corrupting tendency of power. The vulnerability of the second administrative state lay in blind and inflated expectations of its crowning achievement, the positive administrative state and the classical theories of management which underlay it. By the 1960s the administrative system of the two Roosevelts had become a full administrative government heavily centered in and financed from Washington. The chief executive was expected to manage everything.

Each period has provided its own major remedy for the inadequacies and dangers in the system preceding it. To quote another aphorism, nothing succeeds like success. The medicine found so effective in its day has been applied recently in such overdoses as to make the patient ill again. As Peter Drucker diagnosed in 1969, "Government is sick."[31] He could have added, "again." Put in their worst light, our two patent elixirs have been the bureaucratic force of centralized executive management applied with Hamiltonian relentlessness, and the power wielded by "the vicious and excessive activity of partisans," to quote Dorman B. Eaton in 1879.[32] For each elixir the precise formula has never been quite the same, but the essential ingredients have had much in common.

It is intriguing to find Milton Friedman in 1983 calling for a return to the spoils system through the house organ of the Office of Personnel Management.[33]

From 1945 until the middle 1960s the nation was euphoric. The Korean conflict ended with some honor, an extended prosperity created the longest period of manpower shortages in the nation's history, John F. Kennedy brought glamour back to the Presidency and propelled us to the moon, and Lyndon B. Johnson's Great Society program showed substantial promise for civil rights and the inner city.

Administrative refinement continued apace, largely from earlier motivations. Let us review some of the more important actions in the sequence of the original criteria of the administrative state. The creation in 1948–50 of a Department of Defense, plus related new entities such as the National Security Council and the Central Intelligence Agency, provided a spectacular organizational change. This was rivaled only by the demise in 1970 of the heart of the old patronage system, the Post Office Department, and its transformation into the greatest public corporation ever, the United States Postal Service. The Corporation was mandated a full merit system and given orders to make ends meet. The two Hoover Commissions of 1949 and 1955 stimulated a battery of incremental additions and consolidations. Beginning in 1949 the supergrades were added to the civil service, pay began to be dramatically improved, and expanded entry-level examinations were attracting large numbers of able college graduates. In the early 1960s systems analysis and performance budgeting became a part of decision making, and data processing was transformed into information systems. Kennedy introduced formal labor relations into the public service, and under Lyndon Johnson, came a second and impressive wave of civil rights statutes and enforcement activity.

The Corporation Control Act of 1945 and the Administrative Procedure Act of 1946 were highly significant. More and more funds were allocated through grants-in-aid to state and local governments, ending in general revenue sharing under President Richard M. Nixon for the first time since an embarrassing surplus had been distributed in 1836. While the federal budget grew by leaps and bounds under these two pressures, plus that of a rapidly growing system of transfer payments to individuals, with a variety of cost-of-living escalators, the budget remained unbalanced within reason. An unindexed income tax and the fact that continued prosperity fostered growth of the gross national product proportionally faster than the accumulated deficit made the deficit seem much less threatening. The Budget and Impoundment Control Act of 1974 regularized budget preparation schedules and provided for a more unified approach to the total appropriations process.

Computers and operations research symbolized a resurgence in the importance of quantitative analysis, and it was here that new technology had the heaviest impact on administration in general. Conflict-of-interest rules were tightened, and accountability and responsibility made more secure. There were important actions taken during these years in terms of all of the criteria of an administrative state. Moreover, until about 1967 the system appeared to be holding up well as a total system.

But the roof fell in on the second administrative state in the late sixties and early seventies. As Peter Drucker said in 1969, "We are rapidly moving to doubt and distrust of government, and, in the case of the young, even to rebellion against it. We still, if only out of habit, turn social tasks over to the government. We still revise unsuccessful programs over and over again, and assert that nothing is wrong with them that a change in procedures or a 'competent administrator' will not cure."[34] Sure enough, perhaps the most grandiose dose of classical reform ever devised was offered by Nixon in his 1971 State of the Union address when he proposed to bring the entire federal establishment under the direction of four traditional agencies—State, Treasury, Defense, and Justice—plus four new departments of Natural Resources, Human Resources, Economic Affairs, and Community Development, all under the aegis of the White House and its central staff agencies. This plan failed in the Nixon debacle that soon followed.

What are the symptoms of the current disenchantment with government, equally apparent among almost all the advanced industrial societies, including the Communist Bloc? For Americans the Vietnam War, civil riots, Watergate, President Nixon's near impeachment and resignation, and the first real depression since the 1930s are embedded deeply in our lives. Drucker points to inner cities that are still blighted despite billions in aid, farm programs that were designed to save family farms but that ended up promoting corporate agribusiness, and an increasingly confusing maze of laws and regulations. The Pendleton Act of 1883 was four pages long. The Civil Service Reform Act of 1978 was 116 pages long. "Who could have anticipated," mused President Derek C. Bok of Harvard in 1980, "the 10,000 words of regulatory prose that emerged from just 45 words of legislation requiring adequate opportunities for the handicapped?"[35] Rufus E. Miles, Jr., underscored the sensitivity of the earth's ecosystem, the failure to cope with interdependence, and the vulnerability of complicated technological systems to accident, penetration, and sabotage. Miles' observations of 1976 were to be illustrated by the great New York blackout of 1977 and the escapades of students gaining entry into computer systems in the early 1980s.[36] Procurement lead times are lengthening dangerously, and heavy industry, the backbone of any defense system, continues in deep trouble. In frustration, everyone is suing everyone as Congress and the courts judicialize administration to the point that public employment has become almost a property right once again. The judiciary has also moved in to administer elections and education, as the Supreme Court allows the civil rights amendments to override the rest of the Constitution regardless of the framers' intent.[37] The commonality of the symptoms appears to be not just overload of the judicial system but total system overload compounded by the consequent weariness on the part of all concerned.[38]

Since the middle seventies a main scapegoat has been "the bureaucracy" in Washington. There are indeed problems there, and their source lies mainly in Washington, but the bureaucracy—meaning the great bulk of the federal civil service—is no longer at the national level and has not been for 30 years. Since the Korean conflict the federal civil service has expanded from 2.1 to nearly 2.9 million persons, but with its growth proportionately under that of the population. At the same time, but only partly under the stimulus of increasing federal funds, our state and local public services have trebled, ballooning from some 4 million in 1950 to more than 13 million in 1980. Add to this the fact that nearly 90 per cent of the federal service is not in the Washington, D. C. area and never has been, the federal field service being scattered broadly among us, with 150,000 living in my state of Texas alone. The bulk of "the bureaucracy" is not in Washington! It is right at home where we live! Moreover, with so much of the budget allocated for grants-in-aid to state and local government, for transfer payments to individuals, and for defense, Frederick Mosher has recently estimated that no more than 5 to 7 per cent of the federal budget is "allotted to domestic activities that the federal government performs itself."[39] That is, the nuts and bolts of federal civil government cost us very, very little indeed.

What is the problem then? After the Civil War it was said that the Union war veterans of the Grand Army of the Republic (GAR) had saved the country and now they wanted it. As a result, military pensions became a scandalous adjunct to the spoils system. Under the Jacksonians and Radical Republicans the nation's land and natural resources were also thrown open to the exploitation of all in the name of democratic majoritarianism and economic freedom. Today there are few resources to throw open. Instead, through a lower-key gradualism, Americans have for several decades been voting themselves largess from the public trough beyond any dreams of the past, with the eager assistance of senators and representatives who depend on the people for re-election. Even a popular president such as Dwight D. Eisenhower could not keep the lid on very long. As a result, most of the American civil service is now at home taking care of us. Through grants-in-aid and transfer payments, we the people are receiving almost 60 per cent of the federal budget right where we live for the purpose of improving our local personal lot.

Reform under such circumstances is now, as it was in the late nineteenth century a laborious and Herculean task. Again, we ourselves are the cause of the dysfunction. Yet now, as then, there is a pervasive feeling that something is badly wrong, and there is a deep yearning for corrective guidance. Many parallels exist to the situation in the country a century ago.

The Past Is Prologue

In 1876, our first centennial year, there was no obvious solution to the nation's problems either. Rather, a confusing array of alternatives was being proposed via the Prohibition Party, the Greenback Party, the Liberal Republicans, the Standpatters, the Gold or Silver Democrats, the Single Taxers, the Socialists, the Marxists, and a few Anarchists. The major parties alternated in power in rapid succession as the electorate sought programmatic leadership. Ronald Reagan's electoral success from a minority party base in 1980, like that of Grover Cleveland in 1884, is explained mainly by the fact that for the first time in four administrations—also alternating Republican and Democratic administrations—he had a plan based on historic principle. Cleveland stood for retrenchment and for a return to honesty and integrity in politics, representing important concerns but not basic issues bearing on economics, liberty, or equality. That is, Cleveland's was a "how to do it" not a "what to do" program.

President Reagan's inaugural theme, "Government is not the solution to our problem; government is the problem," set the stage for a serious retrenchment (a good nineteenth century term) fight for the first time in decades. Political skill playing on widespread apprehension has made the old battle cry of economy, efficiency, and decentralization rebound once again.

President Reagan's three-pronged program is quite appropriate for the time, but there are three major flaws in the operational approach to the program and two other difficulties that can cause considerable anguish all around.

The most fundamental flaw lies in the nature of the goals of the new conservatism, for like Cleveland's goals, they emphasize "how," not "what." They provide no guidance about *where* to retrench and where not to retrench, *what* to decentralize and what not to decentralize. They are not substantive goals but procedural, as efficiency is too. For substantive and "what to do" examples I refer again to the period between the presidencies of Grant and McKinley, when the really fundamental struggle in the nation was over whether industrialism would supercede agriculture as a national priority. Industrialism finally won a clear victory in 1896. Then the question became: what kind of industrialism should be pursued? There were three choices: (1) the Marxian state enterprise approach, Marxism then holding its strongest position in our history, (2) the cartelism of the trusts of the day, or (3) dusting off the Sherman Antitrust Act in favor of enforced competition. Under the guidance of Theodore Roosevelt and Woodrow Wilson, the nation chose the third alternative. The battle had been confused by a sound-soft money controversy and other secondary concerns such as those Cleveland represented. The latter needed to be settled, but they were also distractions from the mainstream mission on the political front line. Reagan's program is very much like Cleveland's. It provides no answer to questions about "what to do."

The critical matter is not just controlling government, but controlling or uncontrolling to what ends. Since 1960 it has been apparent that we have entered Daniel Bell's postindustrial era. The question still is: what shall be the kind of wine in that bottle? The query is not as simple as it was in 1900 when industrialism provided an obvious out. Ponder the following bare bones scenario.

Currently, two choices are bruited about in answer to "what to do." One is to follow the high-tech knowledge processing route to world leadership. The other is to re-emphasize and rebuild the American heavy industry base. The nation pursues both alternatives, but in different ways. We let high-tech go where it will with strong research and development backup of our bases of knowledge. About heavy industry, we agree that Felix Rohatyn, catalyst of New York City's financial survival, is dead right: there can be no world power without a solid industrial base. We help this base renovate itself through the kind of support Chrysler received, but from a new version of the old Reconstruction Finance Corporation, so useful earlier.[40] That is, we treat industry today as we did agriculture after the turn of the century. Neither is any longer our primary concern, but both must be kept efficient and viable. Such an approach, combined with continued attention to civil rights and the disadvantaged and to a prudent husbanding of energy and the ecosystem, makes the most substantive sense for now. Economy, efficiency, and decentralization can then be applied to much greater effect, as well as, with care, some further doses of classical economics.

Such a program has something in it for almost everyone, at least enough for strong political support. In return, even moderately astute political leadership should be able to ask for the universal sacrifices necessary for general retrenchment and such higher taxes as may be needed to rescue the nation's faltering fiscal system. To realize such a program will require all the intelligence and finesse we can muster.

Underlying this scenario is an acceptance of Abraham Lincoln's view that a symbiotic and mutually inspiring relationship exists between individual and economic freedom and opportunity, bounded only by sensible limits on the exploitation of each other and our segment of Planet Earth. This theme is clearly within our traditions, including those of both major parties.

I move now to subplots of the scenario. The second flaw in the Reagan approach lies in attacking the organizational structure of the executive branch by means of old-fashioned theories. The main organizational problem now lies within Congress and the party system. Leave the executive alone except for minor tune-ups. We do not need more hierarchy, channels, and paperwork. Classical management is fine, but only to a point, which the nation has long since reached. Now the proper concept to apply to the executive branch is Ashby's Law of Requisite Variety out of cybernetic steersmanship. Put in the simpler language of Stafford Beer, "Only variety in the control mechanism can deal successfully with variety in the system controlled."[41] The executive branch is as well equipped administratively now as the instrument panel of a 747 airplane. The problem lies with the copilots, Congress and the party system.

The third flaw is in the constant flaying of the career civil service at the very time when government needs all the experience and expertise it can get. Personnel difficulties exist, and the Civil Service Reform Act of 1978 can do much to solve them if it is used as it was intended. Even as the career service faces a verbal barrage for inefficiency, portions of it are being politicized with a partisanship not seen since Franklin Roosevelt's first term. Even the criterion of patronage appointments is anything but administrative effectiveness. A related but more basic error in the long run is the tendency of recent presidents to use the White House staff and all other civil personnel available to create a kind of President's personal party divorced from the rest of the political system.[42] This does not ensure a supportive Congress, and the practice has been diverting much of the capacity of the White House staff, as well as that of the Office of Management and Budget, away from their administrative and policy control functions. Some diversion is appropriate, but a return to the spoils system can only be self-destructive.

The political parties are still quite viable if presidents will use them, as Franklin Roosevelt, Lyndon Johnson, and Richard Nixon demonstrated. Perhaps then a combined party and president, with a sympathetic Congress beholden to them, can work on the organizational fragmentation of the legislative branch. This is a problem little dealt with since 1946. The catch is that for Congress to gain power through unifying itself, individual congressmen must give up power. This is as difficult a conversion as persuading the mass of voters to give up individual benefits. There is a possibility if all share the benefits and all share the sacrifices. Regardless, some attempt must be made in this direction before it is too late!

Reagan's ancillary problems began with the constant harrassing of the administration by its right-wing supporters, fervently and righteously seeking to establish their various theologies, secular or religious, often under the guise of promoting retrenchment. A president who has a program with wide support need not fear such fragments of the body politic. Of course, morality, principle, and honesty in office are as desperately needed as they were at the turn of the century, but what is really needed is a reapplication of our long-standing and general social ethic on a pragmatic basis, not rigid ideo-theology of any kind.

More trouble can come if the administration is sidetracked by frequent military forays abroad. There is enough of that already. The Communist threat is real, but clearly the first requirement is to strengthen our domestic base of operations.

Whether the Reagan or any Republican administration can metamorphose from the ideas of Cleveland to the higher levels of Roosevelt or Wilson is doubtful. The forces to contend with are formidable, and Reagan's programmatic armament is not very impressive. However, the programmatic quality of the Democratic opposition holds little more promise. One can only hope that the nation will be spared a succession of Harrisons and McKinleys until a worse crisis confronts us.

Politics, Administration, and History

Politics and administration are inextricably intertwined. Both are central to effective action. One problem is how to bring them together in symbiotic association while keeping each in its proper place. The other problem is to understand that the proper place of each will vary through time. There is no permanent solution, no fixed paradigm, for this or any other ends-means continuum. But there is an ebb and flow in a politico-administrative, love-hate marriage that, with persistence and practice, can be perceived and used to change the course of events.

My principal intent has been to illustrate this ebb and flow by trying to make intelligible the evolving trends and tendencies of the American administrative state through four notable periods of history. A secondary intent can be summarized by Waldo's warning in 1948 that "the formal analysis of organizations without regard to the purposes that inspire them (is) but a tedious elaboration of the insignificant."[43] I have also meant to underscore Harry S. Truman's prescient remark that "most of the problems a President has to face have their roots in the past."[44] A suggestive framework of solutions can often be found there as well.

Endnotes

1. I presume familiarity with citations to the 1887 and 1941 printings of Wilson's essay. Moreover, as was the custom in the earlier times I am mainly writing about, I have given a minimum of citations generally and none at all for information available in standard works. Nor do I cite well-known materials of any kind. Quotations are credited as are materials that the author has found especially helpful. A few citations are by way of example.
2. Waldo (New York: Ronald Press, 1948); Morstein Marx (Chicago: University of Chicago Press, 1957).
3. Waldo, op. cit., pp. v and vi; Morstein Marx, op. cit., note 1, p. 2. As Waldo has suggested to me, it is likely that Morstein Marx was referring only to the large size of modern administrative mechanisms in comparison to other governmental institutions.
4. I cite only one work as an example, relevant for other reasons as well. It is William E. Nelson, *The Roots of American Bureaucracy, 1830–1900* (Cambridge: Harvard University Press, 1982), pp. 4–5.
5. Ralph P. Hummel, 2nd ed. (New York: St. Martin's Press, 1982).
6. Here I would argue with Ferrel Heady, who in the second edition of his *Public Administration: A Comparative Perspective* (New York: Marcel Dekker, Inc., 1979), chapters 5 and 6, lists only France and Germany as having "classic" administrative systems in this period and makes no reference to the Federalist effort.
7. The full findings are presented along with related materials as Chapter 11 of the volume by Jack Rabin and James S. Bowman, eds., *Politics and Administration: Woodrow Wilson and Contemporary Public Administration* (New York: Marcel Dekker, Inc., 1984), pp. 203–218. I am indebted to the publisher and editors for permission to include the summary here.
8. (Washington, DC: Government Printing Office, 1879), p. 13. Eaton makes similar asides here and there, especially in Chapter 1. The relevant comments by Waldo on Eaton and Wilson are, op. cit., pp. 26 and 40–41.
9. Eaton wrote his piece on "Civil Administration" for J. J. Lalor, the editor, in 1881. (Chicago: Rand, McNally, 1882), Volume 1, pp. 473–475.
10. *Ground Under Our Feet* (New York: Macmillan, 1938), p. 114.
11. Better known is the fact that Max Weber's essay on bureaucracy was of almost no influence in the United States until about this time.
12. I have italicized the mention of each criterion to assist the reader in following the subelements of the discussion in this section.
13. Charles Warren, *The Making of the Constitution* (Boston: Little, Brown, 1928), p. 174 and passim. For an intriguing interpretation of the parliamentary process by which the decision on the Presidency was reached see William

H. Riker, "The Heresthetics of Constitution-Making: The Presidency in 1787, with Comments on Determinism and Rational Choice," *The American Political Science Review* 78:1–16 (March) 1984.

14. For a discussion of departmental development in Great Britain see Bernard Schaffer, *The Administrative Factor* (London: Frank Cass, 1973), chapter 1, entitled "The Idea of the Ministerial Department."

15. Leonard D. White, *The Federalists* (New York: Macmillan, 1948), p. 124.

16. See Patricia Cline Cohen, *A Calculating People: The Spread of Numeracy in Early America* (Chicago: University of Chicago Press, 1983).

17. Association of the Bar of the City of New York, *Conflict of Interest and Federal Service* (Cambridge: Harvard University Press, 1960), note 3, pp. 27–28.

18. Op. cit., p. 514.

19. Ibid., pp. 511–512.

20. Ibid., p. 512. Reprinted with permission of the Macmillan Publishing Company from *The Federalists: A Study in Administrative History* by Leonard D. White, copyright 1948 by Leonard D. White.

21. White, ibid., pp. 126–127; Lynton K. Caldwell, *The Administrative Theories of Hamilton and Jefferson* (Chicago: University of Chicago Press, 1944), chapter XIV. See also the two extraordinarily insightful lead essays in the bicentennial issue of the *Public Administration Review*. For further background on the Federalist period see Caldwell, "Novus ordo Seclorum: The Heritage of American Public Administration," *The Public Administration Review* 36:476–488 (September/October) 1976. For an analysis of the second century see Barry K. Karl's essay that follows Caldwell: "Public Administration and American History: A Century of Professionalism," pp. 489–503.

22. For most of the information about civil service reform and public personnel management I have relied on my own work. See especially my *History of the United States Civil Service* (Evanston, IL: Row, Peterson, 1958) and "The Tap Roots of American Public Personnel Management," *Personnel Administration* 25:12–16, 32 (March/April) 1962. See also David H. Rosenbloom, *Federal Service and the Constitution* (Ithaca, NY: Cornell University Press, 1971).

23. J. D. Hittle, *The Military Staff* (Harrisburg, PA: Stackpole, 1961), p. 201. See also Stephen Skowronek, *Building a New American State: The Expansion of National Administrative Capacities, 1877–1920* (New York: Cambridge University Press, 1982), Chapter 7, "Reconstituting the Army." This volume and that by Robert H. Wiebe, *The Search for Order, 1877–1920* (New York: Hill and Wang, 1967) both provide important additions to the administrative history of the period.

24. See Mohammad Afzal, "Management Analysis: An Emerging Staff Function" (unpublished Ph.D. dissertation, Graduate School of Business and Public Administration, Cornell University, 1962) for the history of the management analysis function. In 1983 Afzal was appointed Minister of Education in Pakistan.

25. See the National Academy of Public Administration and Office of Management and Budget, *Report on Government Corporations* (Washington, DC: The National Academy of Public Administration, 1981), Volume 1, pp. 6–15, for a brief history.

26. Richard Hofstadter, *Anti-Intellectualism in American Life* (New York: Knopf,

1966), pp. 211–212. Hofstadter considers the role of intellectuals in public life in some detail throughout the work.

27. For the early history of public employee unions, see Sterling Spero, *Government as Employer* (New York: Remsen, 1948).

28. A. B. Stone and D. C. Stone, "The Early Development of Education in Public Administration," in *American Public Administration: Past, Present, Future,* F. C. Mosher, ed. (University, AL: University of Alabama Press, 1975), p. 27.

29. See Alfred P. Chandler, Jr.'s essay on "Theodore Roosevelt and the Panama Canal: A Study in Administration," in *The Letters of Theodore Roosevelt,* Elting B. Morison, ed. (Cambridge: Harvard University Press, 1952), Volume VI, pp. 1547–1557. See also David McCullough, *The Path Between the Seas* (New York: Simon and Schuster, 1977).

30. Quoted in Van Riper, *History,* op. cit., p. 206.

31. "The Sickness of Government," *The Public Interest* 14:3 (Winter) 1969.

32. Op. cit., p. 4.

33. "Sticking Price Tags on Job Performances in Government," *Management* 4:11 (August) 1983.

34. Op. cit., p. 4.

35. Derek C. Bok, "The Federal Government and the University," *The Public Interest* 48:86 (Winter) 1980.

36. Rufus E. Miles, Jr., *Awakening From the American Dream: The Social and Political Limits to Growth* (New York: Universe Books, 1976). Miles is a former Assistant Secretary for Administration in the Department of Health, Education, and Welfare, and later associated with Princeton University. This is a first-rate analysis of our current technological condition.

37. See Jeremy Rabkin, "The Judiciary in the Administrative State," *The Public Interest* 71:62–84 (Spring) 1983, for an excellent discussion of the judiciary's meddling in almost everything and its "cavalier attitude toward the law."

38. See Richard Rose, ed., *Challenge to Government: Studies in Overloaded Politics* (Beverly Hills, CA: Sage Publications, 1980), and Rose's illuminating comparative essay on fiscal overload in Western nations, "Meta-policies for Megagovernment," *The Public Interest* 75:99–110 (Spring) 1984.

39. Frederick C. Mosher, "The Changing Responsibilities and Tactics of the Federal Government," in *American Public Administration: Patterns of the Past,* James W. Fesler, ed. (Washington, DC: American Society for Public Administration, 1982), pp. 198–212. This article provides a superb summary of its topic in a first-rate collection.

40. Rohatyn's analysis is much more complicated and complete than my brief extraction here implies. See "Time for a Change," *The New York Review* 30:46–49 (August 18) 1983, and "American Roulette," *The New York Review* 31:11–15 (March 29) 1984. There is an earlier summary of some of Rohatyn's views by Neal R. Peirce, "Felix Rohatyn's Warning Bell in the Night," *Public Administration Times,* March 1, 1981.

41. W. Ross Ashby, *An Introduction to Cybernetics* (New York: John Wiley, 1956), pp. 206–218 and 245; Stafford Beer, *Cybernetics and Management* (New York: John Wiley, 1959), p. 50. Beer is an especially important source for organization theorists.

42. On current conditions within the White House entourage see the beautifully researched and articulated essay by Chester A. Newland, "A Mid-Term Appraisal—The Reagan President: Limited Government and Political Administration," *Public Administration Review* 43:1–21 (January/February) 1983.

43. Waldo, op. cit., p. 211.

44. Memoirs, Vol. 11, *Years of Trial and Hope* (Garden City, NY: Doubleday, 1956), p. 1.

CHAPTER 2

The Emergence of Public
Administration as a Field of Study

Nicholas Henry
ARIZONA STATE UNIVERSITY

*NICHOLAS HENRY is Professor of Public Affairs and Dean of the College
of Public Programs at Arizona State University. He has authored, co-authored, or edited some ten books, including* Public Administration and
Public Affairs, *and has published articles in several journals. Dean Henry
has served as consultant to a wide range of public and private organizations,
among which are the United States Office of Management and Budget, the
National Science Foundation, and the Hudson Institute.*

Nicholas Henry here constructs an intellectual history of American public
administration. He organizes his description of the evolution of the field
around a succession of five overlapping paradigms, each phase of development characterized by whether it attends primarily to *locus* or *focus*. Locus
is the institutional *where* of the field, such as its location in the apparatus
of government in Paradigm 1, and focus is the specialized *what* of the
field, such as its emphasis on principles of management in Paradigm 2.
The five paradigms are: (1) the politics/administration dichotomy, 1900–
1926, (2) the principles of administration, 1927–1937, (3) public administration as political science, 1950–1970, (4) public administration as management, 1956–1970, and (5) public administration as public administration,
1970 to the present.

The distinguishing characteristic of Paradigm 1 was the idea of a distinct
politics/administration dichotomy related to a corresponding value/fact
dichotomy. Orthodoxy included the beliefs that politics should not intrude
upon administration, management lends itself to scientific study, public

37

administration is capable of becoming a value-free science, and the mission of administration is to assure economy and efficiency.

Paradigm 2 assumed that certain scientific principles of administration exist. They can be discovered and described, and it is the proper role of administrators to be expert in their application. The focus of the field was on managerial knowledge that could be applied in any administrative setting, regardless of locus, and without exception. The acronym POSDCORB summarizes the activities of a manager following the sacred principles: planning, organizing, staffing, directing, coordinating, reporting, and budgeting.

An effective challenge to the principles paradigm came from practitioners who confessed that what often appeared to be value-free administration was actually value-laden politics, and from such academic writers as Herbert A. Simon, who argued in 1947 that scientific principles cannot apply when decision makers are in fact limited by suboptimizing organizational and personal constraints. Rather than apply principles, Simon suggested, decision makers "satisfice." They select the alternative that meets their minimum standard of satisfaction in a system of bounded rationality.

Paradigms 3 and 4 ran concurrently and represented an effort by public administrationists to find a place for themselves in other disciplines. In the era of Paradigm 3 many of them tried to re-establish their conceptual linkages with the mother discipline of political science. In the era of Paradigm 4 other public administrationists tried to work out a housing arrangement with a foster parent, management. Neither plan worked. Political science relegated public administration to the status of an "emphasis" in political science departments, and management made public administration a "subfield" in generic schools of management. Public administration lost its identity in both cases.

Two developments saved the field from obscurity. One was the rise of interdisciplinary programs in science, technology, and public policy. The other was the new public administration movement growing out of the Minnowbrook Conference of 1968. The interdisciplinary programs gave public administration a legitimate claim to intellectual distinction, because public administration often dominated the interface areas of knowledge and power, bureaucracy and democracy, and technology and management. The new public administration gave public administration a counterpart movement to the new political science, which was also calling for a return to more normative concerns. By rejecting the current technical emphases of both the political science and management establishments, the new public administration laid the groundwork for separation from both.

The final paradigm, Paradigm 5, is the model currently in place. Public administration finds itself an independent and self-aware field with its own definition of what "public" means in public administration, its own methodologies, its own educational goals, its own core curriculum, and its own survival techniques.

The Patrick Henry of public administration, Dwight Waldo, who was among the first and certainly the more articulate of the public administration scholars to cut ties with the aging empire of political science and issue a clarion call for independence, has written of what he calls "self-aware Public Administration." Waldo observes that in its evolution as a self-aware academic field, "choice of ancestry and family is always fateful."[1] The ancestry of choice for public administration was, by and large, political science. In this chapter we review the relationship of public administration to this parentage and to another field that became the initial foster parent of public administration, administrative science.

Public administration has developed as an academic field through a succession of five overlapping paradigms. As Robert T. Golembiewski has noted in a perceptive essay,[2] each phase may be characterized according to whether it has *locus* or *focus*. Locus is the institutional *where* of the field. A recurring locus of public administration is the government bureaucracy, but this has not always been the case, and often this traditional locus has been blurred. *Focus* is the specialized *what* of the field. One focus of public administration has been the study of certain "principles of administration," but again, the foci of the discipline have altered with the changing paradigms of public administration. As Golembiewski observes, the paradigms of public administration may be understood in terms of locus or focus; when one has been relatively sharply defined in academic circles, the other has been conceptually ignored, and vice versa. We use the notion of loci and foci in reviewing the intellectual development of public administration.

The Beginning

Woodrow Wilson largely set the tone for the early study of public administration in an essay entitled "The Study of Administration," published in the *Political Science Quarterly* in 1887. In it, Wilson observed that it "is getting harder to run a constitution than to frame one," and called for the bringing of more intellectual resources to bear in the management of the state.[3] Wilson's seminal article has been variously interpreted by later scholars. Some have insisted that Wilson originated the "politics/administration dichotomy"—the naive distinction between "political" activity and "administrative" activity in public organizations that would plague the field for years to come. Other scholars have countered that

Portions of this chapter have appeared in *Public Administration and Public Affairs,* 3rd edition, Prentice-Hall, and are used with the permission of Prentice-Hall.

Wilson was well aware that public administration was innately political in nature, and he made this point clear in his article. In reality Wilson himself seems ambivalent about what public administration really is. Wilson failed

> to amplify what the study of administration actually entails, what the proper relationship should be between the administrative and political realms, and whether or not administrative study could ever become an abstract science akin to the natural sciences.[4]

Nevertheless, Wilson unquestionably posited one unambiguous thesis in his article that has had a lasting impact on the field: Public administration is worth studying. Political scientists would later create the first identifiable paradigm of public administration around Wilson's contention.

Paradigm 1:
The Politics/Administration Dichotomy, 1900–1926

Our benchmark dates for the Paradigm 1 period correspond to the publication of books written by Frank J. Goodnow and Leonard D. White; these dates, like the years chosen as marking the later periods of the field, are only rough indicators. In *Politics and Administration* (1900), Goodnow contended that there were "two distinct functions of government," which he identified with the title of his book. "Politics," said Goodnow, "has to do with policies or expressions of the state will," whereas administration "has to do with the execution of these policies."[5] Separation of powers provided the basis of the distinction. The legislative branch, aided by the interpretive abilities of the judicial branch, expressed the will of the state and formed policy; the executive branch administered those policies impartially and apolitically.

The emphasis of Paradigm 1 was on locus—where public administration should be. Clearly, in the view of Goodnow and his fellow public administrationists, public administration should center in the government's bureaucracy. Although the legislature and judiciary admittedly have their quanta of "administration," their primary responsibility and function remain the expression of the state will. The initial conceptual legitimation of this locus-centered definition of the field, and one that was increasingly problematic for academics and practitioners alike, became known as the politics/administration dichotomy.

The phrase that came to symbolize this distinction between politics and administration was, "There is no Republican way to build a road." The reasoning was that there could be only one "right" way to spread tarmac—the administrative engineer's way. What was ignored in this statement, however, was that there was indeed a Republican way to decide whether the road needed building, a Republican way to choose the location for the road, a Republican way to purchase the land, a Republican way to displace the people living in the road's way, and most certainly a Republican way to let contracts for the road. There was also, and is, a Democratic way, a Socialist way, a Liberal way, even an Anarchist way to make these "administrative" decisions. In retrospect the politics/administration dichotomy posited by Goodnow and his academic progeny was, at best, naive. But many years would pass before this would be fully realized within public administration's ranks.

Public administration received its first serious attention from scholars during this period largely as a result of the "public service movement" that was taking place in American universities in the early part of this century. Political science, as a report issued in 1914 by the Committee on Instruction in Government of the American Political Science Association stated, was concerned with training for citizenship, preparations for professions such as law and journalism, training "experts and [preparing] specialists for governmental positions," and educating for research work.[6] Public administration, therefore, was something more than a significant subfield of political science; indeed, it was a principal reason of being for the discipline.

As an indication of public administration's importance to political science, a Committee on Practical Training for Public Service was established in 1912 by the American Political Science Association, and in 1914, its report recommended with unusual foresight that special "professional schools" were needed to train public administrators, and that new technical degrees might also be necessary for this purpose.[7] This committee formed the nucleus of the Society for the Promotion of Training for the Public Service, founded in 1914—the forerunner of the American Society for Public Administration, which was established in 1939.

Public administration began picking up academic legitimacy in the 1920s; notable in this regard was the publication of Leonard D. White's *Introduction to the Study of Public Administration* in 1926, the first textbook entirely devoted to the field. As Waldo has pointed out, White's text was quintessentially American Progressive in character and, in its quintessence, reflected the general thrust of the field: Politics should not intrude on administration; management lends itself to scientific study; public

administration is capable of becoming a "value-free" science in its own
·right; the mission of administration is economy and efficiency, period.[8]

The net result of Paradigm 1 was to strengthen the notion of a distinct
politics/administration dichotomy by relating it to a corresponding value/
fact dichotomy. Thus, everything that public administrationists scrutinized in the executive branch was imbued with the colorings and legitimacy of being somehow "factual" and "scientific," while the study of
public policy-making and related matters was left to the political scientists.
The carving up of analytical territory between public administrationists
and political scientists during this locus-oriented stage can be seen today
in universities: It is the public administrationists who teach organization
theory, budgeting, and personnel; political scientists teach such subjects
as American government, judicial behavior, the presidency, state and
local politics, and legislative process, as well as such "non-American"
fields as comparative politics and international relations. A secondary
implication of this locus-centered phase was the isolation of public administration from such other fields as business administration, which had
unfortunate consequences when these fields began their own fruitful
explorations into the nature of organizations. Finally, largely because
of the emphasis on "science" and "facts" in public administration and
the substantial contributions by public administrationists to the emerging
field of organization theory, a foundation was laid for the later "discovery"
of certain scientific "principles" of administration.

Paradigm 2:
The Principles of Administration, 1927–1937

In 1927, W. F. Willoughby's book, *Principles of Public Administration*,
was published, the second fully fledged text in the field. Although Willoughby's *Principles* was as fully American Progressive in tone as White's
Introduction, its title alone indicated the new thrust of public administration: Certain scientific principles of administration existed; they could
be discovered; and administrators would be expert in their work if they
learned how to apply these principles.

It was during the phase represented by Paradigm 2 that public administration reached its reputational zenith. Public administrationists were
courted by industry and government alike during the 1930s and early
1940s for their managerial knowledge. Thus the focus of the field—its
essential expertise in the form of administrative principles—waxed, while
no one thought too seriously about its locus. Indeed, the locus of public
administration was everywhere, inasmuch as principles were principles

and administration was administration, at least according to the perceptions represented by Paradigm 2. By the very fact that the principles of administration were indeed *principles*—that is, by definition, they "worked" in any administrative setting, regardless of culture, function, environment, mission, or institutional framework, and without exception—it therefore followed that they could be applied successfully anywhere. Furthermore, because public administrationists had contributed as much if not more to the formulation of "administrative principles" as had researchers in any other field of inquiry, it also followed that public administrationists should lead the academic pack in applying them to "real-world" organizations, public or otherwise.

Among the more significant works relevant to this phase were Mary Parker Follet's *Creative Experience* (1924), Henri Fayol's *Industrial and General Management* (1930), and James D. Mooney and Alan C. Reiley's *Principles of Organization* (1939), all of which delineated varying numbers of overarching administrative principles. Organization theorists often dub this school of thought "administrative management," as it focused on the upper hierarchical echelons of organizations. A related literature that preceded the work in administrative management somewhat in time, but that was under continuing development in business schools, focused on the assembly line. Researchers in this stream, often called "scientific management," developed principles of efficient physical movement for optimal assembly-line efficiency. The most notable contributions to this literature were Frederick W. Taylor's *Principles of Scientific Management* (1911) and various works by Frank and Lillian Gilbreth. Although obviously related in concept, scientific management had less effect on public administration during its principles phase because it focused on lower-level personnel in the organization.

The lack of locus, if not, perhaps, the sharpening new focus of public administration during this period, made itself evident within the university community. In 1935, the Public Administration Clearing House held a conference at Princeton University, and the conference's report was radically different from the report issued by the Committee on Practical Training for Public Service of the American Political Science Association in 1914. Suddenly, political scientists had great difficulties with the idea of founding separate schools of public administration and believed instead that existing courses in political science departments and in other relevant disciplines, such as law, economics, and management, provided, if they were correctly combined, an education that was entirely adequate for budding government bureaucrats. The conference, therefore, found itself "unable to find any single formula which warrants the establishment of an isolated college or university program which alone will emphasize preparation exclusively for the public service." Only a "university-wide approach" would be satisfactory, because the problem of public administration education exceeded the "confines of any single department or special institute or school."[9]

As a more modern scholar has since observed, "A logical consequence of this reasoning could have been the elimination of public administration as a discrete field of study within the universities."[10] Such were the dangers of not having a firm and stationary intellectual locus from which to build a curriculum.

Despite these difficulties, however, scholars who identified with the study of public administration nonetheless found it useful to establish, four years after the publication of the Princeton report, the American Society for Public Administration (ASPA), which continues to function as the nation's primary association of scholars and practitioners of public administration, and as the sponsoring organization of the field's premier journal, *Public Administration Review*. But the creation of ASPA was less a response to the difficulties that public administration was having within universities generally and more a reaction to what public administration-ists were experiencing within political science departments specifically. As Waldo has put it, "The sense that political science as an academic discipline did not adequately represent and nurture the needs of those interested in improving performance in public administration was a strong motivating force in creating the new organization. In retrospect, it is clear that ASPA represented above all an attempt to loosen public administration from the restraints of political science. . . ."[11]

As with any proposed secession, its execution was not easy. Public administrationist Donald C. Stone recalled the emotions involved at ASPA's founding: "Questions of loyalty, sedition, intrigue, separatism, and schism kindled emotions."[12] Golembiewski has summed it up: The birth of ASPA was "an expression of the felt needs of the burgeoning graduates and faculty of suddenly virile programs of public administra-tion. So much was at stake, practically as well as intellectually."[13]

The "high noon of orthodoxy," as it often has been called, of public administration was marked by the publication in 1937 of Luther H. Gulick and Lyndall Urwick's *Papers on the Science of Administration*. This landmark study also marked the high noon of prestige for public adminis-tration. Gulick and Urwick were confidantes of President Franklin D. Roosevelt and advised him on a variety of matters managerial; their *Papers* was a report to the President's Committee on Administrative Science.

Principles were important to Gulick and Urwick, but where those principles were applied was not; focus was favored over locus, and no bones were made about it. As they said in the *Papers:*

> It is the general thesis of this paper that there are principles which can be arrived at inductively from the study of human organizations which

should govern arrangements for human association of any kind. These principles can be studied as a technical question, irrespective of the purpose of the enterprise, the personnel comprising it, or any constitutional, political or social theory underlying its creation.[14]

Gulick and Urwick promoted seven principles of administration and, in so doing, gave students of public administration that snappy anagram, POSDCORB. POSDCORB was the final expression of administrative principles. It stood for:

P   lanning
O   rganizing
S   taffing
D   irecting
C
O   ordinating
R   eporting
B   udgeting

That was public administration in 1937.

The Challenge, 1938–1947

In the following year, mainstream public administration received its first real hint of conceptual challenge. In 1938 Chester I. Barnard's *The Functions of the Executive* appeared. Its impact on public administration was not overwhelming at the time, but it later had considerable influence on Herbert A. Simon when he was writing his devastating critique of the field, *Administrative Behavior*. The impact of Barnard's book may have been delayed because, as a former president of New Jersey Bell Telephone, he was not a certified member of the public administration community.

Dissent from mainstream public administration accelerated in the 1940s in two mutually reinforcing directions. One objection was that politics and administration could never be separated in any remotely sensible fashion. The other was that the principles of administration were something less than the final expression of managerial rationality.

Demurring to the Dichotomy

Although inklings of dissent began in the 1930s, a book of readings in the field, *Elements of Public Administration*, edited in 1946 by Fritz Morstein Marx, was one of the first major volumes to question the assumption that politics and administration could be dichotomized. All fourteen articles in the book were written by practitioners and indicated a new awareness that what often appeared to be value-free "administration" actually was value-laden "politics." Was a technical decision on a budgetary emphasis or a personnel change really impersonal and apolitical, or was it actually highly personal, highly political, and highly preferential? Was it ever possible to discern the difference? Was it even worth attempting to discern the difference between politics and administration if, in reality, there was none? Was the underpinning politics/administration dichotomy of the field at best naive? Many academics and practitioners alike were beginning to think so.

In his superb analysis of "The Trauma of Politics" and public administration, Allen Schick observed that the intellectuals' abandonment of the politics/administration dichotomy in the 1940s has been overstated in more recent years, and that those advocating its abandonment never intended to argue that something called administration and something called politics were totally inseparable. The challengers of the forties only wished to emphasize that public administrators, as well as legislators, made political decisions and public policies:

> Public administration always has served power and the powerful. . . . the service of power was pro bono publico, to help power holders govern more effectively. The presumption was that everyone benefits from good government . . . the constant concern with power was masked by the celebrated dichotomy between politics and administration. But the dichotomy, rather than keeping them apart, really offered a framework for bringing politics and administration together . . . the dichotomy provided for the ascendancy of the administration over the political: efficiency over representation, rationality over self-interest. . . . In the end, the dichotomy was rejected not because it separated politics and administration but because it joined them in a way that offended the pluralist norms of postwar political science.[15]

Puncturing the Principles

Arising simultaneously with the challenge to the traditional politics/ administration dichotomy of the field was an even more basic contention: that there could be no such thing as a "principle" of administration. In 1946 Simon gave a foreshadowing of his *Administrative Behavior* in an article entitled, appropriately, "The Proverbs of Administration," published in *Public Administration Review*. The following year, in the same journal, Robert A. Dahl published a searching piece, "The Science of Public Administration: Three Problems." In it he argued that the development of universal principles of administration was hindered by the obstructions of values contending for preeminence in organizations, differences in individual personalities, and social frameworks that varied from culture to culture. Waldo's major work also reflected this theme. His *The Administrative State: A Study of the Political Theory of American Public Administration* (1948) attacked the notion of immutable principles of administration, the inconsistencies of the methodology used in determining them, and the narrowness of the "values" of economy and efficiency that dominated the field's thinking.

The most formidable dissection of the principles notion, however, appeared in 1947: Simon's *Administrative Behavior: A Study of Decision-Making Processes in Administration Organization.*

Simon understood that administrative decision makers wanted to make rational choices (i.e., the single "best" choice) but that there were a lot of variables standing in the way of locating the single most rational decision. In his book, Simon made the field aware that there were limits on information and computational abilities within any human institution. Where the purveyors of administrative principles had erred, in Simon's view, was in their assumptions that all alternatives were known, that the consequences of choosing any one of those alternatives were equally known, and that decision makers doggedly searched until they found the single best alternative from the standpoint of their own preferences. In questioning these assumptions, Simon argued that choices had to be discovered by searching for them; that typically only a relatively few alternatives could be considered; that information also had to be sought through a search process; and that decision makers did not select the single best alternative, but instead "satisficed," or chose the alternative that both satisfied and sufficed from their point of view.

Simon's perspective was less economic than behavioral. In contrast to the literature that argued for principles of administration, Simon suggested a more human process of decision making. Hence, Simon argued that the constraints on organizational choices not only should include those external factors found in the task environment of organizations but should include as well those constraints that existed as part of the human condition, such as limits on memory, rationality, and information. These notions ultimately waxed into Simon's theory of "bounded rationality," or the idea that people are rational decision makers—within limits. The ultimate effect of Simon's *Administrative Behavior* (other than earning him the Nobel Prize in 1978) and related critiques appearing in the late 1940s was to bury the belief that principles of administration, public or otherwise, could be discovered in the same sense that laws of science and nature could be.

By midcentury the two defining pillars of public administration—the politics/administration dichotomy and the principles of administration—had been abandoned by creative intellects in the field. This abandonment left public administration bereft of a distinct epistemological and intellectual identity.

Reaction to the Challenge, 1947–1950

In the same year that Simon decimated the traditional foundations of public administration in *Administrative Behavior*, he offered an alternative to the old paradigms. For Simon, a new paradigm for public administration meant that there ought to be two kinds of public administrationists working in harmony and reciprocal intellectual stimulation: those scholars concerned with developing "a pure science of administration" based on "a thorough grounding in social psychology," and a larger group concerned with "prescribing for public policy." This latter enterprise was far-ranging indeed. In Simon's view, prescribing for public policy "cannot stop when it has swallowed up the whole of political science; it must attempt to absorb economics and sociology as well." Nevertheless, both a "pure science of administration" and "prescribing for public policy" would be mutually reenforcing components: "There does not appear to be any reason why these two developments in the field of public administration should not go on side by side, for they in no way conflict or contradict."[16]

Despite a proposal that was both rigorous and normative in its emphasis, Simon's call for a "pure science" put off many scholars in public administration. For one thing, there already existed a growing irritation in the field with POSDCORB and other "principles of administration" on the basis of their implicit claims of representing a "pure science"; the challengers of the late 1940s had shown that the "principles of administration" were hardly the final expression of science, and consequently public administrationists were increasingly skeptical that the administrative phenomenon could be understood in wholly scientific terms. Second, Simon's urging that social psychology provided the basis for understanding administrative behavior struck many public administrationists as foreign and discomfiting; most of them had no training in social psychology. Third, because science was perceived as being "value-free," it followed that a "science of administration" logically would ban public administrationists from what many of them perceived as their richest sources of inquiry: normative political theory, the concept of the public interest, and the entire spectrum of human values. Although this interpretation may well have rested on a widespread misinterpretation of Simon's thinking (understandable, perhaps, given the wake of *Administrative Behavior*), as Golembiewski contends,[17] the reaction nonetheless was real.

The threat posed by Simon and his fellow challengers of the traditional paradigms was clear not only to most political scientists but to many public administrationists as well. For their part the public administrationists had both a carrot and a stick as inducements not only to remain within political science but to strengthen the intellectual linkages between the fields. The carrot was the maintenance of the logical conceptual connection between public administration and political science—that is, the public policy-making process. Public administration considered the "internal" stages of that process: the formulation of public policies within public bureaucracies and their delivery to the polity. Political science was perceived as considering the "external" stages of the process: the pressures in the polity generating political and social change. There was a certain logic in retaining this linkage in terms of epistemological benefits to both fields. The stick, as we have noted, was the worrisome prospect of retooling only to become a technically oriented "pure science" that might lose touch with political and social realities in an effort to cultivate an engineering mentality for public administration.

As we also have noted, political scientists, for their part, had begun to resist the growing independence of public administrationists and to question the field's action orientation as early as the mid-1930s. Political scientists, rather than advocating a public service and executive preparatory program as they had in 1914, began calling for, in the words of Lynton K. Caldwell, "intellectualized understanding" of the executive branch rather than "knowledgeable action" on the part of public administrators.[18] In 1952 Roscoe Martin wrote an article appearing in the *American Political Science Review* calling for the continued "dominion of political science over public administration."[19]

By the post–World War II era political scientists were well under the gun and could ill afford the breakaway of their most prestigious subfield. The discipline was in the throes of being shaken conceptually by the "behavioral revolution" that had occurred in other social sciences. The American Political Science Association was in financially tight straits. Political scientists were aware that not only had public administrationists threatened secession in the past but now other subfields, such as international relations, were restive. And in terms of both science and social science, it was increasingly evident that political science was held in low esteem by scholars in other fields. The formation of the National Science Foundation in 1950 brought the message to all who cared to listen that the chief federal science agency considered political science to be the distinctly junior member of the social sciences, and in 1953 David Easton confronted this lack of status directly in his influential book, *The Political System.*[20]

The capitulation of the public administrationists to pressures brought on them by political scientists and their own self-doubt about where the field was and should be going was expressed beyond cavil in the major public administration journal in 1950. John Merriman Gaus, a prestigious public administration scholar, penned his oft-quoted dictum in the tenth anniversary issue of *Public Administration Review:* "A theory of public administration means in our time a theory of politics also."[21] The die was cast.

Paradigm 3:
Public Administration as Political Science, 1950–1970

As a result of these essentially political concerns and the icy intellectual critiques of the field, public administrationists leaped back with some alacrity into the mother discipline of political science. The result was a renewed definition of locus—the governmental bureaucracy—but a corresponding loss of focus. Should the mechanics of budgets and public personnel policies be studied exclusively? Or should public administrationists consider the grand philosophic schemata of the "administrative Platonists" (as one political scientist called them),[22] such as Paul Appelby? Or should they, as urged by Simon, explore quite new fields of inquiry such as sociology, business administration, and social psychology as they related to the analysis of organizations and decision making?

In brief, this third phase of definition was largely an exercise in reestablishing the conceptual linkages between public administration and political science. But the consequence of this exercise was to "define away" the field, at least in terms of its analytical focus, its essential "expertise." Thus, writings on public administration in the 1950s spoke of the field as an "emphasis," an "area of interest," or even as a "synonym" of political science.[23] Even long-standing friends of public administration expressed their concern during this period. Frederick Mosher, for example, concluded, "Public administration stands in danger of . . . senescence,"[24] while Martin Landau stated his deeply held worry that public administration, "that lusty young giant of a decade ago, may now 'evaporate' as a field."[25]

These concerns, which focused largely on the research agenda of the field, were reflected in the curriculum of public administration as well. A survey conducted in 1961 of graduate education in public administration found such enormous diversity of forms and emphases in university programs[26] that one observer could accurately state, "The study of public administration in the United States is characterized by the absence of any fully comprehensive intellectual framework."[27] Public administration, as an identifiable field of study, began a long, downhill spiral.

Things got relatively nasty by the end of the 1950s and, for that matter, well into the 1960s. In 1962 public administration was not included as a subfield of political science in the report of the Committee on Political Science as a Discipline of the American Political Science Association. In 1964 a major survey of political scientists indicated a decline in faculty interest in public administration generally.[28] In 1967 public administration disappeared as an organizing category in the program of the annual meeting of the American Political Science Association. Waldo wrote in 1968 that "many political scientists not identified with Public Administration are indifferent or even hostile; they would sooner be free of it," and added that the public administrationist has an "uncomfortable" and "second-class citizenship."[29] Between 1960 and 1970 only 4 per cent of all the articles published in the five major political science journals dealt with public administration.[30] In the 1960s "P.A. types," as they often were called in political science faculties, often found themselves cast as "untouchables" in a caste system populated by self-designated Brahmins.

At least two developments occurred during this period that reflected in quite different ways the gradually tightening tensions between public administrationists and political scientists: the growing use of the case study as an epistemological device, and the rise and fall of comparative and development administration as subfields of public administration.

Case Studies

The development of the case method began in the 1930s, largely under the aegis of the Committee on Public Administration of the Social Science Research Council.[31] Typically, cases were reports written by practicing public administrators on managerial problems and how they solved them. This framework gave way in the mid-1940s to a new version conceived in the Graduate School of Public Administration at Harvard University, which followed the lines of the public administration case as we know it today. A joint, four-university program with foundation support resulted, called the Committee on Public Administration Cases. The Committee, in turn, engendered sufficient interest in the case method to encourage the establishment in 1951 of the Inter-University Case Program.

The Inter-University Case Program began to falter in the 1970s, but the cause of the case study was taken up in 1977 by the newly formed Education for Public Service Clearinghouse Project, supported by grants from the Ford and Sloan Foundations. The Project lasted only a year but succeeded in publishing a useful bibliography of public administration cases. In 1978, a successor organization, the Public Policy and Management Program for Case/Curriculum Development, was created via grants provided by the Sloan and Exxon Education Foundations, and was housed in the Intercollegiate Case Clearinghouse, a group that had been founded in 1957 with the purpose of developing case studies for business schools. The Intercollegiate Case Clearinghouse expired in 1980, but the Public Policy and Management Program for Case/Curriculum Development survived (and thrived) until 1985; it ultimately published three additional bibliographies of case studies, and developed a number of new cases. Currently, case development in public administration is conducted by the Association for Public Policy and Management, which took over the activities (but not the grants, which terminated in 1985) of the Public Policy and Management Program for Case/Curriculum Development.[32]

The significance of the case study to the development of the field of public administration is a somewhat peculiar one, quite aside from the innate value of the case method as a simulation-based teaching device and as an extraordinarily effective vehicle for illuminating questions of moral choice and decision-making behavior in the administrative milieu. Waldo believes that the emergence of the case method in the late 1940s and its growth throughout the 1950s reflect the response of public administrationists to the "behavioral revolution" in the social sciences generally. On the one hand, the traditional public administrationists, particularly those who entered the field in the 1930s, welcomed the case method as a means of being empirical and "behavioral," and thus provided an additional way of re-establishing the linkages between their field and political science. The case study also offered a comfortable alternative to Simon's call for a rigorous, "pure science of administration" that could—probably would—necessitate a methodological retooling on their part. On the other hand, those public administrationists who entered the field later, and who had been academically reared in political science departments when behaviorism was very much in vogue, were not especially at home with the case study as public administration's answer to the challenge of the behaviorists but temporarily agreed to the case method as an uneasy compromise. There was also a third grouping of public administrationists in the fifties and sixties who embraced the case study: the retired government bureaucrats, who occasionally were hired by political science departments when public administration was held in low professional esteem but in relatively high student demand. This group appreciated an academic approach to the field that identified closely with administrative experience.

The intellectual uneasiness surrounding the use of the case method reflects the condition of public administration at the time: a band of dispirited scholars, isolated from their colleagues but trying to cope in the only way they knew how. But this generalization did not apply to another group of "P. A. types": those who tilled the modish (and financially fertile) fields of comparative and development administration.

Comparative and Development Administration

Cross-cultural public administration, as the comparative approach also is called, is a fairly new development in the field. Prior to the abandonment of the principles of administration, it was assumed that cultural factors did not make any difference in administrative settings because principles, after all, were principles. As White said in 1936, a principle of administration "is as useful a guide to action in the public administration of Russia as of Great Britain, of Irak as of the United States."[33] But as Dahl and Waldo, among others, would later point out, cultural factors could make public administration on one part of the globe quite a different animal from public administration on another part.[34] By the late 1940s, in fact, courses in comparative public administration were appearing in university catalogs, and by the early 1950s the American Political Science Association, the American Society for Public Administration, and the Public Administration Clearing House were forming special committees or sponsoring conferences on comparative public administration. The real impetus came in 1962 when the Comparative Administration Group (CAG, founded in 1960) of the American Society for Public Administration received financing from the Ford Foundation that eventually totaled about $500,000.

The Ford Foundation's support of comparative administration (which has since stopped) appears to have stemmed from an altruistic interest in bettering the lot of poor people in the Third World through the improvement of governmental efficiency in the developing nations, and from a political interest in arresting the advance of communism, especially in Asia, by entrenching bureaucratic establishments composed of local elites—remember, the Ford Foundation's initial decision to support the field in a big way came at the height of the Cold War. The Foundation's emphasis on the Third World was especially enriching to a semiautonomous subfield of comparative public administration called development administration, which concentrates on the developing nations. Ironically, as we shall shortly see, the practical (if somewhat naive) motivations of the Ford Foundation underlying its funding of comparative and development administration were seldom shared by the recipients of the Foundation's grants.

Comparative public administration, as Ferrel Heady has explained, addresses five "motivating concerns" as an intellectual enterprise: the search for theory; the urge for practical application; the incidental contribution of the broader field of comparative politics; the interest of researchers trained in the tradition of administrative law; and the comparative analysis of ongoing problems of public administration.[35] Much of the work in comparative public administration revolves around the ideas of Fred W. Riggs, who "captured" (to quote one assessment)[36] the field's early interest in public administration in the developing nations, and who was simply a very prolific writer and substantial contributor to the theoretical development of the subfield in its early stages. From 1960 to 1970, when the subfield of development administration dominated comparative public administration, Riggs chaired ASPA's Comparative Administration Group.[37]

It was and is Riggs's intention and the intention of the comparative public administrationists generally to use their field as a vehicle for stiffening and strengthening theory in public administration. To borrow Riggs's terminology, comparative public administration is to do this by being empirical, nomothetic, and ecological; that is, put crudely, by being factual and scientific, abstracted and generalizable, systematic and nonparochial. In this emphasis, there always was a quantum of distaste in the ranks of CAG for studies that are rooted solely in the American experience.

Public administration has two differences with its comparative subfield. One is that the larger field is forthrightly and frankly culture-bound. The defense of American public administration's "parochialism" is much the same as that for "parochialism" of the behavioral sciences generally, and it is comprised of four main points:

1. All empirical theory rests on the values of science that guide the conduct of the scientific method;
2. The choice of subjects to study usually reflects the researcher's socialization in and the needs of his or her own society;
3. Because humankind is the object of study in the behavioral sciences, then humanity's values, viewpoints, and culture must be included as part of the theory to be developed, notably as intervening variables in correlational analyses;
4. The uses to which public administration theory and data are put in practice inevitably must be culture-bound.

A second difference that public administration generally has with comparative public administration specifically is the question of action versus theory. From its origins, American public administration has attempted to be "practitioner-oriented" and to be involved with the "real world," while comparative public administration, from its origins, has attempted to be "theory-building" and to seek knowledge for the sake of knowledge. Increasingly, this purely scholarly (as opposed to professional) thrust of comparative public administration has boded ill for the subfield. A spokesperson for the chief financier of CAG, the Ford Foundation, asked what "all this theorizing and all this study will amount to" in terms of improving the practice of public administration, and no one in comparative public administration ever really answered him.[38] In fact, the dominant theme among the members of CAG (although perhaps less emphatically among those involved in development administration) seemed to be to stick to their intellectual guns and to keep building theory as they perceived it. A survey of the CAG membership conducted in 1967 revealed that there was not a

> strongly stated appeal for linking the theoreticians with the practitioners . . . nor for an investment of resources in stimulating empirical research, nor for pursuing the work of the CAG into such practical realms as training and consulting. . . . [P]roposals to channel CAG efforts into the sphere of action received very short shrift among respondents.[39]

Not surprisingly, perhaps, the Ford Foundation terminated its support of CAG in 1971.

Comparative public administration has been productive and active as a subfield; reports of its death are premature, although comparative public administration does appear to have reached a critical point of development. Although CAG had achieved a membership of more than 500 by 1968, in 1973 it was disbanded and merged with the International Committee of the American Society for Public Administration. Relatedly, the field's major journal, *The Journal of Comparative Administration,* was terminated in 1974 after five years of publication. Analyses of core course requirements in Master of Public Administration degree programs across the country found that by the mid-1970s courses in comparative and development administration were virtually never required in the core MPA curriculum, and were almost never taken by students.[40]

Perhaps Golembiewski best sums up the dilemma (or what he calls the "fixation") of comparative and development administration in the eighties by noting, "Public administration should take full notice of the fact that comparative administration's failure rests substantially on a self-imposed failure experience. It set an unattainable goal, that is, in its early and persisting choice to seek a comprehensive theory or model in terms of which to define itself."[41]

Paradigm 4:
Public Administration as Management,
1956–1970

Partly because of their second-class citizenship status in a number of political science departments, some public administrationists began searching for an alternative. Although Paradigm 4 occurred roughly concurrently with Paradigm 3 in time, it never received the broadly based favor as a paradigm that political science garnered from public administrationists. Nonetheless, the management option (which sometimes is called "administrative science" or "generic management") was a viable alternative for a significant number of scholars in public administration, and for some, it still is. But in both the political science and management paradigms, the essential situation was one of public administration losing its identity and its uniqueness within the confines of some "larger" concept.

Management is a field that covers organization theory and behavior, planning, decision making, various techniques of "management science," such as path analysis and queuing theory, personnel administration, leadership, motivation, communication, management information systems, budgeting, auditing, productivity, and, occasionally, marketing.

As a paradigm, management provides a focus but not a locus. It offers techniques, often highly sophisticated techniques, that require expertise and specialization, but in what institutional setting that expertise should be applied is undefined. As in Paradigm 2, management is management wherever it is found; focus is favored over locus.

A number of developments, many stemming from the country's business schools, fostered the alternative paradigm of management. In 1956 the important journal *Administrative Science Quarterly* was founded by a public administrationist on the premise that public, business, and institutional administration were false distinctions—that administration was administration. Public administrationist Keith M. Henderson, among others, argued in the mid-1960s that organization theory was, or should be, the overarching focus of public administration.[42] And it cannot be denied that such works as James G. March and Herbert Simon's *Organizations* (1958), Richard Cyert and March's *A Behavioral Theory of the Firm* (1963), March's *Handbook of Organizations* (1965), and James D. Thompson's *Organizations in Action* (1967) gave solid theoretical reasons for choosing management, with an emphasis on organization theory, as the paradigm of public administration.

In the early 1960s "organization development" began its rapid rise as a specialty of management. As a focus, organization development represented a particularly tempting alternative to political science for many public administrationists. Organization development as a field is grounded in social psychology and values the "democratization" of bureaucracies, whether public or private, and the "self-actualization" of individual members of organizations. Because of these values, organization development was seen by many younger public administrationists as offering a very compatible area of research within the framework of management: democratic values could be considered, normative concerns could be broached, and intellectual rigor and scientific methodologies could be employed.

From the late fifties through the mid-sixties, a spate of scholars writing in a variety of management journals accelerated the drumbeat of generic management as the logical successor to more "parochial" paradigms, such as public administration and business administration.[43] Weighing heavily in the value structure of these scholars were the interdisciplinary nature of management studies and the necessity that university policymakers recognize this aspect and reorganize their management curricula accordingly.

These intellectual currents had a genuine impact on the curricula of universities. A 1961 survey of graduate study in public administration in the United States found that although the great majority of public administration programs were still located in political science departments, there was nonetheless "a ground-swell development that tends to pervade all others," and this was the idea of "administration" as a unifying epistemology in the study of institutions and organizations, both public and private.[44] Similarly, by 1962, as many as a fifth of the business administration programs in the United States, Canada, and Mexico joined the study of business administration with economics, public administration, and other social sciences.[45]

The first institutional expression of the management "ground swell" came in the 1950s with the founding of the School of Business and Public Administration at Cornell University, and over the years three models of the generic management school developed.[46] The "purest" of these were those schools of administrative science that were created consciously (indeed, on occasion, ideologically) as generic, and offer master's degrees only in "administration" or "management." The Graduate School of Management in the University of California at Irvine, founded in the mid-1960s, was the first edition cast in this mold, and the University of California at Riverside, Willamette, and Yale soon followed. Perhaps the most striking feature of these schools of administrative science is their size, or lack of it. The four extant examples have, on the average, fewer than twenty-two faculty each, or considerably fewer than a typical department of political science or management at a major university. In fact, if Yale University is excluded from the list, the average size of the remaining three (all of which are exclusively graduate) programs is fourteen full-time faculty members per school.[47]

Closely related to the school of administrative science is the school of management. In this version, a business ethic prevails, and little or no attempt is made to understand the phenomenon of public administration, which is perceived as an extension of business management; education that is good for business is good for government. Masters of Management or Masters of Business Administration are the only graduate degrees offered, and "public management" is offered as a minor option within these degree programs. The University of California at Los Angeles, Stanford, and Northwestern are examples.

The third variant of the generic management model is the combined school of business and public administration. Typically, these schools offer a common core curriculum for all students but house separate departments of public administration that offer their own degree programs. Examples include the Universities of Alaska and Missouri at Kansas City.

During the sixties and early seventies in particular, the generic management concept was especially modish. Suddenly it seemed that a number of public administrationists were discovering the line in Woodrow Wilson's seminal essay of 1887, "The field of administration is a field of business. It is removed from the hurry and strife of politics. . . ."[48]

The appeal of the generic management school is clear. But what is the basis for its appeal?

The appeal of the generic management school (aside from simply offering an alternative to departments of political science) rests on certain beliefs about the nature of the administrative phenomenon and how the study of administration should be implemented.

For example, one tenet of the management model is that there are significant phenomena common to all fields of management and that, therefore, a body of knowledge exists that is common to all fields of management. The first part of this statement—that there are significant phenomena common to all fields of management—is problematic at best, and the second part—that an agreed-upon body of knowledge exists that is common to all fields of management—appears to be denied by empirical research.

Are all kinds of management really that alike? The (admittedly fragmentary) indications are that they are not. Those successful businesspersons who have become public managers are among the first to deny that there are significant similarities between the public and private sectors, and public administrators who enter the corporate world experience comparable difficulties of transition.[49] In addition, those few attempts at empirically comparing public and private organizations also indicate a growing doubt that the public and private administrative sectors can be fruitfully approached as a single entity.[50] The emerging consensus of public administrationists increasingly appears to be that public and private management are, to cite the old saw, fundamentally alike in all unimportant respects. This conclusion appeals to common sense: business executives, after all, are not subject to the same constitutional constraints as are public executives.

We do not mean to imply in this conclusion that there are not undeniable commonalities among certain specialized areas that students of public and business administration do—and should—study. Organization theory, information theory (including computer science), and basic statistics are obvious examples, and there may be others (although one becomes increasingly hard-pressed to find "obvious" examples in addition to those just listed). But the point stands that there are more differences than similarities between public and private administration. For example, courses on finance, as conducted in public administration programs, are entirely different creatures from their counterparts in the business schools. Moreover, both the public administration and business administration curricula offer numerous courses that constitute terra incognita for one or the other. What, for instance, does public administration know about marketing? What does business administration know about intergovernmental relations? Why should either field care?

It follows that if public and private management are alike in all unimportant respects, then those disciplines that attempt to understand these separate managerial sectors must rely to a significant degree on different sets of knowledge. And research indicates this to be the case. A careful study of eight major, representative generic schools of management found that there were a total of thirty different courses comprising the "common" core of courses for a masters degree. Although there was some limited agreement among the generic schools with regard to eight courses that emphasized operations research, statistics, economics, accounting, finance, and organization theory, there nonetheless remained a "substantial amount of disagreement about the commonality of administrative tools and techniques."[51]

Beyond the basic rationale for generic schools of administration, there are certain arguments dealing with the implementation of the concept itself. One of these arguments is that faculty resources are likely to be equitably distributed among faculty teaching core courses and faculty teaching in more specialized areas, such as public administration. Yet the equitable allocation of resources among faculty in generic schools appears not to be the case. One reason why appeals to common sense. In a generic school, there often are as many viewpoints concerning fields that "need" management (e.g., business, government, education, health—the list is potentially endless) as there are faculty. Hence, in small schools in particular, it is difficult to acquire a critical mass of faculty in any given area, including public administration. Typically, this situation works against those faculty in generic schools who identify with public administration. One reason why is that the ratio of students enrolled in generic schools who are on a business administration track, in contrast to public administration, is approximately six to one.[52] Hence, according to one study, "the resultant tension between programmatic integrity and student demand naturally creates internal tensions among faculty assigned to the various programmatic elements, especially public administration. The resolution of these tensions has traditionally been to the detriment of public administration more than any other component of the generic program."[53]

Similarly, it is argued that the recruitment of students and placement of graduates in generic schools do not need to be differentiated among client groups. Again, this proposition must be viewed in the light of common sense. Certainly one difference between placement programs in business administration and in public administration is the fact that businesses typically blanket a major campus in their search for promising new graduates. Few government agencies, however, emulate this practice. Second, there are status problems between business administration students and those majoring in public administration. According to Michael A. Murray, "typically, public administration students are offered anywhere from $2,000 to $5,000 less for starting positions. The blow to the students' self worth can be devastating."[54]

Under such circumstances, it follows that students entering generic schools may be drawn disproportionately toward the private sector. Fragmentary data from generic schools of administration indicate that students who initially have career goals aimed at government switch over in large numbers to majoring in curricular tracks that redirect them toward a career in private enterprise.[55] It has been speculated that students who are initially interested in public administration careers when they enter generic schools switch to a business administration focus because the ambience of generic schools of management is fundamentally pro–private sector. Certainly those few courses that seem to be common among the core curricula at generic schools indicate a high sensitivity to the problems of business organizations and the workings of the economy, and therefore provide some nominal evidence underlying this concern. In any case, at least one public administrationist who has been associated with a generic school of management has concluded that students interested in the public sector suffer from a "second citizen syndrome" in generic schools.[56]

If the public administration students in generic schools of management are ultimately "captured" by the "B school" types, then a parallel phenomenon appears to happen with faculty as well. Although smaller generic schools appear to be more successful in integrating faculty than larger ones, a problem that frequently occurs within generic schools is a widening gulf between those faculty associated with the core curriculum and those faculty specializing in various kinds of management fields, such as public administration. Regrettably, at least for public administrationists and other "specialized" faculty, those faculty associated with the core curriculum "tend to set the standards for promotions and rewards within the school. Publication in the top rated business or public administration journals may come to be viewed less highly than publication in the *Administrative Science Quarterly* or any of the purely disciplinary journals. . . . The net result is that the faculty who are not aligned with the core disciplines face greater pressure in gaining acceptance by their colleagues and in achieving promotion and advancement within the school."[57]

The upshot of Paradigm 4 insofar as many public administrationists were and are concerned is that the field of public administration would exchange being, at best, an "emphasis" in political science departments for being, at best, a subfield in generic schools of management.

The Forces of Separatism: "Science and Society" and the "New Public Administration," 1965–1970

Even at its nadir during the period of Paradigms 3 and 4, public administration was sowing the seeds of its own renaissance. This process—quite an unconscious one at the time—took at least two distinct but complementary forms. One was the development of interdisciplinary programs in "science, technology, and public policy" (or similar titles) in major universities, and the other was the appearance of the "new public administration."

"Science and Society"

The evolution of "science and society" curricula in universities occurred largely during the late 1960s. These were the intellectual forerunners of a later and deeper scholarly interest in the relationships between knowledge and power, bureaucracy and democracy, technology and management, and related "technobureaucratic" dimensions.[58] These programs, although broadly interdisciplinary, often were dominated by public administrationists located in political science departments. By the late 1960s, there were about fifty such programs, and they were situated for the most part in the top academic institutions of the country. It was largely this new focus of science, technology, and public policy that gave those public administrationists connected with political science departments any claim to intellectual distinction during the 1960s, and helped offset the loss of a disciplinary identity that then beset public administration. This renewed identity came in part because the focus of science, technology, and public policy did not (and does not) rely conceptually on the pluralist thesis favored by political science. Instead, the focus is elitist rather than pluralist, synthesizing rather than specializing, and hierarchical rather than communal.

The "New Public Administration"

The second development was that of the "new public administration." In 1968, Waldo, as Albert Schweitzer Professor in Humanities of Syracuse University, sponsored a conference of young public administrationists on the new public administration, the proceedings of which subsequently were published as a book in 1971, entitled *Toward a New Public Administration: The Minnowbrook Perspective.* The volume remains the key work in this focus.

The focus was disinclined to examine such traditional phenomena as efficiency, effectiveness, budgeting, and administrative techniques. Conversely, the new public administration was very much aware of normative theory, philosophy, and activism. The questions it raised dealt with values, ethics, the development of the individual member in the organization, the relation of the client with the bureaucracy, and the broad problems of urbanism, technology, and violence. If there was an overriding tone to the new public administration, it was a moral tone.

In one respect, the new public administration paralleled the "new political science," a movement that was occurring simultaneously and that represented a desire by younger political scientists to call an end to the now-stultified "behavioral revolution" and broach more normative concerns. Nevertheless, with hindsight the "new public administration" can be viewed as a call for independence from both political science (it was not, after all, ever called the "new politics of bureaucracy") and administrative science (because administrative science always has been emphatically technical rather than normative in approach).

The science-and-society and the new-public-administration movements were short-lived. Science, technology, and public policy programs eventually devolved into specialized courses on such topics as information systems, growth management, and environmental administration, while the new public administration never lived up to its ambitions of revolutionizing the discipline. Nevertheless, both movements had a lasting impact on public administration in that they nudged public administrationists into reconsidering their traditional intellectual ties with both political science and administrative science, and contemplating the prospects of academic autonomy. By 1970, the separatist movement was underway.

Parent Versus Foster Parent: Assessing the Impact of Paradigms 3 and 4

Political science, the intellectual "parent" of public administration, and administrative science, its "foster parent," were major influences on the evolution of the field. Conversely, the development of public administration as a field within both of these paradigms had certain effects not only on public administration but on political science and administrative science as well. What were some of these effects?

Paradigm 3: The Mutual Impact of Progeny and Parent

Political science clearly has had more profound effects on the field of public administration than has administrative science. Public administration was born in the house of political science, and its early rearing occurred in its backyard. The fundamental precepts of American political science—the self-evident worth of democracy, a pluralistic polity, political participation, equality under law, and due process are examples of these precepts—continue to hold sway among even the most independently minded public administrationists. Although it can be convincingly argued that the American civic culture inculcates these values among all its intellectuals, and that American public administrationists would cherish democratic values regardless of their experiences in political science, it nonetheless seems valid that the environment of political science sharpened and deepened the commitment of public administrationists to the country's core constitutional concepts. If, to indulge in speculation, public administration had been born and bred in the nation's business schools, would we have the same kind of academic field that we have today? Perhaps not. In any case, one can argue that political science was a salutary former of the field in laying its philosophic and normative foundations.

Beyond this important point, there are more specific effects that the two fields have had on each other, and two of them are considered here. One is, for want of a better term, the "problem" of public policy. The other is less an "effect" and more a condition of political science that has been illuminated by the departure of public administration: the self-destructive impulses of political science as a field of study.

THE PROBLEM OF PUBLIC POLICY. Occurring concurrently with the evolution of "self-aware" public administration was the development of the subfield of "public policy" within political science departments. And the subfield emerged for many of the same reasons that motivated public administration to secede from political science, particularly the concern shared by some political scientists that their field was far more concerned with science than politics. One of the early contributors to the public policy subfield, Austin Ranney, put it well: "At least since 1945 most American political scientists have focussed their professional attention mainly on the *processes* by which public policies are made and have shown relatively little concern with their *contents*."[59] Ranney and his colleagues took issue with this emphasis and believed that a more substantive approach was needed. From its beginnings, in short, the subfield of public policy has been an effort to "apply" political science to public affairs; its inherent sympathies with the "practical" field of public administration are real, and many of those scholars who identify with the public policy subfield find themselves in a twilight zone between political science and public administration.

Perhaps the first formal recognition by political scientists of the importance of public policy was a small meeting held in 1965 under the auspices of the Committee on Governmental and Legal Processes of the Social Science Research Council. Out of this meeting emerged "a consensus that the most timely and urgent question . . . is: What professional expertise and obligations, if any, have political scientists to study, evaluate, and make recommendations about the contents of public policy?"[60] Two Committee-sponsored conferences on the question followed in 1966 and 1967, and the papers presented at them were published in the following year.[61]

Also in 1967, the American Political Science Association's Annual Conference featured a panel on public policy under its American Politics section, and four papers on public policy were presented at the meeting. In 1970, the Association granted public policy its first section at its annual conference; by now the number of papers on the topic exceeded thirty. By 1982, 140 papers on public policy analysis were given at the annual meeting, involving thirty-six panels.[62]

Public policy was even more popular among political scientists than the proliferating presentations of papers on the topic indicate. During this period the Policy Studies Organization was founded (in 1972), and it provided additional outlets for political scientists interested in public policy—within a decade of its creation, the Organization had more than 2,000 members. The Policy Studies Organization publishes *Policy Studies Review*, which reflects a more public administration hue, and *Policy Studies Journal*, which casts a longer shadow in political science. But the Organization's membership appears to be dominated by political scientists—more than two thirds are political scientists.[63]

The Policy Studies Organization, of course, is not the only association of scholars with an interest in public policy. The Association for Public Policy Analysis and Management and the Public Choice Society are examples of others, and there are more. But most of these groups have an intellectual cast that is distinctly economic or operations research in nature. Those political scientists who belong to such associations seem to be repentant about their original choice of a field and often are found delivering papers at professional conferences on the subject of how they really wanted to be economists.

An important component of the public policy subfield is comparative, or cross-national, public policy. The specialization began to emerge in the early 1970s, and in 1975 a book on the topic received the Gladys M. Kammerer Award from the American Political Science Association.[64] More than a quarter of the public policy papers presented at the annual conferences of the American Political Science Association are in the comparative area.[65]

Public policy as a subfield can be viewed as bisecting along two increasingly distinct intellectual branches. One is the substantive branch. The dominant mode of public policy as a subfield of political science has always been and continues to be substantive issues—what Ranney called "contents," and what Simon, years earlier, called "prescribing for public policy." Roughly half of the papers presented at the American Political Science Association's annual conference in any given year deal with substance, such as the environment, welfare, education, or energy. The journals and papers published by the Policy Studies Organization also reflect this substantive bias. Paramountly, the substantive branch of public policy means a paper, article, book, or course on "The Politics of" some current event.

The other, less leafy but nonetheless supple branch of public policy is the theoretical branch. Susan B. Hansen has usefully categorized the literature comprising this branch (which she calls "three promising theoretical trends") in terms of political economy, organization theory, and program evaluation and implementation.[66]

The "problem" of public policy as a subfield of political science is what it symbolizes for both political science and public administration.

First, political scientists and public administrationists seem to have different definitions of what they are doing in the subfield and why. To generalize is always dangerous, and particularly so in this case, but those public policy researchers who identify primarily with political science seem to be those who, by and large, work on the subfield's substantive branch ("The Politics of" something), while those who identify with public administration seem to be found more frequently on its theoretical branch and are more concerned with problems of research design, public choice, implementation, organization, efficiency, effectiveness, productivity, and those kinds of public policy questions that are only incidentally related to matters of substance, prescription, and content. The differences in these two approaches parallel the differences that the field of public administration has with political science: Public administrationists have always preferred studying questions of public policy that relate to "knowledgeable action" as opposed to an "intellectualized understanding" of public issues.

Regarding these two approaches to the study of public policy, the future seems fairer for that preferred by public administrationists. Although there will always be both room and need for each tack, the substantive one has a deadly deficiency in the longer haul: It is, by dint of its structure, essentially atheoretical. One cannot "build" theory on the basis of ultimately transitory public events. True, there will always be public policies for health, energy, environment, welfare, or whatever, but how does understanding these issues as discrete phenomena get us very far in understanding the global process of public policy—its formulation, execution, and ongoing revision—so that we can develop ideas that enable us to make more responsive policies in all areas and deliver them more effectively? Individual studies of individual public issues often yield us an appreciation of the issues involved, and this is important and useful; but aside from their utility as case histories, these studies cannot really address the larger theoretical questions, the answers to which can, one hopes, be of use to public decision makers regardless of the policy arena in which they find themselves.

A more worrisome aspect of political science's preference for the substantive approach to policy studies is that its intellectual evolution will parallel that of comparative public administration, in that it will try to do too much and end up, to requote Golembiewski on the dilemma of comparative public administration, creating "a self-imposed failure experience . . . an unattainable goal."[67] Certainly this dreary prospect at least seems possible when we appreciate the number of public policies extant, all of them fairly panting to be analyzed, and the problem is especially evident in the area of comparative public policy. The literature of comparative public policy is heavily substantive,[68] but as Elliot J. Feldman points out, the specialty has yet to develop a "guiding theory" of its own to focus research.[69]

A second problem of public policy analysis in its political science mode is that it smacks of an effort by political scientists to fill the vacuum created by the departure of public administration—a last gasp, croaked in the general direction of "hands-on" political science and, of course, "relevance." In this fashion, political science, symbolically at least, retains public administration without admitting it. The fact that the explosive growth of the public policy subfield correlates remarkably in time (i.e., the 1970s) with the secession of public administration lends some credence to this notion.

There is nothing sinister in this effort to re-establish within political science a concern with what is "applied" and "relevant" under a new guise called public policy, but if this is the motivation, then it seems unlikely to succeed. Public policy in its substantive mode may not be, as we have noted, a vehicle ready for long journeys. It is no replacement for public administration. An understanding of education policy, for example, is no substitute for an understanding of public personnel administration, public budgeting and finance, organization theory, intergovernmental management, program evaluation, and the several other interrelated areas that comprise the public administration field.

POLITICAL SCIENCE AND THE DESTRUCTION OF DOMESTICUS. The subfield of public policy highlights the ambivalence of attitudes that many political scientists hold about addressing problems of action, practice, and the grass roots. But the opinions held among political scientists about these values—which can be encapsulated in the phrase, "education for knowledgeable action"—may actually be stronger than mere ambivalence. At root, the field of political science may be hostile to such concerns.

It is noteworthy in this respect that political science has accepted the secession of public administration with remarkably good grace. A review of the discipline published by the American Political Science Association in 1983 contains no discussion of public administration as a subfield in a compendium that covers nineteen chapters and more than 600 pages.[70] The volume itself stands as testimony not only to the reality of public administration's emergence as a separate field but to the quiet acceptance (perhaps relief) by political scientists over its departure.

Despite the equanimity of political scientists, however, the effects of public administration and its subsequent secession on political science are both profound and disquieting. A recent assessment of "the state of the discipline" conducted by political scientists made the following points: "The growth in Masters in Public Administration programs also drained off some of the bright career oriented students. About a third of political science departments had reported a decline in the quality of new Ph.Ds. . . ."[71] The assessment further concluded that public administration was one of only two "pockets of optimism" among political science faculty. Most political scientists had experienced a "statistically significant deterioration in career satisfaction from 1963 to 1976."[72]

Although it would be difficult to prove that the departure of public administration from political science has resulted in a lower quality of graduate students and an emotionally depressed faculty in political science departments, to speculate on such causalities does not stretch the bounds of reason. What may stretch the bounds of reason, however, is the apparent determination of political scientists to disassociate themselves from programs that have long been central in subsidizing political science departments through high enrollments, and that increasingly are evidencing renewed intellectual vitality and a sense of academic purpose. Public administrationists should not forget that they were not, and often are not, the only ones who want them to get out of political science departments; typically, political scientists also want public administrationists to get out of political science departments. In fact, in many cases, particularly in the 1970s, public administrationists and political scientists *mutually* decided that separation was in the best interest of both fields.

We have reviewed why public administrationists thought it was in their best interest to disassociate themselves from political scientists, but a remaining question is why political scientists also agreed—often readily. I do not know the answer, but there seems to be more to the eagerness among political scientists to divest themselves of public administration than merely their desire to distance themselves from a field that has always taken pride in having a practical turn of mind. This eagerness seems to stem also from an inclination among political scientists to put daylight between themselves and any kind of academic enterprise that deals with domestic concerns. After all, not only has public administration been bid a fond adieu by political scientists, but so have related fields that have a distinctly American cast, such as urban politics and criminal justice.

Now we are beginning to hear reports that such baseline courses (certainly insofar as student enrollments are concerned) as American government and state and local politics are being given increasingly short shrift within the nation's major political science departments. If these reports are at all accurate, then they constitute impressive evidence indeed to the capacities for self-destruction among America's political scientists.

Paradigm 4: The Favorable Factor of a Foster Parent

If political science was profoundly influential on the evolution of public administration, management was less so. But, in many ways, the impact of management on public administration was also more positive. In part, this was because the field of management entered into the upbringing of public administration when the field was beginning its adolescence and, unlike political science, it was not a blood relative; consequently, public administration was granted more independence and breathing room to grow and develop on its own. This is not to say that the household environment created by management for public administration was one of warmth and succor. It was not. But instead of treating public administration like an abusive parent, as political science occasionally did, management let public administration stay in its house, like an absent-minded aunt who was never quite sure who was living in which room and who often forgot to serve meals.

Management had at least three distinct and beneficial influences on public administration: It forced public administration to examine more closely what the "public" in "public administration" meant; it convinced many public administrationists that a whole new set of methodologies was needed; and it provided public administration with a model of how to assess what, as a field, it was teaching and why.

UNDERSTANDING THE "PUBLIC" IN PUBLIC ADMINISTRATION. One of the principal effects of the management paradigm on public administration concerned the distinction between "public" and "private" administration. When public administrationists had thought about this distinction at all (as some had done in the eras of Paradigms 1 and 3, when the notion of locus was emphasized over focus), *public* administration was defined largely in institutional terms—i.e., the government bureaucracy. But the experience of public administrationists who participated in Paradigm 4 (and to some degree in Paradigm 2) forced them to reconsider what the "public" in public administration really meant.

These public administrationists saw, perhaps more clearly than did others whose experiences related more to political science, that the field had to be defined in something other than institutional terms. "Real world" phenomena were and are making the public/private distinction an increasingly difficult one to define empirically. The research and development contract; the military-industrial complex; the roles of regulatory agencies and their relations with industry; the emergence of "third sector," or nonprofit, organizations; and the developing awareness of what one author has called "the margins of the state"[73] in reference to such phenomena as the expansive growth of government corporations and the privatization of public policy, all have conspired to make *public* administration an elusive entity.

To deal with these problems, public administrationists began to desert the traditional paradigms that defined public administration in terms of institutional locus and began to cast the field into terms of philosophic, normative, and ethical concepts. Hence, in this new, more dynamic approach, the "public" in public administration became those phenomena that affected the public interest. Thus, rather than concentrating on the Department of Defense, for example, as its proper public locus and leaving, say, Lockheed Corporation to students of business management, public administrationists began to understand that the Department's contractual and political relationships with Lockheed should now be their central object of study, inasmuch as these relationships clearly involved the public interest. This new, noninstitutional and normative definition of the "public" in public administration was brought about in large part by the difficulties encountered by public administrationists who were working within the confines of generic schools of management in explaining their field to their academic colleagues—who, on occasion, were somewhat less than sympathetic to the role of government in society and even to the notion of the public interest.[74]

THE NEW METHODOLOGIES. A second impact that Paradigm 4 had on public administration was methodological. Public administrationists associated with political science departments had long known (or at least it was dawning on them with accelerating speed) that the methodologies of political science were inappropriate to the concerns of public administration. Often these scholars looked to the management schools for illumination and guidance. In many cases, because the public administrationists of Paradigm 3 did not fully understand the methodologies employed by the management scientists, they put great (and frequently inappropriate) stock in their potential utility. In other instances, public administrationists of the Paradigm 3 mode rejected the methodologies of management out of hand because they found them threatening, or were ignorant of them.

The combined consequence of these reactions to the management methodologies was the ultimate recognition by the more committed public administrationists (whether they were found in political science departments or in management schools) that wholly new methodologies were needed for the field. Indeed, the development of these methodologies was central to the emergence of "self-aware" public administration.

In some cases, adapting on a selective basis existing methodologies of both political science and administrative science—such as survey research (from political science) and operations research (from management)—was appropriate. But, by and large, new methods were needed, and *evaluation research* or *program evaluation* have become the terms that we presently associate with many of the developing bundles of methodologies that public administration calls its own.[75] The emphasis on these methodologies is on whether public programs are effective, efficient, and increasingly, whether they are needed. They borrow techniques from a variety of disciplines and have a clearly "applied research" cast.

Closely related to evaluation research are the continually evolving methods of budgeting, ranging literally from A (administrative accounts budgeting) to Z (zero-base budgeting). Increasingly, these "budgetary" concepts are becoming management control strategies that use the methodologies of program evaluation in determining budget allocations.[76]

Finally, there is a plethora of existing quantitative techniques that fall under the general (and unsatisfactory) rubrics of "public decision making" or "public management," and that are being increasingly transformed and adapted to a governmental context. These include probability theory, statistical comparisons, linear correlations and linear programming (particularly sensitivity analysis and the simplex method), critical path method, benefit-cost analysis, decision trees, queuing theory, public choice theory, simulations, and management information systems, among others. There have been a number of recent works that do a fine job in applying these and other methods to problems of the public sector.[77]

LEARNING HOW TO TAKE ONESELF SERIOUSLY. A final area in which the management paradigm influenced the evolution of public administration as a field of study was the relatively serious way in which the business schools took their enterprise. Compared to political science departments, at least, the process of educating students in generic schools of management and in business schools was and is far more focused, self-analytical, systematic, and, well, *serious.* This is not to say that individual political scientists or public administrationists take their classroom responsibilities lightly; by and large, they do not. But as a field, political science has never put itself through the long-term self-examination and critical assessment that management education has.

During the decade of the 1950s, business educators inflicted upon themselves a well-financed and searching examination of their curricula and instructional programs. The resulting reports—two thick volumes often containing sharp criticism of current practices—had profound effects on business education.[78] By contrast, the only comparable effort conducted by political science during this period resulted in a book that has been dismissed by political scientists themselves as one whose "very triteness and superficiality . . . made it important."[79] A later attempt to redress this problem focused more specifically on public administration education but still as it was conducted within the environment of political science, and the results were much the same.[80] Public administrationists criticized the report as dealing with "venerable and eminently fatiguing issues,"[81] and its only lasting impact seems to have been that it led to the field's concern with a "new public administration."[82] The major opus borne by the "new public administration" (Frank Marini's *Toward a New Public Administration* of 1971), however, ultimately had little impact on the public administration curriculum beyond, perhaps, sensitizing the field to the importance of educating for ethics.

These reports on education for the public service appeared between 1951 and 1967, when public administration was dominated by political science, and their superficiality in dealing with the problems they sought to address was rendered all the more stark when compared to the reports of 1958 that had been prepared by business educators. This lesson has not been lost on public administrationists of the 1980s. A proliferating number of analyses of all aspects of public administration education by individual scholars have appeared since the mid-1970s (only a few of which have been cited in this chapter), indicating a renewed concern with the problem. More significantly, however, the National Association of Schools of Public Affairs and Administration has grown into a body of more than 220 member institutions, is enviably well funded, and is maturing into an organization that has the greatest likelihood of producing a self-evaluation of public administration education that parallels in scope and quality the analyses of business education conducted in the 1950s.[83] Perhaps the model of a searching and systemic self-assessment that has been provided by the business education community may become the single most constructive effect that Paradigm 4 ultimately has on the field of public administration.

Paradigm 5:
Public Administration as Public Administration:
1970–?

In 1970, the National Association of Schools of Public Affairs and Administration (NASPAA) was founded. The formation of NASPAA represented not only an act of secession from the field of political science and management by public administrationists but a rise of self-confidence as well.

NASPAA's origins lay in the Council on Graduate Education for Public Administration, which had been founded in the 1950s by a small group of graduate programs in the field. The decision in 1970 to dramatically expand the scope of this unusually cozy group (and later, in 1983, the decision to become a formal professional accrediting agency for public administration programs) indicated a determination by public administration educators to take public responsibility for upgrading the educational backgrounds and technical competence of the nation's government managers. By 1970, as represented by the founding of the National Association of Schools of Public Affairs and Administration, public administration could properly call itself, and increasingly be recognized as, a separate field of study.

The profile of public administration as a "self-aware" field reflects in many ways what Simon predicted it should become in 1947. Although there is not yet a focus for the field in the form of a "pure science of administration," progress, particularly in the area of organization theory and information science, has been made in this direction. Additionally, considerable progress has been made in refining the applied techniques and methodologies of public administration. There has been, perhaps, less movement toward delineating a locus for the field, or what Simon called "prescribing for public policy." Nevertheless, public administration does appear to be emphasizing such areas as state and local government, executive management, administrative law, and all those questions that seek to explain what "the public interest" is in a technobureaucratic "Big Democracy."

The emerging curriculum of graduate public administration education reflects these emphases. A more or less agreed-upon core curriculum seems to have developed for public administration education at the graduate level, and it centers on the environment of public administration (i.e., general introductory courses that focus on the role of the bureaucracy in a democracy), quantitative methods, public budgeting and financial management, organization theory, and personnel administration. The average number of required hours in these core areas grew from fewer than thirty-nine in 1974–75 to more than forty-one in 1980–81, with the primary expansion being quantitative methods and public budgeting and financial management. It appears that this increase in the required number of hours taken in the core curriculum occurred at the cost of electives that students might otherwise take.[84]

The increase in required courses in the core curriculum reflects to some degree the growing clout of the National Association of Schools of Public Affairs and Administration, which strongly favors a common core curriculum at the graduate level. By 1983, seventy universities had been granted the functional equivalent of accreditation by NASPAA, and one survey found that nearly two thirds of the directors of masters programs in public administration believed that those programs approved by NASPAA had higher prestige. Moreover, a plurality of respondents felt that a program approved by NASPAA was in a better position to recruit higher-quality faculty and higher-quality students, and to offer a higher-quality curriculum.[85]

More than 5,000 regular faculty members are teaching in graduate public administration programs. For the most part, these are highly interdisciplinary programs, although approximately a quarter of the public administration faculty have earned their degrees specifically in the field of public administration. The second largest group (about 16 per cent) are political scientists teaching in public administration programs; most of this group have their faculty appointments in political science departments. The remaining faculty come from economics, business administration, planning, statistics, computer science, urban affairs, sociology, psychology, health, law, social work, engineering, history, geography, and criminal justice, in roughly that order.[86] Most of these 5,000 faculty members do not have full-time appointments in public administration; fewer than 1,000, in fact, can make such a claim. Most of these graduate programs are also quite small, averaging slightly more than five professors per program, and the average number of full-time faculty in the programs is only four. A 1980 study determined that only 11 per cent of graduate public administration programs had more than ten full-time faculty in them.[87]

Table 2.1 details the organizational pattern of public administration programs from 1973 through 1983, as determined by surveys conducted of institutional members of the National Association of Schools of Public Affairs and Administration. The number of public administration programs that were members of NASPAA nearly doubled during those

TABLE 2.1 Organizational Patterns of Public Administration Programs, 1973–1983

Organizational Pattern	1973	1975	1977	1979	1981	1983
1. Separate Professional Schools	25(25%)	29(25%)	32(20%)	29(15%)	32(16%)	26(14%)
2. Separate Departments in Large Unit	23(23%)	35(25%)	49(31%)	64(34%)	63(33%)	64(34%)
3. P.A. Program Combined with Another Professional School or Department (e.g., Business Admin.)	17(17%)	22(16%)	16(10%)	20(10%)	20(10%)	26(14%)
4. P.A. Program within Political Science	26(36%)	52(37%)	62(39%)	70(37%)	74(40%)	70(38%)
5. Unclassified Department	—	—	—	8(4%)	3(1%)	0
Total	101(100%)	138(100%)	156(100%)	185(100%)	192(100%)	186(100%)

Source: Data from the 1974, 1976, 1978, 1980, 1982 and 1984 NASPAA Directories. Percentages have been rounded.

74

ten years, and those programs organized as separate professional schools or departments burgeoned by nearly 50 per cent; the most impressive growth rate among all types of organizational alternatives occurred among separate departments of public administration—an increase of almost two thirds. Nevertheless, public administration programs located in political science departments, as Table 2.1 shows, account for 38 per cent of all public administration programs (actually up slightly from ten years earlier), and they grew by 62 per cent from 1973 through 1983.

If public administration has really seceded from political science, then why are NASPAA members situated in political science departments proliferating so rapidly and continuing to comprise such a large plurality of public administration programs? Although the answers to this question must be speculative, they are not unreasonable. For one, NASPAA's prestige (and, indeed, public administration's prestige) has developed over the years, and more public administration programs—even those located in political science departments—are finding it judicious to shoulder the not insubstantial costs of joining NASPAA.

Second, those departments of political science that are joining NASPAA, especially in recent years, seem to be relatively small but with active public administration faculties. Hence, the growth of public administration programs in political science departments among NASPAA's members may well reflect, unlike the situation of the fifties and sixties, the growth of public administration programs that are relatively powerful within their academic units and have enough clout to get their department heads to pay the annual dues needed to join NASPAA, even in a time of tight budgets.

Finally, the most striking trend shown in the table should not be overlooked: The growth of separate departments of public administration. After 1975, virtually all these units were newly created and joined NASPAA almost immediately after being founded, in contrast to long-standing political science departments that finally decided joining NASPAA would be a good idea. The secession, in short, is real.

There are some 21,000 students enrolled in masters degree programs in public administration across the country. Forty-two per cent are women, 12 per cent are black, and 4 per cent are of Hispanic origin.[88]

Students in MPA programs are an unusual group. Sixty-eight per cent have jobs, and 17 per cent are taking courses at off-campus sites.[89] Sixty-five per cent are part-time students,[90] and more than half of the students are twenty-five years of age or older.[91] There are also approximately 8,000 undergraduates registered as public administration majors, of whom 24 per cent are part-time students,[92] in contrast to the nearly two thirds of the graduate students who attend MPA programs on a part-time basis.

To meet the needs of part-time students who have jobs often requires some innovative teaching methods. For the most part, public administration faculties have developed delivery systems for their programs that involve greater convenience for their student clienteles without sacrificing educational quality. About three fourths of public administration programs offer courses during the evening, and a number hold late-afternoon classes, lunchtime classes, and courses on weekends.[93] Nearly 60 per cent offer courses away from the main campus in an effort to take the classes to where the students are. Typically, these courses are offered for credit at the graduate level, but workshops, in-house training programs, and nondegree programs are also offered, as well as a few undergraduate courses. These courses are not a different kind of specialized degree program but are an integral part of the regular MPA degree program that is offered on the main campus. The off-campus component of the MPA degree appears to be growing and involves approximately 10,000 students.[94]

Despite a genuine and sincere effort by faculty to meet the needs of an adult student and professional student clientele, there seems to be some difference of opinion between students and the faculty about what kinds of classes should be offered. A number of studies have concluded that practitioners of public administration want more courses in budgeting, economics, and financial management and fewer courses in research methods, an area that is becoming increasingly required among public administration programs.[95]

The response of public administration educators to this difference of opinion appears to have been a compromise of sorts: *Both* quantitative methods and budgeting and financial management have increased their share of the core curriculum at the expense of electives in the typical MPA program.[96] Hence, educators in public administration have responded to both what students have expressed themselves as wanting and what, apparently, the educators themselves believe to be what their students need. Whether this compromise is completely in the best interest of the field is open to debate. As one observer of the public administration education scene has asked, in the context of the growing emphasis on quantitative methods:

> Does the public sector really need whiz kids? Perhaps in a few places. For the much greater part, the analytic ability must be coupled with the ability to get things done. Paper and people must be coordinated and cajoled. Good algorithms for this are very scarce. . . . Those who advance in the bureaucracy are generally those with staying power. Those who come to a large public organization mainly to achieve lofty, programmatic goals, to make important changes in the lives of their times, do not often become bureaucratic successes. They and their techniques tire and go away to universities, to professions, to educational television.[97]

Finally, there appears to be one longer-range problem that ultimately must be addressed by public administrationists in their "self-aware" mode. This is the question of education for new professors of public administration. It is not necessarily good, for example, that fewer than a quarter of the regular faculty members in public administration programs have their terminal degrees in public administration, and that fewer than a fifth of the estimated 5,000 regular faculty teaching in public administration programs do so on a full-time basis.[98] Yet the number of new doctorates entering the public administration education field is relatively small. Approximately 200 earned doctorates in public administration are awarded each year.[99] We can gain some notion of how small the potential pool of doctorates in public administration is when we realize that the field of political science, for example, is turning out almost as many Ph.D.s as public administration programs are turning out terminal masters degrees![100] Moreover, many of the recipients of new D.P.A.s and Ph.D.s in public administration do not plan to enter the cloisters of academic life but to use their doctorates in the pursuit of different kinds of professional objectives.

Adding to the problem are questions about the academic quality of some of these doctoral programs. Roughly 30 per cent of *all* the new doctorates in public administration are awarded by a single institution, Nova University. Nova conducts D.P.A. programs across the country and has only nine full-time faculty. It relies heavily on part-time faculty and intensive off-campus instruction, and does not specialize in encouraging extensive contact between its roving instructors and their students.[101]

Are these the kinds of programs we want to develop the public administration professoriate of the next generation?

A Note About the Next Century

Public administration has come a long way since 1887; during the last hundred years, it became an academic field. In doing so, it was forced to wage some of the toughest political battles that have ever been fought on American campuses, and wrestle with some of the most confounding intellectual dilemmas confronting professional education. But the field nonetheless emerged.

Perhaps the single most critical challenge now facing public administration is that of faculty for the future. It is faculty who define intellectual paradigms, shape and direct academic fields, and nourish the professions that they support. Developing more doctoral programs of high quality is absolutely central to the future of public administration as a field of study, and vital to the health of democratic government.

Good public servants are less likely to serve unless they have good professors.

Endnotes

1. Dwight Waldo, "Introduction: Trends and Issues in Education for Public Administration," in *Education for Public Service: 1979,* Guthrie S. Birkhead and James D. Carroll, eds. (Syracuse: Maxwell School of Citizenship and Public Affairs, Syracuse University, 1979), pp. 13–14.
2. Robert T. Golembiewski, *Public Administration as a Developing Discipline. Part I: Perspectives on Past and Present* (New York: Marcel Dekker, Inc., 1977).
3. Woodrow Wilson, "The Study of Administration," *Political Science Quarterly* 2:197–22 (June) 1887; reprinted 50:48–506 (December) 1941.
4. Richard J. Stillman, II, "Woodrow Wilson and the Study of Administration: A New Look at an Old Essay," *American Political Science Review* 67:587 (June) 1973.
5. Frank J. Goodnow, *Politics and Administration* (New York: Macmillan, 1900), pp. 10–11.
6. *Proceedings of the American Political Science Association, 1913–1914,* p. 264, as cited in Lynton K. Caldwell, "Public Administration and the Universities: A Half-Century of Development," *Public Administration Review* 25:54 (March) 1965.
7. Committee on Practical Training for Public Service, American Political Science Association, *Proposed Plan for Training Schools for Public Service* (Madison, WI: American Political Science Association, 1914), p. 3.
8. Dwight Waldo, "Public Administration," in *Political Science: Advance of the Discipline,* Marian D. Irish, ed. (Englewood Cliffs, NJ: Prentice-Hall, 1968), pp. 153–189.
9. Morris B. Lambie, ed. *Training for the Public Service: The Report and Recommendations of a Conference Sponsored by the Public Administration Clearing House* (Chicago: Public Administration Clearing House, 1935).
10. Caldwell, "Public Administration and the Universities," p. 57.
11. Waldo, "Introduction," p. 15.
12. Donald C. Stone, "Birth of ASPA—Elective Effort in Institution Building," *Public Administration Review* 35:87 (January) 1975.
13. Golembiewski, *Public Administration as a Developing Discipline,* p. 23.
14. Lyndall Urwick, "Organization as a Technical Problem," in *Papers on the Science of Administration,* Luther Gulick and L. Urwick, eds. (New York: Institute of Public Administration, 1937), p. 49.
15. Allen Schick, "The Trauma of Politics: Public Administration in the Sixties," in *American Public Administration: Past, Present, Future,* Frederick C. Mosher, ed. (Syracuse: Maxwell School of Citizenship and Public Affairs and the National Association of Schools of Public Affairs and Administration, 1975), p. 152.

16. Herbert A. Simon, "A Comment on 'The Science of Public Administration,'" *Public Administration Review* 7:202 (Summer) 1947.
17. Golembiewski, *Public Administration as a Developing Discipline*, pp. 20–22.
18. Caldwell, "Public Administration and the Universities," p. 57.
19. Roscoe Martin, "Political Science and Public Administration—A Note on the State of the Union," *American Political Science Review* 46:665 (September) 1952.
20. David Easton, *The Political System* (New York: Knopf, 1953). Easton pulls no punches in his appraisal of the status of political science. As he notes (pp. 38–40), "With the exception of public administration, formal education in political science has not achieved the recognition in government circles accorded, say, economics or psychology." Or, "However much students of political life may seek to escape the taint, if they were to eavesdrop on the whisperings of their fellow social scientists, they would find that they are almost generally stigmatized as the least advanced."
21. John Merriman Gaus, "Trends in the Theory of Public Administration," *Public Administration Review* 10:168 (Summer) 1950.
22. Glendon A. Schubert, Jr., "'The Public Interest' in Administrative Decision Making," *American Political Science Review* 51:346–368 (June) 1957.
23. Martin Landau reviews this aspect of the field's development cogently in his "The Concept of Decision-Making in the 'Field' of Public Administration," *Concepts and Issues in Administrative Behavior*, Sidney Mailick and Edward H. Van Ness, eds. (Englewood Cliffs, NJ: Prentice-Hall, 1962), pp. 1–29. Landau writes (p. 9), "Public administration is neither a subfield of political science, nor does it comprehend it; it simply becomes a synonym."
24. Frederick C. Mosher, "Research in Public Administration," *Public Administration Review* 16:171 (Summer) 1956.
25. Landau, "The Concept of Decision-Making in the 'Field' of Public Administration," p. 2.
26. Ward Stewart, *Graduate Study in Public Administration* (Washington, DC: U. S. Office of Education, 1961).
27. William J. Siffin, "The New Public Administration: Its Study in the United States," *Public Administration* 34:357 (Winter) 1956.
28. Albert Somit and Joseph Tanenhaus, *American Political Science: A Profile of a Discipline* (New York: Atherton, 1964), especially pp. 49–62 and 86–98.
29. Dwight Waldo, "Scope of the Theory of Public Administration," in *Theory and Practice of Public Administration: Scope, Objectives, and Methods*, James C. Charlesworth, ed. (Philadelphia: American Academy of Political and Social Science, 1968), p. 8.
30. Contrast this figure with the percentage of articles in other categories published during the 1960–1970 period: "political parties," 13 per cent; "public opinion," 12 per cent; "legislatures," 12 per cent; and "elections/voting," 11 per cent. Even those categories dealing peripherally with "bureaucratic politics" and public administration evidently received short shrift among the editors of the major political science journals. "Region/federal government" received 4 per cent, "chief executives" won 3 per cent, and "urban/metropolitan government" received 2 per cent. The percentages

are in Jack L. Walker, "Brother, Can You Paradigm?" *PS,* 5:419–422 (Fall) 1972. The journals surveyed were *American Political Science Review, Journal of Politics, Western Political Quarterly, Midwest Political Science Journal,* and *Polity.*

31. This discussion relies largely on Waldo, "Public Administration," pp. 176–179.

32. Christopher E. Nugent, "Introduction," in *Cases in Public Policy and Management: Spring, 1979* (Boston: Intercollegiate Case Clearing House, 1979), p. v; and Colin S. Diver, "PPMP's Swan Song," *Public Policy and Management Newsletter* 7:1 (May) 1985.

33. Leonard D. White, "The Meaning of Principles of Public Administration," in *The Frontiers of Public Administration,* John M. Gaus, Leonard D. White, and Marshall E. Dimock, eds. (Chicago: University of Chicago Press, 1936), p. 22.

34. See, for example, Robert A. Dahl, "The Science of Public Administration: Three Problems," *Public Administration Review* 7:1–11 (Winter) 1947; and Dwight Waldo, *The Administrative State* (New York: Ronald Press, 1948).

35. Ferrel Heady, "Comparative Public Administration: Concerns and Priorities," in *Papers in Comparative Public Administration,* Ferrel Heady and Sybil Stokes, eds. (Ann Arbor: Institute of Public Administration, 1962), p. 3. But see Heady's excellent work, *Public Administration: A Comparative Perspective,* 2nd ed. (New York: Marcel Dekker, Inc.), 1979, especially pp. 1–48.

36. Keith M. Henderson, "A New Comparative Public Administration?" in *Toward a New Public Administration: The Minnowbrook Perspective,* Frank Marini, ed. (Scranton, PA: Chandler, 1971), p. 236.

37. Heady, *Public Administration,* pp. 15–16. Riggs's classic work in development administration remains his *Administration in Developing Countries: The Theory of Prismatic Society* (Boston: Houghton:Miflin, 1964), but see also Riggs' *Prismatic Society Revisited* (Morristown, NJ: General Learning Press, 1973).

38. George Grant, as quoted in Henderson, "A New Comparative Public Administration," p. 239.

39. *CAG Newsletter* pp. 12–13 (June) 1967.

40. Nicholas Henry, "The Relevance Question," in *Education for Public Service: 1979,* Birkhead and Carroll, eds., p. 42.

41. Golembiewski, *Public Administration as a Developing Discipline,* p. 147.

42. Keith M. Henderson, *Emerging Synthesis in American Public Administration* (New York: Asia Publishing House, 1966).

43. See, for example: Edward H. Litchfield, "Notes on a General Theory of Administration," *Administrative Science Quarterly* 1:3–29 (June) 1956; John D. Millett, "A Critical Appraisal of the Study of Public Administration," *Administrative Science Quarterly* 1:177–188 (September) 1956; William A. Robson, "The Present State of Teaching and Research in Public Administration," *Public Administration* 39:217–222 (Autumn) 1961; Andre Molitor, "Public Administration Towards the Future," *International Review of Administrative Sciences* 27:375–384 (No. 4) 1961; Ivan Hinderaker, "The Study of Administration: Interdisciplinary Dimensions," *Summary of Proceedings of the Western Political Science Association,* Supplement to *Western Political Quarterly* 16:5–12 (September) 1963; Paul J. Gordon, "Transcend the Current

Debate in Administrative Theory," *Journal of the Academy of Management* 6:290–312 (December 1963; and Lynton K. Caldwell, "The Study of Administration in the Organization of the University," *Chinese Journal of Administration:* pp. 8–16 (July) 1965.

44. Stewart, *Graduate Education in Public Administration*, p. 39.
45. Delta Sigma Pi, *Eighteenth Biennial Survey of Universities Offering an Organized Curriculum in Commerce and Business Administration* (Oxford, OH: Educational Foundation of Delta Sigma Pi, 1962).
46. Much of the following discussion is drawn from Kenneth L. Kraemer and James L. Perry, "Camelot Revisited: Public Administration Education in a Generic School," *Education for Public Service: 1980*, Guthrie S. Birkhead and James D. Carroll, eds., (Syracuse: Maxwell School of Citizenship and Public Affairs, Syracuse University, 1980), pp. 87–102.
47. National Association of Schools of Public Affairs and Administration, *1982 Directory: Programs in Public Affairs and Administration* (Washington, DC: NASPAA, 1982), pp. 28, 30, and 178; and the 1982 Yale *Catalog*. Yale is not included in the NASPAA *Directory*.
48. Wilson, "The Study of Administration," p. 209.
49. See, for example, Michael Blumenthal, "Candid Reflections of a Businessman in Washington," *Fortune* (January 29, 1979); Donald Rumsfeld, "A Politician Turned Executive," *Fortune* (September 10, 1979); and A. J. Cervantes, "Memoirs of a Businessman-Mayor," *Business Week* (December 8, 1973).
50. See, for example, Hal G. Rainey, Carol Traut, and Barry Blunt, "Reward Expectancies and Other Work-Related Attitudes in Public and Private Organizations: A Review and Extension," and James L. Perry, Hal G. Rainey, and Barry Bozeman, "The Public-Private Distinction in Organization Theory: A Critique and Research Strategy." Papers presented at the 1985 Annual Meeting of the American Political Science Association, New Orleans, LA, August 19–September 1, 1985; Hal G. Rainey, Robert W. Backoff, and Charles H. Levine, "Comparing Public and Private Organizations," *Public Administration Review* 36:233–244 (March/April) 1976; Bruce Buchanan, II, "Government Managers, Business Executives, and Organizational Commitment," *Public Administration Review* 34:339–347 (July/August) 1974; and Bruce Buchanan II, "Red Tape and the Service Ethic: Some Unexpected Differences Between Public and Private Managers," *Administration and Society* 6:423–444 (February) 1975. Graham T. Allison, Jr., observes the slimness of research comparing public and private management, stating there is "virtually none." However, Allison does a good job in describing what there is. See his "Public and Private Management: Are They Fundamentally Alike in All Unimportant Respects?" Paper presented to the Public Management Research Conference, Washington, DC: Brookings Institution, November 1979.
51. Kraemer and Perry, "Camelot Revisited," p. 92. The investigators found twenty-two universities by their own count that used a generic model in teaching management. This was somewhat higher than the official statistics supplied by the National Association of Schools and Public Affairs and Administration, which in 1978 (when Kraemer and Perry conducted their

study) identified thirteen programs in which public administration was combined with business management.

52. Ibid., p. 95.
53. Ibid.
54. Michael A. Murray, "Strategies for Placing Public Administration Graduates," *Public Administration Review* 35:630 (November/December) 1975. See also Jan Orloff, "Public Management Program Graduates: Public or Private Sector Bound? *Civil Service Journal* 19:14–17 (July/September) 1978.
55. Kraemer and Perry, "Camelot Revisited," p. 97. The authors interviewed the dean of the Graduate School of Administration at the University of California at Irvine and the former dean of the School of Organization and Management at Yale University, and found that perhaps as many as three quarters of those students initially interested in public administration switched to a private enterprise track.
56. Murray, "Strategies for Placing Public Administration Graduates," p. 630.
57. Kraemer and Perry, "Camelot Revisited," p. 99.
58. Representative works of the Science, Technology, and Public Policy movement that had lasting impacts include: Michael D. Reagan, *Science and the Federal Patron* (New York: Oxford University Press, 1969) and Lynton Keith Caldwell, *Environment: A Challenge to Modern Society* (Garden City, NY: Natural History Press, 1970).
59. Austin Ranney, "The Study of Policy Content: A Framework for Choice," *Political Science and Public Policy*, Austin Ranney, ed. (Chicago: Markham, 1968), p. 3. Emphases are original.
60. Austin Ranney, "Preface," in ibid., p. vii.
61. Ibid.
62. Susan B. Hansen, "Public Policy Analysis: Some Recent Developments and Current Problems," *Political Science: The State of the Discipline*, Ada W. Finifter, ed. (Washington, DC: American Political Science Association, 1983), pp. 217–245.
63. Ibid., p. 239. In 1979, 68 per cent of the members of the Policy Studies Organization were political scientists, although this figure may include academics who identify with public administration as well.
64. The book was Arnold J. Heidenheimer, Hugh Heclo, and Carolyn Teich Adams, *Comparative Public Policy: The Politics of Social Choice in Europe and America* (New York: St. Martin's Press, 1975).
65. Hansen, "Public Policy Analysis," p. 219. In 1982, 27 per cent of the public policy papers took a comparative approach.
66. Ibid., pp. 220–229. Some license has been taken with Hansen's categories. Hansen calls the literature of program evaluation and its attendant case studies "changing conceptions of policy failure," which strikes me as a somewhat idiosyncratic descriptor.
67. Golembiewski, *Public Administration as a Developing Discipline*, p. 147.
68. Bibliographies dramatizing this point include: B. Guy Peters, "Comparative Public Policy (A Bibliography)," *Policy Studies Review* 1:183–197 (August) 1981; and Douglas E. Ashford, Peter J. Katzenstein, and T. J. Pempel, eds. *Comparative Public Policy: A Cross-National Bibliography* (Beverly Hills, CA: Sage Publications, 1978).

69. Elliot J. Feldman, "Comparative Public Policy: Field or Method?" *Comparative Politics* 10:287–305, 1978.

70. Finifter, ed., *Political Science.*

71. Naomi B. Lynn, "Self Portrait: Profile of Political Scientists," in ibid., p. 102. Lynn is citing a study by Sheilah Mann, "Placement of Political Scientists," *PS* 15:84–91, pp. 84–91.

72. Walter B. Roettger, "I Never Promised You a Rose Garden: Career Satisfaction in an Age of Uncertainty." Paper presented to the Iowa Conference of Political Science, 1977, p. 33, as cited in Lynn, "Self Portrait," p. 113. The other "pocket of optimism" was political philosophy.

73. Ira Sharkansky, *Wither the State? Politics and Public Enterprise in Three Countries* (Chatham, NJ: Chatham House, 1979), p. 11.

74. An admittedly unfair (and possibly fictitious) example of this problem is provided by my own university, which, it is alleged, houses the largest business school in the free world. (It has some 12,000 students.) The story goes that a lone student stood up in the back of a lecture hall containing several hundred business administration students and asked the instructor, "Sir, what is the social responsibility of business?" The professor replied unhesitatingly, "Son, business has no social responsibility." On hearing the answer, the class burst into applause.

75. Perhaps the seminal statement of evaluation research as it has been adopted by the field of public administration is Carol H. Weiss, *Evaluation Research: Methods of Assessing Programs* (Englewood Cliffs, NJ: Prentice-Hall, 1972). For a review of the evolution of these methodologies, see Nicholas Henry, *Public Administration and Public Affairs*, 3rd. ed. (Englewood Cliffs, NJ: Prentice-Hall, 1986), pp. 143–163.

76. A detailed and excellent study of this process at the federal level is contained in Hugh Heclo, "Executive Budget Making." Paper presented to the Urban Institute Conference on Federal Budget Policy in the 1980s," Washington, DC, September 29–30, 1983. But see also Joseph White, "Much Ado About Everything: Making Sense of Federal Budgeting," *Public Administration Review* 45:623–630 (September/October) 1985.

77. Five good examples of this emerging literature are: Susan Welch and John C. Comer, *Quantitative Methods for Public Administration: Techniques and Applications* (Homewood, IL: Dorsey, 1983); E. S. Quade, *Analysis for Public Decisions*, 2nd ed. (New York: North Holland, 1982); Christopher K. McKenna, *Quantitative Methods for Public Decision Making* (New York: McGraw-Hill, 1980); Richard D. Bingham and Marcus E. Etheridge, eds. *Reaching Decisions in Public Policy and Administration: Methods and Applications* (New York: Longman, 1982); and John Kenneth Gohagan, *Quantitative Analysis for Public Policy* (New York: McGraw-Hill, 1980). For an applied version of some of these techniques, see Nicholas Henry, ed. *Doing Public Administration: Exercises, Essays, and Cases*, 2nd ed. (Boston: Allyn and Bacon, 1982).

78. Robert Aaron Gordon and James E. Howell, *Higher Education for Business* (New York: Columbia University Press, 1959); and Frank Pierson, *The Education of American Businessmen* (New York: Carnegie Corporation, 1959).

79. Albert Somit and Joseph Tannenhaus, *The Development of Political Science*

(Boston: Allyn and Bacon, 1967), p. 188. Somit and Tannenhaus are referring to Committee for the Advancement of Teaching, American Political Science Association, *Goals for Political Science* (New York: Sloane, 1951).

80. John C. Honey, "A Report: Higher Education for Public Service," *Public Administration Review* 27:301–319 (November) 1967.

81. Peter Savage, "What Am I Bid for Public Administration?" *Public Administration Review* 28:391 (July) 1968. See also James S. Bowman and Jeremy F. Plant, "Institutional Problems of Public Administration Programs: A House Without a Home," *Public Administration Education in Transition,* Thomas Vocino and Richard Heimovics, eds. (New York: Marcel Dekker, Inc., 1982), p. 40.

82. Schick, "The Trauma of Politics," p. 162.

83. As this is written, in fact, NASPAA continues to struggle with an in-depth examination of the public administration curriculum. The funding for this project is provided by the Mellon Foundation and is being conducted largely at Princeton University's Woodrow Wilson School of Public and International Affairs. However, it is unclear at this point if the final product will be comparable in depth and thoroughness to the studies of business education conducted in the fifties.

84. Khi V. Thai, "Does NASPAA Peer Review Improve the Quality of PA/A Education?" unpublished paper, pp. 7, 11.

85. M. R. Daniels, "Public Administration As An Emergent Profession: A Survey of Attitudes About the Review and Accreditation Programs." Paper presented at the National Conference of the American Society for Public Administration, New York, April, 1983.

86. James F. Wolf, "Careers in Public Administration Education," in Vocino and Heimovics, eds. *Public Administration Education,* p. 119.

87. Ibid., p. 121. This estimation was drawn from a random sampling of fifty representative institutions.

88. National Association for Schools of Public Affairs and Administration, *1984 Directory: Programs in Public Affairs and Administration* (Washington, DC: National Association of Schools of Public Affairs and Administration, 1984), p. xi. Figures are for 1983.

89. Ibid.

90. Ibid.

91. Deborah J. Young and William B. Eddy, "Adult Learning Methods in Public Administration Education," in Vocino and Heimovics, eds., *Public Administration Education,* pp. 59–61.

92. National Association of Schools in Public Affairs and Administration, *1982 Directory,* p. iv.

93. Young and Eddy, "Adult Learning in Public Administration Education," p. 67.

94. Mark R. Daniels, Robert Emmett Darch, and John W. Swain, "Public Administration Extension Activities by American Colleges and Universities," *Public Administration Review* 42:56, 58, 65 (January/February) 1982.

95. Michael A. Murray, "Education for Public Administrators," *Public Personnel Management:* pp. 239–249 (July–August) 1976, pp. 239–249; Henry, "The Relevance Question," pp. 27–43; John F. Kerrigan and David W. Hinton,

"Knowledge and Skills Needs of Public Administrators," *Public Administration Review* 40:469–473 (September/October) 1980; and Khi V. Thai, "Public Administration Education: The Current Status and Perceived Needs," unpublished paper, 1981.

96. Thai, "Does NASPAA Peer Review Improve the Quality of PA/A Education?" p. 11.
97. Harry Weiner, "Policy Analysis and Public Administration: Convergent Courses?" in Birkhead and Carrol, eds. *Education for Public Service, 1980*, p. 15.
98. Wolf, "Careers in Public Administration Education," p. 119.
99. Ibid., p. 118.
100. National Association for Schools of Public Affairs and Administration, *1982 Directory*, p. iv; and Lynn, "Self-Portrait: Profile of Political Scientists," p. 108. In 1981–82, political science awarded nearly 5,500 Ph.D. degrees to its graduate students, whereas public administration programs awarded slightly more than 6,000 masters degree of all types, including 5,009 MPA degrees.
101. William Earle Klay, "Innovations and Standards in Public Administration Education," in Vocino and Heimovics, eds. *Public Administration Education*, pp. 2–3; Wolf, "Careers in Public Administration Education," pp. 118 and 120; and National Association of Schools of Public Affairs and Administration, *1982 Directory*, p. iv.

PART II

Theoretical Considerations

CHAPTER 3

Politics and Administration: On Thinking about a Complex Relationship

Dwight Waldo
SYRACUSE UNIVERSITY

C. DWIGHT WALDO is Professor Emeritus of Political Science and Public Administration and Albert Schweitzer Professor Emeritus in the Humanities at Syracuse University. His publications list goes to five pages of the most distinguished work in the history of American public administration, including the seminal The Administrative State, *and his latest book,* The Enterprise of Public Administration: A Summary View. *Professor Waldo's writings have been translated into Arabic, French, German, Hindi, Indonesian, Italian, Japanese, Korean, Persian, Portuguese, Spanish, and Vietnamese. Not the least of his achievements was being named Hog Calling Champion of Saline County, Nebraska, in 1931.*

Dwight Waldo helps us understand the complex relationships between politics and administration. Those who think the issue was settled when the dichotomy was rejected by public administrationists after World War II must think again. Waldo says the distinction is a fundamental construct in the history of governmental institutions, and Americans should give up the feeling of responsibility for inventing it or refuting it. The distinction will not go away. It has become a permanent part of the complicated field of forces in which the study and practice of public administration must take place.

The perceived differences between politics and administration turn on the fact that history presents us with two governmental traditions that are significantly different from each other. One is a civic culture tradition that arises in the thought and experience of classical Greece and draws from the Roman Republic and some of the medieval and early modern city-states. The other is an imperial tradition arising in the ancient empires of the Middle East and the Mediterranean basin. Rome was the latest and greatest of these empires and gave many of the administrative technologies of the *imperium* to the strong princes who created the modern state.

The United States reflects both traditions. Our politics are Greek, but our administration is Roman. Thinking about government and deciding what it should and will do are primarily associated with the civic culture tradition. This is the realm of politics, political theory, political science, and, when it developed, democracy. Organizing and executing government functions are primarily associated with the imperial tradition. This is the realm of administration and management. The perception of a distinction between politics and administration is not simply an accidental result of a period of reformism in American history, to be put aside as fiction or nonsense.

How the United States appropriated the civic culture and imperial traditions is largely a function of the English antecedents to the American experiment in government. England's mixed constitution was itself a blending of the two traditions. It was at once royal and popular, authoritative and consensual, centralized and decentralized, and effective but restrained in its exercise of authority. England developed both a substantial civic culture tradition and an empire. The American colonies objected to the imperial side of that equation, however, and created a system of government that the framers thought was weighted on the side of civic culture.

The extended republic the Constitution makers devised was based on the hope that republican ideas could be maintained despite the vast geographical area to be governed. Republican governments historically had been small-scale, so principles were adopted to forestall the imperial. These included limited and enumerated powers allowed to the government, separated and balanced powers among the organs of government, and federated and territorial divisions of sovereignty. Yet the republican ideas of widely but unequally shared powers were overtaken by democracy. With growing enfranchisement, the people demanded and got government attention to problems and functions beyond late eighteenth century republican imaginings. Democracy then called forth imperial mechanisms of government in the most splendid irony of American history.

Yet the disjunction between the rhetoric of civic culture and the demands of imperial administration is probably not as important in the modern world as the economization doctrines and practices that diminish and denigrate the public sphere. Capitalism and its institutions view government as an obstacle to the pursuit of private interests. Government should be a source of enrichment and a general utility-maximizing mechanism. Economization makes the public interest a fiction and promotes the view that life finds its central meaning in the consumption of goods and services. Such privatism threatens to bankrupt the public bank.

The concomitant forces of liberalism and democracy mean in the first instance that one person's right to liberty may be viewed as another person's condemnation to penury, and in the second that citizenship may diminish in prestige to the point where it is little more than a collection of legal rights. The idea that citizenship implies a duty to participate actively in civic life strikes most citizens in modern America as strange and perhaps un-American.

Waldo says that to understand the United States as an intricate mixture of the civic culture and imperial traditions, and to appreciate the problematic relationship between economics and public responsibility, is to begin to comprehend some of the problems and dilemmas of public administration in the 1980s.

Nothing is more central in thinking about public administration than the nature and interrelations of *politics* and *administration*. Nor are the nature and interrelations of politics and administration matters only for academic theorizing. What is more important in the day-to-day, year-to-year, decade-to-decade operation of government than the ways in which politics and administration are conceptualized, rationalized, and related one to the other?

This chapter is an exercise in trying to understand the relationship of politics and administration. The first part of the essay sketches the relationship as it developed in reformism and self-aware public administration. The second part argues that a historical disjunction of politics and administration is germane to both present problems and present opportunities. The third part discusses the manner in which some potent late-modern forces affect the relationship. The fourth part presents some summary observations and reflections about the present status and future prospects of public administration.

The Dichotomy and After

Why are the identities and relationships of politics and administration problematic? Why are they a matter of central importance in public administration? Where are we now in relation to the matter? I shall try to construct a brief answer to these questions for those unacquainted with the terrain.

In the currents of reformism in the late nineteenth and early twentieth centuries there emerged a belief that the institutions and processes of government are best understood as resolvable into the basic acts of decision and execution. Further, decision came to be equated with politics, and execution with administration.

These beliefs were formulated in and related to a national-historical matrix that included the following: (1) a rapid rise of industrialization and urbanization, with a concomitant movement from yeoman-amateur to specialist-professional in relative numbers and as an ideal, (2) a vigorous movement for governmental reform and improvement, in reaction to what was perceived as confusion, corruption, incompetency, and waste in government so widespread as to endanger the republic, or the democracy, as it was coming to be called, (3) emergence of self-aware social studies, especially political science, and their search for structuring beliefs and useful methodologies, and (4) increased faith in the efficiency of science, however loosely interpreted, which caused the emerging social studies to be thought of as sciences and gave impetus and a name, scientific management, to a movement that attempted to make the management of business enterprises a specialized and professional pursuit.

Reformers in and out of academia concluded that the way to improve, perhaps literally to save, our political beliefs and institutions lay in application of the distinction between decision and execution, politics and administration. In the sphere of politics the popular will found its legitimate role and proper fulfillment. When this will was determined, then administration, guided by scientific knowledge of proper means of implementation, should take over. It was concluded that a governmental system properly arranged and guided can simultaneously be democratic, that is, responsive to the popular will via election and representation, and effective and efficient, that is, responsive to the procedures dictated by scientific knowledge as interpreted by experts.

This way of looking at things governmental was prominent for more than a generation, peaking in the late 1920s and early 1930s. The conclusions thought to result when government was viewed this way tended to be stated as "principles." These principles had both a scientific sanction and an element of moral imperative. In general, the principles prescribed governmental arrangements on the "overhead democracy" or "two pyramids" plan. Politics-democracy proceeds upward to an apex at which the popular will is determined by law or otherwise, and then is bridged over to administration. Thereupon the will is realized downward through an organization that is hierarchical, functionally rational, professional, informed by science, and committed to efficiency. Responsibility, responsiveness, and accountability are then brought about by the same structures, but the direction is reversed. They go up the administrative pyramid to the apex, bridge over, and go down this structure to the voters.

There is no doubt about the force and effectiveness of the set of beliefs I have roughly sketched. They have affected the government of the United States in many ways and at all levels. But it is possible to oversimplify and caricature the principles period. Not everyone identified with public administration was an ideologue, and the principles were often applied with a large dose of pragmatic adjustment to circumstances and in recognition of counterprinciples of various kinds. As the 1930s advanced, doubt and dissent increased. In the 1940s refutation and repudiation came to the fore. By the 1950s it had become common to refer to the politics administration dichotomy as an outworn if not ludicrous creed.

The criticisms that were leveled against the dichotomy and its prescriptions were many and included at least the following points: (1) the sanction of science claimed for the principles could not be sustained because, on critical examination, the principles were revealed to be rules of common sense at best and contradictory nonsense at worst; (2) the perspective attempted to implant into American government inappropriate and alien elements from foreign governments and/or business practice that conflicted both with a constitutional scheme of divided powers and with a federal division of delegated functions; (3) anything like an effective separation of politics and administration did not exist and is impossible of achievement; and (4) to proceed very far in the direction of separation raises both practical problems and ethical questions of multiple and conflicting obligations applied to administrative acts, the extreme example being the Nuremberg-Eichmann scenario. The rule-making and case-deciding activities of administrative agencies cannot be returned wholesale to legislatures and courts, nor can they simply be abandoned.

The general rejection of the politics administration dichotomy had two distinguishable but related consequences. One was the dimming of belief in and commitment to a formula for administrative reform. The principles of simplicity and unity, of centralization and hierarchy, of integration and control served for more than a generation as guidelines for reform and reorganization at all levels of government. By the time of the Second Hoover Commission in 1955, however, they were losing their power to command credence and motivate action. Since that time, reform efforts such as Planning, Programming, Budgeting Systems (PPBS), Management by Objectives (MBO), and Zero-Base Budgeting (ZBB) have all tended to reform process rather than structure. The Civil Service Reform Act of 1978, however, did owe a significant debt to the old formula.

The other consequence was what came to be referred to as a crisis of identity for both academics and practitioners who placed themselves in the field of public administration. What could command belief now? What could justify a claim to authority and legitimacy? What phenomena should be studied? What objectives should be in view, and what methods should be used to achieve them?

Despite the fact that public administration had been brought to self-awareness by professors of political science, the role and status of public administrationists in departments of political science tended from the beginning to be anomalous. From one side they were suspect because they purported to train persons for government employment. This was offensive to the liberal arts humane learning ethos, which viewed genuine education as something to enlarge the intellect and free the spirit, not to prepare one for employment. (Today I read that former British Prime Minister Clement Atlee attended a "philistine" school, Haileybury, which specialized in preparing for the India Service.) From another side public administrationists were suspect because the principles for which they claimed scientific legitimacy were regarded as wrong-headed and perhaps fraudulent. From all sides public administrationists were thought to be odd because they were seen as concerned, as they often claimed, with the nonpolitical. This in a department of political science! To make matters worse, public administrationists sometimes talked about the "business" of government, and they openly borrowed from business sources.

In the post–World War II years there was an impulse to make political science genuinely scientific. The behavioral movement became dominant over the liberal arts component of political science and over continuing justifications of political science as the vehicle of education for citizens and politicians. By the early 1960s the behavioralists were capturing the dominant academic positions in the discipline. Public administrationists were influenced only marginally by this current in political science, however, and this made their position even more anomalous and uncomfortable. Public administrationists had the task of preparing students for employment, and they had other practical interests as well. This helps explain why they did not join the behavioral movement in force. For whatever reasons, they did not. Increasingly in political science departments, public administration came to be viewed as something useful at budget time at best and as an embarrassing anachronism at worst.

Thus there was a subdiscipline of political science that relied on a distinction between politics and administration and claimed scientific status for the administrative part of its distinction. It stood to be in serious trouble when the distinction was challenged and the claim to science repudiated. Its map of intellectual interests, professional objectives, and organizational boundaries would have to be redrawn. Indeed, it has been—not fundamentally, for this would indicate that insoluble problems have been solved—but extensively. The following seem to be major developments in the new cartography:

1. A reaching out by public administrationists for ideas and techniques not available in political science. The other social sciences have been seen as relevant and useful, more so than political science, and have been drawn upon significantly. The more or less interdisciplinary cluster of ideas housed largely in schools of business and known there as administrative science have been consulted extensively. More behavioral and scientific findings and methods were absorbed into public administration in this manner than were taken from political science.

2. A notable degree of migration of programs in public administration and/or public affairs from departments of political science. Such programs are likely to reflect their political science background but to draw importantly on other disciplines.

3. The establishment of programs in policy studies, policy science, and policy analysis.[1] These programs have been a response to the view that policy is made, perhaps desirably but in any event inevitably, in administrative settings. There is no hesitation, however, in offering such expertise to legislators and others.

4. The establishment of new programs or the enlargement of older ones in public administration, public affairs, or management in schools of business administration and in the newer generic schools that regard administration and management as essentially the same wherever practiced. In such settings it is unlikely that much will be drawn from traditional public administration or from the old or new political science.

5. Despite an obvious picture of scatter and diversity in settings and nomenclature, a significant amount of homogenization in terms of what is taught. Programs in policy studies are likely to pay attention to implementation, that is, administration broadly and imaginatively interpreted. On the other hand, programs in public administration and public affairs are likely to include instruction in policy analysis. Subjects such as quantitative and analytical techniques and organization theory are presumed to be universal curriculum requirements.

Several further generalizations can be made concerning the educational response to the discrediting of the politics/administration dichotomy and the accompanying principles. One is that despite what has been referred to as homogenization there is still a wide discrepancy in studies undertaken in what with purposeful vagueness I shall designate "this area." A degree in public administration awarded by a political science department may mean only that the recipient has a "concentration" of two or three courses regarded as public administration. On the other hand, a public management program in a school of business

administration may make no appreciable change in its requirements
from the business administration offerings. I have had business administration faculty members tell me confidently and serenely that no changes
are necessary. For certain types of government employment they are
essentially correct.

Another generalization is that there has been accumulation or increasing mass along with homogenization. As new ideas, techniques, and
presumed needs have come along, such as the case method, quantitative
analysis, interpersonal skills, and ethical sensitivity, there has been a
tendency to add these areas to the curriculum without dropping others.
An obvious reason for this is that interest in teaching existing courses
is vested in tenured faculty members who are either loath or ill-prepared
to teach new courses. It is also thought that employment and career
possibilities for students may be enhanced by fashionable additions to
the curriculum. Because it is by no means predictable *what* will enhance
employment and promotion possibilities, a broad-spectrum and bet-
hedging strategy has often been rationalized.

It needs to be added that although the politics/administration dichotomy has been repudiated and its accompanying principles discredited,
we do not write on a clean slate. The following section bears importantly
on this matter.

A Historical Disjunction?

I wish now to argue a thesis that I judge to be relevant in thinking
about the relationship of politics and administration. In brief, it is that
history has given us two governmental traditions that are significantly
different from each other and between which there are problems of
congruence and communication. Our government draws on both traditions, and some of our problems, as well as certain advantages and
opportunities, are drawn from this fact.

If we think of the government of the United States as an amalgam
of politics and administration, these two aspects of our government
have rather different sources. Put bluntly in thesis form, our politics
are Greek, but our administration is Roman. This statement greatly
overstates and oversimplifies, of course, but it calls attention to important
considerations that have long been ignored.

Politics embraces a wide spectrum of phenomena, and many varieties
of politics, such as office politics, harem politics, and court politics, may
have nothing to do with Greece.[2] But self-aware politics, politics practiced
and studied *as* politics, owes a large debt to the experience and thought
of classical Greece. To an amazing degree, the concepts, theories, and

values of politics can be traced to a brief period in the history of the small city-state of Athens. Even the contemporary empirical-behavioral approach to politics owes some debt to Aristotle and Hellenic natural philosophy.

Yet the development of administration, its concepts, techniques, and institutions, has little to do with Greece. The main stream of development arises in the ancient empires of the Middle East and the Mediterranean basin. Rome was the latest and greatest of these empires. The Roman *imperium* endured for centuries and at its height embraced an area now organized into forty independent states. When government was in effect recreated in Europe after the Dark Ages and the feudal period, the inspiration and model was overwhelmingly Roman. "The king is emperor in his own realm" was the operational code of the strong princes who created the modern state.

The polity of classical Greece, the city-state, was approximately the size of a medium-small American city. Its administrative needs were modest and its administrative technology simple. While some administrative tasks were performed by slaves or for compensation, citizens participated in government to a marked degree by assuming responsibility for some public activity, either civil or military, for a limited period of time. The citizen exercised his citizenship. He was not a functionary, a bureaucrat, or an expert. He was seen as acting in a political role, not a professional one. He was performing as one of the elite and demonstrating his virtue in the process. He was not "working."

The ancient empires, however, required and developed an extensive administrative apparatus. How else could large territories be controlled and large populations sustained and governed? By contemporary standards the tasks of government were few, and the bureaucracies that performed them would not rate very high on the Weberian scale of legal-rational decision making. Working in and for government became regular employment for many, however, and government-related skills were developed and formally taught. Beyond question the mainstream of administrative technology has flowed from the ancient empires, through Rome, and into the modern state as it developed in Europe.

In the transition from the decline of Rome to the rise of the modern state the Roman Catholic Church played an important role.[3] For centuries it provided some semblance of government for much of Europe, more so than did the Holy Roman Empire. It carried forward the Roman aura and some of the Roman administrative technology. Vicars and dioceses were Roman first. The Church added some distinctive features as well. To study the origins of the modern state, for example, is simultaneously to appreciate the role of the cleric, whence *clerk*, whether he was a prince of the Church functioning as an aide to a monarch or a humble scribe copying texts of Aristotle.

In broad brush, there is a civic-culture tradition that arises in the experience and thought of classical Greece and includes the experience and thought of the Roman Republic and some of the medieval and early modern city-states. There is also an imperial tradition that is associated with the experience and institutions of the Roman Empire and that was highly influential in shaping the modern state.[4] The modern state in the West is fundamentally imperial but modified according to time, place, and circumstances by the influence of civic culture. Thinking about government and deciding what it should and will do are primarily associated with the civic-culture tradition. This is the realm of politics, political theory, political science, and when it developed, democracy. Organizing and executing government functions are primarily associated with the imperial tradition. This is the realm of administration and management. In sum, the perception of a distinction between politics and administration is not simply an accidental result of a certain period of American history, to be put aside as fiction or nonsense. The distinction is writ deep in several millenia of Western history.

This argument briefly made can be developed at length and in depth, but it is appropriate now to take note of some complications and necessary qualifications. The following items are also part of the story: (1) the input of Germanic ideas, values, and customs during and following the decline of Rome, (2) the development of feudal institutions, some of which were transmuted into parts of the modern state,[5] (3) the rise of the idea of a moral order that is universal, not local, parochial, or ethnic, (4) the enunciation and popularization of political theories that, though they drew on antique inspiration via Machiavelli, Montesquieu, and Rousseau, in other ways were new in their expression of the notions of pre- or extrapolitical rights and the idea of government formed and legitimated by contract, and (5) the rise of capitalism and the economic as spheres of thought and activity that in an unprecedented way challenged the political and governmental, whether civic-culture or imperial, for attention and loyalty. This matter is given some attention below in the discussion of Complicating Late Modern Developments.

Each of these additional and complicating themes could be developed at length, and of course, they have been. A respectable library can be assembled for each item. Such is the strength of the two streams of thought and institutions, the civic-culture and the imperial, that they continue to shape and direct contemporary governments in crucial ways. I turn now to indicate briefly how this is true in the United States.

The immediate and critically important antecedent of the American experiment in government was the English experience in developing government of a particular kind.[6] The essence of the matter can be put in the form of summary statements. Following the Norman Conquest and especially after the Wars of the Roses and the Tudor accession, a government was developed for England. This government was unified and centralized considering the time in which it was constructed. Certainly it was unified and centralized in comparison to what had immediately preceded it and to almost anything with which it might be compared on the continent. In the seventeenth century, with the Stuart accession, the centralization and rationalization of power was arrested. Arrested but not reversed. The result of the Settlement and its sequel was the development of a government that in a unique fashion mixed the old and the new. It was at once royal and popular, authoritative and consensual, centralized and decentralized, and effective but restrained in its exercise of authority.

England's mixed constitution represented a blending of the civic-culture and the imperial traditions. Much can be attributed, of course, to certain accidents of history and to unique circumstances such as the combination of strong and weak rulers and England's geographical characteristic of being both a part of Europe and an island separated from it. For whatever reasons, England developed what most would judge to be a substantial civic culture and what no one would deny was an empire.

Three generalizations seem appropriate: (1) the American experiment with independent government began as a reaction to what was perceived as the growing imperialism of the mother country; (2) the United States in turn became subject to imperial tendencies itself as it developed as a nation and turned westward; and (3) the United States is to be understood most basically as a mix on fairly equal terms of the two traditions of civic culture and imperial administration.

Samuel Huntington has developed the thesis that what was actually transferred to American soil was a set of Tudor institutions and expectations. The American Revolution is to be viewed as the result of a mingled misunderstanding of, and objection to, the exercise of increasing royal power. The Constitution may then be understood as a restatement or reassertion of Tudor-type institutions and values.[7] No single scheme explains the complicated matters in view here, but this one has much validity. The Americans who led the Revolution *thought* they were resisting increasing royal, that is, imperial, power. The Americans who framed the Constitution *thought* they were creating a system of government weighted on the side of civic culture.

No single phrase so well captures the intent of the framers as "extended republic."[8] They were inspired by a tradition and a literature of republican government in which power is widely, but hardly ever equally and universally, shared.[9] Republican governments historically had been small-scale. This was an experiment in *extending* republican ideas, institutions, and values over a vast area. The experiment was pronounced a New Order of the Ages, the Novus Ordo Seclorum of the Great Seal of the

United States. The principles on which the experiment was based were those of limited and enumerated powers to the governments recognized or created, the separation and balancing of powers among organs of government, and the federative, territorial division of sovereignty. To be sure, the governments recognized or created were to administer the powers granted to them, but given the total setting of ideas and institutions, and geography and population, administration was a matter of important concern only to a few of the framers.[10]

A crude but simple indicator of the movement of American government in the direction of the imperial is the fact that there are now approximately four times as many government officials and employees as the entire population in the 1780s. The reasons are obvious. The general population is about seventy-five times greater, the United States has expanded from the Atlantic to the Pacific Oceans, *into* the Atlantic and the Pacific Oceans, and concomitantly, the United States has become predominately urban and industrial. For these and other reasons it has become vastly more complex in socioeconomic terms. Democracy as an ethos and set of institutional arrangements also stimulated the growth of government. With growing enfranchisement the people demanded and got government attention to problems and functions beyond eighteenth-century anticipation, if not eighteenth-century imagination.

Contemporary government in the United States is a mixture of the civic-culture tradition and the imperial tradition, added to and complicated by other factors not prominent in either tradition as it formed in antiquity or as it emerged in the early modern era. When John Quincy Adams declared that the United States had "the most complicated government on the face of the globe" he had seen only the beginning of the complications. The American mixture has no close parallel even among the liberal-democratic governments that use the federal principle. The complex is difficult for Americans to understand, even when they try, and it is difficult for foreigners to understand, even when they try hard. Foreigners hear many voices and cannot find *the state*.

I now offer two sets of observations related to the civic-culture–imperial tradition thesis that has been sketched here.

1. The thesis is the product of my personal intellectual-professional experience. This may signify that it has no significance beyond the biographical. Or perhaps by accident I have developed a binocular view that supplies a useful perspective. I came by my binocular view in the following fashion.

    First, my initial intellectual-professional interest was in political theory, but I found myself more and more engaged with public administration. Both of these areas of specialization were regarded as part of political science, but neither field spoke to the other.

Political theory as conventionally defined began with the Greek experience and its articulation. The Greeks discovered or invented The Political, brought it to self-awareness, and naturally perceived and defined it in their own image. In the histories of political theory Rome is noted only briefly and then attention is focused on Polybius, who was a transplanted Greek. Most general treatments of political theory do not contain even an index reference to administration, public administration, management, or bureaucracy. Public administration, for its part, was content to view itself as a set of recently developed professional techniques. Even when it developed an interest in theory, the interest did not run to a union with conventional political theory, American constitutional theory aside, but in other directions. How could we account for these two separate worlds?

Second, I have written about political science in the round three times. That is, I have tried to portray this peculiarly American field or discipline in terms of its origins, components, and methods.[11] Each time I have puzzled over a certain rootlessness. In the United States, political science became a name, a movement, and a putative discipline in the late nineteenth and early twentieth centuries. It could be related to various currents of American life, both popular and scholarly, as well as to some European philosophic movements. But it seemed to have no important history other than political theory, at least history that was regarded as respectable after repudiation of certain nineteenth-century notions of political evolution associated with Hegelianism and Darwinism.

Third, I became interested in the history of administration in general and of governmental administration in particular. From my reading I came to these conclusions: (1) that what can legitimately be designated government[12] predates classical Greece by at least two millenia, (2) that without exception, from antiquity to the present, government has implied an administrative apparatus that can perform at least the enduring core functions of government, such as defense, peacekeeping, and public works, and (3) that the brilliance of the Greek achievements in general, including Greek contempt for the ancient empires, led to a systematic bias in the interpretation of government experience overall. It inclined subsequent analyses toward a political/philosophical, as against an administrative/institutional, interpretation. In terms of this essay, it biased us toward a civic-culture experience as against an imperial experience.[13]

2. My second observation about the civic-culture—imperial traditions thesis is that there are causal factors involved when an earlier pattern of ideas and institutions is replicated, but to some extent the usage is metaphorical and ideal-typical. One can speak meaningfully of

civic-culture and imperial styles of government even if no important or direct historical cause is discernible. Similar impulses and situations may produce similar results without conscious imitation.

The influence of imperial Rome in the emergence of the modern state is indisputable.[14] The idea of Rome was itself important as inspiration, and the revival of Roman law, sometimes referred to as the Reception, supplied concepts and techniques for shaping the emerging order. This is especially true for the continent, but it is also true to a significant degree for England. It has been put this way: By way of the Conquest the developing English government received an early innoculation of the Roman influence, and this innoculation, plus the English Channel, prevented the disease of the strong Roman influence present on the continent. (This view is English, of course.) The Church, as noted, was a source of influence of things Roman, before and after the Act of Supremacy.

But discontinuities and reinventions, adaptations to local conditions and interactions with changing physical and social technologies, must also be recognized. The American repudiation of the imperial tradition and embrace of the republican tradition, plus the strong democratic currents flowing in the nineteenth century, meant that when the United States nevertheless became imperial in terms of size and complexity, it could not simply import an administrative technology from Europe. Although a few items such as written examinations, executive budgets, and the military staff organization were borrowed and modified to fit the American setting, on the whole American administrators invented new management techniques. The management on which Leonard D. White proposed to rest public administration when he wrote its first textbook in 1926 was at center the techniques of the new scientific management movement.

Complicating Late-Modern Developments

Some major developments of the late-modern period have served to diminish the importance of both the civic-culture and imperial traditions in the public realm and to complicate the relationship of the political and the administrative. They deserve attention in our effort to understand the political/administrative complex.

One major development is what I shall call the economization of the world. The second is the rise of liberalism, and the third is the rise of democracy.

Major aspects of the economization of the world include: (1) the rise of capitalism as an ethos and complicated set of related institutions, (2) the emergence of economics as a field of specialization and a preeminent social science, (3) the enunciation and wide acceptance of the idea that society exists apart from government and indeed is prior to and greater than government, (4) a vast increase in productivity achieved by the dynamics and organization of capitalism and by putting a great historic quickening of science and technology at the service of capitalism, (5) the ascendance of the point of view that life finds its central meaning in the consumption of goods and services, and (6) a large and varied literature of justification for the values and mechanisms of economization.

The result of these developments has been to diminish and even denigrate the public sphere. Government has come to be viewed as an obstacle to the pursuit of private interests, a source of enrichment, or a general utility-maximizing mechanism. The public interest has become something of a fiction, something that custom and law dictate must be invoked at certain times but that proves ghostlike upon close examination. Public vocations, whether political or administrative, have been devalued. Both the civic-culture and the imperial traditions have been eroded. The United States is at far remove indeed from the sense that to engage in public life in the polity is one's highest achievement and from the sense that to serve the emperor or the state is a source not only of livelihood and authority but of dignity and honor.

There are many implications of the economization of the world for the relationship of politics and administration. One of the most important is the concept of efficiency. This idea, seemingly so denotative and hard, but also so vaporous and protean, has in the last two centuries become a sacred concept in both the American political and administrative cultures. We philosophize and debate about whether efficiency is a *measure* of value only. If so, what is valuable? Is efficiency a value in itself? If so, what kind of value is it, and how valuable is it, and in relation to what? The concept is so important in an economized culture that it cannot be avoided, but it is so difficult to accommodate to either the civic-culture or the imperial tradition that we fumble with and dispute it. So efficiency is not yet naturalized in the public realm, and it is not clear that it can be and will be.[15] Can we turn efficiency on itself and subject it to a cost-benefit analysis?

Liberalism and economization are closely joined and intricately related. They developed in the same historical matrix, and over a large area one supports and forwards the other, as the names John Locke, Adam Smith, and David Ricardo signify. But as such names as Jeremy Bentham, John Stuart Mill, and John Maynard Keynes also signify, the relationship is complicated and controversial. Liberalism is subject to qualifying, differentiating adjectives. One brand of liberalism is distinguished from another and is even held antagonistic thereto. And these are not just academic debates. They are the verbalization of contests in a very real world, contests in which one person's right to liberty may be viewed as another person's condemnation to penury and servitude.

The conceptual and institutional world in which the public administrator must deal with varying interpretations of liberalism is further complicated by the concepts and institutions of democracy. Democracy arises as a significant force *pari passu* with liberalism and in response to some of the same causes. In many ways liberalism and democracy are parallel, complementary, and reinforcing, as the familiar label "liberal-democratic countries" attests. But again, there is an area of confusion and antagonism between them. Indeed, much in our public life, political and administrative, can be interpreted as a conflict between some variety of liberalism and some variety of democracy such as populist, representative, direct, participatory, or pluralist.

There is an important problematical interaction not only between liberalism and democracy but also between citizenship and democracy. In its origins the civic-culture tradition was republican but not democratic.[16] In Greece and in the Roman Republic citizenship was highly meaningful and reflected an elite status. Women, slaves, those of foreign origin, and those of low status were excluded. Citizenship was strongly participatory. To participate in the civic life was a privilege and a duty. Membership in an imperial community was generally less meaningful, at least below the ruling groups. The status of "subject" might carry certain prerogatives or offer certain advantages in the imperial tradition, but it did not generally carry the elite and participatory meaning of classic citizenship.

Although the American Constitution refers to citizenship a number of times and confers on Congress the power to establish "an uniform rule of naturalization," only with the Fourteenth Amendment in 1868 were some troublesome questions settled. As a practical matter, citizenship in the new extended republic meant in the beginning about the same thing it had meant historically in other republics. Given restrictions on the franchise, and the importance of wealth, education, and status, government in the United States was an affair of the elite.

With the progressive enlargement of the franchise and the growth of democratic sentiment and ideas, the government established by the framers has been greatly changed. The republic has become a democracy. The United States went to war in 1917 to make the world safe for democracy, not for republicanism. But as democracy advanced, the concept of citizenship diminished in prestige and in the expectations attending it. Citizenship is hardly a negligible status, as millions can attest. It can mean the difference between poverty and affluence and even life and death. Yet for most purposes it has become a bundle of legal rights, most of which resident aliens share, and rights that may never be challenged or exercised. The idea that citizenship implies a duty to participate actively in civic life would strike most citizens as strange and perhaps un-American.

It may go too far to say that citizenship in its full classical sense and democracy in its modern interpretation are incompatible, but experience would indicate serious difficulties in trying to meld the two.[17] It is a strange joining of ancient and modern ideals for citizens to be legally obligated to vote, as they are in some democracies.

To understand the United States as an intricate mixture of civic-culture and imperial traditions, and to understand the problematic relationship between democracy and citizenship, is to arrive at the threshold of understanding some of the problems and dilemmas of public administration. It will help in understanding, for example, how a highly placed civil servant can be simultaneously more and less a citizen than his or her fellow citizens. The civil servant is more than fellow citizens with respect to the authority vested in the office and less than fellow citizens with respect to the political prerogatives he or she enjoys.

In sum: the government of the United States was founded in the civic-culture tradition. Constructed as an extended republic, it was not only a government of limited powers but it embodied both a territorial and a functional separation of powers. Increasingly, the government assumed imperial obligations, however, through an increase of territory and population, as a consequence of growing complexity, through demands of the new democratic politics, and as a result of the transformation of its geopolitical situation in the world. The forces of economization, liberalism, and democracy pushed and pulled it in varied directions. The result is a government of extreme complexity. Overall, one does not know whether to lament what often appears to be overload and confusion, or to praise the seemingly endless American capacity for adapting and coping.

Some Observations and Reflections

If what has been set forth here represents a rough sketch of some of the major features of the relationship between politics and administration, and the field of forces in which the relationship must be worked out, then the conclusion can be put in a good news/bad news report. The good news is that the unsolved problem of finding a satisfactory relationship between politics and administration is not just a public administration problem, a badge of singular incompetence, but a problem for society generally. The bad news is that the problem is so complex that society generally will not be able to find a simple and widely acceptable solution.

It must quickly be added that the bad news is really good news. In a situation in which there is principled as well as practical lack of congruence between politics and administration there are opportunities as well as problems, freedoms as well as frustrations. It is close to the mark to say that problems of congruence are a defining characteristic of liberal-democratic institutions. Put the other way around, the term *totalitarian* might best fit an entity in which politics and administration are a seamless robe. In the real world, empirically, such are the practical difficulties of joining the political and the administrative that even when principle endorses the joining no entity has ever been completely totalitarian. The difficulties experienced by communist regimes illustrate the point.

All considered, the idea that a distinction can be made between politics and administration is simplistic but not absurd. It is simplistic because so many governmental phenomena are a mix of some variety of politics/policy and administration/management. It is not absurd because often there is enough of a distinction to have analytic and prescriptive importance. The distinction is important enough to justify institutional structures and operating procedures. Retrospectively, it is clear that the dichotomy served the purposes of the generation in which it was prominent. In a time of reform and the growth of science, it served as a shield behind which the sanction of science could be asserted for administrative study and the claims of economy and efficiency could be advanced for simplifying and centralizing the reforms that were presumed to be justified by administrative study.

It is plain that the related politics/administration and decision/execution distinctions must be accepted as permanent parts of the complicated field of forces in which the study and practice of public administration take place. If my thesis is valid that history has presented us with a dichotomy between politics and administration, then presumably the distinction is deeply grounded indeed. In any case, the related distinctions have a commonsense logic, a general acceptance, and a pragmatic usefulness. They are pervasive in our language and institutions. They cannot be discarded.[18]

If they cannot be discarded, they must be accommodated to an American constitutional system that ordains that government shall be organized under three rubrics, not two.[19] They must consider the complications presented by a federal-territorial division of powers and functions, as well as the various and complicating forces reviewed previously.[20]

How well are we doing in this endeavor? This is difficult to answer honestly because answers are inevitably colored by the viewer's experience and values. It is difficult to answer meaningfully because an answer implies a comparative standard. What comparison would be realistic and fair?

In the opening section I mapped post–World War II developments in self-aware public administration and in pedagogical-institutional terms. It would be a great service if someone gave us not just a better map but a rather different one, a map showing conceptual-theoretical developments. We need an overview that relates such developments to their contexts, takes note of their uses and consequences, evaluates them critically but fairly, and attempts a synthesis of them or concludes that a synthesis is impossible and explains why.

What would be included in such map making? It would treat major events in public life, major currents in philosophy, major socioeconomic trends, major developments in the social sciences, and whatever else constitutes a significant context. Primarily, it would consider the responses in public administration. I have in mind, for example, (1) Herbert Simon's proposal to focus attention on decision making, using a fact/value distinction instead of a politics/administration distinction, (2) the comparative/development administration movement, (3) the new public administration movement, (4) the public choice movement, and (5) the policy studies/analysis/science movement and its implementation extension.

No one would deny that these matters deserve attention in describing the developments in public administration during the past four decades. By listing them I have not meant to construct an agenda or to establish priorities. Other less global, less publicized, or newer initiatives may prove more significant. A map of the whole would help us understand where we are and help us decide the direction in which we can move forward.

In concluding I suggest, as I have on previous occasions, that a useful comparison can be made with the field of medicine, the image of which is generally favorable. Medicine is presumed to be a field in which science and art, individual skills and institutional arrangements, are joined to produce generally satisfactory results even if at exorbitant costs. No month passes without news of a promising research discovery and an improved therapy. Health improves and life lengthens.[21] What impresses me as I survey and reflect on the field of medicine is its sprawling, heterogeneous, and shifting nature. Its theories of causation and its therapies are many, varied, changing, and rather frequently in conflict. It draws not only on biology and chemistry but upon any and every source of putative knowledge that has a gleam of promise. Boundaries are not distinct and border wars are incessant. It is a melange of professions, specializations, occupations, skills, and roles, the whole given a semblance of unity by a focus on . . . on what? I invite the reader to write an unchallengeable conclusion to the sentence.

Is it realistic to expect that the administration of government, *our* government in present and anticipated circumstances, can be less complicated and problematic than medicine? The answer is clearly negative. The body political is not less complicated but more complicated than the body biological.

Taking all of this into account I conclude that, like medicine, public administration is properly served by multiple theories, perspectives, strategies, and roles, and by a situational, pragmatic adaptation of means to ends. As a broken ankle is not set by a typhoid vaccine, agency accounts are not audited by an appeal to social equity. As a contact dermatitis is not soothed by removal of the appendix, a confusing or vague regulation is not clarified by a transfer of funds.

The possibility must be allowed, of course, that I am only rationalizing and seeking to justify the chaotic situation in public administration as it has evolved in the past four decades. But, right or wrong, I conclude that our diversity is functional.[22] Our conflicts serve the useful purpose of exposing error and keeping us honest and sharp. Let us advance together and apart.

Endnotes

1. Adoption of the terms *public affairs* and *management* in the naming or renaming of pedagogic and research programs has represented an attempt to go beyond the old public administration, or to project an image of innovation, or both. *Public affairs* has suggested a movement in the politics/policy direction. *Management,* the preferred term of business, has suggested a movement in the science/techniques/efficiency direction. The new *policy* units plainly wished to be dissociated from what was viewed as a sterile and unprestigious identification.

2. The presentation at this point follows closely one I made earlier in a piece for the September/October 1982 issue of *Dialogue,* an organ of the Public Administration Theory Network.

3. A good summary presentation of the role of the Church in bridging the ancient and modern administrative organization is Maureen Miller, "From Ancient to Modern Organization: The Church as Conduit and Creator," *Administration and Society* 15:275–293 (November) 1983.

4. I use *imperial* in a descriptive, denotative sense, not as a term of opprobrium. As used in this essay *imperial* means rule over a large territory and a sizable population. Of course, imperial rule has often, even characteristically, been harsh for a large part of the population ruled. But this is true regardless of time, place, and ideology. Put another way, I do not use *imperial* and *imperialism* in their Marxist sense of oppressive rule over other peoples by capitalist regimes.

5. An important example is the now democratic representative assembly that evolved from a convocation of magnates or the estates.
6. The significance of the English antecedent is indicated by asking, for example, what might have resulted if our mother country had been Spain or Russia, both of which colonized in the Americas?
7. Samuel P. Huntington, *Political Order in Changing Societies* (New Haven, CT: Yale University Press, 1968), p. 110. "America perpetuated a fusion of functions and a division of powers, while Europe developed a differentiation of functions and a centralization of power." The point is well taken, although, as Huntington knows, settlement began only after the Tudor period had ended. This historical view helps to explain the judiciary in the United States, because courts in Tudor England exercised important administrative functions.
8. Interpretation and reinterpretation of the idea and motives of the framers is endless, of course, but I believe there would be general agreement with this statement before qualifications were made. The influence of Montesquieu's (mis)interpretation of the English Constitution and of Newtonian ideas of balance and reciprocal action are old standard items in the interpretive literature.
9. The republican influence is well symbolized by the formation of the Society of the Cincinnati by officers of the Revolution. Cincinnatus, a semilegendary figure of early republican Rome, twice left the plough to lead the republic to victory against its enemies.
10. There is another point of view with highly respectable proponents. In summary and perhaps in too crude a form, the opinion is that the framers were very much aware of administration. But they did not view it as a separate function of government. They saw it rather on a continuum with, or inextricably mixed with, the political. The separation of function created by later events and ideas is contrary to the thought and intent of the framers. The nation should seek to return to a scheme closer to their intention.

   The late Herbert J. Storing argued this position cogently. See "Herbert J. Storing and the Study of Public Administration" in Kent A. Kirwan, *The Political Science Reviewer* XI:193–222 (Fall) 1981. The position is also presented skillfully by John A. Rohr in his essay in this volume. And it is advanced by Vincent Ostrom in *The Intellectual Crisis of American Public Administration* in his critique of a public administration premised on the dichotomy and the principles.

   The scholarship apparent in writings that develop this point of view is impressive and the arguments are well made. How realistic it is to suppose that we have strayed from the views of the framers and ought generations later to return to them remains to be demonstrated.

   I can hardly claim to be the first to observe the academic separation of theory and practice. Consider the following quotation:

   > It has been a mistake to declare that the principles of administration apply under any form of government and to assume that administration (or governance) is not concerned with political theory. Since special efforts are required to get the political theorist past Machia-

velli, the quarantining of theory has had unfortunate consequences. Theorists have been deprived of the invigorating influence of close participation in and observation of governmental processes, and the study of administration has been denied the insight and sense of the significant which the good theorist could bring to the job. Political theory, instead of being the core of the study of administration, is relegated to the position of an irrelevant subject connected with administration only in the sense that both are about government. Research and writing in administration continue to be atomistic, first, because there are no recognized principles which are peculiar to administration, and, second, because students of administration have not availed themselves of the continuity which theory might provide.

To put the matter succinctly, the subject matter of public administration has been defined so as to leave a no-man's land of significant problems, flanked on one side by the students of administration and on the other by political theorists. (Donald Morrison, "Public Administration and the Art of Governance," *Public Administration Review* 5:83–87, 85 (Winter) 1945.

No one has said it better.

11. My most recent effort is "Political Science: Tradition, Discipline, Profession, Science, Enterprise," in Fred Greenstein and Nelson Polsby, eds., *Handbook of Political Science,* Vol. 1 (Reading, MA: Addison-Wesley, 1975), pp. 1–130.

12. There is a terminological problem to which I am increasingly sensitized, one I judge to be related to the disjunction. It is a conundrum in and for political science, or it should be. It can be put this way: What is the name for "it," the phenomenon or cluster of phenomena that is or should be at the center of government attention?

Polity is often used as a generic term for independent political entities, but its derivation from *polis* means that it carries associations quite inappropriate in some cases. Neither the United States, the U. S. S. R., nor, for that matter, France or contemporary Greece, would be polities to the Athenians. *State* as a generic term suffers two handicaps. One is its close association with modern history. The other is its association with philosophies judged fanciful or pernicious. *Country* and *nation* suffer from obvious handicaps of lack of precision or generalizability.

For most purposes, *government,* deriving via Latin from the Greek root which also gives us *cybernation,* is the most appropriate term for analysis in my opinion. The ancient empires *and* the city states unquestionably had government, as do both contemporary liberal democracies and communist regimes.

13. If there is a literature that can be designated "the history of government" I have not been able to identify it. Of course, there are treatments of *a* government or of government in general in particular eras. The rise of the modern state is well covered, as is the evolution of American government. But the history of government, in general and as such, has not to my knowledge engaged the attention of historians. Archeologists, anthropologists,

and sociologists contribute significantly to understanding the evolution of government, but to political scientists the history of government is a nonsubject.

I will put my point another way. E. N. Gladden's *A History of Public Administration* (London: Cass, 1972), two volumes, is as close to a history of government as anything of which I am aware. I believe the disjunction relates to a matter that has long puzzled me and on which I have commented twice in print, the last time in "Organizational Theory: Structural and Behavioral Analysis," *Public Administration Review* 38:589–597 (Nov./Dec.) 1978. There is a literature of organization theory that has been produced by, and can be identified with, the disciplines of anthropology, economics, and sociology. But there is no body of organization theory that can be identified with political science, unless it is invisible to my eyes. The literature that is identified with public administration, the principles and related concepts, for example, as well as later behavioral theory, did not come from political science.

14. The best brief treatment of the development of the modern state is Gianfranco Poggi, *The Development of the Modern State: A Sociological Interpretation* (Stanford, CA: Stanford University Press, 1978). In his preface, Poggi remarks, "As for political science, over the past thirty years or so it seems to me to have gone to incredible lengths to *forget* the state," p. xiii (emphasis in original). In 1982 the American Political Science Association took as the theme of its annual meeting The State. This is rather like the American Medical Association taking as the theme of its annual meeting The Body.

15. When I wrote *The Administrative State* (New York: Ronald Press, 1948) as an attempt to view the literature of public administration through the lens of political theory, I puzzled over the concept of efficiency in Chapter 10. Plainly, efficiency was being used as premise and value in arguments that could only be construed as arguments in political theory. But, unlike other concepts on which I focused, it had no place in the history of political theory. How had this happened? I now understand the matter better if the arguments set forth in this essay are tenable.

16. The popular idea that democracy was a Greek invention must be severely qualified. The Greeks gave us the name, and the Greek literature extolling democracy certainly has played an inspiring and motivating role in its development, but Greek democracy was not very democratic, or very liberal, by American standards. For most purposes democracy is a late-modern phenomenon.

17. The efficient citizenship movement of the Progressive period represents our closest approach to combining the classical, activist type of citizenship and modern equalitarian democracy. Its success was modest, its scope was limited, and its time was brief.

18. I have speculated that dichotomies or paired opposites have a base in the biology of the brain, given their prominence in our thought ways. Certainly they are prominent in other cultures as well as our own. But monisms and triads are also prominent, and beyond these, pluralisms. Christianity exhibits the full range.

19. The ways in which simultaneous use of triparte and dual schemes of conceptu-

alizing and rationalizing government can be in conflict are various, but two have been obvious and troublesome. One is the third branch, the judiciary. It can hardly be ignored, but how can it be rationalized? The other is the elected chief executive who competes with the legislature as the representative of the popular will. This complicates the overhead or two-pyramid conceptualization, as well as presenting an anomaly if the chief executive is thought of as the chief administrator. As the old reform slogan had it, "For representation, elect; for administration, appoint." The council-manager scheme presents no problem of this kind as a matter of principle, although it presents major problems at the points where politics and administration meet.

20. A complicating force that was not mentioned is religion. In both the civic-culture and imperial traditions government has been sacred, that is, at the center of, perhaps the source of, what is claimed and generally accepted as sacred. The United States is engaged in an experiment in separating what millenia of governmental experience have joined. It is hardly surprising that complications and controversy attend the experiment.

21. I share the favorable view of medicine and surrender myself to the White Coat with only minor misgivings. I note, however, that (1) it is estimated that 80 per cent of diseases are self-limiting ("God heals and the doctor takes the fee"), (2) a significant amount of disease is iatrogenic, that is, caused by medical treatment, and (3) despite all, eventually everyone dies. Would the reader care to qualify what he or she has been saying about the Postal Service?

22. I have been chided for soft-headedness and for an irresponsible ecumenism. I am not against rigor where it is appropriate, and I am on the record as favoring more careful research on matters that lend themselves to careful research. But, yes, I am against sectarianism and for ecumenism.

CHAPTER 4

The Administrative State
and Constitutional Principle

John A. Rohr
THE VIRGINIA POLYTECHNIC INSTITUTE AND STATE UNIVERSITY

JOHN A. ROHR is Professor of Public Administration at the Virginia Polytechnic Institute and State University. His articles on constitutional themes related to public administration have appeared in the Public Administration Review, *the* Review of Public Personnel Administration, *the* Public Administration Quarterly, *the* American Journal of Public Administration, *and the* International Journal of Public Administration. *He has written three books, the most recent being* To Run a Constitution: The Legitimacy of the Administrative State. (*Lawrence, Kansas: University Press of Kansas, 1986.*) *In that book he develops more fully the themes treated in the present chapter. Professor Rohr is Managing Editor of* Administration and Society *and a former member of the Editorial Board of the* Public Administration Review. *He is a leading authority on administrative ethics.*

Theory is grounded in particular history as John A. Rohr offers an important study of the administrative state and constitutional principle. In Endnote 10 of the previous essay in this volume, Dwight Waldo discusses the literature that argues for the commitment of the founders to administrative application as well as administrative energy. Waldo cites Rohr's work as a skillful presentation of the point of view of Herbert A. Storing, Vincent Ostrom, and others to the effect that the nation has strayed from the unity of function the founders intended for American government.

Rohr does represent this point of view, but he does considerably more than that. His intellectual debt to Storing and Ostrom is obvious and acknowledged. He moves beyond them, however, to suggest that the modern administrative state is not just a return to federalist principles. It is also a correction of the dysfunctions in the constitutional system the federalists and anti-federalists devised. The bureaucracy, for example, embattled as it is by those who do not understand its legitimate place in constitutional principle, is probably more representative of the people than the House of Representatives itself. Further, the functions of the higher reaches of today's career civil service are a reasonable approximation of what the framers envisioned to be the functions of the Senate in the regime they proposed. Those who argue that administrative agencies such as independent regulatory commissions act unconstitutionally because they violate the separation of powers do not know their Constitution. More precisely, they do not know the intent of the framers.

Rohr says the legitimacy problem stems from a traditional theory of public administration that developed independently of and at times in opposition to the primary symbol of legitimacy in American politics, the Constitution of the United States. Woodrow Wilson himself must bear some of the responsibility for this, along with Frank J. Goodnow and the Civil Service Reformers. Wilson's instrumental view of administration in his 1887 essay was at odds with the Constitution to the extent that it emphasized a separation of function whereby only the legislature embodied the will of the state. In saying administrators merely execute policy, Wilson set aside his knowledge that in American constitutional theory the legislature does not possess the totality of governmental power. It does not embody the entire will of the state. The Constitution-makers won an argument with John Adams on that point.

The Civil Service Reformers overcorrected the dysfunction of Jacksonian democracy by ignoring the fact that the balance of power in American government is struck in the Constitution itself, not in the legislature. Congress is part of the balance. The executive and judicial branches cannot be subordinate to the legislative branch or the balance to which the people consented when they ratified the Constitution is destroyed. In constitutional theory checks are intended to preserve the constitutional equilibrium that the doctrine of separation of independent powers represents. Wilson developed a rich polemic against such a separation in *Congressional Government* (1885). His intellectual progeny also stand outside American constitutional principle when they call for changes to the Constitution to accommodate administrative needs. Administrative needs can be met and the administrative state legitimated *within* existing American constitutional theory and design. Attention to the founding event itself, including the great public debate surrounding ratification of the Constitution, facilitates a more complete understanding of the constitutional principles agreed upon. With that understanding, perhaps some healing of the diseased body politic can take place.

Most foundings are shrouded in myth, and political foundings are no different. For the Greeks Plato fashioned the myth of Er to enlist cosmic order in support of virtue. For Romans the stories of Aeneas and Romulus illustrated the decisive normative event of the founding of the city of Rome. Americans, too, have built a civil religion around the founding period. But, unlike the Greeks and Romans, we have more than myths at our founding. We have a founding document, notes from the participants of the convention that wrote the document, and summaries of the speeches at the subsequent ratifying conventions in the several states. We also have carefully edited texts of the pamphlets and newspapers attacking and defending the proposed Constitution.

Rohr has consulted these materials extensively, and he understands their relevance for modern public administration in a profound way. The conclusion of his work is deceptively simple, however. He says that American administrative institutions are compatible with and even enhance constitutional design. Public administrationists who call for changes in the design are impatient with a resource richer than they know. The Constitution is both the real and the symbolic source of the legitimacy of the administrative state.

Public administration cannot inherit the founders' intent unless it realizes the extent to which Woodrow Wilson and others of the Progressive Era fathered it out of wedlock with the Constitution. The real fathers of the administrative state are the founders themselves, both federalists and anti-federalists. It was a long and ecstatic night in the summer of 1787 when more brilliance was gathered for a single act of political creation than had ever occurred before. Rohr and Van Riper agree that the result was not a bastard child that ought to struggle for legitimacy today. It was an heir to the constitutional purple. When American politicians today invoke "the spirit of the founding fathers" in order to denigrate administrative institutions, they are wide of the mark of both the theory and the letter of the Constitution of the United States.

It [the Federal civil service] continues to play an essential role in ensuring the stability of the world's largest and most successful democracy. Our ability to function effectively in times of trial and upheaval and to prosper when various national crises have passed depends in no small degree upon the contributions of those who make up our civil service system.

— *Ronald Reagan*
January 10, 1983

A decade ago Vincent Ostrom presented an important study in administrative theory that went beyond Woodrow Wilson to a view of government "that Wilson rejected in establishing the foundations for his political science."[1] The rejected view was that of *The Federalist Papers*. In this essay I shall follow the path Ostrom opened because I share his belief that contemporary students of public administration have much to learn from the *Federalist* and indeed from the entire founding period. Because I tread this path with questions in mind and goals at hand quite different from Ostrom's, my interpretation of the *Federalist* and the founding period is quite different from his.

Introduction

> I think it may be laid down as a general rule, that their [the people's] confidence in and obedience to a government, will commonly be proportioned to the goodness or badness of its administration.
>
> — *The Federalist* 27

My goal in writing is to contribute to the important effort of legitimating the contemporary administrative state. The question I ask is how a close examination of the founding period might help in this legitimating endeavor. Before getting into the substance of my argument, I shall state the postulates of my inquiry:

1. We live in an administrative state and will continue to do so for the foreseeable future.
2. This administrative state is not well managed.
3. One of the reasons the administrative state is not well managed is that its institutions and procedures are looked upon as illegitimate.
4. This lack of legitimacy is due in part to the questionable constitutional status of administrative institutions in a regime organized around the principle of separation of powers and intended to preserve individual rights.

These are my postulates. My hope is that a justification of administrative institutions in terms of constitutional principle will make a modest contribution to the effectiveness of their performance. I use the language of hope and postulate to bypass the demands of rigorous argument. The argument will come later when I try to demonstrate that the administrative institutions are compatible with—and indeed enhance—constitutional design. At the outset, however, I rely on hope and postulate to explain why the argument is worth making. One must begin any task somewhere unless one emulates Descartes in thought or the Creator in action. I believe my hope and postulates do not outrage common sense. The first two postulates are platitudinous. The other two, as well as my hope, are supported in well-established literature.[2]

The Problem

If it be true that all governments rest on opinion, it is no less true that the strength of opinion in each individual, and its practical influence on his conduct, depend much on the number which he supposes to have entertained the same opinion. The reason of man, like man himself, is timid and cautious when left alone and acquires firmness and confidence in proportion to the number with which it is associated. When the examples which fortify opinion are *ancient* as well as *numerous* they are known to have a double effect. In a nation of philosophers this consideration ought to be disregarded. A reverence for the laws would be sufficiently inculcated by the voice of an enlightened reason. But a nation of philosophers is as little to be expected as the philosophical race of kings wished for by Plato. And in every other nation the most rational government will not find it a superfluous advantage to have the prejudices of the community on its side.

— *The Federalist* 49

In using the word *legitimacy,* I do not mean mere legality. Administrative institutions are quite legal, but so are the American Nazi Party, the Flat Earth Society, and *Hustler* magazine. By *legitimacy* I mean more than a grudging acceptance of the inevitable. To me the word suggests at least confidence and respect and at times even warmth and affection. Hamilton was speaking the language of legitimacy when he noted the connection between sound public administration and widespread popular support in *Federalist* 27. His point was that a well-administered government would win the affection of the people. I suggest that we stand Hamilton's argument on its head and say that governmental institutions with weak legitimacy will not be well administered.

The link between legitimacy and the founding period needs a word of explanation. The Constitution is not the only source of legitimacy in American politics. Consider, for example, the Declaration of Independence, Washington's Farewell Address, and Lincoln's profound remarks at his second inauguration. The legitimacy of administrative institutions, however, is particularly vulnerable to *constitutional* attack. At a very simple level, campaign oratory that calls for a return to the ways of the founding fathers is usually a thinly veiled attack on the administrative state. Such language should not be dismissed lightly. As Marvin Meyers has reminded us, "Political talk has mattered in America."[3] It tells us a great deal about our politics if an elected official can rally support by shouting "Who elected Paul Volcker?"

Coming closer to home, we find at times in public administration literature a plausible but embarrassing impatience with a constitutional design that severely inhibits economy, efficiency, and effectiveness, the hallmarks of our calling. Dramatic calls for far-reaching constitutional reform are no strangers to the corpus of public administration literature. Fortunately for our profession, these calls are frequently buried in academic publications where they are likely to escape the notice of elected officials who have always suspected that we are wayward sons and erring daughters of our founding fathers.[4]

The most direct link between the administrative state and constitutional illegitimacy, however, can be found at the very beginnings of self-conscious American public administration, in the work of Wilson, Goodnow, and the Civil Service Reformers. For our purposes, Wilson's work is the most interesting. In the second section of the centennial essay, Wilson states his famous instrumental view of administration. The constitutional background of Wilson's understanding of administration can be found in his 1885 book, *Congressional Government,* where he develops a rich polemic against separation of powers. What is remarkable, however, is that neither in the book nor the essay does Wilson call for the constitutional amendment that was absolutely essential for the reforms he had in mind. In his earlier writings, Wilson had not been so reserved. In an article written in 1884, Wilson issued a straightforward call for an American version of cabinet government. He offered specific language to amend the Constitution to bring about the desired change. Article I Section 6, now reading ". . . and no person holding any office under the United States shall be a member of either House during his continuance in office," would have been changed by Wilson to read "and no person holding other than a Cabinet Office under the United States shall be a member of either House during his continuance in office." Thus the addition of four words, "other than a Cabinet," would introduce members of the President's cabinet into Congress and thereby destroy separation of powers.[5]

I have discussed elsewhere some possible explanations for Wilson's decision to omit the call for a constitutional amendment in *Congressional Government.*[6] What is important for our purposes here is to note that Wilson's instrumental view of administration in the second part of his 1887 essay was at odds with the Constitution of the United States, and Wilson knew it. Wilson, like Goodnow and many of the civil service reformers, preferred separation of functions to separation of powers.

The legislature embodied the will of the state. Administration, which must be separated from the legislature, executes that will. This separation of functions is the familiar instrumental model of public administration, but it is not the constitutional theory of separation of powers. In constitutional theory the legislature does not embody the will of the state. It does not possess the *totality* of governmental power. The people in ratifying the Constitution conferred governmental power on *each* of the three great branches in such a way that each is independent of the other. As Wilson read his times, this arrangement led to the sorry state of affairs he lamented so eloquently in *Congressional Government* and which he tried to correct in his essay of 1887.

The point of all this is that if we trace the birth of the administrative state to Wilson's essay, we find that it was conceived out of wedlock with the Constitution of the United States and hence we should not wonder at subsequent attacks upon its legitimacy. Its presence has always been something of an embarrassment at patriotic reunions. How can a real American love the Occupational Safety and Health Administration? Unlike political parties, congressional committees, and judicial review of acts of Congress, all of which are strangers to the Constitution, the administrative state has never been at ease in our constitutional design.[7]

In tracing the legitimacy problem to Wilson, I do not propose to make him the posthumous recipient of unsolicited advice on how he might have accommodated his ideas on administration to American constitutional theory. Instead, I propose to follow Ostrom back to the founding of the republic to see what congruence we might find between what the framers envisioned and what we know today as the administrative state.

Foundings

At the birth of societies, the rulers of republics establish institutions; and afterwards, the institutions mould the rulers.

— *Montesquieu*

If it is important to legitimate the administrative state, one might wonder why we must return to the Constitution to do so. The question is particularly germane if legitimacy means more than legality. If the administrative state can be squared with the principles of the Constitution, what surplus value above legality is thereby conferred? The answer to this question lies in the symbolic importance of the Constitution in American politics.

At a descriptive level it is obvious that the Constitution is of enormous public interest. As these sentences are being written, plans are afoot to mark the Constitution's bicentennial in a variety of ways. Serious books on the Constitution abound: Kent, Story, Curtis, Thayer, Cooley, Beard, Corwin, Warren, Pritchett, Swisher, Crosskey, Bickel, Kurland, Tribe, and Ely. The list goes on and on. Social scientists who have never read the Constitution can tell us about Beard's interpretation of it. Recently a popular interpretation of the *Federalist* was promoted by the Book-of-the-Month Club.[8]

More important than the writings about the Constitution, however, is the habit of American statesmen of invoking its spirit to support the policies of the day. For our purposes, it is particularly important to note that the invocation usually takes place in a context that is hostile to the ways of the administrative state. "Getting back to the spirit of the founding fathers" is usually an easily deciphered code for reducing the scope of government. The assumption is that the framers of the Constitution would disapprove of the power of our contemporary federal government. In allowing it to become so powerful we have somehow betrayed them.

There is no doubt the framers would be amazed at what the government they created has become, but it is not clear they would disapprove. The framers were unalterably committed to the preservation of individual rights as the purpose of government, but they did not see such rights in competition with governmental power in a zero-sum game. In the *Federalist* and in the secret debates in Philadelphia, one of the major arguments in favor of the new Constitution was that a strong government is needed to protect individual rights. This is precisely what was wrong with the Articles of Confederation: Individual rights were not being protected.[9]

The framers of the Constitution might be somewhat sympathetic with those whose efforts to fashion new institutions of government are criticized on grounds of their legitimacy. They faced legitimating problems themselves. The 1787 Convention in Philadelphia was the creature of congressional approval of a recommendation from the Annapolis Convention of the previous year. There a handful of delegates issued a call for a convention "to devise such further provisions as shall appear to them necessary to render the Constitution of the Federal Government adequate to the exigencies of government and the preservation of the Union."[10] Congress approved this call but added an important qualification: The convention was to meet "for the sole and express purpose of revising the Articles of Confederation."[11]

During the debate over ratification of the Constitution the Anti-Federalists scored some telling points against the proposed document by noting that the framers had exceeded their congressional mandate. Having been told to convene "for the sole and express purpose of revising the Articles of Confederation," they proceeded to bring forth a new government. The Anti-Federalists had a good point, but the Federalists were ready with a reply that might well serve as the keynote for those Americans who support a powerful federal government. The Federalists said it was more important to achieve the ends of the congressional mandate as stated at the Annapolis Convention—"to render the Constitution of the Federal Government adequate to the exigencies of government and the preservation of the Union"—than to scruple too nicely over the specified means ("of revising the Articles of Confederation"). They maintained that once it was clear that revision of the Articles could not meet the exigencies of government and preserve the union, it was incumbent upon them to propose a new government.

In emphasizing the ends–means rationality of the framers' defense of a powerful government in support of individual rights, I do not suggest that they were so far removed from the Revolution as to have grown complacent about tyranny. Their fears of government abuse are well known, and it is this aspect of the framers' thought that is stressed almost to the exclusion of everything else they had to say when their spirit is called upon in contemporary political discourse. The framers are inaccurately presented as implacable foes of the wide-ranging activities of modern government. If we are to legitimate the administrative state, we must at least neutralize the framers. I say *at least* neutralize, because I think we can do better. I believe they can be enlisted in support of the modern administrative state. For the present, however, let us be content with neutralizing them so that opponents of the administrative state do not win cheap victories by exploiting the symbolic power of the Constitution. This neutralization is the first of two answers to the question I raised at the beginning of this section, viz., if legitimacy means more than legality, why return to the Constitution to legitimate the administrative state?

The second answer is that the Constitution is the symbol of the founding of the republic, and in politics foundings are normative. Here I follow Hannah Arendt's treatment of "authority," which she sees as originally a Roman idea, but one that is quite pertinent to American politics. Plato had no equivalent for the Latin word for authority, *auctoritas*. The Greeks saw public life in terms of either persuasion or coercion. Coercive regimes were not "political." Life in the polis demanded a public order based on persuasion and argument among equal citizens. The democratic execution of Socrates led Plato to despair of the politics of persuasion and to look for an alternative to coercion. He found it in philosophy for the few who would rule and myth for the many who would be ruled.[12]

Although the Romans reverently accepted the Greek sages as their teachers, their public order rested on a different set of principles. For the Romans, the founding of the city was the decisive political event. Their years were numbered from that event, *ab urbe condita,* from the founding of the city, as ours are numbered from the birth of Jesus. Their great political myths, the stories of Aeneas and Romulus, were related to the founding of Rome and, in this respect, contrasted sharply with Plato's political myth of Er that enlisted cosmic order in support of virtue.[13] The emphasis on the unique character of the founding of Rome explains why the Romans, unlike the Greeks, never had a foreign policy of colonization. The Greeks frequently set out to establish new settlements in the belief that the polis was in their persons regardless of geography. Instead of founding new cities, the Romans expanded their rule by adding to the original foundation "until the whole of Italy and eventually the whole of the Western world were united and administered by Rome as though the whole new world were nothing but Roman hinterland."[14]

Underlying this emphasis on the founding of the city was the Roman idea of authority. Authority is a difficult concept for contemporary social scientists to grasp because we have been taught to think in terms of function and behavior rather than nature and essence. When those in authority succeed in getting their subordinates to obey, we find it hard to see any meaningful distinction between authority and coercion. The distinction, however, was crucial for the Romans.

Theodore Mommsen, acknowledging the difficulty in arriving at a clear concept of Roman authority, describes it as "more than advice and less than a command, an advice which one may not safely ignore."[15] Arendt suggests looking at the political language of the Romans to understand that authority meant something that is powerful without being coercive. The word *auctoritas* is derived from the verb *augere,* "to increase," whence the English "augment." Roman politics was looked upon as the augmenting of the great decisive act of founding the city.[16]

This reverence for the past is reflected in the use of the word *majores,* "the greater ones," for those we call ancestors. The great governing body of the Roman Republic was the Senate, from *senior,* "an elder." The well-known Roman regard for the father as head of the family, *paterfamilias,* had its political counterpart in veneration for the *patria,* "fatherland," from *pater,* "father." Ancestors, elders, and fathers were revered not just because they were old but because they were closer to the founding that gave meaning and purpose to public life.

Arendt notes that authority for the Romans was closely related to tradition and religion. *Traditio* means a handing down from generation to generation and explains in part the extraordinary—though at times quite dysfunctional—Roman tendency to preserve archaic forms of government. If tradition stresses the action of ancestor upon descendents, religion connotes action in the opposite direction. The noun *religio* is from the verb *religare*, which means "to tie back," hence, to bind oneself to the past. Authority *augments* the founding by *tradition* and ties back the citizen to his past through *religion*.

As a telling summary of this linguistic examination, we should note that the Latin *principium* has the double meaning of both "beginning" and "a principle." It thereby captures the normative dimension of political foundings and brings us back to our own Constitution. It is the moral vitality of the Constitution as the great work of the founding period of the republic that makes it so powerful a symbol in our politics. This aspect of the Constitution, the product of the normative event of founding, provides my second answer to the earlier question of why we should return to it to legitimate the administrative state. It explains why it was so unfortunate for American public administration that Woodrow Wilson was unable or unwilling to ground his theory of administration in American constitutional principle and why it is so unwise for his intellectual progeny to call for constitutional changes to accommodate administrative needs.[17]

The sanctity of the founding period for Americans is quite clear to anyone who reflects on the paths tourists follow when they visit Philadelphia or the nation's capital. The salience of American civil religion is obvious. It is no accident that our heroic statues are larger than life. Like all peoples, we need our myths. Like the Romans, our myths are related to our founding, but, unlike the Romans, we have more than myths at our founding. We have written records that surround the event: notes from the participants at the Philadelphia Convention, summaries of the speeches at the ratifying conventions in the several states, and carefully edited texts of the pamphlets and newspapers defending and attacking the proposed Constitution. We can have it both ways. We can have our Constitution as the object of civil religion, and we can have it as an object of close scrutiny and critical evaluation.

Throughout the remainder of this essay, I shall emphasize this second aspect of the Constitution and the founding period. To legitimate the administrative state in constitutional terms, we must *examine* the Constitution rather than simply revere it. We shall examine it less as the product of the framers' will than as the centerpiece of the great public argument of 1787–88. Our task is to see how the administrative state can fit into American political orthodoxy, an orthodoxy that is found not in a set of approved propositions but in the dynamism of the public argument itself. In emphasizing the public argument of 1787–88, careful attention must be given to the vanquished Anti-Federalists. They were important participants in the debate. They lost the argument, but in doing so they pointed out the glaring weaknesses in the Constitution, some of which are still with us today. In stressing the *argument* of the founding rather than its outcome, we follow Arendt's observation on American politics that more fundamental than the written Constitution itself is the "principle of mutual promise and common deliberation"[18] that made it possible.

Specifically, three points will be made concerning the administrative state and the Constitution: (1) that administrative institutions are not inconsistent with the constitutional principle of separation of powers, (2) that the higher reaches of the career civil service fulfill the framers' original intent for the Senate, and (3) that the entire career civil service provides a remedy for a serious defect in the Constitution, namely the inadequate representation that so distressed the Anti-Federalists of 1787–88. Thus I shall argue that the administrative state is consistent with the Constitution, fulfills its design, and heals a longstanding, major defect.

The Founding Argument: 1787–88

> Upon the whole I doubt whether the opposition to the Constitution will not ultimately be productive of more good than evil.
>
> — *George Washington*

Preliminary Comment

Before addressing the substantive points of the founders' arguments over separation of powers, the Senate, and representation, a preliminary comment is in order. Some of the sources cited in the discussion that follows may be unfamiliar to the reader. The text of the Constitution itself and the *Federalist* are well known, but the corpus of the Anti-Federalist writings is less familiar. Nevertheless, the Anti-Federalist position is crucial for our purposes in examining the argument over the Constitution. Unfortunately, the *Federalist* and other writings in support of the Constitution are often read simply as authoritative expositions of the true meaning of the document. History has conferred victors' laurels on these authors. When they were writing, however, their purpose was more to persuade than to expound. To understand the arguments in *support* of the Constitution, we must understand the arguments *against* it as well. Publius and the other writers supporting the Constitution shaped their arguments to meet the attacks of the Anti-Federalists.

We are fortunate to have a critical and comprehensive edition of the Anti-Federalist writings, Herbert J. Storing's seven-volume work, *The Complete Anti-Federalist*. In his introductory essay, Storing argues that the Anti-Federalists should be counted *among* the founding fathers because of their contribution "to the dialogue of the American Founding."[19]

As Storing puts it, "The Constitution that came out of the deliberations of 1787 and 1788 was not the same Constitution that went in."[20] Under stern Anti-Federalist pressure, the Constitution was ratified on the understanding that a Bill of Rights would be added immediately. In addition to securing a Bill of Rights, the Anti-Federalists initiated the main lines of constitutional debate that dominated the early years of the republic and, to a certain extent, the constitutional debate of today. The Anti-Federalists gave us the first warnings of where the polity was most vulnerable. It was a service no less patriotic, although far less celebrated, than the service of those who have told us where we excel.

In examining the founding arguments for hints of what we call the administrative state, I will look to Publius and others who supported the Constitution to determine (1) what it was they wanted from the new Constitution, and (2) what they thought they were providing. Conversely, the writings and speeches of the Anti-Federalists will tell us (1) what they feared from the new Constitution, and (2) what they thought they were getting. The contrast between Federalists and Anti-Federalists, however, is not quite as neat as the previous sentences suggest. The Anti-Federalists were not merely opponents of the Constitution. Many of them saw considerable merit in the proposed Constitution but withheld support in order to force a second convention that would amend the proposed Constitution to meet certain, and in some cases very limited, objectives. Thus some portions of the Anti-Federalist literature can correctly be read as supporting specific aspects of the Constitution, for example, federal regulation of commerce, equal representation of the states in the Senate, and life tenure for federal judges.

A final word on sources concerns the notes taken by participants at the Philadelphia Convention, especially the exhaustive notes of James Madison. The speeches given at the Convention are not part of the argument for or against the Constitution. Rather, they are arguments over what the Constitution would be. These arguments are important for determining the intent of the framers for specific parts of the Constitution. In discussing the executive powers of the Senate, for example, it is important to know that at several points in the deliberations at Philadelphia the Senate was to have complete power over treaties and the appointment of ambassadors, consuls, and federal judges. This tells us that when the framers finally decided that the President was to share these executive powers with the Senate, they had in mind far more than a legislative check on the executive power of the President. The development of the Philadelphia document clearly indicates that the framers intended the Senate to be not only a second house of the legislature but an executive institution as well. Neither the text of the Constitution nor subsequent institutional history suggests the extent to which the framers looked to the Senate as part of the executive establishment.

Separation of Powers

> To what purpose separate the executive or the judiciary from the legislative
> if both the executive and the judiciary are so construed as to be at the
> absolute devotion of the legislative? Such a separation must be merely
> nominal and incapable of producing the ends for which it was established.
> It is one thing to be subordinate to the laws and another to be dependent
> on the legislative body. The first comports with, the last violates, the funda-
> mental principles of good government, and whatever may be the forms
> of the Constitution, unites all power in the same hands.
>
> — *The Federalist* 71

One of the earliest criticisms of the governmental institution considered
by some to be the harbinger of the administrative state—the independent
regulatory commission—was that it violated the principle of separation
of powers. Interestingly, Publius had to answer a similar attack against
the Constitution. "One of the principal objections inculcated by the more
respectable adversaries to the Constitution is its supposed violation of
the political maxim that the legislative, executive, and judiciary departments ought to be separate and distinct."[21] Our task of defending the
blending of powers in administrative institutions is much easier than
Madison's. We need only show that such blending is not contrary to
the spirit or letter of the Constitution, whereas Madison had the more
fundamental task of defending the blending in the Constitution itself.
Our task is made simpler by maintaining that the Senate is a body that
exercises all three powers. It is legislative when it joins the House of
Representatives in endorsing a bill, it is executive when it advises and
consents to treaties or to appointments of high-ranking federal officials,
and it functions in a judicial capacity when it acts as a court to try
impeachment charges.

The blending of powers in the Senate was a cause of considerable
concern to the Anti-Federalists.[22] History has taught us to look upon
the Senate as almost exclusively a legislative body. This was not what
the framers had in mind. The development of the executive agreement
in foreign affairs and the merit system in personnel management have
substantially reduced the significance of the Senate's constitutional powers over treaties and appointments. Because impeachments have been
rare we hardly ever think of the Senate as a judicial body. The judicial
character of the Senate is dramatically clear, however, in the provision
in Article I that the Chief Justice will preside over the Senate when it
tries a presidential impeachment.[23] In as much as this has happened
only once in our history, the awesome scene of a Chief Justice presiding
over the Senate to remove a President from office is more a majestic
museum piece than an operating principle of government.

This was not the case for the framers. Impeachment was discussed in remarkable detail at the Constitutional Convention and during the ratification debate. It is surprising to note that the impeachment power was a major consideration in the creation of the electoral college. Throughout the Convention, the method of selecting the President was a matter of stormy controversy. At various times the Senate or the Congress as a whole were among the possible candidates considered for this responsibility.[24] Toward the end of the Convention, a committee came forward and presented the model for what was to become the electoral college. When Edmund Randolph and Charles Pinckney asked "for a particular explanation and discussion of the reasons for changing the mode of electing the Executive," Gouverneur Morris responded with an account worthy of the complexity of the college itself.[25] He began by stating the committee's reasons for deciding that the Senate was the proper institution to try causes of presidential impeachment. This power could not be given to the Supreme Court because a President removed from office might still be tried in the federal courts for the offense that led to his removal. Because the Senate would try the impeachment, the House of Representatives should bring the charges. Because both houses of Congress would be involved in the removal of the President, neither should be involved in selecting him. Here the Convention's reasoning seems to have been that a body that had chosen an officer would be likely to consider impeachment and conviction an adverse reflection on its earlier judgment. Hence, the committee recommended that a body of special electors chosen by the people, the electoral college, should select the President. Only if this body failed to agree upon one person should the legislature be permitted to enter the presidential selection process.

I mention this arcane point only to support my contention that the judicial power of the Senate was not a bizarre aberration but an aspect of constitution making that was solidly integrated into the overall design of the document. The framers found it easier to achieve consensus on how to oust a President from office than on how to select one.

The salience of the impeachment power in the constitutional design provides textual evidence that the framers were quite willing to place all three powers of government in one institution when circumstances so required. Hence any argument that administrative agencies act in a constitutionally suspect manner simply because they exercise two or even all three governmental powers can be refuted from the intent of the Constitution itself.[26]

The separation-of-powers attack on administrative agencies is usually based on an excessively rigid interpretation of this venerable doctrine. One careful student of the history of separation of powers has described the "pure position" as separation of *functions*, exercised by separate organs of government with no overlap.[27] This is helpful as an ideal type, but it is far removed from the common understanding of the principle of separation of powers discussed by the framers.

Madison's position is instructive. He acknowledges the importance of the principle of separation of powers when he allows that "the accumulation of all powers legislative, executive, and judicial in the same hands may justly be pronounced the very definition of tyranny."[28] After acknowledging "the celebrated Montesquieu" as "the oracle who is always consulted and cited on this subject," Madison maintains that Montesquieu "did not mean that these departments ought to have no *partial agency* in, or control over, the acts of each other." He meant "no more than this, that where the *whole* power of one department is exercised by the same hands which possess the whole power of another department, the fundamental principles of a free constitution are subverted."[29] This is not the place to evaluate Madison's reading of Montesquieu.[30] What is important for our purposes is that no less an authority than James Madison in *The Federalist Papers* subscribes to a remarkably relaxed view of separation of powers. Clearly no administrative agency ever has functioned or ever could function as a department that exercises the whole power of another department.[31] In effect, Publius has defined any possible violation of separation of powers out of existence for the entire government as well as for any administrative agency we know today. Even Abraham Lincoln during the darkest days of the Civil War did not come close to appropriating the "whole power" of either Congress or the courts.

In making this point, I do not suggest that Madison is the most reliable guide on the correct understanding of separation of powers. Nor do I suggest that his position is representative of the framers. Certainly he is not alone in his relaxed point of view, but other framers were more moderate. Rufus King and James Wilson, for example, stressed the independence of one department from another as the heart of the separation-of-powers doctrine.[32] This follows Madison's position without going to the extreme of saying the principle is breached only when the "whole power" of one branch has been taken over by another. Hamilton too is less exuberant than his *Federalist* co-author on the point of separation of powers. In *Federalist* 66 he rendered a subdued summary of Madison's earlier statement:

> The true meaning of this maxim [of separation of powers] has been discussed and ascertained in another place and has been shown to be entirely compatible with a partial intermixture of those departments for special purposes, preserving them in the main distinct and unconnected. This partial intermixture is even in some cases not only proper but necessary to the mutual defence of the several members of the government against each other.

Madison would agree with Hamilton that a "partial intermixture" of the departments' powers is at times a good thing. Indeed, the main point of *Federalist* 48 (written by Madison) is a positive defense of a blending of powers to preserve the principle of separation. It is not enough to rely on "parchment barriers" to keep the great branches independent of one another. The Constitution wisely preserves its intended balance by an elaborate series of checks that allow one branch to exercise in part the powers of another. An example is the President's legislative power of a conditional veto over acts of Congress. Thus for Publius a discreet blending of powers is the best way to preserve their sensible and effective separation.

With this relaxed teaching of the framers in mind, we can see how wide of the mark formalistic attacks on the administrative state are when they are aimed at the mere existence of a combination of powers in administrative agencies. The problem is not one of doctrine but of prudence. A partial blending of powers does not violate separation of powers, and according to Publius, it may at times enhance it.[33]

During the ratification debate there was considerable confusion over the theory of separation of powers that undergirds the Constitution. The confusion stemmed from Anti-Federalist allegations that the framers at Philadelphia patterned their work on John Adams' *Defense of the Constitutions of Government of the United States of America*. There is little evidence that this is the case, although we do know that the first volume of Adams's book reached Philadelphia in the spring of 1787.[34]

Regardless of what the framers thought of Adams's work, it is clear that their endeavor rested on a theoretical understanding of separation of powers that was quite different from that of Adams. It is no less clear, however, that in the heated debate after the Convention, the similarities between such ideas as "checks and balances," "mixed government," "balanced government," and "separation of powers" blurred the theoretical differences that separated Adams and the framers. The upshot of this confusion was that many Anti-Federalist writings missed their mark. They were aimed at the Constitution, but they hit Adams's *Defense* instead. The misdirected arguments of the Anti-Federalists are important for our purposes because they have a direct bearing on the understanding of administrative responsibility that was developed by the civil service reformers a century later. First, let us examine the differences between Adams and the framers, and then let us turn to the importance of this difference for public administration.

Adams's discussion of balanced government was profoundly influenced by the British experience with the mixed constitution of the limited monarchy at the end of the seventeenth century as well as by his personal observation of British government in practice in the late eighteenth century. King, Lords, and Commons were all present in Parliament, and that is where the checking and balancing went on. In applying this model to America, Adams saw the various orders in society being represented *in the legislature*. He supported separation of powers, but the executive and judicial powers were clearly subordinate to the legislature. They were not a check on the legislature because the legislature embodied the entire society and therefore had all the appropriate checks built into it. Despite his spirited defense of a vigorous executive, Adams's version of separation of powers rested on legislative supremacy. His frequent attacks on legislatures were not aimed at legislative power as such. His target was a unicameral legislature with no internal checks.

The Constitution does not rest on the principle of legislative supremacy. The balance of power is struck in the Constitution itself, not in the legislature. The legislature, Congress, is part of the balance. One branch may exercise powers ordinarily considered appropriate for another branch, as when the Senate shares the executive power of appointment with the President. This is a check that is intended to preserve the overall balance of the constitutional separation of powers. The executive and judicial branches cannot be subordinate to the legislature, for that would destroy the balance to which the people consented when they ratified the Constitution.

Thus, in constitutional theory checks are intended to preserve the constitutional balance, which is a separation of independent powers. For Adams, the checks balance the orders in society that are represented in a legislature that, in turn, is superior to but separate from the executive and judiciary. One of the most frequent criticisms of Adams's position was that a balanced legislature made sense only in a country such as England where there is a monarch and an hereditary nobility. In a republic there are no similar orders in society to check and balance each other in the legislature. Adams' reply was his famous discussion of a natural rather than an hereditary aristocracy that had to be managed in a balanced constitution.

The supporters of the Constitution did not need to resort to that argument. Their starting point was the solid republican ground that there was but one social order—the people—and their will was expressed in the Constitution they created. To preserve this Constitution, Publius would rely on *interest* to do for the Constitution what social orders do for the British. The famous lines of *Federalist* 51 occur in the context of preserving separation of powers: "Ambition must be made to counteract ambition. The interest of the man must be connected with the constitutional rights of the place."

It is no wonder that in the ratification debate the Constitution's President, Senate, and House of Representatives should be confused with Adams's version of King, Lords, and Commons. Nor is it surprising that the powerful constitutional Senate should be incorrectly regarded as the intended home of Adams's natural aristocracy.

The importance of the confusion in the debate is that Adams's idea of legislative supremacy reflected a strong conviction of many Americans. It had a lasting effect on our politics. If his position is purged of its natural or hereditary social orders,[35] the upshot is a legislature, rather than an elaborate constitutional design, that embodies the will of the people and that is distinct from but superior to both the executive that carries out its commands and the courts that adjudicate them. This is quite similar to the model of government favored by the civil service reformers. It gives a clear rationale for an instrumental view of administration that prizes above all else responsibility to the *elected* leadership. This may be a fine theory of public administration, but it is not the theory of the American Constitution. It was, however, a theory that fit nicely with the rising democratic spirit of the nineteenth century, and it is not surprising that it was defended by Woodrow Wilson, Frank Goodnow, and the other "founding fathers" of public administration.

Many Anti-Federalists found Adams's defense of legislative supremacy quite attractive. They were less impressed with his reliance on checks and balances, an opinion he shared with Publius. This was true regardless of whether the checks balanced the social orders in Adams's legislature or the three great branches of Publius's Constitution. The Anti-Federalists were more inclined to rely on civic virtue to preserve liberty. They believed in separation of powers, but, like Adams and unlike Publius, they linked this principle with legislative supremacy and valued it more for its efficiency than for its capacity to preserve liberty. For these higher matters the Anti-Federalists looked to the heart of the citizen rather than to the sophisticated checks and balances of either Adams or Publius. Civic virtue could best be inculcated in a small, homogeneous republic. This opinion was also generously supported in the political science of the day but was directly challenged by the bold Publius with his grand vision of a great commercial republic wherein interest would do the work of virtue.

The small republic with its capacity to promote civic virtue is a crucial point in the Anti-Federalist argument. They were not simply "states' righters." They were enamored of the states because the states were in fact small republics wherein a virtuous people with a common religion and homogenous culture could know their elected representatives who in turn would be responsible to the people. The fabric of the Anti-Federalist argument is woven with the strands of responsibility, religion, civic virtue, homogeneous culture, small republic, states' rights, and representatives close to the people. The point to stress is the Anti-Federalist belief in responsibility to the people as an overriding theme in their understanding of sound government. In 1787 this meant for the most part the responsibility of elected legislators to their electors. When the civil service reformers a century later insisted on the responsibility of administrators to the legislature, they were faithful heirs of the legislative-supremacy position of the Anti-Federalists. For the reformers and for the Anti-Federalists, the legislature was free of Adams's checks and balances because, good republicans that they were, they knew there was but one order in society—the people—and hence there was nothing to balance.

All this was at odds with the theory of the Constitution that Publius proposed. First, he understood responsibility in terms of the obligation of constitutional stewards to preserve the constitutional order the people had created. Government was responsible to the people, but only in the ultimate sense that the people had created a Constitution that is the immediate and practical object of political obligation and of the moral obligation announced in one's oath of office. Second, Publius would hotly dispute any hint of legislative supremacy. Indeed, he saw the "legislative vortex" as the great threat to the constitutional order he hoped the people would approve. He generously sprinkled the *Federalist* with hostile comments on legislatures. The fact that one steward is elected and another appointed suggests no preference for the former. Election is simply one of several ways of attaining a constitutional office. Like the later civil service reformers, Publius insisted upon responsibility from administrative officials, but it is responsibility to the President and emphatically not to the Congress.[36] For Publius the administrator is enlisted in the cause of helping the President maintain the constitutionally sanctioned balance among the separate constitutional branches.

When the civil service reformers came along with their principles of separation of powers, legislative supremacy, and administrative responsibility, they acknowledged their debt to their European mentors, but they also touched on ideas deeply rooted in American political experience. Although these ideas were embedded in our politics, they were not enshrined in either the letter or the theory of the Constitution. There a different set of ideas had triumphed a century earlier. The congruence between the reformers' principles and the American political experience may help to explain their success, but the constitutional dissonance surely helps explain the severe embarrassment they suffered at times. Perhaps the most notable embarrassment was the problem of what to do with the President in a plan based on administrative responsibility to a supreme legislature. Recall that Wilson once wondered in print about the consequences of making the President part of the civil service.[37] Instrumental administration tended to drag constitutional executive power down to its own level.

Then there is the problem of bicameral legislatures. If the legislature represents the will of the people, why have two houses? Publius would answer the question by denying its premise. It is the Constitution, not the legislature, that represents the will of the people. More precisely, it represents their considered judgment and deliberate choice. In that fundamental law the people had the good sense to create a bicameral legislature in which one body of their elected officials would check the other, and the President with his veto and executive subordinates would check both of them.

Adams could answer the question of bicameralism by saying it is part of the process of balancing the social orders in the legislature. For the civil service reformers and the Anti-Federalists who went before them, however, the bicameral legislature did not make a lot of sense.[38]

Our discussion of separation of powers began with an examination of the common charge that administrative agencies are illegitimate because they combine legislative, executive, and judicial powers. We saw that this charge is easily refuted because (1) the Constitution itself joins all three powers in the Senate, and (2) the understanding of separation of powers advanced by Publius, the foremost theoretician of the Constitution, readily accommodates the sort of blending of powers we find in modern administrative agencies.

The more serious separation-of-powers problem is that American public administration has developed around a model of responsibility to elected officials that puts severe pressure on both the letter and the theory of the Constitution's separation of powers. Elected officials head two branches that are separate without one being subordinate to the other. I suggest this is where we find a legitimacy problem more serious than that of the blending of powers. There is nothing illegitimate about the institutions of the administrative state in the formal powers it exercises. The problem lies with a traditional theory of public administration that has developed independently of and at times in opposition to the primary symbol of legitimacy in American politics, the Constitution of the United States.[39]

The Senate

And when I behold the Senate wielding in the one hand the strong powers of the Executive, and with the other controlling and modifying at pleasure the movements of the legislature, I must confess that not only my hopes of the beneficial effects of the government are greatly diminished, but that my apprehensions of some fatal catastrophe are highly awakened.

— James Monroe

The discussion in the previous section was intended to show that the blending of powers in administrative agencies is not inconsistent with the principle of separation of powers. The focus of this section is on the Senate. Here I shall escalate my position from the negative statement that the administrative state is not inconsistent with the framers' intent to the positive affirmation that it fulfills their design. I shall do this by examining the sort of institution the participants in the founding debate had in mind when they discussed the merits and defects of the proposed Senate. With allowance in mind for the havoc 200 years will wreak on anyone's intent, my point is that the function of the higher reaches of today's career civil service is in broad outline a reasonable approximation of what the framers envisioned as the function of the Senate in the proposed regime. The section has two parts. The first maintains that the Senate was intended to be part of an executive establishment and not simply a second house of a national legislature. The second examines certain salient characteristics the proposed Senate was expected to have that, when combined with its participation in the executive establishment, suggest some striking similarities to today's higher civil service.

EXECUTIVE ESTABLISHMENT.   The first point in establishing the executive character of the Senate is to note that it was not seen by anyone as simply a second house of the national legislature. This perception was universal. It was shared by friend and foe alike. Publius was unequivocal on the point,[40] and so were the Anti-Federalists. At times the latter list the legislative function of the Senate as but one of several powers they found objectionable.[41] At other times they used such terms as *veto* and *negative* to describe the Senate's legislative role. This language appears not only in the context of money bills, which must originate in the House of Representatives, but in general discussions of the Senate's legislative powers as well.[42] Perhaps the clearest Anti-Federalist statement on the nature of the Senate's legislative power appears in the quotation from James Monroe cited at the head of this section. He described the Senate as "wielding in the one hand the strong powers of the Executive, and with the other controlling and modifying at pleasure the movements of the legislature."[43] For Monroe, the House of Representatives is the real legislature. The Senate's role is to control and modify the House.

This view of the Senate can be found in the language of the framers of the Constitution at Philadelphia. Roger Sherman,[44] Gouverneur Morris,[45] and James Madison[46] were explicit on the point.[47] The Senate is part of the legislative branch, but the nature of its legislative power is different from that of the House. Bicameralism did not mean simply that one house would check the other. As Gouverneur Morris put it, the Senate was to be "the checking branch" of the legislature.[48] The reason this function fell to the Senate was because of its executive character. Just as the President, the Chief Executive Officer, had a conditional veto over both houses, so also his executive partner, the Senate, had a more extensive veto over the House of Representatives.

Thus far I have tried to show that the Senate was intended to be more than a second house of a national legislature. Was it also seen as part of an executive establishment? A strong indication that this is the case appears in the development of the text of the Constitution during the Convention. On August 6, 1787, the Committee of Detail reported a draft of the Constitution that referred to the Senate "when it shall be acting in a legislative capacity."[49] This clearly implies that legislation was but one of its functions.[50] The same draft gave the Senate exclusive power over treaties and the appointment of ambassadors and judges of the Supreme Court. When the Senate exercised these powers, the August 6 draft would have exempted it from a prohibition against adjourning "to any other place than that at which the two Houses are sitting."[51] Thus the August 6 draft would have allowed the Senate to meet in a place other than its ordinary legislative location to conduct its executive affairs. The language of the Constitution itself is not explicit on this point, but it does allow this interpretation. The fourth clause of Article I, Section 4, reads: "Neither House, during the Session of Congress, shall, without the Consent of the other, adjourn for more than three days, nor to any other place than that in which the two Houses shall be sitting." The immobility of the two houses applies only when Congress is in session. It is possible, of course, for the Senate to be in session without Congress being in session, as when the Senate conducts its executive affairs. If such business were conducted in a place other than the chamber in which the Senate legislates, its executive character would be dramatically heightened. An early draft of the Constitution would have made an explicit provision for this possibility, and the final version at least implies it. This textual argument is offered to support the point that the executive character of the Senate was not simply an afterthought but was an integral part of the earliest constitutional plan. It is not as though the Senate were given a share in the treaty and appointing powers simply to provide a legislative check on the President. It was the other way around. The President was eventually given a share in the Senate's hitherto exclusive power over treaties and the appointment of ambassadors and Supreme Court justices.[52]

A profile of the Senate as an executive establishment emerges with striking clarity in the arguments of the Anti-Federalists. This is true even though the Anti-Federalists differ sharply in what they find offensive about the Senate. One group feared a Senate-Presidential cabal. For William Grayson, the senators were the President's "counsellors and partners in crime."[53] To gain his favor, the senators would support him and would unite with him "to prevent a discovery of his misdeeds."[54] Cato complained that in trying an impeached President the senators "are to determine as judges the propriety of the advice they gave him as senators." They will not be "an impartial judicature." Instead, they will serve as a screen for great public defaulters.[55] Luther Martin[56] and James Monroe[57] voiced similar concerns.

A second group of Anti-Federalists feared the executive powers of the Senate were so great that they would overwhelm the President.[58] The Federal Farmer, for example, feared that "this sexennial senate of 26 members will not, in practice, be found a body to advise, but to order and dictate in fact, and the President will be a mere *primus inter pares*."[59] Centinel saw the Senate as "the great efficient body in this plan of government," with the result that "the President, who would be a mere pageant of state, unless he coincides with views of the Senate, would either become the head of the aristocratic junta in that body, or its minion."[60] The Anti-Federalist minority at the Pennsylvania Ratifying Convention voiced a similar concern. "The president-general is dangerously connected with the senate. His coincidence with the views of the ruling junta in that body is made essential to his weight and importance in the government, which will destroy all independency and purity in the executive department."[61]

A third group of Anti-Federalists criticized the Constitution for failing to provide an executive council to the President.[62] The Senate, they maintained, is a poor substitute. At the Virginia Ratifying Convention, George Mason, after noting his fear of Senate-President conspiracies against the people, proposed a remedy: "A constitutional council, to aid the President in the discharge of his office." The Senate should have the power to impeach the President and his council. "Then we should have real responsibility. In the present form, the guilty try themselves. The President is tried by his counsellors."[63]

Mason's position on the executive council issue is interesting. As a delegate to the Philadelphia Convention, he had originally favored a plural executive. When this measure failed,[64] he took as his backup position an executive council that would not only assist the President but would check him as well.[65] In desiring to put the check *within* the executive branch, Mason seems to have judged this to be the best way to recoup some of his losses from having the plural executive rejected. The idea of a council within the executive branch serving as a check on the President suggests interesting parallels with contemporary bureaucracy. For the present, however, our main point is that Mason saw the Senate as a close executive partner of the President. "The Constitution has *married* the President and Senate,"[66] he complained. A similar position is taken by Anti-Federalist Richard Henry Lee in a letter to Governor Randolph[67] and by Judge Samuel Spencer at the North Carolina Ratifying Convention.[68]

From a variety of adherents to the Anti-Federalist persuasion, the image of the Senate as an executive establishment clearly emerged, and the Federalists did not contest the point. They granted it. Their counter-attack was aimed at Anti-Federalist positions that found the Senate's role in executive matters excessive, unwise, or inappropriate.[69] Thus there was no dispute in 1787–88 over the *fact* that the Senate was intended to serve as part of the executive. The dispute centered on the propriety of the arrangement.[70]

ATTRIBUTES OF THE SENATE.   The founding argument highlights certain attributes of the Senate. Again, the argument was not so much over what they were but over whether they were desirable. The attributes important for our consideration are duration, expertise, and stability. Each one was seen by Publius as leading to the other, and he discussed them all in the *Federalist* 62.

DURATION, EXPERTISE, STABILITY.   The six-year term of office would give the senators the duration they needed to resist "the impulse of sudden and violent passions" by which "factious leaders" might try to induce them to approve "intemperate and pernicious resolutions." The Senate must "possess great firmness and consequently ought to hold its authority by a tenure of considerable duration." The six-year term would also give the senators time to develop the expertise they would need to master the intricacies of public life, especially the complexities of foreign affairs.[71] When the Anti-Federalists examined the six-year term, they tended to emphasize the indefinite re-eligibility of senators. To ignore this factor would lead to a senator's lifetime in office that would lay the foundation for an American aristocracy. The Anti-Federalists argued that because senators can be chosen again and again by their state legislatures, it is inevitable that they would be. For Centinel, this inevitability would come from "their extensive means of influence."[72] Brutus feared that "it will before long be considered disgraceful not to be reelected. It will therefore be considered as a matter of delicacy to the character of the senator not to return him again." Senators will in effect serve during good behavior. They will always be returned "except in cases of gross misconduct."[73]

Melanchthon Smith, Hamilton's great adversary at the New York Ratifying Convention, conceded the importance of stability in the Senate and agreed that a six-year term was not excessive. Re-eligibility was the problem for Smith, and consequently, he proposed an amendment that would enable a state legislature to recall any senator it had chosen and prohibit the legislature from selecting any one man to serve for more than six years out of any twelve. This would prevent the possibility of the Senate becoming "a fixed and unchangeable body of men."[74]

The Federalists could not deny the possibility that a senator might serve for a lifetime. The text of the Constitution clearly allowed it. Instead the Federalists spoke warmly of the lifelong tenure in the venerable senates of Sparta and Rome. At the convention, not only did both Hamilton and Gouverneur Morris support life tenure for senators,[75] they did so without any admission of embarrassment on the issue.

CONTINUING BODY.   The Anti-Federalists feared the Senate would become a continuing body. Section 3 of Article II states that the President "may, on extraordinary occasions, convene both Houses, *or either of them*" (emphasis added). The most obvious situation in which the President would want to convene one house but not the other is when he wanted the advice and consent of the Senate on a treaty or an appointment. The Anti-Federalists maintained that the "extraordinary occasion" of Section 3 would in practice become quite routine, and, as a result, the Senate would be in session permanently.[76] Thus for George Mason, the Senate would be "a constant existing Body almost continually sitting."[77] For Luther Martin, it would be "in great measure, a permanent body, constantly residing at the seat of government."[78] Cato maintained that the powers of the senators were so extensive "that it would be found necessary that they should be constantly sitting."[79]

PERSONNEL MANAGEMENT.   The Senate's role in appointments received considerable attention during the founding debate. As we have seen, early drafts of the Constitution had given the Senate exclusive power over the appointments of ambassadors and Supreme Court justices. Thus the framers were quite serious about including the Senate in the appointing power. Indeed, it was not until the penultimate session of the Convention on September 15 that the framers got around to giving Congress the power to vest "the appointment of such inferior officers as they think proper in the President alone, in the courts of law, or in the heads of departments." Had this clause not been added to the second section of Article II, a literal reading of the Constitution would require senatorial approval for every federal appointment.[80]

The Federal Farmer was one of the strongest critics of the Senate's role in appointments. He feared the Senate would not approve legislation vesting the appointing power in department heads but would jealously guard that power for itself. He did not think the Senate itself would constantly be in session, but the demands of its personnel responsibilities would prompt it to select from its members a "council of appointment" that "must very probably sit all, or near all, the year."[81]

The Anti-Federalists tended to emphasize the extensive intervention of the Senate in what we have come to know as personnel management. Hamilton took some trouble to deny this. Such senatorial intervention would run counter to his cherished principle of unity within the executive.[82] In his eagerness to downplay the Senate's role in appointments, however, Hamilton proved a poor seer. He noted that the Senate's power to advise and consent referred only to appointments, not to nominations.[83] Thus, while the Senate can approve or reject, it cannot choose. Hamilton would not have approved of what we have come to know as senatorial courtesy.

There was another matter touching the Senate's power over personnel matters in which history clouded Hamilton's crystal ball. This was the issue of removal from federal office. The Constitution is silent on this topic, but Hamilton argued in *Federalist* 77 that the Senate would have to concur in a presidential decision to remove a federal officer. In making this argument, however, Hamilton compromised his belief in unity in the executive branch. In this case it was a good bargain. Hamilton's commitment to stability in public administration triumphed over his belief in unity. Presidents, especially after Washington, would come and go, but the Senate, with its staggered six-year terms, would provide stability. The passage is worth quoting in its entirety:

> It has been mentioned as one of the advantages to be expected from the co-operation of the Senate, in the business of appointments, that it would contribute to the stability of the administration. The consent of that body would be necessary to displace as well as to appoint. A change of the chief magistrate therefore would not occasion so violent or so general a revolution in the officers of the government as might be expected if he were the sole disposer of offices. Where a man in any station had given satisfactory evidence of his fitness for it, a new President would be restrained from attempting a change, in favour of a person more agreeable to him, by the apprehension that the discountenance of the Senate might frustrate the attempt and bring some degree of discredit upon himself. Those who can best estimate the value of a steady administration will be most disposed to prize a provision which connects the official existence of public men with the approbation or disapprobation of that body which from the greater permanency of its own composition will in all probability be less subject to inconstancy than any other member of the government.

Hamilton's image of the civil servant whose tenure rests on "satisfactory evidence of his fitness" is instructive for our purposes. It fits neatly with the views of one of Hamilton's most formidable adversaries, the Federal Farmer. The latter, as we have seen, objected to the Senate's role in appointments because he thought it unlikely that the senators would yield their appointing power to department heads, which the Constitution permits but does not command. The Federal Farmer found this unfortunate because he envisioned the department heads as "well informed men in their respective branches of business," who "will, from experience, be best informed as to the proper person to fill inferior offices." Appointments of department heads "will not often occur." The Federal Farmer thinks we can count on the department heads to make "impartial and judicious appointments of subordinate officers." In addition, he finds in the presence of these well-informed, experienced, stable, impartial, and judicious department heads a further but decidely un-Hamiltonian advantage. "An executive too influential may be reduced within proper bounds by placing many of the inferior appointments in courts of law and heads of departments."[84]

The idea of subordinate executive officers checking the President is strictly Anti-Federalist.[85] Hamilton would reject it out of hand. Despite this important difference, however, Hamilton and the Federal Farmer agree on a rather lofty image of the civil service. The agreement is somewhat remarkable inasmuch as the contexts of the discussions are, according to the Federal Farmer, how to get the senators out of appointments and, according to Hamilton, how to get them into removals. Their agreement on the common end of a stable and competent civil service is all the more instructive because of their total disagreement over how to achieve it. A high-minded civil service is the intent of both supporters and opponents of Senate activism in personnel administration.

"DUE SENSE OF NATIONAL CHARACTER."   In *Federalist* 63, Madison looks to the Senate to fill the need for "a due sense of national character." The expression occurs in the context of foreign affairs, but similar language in other parts of the *Federalist* and in speeches by both Madison and Hamilton at Philadelphia suggests a broader application of this intriguing idea. In discussing the power to try impeachments, Hamilton refers to senators as "the representatives of the nation."[86] At the Philadelphia Convention, Hamilton had looked to the Senate, whose members in his plan would serve for life,[87] as embodying "a permanent will" and a "weighty interest" in the government that would give them a reason to endure "the sacrifice of private affairs which an acceptance of public trust would require."[88] Also at the Convention, Madison had looked to the Senate as an institution that would "protect the people against their rulers."[89] By "ruler," the context makes clear, he meant the elected representatives in the House. Madison echoes this theme in *Federalist* 63, where he looks to the Senate for that "cool and deliberate sense of the community" that will safeguard against the danger that the country "may possibly be betrayed by the representatives of the people."

There is some special significance in these references to the Senate as providing a "due sense of national character," embodying a "permanent will," and enjoying some special insight into "the cool and deliberate sense of the community." It was these characteristics that prompted

Publius to use the rather extraordinary image of senators as "the representatives of the nation." This language is extraordinary not only because of the rather exalted position it suggests for the Senate—a position not easily squared with Publius's understanding of checks and balances[90]—but also because it implicitly denies a role for senators as representatives of the states. Clearly the Senate does not "represent" the people. All are agreed on that, but interestingly, many Anti-Federalists joined Publius in denying that the Senate represents the states. Inasmuch as senators will vote *per capita,* as individuals, they cannot be said to represent their respective states. One senator may cancel the vote of his colleague who has been chosen by the legislature of the same state. The state legislature cannot dismiss, impeach, or recall senators whose votes fail to reflect the state's interests. As a leading Pennsylvania Anti-Federalist put it, "It is not the power of choosing to office merely that designates sovereignty, but the power of dismissing, impeaching, and the like those to whom authority is delegated."[91] In an effort to make sure the senators did represent their states, Anti-Federalist George Livingston introduced an amendment at the New York Ratifying Convention that provided in part

> that it shall be in the power of the legislatures of the several states to recall their senators, or either of them, and to elect others in their stead, to serve for the remainder of the time for which such senator or senators, so recalled, were appointed.[92]

This amendment was eloquently defended by Melanchthon Smith on the grounds that it would ensure the Senate would be an institution that represented the states.

If, as all agree, the Senate does not represent the people and if, as the Anti-Federalists maintained, it fails to represent the states as well, then who or what does the Senate represent? Perhaps Hamilton's expression, "representatives of the nation," is meaningful.

In reviewing our examination of the Senate in the founding debate, what emerges is an institution:

1. in which legislative, executive, and judicial powers are combined,[93]
2. which functions as part of an executive establishment, working (or conspiring) with the President and checking him as well,
3. whose members will serve for a long period and possibly for life or during good behavior,
4. whose members are expected to have an expertise not found in the House of Representatives,[94]
5. whose members will have the institutional support to resist popular whims of the moment,
6. which is constantly in session,

7. which may conduct its affairs in a place other than the legislative chamber,
8. which exercises supervisory power over the federal personnel system, and
9. which expresses a permanent will and national character.

I do not suggest that all the participants in the debate anticipated any one of these characteristics, nor that any one of the participants saw all of them. What I do contend is that an institution with these characteristics can be found in the great normative act of founding the republic.

Today's Senate, of course, resembles hardly at all the institution envisioned in the debate of 1787–88. The adoption of the Seventeenth Amendment mandating direct election of senators, a wise and long overdue recognition of the democratic spirit of the United States, formalized the role of the Senate as almost exclusively a second legislative chamber. It was a role that had characterized the Senate long before the amendment's adoption in 1916. Executive agreements in foreign affairs and a merit system in personnel administration considerably reduced the Senate's executive powers under the Constitution as well. Today's Senate is not an executive council in any sense. Its judicial powers are hardly ever exercised. It is not particularly more effective at resisting popular whim than the House. It is not constantly in session. Relatively few of its members serve for more than twenty years. Its expertise is not noticeably greater than that of the House. In a word, today's Senate is not the sort of institution the Federalists wanted and the Anti-Federalists feared.

The closest approximation to such an institution as the Federalists wanted and the Anti-Federalists feared can be found in the career civil service, especially at its higher levels. I resist the temptation to point to the Senior Executive Service (SES) because I do not want to burden my argument with all the problems facing that unhappy institution. The pre-SES writings on some sort of senior civil service seemed closer on paper than the SES does in fact to the sort of institution that is identified in the founding argument.[95] This is not the place to call for specific institutional reforms, however. My argument has been aimed at legitimacy, not reform. Neither a Senate nor a bureaucracy that resists popular whim is a likely candidate for plaudits today. We tend to call such institutions unresponsive. I am not addressing the issue of how to make bureaucracy more responsive nor even whether it should be. What I do suggest is that there are aspects of the administrative state that roughly fulfill the vision of the framers. Today's administrative state is fair game for criticism but not on grounds of constitutional legitimacy.

Representation

> To make representation real and actual, the number of representatives ought to be adequate. They ought to mix with the people, think as they think, feel as they feel, be perfectly amenable to them, and thoroughly acquainted with their interest and condition.
>
> — *George Mason*

The third aspect of the founding argument that we shall consider is the debate over the number of representatives in the House. The Anti-Federalists had a powerful argument, and they knew it. The Federalists knew it too. They put up only token resistance.

The Constitution provided that when the First Congress met there should be sixty-five men in the House of Representatives apportioned as follows: New Hampshire 3, Connecticut 5, New York 6, New Jersey 4, Pennsylvania 8, Delaware 1, Massachusetts 8, Rhode Island 1, Maryland 6, Virginia 10, North Carolina 5, South Carolina 5, and Georgia 3. The text of the Constitution made it clear that this distribution was merely provisional. "Within three years after the first meeting of the Congress" there was to be an "actual enumeration" that would redistribute representatives and liability for direct taxes in accordance with the standards of apportionment mentioned in Article I, Section 2.[96] The process of reapportioning representatives was to be taken up every decade after the constitutionally mandated decennial census. The ultimate size of the House was not fixed in the Constitution. The only provision was that "the Number of Representatives shall not exceed one for every thirty Thousand, but each State shall have at least one Representative."

The Anti-Federalists attacked this arrangement. They maintained that there were too few members in the House to provide adequate representation and that the provision that there can never be more than one representative for 30,000 persons insured the perpetuation of the problem. Their argument was solidly grounded in a theory of representation that was held by nearly all Anti-Federalists who addressed the issue and, at times, by Federalists as well.[97] The theory held that a representative assembly should be a microcosm of the society as a whole. With so few representing so many, it was likely that very few men "of the middling sort" would ever be elected. This basic theme is captured in the quotation from George Mason at the heading of this section to the effect that representatives ought to think and feel the same as those they represent. The theme is played throughout the Anti-Federalist literature with only minor variations.

Centinel linked numbers of representatives with safeguards against corruption:

The number of the representatives (being only one for every 30,000 inhabitants) appears to be too few either to communicate the requisite information of the wants, local circumstances, and sentiments of so extensive an empire, or to prevent corruption and undue influence in the exercise of such great powers.[98]

The Federal Farmer connected the representation issue with the Constitution's failure to provide for jury trials in civil cases:

The essential parts of a free and good government are a full and equal representation of the people in the legislature and the jury trial of the vicinage in the administration of justice. A full and equal representation is that which possesses the same interests, feelings, opinions, and views the people themselves would were they all assembled. A fair representation, therefore, should be so regulated that every order of men in the community, according to the common course of elections, can have a share in it. In order to allow professional men, merchants, traders, farmers, mechanics, etc. to bring a just proportion of their best informed men respectively into the legislature, the representation must be considerably numerous.[99]

Brutus found it impossible to have adequate representation in a nation as large as the proposed United States and gave this as one of his reasons for opposing the Constitution:

If the people are to give their assent to the laws by persons chosen and appointed by them, the manner of the choice and the number of the chosen must be such as to possess, be disposed, and consequently qualified to declare the sentiments of the people. For if they do not know, or are not disposed to speak the sentiments of the people, the people do not govern. The sovereignty is in a few. Now in a large extended country it is impossible to have a representation possessing the sentiments and integrity to declare the minds of the people without having it so numerous and unwieldy as to be subject in great measure to the inconveniency of a democratic government.[100]

Samuel Chase feared that the House of Representatives would be dominated by the rich:

I object because the representatives will not be the representatives of the people at large but really of a few rich men in each state. A representative should be the image of those he represents. He should know their sentiments and their wants and desires. He should possess their feelings. He should be governed by their interests with which his own should be inseparably connected.[101]

Anti-Federalist literature abounds with similar attacks on representation in the Constitution.[102] As we have just seen, the argument may be paired with fear of corruption and opposition to an extended republic. But the common thread in the Anti-Federalist attack is the need for representation to reflect properly the society as a whole. "The representation ought to be sufficiently numerous to possess the same interests, feelings, opinions, and views which the people themselves would possess, were they all assembled."[103]

The Federalist reply to this argument was weak, confused, and disorganized. The reason was that many Federalists were quite sympathetic with their opponents on this issue. This was true even of Madison, whose view of representation as "filtering" and "refining" public opinion was the most serious principled reply to the Anti-Federalist microcosm theory.[104] Despite Madison's theoretical differences with the Anti-Federalist position on representation, as a practical matter he agreed that the number of representatives in the proposed House was too small; there were limits to filtering and refining.[105] At the Philadelphia Convention, Madison had argued on several occasions that the number of representatives ought to be substantially increased.[106] Hamilton agreed with him. As Madison related in his notes:

> Colonel Hamilton avowed himself a friend to a vigorous government but would declare at the same time that he held it essential that the popular branch of it should be on a broad foundation. He was seriously of the opinion that the House of Representatives was on so narrow a scale as to be really dangerous and to warrant a jealousy in the people for their liberties. He remarked that the connection between the President and Senate would tend to perpetuate him by corrupt influence. It was the more necessary on this account that a numerous representation in the other branch of the legislature should be established.[107]

As both Hamilton and Madison were displeased with the size of the House,[108] it is no wonder that as Publius they approached the defense of the actual number of representatives with little zest. Madison's discussion of representation in the *Federalist* is brilliant and justly famous,[109] but on the sixty-five-member House he is disappointing.

Concern over the size of the House was widespread at the convention. James Wilson explicitly defended the microcosm theory of the legislature.[110] So did George Mason, who, as an Anti-Federalist after the convention, mercilessly hammered away at the representation issue. Having been one of the most active delegates at the Convention, he knew the weak spots of the Constitution better than any other Anti-Federalist.[111] The most dramatic moment in the Convention's discussion of representation came on the very last day, September 17. The final version presented to the delegates provided that there could not be more than one representative for every 40,000 persons. With a motion on the floor to approve the entire document, Nathaniel Gorham of

Massachusetts said that "if it was not too late," he would like to see the number 40,000 reduced to 30,000 "for the purpose of lessening objections to the Constitution."[112] The reduction would not affect the sixty-five members approved for the first Congress, but it would give Congress greater discretion to increase the size of the House in the future. One can imagine the anger of the weary delegates when literally at the last moment Gorham raised this intractable issue that, by his own admission, "had produced so much discussion."[113]

Whatever restlessness the delegates might have felt was summarily quashed when General Washington, the President of the Convention, rose and, for the first time during the four months of the Convention, expressed his opinion on a substantive matter on the floor. Madison reported Washington as stating that "the smallness of the proportion of Representatives had always appeared to himself [Washington] among the exceptionable parts of the plan and late as the present moment was for admitting amendments, he thought this of so much consequence that it would give him much satisfaction to see it adopted."[114] Madison hastened to add: "No opposition was made to the proposition of Mr. Gorham and it was agreed to unanimously."[115]

The consensus that settled around the inadequate representation in the House of Representatives has a normative bearing on today's administrative state. No one would seriously contend that today's House of Representatives is in any sense a microcosm of American society. Its elite character is obvious. It has developed in a manner consistent with the worst fears of the Anti-Federalists.

The House appears in a better light if one follows Madison's filtering and refining view of representation. A charitable observer of American politics might find a certain human excellence in the men and women who sit in the House today. Even if this point is conceded, however, the current House with its 435 members representing over 200 million people does not meet an important precondition of Madison's filtering theory. In *Federalist* 58, Madison argued convincingly against a legislature that is too large. Without deciding how large is too large, he warned against adding members to the legislature. But he cautioned that his warning should be observed only *"after securing a sufficient number for the purpose of safety, of local information, and of diffusive sympathy with the whole society."* The italics are Madison's. It is his generous concession to the Anti-Federalist microcosm argument. A concession, but not a surrender. Information and sympathy in the representatives is not the same as thinking as the people think and feeling as they feel. Throughout the representation debate, Madison tended to stress the knowledge the representatives should have of the people's circumstances. The Anti-Federalists tended to stress their feelings and character. Madison's reference to "sympathy" in *Federalist* 58 is not as common in his writings on representation as his references to knowledge and information.[116]

Given a ratio of 435 to over 200 million, it is quite doubtful that today's representatives could meet the Madisonian criteria of information *and* sympathy. Indeed, it is doubtful they could meet the criterion of information alone. It is absolutely certain they cannot meet the Anti-Federalist standard of feeling and character.

If one takes the founding argument as normative, it seems fair to conclude that the House of Representatives presents a serious defect in the Constitution, a defect that has been with us from the very beginning. There is a certain illegitimacy about the House of Representatives; not in a technical, legal sense, of course, because the House exists as the text of the Constitution clearly permits. The illegitimacy is at a deeper level. The formal constitutional provision for apportionment belies the principles of representation that dominated the founding debate. The House of Representatives is at odds with what the founding generation thought representation should be. This defect is serious and perennial.

Calling for a larger House of Representatives is not the answer. Madison argued convincingly against that approach. "The countenance of the government may become more democratic, but the soul that animates it will be more oligarchic."[117] Any freshman congressman would surely understand Madison's point. In calling for a larger House of Representatives in 1788, the Anti-Federalists knew there was an outer limit. A mob was not what they had in mind. As Melanchthon Smith noted, "Ten is too small and a thousand too large."[118] The Anti-Federalists had no intention of destroying the deliberative character of the legislature. They would probably have been appalled at a House of Representatives with 435 members.

If the House is too small and yet cannot be increased, the solution to the representation problem may lie elsewhere. During the past two decades, considerable professional attention in public administration has been given to the idea of representative bureaucracy.[119] The literature is rich and varied. Sometimes it raises questions of equity, as with the argument that the distribution of jobs in the career public service should bear some resemblance to the makeup of society as a whole. This is an interesting reprise on the Anti-Federalist microcosm theme. Sometimes the advocates of representative bureaucracy stress control. That is, a truly representative public service is the most effective safeguard against a runaway bureaucracy. Again, the echo of the Anti-Federalists is heard when representative bureaucracy advocates say it is important to have in *government,* if not in the legislature, people who think as we think and feel as we feel. Sometimes the literature makes the bold claim that in certain circumstances the bureaucracy can *govern* more effectively than Congress because it represents important interests and attitudes that are nearly always excluded from Congress.[120]

If one combines the representative-bureaucracy literature with the literature that stresses the discretionary power of the modern administrative state,[121] what begins to emerge is the image of a governing institution whose personnel distribution comes much closer to the microcosm the Anti-Federalists had in mind than the House of Representatives has ever done. This is not to say the bureaucracy *is* a microcosm, only that it comes closer to being one than the House of Representatives. Although the bureaucracy is not, and perhaps should not be, a microcosm of American society in any exact sense, it may be the sort of microcosm the Anti-Federalists had in mind. The Anti-Federalists were not doctrinaire. They were more interested in making the statement that the House of Representatives is *not* a microcosm than in arguing the fine points of what they meant by thinking as the people think and feeling as they feel. There was no need for them to develop the point. The Federalist attack was not coming from that side. A careful review of the Anti-Federalist literature suggests a rather clear middle-class idea of microcosm. They feared "the better sort" as a potential aristocracy, while they favored "the middling sort."[122] Little is said about the poor.

Thus, even if today's bureaucracy can be justly faulted for not being truly a microcosm, it may well meet the more relaxed, middle-class standards of the Anti-Federalists. With its merit system it aspires at least in principle to achieve the filtering and refining effect of representation that Madison envisioned without sacrificing the "diffusive sympathy" with society as a whole that was also part of Madison's view. With its affirmative action policies, it is driven, at least in principle, to seek out those qualified persons who have been excluded from serving in a governing institution where they *and people like them* will have a voice, not just a job, in the public service. The House of Representatives simply cannot do this. For this reason, I would suggest that the administrative state, with its huge career public service, heals and repairs a defect in the Constitution of the United States.[123]

Conclusion

There has been just opposition enough to produce probably further guards to liberty without touching the energy of government, and this will bring over the bulk of the opposition to the side of the new government.

— *Thomas Jefferson*

In his 1887 essay Woodrow Wilson said it is becoming more difficult to run a Constitution than to frame one. Without deciding which of the two activities is the *more* difficult, we can readily assert that both are hard enough. Today's administrators "run a Constitution." The Constitution does not simply interface with public administration. The two are inextricably intertwined. He or she who studies constitutional law today studies public administration as well. It should not be otherwise in the administrative state.

This essay began with the expression of hope that legitimating the administrative state would enable it to perform more effectively. I shall close with another hope, that legitimation will tame the excesses of the administrative state. Legitimation has a civilizing aspect about it. In grounding the nature and function of the administrative state in constitutional principle, administrators are invited to assimilate the values salient in their constitutional heritage. If they do so, they will find at the center of this heritage a profound belief in individual rights and in the securing of these rights as the great overarching purpose of government. If administrators thus legitimate their activities, they will find not only what they seek but much more besides. They will find principles that will enable them to avoid the worst excesses of the administrative state. To legitimate is to tame and to civilize.

Endnotes

1. Vincent Ostrom, *The Intellectual Crisis in American Public Administration* (University, AL: University of Alabama Press, 1973), p. 81.
2. James O. Freedman, *Crisis and Legitimacy: The Administrative Process and American Government* (Cambridge: Cambridge University Press, 1978), p. 10; Rexford Tugwell, *The Emerging Constitution* (New York: Harper's Magazine Press, 1973), pp. 573–574; Peter W. Colby and Patricia Ingraham, "Individual Motivation and Institutional Change Under the Senior Executive Service," *Review of Public Personnel Administration* 2-108 (Spring) 1982; Kenneth Warren, *Administrative Law in the American Political System* (St. Paul, MN: West, 1982), p. 66; Hugh Heclo and Lester Salamon, *The Illusion of Presidential Government* (Boulder, CO: Westview Press, 1981); Charles L. Black, *The People and the Court* (New York: Macmillan, 1960), p. 36.
3. Marvin Meyers, *The Jacksonian Persuasion: Politics and Belief* (Stanford, CA: Stanford University Press, 1957). The quote is from p. viii of the Preface to the 2nd edition.
4. A. C. Millspaugh, *Toward Efficient Democracy* (Washington: Brookings, 1949) and *Democracy, Efficiency, Stability* (Washington: Brookings, 1942); Conley Dillon, "American Constitutional Review: Are We Preparing for the 21st Century?" *World Politics:* 5–24 (1977); Charles M. Hardin, *Presidential Power*

and Accountability: Toward a New Constitution (Chicago: University of Chicago Press, 1974); Rexford G. Tugwell, *Model for a New Constitution* (Santa Barbara: Center for the Study of Democratic Institutions, 1970); Conley Dillon, "Recommendation for the Establishment of a Permanent Commission on Constitutional Review," *The Bureaucrat:* 211–214 (July) 1974; 214 Herbert Croly, *Progressive Democracy* (New York: Macmillan, 1914).

5. Woodrow Wilson, "Committee or Cabinet Government," *Overland Monthly* 2nd sec. 3:17–33 (January) 1884. This article is reprinted in *The Papers of Woodrow Wilson,* edited by Arthur S. Link, Volume II, pp. 614–640, Princeton University Press, 1966. For a recent version of Wilson's proposal see Lloyd N. Cutler, "To Form a Government," *Foreign Affairs* 59-140 (Fall) 1980.

6. John A. Rohr, "The Constitutional World of Woodrow Wilson," in Jack L. Rabin and James S. Bowman, eds., *Politics and Administration: Woodrow Wilson and American Public Administration* (New York: Marcel Dekker, Inc., 1983), pp. 31–49.

7. James O. Freedman mentions parties, committees, and judicial review as examples of extraconstitutional institutions that have attained legitimacy in American government. See his *Crisis and Legitimacy: The Administrative Process and American Government* (London: Cambridge University Press, 1978), pp. 127–29.

8. Garry Wills, *Explaining America: The Federalist* (Garden City, NY: Doubleday, 1981).

9. Theodore Bland, a staunch anti-Federalist, reported that the Virginia Ratifying Convention was evenly divided, with "one-half of her crew hoisting sail for the land of *energy* and the other looking with a longing aspect on the shore of *liberty*." Robert Rutland, *The Ordeal of the Constitution: The Anti-Federalists and the Ratification Struggle of 1787–88* (Norman, OK: University of Oklahoma Press, 1966), p. 231. The sharp dichotomy Bland draws between liberty and energy in government was precisely what Publius attacked in *The Federalist.*

10. Charles C. Tansill, ed., *Documents Illustrative of the Formation of the Union of the American States* (Washington, DC: Government Printing Office, 1927), p. 43.

11. Ibid., p. 46.

12. This comment applies more to *The Republic* than to Plato's *Laws.* The latter work puts considerable stress on the art of founding a regime, even though there is nothing in the *Laws* comparable to what Arendt describes as the Roman meaning of *auctoritas.*

13. Plato, *The Republic: Book X,* 614a–618a.

14. Hannah Arendt, "What Is Authority?," *Between Past and Present* (New York: Viking Press, 1961), p. 120.

15. Ibid., p. 123.

16. *Auctor* ("author") is also from *augere* and is used synonymously with *conditor* ("founder") for those who established the political order. Like literary authors, authors of regimes have their work live after them. Authority thus augments the work of political authors.

17. See note 4 above.

18. Hannah Arendt, *On Revolution* (New York: Viking Press, 1963), p. 214. In stressing the "principle of mutual promise and common deliberation" as a founding principle, Arendt invites the reader to think of the Constitution more in terms of a covenant than a contract. That is, it brings a people into being, and to this day sustains them in being. Arendt's invitation is eloquently accepted in Milner S. Ball, *The Promise of American Law* (Athens, GA: University of Georgia Press, 1981), pp. 7–15.

19. Herbert J. Storing, ed., *The Complete Anti-Federalist*, 7 Volumes (Chicago: University of Chicago, 1981). The first volume of *The Complete Anti-Federalist* is Storing's brilliant introduction to the writings he edited so carefully. It is published in paperback under the title, *What the Anti-Federalists were FOR: The Political Thought of the Opponents of the Constitution*. The quotation in the text can be found on p. 3 of Volume 1. Discussions of the seven-volume work can be found in Leonard J. Levy, "Against the Union," *New York Times Book Review* (February 21, 1982), Edmund S. Morgan, "The Argument for the States," *The New Republic* (April 28, 1983), and John A. Rohr's review essay of *The Complete Anti-Federalist* in *America* 148 (January 15) 1982.

20. Ibid.

21. *The Federalist* 47.

22. Storing, *The Complete Anti-Federalist* (CAF); Brutus 2.9.197, 202; Mason 2.2.7–8; Federal Farmer 2.8.86, 175; Old Whig 3.3.31; Officer of the late Continental Army 3.8.3; DeWitt 4.3.12–14; Agrippa 4.6.73; Brutus 5.15.1; Henry 5.16.7–14; Cincinnatus 6.1.26–32; Plebeian 6.11.16. For a more relaxed anti-Federalist stance on separation of powers, see Penn 3.12.16–17 and Watchman 4.22.4. Subsequent reference to *The Complete Anti-Federalist* will be listed as Storing, CAF. This reference will be followed by the name of the anti-Federalist author and three arabic numbers. The first number indicates volume, the second the author's position in the volume, and the third is the paragraph in the author's pamphlet or speech. Thus, Federal Farmer 2.8.86 refers to the Anti-Federalist writer who calls himself the Federal Farmer. He is the eighth author to appear in the second volume. The statement cited can be found in the eighty-sixth paragraph of his writings. All paragraphs in the CAF are numbered. References to Volume 1 (Storing's introductory essay) and to Storing's notes will be by volume and page.

23. Because the Vice-President of the United States is President of the Senate, it was essential to go outside that body for a presiding officer at the impeachment trial of a President. Otherwise the Vice-President would find himself in a severe conflict of interest.

24. In his remarks of July 26, George Mason provided a nice summary of the Convention's efforts to find a suitable way to elect a President. See "Debates in the Federal Convention of 1787 as reported by James Madison." Tansill, op. cit., pp. 456–457.

25. Tansill, op. cit., pp. 662–663.

26. This is not to say that separation of powers can be disregarded at will. My point is simply that the mere presence of all the powers of government in one agency is not of itself constitutionally suspect. The responsible excr-

cise of these powers is another matter. See *Wong Yang Sung* v. *McGrath*, 339 U. S. 33 (1950).

27. M. J. C. Vile, *Constitutionalism and Separation of Powers* (New York: Oxford University Press, 1967), p. 13.

28. *The Federalist* 47.

29. Ibid. Madison's position on separation of powers in *The Federalist* is quite consistent with his remarks at the Philadelphia Convention. See Tansill, op. cit., pp. 423–424; p. 166, 397–398, 412–413, and 423–424.

30. For a full discussion of the principle of separation of powers, see Vile, op. cit. and W. B. Gwyn, *The Meaning of the Separation of Powers* (New Orleans: Tulane University, 1965).

31. By "department" Publius here means the three great constitutional branches of government, not the executive departments of Article II.

32. For Rufus King's position, see Tansill, op. cit., p. 419. For James Wilson's position, see Tansill, op. cit., pp. 444–445.

33. The powers of administrative agencies, unlike those of Congress, the President, and the courts, are always partial in the sense that they are exercised over a narrowly defined scope of governmental activity. Examples are television licenses, railroad rates, and food stamps. Not only are these powers partial, but unlike those of Congress, the President, and the courts, they are formally and entirely subordinated to one or another of the traditional constitutional branches. Thus even egregious abuses by administrative agencies are far removed from tyranny. There is, of course, a great difference between avoiding tyranny and providing good government. When the attack on the administrative state is launched from the high ground of separation of powers, the entire argument has an upward tilt toward high politics, as do questions of tyranny. If administrative agencies were spared the sort of attack that questions their legitimacy, they might be as successful in providing good government as they are in avoiding tyranny.

34. Storing, I, op. cit., p. 35.

35. Adams would argue that such a purge is impossible because of the *inevitable* tendency toward aristocracy in government. Some anti-Federalists would reluctantly agree. See Storing, CAF: 1, op. cit., pp. 56–59.

36. Good discussions of Hamilton's thought on administrative responsibility during his tenure as Secretary of the Treasury can be found in David E. Marion, *Toward A Political Theory of Public Administration: The Place and Role of Federal Public Service Personnel in the American Democratic Republic* (Ann Arbor: University Microfilms International, 1978), pp. 78–87, and in Lynton Caldwell, *The Administrative Theories of Jefferson and Hamilton* (Chicago: University of Chicago Press, 1944), Chapters I–VI.

37. Woodrow Wilson, *Congressional Government: A Study in American Politics* (New York: Meridian Books, 1967), p. 170.

38. Storing, CAF: Centinel 2.7.9; Luther Martin 2.4.40.

39. It is the theory of the reformers that sends us off on the will-of-the-wisp of defining administrative responsibility in terms of control by elected officials. Their true responsibility is to maintain the constitutional order by using their statutory powers to favor whatever branch of government needs their help at a given time in history. Publius made them all the President's

men, but he did not envision the President as a democratically elected man of the people. This would have made him too powerful for the framers. One reason they agreed to a one-man Presidency was precisely because he was *not* democratically elected. If the legislative vortex switches to the executive, the administrative officers must strive to keep the balance.

40. *The Federalist* 65.
41. Storing, CAF: Mason 2.2.4.
42. Storing, CAF: Monroe 5.21.32; Montezuma 3.4.2. See also the comments of William Grayson on June 14, 1788 at the Virginia Ratifying Convention. Jonathan Elliot, ed., *The Debates in the Several State Conventions on the Adoption of the Federal Constitution as Recommended by the General Convention at Philadelphia in 1787*, 5 Volumes, 2nd Ed. (Philadelphia: J. P. Lippincott, 1836). Grayson's comments appear in Volume III, pp. 375–377. Subsequent references will be listed as "Elliot" followed by volume and page. See also the comment of Fisher Ames at the Massachusetts Ratifying Convention in Elliot.
43. Storing, CAF: 5.21.37.
44. Tansill, op. cit., p. 609.
45. Tansill, op. cit., p. 319.
46. Tansill, op. cit., p. 324.
47. Note the colloquy between Edmund Randolph and George Mason in Tansill, op. cit., pp. 528–529.
48. Tansill, op. cit., p. 319.
49. Tansill, op. cit., p. 474.
50. When this clause was eventually deleted, it was not because of any hesitation over the nonlegislative character of the Senate. The reason was to include the executive functions of the Senate in the general congressional rule that a journal of proceedings should be published. Some framers wanted to exempt the Senate from this obligation when it was acting in a nonlegislative capacity. See Tansill, op. cit., p. 519.
51. Tansill, op. cit., p. 474.
52. Ibid., p. 661.
53. Elliot: III, op. cit., p. 491.
54. Ibid.
55. Storing, CAF: Cato 2.6.45.
56. Ibid. Martin 2.4.42 and 2.4.48.
57. Ibid. Monroe 5.21.35 and Elliot: III, op. cit., pp. 220–222.
58. Some supporters of the Constitution also shared this fear. See the remarks of James Wilson in Tansill, op. cit., p. 674.
59. Storing, CAF: Federal Farmer 2.8.170.
60. Ibid. Centinel 2.7.23.
61. Ibid. Minority of Convention of Pennsylvania 3.11.45. Several anti-Federalists referred to the President as "president-general" because of his constitutional position as commander-in-chief of the army and navy. For a further discussion of the Anti-Federalists who favored a strong executive, see Storing, CAF I, p. 49, and note 5 on p. 94. The Federal Farmer was one of the staunchest Anti-Federalist champions of a strong executive. See 2.7.128 where the Farmer follows Adams closely.

62. Some Federalists shared this concern. See Wilson's comments in Tansill, op. cit., p. 684, and Elseworth, op. cit., p. 537.
63. Elliot: III, op. cit., p. 494.
64. Tansill, op. cit., p. 671.
65. Tansill, op. cit., pp. 686–687.
66. Elliot: III, op. cit., pp. 493–494.
67. Storing, CAF: Lee 5.6.5.
68. Elliot: VI, op. cit., pp. 116–117.
69. *The Federalist* 62–65.
70. A final indication of the executive character of the Senate can be seen in the evolution of the office of Vice-President. He was a latecomer to the convention. No mention of the office was made until September 4, less than two weeks before the four-month convention adjourned. Today we tend to think of the Vice-President's role as President of the Senate as rather unusual, but it made good sense to the framers. An earlier draft of the Constitution had the Senate selecting the President. This arrangement was rejected as an excessive threat to the independence of the President. The Senators would too likely select one of their own number and then control the man they had selected. This concern led eventually to the complicated arrangement we know as the electoral college. Because the President was not to be elected by the Senate, the framers logically concluded that the Vice-President should not be elected in this manner either. Since, however, they had given some thought to the Senate as a possible institution for selecting the President, it was natural that they should look in this direction for a successor to a deceased President. So natural was it that Gouverneur Morris could assure critics of the office of Vice-President that if no such office existed, the President of the Senate would become a "temporary successor" to the President in any event. Roger Sherman agreed and supported the creation of the office of Vice-President in order to avoid the risk of one state losing the full voting power of one of its senators if he were elected President of the Senate. Tansill, op. cit., pp. 659–664; and pp. 682–683.

Throughout the Convention there was no discussion of the Speaker of the House succeeding to the Presidency. If the successor was to have any connection with Congress, it would only be with the Senate. The fact that the Presidential Succession Act of 1947 put the Speaker of the House immediately after the Vice-President and before the President pro tempore of the Senate is consistent with the democratic evolution of the office of President and the decline in awareness of the executive character of the Senate. It is interesting to note that in the Succession Act of 1792 the President pro tempore of the Senate was placed ahead of the Speaker of the House and right after the Vice-President of the United States. This suggests that the executive character of the Senate was quite clear to the men of the founding generation.

71. This point is also made by Rufus King at the Massachusetts Ratifying Convention, Elliot: IV, op. cit., pp. 47–48, and by James Iredell at the North Carolina Ratifying Convention, Elliot: IV, op. cit., pp. 41, 133.
72. Storing, CAF: Centinel 2.7.23.

73. Ibid. Brutus 2.9.201.
74. Ibid. M. Smith 6.12.27.
75. Tansill, op. cit., pp. 222, 319. Enough senators have served for twenty or even thirty years that the lifetime Senate of Hamilton and Morris has not proved altogether fanciful. Because, however, the Senate never achieved its potential as an *executive* institution, this senatorial longevity has done little for executive stability. The Twenty-second Amendment, which prohibits a third presidential term, is a further limitation on executive stability. Today the career civil service is the most likely institution to fulfill Hamilton and Morris's view of executive stability through a lifelong career.
76. The fear of the Senate's treaty power was the basis of another anti-Federalist argument. Article VI of the Constitution provides that treaties shall be the "Supreme Law of the land." The Anti-Federalists maintained that this could lead to legislation without concurrence from the House of Representatives. A generous definition of "treaty" could put the entire legislative power in the hands of the Senate. This danger was combined with the fear of the proposed "Federal city" where the Senators would live all year round. Their distance from home and their six-year term would threaten republican virtue. On the dangers of the Federal city, see the following anti-Federalist writings in Storing, CAF: Federal Farmer 2.8.222–223; Aristocrotis 3.16.2; Brutus 2.9.200; Columbian Patriot 4.28.8; Cato Uticensis 5.7.7.
77. Storing, CAF: Mason 2.2.24.
78. Ibid. Martin 2.4.42.
79. Ibid. Cato 2.6.45.
80. See the colloquy between Madison and Morris in Tansill, op. cit., p. 733.
81. Storing, CAF: Federal Farmer 2.8.170.
82. *The Federalist* 66 and 76.
83. *The Federalist* 66.
84. Storing, CAF: Federal Farmer 2.8.173.
85. George Mason is the leading anti-Federalist on this point. See his remarks at the Virginia Ratifying Convention, Elliot, op. cit., pp. 494–496.
86. *The Federalist* 65. The quotation appears in the fifth paragraph of 65. The references to the Senate in the two preceeding paragraphs and the one following the quotation suggest that Hamilton was referring to the Senate and not to the entire Congress when he speaks of "representatives of the nation."
87. Tansill, op. cit., p. 222. But see also p. 283, where Hamilton compromised on a shorter term for senators.
88. Tansill, op. cit., p. 222.
89. Tansill, op. cit., p. 279.
90. See pp. 000–000 above for a discussion of Publius on the separation of powers. "Representatives of the nation" sounds like Adams's legislature. Also see pp. 000–000.
91. Storing, CAF: A Farmer 3.14.15.
92. Ibid. Livingston 6.12.25.
93. The combination of powers in the Senate was a major point made earlier in this paper when separation of powers was discussed. The power of

the Senate to try impeachments was considered judicial power by all participants in the debate. The impeachment process was given strong attention
throughout the discussions.

94. For further remarks on the Senate's expertise in foreign affairs see John
    Jay's comments in the *Federalist* 64.

95. An excellent discussion of this literature can be found in Chester A. New-
    land, "Professional Public Executives and Public Administration Agendas,"
    in *Professional Public Executives,* Chester A. Newland, ed. (Washington, DC:
    American Society for Public Administration, 1980), pp. 1–29.

96. The full text of Article I, Section 2 reads as follows:

    Section 2. [1] The House of Representatives shall be composed
    of Members chosen every second Year by the People of the several
    States, and the Electors in each State shall have the Qualifications
    requisite for Electors of the most numerous Branch of the State
    Legislature.

    [2] No Person shall be a Representative who shall not have attained
    to the Age of twenty five Years, and been seven Years a Citizen of
    the United States, and who shall not, when elected, be an Inhabitant
    of that State in which he shall be chosen.

    [3] Representatives and direct Taxes shall be apportioned among
    the several States which may be included within this Union, according
    to their respective Numbers, which shall be determined by adding
    to the whole Number of free Persons, including those bound to
    Service for a Term of Years, and excluding Indians not taxed, three
    fifths of all other Persons. The actual Enumeration shall be made
    within three Years after the first Meeting of the Congress of the
    United States, and within every subsequent Term of ten Years, in
    such Manner as they shall by Law direct. The Number of Representa-
    tives shall not exceed one for every thirty Thousand, but each State
    shall have at Least one Representative; and until such enumeration
    shall be made, the State of New Hampshire shall be entitled to
    chuse three, Massachusetts eight, Rhode Island and Providence Plan-
    tations one, Connecticut five, New York six, New Jersey four, Pennsyl-
    vania eight, Delaware one, Maryland six, Virginia ten, North Carolina
    five, South Carolina five, and Georgia three.

    [4] When vacancies happen in the Representation from any State,
    the Executive Authority thereof shall issue Writs of Election to fill
    such Vacancies.

    [5] The House of Representatives shall chuse their Speaker and
    other Officers; and shall have the sole Power of Impeachment.

97. See the comments of James Wilson in Tansill, op. cit., p. 160.

98. Storing, CAF: Centinel 2.7.22. Centinel weakens his argument by assuming
    that the Constitution required one representative for every 30,000 persons.
    Article I, Section 2 provides that there cannot be *more* that one representative
    for every 30,000 persons. Thus the situation, from Centinel's point of
    view, was even worse than he thought.

99. Ibid. Federal Farmer 2.8.15. The Federal Farmer's reference to jury trials
    in the vicinage touches on another important Anti-Federalist theme. Article

III, Section 2 of the Constitution provides for a jury trial in criminal cases but not in civil cases. This was changed by the Seventh Amendment. Article III, Section 2 also specifies that jury trials shall be held "in the state where the said crimes shall have been committed." Many Anti-Federalists found this provision inadequate. They demanded a trial in the "vicinage" of the offense, not merely within the state where the offense occurred. Modern readers might be surprised at the Federal Farmer's willingness to rank trials in the vicinage as one of the two essentials of a free government. Many of the writers of the founding period stressed the important *political* functions of juries. It was a way of including the people at the termination of the governmental process where laws are being applied to individual situations, just as the representatives of the people can be found at the beginning of the political process when the laws are made. If we were to use a contemporary analogy, the jury of the 1780s might be defended on the same grounds as popular participation in governmental decisions, as, for example, rule making under the Administrative Procedure Act is defended today. There is an important difference, however. In contemporary rule-making procedures the participants are usually interested parties. The jurors were supposed to be disinterested. DeTocqueville saw great possibilities for the jury as an institution that develops civic virtue in the citizens because of the disinterested judgments they are asked to make. We seem to have lost something important along the way. Today jury duty is looked upon as a burden that shrewd citizens skillfully avoid. Nowadays popular participation in government decision making is justified on grounds of self-interest, not disinterested judgment.

Nonetheless, the jury of the 1780s assists those who look to the framers to support a modern argument for participatory democracy. The view many Anti-Federalists had of juries might somewhat soften the harsh language of Madison in the *Federalist* 63, where he celebrated "*the total exclusion of the people in their collective capacity* from any share in [America's governments.]" (Madison's italics.)

100. Ibid. Brutus 2.9.14. Obviously Brutus would not be reconciled to the Constitution if a few more representatives were added to the House. His point is that republican principles cannot be satisfied in an extended republic, a point Publius attacked brilliantly in the *Federalist* 10. George Mason made a somewhat similar argument when he used the impossibility of meeting republican standards as the basis for his position that the Federal government should have less power in matters such as navigation. CAF: 5.17.1.
101. Ibid. Chase 5.3.20.
102. Melanchthon Smith is perhaps the most effective Anti-Federalist spokesman on representation. See CAF: 6.12.1–40 passim. See also CAF: 5.14.27–34 and Storing's introduction to "Essays by A Farmer," CAF: 5., p. 6. For further statements by the Federal Farmer, see CAF: 2.8.97, 106–107, 114, 117–118. For statements by George Mason, see CAF: 2.2.2., 5.171, Tansill, op. cit., p. 161, and Elliot: III, op. cit., pp. 262; 265–266.
103. Storing, CAF: Minority of Convention of Pennsylvania 3.11.33.
104. For a recent discussion of Madison's views on representation, see Garry Wills, *Explaining America: The Federalist* (Garden City, NY: Doubleday, 1981),

pp. 177–264. Wills argues that Madison looked to representation as the governmental institution that would refine not only public opinion but civic virtue as well. Wills finds in Publius a more generous attitude toward the ordinary citizen than most other commentators have found.

105. At the Virginia Ratifying Convention, Patrick Henry offered the following reductio ad absurdum to Madison's filtering and refining idea: "If ten men be better than one hundred seventy, it follows of necessity that one is better than ten. The choice is more refined." Elliot: III, op. cit., p. 167.

106. Tansill, op. cit., pp. 349–350; 694.

107. Tansill, op. cit., p. 694. Hamilton's candid fears of presidential corruption may stand as a monument to the wisdom of secrecy in some forms of decision making.

108. Tansill, op. cit., p. 349.

109. See the *Federalist* 10 and 55–58 and Tansill, op. cit., pp. 162–163.

110. Tansill, op. cit., pp. 160–161. See also the statements by John Dickenson (Tansill, op. cit., p. 168) and Hugh Williamson (Tansill, op. cit., pp. 668, 694, 720). Williamson raised the issue of representation on three occasions at Philadelphia. He seems to have been more interested in increasing the size of North Carolina's delegation than in a theory of representation, however.

111. George Mason, Elbridge Gerry, and Edmund Randolph were the only members of the Convention who stayed until the end but refused to sign the Constitution. All three were active participants, but Mason was more effective after the convention than either Gerry or Randolph.

112. Tansill, op. cit., p. 741.

113. Ibid.

114. Ibid.

115. Ibid.

116. For examples of Madison's emphasis on knowledge and information, see the *Federalist* 10, 35, 36, and 57.

117. *The Federalist* 58.

118. Storing, CAF: M. Smith 6.12.14.

119. Harry Kranz, *The Participatory Bureaucracy* (Lexington, MA: Lexington, 1976); Kenneth Meier, "Representative Bureaucracy: An Empirical Analysis," *American Political Science Review* 69:526–542 (June) 1975; Kenneth Meier and Lloyd Nigro, "Representative Bureaucracy and Policy Preferences," *Public Administration Review* 36:458–469 (July/August) 1976; V. Subramaniam, "Representative Bureaucracy: A Reassessment," *American Political Science Review* 61:1010–1019 (December) 1967; and Samuel Krislov and David H. Rosenbloom, *Representative Bureaucracy and the American Political System* (New York: Praeger, 1981).

120. Norton Long, "Bureaucracy and Constitutionalism," *American Political Science Review* 46:808–818 (September) 1952.

121. Kenneth C. Davis, *Discretionary Justice: A Preliminary Inquiry* (Baton Rouge, LA: Louisiana State University Press, 1969); Jeffrey L. Jowell, *Law and Bureaucracy: Administrative Discretion and the Limits of Legal Action* (Port Washington, NY: Dunellen, 1975).

122. Storing, CAF: M. Smith 6.12.16–17.
123. Further healing may come from congressional staffs. By a judicious use of patronage a public-spirited congressman can come into close contact with those who think the way the people think and feel the way the people feel.

CHAPTER 5

The Pluralist Legacy in American Public Administration

William L. Morrow

THE COLLEGE OF WILLIAM AND MARY

WILLIAM L. MORROW is Professor of Government at the College of William and Mary. Previously he served on the faculty of DePauw University and on the visiting faculties of the University of Iowa, Indiana University, and the University of North Carolina. Professor Morrow holds the doctorate from the University of Iowa. He has served as a Congressional Fellow of the American Political Science Association and as a Public Administration Fellow of the National Association of Schools of Public Affairs and Administration. He has published numerous monographs, articles, and essays in leading journals and anthologies, and he has authored three books, including the acclaimed Public Administration: Politics, Policy and the Political System.

William L. Morrow presents a unique analysis of the place of pluralism in the development of the American administrative state. James Madison, John C. Calhoun, and Alexis de Tocqueville all argued from the theoretical base that majority rule has no absolute claim on standards of right merely because it is the opinion of the majority. Madison also warned against the use of moral propositions as the basis of the formulation of public policy because the question of *whose* moral propositions are superior can never be settled in the extended and commercial American republic.

The founders' hope that interest would play the role of virtue in the new republic has been realized beyond their wildest expectations. The norms of political pluralism have in fact displaced both classical democratic theory and classical administrative theory in the real world of American government. Pluralist norms view the institutions of government as arenas for the expression of self-interest. They see the processes of government as bargaining bazaars for the negotiation of interest group conflicts. The bureaucracy is the linchpin of the pluralist system because it is the focal point of representation. It provides access to the decision centers of government.

The bureaucracy has had a hidden history in the United States. Its actual role has always been subordinated to official doctrines, masking the essential representativeness of administrative institutions. Until about 1829 the bureaucracy was expected to represent the body politic through the President. It had virtually no autonomy to develop its own standards of accountability because it was subservient to him. During the Jacksonian era and until about 1869, the idea that public administrators would represent the people via the presidency did not change, but the means of achieving this objective changed drastically. The Jacksonians sought the literal integration of politics and administration through what came to be called the spoils system.

The widespread incompetence resulting from the spoils system led to the fusion of administrative decision making and pluralist democracy that still characterizes the administrative state. The seeds of integration were in Jacksonianism itself. The movement's commitment to decentralized administration made it vulnerable to the influence of the interest groups dominant in party activities at the state and municipal levels where the Jacksonians went for nominations to administrative positions. The legal constraints placed on executive control of subordinate administrators during the era made administration even more vulnerable to co-optation by political, economic, and cultural interest groups.

The reform movement of the 1870s and 1880s unwittingly completed the fusion process through the neutrality crusade. The new science, the new morality, and the new professionalism all marched under the neutrality banner in an attempt to insulate administration against the tyranny of majoritarian government made more ominous by the threats of immigration and industrialization. The idea that consensus about good public policy could be developed by professionally trained elites who would serve as registrars of public opinion played directly into the hands of the forces of pluralism.

The theory of neutrality, the nonhierarchical components of professional obligation, and ambiguity about whether the executive or the legislative branch should control administrators, together constituted a screen behind which administrators could seek alliances in the pluralist system for their own purposes. These arrangements, variously called "triple alliances," "subsystems," and "iron triangles," are typically formed among bureau-tier agencies, congressional subcommittees, and interest groups, all of which share similar objectives. Perhaps the best known of these alliances is the military-industrial complex, consisting of agencies within the Defense Department, the House and Senate Armed Services Committees and their subcommittees, and interest groups representing the aerospace and armaments industries.

Four factors encourage administrators to seek agency security and policy continuity outside the norms of classical administrative theory. They are: (1) the fragmentation of power represented in fiscal federalism, (2) the independence of bureau-tier agencies that often have their own budgets and personnel systems, (3) a marketplace ideology that makes distributive and regulatory policy decisions a matter of intense bargaining and negotiation, and (4) confederal political parties that can neither define an authoritative direction for policy making nor enforce party discipline.

The coordination of public policy is one of the major casualties of the pluralist system. Efficiency is made more difficult because legislators often send vague policy mandates to administrative agencies as a function of the necessary compromises within legislative committees when bills are discussed and votes taken. The technology may not exist to accomplish the goals specified, and the goals themselves may be only moral commitments: to clean up the environment, control the spread of poverty, or provide adequate housing for the poor, for example.

To survive in such an environment, public administrators must develop a procedurally shrewd political style. They are more regularly rewarded for being open, flexible, and accommodative to the centrifugal forces expressing interest in their policy decisions than they are for being conscientiously concerned about the quality and relevance of their decisions. Dealing with accountability pressures means administrators must document, report, explain, and consult with their clients to the extent that administrative agencies themselves often display the excessive proceduralism associated with bureaupathology.

Pluralism forces public administration to forfeit its ability to do rational, comprehensive planning because planning and pluralism are rooted in different assumptions about government. Planning is substantive in nature and focuses on the ends of governmental activity. Pluralism is procedural in character and focuses on providing interest group access to centers of decision. As long as pluralism is the major operating norm of American public administration, planning, efficiency, and cooperation must yield to the requirements of representation. It is ironical that the structural manifestations of neutrality make the modern administrative state a form of Jacksonian democracy.

Classical democratic theory asks that citizens be enlightened and public-spirited, and that mechanisms be available to transmit this enlightened public spirit into public policy. In democracy's ideal state, institutions of government serve as registrars, forums of expression, and legitimizers of public opinion. These responsibilities are essentially procedural in character, having little to do with the substance of policy itself.

The real world of government and politics has never reflected democratic theory in practice. As a rule, the public has not been either enlightened or public-spirited. Institutions of government have rarely served as neutral transmitters and legitimizers of public opinion. Rather, public opinion has often been dominated by interest groups that contribute a distinct "self-interest" flavor to their claims on governmental institutions. The institutions have generally followed suit. The effect of these practices has been to reject morality as a standard to be applied consistently to the development of public policy. "Morality" refers to concepts of the "public interest" that overcomes the influence of interest groups, replacing such influence with a more inclusive, or "common good" policy perspective. Classical democratic theory maintains that morality can surface in the political process. Experience has shown this to be the exception rather than the rule.

The hopes of classical democracy have been displaced, by and large, by the norms of political pluralism, a doctrine that replaces enlightened and public-spirited policies with the compromises resulting from interest group conflict. Under such conditions the institutions of government tend to become arenas for the expression of self-interest.

The purpose of this essay is to analyze the nature and extent of the ties between public administration and the pluralist legacy in American politics. The essay's basic assumption is that bureaucracy is a key representative institution in the American political system. Administrative institutions embody and express most of the tenets of political pluralism in both its positive and negative dimensions. Like democracy, however, pluralism as a theory rarely performs according to script in the real world of government.

The Pluralist Tradition in American Politics

Pluralism is largely unchallenged as a theory that describes decision making in American politics. It views the political system as a balance of power among economic, religious, professional, geographic, and ethnic groups whose memberships often overlap. These groups seek to impose their will on public policy, but each one is limited in its influence because each must relinquish some of its claims to accommodate the demands of other groups. Disagreements among interest groups over the character of public policy are often easy to resolve because most groups share a fundamental commitment to the goals and processes of the American political system. This facilitates compromise.

Pluralism is also defended as a normative theory and laudable goal of the American political system. It is said to promote individual growth through membership in a number of groups. Such membership provides the individual with access to government that he would otherwise not experience. In addition, pluralism is said to have a stabilizing effect on society. The existence of multiple group pressures on government virtually guarantees that the most important policy questions will be transmitted to government for resolution. Individual activity within groups helps cultivate a sense of appreciation for the political system, which in turn fosters stability. It is reinforced even further by the tendency of public policies to reflect the accommodation of multiple group pressures. Thus, most interests are partially satisfied, but none are satisfied exclusively.

Major policy changes are possible in a pluralist society, however. Newly formed groups are able to gain avenues of access to government, articulate their views, and eventually help shape the character of public policy by forcing established groups to compromise with them. Thus, pluralism is heralded as a credo that develops human potential, protects individual rights, and encourages incremental change, while simultaneously identifying important policy issues.

Pluralism does battle with the most fundamental objective of classical democratic theory, majority rule. In place of majority rule, pluralism proposes rule by a consensus developed from competing factions. A justification of rule by minorities can be found in the works of James Madison, Alexis de Tocqueville, and John C. Calhoun.[1] Each of these theorists feared majority rule because, in their opinion, a majority's policy position does not have any claim on abstract standards of the public good merely because it is the opinion of the majority. Public interest rhetoric can be a smoke screen that hides a self-interest–oriented government. Majority support for a given policy does not make it intrinsically correct. Pluralist theory argues therefore that all groups must be tolerated equally by government, and that government is obligated to provide an opportunity for all groups to gain access to government decision centers. Policies reflecting a balance of group positions will then result. Madison argued that this outcome could be achieved by a constitutional check-and-balance system, and through the policy decisions of elected representatives whose judgment would be more rational than that of the general public.

Rejecting the notion that group equilibrium could ever be achieved with certainty, Calhoun reinforced and extended Madison's argument by offering the doctrine of the concurrent majority. This theory argued that the universal consent of all rival interests concerned with a particular policy furnishes the only legitimate basis for determining the public interest on that issue.[2]

Unable to agree on concepts of morality in public policy, but able to agree that the expression of self-interest through interest groups, is natural and inevitable in a democratic system, the pluralist tradition has categorically rejected the idea of majority rule and replaced it with the idea of balanced rule by minorities. Therefore, public policy is legitimate if it accommodates all concerned interest groups through compromise.

In pluralist theory, the effective response by government to citizen demand is heavily dependent upon the role of an elite. Classical democratic theory stresses participation by informed citizens as the key mechanism that holds government accountable to majority opinion. The pluralist tradition assumes on the other hand that most citizens are uninformed or apathetic. They are always motivated by self-interest in any event. Accordingly, elected officeholders become important representative mechanisms. Because they are driven by the ambition to remain in office and accrue power, they and their rivals compete for interest group support. Such competition leads to a responsive government, one that reflects the opinions of both the active and the inactive citizenry. The net result is the effective representation of all major groups, both existing and potential, in the political system. Pluralist theory posits a political system led by a responsive elite who make decisions that are eventually approved by the people, rather than a system of direct citizen participation.

The pluralist tradition has sought to defend elitism in politics and policy-making by expecting elites to exploit ambition and self-interest in order to check the negative side effects of each. In this model, a politician must be a professional who is motivated by ambition and the desire to gain and maintain office. This makes the politician a natural power broker among his constituency's existing and potential interest groups. Failure to play the broker role effectively would result in loss of office. Success in this venture not only enhances one's chances of holding onto an elected position, but it constitutes a natural and effective means of representing citizens and enforcing governmental accountability.

This brief outline of the pluralist model presents pluralism in its ideal, not its operational, state. The model envisions politics as essentially a struggle for power in which the major forces are organized interest groups. It argues that existing and potential interest groups furnish the foundation for social and political stability because of their number and heterogeneous character. The argument is reinforced by the overlapping membership of most groups and by ambitious politicians who try to secure their careers by representing as many group elements as possible.

However, pluralism in its ideal form is mirrored only rarely in practice. As is the case with most decision-making models, gaps exist between conceptualization and operation. The nature and consequences of these gaps between form and fact in pluralism will be discussed later. For the time being, it is important to note that public administration has fundamental linkages to both the theoretical and practical sides of pluralism. First, our focus will be on what might be termed the natural, or environmental factors that link the administrative state to the expectations of the pluralist model.

The Public Bureaucracy: Roles and the Pluralist Tradition

In examining the administrative roles that reflect principles of pluralist democracy, our attention must necessarily be directed to the roles administrative agencies play in response to the political system. As a representative institution, the public bureaucracy embodies not only American social and political philosophy but the structural characteristics of the Constitution as well. The bureaucracy also has traditional responsibilities in organization and management. However, the clearest correlations between public administration and the pluralist tradition are to be found in the bureaucracy's role as a representative institution.

Representativeness

Although the Constitution is virtually silent on the subject of administrative institutions, the first vestiges of the administrative state were put in place with the expectation that administrative agencies would be representative organizations. Between 1789 and the post–Civil War period, however, agencies were assigned little discretionary power to pursue the goals of representation on their own. During the period 1789 to 1828, the national bureaucracy was viewed as the servant of the President. He was the only official with a national constituency, and Presidents of this period worked assiduously to establish the presidency as the premier institution of policy leadership. This was true for both the Federalist and Jeffersonian movements. The former stressed the moral leadership of the President, whereas the latter stressed the President's political leadership.[3] In both instances the bureaucracy was expected to represent the body politic through the President. It had virtually no autonomy to develop its own standards of accountability to the people. The period was one of representativeness through subservience.

The expectation that administrators would represent the people via the presidency did not change during the Jacksonian era (1829–69), but the means of achieving the objective changed drastically. In effect, Andrew Jackson was an "operational" Jeffersonian, elected by society's plebian interests. He embodied the spirit of frontier individualism that had surfaced during the 1820s. Jackson felt that representativeness in administration meant not only accountability to the views of citizens as interpreted by the President but also the responsibility of administration to reflect the body politic demographically. Agencies were to be staffed not only with personnel who embodied the people's will but with personnel who were expected to be a mirror image of the majority party. Once the party loyalty of aspirants to office had been established, appointments to office were not difficult to obtain. In contrast to the Hamiltonian and Jeffersonian periods, when "fitness of character" and professional competence were the major qualifications for administrative positions, the Jacksonians sought the literal integration of politics and administration via what came to be called the spoils system. The new system led to widespread incompetence in administration, for with few exceptions it substituted administration by novice party loyalists for administration by professionals.

The Jacksonian brand of representation laid the groundwork for the fusion of administrative decision making with pluralist democracy in three distinct ways. First, although the spoils crusade was led by a President, its effect was to limit presidential control over the bureaucracy. It made administrative agencies vulnerable to the enticements of pluralism. This was because the appointment of party loyalists to administrative positions at the national and state levels usually had to be cleared with party officials at the government level affected by the appointment. Often the appointees were selected by the party cadres themselves. The President and the national party leaders were not infrequently denied any role in the choice.

The result of this practice was to decentralize administration and make it vulnerable to the influence of the interest groups dominant in party activities in the various states and municipalities. Although it would be some time before the forces of pluralism were well ingrained in American society, the structural byproducts of Jacksonianism made the merger possible. Jackson was a strong and assertive President, but his presidency was followed by a period of legislative supremacy that endured until the Civil War. The idea of plebian majoritarianism voiced through a strong party mechanism remained popular throughout the era, but its champion was the elected legislature, not the elected chief executive. The party in the legislature did not focus on comprehensive policy formulation but on the dispensation of political favors to party members through the patronage system.

The second relationship between the Jacksonian movement and pluralism in administration was the influence of pluralism on the formation of the weak executive system of government adopted by many state and local jurisdictions during the Jacksonian era. The concept of the weak executive sought to discourage tyranny by (1) placing statutory limitations on tenure of office, (2) providing for overlapping terms of office, (3) subjecting to popular election officers organizationally subordinate to governors and mayors, and (4) imposing strict limitations on the ability of chief executives to remove lower officers. The effect of these legal constraints on executive control of subordinate administrators was to polarize administration by making its component parts vulnerable to co-optation by interest groups. Pluralist democracy began its infiltration of administration when elected executives were denied substantial control over their subordinates.

In the third place, Jacksonian democracy promoted ties between pluralism and public administration by the problems it created. The incompetence and conflict of interest that characterized national, state, and local bureaucracies in the 1860s and 1870s were connected, with good reason, to the exploitation by politicians of the spoils system. The reforms begun in the 1880s to neutralize and professionalize the bureaucracy served further to fragment the administrative landscape and further to reduce the control of chief executives over their subordinates. By considering employees as neutral implementors of public policy, and agencies as objective purveyors of the public interest, the reformers assumed that law could remove politics from administration. This assumption was never realized. The introduction of the neutrality doctrine into public administration made administrative institutions more, not less, vulnerable to the forces of pluralism.

Neutrality

The promotion of neutrality as an administrative standard began in the 1880s at a time when it was popular to view science as the route to morality. According to William E. Nelson, during this period science commended itself as a way to preserve pluralist society against the challenges posed by majoritarian government. Majoritarianism, argued the reformers, had produced a kind of tyranny engineered through a strong party system.[4] In politics and government, the reformers considered the excesses of Jacksonianism as merely one example of how society would suffer if a single President backed by a strong party could dictate not only the character of government but a way of life as well. Although Jacksonian democracy resulted in the de facto weakening of executive control over administrative institutions, the movement itself was energized by a strong President and Congress employing a well-disciplined party structure to work their joint will. The quest for a pluralist social, economic, and political structure in society was seen therefore as an anti-Jacksonian, anti-majoritarian enterprise.

As noted previously, a basic premise of pluralist democracy is the substitution of rule by minorities for rule by the majority. Reformers were interested in rule by minorities not only because they had been alienated by the poor quality of Jacksonian majoritarianism, but because they feared that urbanization, immigration, and industrialization would further threaten the quality of majoritarian government. In response to such a threat, the reformers sought to fragment and professionalize government, thereby insulating it from the majoritarian tide. This deliberate fragmentation of power ultimately became the operational base of pluralist democracy. Consequently, the revolt against partisanship during the last third of the nineteenth century laid the foundation for a natural synthesis of pluralism and public administration in the American administrative state.

The science-based search for morality in government was based on discovering the causes of major social problems and on developing policies to deal with those problems. This approach was employed by political scientists, historians, economists, and lawyers alike in the late nineteenth century.[5] As a disciple of the movement, Woodrow Wilson argued that administration was the business dimension of government and should be distinctly separate from politics.[6] Politics was concerned only with establishing the ends of government. Administration was to provide the means. Administrators were to study and perfect techniques of organization and management to ascertain the most efficient way to implement the policy mandates given to them. The field of public administration was therefore a field of scientific inquiry. Furthermore, and reminiscent of the Federalist era, administrators themselves were members of an elite class of well-educated, skilled leaders. Not only would such professionals conduct the affairs of state scientifically, they would also be repositories of "communitarian" wisdom.[7]

Communitarianism equated morality in government with local community values. Reformers such as Wendell Phillips, Herbert B. Adams, and Josiah Royce championed the vision of solidarity, democracy, and wholesomeness that they believed characterized small communities in early nineteenth-century America. These virtues enabled communities to examine major social and political issues from the perspective of shared values. Although communities were different, each worked at developing toleration for the values of other communities. Communitarianism was a distinctly antimajoritarian point of view because it stressed the development of consensus. Its attitude toward consensus-building had much in common with the pluralist creed. It also reflected the conditions de Tocqueville described in his examination of American society at the zenith of the Jacksonian era.

Well-educated and experienced administrative elites were considered by the reformers to be well qualified to measure and appreciate the nature and worth of communitarian values. They were also able to undertake initiatives to incorporate those values into public policy. The neutrality movement carried with it the conviction that the registration of consensus could best be accomplished through administrative elites. Further, these elites should be expected to seek out and apply policy morality by employing the scientific method. This could best be achieved if administrators were annointed with the oil of neutrality and if their agencies were vested with statutory independence.

The primary goal of the morality movement in public administration was to permit administrators to make objective decisions by separating politics from administration. The movement intended not to challenge the idea of representativeness but to fulfill it. The argument went something like this: Elected executives had lost control over government because of the fragmenting effects of legislative supremacy, the spoils system, the long ballot, and the corruption and incompetence resulting from these conditions. If government and administration were neutralized and professionalized, chief executives would be better able to resume the role of policy leadership. Neutrality would result in better representation of the public's policy needs.

The formal marriage of the neutrality doctrine to the administrative state was triggered by the assassination of President James A. Garfield by a frustrated office seeker in 1881. This event dramatically shifted public opinion in favor of abolishing the spoils system. The result was the Pendleton Act of 1883. This Act created a Civil Service Commission instructed to divide the public service into classified and unclassified sections, and to devise a system of selecting members of the classified service on the basis of merit. The Act sought to change the process of governmental decision making from one in which government officials assigned the spoils of office to party loyalists into one that required administrators to make decisions in accordance with moral and scientifically determined standards of management. In 1887, the Interstate Commerce Commission (ICC) was created, composed of commissioners serving fixed and staggered terms. It was granted statutory independence from both the President and Congress. Its mandate was to eliminate the abuses in rate setting by railroads through the issuance of rules and regulations that guaranteed just and reasonable rates. The ICC's status as an "independent" regulatory agency was a means of ensuring objectivity in its decisions. It was the first of many similar agencies established during the ensuing decades. Most of them have counterparts in the states. State and local government policies affecting parks, police protection, health, finance, education, and utilities are often made by such independent bodies rather than by agencies led by a single administrator.

On another front, the council-manager form of municipal government was introduced in Staunton, Virginia, in 1906. This innovation also illustrated the politics administration dichotomy by mandating that city councils be responsible for all policy decisions and that professionally trained city managers be responsible only for the administration of those policies. The influence of the neutrality crusade is apparent in the system, which remains popular today.

A major effect of the neutrality movement on public administration was to reinforce the subjugation of administrative institutions to the forces of pluralist democracy. The antimajoritarian goals of the movement, together with its stress on consensus development by professionally trained elites, are highly compatible with the assumptions of pluralism. The stress on neutrality and professionalism within an already atomized governmental structure weakened the control of both chief executives and legislatures over administrative agencies and made them vulnerable to co-optation by interest group forces. The fact that morality was associated with the successful application of the scientific method to policy problems bred into agencies the idea that constituencies should be inclusive, or broad, rather than exclusive, or narrow, in character.

Regulatory agencies such as the Interstate Commerce Commission were expected to uncover the facts affecting all interested parties in their issue areas and to make decisions that balanced the needs and expectations of the interested parties. Administrative institutions thus assumed the role of the ambitious politician in the pluralist model, although the motive behind the balancing effort was different in each case. The motive for regulatory commissions was to make balance forces and make the most scientific decision, which by definition was the best one possible, while the motive for the ambitious politician, as he sought to represent a balance of interests in his constituency, was survival.

Hierarchy and Executive Leadership

Chief executives were among the most prominent advocates of the neutrality movement in public administration. They were convinced that the formal insulation of administrators from partisanship would bring with it a willingness on the part of administrators to renew their allegiance to classical administrative norms, especially those related to hierarchy and leadership. If the neutrality mandates were taken seriously, the chief executives thought, administrators would have no other moral choice but to follow the directives of their superiors in the hierarchy. Such practice would strengthen executives both administratively and politically.

Success in this venture was limited. For about four decades between the turn of the century and the New Deal era, principles of scientific management were popular in both the public and corporate sectors because they were clearly compatible with the profit motive. The principles were popular in the public sector because of the perceived need to control costs in response to the increased involvement of government in a rapidly urbanizing and industrializing society. Several concurrent developments in public sector administration underscored the concern for efficiency. Introduction of the council-manager form of government at the municipal level was one example. The establishment of the Taft Commission on Economy and Efficiency in 1912 was another. The Taft Commission, along with similar commissions in the states, worked to centralize executive control over both policy-making and management by introducing executive budget making, reorganization proposals, and enlarged executive staffs to help chief executives deal more effectively with the requirements of modern government.

The stress on principles of scientific management was popular in the public sector for yet another reason rooted in one of the unintended consequences of the neutrality crusade itself, and it signaled trouble for chief executives who were interested in exerting tight administrative control over agency behavior. Contrary to the hopes and expectations of the reformers, administrators soon discovered that their neutrality allowed them to profess allegiance to institutions and standards other than those in the hierarchical system. Neutrality was equated with professionalism, and some interpretations of professional obligations have distinct nonhierarchical components. Civil servants found it convenient to adhere to professional norms rather than subjugate themselves to executive direction. The fact that regulatory agencies were expected to conduct business independently, therefore to be free from executive and legislative politics, underscored the fundamental nonhierarchical possibilities in the neutrality mandate.

By far the most important unintended result of the neutrality movement was the introduction of clientism. Clientism may be defined as the tendency of administrative agencies to consider the positions or claims of nongovernment "clients" as major inputs into administrative policy-making. Most of the clients are interest groups, but they may also be government officials, foundations, or citizens, for example, who want some form of support or concession from government. Usually concessions involve grants of money, but they may also involve awards of authority or privilege to pursue certain activities with the legal sanction of government. The right to own and operate a radio or television station is one example of such an activity.

The cause of clientism was bolstered during the neutrality period by moves to transfer policy discretion from legislative to administrative arenas. Part of the motivation for this was to respond to the complex problems that accompanied the urbanization of America. Another part of the motivation was related to the nature of the neutrality crusade itself. Because neutrality officially mandated the application of professional standards to administrative decisions, such decisions were largely managerial at the beginning of the neutrality period. However, they gradually became more substantive. They began to deal more and more with the nature of policy itself. Reformers saw no danger in this as long as professional and public interest standards were applied to discretionary decisions by administrators. After all, the purpose of the merit system and regulatory agency independence was to make administrators professional and objective.

This was administration in its ideal form but not in its real one. The fusion of agency-centered policy discretion and neutrality-nurtured agency independence made it inevitable that agencies would seek out and follow nonhierarchical decision-making strategies. Agencies followed the course of least resistance, one that helped employees secure their careers, one that was well received by legislatures, and one that guaranteed policy continuity for years to come.

Clientism could provide policy continuity that executive leadership could not. Interest groups had their allies in Congress, and Congress was responsible for agency budgets. The policy commitments of interest groups remain constant. They outlast more transient presidential policy preferences. The professional norms championed by the reform movement of the 1870s and 1880s did not prove to be so popular that they could outlast the more client-centered programs that dispensed money, authority, and services. Clientism, therefore, became a natural substitute for the decisional premises of classical administration. Ironically, clientism was encouraged by the reform attempts to foster greater, not less, attention to these classical norms.

In 1912, the Taft Commission on Economy and Efficiency reflected the frustration encountered by chief executives, especially the President, over the centrifugal outcomes of the neutrality crusade. The Commission recommended an executive budget system, whereby Presidents would submit a comprehensive budget to Congress, to replace the existing system, under which agencies submitted requests directly to congressional committees. It recommended the enlargement of the presidential staff, more presidential authority over administrative reorganization, and the merger of agencies and operations that had similar purposes. The Taft Commission's stated goal was to improve efficiency in government. State commissions operating concurrently with the Taft Commission had similar official purposes.

The underlying purpose of the commission activity was to make neutrality work, not necessarily to grant Presidents, governors, and mayors more control over policy. Neutrality would simply work better with more chief executive control over an atomized bureaucracy. Allegiance to the classical principles of hierarchy, merit, and rational definition of administrative responsibilities went unquestioned. The reformers saw no contradiction between expanded executive control over administration on the one hand and the fulfillment of the goals of the neutrality crusade on the other.

Later administrative reforms were inspired by the original work of the Taft Commission. An executive budget system was finally adopted by the federal government in 1921. The Reorganization Act of 1939 enlarged the presidential staff system by creating the Executive Office of the President. That institution has expanded regularly since its creation. Several reorganization commissions, notably the Hoover Commissions of 1949 and 1953, centered their attention on the restructuring of the executive establishment to give the President more policy-making and managerial control. Several states had their own "Little Hoover" commissions. More recently, Presidents Nixon and Carter each advanced major reorganization plans that sought to eliminate overlapping agency jurisdictions and to merge specified cabinet-level agencies to make them more functionally homogeneous. The efforts of both Presidents were largely unsuccessful, however. Their plans were rejected by a Congress that preferred its own way of accessing agencies and participating in policy-making. Organizational fragmentation better suits the purposes of pluralist democracy.

The movement favoring hierarchy and executive leadership had its roots in both administration and politics. The ties between neutrality and classical administrative principles are clear, but neutrality's connections with politics may be less so. Elected executives representing broad-based constituencies make policy pledges that cannot be engineered through a client-oriented, decentralized policy system nurtured by alliances among interest groups, legislative subcommittees, and administrative agencies. To serve their constituencies, therefore, elected executives seek administrative reorganization and management changes that will better fulfill the needs of their constituencies. The elected executives champion the structural implications of classical administration because the principles serve the political objectives of the executives. The goals of administration and politics are one and the same in this case. Yet within such a scenario, organization is not considered a means to facilitate the implementation of predetermined policy. It is a mobilization of bias.[8] It is related to a concern over the substance of public policy, not over how that policy can best be implemented. The marriage of hierarchy and politics is natural, not accidental.

The mobilization of bias serves as a convenient theme to link the notion of representativeness to the influence of pluralist democracy on the administrative state. The representation movement was dedicated to incorporating the biases of frontier America into public administration through the party system. Jacksonianism maintained that the spoils system was the best way to represent society's plebian interests. The neutrality movement sought to replace such a standard with scientific principles.

Although this is surely a bias toward a particular decision-making scheme, its ties with representativeness are important if one considers what the neutrality movement tried unsuccessfully to reject. The neutrality movement was an antidemocratic movement. It turned away from the homogenization of politics and administration, but it failed to establish the dichotomy it preferred. Because of the structural manifestations of neutrality, it actually facilitated the infiltration of administration by the interest group forces that are a modern form of Jacksonian democracy.

In attempting to separate politics from administration, the neutrality crusade tacitly confirmed that public administration is inherently a political process. The hierarchy and executive leadership movement attempted to regroup estranged agencies and their neutral employees under the command of one politically elected leader and his appointees. The President represented a broad-based and inclusive constituency. The presidency as an institution viewed the public interest from a macroscopic point of view, one that equates a synthesis of interest group values with the common good in much the same way that pluralist theory equates compromise among interest groups with the common good. The mobilization of bias under an administrative system that stresses hierarchy and leadership as a means of controlling autonomous enclaves of political and administrative power is a bias that favors the general over the particular. It controls the excesses of factionalism while it acknowledges that factions are a major source of representation in the system. It is an example of Madison's advocacy of large constituencies that "extend the sphere and take in a greater variety of parties and interests."[9] Whether hierarchy and leadership are advanced for reasons that are political or administrative, the result of such advocacy is to widen the scope of interest group representation by enlarging constituency networks within the bureaucracy. If successful, such advocacy facilitates the access of factions to decision-making arenas. It creates a balance of power among them.

Pluralism and Administration: The Situational Forces

This analysis has been directed toward linking the evolution of selected roles of public sector administrative agencies to the absorption by those agencies of key tenets of pluralist democracy. If administration is expected to be responsive and democratic, and if pluralism is a natural form of value expression, then the cooperation of administration and pluralism on a number of fronts is probably inevitable. If a government is democratic and its society is pluralistic, the institutions of government will absorb and reflect the elements of pluralism.

There are other forces peculiar to American society that make the marriage of public administration and pluralism more complete than is the case in other democracies. These forces are (1) a Constitution that fragments power among three distinct branches of government at the national level and between two strata of government geographically, (2) an economic system heavily influenced by a technology that makes it administratively logical and politically expedient to delegate vast amounts of policy discretion, (3) a commitment to the marketplace as a way of measuring social and economic success, and (4) a weak political party system that rewards constituency service much more than policies that sacrifice expediency for long-term objectives. The effect each of these forces has on cementing ties between public administration and pluralism is discussed in the following sections.

The Fragmentation of Constitutional Power

The constitutional fragmentation of power is illustrated in two structural features of the Constitution of the United States: separation of powers and federalism. By dividing policy-making power between the presidency and Congress, the Constitution requires that these two institutions cooperate to produce public policy. Each branch has a distinct, constituency-oriented stake in the character of the policies it allows to be created. Each must agree on the finished product, so major compromises usually precede the official legitimization of policies.

Insofar as the bureaucracy is concerned, the separation-of-powers principle introduces what Norton Long has called a "who is boss" issue.[10] Congress establishes and funds agencies and their programs, but the President is the chief executive. Theoretically, the bureaucracy is subordinate to the President. He has a legitimate claim on the bureaucracy's loyalty. *Both* the President and Congress have legitimate claims on the bureaucracy's loyalty, however. Because both branches act from different constituency orientations, the stage is set for conflict over who actually bosses and should boss the bureaucracy. Agencies exploit the ambiguity. They do so by searching for allies who will reinforce their desire for security and growth, and they tend to find dependable allies in the interest group system. Interest group support is continuous, it frequently generates the same objectives that the agencies have, and both parties find that their common objectives are shared by influential members of congressional subcommittees who have control over the authorization of agency programs and the appropriation of agency funds. The result is that agencies often embrace pluralist democracy via alliances with congressional subcommittees and interest groups. These arrangements have been called "triple alliances," "subsystems," and "iron triangles." They enable all actors to realize at least some of their policy goals in a manner that the formal distribution of constitutional power does not permit. The Constitution fragments power while the triple alliances unify power.

Some of these alliances have been subjected to careful and critical analysis. Probably the best known of them is the military-industrial complex. It consists of agencies within the Defense Department, the House and Senate Armed Services Committees and their subcommittees, and interest groups representing the aerospace and armaments industries. Another well-known subsystem includes congressional agriculture subcommittees, major farm organizations, and bureaus within the Department of Agriculture. Yet another example is the alliance between the Bureau of Indian Affairs, congressional subcommittees dealing with policies on Indians, and the Association on American Indian Affairs. Administrative agencies become parties to such arrangements simply by following a course that will provide them the security and policy relevance they naturally seek. The "who is boss" condition makes the pluralist-based triple-alliance alternative a safe strategy.

The second major institutional manifestation of the constitutional fragmentation of power is federalism. Federalism divides governmental authority geographically between a national level and smaller state levels. Each state has constitutionally guaranteed autonomy and is therefore not the child of the central government. Nevertheless, there is a good deal of policy-making and managerial interaction between administrative officers at each level of government, and officials at each level deal directly with their counterparts in urban areas. Many policy issues are of common concern to administrators at all three levels: federal, state, and urban. National agency personnel frequently must attempt to supervise and coordinate dispensations to officials in jurisdictions over which they have no coercive authority. Although organization charts may specify a hierarchical relationship, in fact it is more horizontal than vertical, and it is characterized by negotiation. The grant-in-aid system has provided national officials some leverage over states and localities when grants are allocated by category, for example, when the national government can require its monies to be used for a specific purpose. When grants are allocated on "block" terms, however, no such specificity is a part of the transaction, and states and localities are allowed considerable discretion in deciding how to use federally granted funds. Under these conditions, national agency influence results almost exclusively from bargaining rather than from legal requirements.

This means that the interest groups that dominate state and local politics are highly influential in determining how grant-in-aid money is spent. Such influence would be heavily diluted by the claims of other groups if the same policy decisions were made by national agencies. The focus in states and communities is typically on the strength of one or a few interest groups instead of on the compromises that must inevitably be struck if a decision is made at a higher level. Decentralization of policy-making provides access opportunities for interest groups.

Salience of the Bureau

Another characteristic of the administrative state that enhances the influence of interest groups is the policy-making dominance of the bureau. Within executive departments, bureaus are typically the first-level subordinates to the politically appointed cabinet secretaries and their assistants. Cabinet officers spend much of their time attempting to assert administrative and policy control over the bureaus.

Wallace S. Sayre once argued that the term "bureau" should be employed in a generic sense.[11] All subcabinet agencies that have a clearly prescribed policy jurisdiction in distributive and regulatory areas may be described as "bureau-tier" agencies regardless of where they appear on the organization chart. Included would be bureaus within cabinet-level departments, such as the Bureau of Land Management (Department of the Interior) and the Federal Bureau of Investigation (Department of Justice), as well as some agencies officially designated as "services," such as the General Services Administration; "administrations," such as the Veterans Administration; and "commissions," such as the Federal Trade Commission and the Federal Maritime Commission. Some of these services, administrations, and commissions are located within cabinet-level departments, some are independent, some are regulatory, and some have corporation status, but they are all bureau-tier agencies. They are important to policy-making and administration because they possess significant policy discretion, they have their own budget and personnel systems, and their leaders interact regularly with career civil service employees as well as hierarchically superior political appointees. Because bureaus are pivotal partners in the policy-making process, they are primary targets of interest group activity. They are often the administrative parties to the triple alliances or iron triangles described earlier. The ties these bureaus have with interest groups make them an obvious part of the pluralist system.

The bureau gains its importance from the constitutional system of fragmented power. Because one result of the separation of powers is conflict among the branches of government, compromise must precede the formalization of policies. The process of compromise is viewed by the forces seeking to maximize their leverage over policy as an opportunity to dominate policy-making procedures. Triple alliances among bureaus, interest groups, and legislative subcommittees are the natural result of the process because they generate cooperation among the forces that support the same policies. These policies would be diluted if more comprehensive and macroscopic elements dominated decision making within Congress and the bureaucracy. Triple alliances bypass the effects of the check-and-balance system by enhancing the influence of group politics on administrative decision making. Thus, a structurally fragmented constitution triggers a devolution of power within both Congress and the bureaucracy. The bureau-tier agencies and congressional subcommittees are the principal beneficiaries of such a condition.

Marketplace Ideology

Americans are fond of the challenges and rewards of the marketplace. Many believe that capitalism, free enterprise, and other types of nonviolent civil conflict are healthy. From one point of view, such "creative" conflict is selfish because those who win reap large rewards. From another point of view it is stimulating because it "brings out the best" in those who compete economically, athletically, and intellectually. The ideology typically does not allow for those who do not have the strength to compete.

In political theory, marketplace ideology can be traced to the doctrine of individualism held sacred by John Locke and Thomas Jefferson, and to the impact of the frontier on American culture as analyzed by de Tocqueville and Frederick Jackson Turner. The spirit of the marketplace can also be found in the system of constitutionally fragmented power already discussed in this essay. Madison's major mission in *The Federalist* was to harness the excess energy of the marketplace for public purposes.

The public bureaucracy reflects marketplace ideology in both management style and policy-making procedures. According to William E. Greider, this identification occurs because policy decisions in administrative agencies tend to slight the public interest in order to accommodate private interests. The ideal of American government is to the contrary, of course, holding that the coercive authority of government suppresses private interests in favor of a more inclusive public interest. Greider argues, however, that most distributive and regulatory policy decisions resemble a "grand bazaar."[12] Within the environment of the grand bazaar, administrative institutions and their bureau-tier components bargain with and dispense money and authority to groups, foundations, and public officials. True to the pluralist creed, intense negotiation precedes such decisions. The Department of Agriculture, for example, negotiates with farmers over commodity prices and acreage allotments. Bureaus within the Department of Commerce and the Department of Housing and Urban Development negotiate with big city mayors over capital improvement projects. Regulatory agencies negotiate with regulated industries over how clear to make the air, how clean to make the water, and how safe to make drugs and automobiles.

The power of bureau-tier agencies represents a potential advantage to the negotiators of all sides. It creates distinct points of access to decision centers, and it increases the chances of realizing both group and agency goals. Overlapping policy jurisdictions increase group opportunities to find a friendly administrative ear somewhere and consequently gain at least some distributive or regulatory policy concession from government.

Theodore J. Lowi has made the bazaar theme the core concept in his theory of interest group liberalism.[13] Lowi observes that most Americans mistakenly assume that the trend toward the centralization of governmental power in the federal system during and following the New Deal signified a corresponding concern by government for more inclusive and general policies directed toward the public interest. Lowi believes such an assumption is a myth. It is true that the *scope* of governmental activity expanded as a result of the New Deal. Legislatures willingly transferred large amounts of policy discretion to the bureaucracy as part of the trend. The results of these procedural alterations, however, did not change the propensity of administrative agencies to identify with society's major interest groups. Changes were made in the scope and level of governmental activity but not in its results. Administrative agencies have actually utilized their increased control over policy to reinforce the impact of marketplace politics on government. The movement has been liberal only in the sense that government has become more centralized in response to citizen demands in the social service state. The effects of the centralizing movement have really been conservative in the sense that they reinforce the power of dominant interest groups, most of whom favor the status quo.

Yet in general the public finds little fault with the absorption by administration of the marketplace ideology. It transplants what is considered to be an appropriate activity from the private to the public sector. The transfer is culturally compatible with the country's commitment to capitalism and individualism. Although its results may be the legitimization of conflict of interest, they are accepted because they represent an extension of values that are considered basic to the creation and strength of the American system. Thus marketplace ideology has hastened the assimilation of the elements of pluralist democracy by the administrative state.

Confederal Political Parties

The two major political parties that have dominated national politics since the Civil War are really confederations of state and local parties. Confederations are characterized by the investiture of authoritative power in small jurisdictions. If these jurisdictions decide to transmit some of their authority to a more central seat of power, they may do so, but the transfer is up to them. Ironically, the American federal constitutional structure has encouraged confederal political parties. Because federalism guarantees the residents of states the right to elect their own officials, political parties in the states feel little or no compulsion to dilute their power and forfeit their sovereignty to national party organizations. National party organizations are therefore conglomerates of fifty state miniparties. Under such a system, the national party becomes a conciliator and synthesizer of the varied demands of the state and local party units.

This situation has a profound effect on the interdependence of public administration and pluralism. Lacking any definitive and authoritative direction from a centralized party system that dominates both houses of Congress and the presidency, administrative agencies are encouraged to seek support from interest groups and congressional subcommittees in their continuing effort to assure policy continuity and agency security. The absence of party discipline places agency leaders in exposed and vulnerable positions and rewards them for developing alliances where they can.

Confederal parties are undisciplined parties. In the United States they serve primarily as vehicles of candidate identification and sources of campaign funds. They do not function effectively as purveyors of distinct and long-term policy goals, nor have they been effective in securing anything like strict party-line votes in Congress. Members of the House and Senate feel little need to follow a party line. Instead they are subjected to intense pressure to follow a constituency line. In theory, there can be as many Democratic and Republican doctrines of party as there are members of each party in Congress.

Such a situation permits personal ambition to displace party ideology as the standard for most decision making in Congress. It may be recalled that pluralist theory considers the ambition of elected officials to be beneficial to society because it encourages them to attempt to represent all the major factions in their constituencies. This doctrine has two clear consequences for public administration. First, bureaus in some ways are agents for legislators assigned to subcommittees that are critical to bureau programs and budgets. Second, it encourages legislators to transfer policy discretion on sensitive issues to bureaus, permitting legislators to blame them in case of policy malfunctions. The conventional explanation for the expansion of administrative discretion is technological. Discretion is given to the bureaucracy because issues are so complicated that Congress cannot deal with them effectively. Legislative avoidance of responsibility for unpopular and poorly conceived policies also explains elements of administrative discretion.

Pluralism and Public Management

Democratic pluralism has its most direct and dynamic influence on public administration in the organizational and policy-making processes. This does not mean that pluralism's influence on the techniques and objectives of public sector management is not also significant. There is a direct relationship between agency policy-making patterns and organizational arrangements on the one hand, and the character of management on the other.

Productive management means efficient and effective coordination of people and policy. Pluralism makes such coordination very difficult. As noted earlier, the fragmentation of constitutional power encourages agencies that are part of the iron triangle system to pursue their policy objectives with little or no regard for the orchestration of their programs with those of sister agencies. Federal grants-in-aid to urban areas, sponsored by the national government with the wholehearted support of agencies whose status in government depends on the continuence of such grants, serve to fragment urban policy rather than integrate it. Some grants go to inner-city housing and business projects to revitalize the center city, whereas others go to the construction and maintenance of interstate highway and mass transit systems that encourage workers and executives to reside in suburban areas. Funds are often dispensed for education, health, welfare, and other social service programs as though the problems they seek to solve exist in isolation from one another. The costs of fragmentation in terms of effective policy management are high. The coordination of urban programs is especially difficult in the American political system.

The same problem exists for the development and systematic exploitation of natural resources, as well as for the subsidization and rehabilitation of basic industries. Fragmentation of power encourages legislatures and managers occasionally to retire from the fray and set unambitious policy objectives that reflect little interest in coordinating policy among actors in the system. Such uninspired efforts often set goals that are estranged from the problems the actors are trying to solve. The result may be long-term waste and inefficiency.

There are at least two dimensions to the study and practice of public administration: policy management and administrative management. Policy management involves efforts to comprehend and apply the often vague policy directives sent to administrative agencies by legislatures. Legislative intent is not always clearly stated, nor are the procedures for implementing legislative intent specified. Laws are often little more than expressions of moral commitment, such as the intent to clean up the environment, control the spread of poverty, or provide adequate housing for the poor. These lauditory goals do not state specific interim objectives, nor do they specify the time frames in which the goals or objectives are to be achieved. Neither do they establish criteria for evaluation. Terms such as "clean environment," "poverty," and "adequate housing" represent problems that vary in intensity from community to community. There can be as many definitions of solutions to them as there are parties concerned about the conditions. Legislative mandates are often sent to administrative agencies without regard for the scope of human and technological resources needed to implement the mandates. Indeed, the appropriate technology for doing so may not exist. Public policy managers are expected nevertheless to serve even nebulous goals, despite unspecified standards of performance and nonexistent technology.

Goal elusiveness may be a function of the ambition of legislators who feel it is politically advantageous to enact vague legislation. Under such conditions, the blame for mistakes can be shouldered by administrators and not by legislators. The latter may avoid the unpleasantness of dissatisfying one or more factions in their constituencies. In addition, vague policy objectives facilitate compromise within legislative committees when bills are discussed and votes taken. The more specific the objectives, the more unattractive they may be to legislators who are attempting to placate as many interests as possible. To the extent that goal elusiveness is a response to the ambition of legislators and to the search for a base of compromise, pluralist democracy has a direct effect on policy management, albeit a negative one.

Public sector policymakers face strong accountability pressures in the pluralist society from the same sources that are responsible for their frustration. According to Herbert Kaufman, appeasing congressional interests is far more time-consuming for federal bureau heads than is obedience to their departmental superiors.[14] Congress speaks with many voices. The President, the press, and interest groups, acting alone or through their legislative allies, all ask that bureaus be responsive to their claims or positions. The result is that policy managers, in their attempt to placate and appease such assorted demands, become politicians themselves. They use unspecified objectives to assure each claimant that there is at least something in the agency's scheme of things for the claimant. Appeasement strategies have their costs, however. The most important of these is the administrator's necessary sacrifice of concern for sound policies in the interest of a procedurally shrewd political style. Public administrators simply have not been rewarded very much for conscientious concern about the quality and relevance of bureau policies. They have been more regularly rewarded for being open, flexible, and accommodative to the centrifugal forces that express interest in their policy decisions. The immediate consequence is the bureaucratization of the administrative process. In their rush to be accountable to the pressure points they face, managers document, report, explain, and consult with each claimant. Thus they promote delay, confusion, excessive paperwork, and the conditions associated with bureaupathology.

These conditions help explain why so many policy reform initiatives of the 1960s and 1970s dealt with the alteration of management style and procedure. Planning-Programming-Budgeting (PPB), Zero-Base Budgeting (ZBB), Management by Objectives (MBO), and the Civil Service Reform Act of 1978 all sought policy reform as a major objective. But each in its own way sought reform by altering the means by which agency officials drafted their budgets, defined their objectives, and motivated their personnel. The managerial overtones of the reform efforts made clear the connection between policy reform and procedural reform.

In contrast to the management of policy, the management of administration is concerned primarily with the traditional techniques of motivating employees to maximize efficiency. Efficiency is more easily facilitated in the private than in the public sector, because the profit motive in corporate sector administration makes goal definition comparatively easy. In the public sector goal ambiguity is the norm, and the forces of pluralism are responsible. Public sector managers find it difficult to develop an incentive system around ambiguous goals in a system that is responsive to a constellation of forces instead of a single imperative. Market-based performance measures cannot be applied to most public sector operations. The influence of interest groups on bureau decision making means that service and accommodation are often more important than efficiency. There are few rewards for improving efficiency if other performance criteria are more important in day-to-day operations. Efficiency simply does not satisfy the forces of pluralism as long as they are interested primarily in access to decision centers and the accommodation of interest group claims. If agencies respond as pluralism asks them to, the results are frequently at odds with the traditional goals of administrative management.

Conclusions

As representative institutions, public sector administrative agencies reflect what Harold Seidman describes as the "values, conflicts, and competing forces to be found in a pluralist society."[15] What is the consequence of this state of affairs for government in general and public administration in particular? First, it means that the administrative state is, and always has been, a highly responsive organism. Because it is first and foremost responsive to the forces of pluralism, however, its behavior incorporates both the positive and negative attributes of pluralist democracy. It does indeed provide arenas of negotiation for a wide variety of social, economic, and political groups. Through devices such as the public budget, it provides opportunity for faction to counteract faction. But perhaps it does not foster as much conflict and bargaining as pluralist theory suggests. Too often interest groups need only to develop points of access to bureau decision centers, and groups are automatically rewarded with concessions from government without having to undergo the stress and strain of the compromise advocated by the pluralist theory. Administrative agencies are not responsible for this state of affairs by themselves. It is encouraged by the entire policy-making process.

Budgets frequently reflect the depth of the system's informal commitment to conflict-of-interest government. Government allows each major interest to find its friends within the system, stake out a claim on subsidies and/or related privileges, and then not infrequently go its way without confronting the requirements of political responsibility. No one asks the interest to make concessions in favor of national policy priorities. Groups in American public administration that have had policy reform as their major goal—policy staff agencies, interagency coordination committees, and reorganization task forces, for example—generally have not been able to foster a synthesized and macroscopic view of the public interest. This is not necessarily because public administration has failed, but because it has succeeded too well in the tasks assigned to it in a pluralist democracy.

A second consequence of pluralism that is reflected in public administration is the forfeiture of the political system's ability to respond to the challenges of rational comprehensive planning. Planning and pluralism are rooted in assumptions that are quite different. They seek contrary objectives. Planning is concerned with policy definition, whereas pluralism is concerned with the representation of social interests. Planning is substantive in nature and focuses on the ends of governmental activity. Pluralism is procedural in character and focuses on providing access to decision arenas. Because administrative agencies are very security-conscious, and their security is achieved in large part through a client-oriented decision posture, they habitually turn a deaf ear to appeals for systematic and long-term policy planning.

Proposals for administrative reorganization and budget reform in recent years have tried to make administrative agencies more effective planning mechanisms. The efforts generally have not been very successful. The extent to which they have succeeded is the extent to which they have been made palatable to the public. California's Proposition 13 and the election of Presidents Carter and Reagan show that the more traditional processes and goals of administration—efficiency and economy—can have great popular political appeal. When good administration is good politics, reforms have a chance. When good administration and good politics collide, reforms have no chance at all. Administrative reform in the past inevitably has done battle with the forces of pluralism. It has succeeded only when the forces of pluralism are rejected by the people as a whole. Future reformers would do well to work out as little disparity as possible between what administrative agencies represent and what the planning process demands. Until then, the representative role will dominate the planning impulse in public administration.

The third and final conclusion offered in this essay is that pluralism has displaced the classical principles of public administration as the major operating norm for American public administration. Administrative institutions cannot embody the expectations of pluralist democracy and simultaneously be efficient, neutral, and hierarchical. If public sector agencies are excoriated because they fail to fulfill the classical goals of administration and fail to embrace scientifically established procedures of sound organization and management, such criticism is voiced with notable insensitivity to the established role of administrative agencies as exponents of pluralist democracy in the United States.

Endnotes

1. Madison stressed the role of constitutional limitations in promoting stability and protecting rights. His ideas appear in *The Federalist Papers,* along with those of Alexander Hamilton and John Jay. *The Federalist* is available in several editions. De Tocqueville concentrated on the sociological roots of pluralism and the role of group associations in the development of individual personality. His ideas are presented in *Democracy in America,* Richard D. Heffner, ed. (New York: Mentor Books, 1956). Calhoun stressed the need for pursuing a universal consensus around public policies. His major work on this subject is "A Disquisition on Government," in *The Works of John C. Calhoun,* Richard K. Kralle, ed. (New York: Appleton-Century-Crofts, 1954).
2. See Kralle, op. cit., Volume 1, pp. 1–107, and Sheldon Wolin, *Politics and Vision* (Boston: Little, Brown, 1960), p. 389.
3. See Leonard D. White, *The Jeffersonians* (New York: Macmillan, 1951), pp. 510–559.
4. William E. Nelson, *The Roots of American Bureaucracy, 1830–1900* (Cambridge, MA: Harvard University Press, 1982), pp. 41–61.
5. Ibid., p. 84.
6. Woodrow Wilson, "The Study of Administration," *Political Science Quarterly* 11:197–222 (June) 1887.
7. Nelson, op. cit., pp. 90–91.

8. E. E. Schattschneider, *The Semisovereign People* (New York: Holt, 1960), p. 96.

9. Clinton Rossiter, ed., *The Federalist Papers* (New York: Mentor Books, 1961), p. 325.

10. Norton Long, "Power and Administration," *Public Administration Review* *9:257–264, 1981.*

11. Walter G. Held, "Decision Making in the Federal Government: The Wallace S. Sayre Model," in *Current Issues in Public Administration,* Frederick S. Lane, ed. (New York: St. Martin's Press, 1982), pp. 39–41.

12. See William E. Greider, "The Grand Bazaar: Coping with the Federal Bureaucracy," *Washington Post* (January 20, 1977), p. JEC 6.

13. Theodore J. Lowi, *The End of Liberalism: The Second Republic of the United States* (New York: W. W. Norton, 1981).

14. Herbert Kaufman, *The Administrative Behavior of Federal Bureau Chiefs* (Washington, DC: The Brookings Institution, 1981).

15. Harold Seidman, *Politics, Position, and Power* (New York: Oxford University Press, 1970), p. 13.

CHAPTER 6

Toward an Ethical Convergence of Democratic Theory and Administrative Politics

Louis C. Gawthrop
INDIANA UNIVERSITY

LOUIS C. GAWTHROP is Professor of Public and Environmental Affairs at Indiana University at Bloomington. He formerly taught at the State University of New York at Binghamton and the University of Pennsylvania. He received the Ph.D. degree from the Johns Hopkins University. Professor Gawthrop was the Editor-in-Chief of the Public Administration Review *from 1978 through 1984. He has written four books:* Bureaucratic Behavior in the Executive Branch, The Administrative Process and Democratic Theory, Administrative Politics and Social Change, *and* Public Sector Management, Systems, and Ethics. *Professor Gawthrop is currently on leave and engaged in research on ethics and public policy at the Harvard University Divinity School, where he is the Henry Luce Senior Fellow in Theology.*

Louis C. Gawthrop challenges modern public administration to devise a politics of being as opposed to a politics of having and doing. He describes two other periods in administrative history in which public confidence in government has been at the same low ebb as exists in the 1980s: in the 1880s, when the excesses of political cronyism had functionally disenfranchised millions of American citizens and in the 1930s, when citizens became

almost comatose as public policy stagnated, the public administrative efficiency machine broke down, and economic collapse resulted.

Faith in democratic government was restored in the first instance by
the emergence of a professional career service and in the second by an
inventive public administration that combined administrative efficiency
with political effectiveness. Public confidence in government was epitomized by the elite status of the Bureau of the Budget in the early 1950s.
In both cases administrative energy made government interesting as it
revitalized the body politic.

But public administration has fallen on hard times since about 1953.
Gawthrop says that "today a once proud profession stands immobile and
virtually mute in the face of an accelerating dynamic of systems change."
Among the factors contributing to "a steady deterioration of administrative
competency" are these: (1) the invidious psychological destructiveness of
McCarthyism, with questions of disloyalty, distrust, and disdain revived
intermittently since 1968; (2) the opening up of congressional committee
oligarchies by television's effects on political campaigning, a major result
being the decline of the influence of the bureau chief component of the
iron triangle of policy-making; (3) the establishment of the supergrades
in 1949, drawing a distinction between policy careerists at the GS-16, 17,
and 18 levels and proceduralists at the GS-15 level, thus fragmenting
political and administrative power; (4) the venture of the Eisenhower Administration into global responsibility for the civil service in implementing
the containment policy, a policy that extended the competency of the
American administrative system beyond its capacity; and (5) the fragmentation of the bureaucracy into a multiplicity of suzerainties, with centrifugal
forces at work caused by single-issue politics, the new politics of litigation,
and a system of intergovernmental relations that defies administrative
control.

In Gawthrop's analysis, "since 1950 the federal bureaucracy has been
stretched and balkanized virtually beyond recognition. It has been politicized in a manner far more invidious than envisioned by the most blatant
spoilsmen." Yet the career service endures and remains the best hope
for inspiring the arcane impulses of democracy in modern America. To
do so it must admit the following characteristics of itself and the larger
society: (1) the administrative artifacts of Rome, particularly those related
to the politics of having and doing, have been so completely absorbed in
democratic ideology that the medieval imprint of ontological ethics, the
politics of being, has been thoroughly repressed; (2) government and society
are paralyzed by a trained incapacity to discern the difference between
means and ends, facts and values, and the processes and purposes of
policy; (3) the career service in carrying out its transfer function in an
exemplary way has had little time to consider the qualitative consequences
of its actions; (4) because of item (3), the individual citizen is currently
defined almost solely in terms of his or her aggregate characteristics; and
(5) qualitative aspects of democracy are understood primarily in terms of
quantitative measurements.

The cumulative result of this pattern is a subtle reconceptualization of the essence of democracy into terms of the greatest good for the greatest number. Thus the capacity of public administrators to convert the transfer of goods for aggregate groups into the qualitative enhancement of individual lives has been seriously diminished. Gresham's law applies: Concern for the mechanics of having and doing drives out concern for being.

If it is true that the reality of any period in history can be captured in the leading fictional characters of its literature, the vacuousness permeating contemporary public administration is depicted summarily in the person of George Smiley. John le Carre's spy hero is a generic model of the modern public administrator. Without sympathy or enthusiasm, but with absolute dedication to his profession, Smiley combines the best of Max Weber and Luther Gulick. In a manner that would have warmed the heart of Louis Brownlow, he is driven by a passion for anonymity, and he makes the science of muddling through a pure art form. But for Smiley and his indistinguishable Soviet counterpart, Karla, means and ends are the same. Means become ends. Process becomes purpose. Higher-order questions are naive. What works becomes the good.

If public administration is to do its part in revitalizing American society, it must redefine its current role. It has been too modest in pointing out its accomplishments and too passive in response to the political abuse it has received. It must speak with a unified, positive, and professional voice to reverse the trend of individual administrators who place prudence before principle in an effort to preserve personal reputations. No longer can public servants make a virtue of disinterest by suspending judgment on the normative consequences of their actions. Neither can they avoid moral responsibility by maximizing their interest in the problems of aggregate policy clusters and projecting their concern to higher and higher levels of analytical abstraction. For many public administrators the Weberian hierarchy of graded ranks of authority has been replaced by a hierarchy of graded ranks of aggregation.

The new professional consciousness will be motivated by the willingness of individual administrators to render critical judgments at the most basic level of policy output: the existence and welfare of individual citizens. Administrators will think larger and act smaller as they try to translate values to a scale much smaller and more directly related to people who have names. Democratic theory and administrative politics will converge at the point of professional ethics where the quality of human relationships is enhanced through the public service apparatus of government.

The soul of the state will then be rediscovered. Public administrators will make government interesting again by converting policy programs into ethical encounters between and among individual citizens. Continuous and reciprocal relationships will forge linkages of trust and loyalty between public servants and citizens, which will provide a dynamic new source of energy for the revitalization of American democracy. Modern public administration has before it no less a task than to create a network of coordinates and parameters for a politics of being. Applied ontological ethics will turn the amorphous body politic into an organic matrix of authentic human relationships.

Viewed from virtually any perspective, public administration can best be appreciated in terms of its enduring character. From the ancient civilizations of China and Egypt to the nation-states of the current world order, the functions of implementing the policy decisions of political leaders and satisfying the needs of the governed have been maintained by public servants with noteworthy consistency. From age to age and culture to culture methods and modes of governing may change, but the management of political enterprises and decisions inevitably involves people who share a common vocation. In short, public administration is an enduring component of all political systems. It illustrates the subtle axiom of B. F. Skinner: "That which survives is survival-worthy."[1]

If survival is the ultimate goal of all organizations, American public administration has adapted remarkably well to its changing environment. It must be considered survival-worthy in much the same way a ship is referred to as seaworthy. To warrant such an appellation is no mean feat. For the past two hundred years the Republic has charted a course through intermittently calm and stormy waters, but the cycles of turbulence have grown more rather than less frequent.

Given the storms encountered by our constitutional ship of state, a modern-day de Tocqueville might conclude that the key to our success can be explained only in terms of the guiding wisdom and firm hand of our helmsmen. As appealing to our pride as such an explanation may be, the fact is that forty Presidents over a period of 200 years is the equivalent of a new helmsman every five years, which is not exactly an impressive record of stability in leadership. Several analogies illustrate the problem. Two hundred years converted into 200 months is the equivalent of 16.6 years. This would return us approximately to the year 1970, when the Office of Management and Budget was established. The comparison would mean a new director of OMB every five months for the past 200 months. If converted into weeks (200 weeks = approximately 4 years), the counterpart would be new congressional elections every five weeks. In terms of days, a new and major piece of legislation would have been passed every five days for the past 200 days. The Office of Management and Budget, Congress, and the public policy process itself would be in shambles. Yet the executive structure of the American ship of state survives. We may love and honor our helmsmen, but a case can be made that we are still afloat today in spite of rather than because of their collective efforts. The explanation of whatever stability there is must be sought elsewhere. Perhaps it is in the cadre of professional public administrators.

The bureaucracy is the bulwark of stability and continuity. The essential ballast of professionalism seems to stay aright when all else seems awry. The cumulative knowledge and expertise of bureau chiefs, for example, frequently exceed the naivete and ineptitude of their political superiors. Moreover, because policy is not policy until it is implemented, it is the administration of it that establishes the public good. We may agree with Woodrow Wilson that "liberty cannot live apart from constitutional principle; and no administration, however perfect and liberal its methods, can give men more than a poor counterfeit of liberty if it rests upon illiberal principles of government."[2] But does it not also follow that no matter how fervently committed to the purest principles of liberty a government may be, it can offer nothing more than a poor counterfeit of liberty if its *administration* rests on imperfect and illiberal methods? Administration is government in action. Just as repression by the most tyrannical regime depends on the effectiveness of its administration, the values of democracy are equally dependent on how career public servants implement public policy.

This proposition may call forth more skepticism than accord. Perhaps history provides too many examples of administrative villainy for us to be seduced by such a vision of administrative virtue. Indeed, some would argue that the captains of our ship of state have labored manfully just to overcome the dead hand of inertia imposed by an encrusted bureaucracy. Or, from an individual citizen's point of view, public administration may frequently appear to resemble a cabal committed solely to the nihilistic mechanics of political expediency. By the same token, the luster of these concepts is no less tarnished by administrators who move only in the name of efficiency. We have experienced the administration of public policy under each set of conditions, and we have found both to be lacking.

The Two Faces of Administration

During its first forty years, the Republic was administered by people whose manner reflected gentlemanly dedication to their tasks in a generalist and scholarly mode. From about 1830 to about 1880, however, public administration reached a zenith of politicization. Aside from the

Civil War years and the Lincoln presidency, this fifty-year period was characterized by the increasing ascendancy of the legislative branch, the debilitating weakness of the presidency, and the initiation, enactment, and implementation of public policy based on crass political opportunism. Under these circumstances public administration came to be viewed as a managerial extension of the political machine. It was inevitable that the blatant corruption that fueled the machine would have its effects on public administration. Operating under the rubric of an absolute commitment to political expediency, public administration was in dismal disarray during most of this period.

In retrospect, it is no exaggeration to say there were serious threats to the survival of American democracy. The Civil War obviously challenged the concept of national sovereignty, but the moral and ethical degeneration seen throughout the political system was both endemic and virulent. In the case of the Civil War the survival of the federal government was threatened by forces external to it, but in the other instance the deterioration of national character undermined the democratic ethos itself. The use of force was the only mechanism available to deal with the first challenge. The response to the second had to be initiated within the body politic itself, and the alternatives available were pitifully few. They amounted to revolution or reform. The period was characterized by both: violent social revolution and extensive political reform.

Two events of the 1880s directly affected public administration. They signaled the start of major reform in the executive branch, although each was preceded by many years of struggle. The first event was the Civil Service Act of 1883.

As early as 1868 *The Nation* had editorialized:

> With a Constitution purified from slavery, with a government under it that has undergone the throes of civil war, of dissentions between its coordinate branches, and with a people honestly and heartily in earnest to maintain both the government and the Constitution, there is still a vice in the administration of the laws which almost palsies them. This mischief lies in the shifting, changing, uncertain, and gradually decaying conditions of our civil service.[3]

On the eve of the 1880 presidential election in which James A. Garfield emerged victorious, *The Nation* was still searching for "an honest and generally efficient and business-like conduct of the departments without scandal or jobbery." Now the editors urged action that would prevent

> eighty thousand officers and their families from retiring at night with much the same feelings as the inhabitants of a beseiged city who know

that in the morning their homes may be given up to pillage if the defence should not hold out. Such a quadrennial terror we have called an Oriental barbarism, and no human man will contend that it ought to be perpetuated, or that Republican or Democratic Executive Committees should be allowed to play on it, on the twofold pretense, first, that the party is the country, and, second, that the civil service is an appanage of party.[4]

Thus the drive for the reform of public administration in the form of a merit system began well before the protestations achieved success.

The second event occurred in 1887. It was the publication of a journal article entitled "The Study of Administration" by Woodrow Wilson, who had just received his Ph.D. degree from the Johns Hopkins University the year before. He advanced an argument for an inherent dichotomy between politics and administration. The latter should be concerned only with the responsibility of applying apolitical and generic operating techniques to the implementation of public policy.[5]

Although a great many interpretations of Wilson's article are currently being advanced on the occasion of its centennial, there can be no question that it was primarily a reform piece written by a reform-minded academician. It was designed to fit into the mainstream of the considerable body of reform literature being generated at the time. The article itself had more symbolic than real impact,[6] and certainly the ideas Wilson expressed were not original with him.

"The field of administration is a field of business," wrote Wilson. "This is why there should be a science of administration which shall seek to straighten the paths of government, to make its business less unbusiness-like." Such a science of administration was essential to improve "the organization and methods of our government offices" and to realize "the utmost possible efficiency at the least possible cost either of money or of energy."[7] These ideas may not have reached the scholarly alcoves of the academic community for a while, but if what *The Nation* printed is any gauge, they were live issues in the popular press.

In the seven years preceding the publication of Wilson's piece, *The Nation* maintained a steady drumfire calling for "an honest and generally efficient and business-like conduct of the departments."[8] It demanded "a change which recognizes human nature in the transaction of Government business to the same extent and by the same arrangements as in private business."[9] People selected for administrative positions were to be chosen on the basis of "their business qualifications."[10] The publication lauded President Grover Cleveland for his firm insistence on "the rule of business principles," and saluted the Galveston [Texas] *News* and the New Orleans *Times-Democrat* for their strong support of "business-like efficiency and singleminded fidelity in the public service." The editors approved public administrators who were "business-like and thorough in their methods, and always to be trusted."[11]

Three months before the appearance of Wilson's article, *The Nation* cited the customshouse and the post office as "the two great business establishments of the Government in New York City [that] are now conducted upon business principles." After expressing some disappointment in Cleveland's administration, the journal continued: "But, making all due allowances for these failures, it still remains true that he has established a firm foothold for the system of a business administration."[12] On April 7, 1887, two months before Wilson's article appeared, *The Nation* ran an editorial headed "Government On Business Principles," in which it praised the Secretary of the Treasury, Charles S. Fairchild, for establishing "a great business institution." The appointment of Fairchild by Cleveland was, according to the editors, "a most notable extension of the system of conducting the affairs of the Government on business principles."[13]

That Wilson capitalized on the temper of his times in no way diminishes either the perceptiveness of his analysis or the long-term significance of his article. Businesslike management and the science of administration were in fact the central themes of a half century of American public administration, from the 1880s through the 1930s. The impact of these themes can be judged by comparing the editorial tones of *The Nation* in the 1880s to the official opinions reflected in the Harding administration by the first director of the Bureau of the Budget, Charles G. Dawes.

"There is no reason why, because the government of the United States does the largest business in the world, it should be the worst conducted," opined Dawes. He would apply "simple business principles in a simple way" to the business organization of government.[14] For Dawes and all other officials in the administrations of Presidents Harding, Coolidge, and Hoover, governmental effectiveness was simply a function of efficiency. Efficiency, in turn, was a function of organizational control, fiscal frugality, and administrative neutrality. Unity, discipline, and loyalty were set in a framework of detachment, impersonality, and professional integrity.

Efficiency was clearly associated with costs during this period, and costs were directly related to the quality of management decisions. Decreasing cost curves were a priori evidence of efficiency and soundly based business administration methods. Management principles judged sound in the private sector were assumed to be just as sound for the public sector. The time-honored dictum of "he who governs least governs best" was modified to "he who governs least expensively governs best." As Budget Director, Dawes established the precedent for focusing exclusively and almost fanatically on cost-reduction methods which were themselves equated with efficiency.

A Different Kind of Demise

The political efficacy and administrative egalitarianism envisioned by Andrew Jackson degenerated into political nihilism, and the science of management and administrative efficiency envisioned by Woodrow Wilson degenerated into economic turbulence and chaos. The fifty-year period of the 1830s through the 1880s proved that government was too powerful to be left to the simple virtues of everyman's values. The following fifty-year period of the 1880s through the 1930s proved government was also too complex to be left to the simple virtues of the scientific method. What remained for the next fifty years, the 1930s through the 1980s, was to fashion a public administration that combined the best features of each of the two prior periods—political effectiveness and administrative efficiency—in a manner that would yield a public policy implementation capacity capable of absorbing rapid sociopolitical and economic change. By 1950, one might conclude that such a challenge had largely been met. Overcoming the turbulence of a global depression and a global war, the United States began the decade of the 1950s with a public administration proficiency worthy of the visions of both Jackson and Wilson.

Building on the base of an expanding social science research capacity, Norton Long wrote in 1952: "Accustomed as we are to the identification of elections with both representation and democracy, it seems strange at first to consider that the non-elected civil service may be both more representative of the country and more democratic in its composition than the Congress."[15] Despite a change in administrations that brought the executive branch under Republican control for the first time in twenty years, the popular perception of public administration as a profession remained very positive in 1952. The perception was epitomized by the Bureau of the Budget, which enjoyed the status of an elite presidential managerial corps. Political efficacy and administrative efficiency had been joined.

Sociopolitical equity prevailed in the fertile deltas of postwar economic growth. In such rich soil, one could afford to be bullish on government, including its administrative apparatus. Yet those halcyon days of the early 1950s also triggered policy decisions that gradually encircled the federal administrative cadre in a constrictive grip. The long-term result is that today a once proud profession stands immobile and virtually mute in the face of an accelerating dynamic of systems change. Now unable to attain either equity or effectiveness, the methods of political efficacy and administrative efficiency have become value-drained techniques of expediency. By the beginning of the 1980s, government in general and public administration in particular were perceived by the people at large in such disturbingly negative terms that a former presidential advisor to Woodrow Wilson was forced to observe:

> No one can look at the modern world with its squabbling nations, lethal arms race, exploding populations, misuse of resources, unjust distribution of justice and welfare, callous disregard of suffering, bankruptcy of constructive ideals, and neglected opportunities without suspecting that the human species is already doomed to extinction in the near future. Yet I am still an optimist. I believe we still have a chance to see the way whereby mankind can work out a noble future destiny before it is too late. [Nevertheless] we are in deep trouble. Our experiment in representative federalism and democratic self-government is not delivering the utopia our forefathers anticipated. We cannot look forward to the future without hoping to find things we can initiate to improve the prospects for our descendents.[16]

One can talk of the failures of bureaucracy *ad infinitum*. The ironical truth of the matter is that our mechanistically contrived governmental structures have fallen victim to the systemic successes of democracy. The history of the explosive expansion of American government since 1950 has also been the history of a steady deterioration of administrative competency. A brief review of the key factors contributing to this decline may be helpful in trying to determine the future direction of American public administration.

For career civil servants in the executive branch of the federal government, the middle 1950s formed a macabre, bête noire scene of bizarre and surrealistic proportions. The impact of Senator Joseph R. McCarthy, his loyalists (McCarthyites), and his methodical techniques (McCarthyism) was an invidious psychological destructiveness that significantly impaired the operations of the federal civil service. The question of national loyalty temporarily receded from the public consciousness during most of the Kennedy and Johnson administrations, but with the advent of Richard M. Nixon, and continuing in a nonpartisan fashion through the Carter and Reagan administrations, questions of disloyalty, distrust, and disdain directed toward professional public administrators were revived with noteworthy success. The steady growth of the Executive Office of the President and the White House staff in every presidency since Eisenhower can be explained largely in terms of the fear accorded executive branch career administrators by the President's advisors. The legacy of McCarthy endures. It has seriously undermined the effectiveness of the federal bureaucracy.

The residue of McCarthyism demonstrates just how vulnerable the federal bureaucracy is to the machinations of politics. McCarthy's attack on the career system was straightforward and direct. Public administrators are equally vulnerable to more subtle attacks. For example, the 1950s also marked the beginning of the use of television on a national scale for political campaigning. Television and national-local networks made it possible for political candidates to establish instantaneous visual and audio contact with the electorate. Television offered opportunities to revolutionize campaign practices despite the substantial limitations and constraints it also imposed. In the early years of television there were large sets with small screens. It offered limited programming at high retail cost, which resulted in limited sales. This amounted to a significant constraint on many political candidates, particularly at the state and local levels. By the end of the 1950s, however, these technological limitations had been overcome and television was a firmly established medium of communication in the majority of American households.

In solving the initial problems of television, the industry imposed a second constraint on politicians. As potential access to a growing number of viewers increased, the cost of gaining access increased as well. Access became a function of cost. This represented a serious limitation for many state and local political aspirants who, despite having formal party organization support, had limited funds to purchase television time. Conversely, the cost factor was not a constraint for people who, even without the endorsement of the party organization, had access to funds. The consequence was immediately apparent. Television afforded any citizen who was financially well off the opportunity to run for public office. The regular party organization could be circumvented. Such a state of affairs was particularly advantageous for certain congressional candidates in presidential election years. Through the adroit staging of television advertising campaigns, they could link themselves to the coattails of popular presidential candidates and transcend inept regular party organizations.

This is not to suggest that the advent of television is the sole explanation for the weakening of American political parties. Given the highly fragmented and decentralized nature of the American political system, political parties have always been relatively weak. The years of the Depression and World War II manifested a wide range of sociopolitical and economic changes that rendered a weak party system even weaker. Television was simply the crowning blow to party control of the nomination stage of the electoral process.

The phenomenal success of television in providing candidates with direct access to the living rooms of the electorate inevitably imposed a third constraint on electoral politics. The magic eye of television, particularly under live conditions, does not treat human imperfections kindly. It sometimes magnifies anatomical characteristics to the point of distortion. In the ideal model of civil democracy voters are asked to *listen* and decide. In televised democracy voters are trapped into *looking* and deciding. The cosmetics of political campaigning represent a major limitation on candidates who cannot project themselves attractively across the wavelengths of television.

What all this means is that television effected major changes in political campaign tactics. It further weakened the influence of regular party organizations in the nominating stages of the electoral process, and it changed the nature of campaigns for the House and Senate. It generated a new breed of officeholder who was elected by the miracle of the tube as opposed to the muscle of the machine. A major result of this phenomenon has been an overall weakening of the managerial effectiveness of the federal bureaucracy.

The operative model of the policy-making process prior to the advent of television was accurately portrayed by J. Leiper Freeman in his classic monograph, *The Political Process*.[17] The iron triangle of policy-making that Freeman described was not a grand interaction between interest groups, *the* Congress, and *the* President, but a much more modest and mundane troika composed of specific lobbyists, individual congressional committee and subcommittee chairmen, and specific bureau chiefs. In Freeman's three-cornered subsystem, committee and subcommittee chairmen were aptly described as the autocrats of Congress, while certainly the same description could be applied to GS-15s in the federal bureaucracy. Prior to the 1950s, bureau chiefs were largely in control of their bureaus, figuratively as well as literally, as politically appointed departmental assistant secretaries, undersecretaries, and even secretaries sometimes learned the hard way. Broad policy considerations could be explored, discussed, debated, and decided at the highest levels of government, but the specific details of policy decisions had to be hammered out in a relatively closed network of insiders including the affected bureau chief, a congressional committee chairman and perhaps one or two other senior members of the responsible committee, and a precisely defined set of interest group leaders.

The implicit assumption of this subsystem was that the actors who composed the elite clusters could enter into policy negotiations without fear of being undercut by their subordinates or overridden by their superiors. The changes in the tactics of political campaigning that began in the 1950s had a cumulative effect on the tensile strength of the iron triangle, however. Congressional committee chairmen were increasingly confronted with a group of members—down to and including the most junior—whose political successes were based on a television image and whose continued political successes depended on high visibility in the policy-making process. The small, tightly controlled congressional committee oligarchies were forced to include an expanding number of committee members in the process of decision. Viewed from the perspective of the GS-15, congressional committee control became more and more fragmented and diffused. As a result the effectiveness of the bureau in policy implementation was significantly impaired. The inability of bureaus to adjust to the new congressional configurations can be explained in part by the increasing variety of forms of communication directed toward the bureaus from the legislative system. The confusion was compounded by establishment of the supergrades in 1949.[18]

Shortly after Dwight Eisenhower was sworn in as President in 1953, it became apparent to top-level administration officials that a problem of major magnitude existed in the federal career service. The dilemma was both administrative and political in nature, and it related to the clogged-up pipelines of positions in the civil service classification system at the GS-12, 13, and 14 levels.

From a purely administrative point of view, the General Schedule managerial ranks, despite the rescission and repeal of numerous wartime operations and programs, were still swollen with people who had entered the career service during the 1930s and 1940s and were now well advanced along the GS career ladder. By the early 1950s the personnel network was simply overloaded with civil servants in the GS-12 through GS-14 ranks.

From a purely political point of view, the situation was grave because after twenty years as the out-party, Republicans across the nation now inundated the Eisenhower administration with requests for positions in government. The prospects of accommodating even a small percentage of these aspirants were slight unless a significant change could be effected in the personnel system of the federal bureaucracy.

The most obvious way to deal with the politics of the situation was through reductions-in-force, or RIFs, which the President immediately ordered in the name of increased efficiency. As a short-term political strategy this move opened up positions that were filled incrementally by Republicans after a prudent waiting period, but it did not provide a long-term solution to the dilemma. The administrative problem was addressed in two ways: (1) by expanding the scope of the federal bureaucracy through the establishment of a new federal Department of Health, Education, and Welfare, and (2) by expanding the number of people authorized for the supergrade ranks of GS-16, 17, and 18.

Each of these initiatives served both political and administrative purposes. The supergrade expansion decision had an especially significant impact on the managerial ethos of professional public administration. As originally authorized by Congress in the Classification Act of 1949, a limit of 300 positions was placed on the GS-16 grade, a limit of 75 on GS-17, and a limit of 25 on GS-18. In each subsequent session of Congress, the authorizations were increased. By the beginning of the Eisenhower administration in 1953, the original 400 positions had been expanded to 786.[19] A few of the supergrade positions could be filled with political appointees, but the great majority of them were assigned to careerists. This development set off a chain reaction of promotions involving all the lower grades, helping to break the logjam at GS-12 through 14. It also undermined the influence of bureau chiefs, however, and it created a high degree of uncertainty about the proper administrative role of the supergrades.

One of the laudable rationales for increasing the number of supergrade positions was to harness the wealth of knowledge existing among GS-15s and to direct it into top-level decision making. The supergrades were to become policy careerists. But as the extent of their policy-making involvement increased, the extent of their line-operating responsibility decreased. Because this change progressed in tandem with the changes in Congress, the net effect was a reconfiguration of the locations of power and influence in both the executive and legislative branches. A fundamental modification of the purposes of public administration emerged. Prior to the creation of the supergrades, responsibility for the day-to-day line operation of bureaus was clearly and explicitly linked to formal authority. Bureau chiefs were able to parlay their administrative power into significant political power. This conjunction of bureaucratic responsibility, authority, power, and influence was fragmented and diffused in the new arrangement. The power of bureau chiefs was dissipated in much the same way that the power of congressional committee chairmen was dissipated under the influence of television.

GS-15s are still viewed as bureau chiefs, but only their procedural authority is left. Substantive authority of the type required to maximize managerial effectiveness is located only in the supergrade positions. Whereas the old GS-15s were the entrepreneurs of policy, current GS-15s are simply midlevel managers of directives. The supergrades, or the Senior Executive Service as the collection of supergrades is now called, are the architects of a large amount of public policy. Although the SES has this responsibility, it has minimal power to insure effective implementation of its decisions. The SES merely enjoys the view from the bridge of the ship of state. No one appears to be in charge. Neither the SES nor the current GS-15s have the sense of purpose and direction, responsibility and authority, and power and influence that the pre-1950 bureau chiefs had. Despite the positive features of the supergrades, the management processes of the federal executive system have suffered measurably since the supergrades were authorized.

The supergrade positions were intended to extend the civil service classification system vertically. The other available options for alleviating the personnel dilemma at the time were to expand the scope of the federal bureaucracy by creating new federal departments and enunciating new foreign policy. The chief architect of the new foreign policy part of the plan was President Eisenhower's Secretary of State, John Foster Dulles.

The Eisenhower administration did not initiate the Cold War, nor did it originate the American foreign aid program, but it did enunciate the policy of containment. Containment was an integral element of the Dulles foreign policy, and foreign aid was the keystone of containment. The success of the multibillion-dollar economic-military-technical assistance program depended in turn on the effectiveness of its administration. This gave rise not only to a new breed of development administrators but also to a new dimension of American public administration. It now had global responsibilities. In a manner more reminiscent of Roman history than American experience, the maintenance of world order through the effective containment of communism came to rest on American administrative shoulders.

The successes and failures of the American foreign aid program need not be recounted here. History may record the extent to which communism was contained and democracy was advanced around the world. Suffice it to say the American administrative venture into global responsibility was placed in a no-win position from the very beginning. It remains so today. Administrative successes were discounted by the political detractors of the foreign aid program, and administrative failures were fully exposed by the news media and diplomatic networks. Unsuccessful Soviet foreign aid efforts were exposed in the same way. For a variety of reasons the tag "ugly American" had a lasting effect on the profession of public administration in the United States. Veteran administrators who had successfully hacked their way through the thickets of domestic politics frequently emerged from the jungles of international politics and diplomatic intrigue bloodied, bowed, and sometimes dead. The competencies of the American administrative system were in fact extended far beyond their capacity. Public administration was certainly not enhanced in this period, and in many respects it was seriously wounded by its foreign experience.

Obviously the decade of the 1950s was neither dull nor uneventful. We have seen that fundamental changes in the character of American public administration were initiated, and most of them were decidedly negative in their impact. The distrust and suspicion heaped on the federal bureaucracy by McCarthy is a hand that has been replayed many times from 1968 through this writing. The changing nature of party politics has continued to run a chaotic course to the point where single-issue politics, accompanied by the new politics of litigation, has fragmented the bureaucracy into a multiplicity of suzerainties. The current status of the Senior Executive Service is no more certain and no less ambiguous than when the supergrades were created in 1949. The question remains unanswered whether the Senior Executive Service will become the proud inheritor of a distinguished legacy of administrative excellence and expertise, as envisioned by Alan Campbell when he designed the Civil Service

Reform Act of 1978, or simply the administrative Gauleiters of whoever controls the White House.

Certainly the experience of careerists in the administration of the foreign aid program should have prepared them for the revenue-sharing, block, and categorical grant programs that were introduced during the Great Society experiments of the Johnson administration and carried forward purposefully by Richard M. Nixon. Yet the system of intergovernmental relations that has emerged during the past two decades appears to defy administrative control and imagination. As with the foreign aid program, American domestic aid programs appear to extend the competency of the federal bureaucracy beyond its capacity.

In short, since 1950 the federal bureaucracy has been stretched and Balkanized virtually beyond recognition. It has been politicized in a manner far more invidious than envisioned by the most blatant spoilsmen. Yet it endures. It endures despite the indignity, distrust, suspicion, and injury that has been visited upon it unremittingly over the past three decades. Moreover, it endures in a manner that suggests that if democracy and civic virtue are to have any meaning in the twenty-first century, these values will have to be realized through the machinery of public management and mediated by public administrators. It has been the enduring genius of public administration that its traditions have intermittently inspired the arcane impulse of democracy to make government of, by, and for the individual citizen interesting.

The Effects of Distorted Reality

It may be argued, as Dwight Waldo does persuasively, that although the American administrative ethos stems from Rome, the political pathos of our democracy is derived from Greece. These two strains of thought pervade the intellectual history of the Western world in a manner that can neither be ignored nor denied. In contrasting the politics of having and doing with the politics of being, our administrative dilemmas lend themselves to description in terms that also characterize the Roman and Greek approaches to life in general and government in particular. One of the disabilities of the Greek part of our heritage is that as our society moves ahead through the good-bye years of the twentieth century, we do so as a nation-state and not as a city-state.

With the emergence of the nation-state as the dominant political entity of Western society, the administrative artifacts of Rome, particularly those related to the politics of having and doing, were absorbed in democratic ideologies. Every nation-state has been forced to address an entirely different notion of being than that which inspired the Greeks. Each has had to confront the medieval imprint of the human soul. For 500 years each has attempted to finesse the theological system in which the ideas of the soul were lodged, and each has been unable to do so. Yet the ontological system of ethics that characterized the medieval mind is very much with us. As we near the twenty-first century, it is that ontological system, the politics of being, that confounds us. We have become increasingly saturated with the technoscientific abundance of the politics of having and doing, and we have come hard on its limitations. Reluctantly, we must admit that the politics of being can only be addressed on a macro-scale through the administrative state. Over forty years ago David M. Levitan concluded his essay on "Political Ends and Administrative Means" with these words:

> An outstanding government administrator once remarked that "administration must have a soul." That, in a way, magnificently summarizes the thesis I have been developing. It needs to be added, however, that administration should contribute to the fuller development of the soul of the state. I have tried to point out that administrative machinery and political and philosophical principles together determine the system of government; that a democratic state must be based not only on democratic principles but also democratically administered, the democratic philosophy permeating its administrative machinery and being manifested in its relations both with the citizen outside the government and the citizen inside the government, the public servant; that administrative procedures are even more important in effectuating the basic principles of government than is substantive law; and that these procedures must therefore constantly be reexamined in terms of the ends they serve and changed when the changing social and economic milieu requires different means to attain these ends.[20]

But how, one may ask, can public administration today hope to carry out such an exalted mandate as the fuller development of the soul of the state? I believe the answer is deceptively simple. Public administration can again make government interesting for citizens by reuniting them with the state in a manner that protects and enhances the essential integrity of each individual being. Government is made interesting both by ending the isolation of and respecting the solitude of individual citizens. This concept is the essence of the politics of being, and it is the ontological basis for the soul of the state.

The first priority is for public administration to assume the responsibility for delineating the distinction between the politics of being and the politics of having and doing. Assessments of the current maladies that plague democracy cover a wide range of analysis, from the humanistic description of the loss of a sense of direction and purpose to the scientific fear that we do not have the capacity to adapt to the realities of a rapidly accelerating cybernetic society. The arguments advanced from both ends of this continuum are cogent and pertinent. Viewed together, they offer a forboding picture of a dismal future. Government and society have lost the sense of vision, direction, and purpose that must pertain to preserve the values of democracy in a technoscientific and systems-integrated society. From a political perspective the problem is that government and society are paralyzed by a trained incapacity to discern the difference between means and ends, facts and values, and programmatic process and the purpose of policy. The polity cannot tell the difference between authentic being and the inauthentic processes of having and doing.

The changing nature of party and electoral politics during the past thirty years makes it unreasonable to expect elected or politically appointed public officials to assume the responsibility of talking about the quality of democratic being as opposed to the quantitative aspects of having and doing. Indeed, it has been argued that given the nature of pluralist democracy, such a responsibility is not proper for legislators or elected and appointed executive branch officials. A correctly balanced pluralist political system should be able to defend *every* public policy program as being good without having to explain what it is good for. Moreover, the central thrust of American jurisprudence is that if the goodness of fit between democratic ends and political means is in question, it is the judicial branch that has the responsibility of rendering authoritative judgments.

The logic of this argument is compelling. The 200-year history of the United States Supreme Court provides a set of landmark decisions that together fully explicate the soul of American democracy. As invaluable as these decisions are, however, it must be recognized that the Court's pronouncements are relatively infrequent and significantly delayed. Neither may it be appropriate to expect the Supreme Court to assume the responsibility of developing the soul of American democracy. If one also discounts the probability that the citizenry is capable of transforming itself, one is left with the only major component of the American political system that could possibly assume a soul-building function, and that is the profession of public administration.

This suggestion will be perceived by many as ludicrous. The political dyslexia that threatens our capacity as individual citizens to adapt effectively to systemic complexity is seen by many as being *caused* by public administration. To assign the virtue of the future to people who are viewed as being responsible for a host of villainies in the past is a gamble that many of us would describe as foolhardy and dangerous. Unfortunately, this argument is well taken. There is evidence for the negative effect the permanent career service has had in contributing to the intellectual distortions currently stifling democracy. From Washington, DC, to the county seats across the nation, public administrators have labored indefatigably to implement public programs. In the process of doing their work, however, they have printed images of reality from reverse negatives. They have created a quasi-schizophrenic administrative world that undermines any sense of value and ethical responsibility. When we assess the wasteland of the politics of having and doing for the past thirty years, there seems to be little to suggest that public administrators can make a positive contribution to the future development of the soul of the state.

If it is true that the reality of any period in history can be captured in the leading fictional characters of its literature, then the vacuousness permeating contemporary public administration is depicted very well in the personality of George Smiley.

Smiley is a career civil servant in the spy novels of John le Carre. For purposes of administrative analysis, the fact that Smiley works for the British government is irrelevant, as is his particular occupational classification. He is a generic model of the modern public administrator. His counterparts can be found at all levels of government on both sides of the Atlantic. The truth of the matter is that those who have followed George Smiley through the twilight years of his career have walked with him in the shadows of most of the internalized traditions of public administration. Proceeding *sine ira an studio*, without sympathy or enthusiasm, but with absolute dedication to his profession, Smiley combines the best of Weber and Gulick. In a manner that would have warmed the heart of Louis Brownlow, he is totally driven by a passion for anonymity. He is the epitome of the kind of public administrator who emerged in the 1930s, combining professional expertise with political astuteness and prudent pragmatism. Smiley makes the science of muddling through a pure art form.

If Smiley represents the best of public administration as it developed from the 1930s through the 1950s, he also represents the worst of the profession as it developed after the 1950s. The legacy of Smiley has frozen the civil service in its current inert, unimaginative, nonresponsive, and ethically vacuous position. In an excellent review of le Carre's hero, Karl O'Lessker notes that Smiley has no difficulty with the operating maxim that means and ends are indistinguishable.[21] In fact, means become ends. Process becomes purpose. Any effort to raise higher-order and more fundamental questions about purpose is dismissed as naive. This is particularly true within the Byzantine model of American pluralist and incremental decision making. In the struggle between the forces of good and evil that has gone on since the 1950s, public administration has been forced to operate somewhere on the other side of midnight, feeling its way through the murky gray of whatever works. What works becomes the good.

Anatole Broyard also examines the genius of George Smiley in his delightful review of le Carre's people. Broyard maintains that Smiley, "short, fat, nearsighted, badly dressed, and unlucky in love, yet stubbornly intelligent and unmistakably moral, represents humanism."[22] But O'Lessker proves to be the more thorough sleuth. Digging back into the pages of *The Spy Who Came in From the Cold,* where Smiley is assigned a minor walk-on role, O'Lessker reminds us that "we hear Smiley sounding remarkably like Senator Goldwater at the 1964 Republican Convention calling upon Western agents 'to be inhuman in the defense of our humanity, harsh in defense of compassion, and single-minded in defense of our disparity.' "[23] It requires some intellectual agility to justify a humanist becoming inhuman in the defense of humanity.

Broyard focuses his attention on the intriguing juxtaposition of the humanist Smiley with his KGB counterpart, Karla, as they deal with the contradictions of the human spirit. Smiley, Broyard writes,

> listens to Ann [Smiley's estranged wife] saying, "I'm a comedian, George. I need a straight man."
>
> Smiley and Karla are both straight men in their separate ways. One mourns and the other murders. Perhaps, Mr. Le Carre suggests, these are the principal coordinates, the parameters, of the human spirit.[24]

But how limp the coordinates become when from behind the mask of the murderous Karla we see him mourning his mentally ill daughter, and when from behind the mournful countenance of the muddling Smiley we see a man who easily condones killing. Straight men provide no coordinates, hence no parameters, when A becomes interchangeable with B. The axes of the human spirit and of being must represent discrete and distinct variables. Comedians can be coordinated with straight men, but straight men cannot be coordinated with each other. They can, however, be correlated along a continuum of straight *types*— the benign Smiley at one end of the continuum and the satanic Karla at the other. Pontius Pilate was at one extreme of this continuum also. He was uncommitted. Karl Adolf Eichmann was at the other end. He was committed with high efficiency. Albert Speer was somewhere in between. Each of the three was a straight man, and each was a public administrator.

The world as seen through the eyes of George Smiley and all public administrators of his caliber is a world of reverse negatives, distorted perspectives, and blurred images. In the universe of the permanent career service, seemingly incongruous criteria are often imposed on administrative behavior as accepted measures of performance. Scholastic aptitude scores become the measure of the quality of one's education. Crime statistics, caseloads, urban renewal grants, and body counts are used as surfeits of performance by straight men all around.

To this may be added Broyard's insight that in le Carre's mind

women become the images of irrationality, and life turns into a tension between love and politics. Though it is contrary to their ideals, Smiley loves Ann, and Karla loves Alexandra, his schizophrenic daughter. Underneath everything we cling to our craziness. We are all double agents with two conflicting identities, always wondering which is the false one.[25]

At the risk of imposing more weight on this analogy than it will bear, there may be elements in it around which a set of coordinates can be fixed. A rational behavior axis can be plotted against an axis of the irrational. Ann and Alexandra are clearly operating in other worlds. They are following the passions of the body in the case of Ann and inner voices in the case of Alexandra. In the eyes of both Smiley and Karla, their women are irrational because they are driven by emotions rather than the disciplined rules of the game. Presumably, both women had the option of fulfilling integral functions in their respective organizational roles in life, but neither carried them out. One veers outside the closed order onto the road of the flesh, while the other drives deeper into the existential inner sanctum of her own mind. The message is clear: In the turbulence of uncertainty and discontinuity some are lost and some are saved by their wits. It is not at all clear among le Carre's people who is saved and who is lost, however, just as it is not clear who is rational and who is irrational. More to the point, however, it is not at all apparent what significant differences exist between Smiley and Karla as related to the implementation of public policy. This in itself should give us some cause for concern.

Methods of governing have evolved over time in cross-national and cross-cultural contexts. The emphasis on techniques of efficiency that began with Woodrow Wilson, and the stress on centralized hierarchical control identified with Max Weber, simply formalized ideas that had been employed by public administration for a very long time. Wilson certainly felt no discomfort when he advised the world to study the murderous fellow who sharpened his knife cleverly and to adopt his techniques if they were superior.[26] The mastery of objective techniques simply created a scientific tool kit of administrative practice. We have followed Wilson's advice very well.

It was American infatuation with the techniques of scientific management that left public administration paralyzed when confronted with the facts of sociopolitical and economic collapse in the early 1930s. Just as faith in democratic government was once restored in the 1880s by the emergence of a professional and efficient career public service as a result of the efforts of the proponents of scientific management, so also was faith in democratic government restored in the 1930s by the emergence of an imaginative and inventive public administration when the efficiency machine broke down. The term "faith" is not used rhetorically here. What is being suggested is that it was the *energy* of public administrators in the 1880s that made government interesting to citizens who had become functionally disenfranchised as a result of the excesses of political cronyism, and it was the *energy* of public administrators in the 1930s that made government interesting to citizens who had become almost comatose as a result of the stagnation of policy. To say that public administrators in both instances restored faith in democracy is to say that they made government interesting by the exertion of their energy.

For reasons already described, the dynamism that energized public administration and revitalized the body politic during the 1930s and 1940s was incrementally defused during the 1950s. From 1960 to the present, the profession of public administration has deteriorated steadily, as has interest and faith in government. Confronted with unremitting global and national turbulence for the past quarter century, government is mesmerized by the continual amplifications of policy. As more time and effort is directed toward policy amplification, less time is left for testing, assessing, explaining, debating, and modifying the impact of the policy amplified either in terms of intent or consequence. The demand that public administration attend to *means* inevitably downplays the attention that should be correlated to ends. Once again, the means become the ends. The politics of having and doing eliminates concern for policy analysis, just as machine politics once eliminated the dedication of the aristocracy to public service.

On two previous occasions in American history when interest in government was reduced to near-zero, public administration emerged as the dominant force of renewal for a moribund democracy. Public administrators demonstrated an intrinsic capacity to make government interesting. An equally serious challenge exists in the 1980s. Does public administration still have the capacity for innovation?

There has to be more to the future of public administration than a cadre of Smileys and Karlas. Our administrative heritage may be drawn from the Romans, but our administrative focus for the year 2000 must go beyond the vision of the new centurions. Public administration has demonstrated in the past that it has a soul. It is that quality that must be harnessed to revitalize the being of the profession and the society.

An Uncertain Pathway to the Future

One of the characteristics of modern public administration is its dramatic success in destroying the sense of isolation that separated citizens from government throughout most of the nineteenth century. A laissez-faire government that represents a negative state is certain to offend or impress no one. An inner-directed society, driven by the rugged individualism of the Protestant ethic, is a perfectly consistent code for people committed to the normative premises of social Darwinism. Such an attitude generally prevailed in the United States during the first hundred years of the Republic while the emerging federal establishment was concerned primarily with resolving basic issues of constitutional law such as slavery, providing military support for frontier expansion, and establishing internal record-keeping routines and procedures. The individual citizen was clearly isolated from the federal government to the extent that his or her well-being per se was not considered a primary responsibility of government.

The beginnings of the independent regulatory commissions in the 1880s and the creation of the Department of Agriculture in 1889 represented the first steps by the federal government in moving beyond a narrowly defined and purely utilitarian sense of responsibility. The Department of Agriculture provided a service designed to benefit an explicitly designated subset of the population. The creation of virtually all federal departments and agencies since 1889 has been intended to decrease the isolation of a number of other subsets. This process advanced slowly through the early years of the twentieth century and then accelerated rapidly from the 1930s through the 1980s. As a result, the old cliche of the womb-to-tomb impact of government on the lives of citizens has become a reality. Few people in American society can escape the ubiquitous network of public administration. Administrators function as transfer agents and have the responsibility of insuring that the target group of every policy program is serviced according to legislative intent. Although it has always been the primary responsibility of public administration in every governmental system to insure maximum congruence between policy formulation and implementation, it is the unique responsibility of public administrators in democratic governments also to be informed about the ways government programs contribute to or detract from democratic ideals. American public administrators have the responsibility to insure not only a high correlation between legislative intent and administrative action but also a high degree of congruence between having, doing, and being.

To fulfill the responsibility of mobilizing and transferring federal policy requirements and resources to appropriately designated recipients is a major challenge of logistics. The performance of American civil servants in this regard has been exemplary. The capacity of public administrators to effect the relatively prompt transfer of goods from the federal government to specified objectives reflects a high degree of applied managerial expertise. Yet considerable costs have been incurred by the career service in carrying out its transfer function.

Time-consuming attention to the effective transfer of goods leaves little time to consider the qualitative consequences of such actions. Gresham's law applies also to line administrators: Concern for the mechanics of having and doing drives out concern for being. Two major consequences have emerged: (1) the individual citizen has been defined solely in terms of his or her aggregate characteristics, and (2) qualitative aspects of democracy have been understood only in terms of quantitative measurements. The cumulative effect of this pattern as it has developed since about 1960 has been to apply increasingly sophisticated quantitative techniques that have resulted in the steady, though subtle, reconceptualization of the essence of democracy in terms of the classical Benthamite doctrine of the greatest good for the greatest number. Democracy has become the means of expression of the majority of a dynamically expanding number of minorities. Thus the capacity of public administrators to convert the transfer of goods for aggregate groups into the qualitative enhancement of individual lives has been seriously diminished. The process of reconstituting the systemic and organic conceptualization of democracy has proved to be one of the most significant developments of the twentieth century.

As a result of this pragmatic redefinition of the democratic process, public administration has consistently defined too narrowly its role and responsibility in American society. It has been too modest in pointing out its accomplishments and too passive in response to the political abuse it has received. History has always accorded an ambiguous role to public administrators. On the one hand they have been expected to demonstrate the characteristics of initiative, competence, efficiency, and loyalty, while on the other they have also been expected to show a passion for anonymity. The nation expects administrators to be on tap rather than on top, to be seen rather than heard, and to be loyal rather than assertive. This may be sound advice for defining the decorum of individual administrators, but it is a doubtful strategy for the profession as a whole. The consequence of such a posture is a servile, complaisant, compliant, and passive career service that presents itself as a window of vulnerability. Through the window bureaucratic cariactures can be projected.

Inversely related to public administration's tendency to understate its role and responsibility is the predisposition of individual administrators to define their role and responsibility too broadly. The irresponsible attacks by political mountebanks on the bureaucracy invariably facilitate a divide-and-conquer strategy. Virtually all such attacks are qualified to exclude the truly dedicated, conscientious, and efficiency-minded career civil servant. But in the absence of a positive, cohesive, and professional voice responding to these political ploys, the strategy of choice for individual public administrators is to save themselves. This means that individual administrators must be prepared to conform to whatever bell-shaped curve of behavior happens to prevail within any given political regime at any given time. Prudence precedes principle when there is no unified profession to insist on the reverse. It should not be surprising, therefore, that individual administrators frequently attempt to minimize risk and maximize certainty in their effort to preserve personal reputations. Nor should it be surprising that individual administrators try to disassociate themselves from the popularly perceived negative image of their profession, and that in carrying out their duties they tend to make a virtue of disinterest by suspending judgment on the normative consequences of their actions. Finally, they are predisposed to project their sense of responsibility to higher levels of analytical abstraction. The net result of all this is a strategy of avoiding responsibility by minimizing one's professional commitment except in the most innocuous terms and maximizing one's interest in the problems of aggregate policy clusters. For many public administrators the Weberian hierarchy of graded ranks of authority has been redefined as a hierarchy of graded ranks of aggregation.

The relationship between the profession and its individual members is integral and reciprocal. Unity in the diversity of public administration can be forged only by the development of a critical professional consciousness. A collective consciousness in turn depends upon the willingness of individual careerists to render critical professional judgments at the most basic levels of policy output. That is the level that discusses the existence of individual citizens. If professional integrity and responsibility are to be more than hollow cliches, individual public administrators must try to translate values on a scale much smaller and more directly related to the well-being of individual citizens than now characterizes their profession. The profession must think larger and act smaller. The most durable amalgam that can bind public servants together in a profession is the reputation they gain from serving individual citizens at the level of being.

Public administration is much more than the implementation of public policy. Policy programs provide the nation with the means to increase its capacity to have and do, and the civil service performs an important role in this process. In a democracy, however, the only real justification of policy programs is the extent to which they enhance the quality of being of individual citizens. The first responsibility of public administration is to forge a system of reliance of one individual being on another. The reality of democracy lies in the quality of the relationships it achieves through its public service apparatus.

Of course this creates an ambiance of anxiety, but it is the tension between anxiety and faith that energizes American democracy and provides the basis for its ethics. H. Richard Niebuhr has written:

Ethics helps us to understand ourselves as responsible beings, our world as the place in which the responsible existence of the human community is exercised. Its practical utility is in its clarification, its interpretation, its provision of a pattern of meaning and understanding in the light of which human action can be more responsible.[27]

Viewed in this context, the ethical self may be seen as a complex system of multiple relations functioning in the midst of countervailing forces that heighten the individual's anxiety and threaten to undermine his or her structure of faith. Caught in this vortex, people need guidance, and such counsel can be provided by the critical consciousness and expertise of career public administrators.

Operating at the core of this complex system of relations, public administrators can establish a network of critical realism. They represent the sole force capable of converting policy programs into ethical encounters among individual citizens, aiding in the development of their sense of reality. Such guidance requires a sense of consciousness "in which correction is forever taking place and in which interpretation never ceases."[28] Responsibility becomes a continuous and reciprocal relationship between public administrator and individual citizen and between citizen and citizen. The basic ethical question, "What should I do?" is no longer just an empirical question. It becomes an existential and relational question based on the anticipated response of another self in a transaction. It involves a continuing process that forces an assessment of the relationship between action, intention, and perception.

The dynamics of democratic government bring individual citizens together with public administrators in necessary and inevitable transactions. The relationship between citizen and administrator always involves the *cause* of the transaction. It is the cause that binds the citizen and the administrator to each other. "The cause sustains and feeds the relation; and a community can be a community only by virtue of such a common and binding cause. It makes interpersonal trust possible."[29] For Neibuhr, faith consists of the elements of trust and loyalty. They are always mixed with varying degrees of distrust and disloyalty. Neither faith in democracy nor faith in a politics of being can be taken as a given. They must be developed and maintained by specific actions that call for response. "I learn to trust in response to evidence of loyalty; I learn to be loyal in response to revelations of trustworthiness."[30] "Faith—the attitude of the self in its existence toward all the existences that surround it, as beings to be relied upon or to be suspected—is fundamentally trust or distrust in being itself."[31]

By forming a triad of faith, trust, and loyalty, public administrators emerge as critical determinants of the fuller development of the soul of the state. As faith emerges more perceptibly from the linkages of trust and loyalty forged in the public service, and as the network of faith expands, the response patterns will point beyond themselves to wider patterns that integrate democratic ideals into larger communities. Such a process cannot be taken for granted, however. The characteristics of faithfulness will be determined by the manner in which loyalty and trustworthiness are applied to the public policy process as the principal coordinates and parameters of a politics of being.

The basic proposition of this essay is that public administration is the primary source of energy for American democracy. Public administration makes possible a dynamic faith in democracy, and the feelings of trust, loyalty, and confidence directed toward it. Faith is manifested not only in such abstract concepts as the state, government, and public policy but also in the essential and existential reliance of one individual human being upon another. The core idea of democracy is not self-government or government of the self, but government of the self as related to other selves. It is the exclusive function and responsibility of public administration to create a network that turns the amorphous body politic into an organic matrix of authentic human relationships.

Endnotes

1. B. F. Skinner, *Beyond Freedom and Dignity* (New York: Knopf, 1971), pp. 127–183.
2. Woodrow Wilson, "The Study of Administration," *Political Science Quarterly* II:20. (June) 1887.
3. *The Nation*, May 28, 1868, p. 425.
4. Ibid., November 11, 1880, p. 336.
5. Wilson, op. cit., p. 200 ff.
6. Paul P. Van Riper, "The American Administrative State: Wilson and the Founders—An Unorthodox View," *Public Administration Review* 43:4–5, 1983. See also Van Riper, "The Policy-Administration Dichotomy: Concept or Reality," in *Politics and Administration: Woodrow Wilson and Contemporary Public Administration,* Jack Rabin and James S. Bowman, eds. (New York: Marcel Dekker, Inc., 1985).
7. Wilson, op. cit., p. 197.
8. *The Nation*, November 11, 1880, p. 336.
9. Ibid., March 17, 1881, p. 180.
10. Ibid., December 29, 1881, p. 506.
11. Ibid., August 13, 1885, p. 128.
12. Ibid., March 10, 1887, p. 202.
13. Ibid., April 7, 1887, p. 288.
14. Charles G. Dawes, *The First Year of the Budget of the United States* (New York: Harper & Row, 1928), p. 170.
15. Norton Long, "Bureaucracy and Constitutionalism," *The American Political*

Science Review 46:812 (September) 1952. The quotation is also contained in Norton Long, *The Polity*, Charles Press, ed. (Chicago: Rand, McNally, 1962), p. 7.

16. Luther Gulick, "The Dynamics of Public Administration Today as Guidelines for the Future," *Public Administration Review* 43:195, 198, 1983.

17. J. Leiper Freeman, *The Political Process: Executive Bureau–Legislative Committee Relations*, rev. ed. (New York: Random House, 1965).

18. The term *supergrade* is applied to the GS-16, 17, and 18 positions added to the General Schedule (GS) grades by the Classification Act of 1949.

19. William C. Torpey, *Public Personnel Management* (New York: D. Van Nostrand, 1953), pp. 53–54; Donald R. Harvey, *The Civil Service Commission* (New York: Praeger, 1970), pp. 187–188.

20. David M. Levitan, "Political Ends and Administrative Means," *Public Administration Review* 3:359 (Winter) 1943.

21. Karl O'Lessker, "Le Carre's People," *The American Spectator* 13:18 (March) 1980.

22. Anatole Broyard, "Le Carre's People," *The New York Times Book Review*, August 29, 1982, p. 23.

23. O'Lessker, op. cit., p. 18.

24. Broyard, op. cit., p. 23.

25. Idem.

26. Wilson, op. cit., p. 221.

27. H. Richard Niebuhr, *The Kingdom of God in America* (New York: Harper & Brothers, Torchbooks, 1959), p. 1. The quotation is also contained in Libertus A. Hoedemaker, *The Theology of H. Richard Niebuhr* (Philadelphia: Pilgrim Press, 1970), p. 61.

28. Hoedemaker, op. cit., p. 67.

29. Ibid., p. 70.

30. Ibid., p. 71.

31. Ibid., p. 72. See also H. Richard Niebuhr, *The Responsible Self* (New York: Harper & Row, 1963), p. 118.

PART III

The Interfaces of Government and Public Administration

CHAPTER 7

A Century of the Intergovernmental Administrative State: Wilson's Federalism, New Deal Intergovernmental Relations, and Contemporary Intergovernmental Management

Deil S. Wright

THE UNIVERSITY OF NORTH CAROLINA AT CHAPEL HILL

DEIL S. WRIGHT is Alumni Distinguished Professor of Political Science and Public Administration; and Research Professor, Institute for Research in Social Science, at the University of North Carolina, Chapel Hill. He has authored eight major publications, including the authoritative Understanding Intergovernmental Relations, *and he has published more than sixty articles in seventeen different scholarly and professional journals. He is the author or co-author of a similar number of unpublished professional papers and research reports. Professor Wright specializes in the fields of state and local executive behavior, organizational theory, and federalism and intergovernmental relations. He holds the Ph.D. from the University of Michigan.*

Deil S. Wright explores three concepts employed to organize and characterize the changing patterns of national, state, and local government interactions over the past century. Each term—federalism, intergovernmen-

tal relations (IGR), and intergovernmental management (IGM)—denotes particular values and expectations about the processes of policy-making and administration in the American political system.

The most direct and memorable expression of Woodrow Wilson's thinking on the subject of federalism is found in his 1887 essay: "To make town, city, county, state, and federal governments live with a like strength and an equally assured healthfulness, keeping each unquestionably its own master and yet making all interdependent and cooperative, combining independence with mutual helpfulness." Wilson's scholarly and political activities provided theoretical and practical benchmarks for the translation of this definition of federalism into intergovernmental relations.

The term *intergovernmental relations* did not originate until the 1930s, and it has attained broad currency only since the 1950s. Both academicians and practitioners needed a phrase that would circumscribe the novel, varied, and complex interactions among public officials. These relationships had become increasingly volatile since the Interstate Commerce Commission Act of 1887 breached the administrative settlement that had existed for a century between the national government and state governments. Prior to this date the national government and state governments had established distinct and largely separate dual systems of administration.

Governmental interactions were inadequately captured by the classic and historic term, *federalism*. The political use of the term throughout American history has encouraged great ingenuity and imagination in choosing adjectives to attach to it. *Dual federalism, cooperative federalism,* and *picket-fence federalism* are but three examples. One student of the subject counted 326 different types of federalism so modified. It is an honorable but muddled and imprecise idea.

The general and selective usage of IGR occurred almost simultaneously with the demise of the politics/administration dichotomy in the 1940s and 1950s. A positive spillover of the dichotomy's discrediting was that IGR could and did comfortably encompass both the policy-making and the administrative dimensions of government action. The scope as well as the originality of the concept made it a useful tool, rather like a new lens or microscope, through which to view and analyze the American political system.

Intergovernmental relations incorporates several distinctive units of analysis. Among them are governmental institutions and officials, especially administrators, the human dimension of management, the persistent patterns and long-term regularities of official interactions, and prominent policy components such as finance and accountability. With these features as focal points for observation, at least four identifiable phases of IGR are discernible from the 1930s through the early 1970s. Wright designates them as *cooperative, concentrated, creative,* and *competitive.*

The third concept Wright explores in this chapter is *intergovernmental management* (IGM). The seeds of IGM were planted in the 1960s and emerged robustly in the 1970s on the occasion of the near bankruptcy of New York City. The movement is largely a product of the scale, scope, depth, and complexity of program implementation activities in the intergovernmental arena. At a theoretical level it has yet to be resolved whether IGM constitutes a major development that transcends IGR, as IGR transcended, but did not replace, federalism, or whether IGM is simply the most recent phase of IGR.

It is apparent that several factors ensure the distinctiveness of IGM. Conscious, deliberate, and calculated managerial behavior is one of them. Pressures toward this type of behavior have been accentuated by cutbacks and retrenchment in the public sector generally, and in the intergovernmental area in particular. Other distinctive features of IGM include emphasis on coping capabilities, problem-solving skills, and networking/communication strategies among practitioners. The strong emphasis on the word *management* shapes the movement.

IGM is a manifestation of the age of organization, in which large administrative institutions have become the primary means through which individuals secure political satisfaction. It is also associated with the escalation of regulation, a phenomenon related to the explosive growth of federal grant law. Conflicts over grants-in-aid and entitlements produced by hundreds of legislative authorizations were so pervasive in 1980 that the District of Columbia Bar Association sponsored a conference entitled "Federal Grant Litigation: Suing the Hand That Feeds You."

The current prominence of the courts in dealing with intergovernmental disputes has prompted James D. Carroll to elaborate the concept of juridical federalism. Carroll sees the increasing role of the federal courts as a response to (1) public distrust of and disenchantment with government, and (2) the mess that is said to exist in the midst of the complexity, confusion, and uncertainty of managing intergovernmental programs. Ironically, juridical federalism may strengthen public administration by imposing new requirements for resource allocations on legislators and other political officials. In this respect intergovernmental management is a legacy of Woodrow Wilson's effort to reconcile administrative practice and constitutional principle.

The concepts of federalism, intergovernmental relations, and intergovernmental management denote as well as connote the shifting and evolving character of the varied and noncentralized system of governance in the United States. The origins, development, and significance of these three terms have been explored elsewhere and will not constitute a major focus of this essay.[1] The nature and use of the concepts are important, however, to the purposes of this discussion. Their respective meaning(s) will emerge in the process of reviewing the historical origins and developmental sweep of the administrative state. Broadly stated, the three terms have been used to describe the reciprocal relationships among national, state, and local governments during the emergence and maturation of an enlarged and sophisticated American governmental system. Elsewhere in this volume, Van Riper offers a related and historically oriented treatment of some of the same material.

Two sets of clarifications, caveats, and contextual comments should be recorded at the outset. The first relates to the *century* theme that underlies this essay (and others) in the current volume. The second involves the use of Woodrow Wilson's 1887 essay as a benchmark for analyzing subsequent historical developments and intergovernmental trends.

A One-Century Focus

Leonard D. White identified and highlighted the year 1887 as the breech-point in the *administrative* settlement between the national government and state governments.[2] By this he meant that the national government and state governments, prior to this date, had established distinct and largely separate dual systems of administration. Conflict in the constitutional realm during America's first century was evident and frequent, but *administrative* conflict was, according to White, rare and coincidental. The amount and extent of intergovernmental administrative interaction was comparatively modest, and cooperation rather than conflict dominated the administrative arena.[3] White marks the Interstate Commerce Commission Act of 1887 as the clear breakpoint from which increased administrative interaction laid the base for increased administrative, as well as political, conflict. Additionally, the growth of conditional grants-in-aid after 1887, White notes, were essentially an expansion of the breakdown in administrative dualism. Administratively, then, the one-century focus for this discussion is grounded in White's broad historical analysis.

Yet the most recent century should be seen in the context of the constitutional conflict and administrative detente of the first century of our political history. The century from 1787 to 1887 was one in which federalism as a concept became uniquely associated with the legal-constitutional arrangements for distributing power within the American political system. Constitutional writers in Europe and in other countries of the Western hemisphere during the nineteenth century used the formal American model for precedent as well as for a point of departure. But those who either duplicated or deprecated various aspects of the American constitutional settlement were largely ignorant of or ignored the administrative settlement to which White referred. It remained for a young academic to write a speech in 1886, later published in 1887, that would formulate the intellectual underpinnings of the emergent federalism and its later progeny, intergovernmental relations and intergovernmental management.[4]

Wilson's Essay

The reams of analysis and the contentiousness of debates associated with Wilson's 1887 essay will not be revisited here. It is pertinent to note, however, some of the givens and the unresolved issues that are part of the legacy of Wilson's essay.

Let us state four assumptions at the outset. One is to recognize the preliminary and provisional character of Wilson's article. It is generally acknowledged that Wilson's thinking about administration was in its formative stages.[5] Link says that Wilson "was reluctant to see his essay go into print" and quotes from Wilson's 1886 letter to the editor of *Political Science Quarterly* that "It [the article] goes critically round about the study, considering it from various outside points of view, rather than entering it and handling its proper topics."[6] Furthermore, despite extensive teaching notes and subsequent plans for a book on administration (essentially administrative law), the 1887 essay was the only substantial piece that Wilson ever wrote primarily on administration.

A second given in this approach to Wilson's essay is the complexity and ambiguity present in his discussion of the relationship between politics/policy and administration. A full, fair, and balanced reading of the entire essay makes it difficult to support the contention that Wilson created and endorsed a neat, simple, unbending dichotomy between politics and administration.[7] Such a reading can be documented by three quotations from passages immediately following Wilson's classic statement that "administration lies outside the proper sphere of politics."[8] On the next two pages Wilson offers the following modifiers:

> One cannot easily make it clear to everyone just where administration resides in the various departments without entering upon particulars so numerous as to confuse and distinctions so minute as to distract. (p. 495)

> No lines of demarcation, setting apart administrative from nonadministrative functions, can be run between this and that department of government

without being run up hill and down dale, over dizzy heights of distinction and through dense jungles of statutory enactment. (p. 495)

The study of administration, philosophically viewed, is closely connected with the study of the proper distribution of constitutional authority. (p. 497)

Such ambiguity produces a third well-acknowledged fact—that later writers react to and interpret Wilson's essay in contradictory ways. Such reactions and interpretations often tell us more about later scholars and events than about Wilson's original analysis and its intent.[9]

A fourth and final assumption about Wilson's essay involves his theory of the state. Miewald[10] has addressed this issue thoughtfully, and Sayre[11] asserted more than a quarter century ago that the role and function of public administration is essentially a problem in political theory. At the time Wilson wrote in the 1880s he was influenced by Germanic and essentially organic theories of the state. The Germanic tradition encouraged Wilson to imagine and argue for a cadre of public administrators who would not be affected by ordinary human weaknesses but would dedicate themselves instead to serve the common good and the public interest.

In addition to these four assumptions about Wilson's essay, it may also be useful to note several unresolved issues buried in the fabric of the essay, in the period when it was written, and in its subsequent treatment. The most obvious and frequently cited issue is the separation of administration from politics. A second is the tension between the public or common good and the claims of special, private, or class interests. A third involves Wilson's political philosophy, which was at this stage, despite Germanic influences, strongly individualistic and interested in classical (Manchester) liberalism. At odds with this philosophical strain in Wilson's environment was the emergence of the social gospel and the collective reform efforts that Wilson would later champion as part of the Progressive Movement.

This constellation of issues was accompanied by several others that were central to the immediate purpose and later uses of Wilson's essay. They turn on the question: Was "The Study of Administration" designed as an academic and intellectual analysis, or was it intended to be a framework for active reform and change? The essay was originally presented as a speech in 1886 at Cornell University under the title "The Art of Governing." Evidence and opinion from varied sources[12] suggest that Wilson at the time was reaching for a firm intellectual grasp of the subject of administration rather than delving into and debating its operational details. Indeed, Wilson took some pride in the fact that he could discuss a topic thoughtfully and perceptively without direct and detailed firsthand observation.[13]

The consensus among scholars is that Wilson at this juncture in his career was more concerned with form than with meaning, with description than with action, and with general principles than with immediate social consequences. Link believes, for example, that "above all, he was one of the first scholars to realize, in all its ramifications, the truth of the generalization that is now commonplace—that all government was destined to be administration."[14]

Wilson's scholarly orientation and single-article attention to administration helps clarify a related question: Was Wilson one of the founders of the field of public administration? Van Riper has developed strong evidence for the thesis that Wilson was not a central or even a peripheral figure in the development and implementation of the administrative state.[15] Wilson's apparent influence, Van Riper contends in his essay in this volume, is a recent phenomenon, dating from the rediscovery of Wilson's 1887 essay in the 1930s.[16] The rediscovery movement reached full fruition in the 1956 centennial of Wilson's birth.

We cannot resolve this issue here. We can observe, however, that Wilson was part of the intellectual and social ferment of the post–Civil War period. That ferment produced groups and individuals who typically attempted to systematize their thinking and organize their actions to cope with a rapidly changing economic and social order. Seen in this context, Wilson was one scholar and systematizer whose ideas should be no less notable because they went largely unrecognized for a half century.

A final point of tension evident in the tenor, content, and timing of Wilson's essay is his focus on a variety of political systems. He remarks the rise of a science of administration in continental European national systems, especially those of Germany and France. But the United States and Great Britain were different because of their more democratic electoral processes, and Wilson said these differences posed special problems for administrative efficiency. To complicate matters further, the United States had a federal system that presented barriers to implementing more effective administrative procedures. Wilson was explicit about the need to Americanize the new science of administration. It "must be adapted to a complex and multiform state, and made to fit to highly decentralized forms of government."[17] In cross-cultural and comparative governmental terms, Wilson was advocating the transfer of a social technology from centralized, authoritarian systems to a decentralized and democratic system. The adaptations and modifications necessary to accomplish a successful transfer across such diverse systems were not specified by Wilson.

Also unspecified were the priorities Wilson attached to the installation of the science of administration in national, as opposed to state and local, government. Wilson's first work, *Congressional Government* (1885), had taken national government as the unit of analysis.[18] The kind of attention given to the federal system in his 1887 essay, however, foreshadowed Wilson's evolving interest in state and local government. In the 1890s he was actively involved with the National Short Ballot Association and the National Municipal League. In 1895 he drafted "one of the first fully developed plans for the commission form of government" for the City of Baltimore.[19] In short, the precise as well as the diverse and problematic aspects of Wilson's thinking prompted him to grapple with linkages between (1) the emergent administrative state, (2) the new science of administration, and (3) the reality of federalism and decentralized governance in the United States.

With these contextual matters in mind, we now turn to the major themes of "The Study of Administration," particularly the ones that explicitly address federalism. These themes anticipate the later emergence of intergovernmental relations and intergovernmental management.

Wilson and Federalism

The extent to which Wilson directly discussed federalism in his classic essay is regularly overlooked or ignored. Three sentences from the closing paragraphs reveal the significance Wilson attached to intergovernmental relations:

> This [American] interlacing of local self-government with federal self-government is quite a modern conception.

> The question for us is, how shall our series of governments within governments be so administered that it shall always be to the interest of the public officer to serve not his superior alone but the community also with the best efforts of his talents and soberest service of his conscience?

> If we solve this problem we shall again pilot the world.[20]

Federalism for Wilson was closely connected to the proper type of influence exerted by the administrator—the administrator should serve not only a hierarchical superior but the community as well. It would not be an inaccurate reading to substitute "public interest" for "community" here. The debate a half century later between Carl Fredrich and Herman Finer over administrative responsibility is anticipated by Wilson's mention of the problem.[21] In the third quotation above, Wilson asserts a solution that is as significant retrospectively as it is prescient prospectively.

Resolving the issue of administrative responsibility in a federal system would again make the United States the flagship country among the family of nations, he said. Thirty years later Wilson would pilot the American ship of state on a course aimed at leading the world, but the markers that misdirected his later course were not the lighthouses of administrative responsibility and federal self-government. Wilson's failure to pilot the world successfully arose from a combination of his own uncompromising moralism and "a little band of willful men" in the United States Senate. But that is another story.

Federalism was clearly a matter of substantial interest to Wilson in 1887. It continued to loom large in his thinking for at least another twenty years. In *Constitutional Government in the United States* (1908) he said: "The question of the relation of the states to the federal [national] government is the cardinal question of our constitutional system."[22]

Federal Features

The prominence of federalism in Wilson's thinking encourages us to pursue two further questions: (1) What characteristics did Wilson associate with federalism? and (2) What were the problems and prospects he saw associated with this form of government? Wilson's writings enable us to extract several factors he saw as descriptive of the American system.

LAW. Wilson's heavy emphasis on constitutionalism resulted in a strong and somewhat conventional legal treatment of federalism. We might recall that he was a lawyer and that he defined public administration as "the detailed and systematic execution of public law."[23] In discussing how we might borrow "the science of administration with safety and profit," Wilson pointed to two distinctive legal features of American federalism. He did so by posing this rhetorical query: "What did we ever originate, except the action of the federal government on individuals and some functions of the supreme court?"[24]

STATE-NATIONAL RELATIONS. Wilson saw federalism prominently but only partially in state-national legal terms. A sentence following the 1908 "cardinal question" reference says, "The general lines of definition which were to run between the powers granted to Congress and the powers reserved to the States the makers of the Constitution were able to draw with their characteristic foresight and lucidity."[25] The state-national focus was far from exclusive, however. It was probably not even preponderant because of three additional features of Wilson's views on federalism: (1) local government, (2) new administrative arrangements, and (3) socioeconomic developments that produced evolutionary political changes.

LOCAL GOVERNMENT.   Local government was an explicit component in Wilson's thinking about federalism from both a positive and a negative point of view. On the negative side Wilson saw systemic shortcomings exemplified by "the poisonous atmosphere of city government" as well as by "the crooked secrets of state administration." On the positive side we have previously noted Wilson's approval of "this interlacing of local self-government with federal self-government." Local self-government had a standing quite distinct from federal self-government. But Wilson went further by referencing "a *federal* organization" (italics in the original), construed as "systems within systems . . . town, city, county, state, and federal governments."[26] Wilson framed his characterization of federalism in uncannily modern terms and included all planes of government in a matrix of governing entities.

ADMINISTRATIVE DEPARTURES.   When we look at the new administrative arrangements discussed by Wilson, we also see the scope of his conception of federalism. We first note the awareness and significance attached by Wilson to what Leonard D. White called the breach in the administrative settlement, namely, the establishment of the Interstate Commerce Commission. Wilson comments:

> Where government once might follow the whims of a court, it must now follow the views of a nation. And those views are steadily widening to new conceptions of state duty; so that, at the same time that the functions of government are every day becoming more complex and difficult, they are also vastly multiplying in number. Administration is everywhere putting its hands to new undertakings. The creation of national commissioners of railroads, in addition to the older state commissions, involves a very important and delicate extension of administrative functions. Whatever hold of authority state or federal governments are to take upon corporations, there must follow cares and responsibilities which will require not a little wisdom, knowledge, and experience.[27]

Wilson was clearly sensitive to the implications and complications of such novel administrative departures as regulatory commissions. Ever the scholar with a detached perspective, however, Wilson noted the academic ramifications of the new administrative arrangements: "Such things must be studied in order to be well done," he opined.[28] Walker and Plant highlight the conjunction of Wilson's essay with several other significant nationalizing political events of the period, for example, cash grants to states, the Sherman Anti-Trust Act, and related Supreme Court decisions.[29]

Later in the 1887 essay, Wilson's legal bent reasserted itself when he said, "The study of administration, philosophically viewed, is closely connected with the study of the proper distribution of constitutional authority."[30] But constitutional questions were no longer preeminent for Wilson. They were being displaced by administrative ones:

> The weightier debates of constitutional principle are even yet by no means concluded; but they are no longer of more immediate practical moment than questions of administration. It is getting harder to *run* a constitution than to frame one.[31] (Italics in original.)

Administration—implementing a constitution—had evolved in the late nineteenth century to a status and level of difficulty greater than that of writing the constitution a century earlier.

In some respects it could be argued that Wilson, writing before 1900, actually saw *too far* ahead in terms of administrative matters overshadowing constitutional ones. The era of dual federalism is often identified as falling between the years 1890 and 1937, a period in which the legal interpretation of the Tenth Amendment was a major barrier to national policy and administrative actions. The Supreme Court revolution of the late 1930s paved the way for major policy shifts in this area over the next half century and for administrative expansion at all levels of government—national, state, and local. Ironically, when Wilson's article of 1887 was reprinted in 1941 it probably predicted more accurately the developments of the subsequent fifty years (1940–1990) than it did the previous fifty (1890–1940).

Wilson's observation that administration was displacing constitutionalism foreshadowed Sheldon Wolin's thesis about the twentieth century in general. Wolin argues that politics has been subsumed in organizations and administration.[32] Wilson could hardly have anticipated the rise of the administrative state to the length, breadth, and depth that we experience it today. He should be given major credit, however, for perceiving it in embryo and for linking it with the changing character of federalism.

EVOLUTIONARY CHANGE. Wilson's views on historical change involving both institutions and federalism deserve brief comment as we conclude this section. In the 1887 essay Wilson set forth a minitheory on the veneration of political institutions. He said the originators of an institutional form typically regard their invention "as only a makeshift approximation to the realization of a principle." The next generation comes to believe that the innovation is "the nearest possible approximation to that principle." The third generation then honors the innovation as the direct embodiment of the principle. "It takes scarcely three generations for apotheosis; the grandson accepts his grandfather's hesitating experiment as an integral part of the fixed constitution of nature."[33]

Wilson did not apply this three-generational, innovation-to-veneration scheme to federalism. Rather, he applied it to the elevation of public opinion and popular sovereignty to top rank in the American process of governance. "Wherever public opinion exists it must rule."[34]

This pattern of perceptual change was one aspect of Wilson's effort to describe historical evolution. It was also indicative of his tendency to search for explanations and to seek solutions in developmental terms. Later he directly addressed the evolving character of federalism. Writing in 1908, Wilson came to a mature and relativistic view of federalism as he discussed the "cardinal question of our constitutional system:"

> At every turn of our national development we have been brought face to face with it, and no definition either of statesmen or of judges has ever quieted or decided it. It cannot, indeed, be settled by the opinion of any one generation, because it is a question of growth, and every successive stage of our political and economic development gives it a new aspect, makes it a new question. The general lines of definition which were to run between the powers granted to Congress and the powers reserved to the States the makers of the Constitution were able to draw with their characteristic foresight and lucidity; but the subject-matter of that definition is constantly changing, for it is the life of the nation itself. Our activities change alike their scope and their character with every generation.[35]

Prospects for Federalism

What did Wilson assert or suggest about the desired and likely trends of American federalism? Here we should realize that we are speculating about Wilson's speculations. Three specific points may be made in this context, the first two coming from the 1887 essay. The third comes from his *Constitutional Government* study of 1908.

LARGE POWERS.   The first point about trends in national-state relations comes from Wilson's view of power in the public sector. Jameson Doig has highlighted "another face" of administration that Wilson confronted in the 1887 essay, namely, the need for larger powers and wider discretion in the hands of public officials.[36] Doig developed this other face in relation to public authorities, but we suggest it has similar if not equal applicability to questions of federalism.

Wilson's position was clear and unmistakeable:

> Large powers and unhampered discretion seem to me to be the indispensible conditions of responsibility. There is no danger in power, if only it be not irresponsible. If it be divided, dealt out in shares to many, it is obscured; and if it be obscured, it is made irresponsible. But if it be centered in heads of the service and in heads of branches of the service, it is easily watched and brought to book. If to keep his office a man must achieve open and honest success, and if at the same time he feels himself intrusted

with large freedom of discretion, the greater his power the less likely is he to abuse it, the more is he nerved and sobered and elevated by it.[37]

Thus Wilson stands Lord Acton's famous epigram on its head. Power perfects rather than corrupts.

Wilson did not explore the implications of this philosophical outlook for changing power relationships in the federal system. He did not link his view of large powers directly or indirectly to federalism. But the logic of his position leads in two directions. First, what formerly may have been legal-constitutional questions are shifted to questions of public policy, administrative discretion, and organization structure. Second, the connection between greater responsibility and increased power could later offer a positive rationale for expanded national action. Wilson's "New Freedom" program in 1913 did in fact fit this mold, as did the first enactment of modern grant-in-aid programs in 1914. Wilson's position was a frontal assault on the Madisonian doctrine of dispersed and fragmented power.

HEALTHY SYSTEMS WITHIN SYSTEMS. If Wilson was challenging, consciously or unconsciously, one or more of the classic doctrines of the founding fathers, he was also staking out a claim to the land where the new doctrines could lead. He was a reformer at heart, with a strong emphasis on practical results. "Doctrinaire devices must be postponed to tested practices," he said. "In a word, steady, practical statesmanship must come first, closet doctrine second." Where did these ideas lead in terms of arrangements in the federal system? The goal was clear to Wilson, although the last sentence in the following quotation reveals that the specific means required careful analysis:

> Our duty is, to supply the best possible life to a *federal* organization, to systems within systems: To make town, city, county, state, and federal governments live with a like strength and an equally assured healthfulness, keeping each unquestionably its own master and yet making all interdependent and co-operative, combining independence with mutual helpfulness. The task is great and important enough to attract the best minds.[38]

Wilson's vision of strong, healthy, self-directing, yet interdependent governmental systems could be inserted appropriately in a recent presidential speech or a current report of the Advisory Commission on Intergovernmental Relations. It would not seem out of place in a variety of other contemporary sources.

The lingering question is whether the subject of governing systems within systems is indeed attracting the best minds. Federalism and its related progeny of intergovernmental relations (IGR) and intergovernmental management (IGM) are not lively and stimulating topics for the average citizen or the student in the classroom. As Washington correspondent Rochelle Stanfield remarked: "Remember when federalism was something dimly recalled as a sleep-inducing segment of a high school civics class?"[39] Whatever may be the pros and cons of President Reagan's New Federalism proposals, there does seem to be broad agreement that New Federalism has in fact focused our attention on the persistent and problematic features of the American system of government. How can we, in Wilson's words, now properly adapt the science of administration to the needs of "a complex and multiform state, and made to fit highly decentralized forms of government?"[40]

EVOLUTION WITHOUT REVOLUTION. We have previously noted the evolutionary changes that Wilson saw in the federal relationship and the attendant controversies for which each generation "makes it a new question." By 1908 Wilson had defined his position regarding the scope of national interests and powers.

> It is clear enough that the general commercial interests, the general financial interests, the general economic interests of the country, were meant to be brought under the regulation of the federal government, which should act for all; and it is equally clear that what are the general commercial interests, what are the general financial interests, and what are the general economic interests of the country, is a question of fact, to be determined by circumstances which change under our very eyes, and that, case by case, we are inevitably drawn on to include under the established definitions of the law, matters new and unforeseen, which seem in their magnitude to give to the powers of Congress a sweep and vigor certainly never conceived possible by earlier generations of statesmen, sometimes almost revolutionary even in our own eyes. The subject-matter of this troublesome definition is the living body of affairs. To analyze it is to analyze the life of the nation.[41]

Congressional action was attaining a sweep and vigor that surpassed both past and current expectations in Wilson's time.

The appropriate direction for adjustment and improvement rested not in consultation with historical principles and legal doctrines, however, but in grappling with "this troublesome definition" of healthy intergovernmental relationships coming from an analysis of "the life of the nation" and "the living body of affairs." These phrases lack guidance and focus, of course. They permit and invite the broad discretion and judgment of political leaders. And, in keeping with his ambiguous approach to administration, Wilson's public manager could enjoy great latitude to assess the life of the nation and to act in an appropriate manner to promote healthy, cooperative, interdependent, and independent systems of government.

A century ago Wilson laid the intellectual foundation not only for the study of administration but also for the continuing assessment of federalism. In the two concluding sections of this essay, we will sketch the conceptual shifts that followed his original and prescient analysis.

From Federalism to Intergovernmental Relations

Federalism

Federalism is a commonplace term, one that enjoys historic significance spanning two centuries from the framers through Woodrow Wilson to the present administrative state. The United States Constitution does not use the term. Conventional references trace it to *The Federalist* papers, where James Madison employed it extensively. Yet Madison and the other framers used *federalism* to describe what we would call today a *confederation*—a compact among independent and sovereign states, similar to the confederation of the United Nations. In *The Federalist* (39) Madison describes the proposed Constitution as "neither wholly national nor wholly federal."[42]

The framers did not have an intermediate concept between "national" and "federal." By calling themselves "federalists," they successfully claimed the undefined middle ground the Constitution was designed to occupy. As a result, we now say the United States Constitution established a "federal" system, a reference that would probably confound Madison and his associates. Furthermore, our present-day dictionaries are inclined to define federal in constitutional terms. It is "a form of government in which a union of states recognizes the sovereignty of a central authority while retaining certain residual powers of government."[43] This definition fits the United States, but it does not fit Canada, for example, for in Canada reserved powers are in the hands of the central government.

The political significance of the word *federalism* has not diminished since the early days of the republic. It is not pertinent to summarize the term's evolution and use. Extensive treatments of the subject are readily available elsewhere.[44] We should, however, offer two relatively recent illustrations of the term's political import.

In conjunction with the Great Society programs of the 1960s, President Lyndon Johnson proposed numerous "creative federalism" policies. These policies included major expansions of federal aid programs and were clearly centralizing in their intent and results. Recently, President Ronald Reagan offered several "New Federalism" proposals aimed at returning programs and tax revenues to state and local governments. Both examples highlight the *political* use of the term *federalism*.

Federalism as a political slogan is not a new or isolated occurrence. Academics as well as politicians have shown great ingenuity and imagination in choosing adjectives to attach to the word *federalism. Dual federalism, cooperative federalism,* and *mature federalism* are but three examples. The proliferation of adjectives has been so frequent and extensive that one student of the subject counted 326 different types of federalism.[45]

Federalism has been expropriated for such varied uses that its meaning has become muddled and imprecise. In Wilson's day the concept had a specific content, but in contemporary society the invent-your-own federalism game has almost fatally politicized the term among politicians, administrators, and academics. The many value-laden adjectives attached to the leading edge of this historic idea have blunted its meaning and altered and diminished its analytic utility. One recent observer commented that federalism

> has begun to show distinct marks of wear and tear. The signs are everywhere: in the many and different approaches to the subject; in the varying attempts to rectify its name; in the contradictory political programs urged in its name; in the alternating arrangements brought within its fold; in the minimal returns of comparative studies; and in the growing disinclination of many scholars to work with the concept. The subject has indeed fallen on hard times.[46]

Although federalism may have fallen on hard times, it does not follow that the concept is completely useless. We shall try to employ it selectively. But the value-related constraints on the term do suggest the utility of alternative ways of referring to the multiple, complex, and interdependent interjurisdictional relationships found in the United States. We will try to help by employing the term *intergovernmental relations,* or IGR.

Intergovernmental Relations: Origins and Phases

Fifty years ago it was unlikely that the term *intergovernmental relations* (IGR) would be used in any newspaper, magazine, public affairs journal, or textbook. It was an unrecognizable term then, and even today it is often not found in standard dictionaries and encyclopedias. It is found in current newspapers, however. More importantly, several major agencies of the national government have an assistant secretary or other top-level official whose title includes the phrase *intergovernmental relations.* All fifty states and hundreds of cities and counties have one or more persons or agencies with a prime responsibility for IGR. At the state level the designation most often used is *state-federal relations coordinator.* At the local level the term *intergovernmental coordinator* is frequently used.

The first statutory use of the term occurred in 1953, when Congress, acting in response to a request from President Eisenhower, created a temporary Commission on Intergovernmental Relations. The commission produced numerous reports and policy recommendations, most of them filed in 1955, and gave IGR a high level of political visibility.[47] Several years passed, however, before the administrative characteristics of IGR were subjected to careful analysis.

Both the policy and the administrative aspects of IGR can be analyzed in four phases of IGR development. These phases span the four decades from the New Deal of the 1930s to the New Federalism of the 1970s.[48] A brief description of each of them follows. A significant overlapping among successive phases is a recognized part of the evolution of the idea.

COOPERATIVE PHASE. The economic distress of the 1930s and the international demands and tension of the 1940s brought public officials together in a spirit of cooperation. Collaboration between the national government and state governments in the welfare field was an obvious result of the Great Depression. Likewise, all governments and officials of government supported the war effort of 1941–45. One perceptive observer said:

> Cooperative government by federal-state-local authorities has become a byword in the prodigious effort to administer civilian defense, rationing, and other war-time programs. . . . Intergovernmental administration, while it is a part of all levels of government, is turning into something quite distinct from them all.[49]

The cooperation among national, state, and local officials did not stop at the end of World War II. The continued intertwining of IGR contacts gave rise to a new metaphor—marblecake federalism.[50]

CONCENTRATED PHASE. IGR increasingly revolved around a rising number of specific federal grant-in-aid programs. More than forty major functional, highly focused grant programs were established in a fifteen-year period following World War II. They included programs for airports, defense education, libraries, sewage treatment, and urban renewal. The number, focus, fiscal size, and specificity of these grant programs produced an incremental but distinct policy shift in intergovernmental relations.

The contacts deeply involved and often were dominated by specialists and professionals in particular fields, such as airport engineering, library science, and health. Administrators, who were also program professionals, became important participants. The rising professionalism of the period was more and more characteristic of the entire public service.

The joining of administrative responsibility and professional expertise is the reason this phase is labeled "concentrated." Frederick Mosher has referred to this era, the 1950s, as "the triumph of the professional state."[51]

Between 1953 and 1955 the temporary presidential Commission on Intergovernmental Relations devoted considerable time to policy and administrative questions involving IGR. Continuing attention to the subject has been assured since 1959, when Congress created the permanent Advisory Commission on Intergovernmental Relations (ACIR). The ACIR is a representative body that conducts studies and makes recommendations to improve the functioning of the entire federal system.

CREATIVE PHASE.   The cooperative and concentrated phases constituted the pilings if not the full foundation on which the creative phase of IGR was built. The word for this phase comes from President Johnson's Great Society program, when he called for numerous policy initiatives under the banner of "creative federalism." The impact of the Johnson influence was stupendous. More than 100 major new categorical grant programs were enacted during his presidency, including over 200 specific legislative authorizations. More significant from an administrative point of view was that about two thirds of the new grant authorizations were *project* grants. Historically, grants had formula provisions that apportioned grant monies generally among the states and occasionally among cities. But project grant funds for programs such as model cities and urban mass transit were available for open competition. They involved specific project approval rather than broad program approval. Large numbers of cities could and did apply with specific and detailed project proposals as required by federal guidelines and regulations. Not only did federal program administrators write the guidelines and regulations, they also made most of the decisions on which projects were approved and funded. State and local administrators were thrust into the policy-making limelight, in part because of the additional resources now available to them and the clientele-building tasks they needed to accomplish to sustain new programs.

The revolution in IGR during the 1960s can be calculated in financial terms. Federal aid to state and local governments more than tripled from $7 billion in 1960 to $24 billion in 1970. A similar increase characterized state aid to local units of government—from almost $10 billion in 1960 to almost $29 billion in 1970. Detailed breakdowns of the intergovernmental flow of funds are important, but they are too numerous and complex for specific comment here. Overall, the amounts show the startling magnitude of the links forged among national, state, and local governments by 1970. Thus the creative phase of IGR produced a highly interdependent and tightly bonded set of relationships. These relationships were sometimes referred to as "fused federalism," and it was said that "when national policy makers sneeze, state and local government officials catch pneumonia."

COMPETITIVE PHASE.   The tight links of the creative phase of IGR overstated reality, however. Even before the creative phase peaked in dollar terms at the end of the 1960s, there were signs of tension, disagreement, and dissatisfaction among many IGR participants, especially those at the state and local levels. Senator Edmund Muskie (D., Maine) perceptively commented on the nature of the tension. He had been a governor, and as a senator he chaired the Subcommittee on Intergovernmental Relations. As early as 1966 Senator Muskie observed: "The picture, then, is one of too much tension and conflict rather than coordination and cooperation all along the line of administration—from top Federal policymakers and administrators to state and local professional administrators and elected officials."[52] An example is the case of a state health department head who supported provisions in national health legislation despite the fact that they differed from the policy position taken by the governor of his state.

The tension and conflict between the "line of administration" and "professional administrators" laid bare a new type of fracture in IGR. This was the split between policy-making generalists, whether elected or appointed, and professional program specialists. Figure 7-1 displays what ex-governor Terry Sanford of North Carolina called "picket fence federalism."[53] This metaphor describes the friction between the vertical functional allegiances of administrators to their specialized programs and the horizontal coordination interests of policy generalists—represented in Figure 7-1 by the position-based associations of the "big seven" public interest groups.

The tolerance and support of officials in the big seven public interest groups had weakened by 1966 in the face of categorical grant programs of both formula and project varieties. The officials referred to "vertical functional autocracies," "balkanized bureaucracies," and the "management morass" that seemed to be associated with categorical forms of federal aid. They shifted toward new policy stances, including support of general revenue sharing (enacted in 1972), broad-based block grants, grant consolidations, and similar proposals. A concise statement about the fragmenting impact of federal aid in the competitive phase of IGR came from a local official who observed in 1969 that "our city is a battleground among warring Federal cabinet agencies."[54] He was referring to the fact that various federal departments were funding, operating, and controlling "their" semiautonomous programs within his city.

Figure 7-1   Picket Fence Federalism: A Schematic Representation.   (Deil S. Wright Copyright 1/7/77)

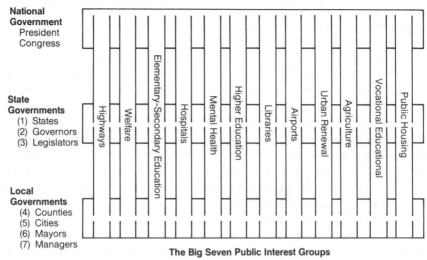

(1) Council of State Governments
(2) National Governors Association
(3) National Conference of State Legislatures
(4) National Association of County Officials
(5) National League of Cities
(6) United States Conference of Mayors
(7) International City Management Association

Intergovernmental Relations: Distinctive Features

Our discussion of the phases of IGR development provides the basis for identifying five major and distinguishing features of IGR. These features, treated at greater length elsewhere,[55] are listed with brief explanatory comments.

ALL GOVERNMENTAL UNITS.   William Anderson once defined IGR as "an important body of activities or interactions occurring between governmental units of all types and levels within the [American] federal system."[56] Whereas federalism emphasized national-state relationships, with occasional attention to interstate concerns, IGR recognizes not only these two boundary-spanning exchanges but also national-local, state-local, national-state-local, and interlocal relations.

A listing of the number of major types of governmental jurisdictions in the United States helps illustrate the variety of IGR relationships.[57] Table 7-1 lists these jurisdictions for the year 1982. When viewed from the standpoint of Anderson's definition, IGR encompasses all the permutations and combinations of possible relationships among the units of government in the American political system. Indeed, IGR suggests that the American system (singular) is in fact a system of systems (plural).

TABLE 7.1   Governmental Units, Elected Officials, and Full-Time Equivalent (FTE) Employment in the U. S. State and Local Governments by Type of Government, 1982

	Number of Governments	Number of Elected Officials*	FTE Employment (000)
State Governments	50	15,294	3,083
Local Governments (*total*)	82,290	474,971	7,746
Counties	3,041	62,922	1,598
Municipalities	19,076	134,017	2,079
Townships	16,734	118,966	245
School Districts	14,851	87,062	3,403
Special Districts	28,588	72,377	421
Grand Total	82,341	490,265	10,829

* Available only for 1977

Source: U. S. Bureau of the Census, *Governmental Organization,* Vol. 1, GC82(1), 1982 Census of the Governments (GPO, 1983), p. vi; *Popularly Elected Officials,* Vol. 1, No. 2, 1977 Census of Governments (GPO, 1979), p. 9; *Public Employment in 1982,* GE82-No. 1 (GPO, 1983), p. 10.

THE HUMAN DIMENSION.   A second distinctive feature of IGR is its human dimension—the attitudes and actions of the people occupying official positions in various units of government. Again Anderson assists in elaborating the idea: "It is human beings clothed with office who are the real determiners of what the relations between units of government will be. Consequently the concept of intergovernmental relations necessarily has to be formulated largely in terms of human relations and human behavior."[58]

Strictly speaking, then, there are no inter*governmental* relations; there are only the relationships among officials who govern different political units. The specific and individual attitudes and actions of public officials are at the core of IGR. Official actions are purposeful—to obtain a federal grant or to secure the enactment of a state law, for example. Furthermore, official actions are strongly influenced by how the official actors perceive the attitudes of other officials.[59] For example, the picket fence diagram involving the competitive phase of IGR represents a set of attitudes, perceptions, and lenses through which one set of participants, the political-administrative policy generalists, view another set of participants, the programmatic professional specialists. The various perspectives of IGR participants have been explored at greater length elsewhere.[60]

REGULAR INTERACTIONS AMONG OFFICIALS.   A third feature of IGR is that exchanges between and among officials are not one-time, occasional occurrences but are characterized by regular and continuous day-to-day interactions. Boundary-spanning actions are not always formal agreements ratified in writing. They often involve *understandings* that may include one or all of the following types of transfers: money, information, intentions, expectations, and attitudes.

This third dimension of IGR focuses on the efforts of public officials to achieve their political, policy, and managerial aims. They do not normally act randomly, capriciously, or arbitrarily. Their activities tend to be targeted, patterned, and repeated to achieve their respective personal, professional, and organizational goals.

ALL PUBLIC OFFICIALS.   The fourth distinguishing feature of IGR is that *all* public officials are actual or potential participants in IGR decision making. Mayors, city/town council members, county commissioners, state legislators, governors, judges, members of Congress, the President—all are actors on a large stage where numerous IGR dramas are played simultaneously.

The IGR stage is even more densely populated than the preceding list would suggest. As Table 7-1 indicates, there are over 490,000 popularly elected officials responsible for governing the 82,000 units of government in the United States.[61] There are also nearly 11 *million* nonelected state and local public officials who are responsible for the day-to-day conduct of the public programs provided by these governments.[62] There are almost 3 million national-level civilian employees.

If we assume that 10 per cent of all elected officials are important IGR actors, the stage for IGR plays would need to accommodate almost 50,000 officials. If we assume that only 1 per cent of the appointed public officials, sometimes called bureaucrats, are important actors, the size of the IGR stage would need to be enlarged to handle an additional 140,000 people.

There is significance to these numbers beyond their density. In the composition of the cast of characters, appointed administrative officials outnumber elected officials almost three to one. These numbers are a function of the percentages applied to the original aggregate figures, and it could be charged that the percentages we have selected are arbitrary. Admittedly, the idea of who constitutes an "important" IGR actor is open to speculation and subjectivity. The selection process should not obscure the larger point that the contrasting totals suggest. Appointed administrators and managers occupy a central and extensive part of the stage on which IGR policies are formulated, ratified, and acted out. By involving *all* officials, then, the concept of IGR focuses prominently on the role played by public managers and administrators, as well as by elected officials.

THE POLICY COMPONENT.   The fifth and final distinctive feature of IGR is its policy component. Policy consists of the intentions and actions or inactions of public officials, elected and appointed, as well as the consequences of their intentions, actions, and inactions. In the context of IGR, policy is generated by and diffuses from the regular and irregular interactions among all public officials. Policy is the plot and includes the subplots spread across the intergovernmental stage.

The backdrops and stage settings that frame intergovernmental policy dramas are in a constant state of flux. This characteristic of constant change makes IGR difficult to study, understand, and practice effectively.

The challenge of coping with change introduces at least two additional elements into the policy component of IGR. One is to raise further the influence and visibility of administrators/managers in the formulation and execution of public policy. The tenure, permanence, skills, experience, and expertise of appointed administrators give them definite advantages over elected officials in mapping strategies to deal with change. Another additional element is the intrusion of greater uncertainty and unpredictability into the process of defining and pursuing public purposes.

These two elements—the prominence of administrators/managers and the intrusion of uncertainty and unpredictability in IGR—were stated concisely in an essay on "Sticking-Points and Ploys in Federal-Local Relations."

> One of the things that is most fascinating and yet most troubling to the student of American intergovernmental relations is the fundamental unpredictability of outcomes. Programs are created on the basis of compromises which frequently leave large areas to the discretion of administrators; the personalities of administrators and those with whom they must interact in order to implement a program create additional indeterminacies; those indeterminacies, in turn, may lead the legislative creators of the program, as well as those administrators charged with its operation, to make changes in the program itself or in the way it is administered. The result of this experimental mode of behavior can be maddening to both the actors involved and to academic observers, whatever benefits it may (or may not) provide in terms of the adaptive capacity of the political system.[63]

At least two types of "maddening" difficulties are indicated. One is the problem that academics have in attempting to arrive at a *systematic* understanding of IGR. A second difficulty is that confronting practitioners who, regardless of their degree of comprehension of IGR, are nevertheless required to function effectively through a maze of governments, officials, and policies. The concept of "system" is foreign to many practitioners, and this unfamiliarity creates a condition that greatly complicates the task of managing IGR.

Our attention is now turned to intergovernmental management (IGM). Before exploring this concept, however, it may be useful to recapitulate the major features of IGR and to offer some concluding comments. IGR encompasses the linkages among all governmental units in the American political system. It emphasizes the human dimension of cross-boundary relationships. It includes exchanges among all officials of government, especially professional public administrators, and it acknowledges that these exchanges are frequent and that they follow regular patterns. It incorporates purposive behavior as a prominent element in the study and practice of the field.

The term *intergovernmental relations* has emerged from the political and administrative experience of the past half century.[64] The concept and features identifying it enable contemporary practitioners and analysts to organize and accumulate knowledge about the governing process that other concepts have failed to clarify. Wilson's early use of such phrases as "systems within systems," "interdependent and cooperative," and "mutual helpfulness" may be construed as describing activities and relationships that were subsequently denoted as aspects of IGR.

Such an interpretation may credit too much omniscience and foresight to Wilson. A careful reading of his 1887 essay and later writings suggests a more modest, yet no less significant, conclusion. It seems clear that Wilson was sensitive and alert to emerging social and political changes. He wrote about these changes in both descriptive and prescriptive terms. He described and prescribed various patterns and relationships of governments that currently we would place within the scope of IGR. His discernment deserves more credit than our latter-day invention of a term that happens to encompass a portion of what he saw and sought.

Contemporary Intergovernmental Management

Federalism is a classic and historic concept of worldwide significance, directly and indirectly attested to by Wilson. Intergovernmental relations is a concept indigenous to the United States. It has enjoyed a half century of increasing use and elaboration.[65] In contrast to these two well-developed concepts, intergovernmental management (IGM) is something of a miniplot on the stage where broad political and policy dramas are played. Its origins date from the late 1960s and 1970s. Its features cannot be fully or clearly specified. We must therefore explore and attempt to describe a phenomenon that seems embryonic in its form. Our discussion will be more descriptive and illustrative than definitive and analytical.[66]

IGR originated in the 1930s, but IGM originated forty years later. Two study group reports and a major publication of the Advisory Commission on Intergovernmental Relations (ACIR) provide some basis for describing IGM. The first report was that of the Study Committee on Policy Management Assistance, sponsored jointly by the National Science Foundation and the Office of Management and Budget (OMB) and issued in 1975.[67] The second report was issued in 1977 as a publication of ACIR and entitled *Improving Federal Grants Management.*[68] Our third source of information about IGM is a two-year OMB study pursuant to the Federal Grant and Cooperative Agreement Act of 1977 (P. L. 95–224). A summary of the OMB study was published in 1980 under the title *Managing Federal Assistance in the 1980s.*[69]

Our subsequent discussion will draw selectively on the contents of these documents, as well as the actions suggested by them. All three reports marched under the banner of *management*. Good management was featured prominently in the recommendations of all three pieces of work. They gave currency, prominence, and meaning to IGM as an operative phrase in the parlance of public managers.[70]

A concise description of IGM was provided in the "Letters" column of the *Public Administration Times* as the 1970s ebbed into history. The December 15, 1979, issue of the *Times* contained the following interpretation of what IGM is all about:

> Whereas intergovernmental relations identifies who the actors are in the system and how they relate, intergovernmental management is the tool needed to understand how and why these levels interrelate the way they do and how we can cope in this system. It is an action-oriented process that allows administrators at all levels the wherewithal to do something constructive. Instead of merely pointing a finger at who is to blame, it provides us with the capabilities to take useful actions. It allows a perspective that looks at networks and communications as positive ways to make things work in intergovernmental systems.[71]

From subsequent events it is not clear whether IGM constitutes a new play on the intergovernmental stage that is largely autonomous and distinct from IGR, or whether IGM is merely a new phase of IGR. Without prejudging the issue, let us expand on two possibilities: (1) IGM as the most current phase of IGR, and (2) IGM as set apart from IGR.

IGM: The Calculative Phase of IGR(?)

Our previous discussion has pointed out that the time periods associated with each phase of IGR are imprecise and approximate. If forced to identify a precise date and event that signaled the rise of what could be the current calculative phase, we would select 1975. The event would be the near bankruptcy of New York City. Telescoped into that episode and the continuing fiscal/social/economic plight of that city were several issues that reflected the core problems of our society. The problems range from accountability, bankruptcy, and constraints on government to dependency, the role of the federal government, and the loss of public confidence in government at any level.

For years it had been difficult for the citizens of New York City to identify and hold accountable the officials who were making major and costly public decisions.[72] For example, bond monies, ostensibly intended for capital construction, were often used for the purchase of equipment and for operating expenses. It finally took the private banking community, not without its share of blame for the condition, to call a halt to such practices. The banks pushed the city to the brink of bankruptcy.

New York City's route into and its provisional route through the crisis is illustrative of a common problem in IGR—dependency. Dependency is attached to a larger problem, and that is the appropriate role of the federal government in state and local administration. What are the boundaries within which the federal government should or should not act? Finally, the crisis of New York City in 1975 was compounded by the lack of citizen confidence and public trust in government as an institution.

What happened in IGR during this period? What were the perceptions of the main participants in IGR processes circa 1975? Three chief perceptions seemed to dominate the decade. They may be called gamesmanship, fungibility, and overload. All three are tied directly to the argument that IGM is the calculative phase of IGR.

The word *calculative* is used in at least three senses. First, it means thinking in advance of taking action and weighing one or more avenues of action. A second meaning is to forecast or predict the consequences of an anticipated action, implying the adoption of a rather sophisticated, quasi-scientific mode of thinking best expressed in the hypothetical statement: "If . . . , then . . . ." Third, calculative means to count, to figure, or to compute in a numerical sense. Quantitative forecasting, usually measured in dollar units, is a prominent but not a universal part of the term's meaning. There are several types of behavior identifiable as calculative in character, and these behavior patterns currently prevail in intergovernmental relations.

One prominent feature of calculation is the increased tendency of state and local officials to estimate the costs as well as the benefits of getting a federal grant. Two illustrations will suffice. In 1976 the Coordinator of State-Federal Relations for New York State reported that New York refused to pursue more than $2 million in funds available to the state under the Developmental Disabilities Act. The Coordinator said:

"It would have cost us more than the two million we would receive to do the things that were required as a condition for receipt of the funds; my recommendation was not to take it and that was a hard one to make."[73] At the local level, the city manager of a town with a population of 30,000 indicated to the author that unless a federal grant exceeded $40,000, he declined to inquire about or pursue it. Only a grant in excess of that break-even amount was sufficient to make it worth seeking. This calculation-based comment was made in 1973. Subsequent inflation and added federal regulations may have doubled or tripled the earlier threshold figure. It is clear from these illustrations that state and local administrators have become more cautious and calculative about their intergovernmental fiscal efforts.

A second type of calculation involves the formula game. This is simply the strategic process of attempting to make more favorable to the applicant one or more formulas by which federal funds are allocated among state and local governments. Increased attention to grant formulas has occurred since 1975 for three reasons. One is the widely heralded conflict between the snowbelt and sunbelt regions of the country. A second is that despite enactment of a large number of project grant programs, older formula grant programs still accounted for nearly 80 per cent of the $96 billion in estimated federal aid distributed in 1981. A third reason is the political necessity for members of Congress to continue to secure more funds for their districts or states.

An example of calculational strategy on a formula grant occurred with the extension of the Community Development Block Grant (CDBG) Program in 1977. The factors used in allocating $3.4 billion in 1978 funds were changed by substituting for "housing overcrowding" the phrase "age of housing," which meant houses built prior to 1940. This formula revision heavily favored older industrial cities in the Northeast and North Central states at the expense of newer, younger, and smaller cities in the Southern and Western states. The stakes involved in this kind of calculative IGR can be huge. We can easily understand why management consultants, statisticians, and computers have become commonplace in the current phase of IGR.[74] A close observer captured these dynamics when he said: "Public interest groups come into Washington with computer printouts with the [formula] weighting and what will happen if a certain weighting is approved."[75]

A third illustration of calculative behavior might be summarized as the risk of noncompliance. This feature derives directly from the rising regulatory dimensions of IGR. We made earlier reference to the Office of Management and Budget study on managing federal assistance. This study identified fifty-nine crosscutting or general national policy requirements.[76] The regulations are called crosscutting because they apply to the national assistance programs of more than one agency or department. In some cases they apply to *all* assistance programs in *every* department or agency doing business with the federal government. An example is the requirements for nondiscrimination because of race, color, national origin, or handicapped status. Supplementing the major crosscutting requirements are several hundred national and state mandates with which local officials are expected to comply. A recent study identified 1,200 national and 3,500 state mandates.[77] Responding to this flood of regulations, a mayor appeared before the United States Regulatory Council in the fall of 1980 to complain that in the previous eighteen months his city had received 2,000 *pounds* of directives from different federal and state agencies.[78]

The relevance of the mandates to the calculative phase of IGR is twofold. One type of cost is the cost of compliance with the regulations by the recipients of federal assistance.[79] The estimated cost of compliance with equal-access provisions for handicapped persons (Sec. 504, P. L. 93–112) in the public transportation field alone is estimated at $4 *billion*. Reagan Administration revisions in these regulations are designed to permit greater local discretion in the provision of services.

The other type of cost associated with crosscutting requirements is the cost of noncompliance or, more accurately, incomplete compliance. It is hard to imagine any recipient of federal assistance being able to comply fully with all the applicable policy mandates. The calculations laid on assistance recipients require trade-offs between and among these mandated obligations, provided the recipient is even aware of all the mandates. The OMB study cited previously described the forced choices and costs of selecting policy mandates with which to comply. It allowed for the possibility that recipients might not know of some requirements because no one in the national government has been charged with knowing what all of them are either.

> Individually, each crosscutting requirement may be sound. But cumulatively the conditions may be extraordinarily burdensome on federal agencies and recipients. They can distort the allocation of resources, as the conditions are frequently imposed with minimal judgment as to relative costs and benefits in any given transaction. Frequently, the recipients must absorb substantial portions of the costs. While the recipients may feel the full impact of these multiple requirements, there has been no one place in the federal government charged even with the task of knowing what all the crosscutting requirements are.[80]

The remaining aspects of what may be the calculative phase of IGR deserve some brief mention and exposure. The perceptions of participants have been summarized with three terms—gamesmanship, fungibility, and overload. The first refers to the way in which actors in various intergovernmental dramas engage in strategic behavior by playing games.

Grantsmanship is a well-established game that local officials have learned to play well.[81]

Fungible means "interchangeable." In intergovernmental terms, fungibility refers to the ability of state and local officials to shift or exchange resources received for one purpose in order to accomplish other purposes. General revenue sharing and block grant funds are noteworthy for their fungible or displacement value. The receipt of such funds may permit the recipient government to reduce the amount of its own resources devoted to the federally assisted program. The funds that are released through this substitution process can be allocated to other objectives, or the process can result in a tax decrease.[82]

Overload is a third dimension of the participant's view of IGR. The term gained considerable currency in the late 1970s, and it fits the tone and temper of IGR as calculation. Overload has been employed to mean that "modern democratic governments [are] overwhelmed by the load of responsibilities they are called upon to shoulder."[83] Applied to the United States as a condemnation of government performance, the word has been interpreted as standing for excessive costs, ineffectiveness, and overregulation.[84] These interpretations, combined with crosscutting requirements, describe the negative connotations of overload.

If IGM is the calculative phase of IGR in the 1970s and 1980s, it is characterized by the roles of public managers being featured even more prominently than they were in previous phases. The cause is a combination of circumstances, including increasing complexity, interdependency, uncertainty, and risk. Such conditions enhance the status of actors with experience, expertise, and knowledge—attributes that appointed administrators and managers generally possess in substantial measure.

IGM: A New Era(?)

Intergovernmental management may be more than a recent phase of IGR. It may be the start of a new and distinct era in the analysis of the nature and functioning of government in the United States. If IGM does represent a significant departure from old organizing ideas, it should be possible to identify characteristics that set it apart from both federalism and IGR. Let us attempt to identify and elaborate the special qualities of IGM.

PROBLEM-SOLVING FOCUS. IGM has been described as "an action-oriented process that allows administrators at all levels the wherewithal to do something constructive."[85] This assertion gives IGM a problem-oriented and problem-solving character. IGM does not consist simply of pointing an accusing finger at who is to blame for bad government. It is a process in which problem identification and strategies for problem resolution are the guiding motifs. Continuing the metaphor of a stage play, the plot of IGM is not that of a Greek tragedy. Instead it pursues the themes of such playwrights as George Bernard Shaw, who is interested in achievement over adversity and victories attained in the face of risk.

USEFUL AND COPING APPROACH. It has also been noted that IGM "is the tool needed to understand how and why these levels [of government] interrelate the way they do and how we can cope in this system. [IGM] provides us with the capabilities to take useful actions."[86] Three aspects of this claim merit further comment.

First, IGM is intended to provide a conceptual framework for explaining how and why interjurisdictional exchanges occur. Second, IGM provides guidance on how to cope with the system. It offers either a script with specific lines for the actors on the intergovernmental stage, or it provides general rules for actors to use in playing their proper roles. Implicit in this second assumption is a third, namely, that the roles played by the actors will produce useful results. Thus IGM is a conceptual tool for guiding the actions of political decision makers and managers to help them cope with the problems they face.

NETWORKING AND COMMUNICATIONS. Another feature of IGM is its emphasis on intergovernmental contacts and the development of communication networks. These contacts and networks are intended to produce positive results. IGM "allows a perspective that looks at networking and communications as positive ways to make things work in intergovernmental systems."[87]

This facet of IGM reflects the theoretical developments of the past decade that emphasize the importance of external and interorganizational relationships. The literature and main conceptual lines of development in interorganizational theory are beyond our scope or purpose here. Conceptual approaches and empirical investigations are readily available.[88] Proper attention to this feature of IGM requires an extensive elaboration of network analysis.

Summary and Concluding Observations

Three concepts have been employed to organize and characterize the changing patterns of national, state, and local government interactions over the past century. Each term—federalism, intergovernmental relations, and intergovernmental management—denotes particular patterns, values, and expectations about the processes of policy-making and administration in the American political system.

For Woodrow Wilson federalism was a fundamental component of American government. Its presence and operation were founded in law, but it was not rigid and legalistic. Wilson's view of the term explicitly recognized the prominence of administration and the significance of evolutionary developments in the meaning and content of federalism.

Wilson also foresaw the need for changes that would improve the functioning of American federalism. The most direct and memorable expression of his thinking on this subject is found in his 1887 essay: "To make town, city, county, state, and federal governments live with a like strength and an equally assured healthfulness, keeping each unquestionably its own master and yet making all interdependent and cooperative, combining independence with mutual helpfulness."[89] This assertion and others similar to it permit an inference about what Wilson's views might have been on contemporary national-state-local interactions. It is reasonable to conclude that he would find these interactions comprehensible and tolerable but in need of constant study, attention, and improvement.

The central question, however, is not what Wilson might think about the current policies and problems of intergovernmental relations. Such a question will remain forever academic and moot. The central question permeating the 1887 essay is how well Wilson related and reconciled constitutional principles with practical politics and pragmatic administration.

Recall that Wilson wrote almost exactly one century after the framers formulated a new constitutional order. He was thoroughly familiar with the conflicts and complexities of the original constitutional debate. He was clearly knowledgeable and insightful about the practical politics that had since produced fundamental shifts in constitutional power and relationships. He knew about the primacy of Congress in his own day. Wilson's 1887 essay can be viewed as an intellectual effort to recodify and redirect the nature of the American *political experience* with regard to both practical politics and constitutional principles.

The term *political experience* is emphasized to highlight a specific and special meaning. Michael Lienesch employs the term in analyzing the historical, philosophical, and scientific perspectives of the framers, as well as their opponents, in creating the American Constitution. He considers the views of both the Federalists and the Anti-Federalists in discussing

> how these competing theories combined to create a contradictory constitution; simultaneously grounded in historical events, constructed according to philosophical principles, and operating with scientific method and precision. It is further suggested that these same contradictions allow for a constitutional theory that has been changeable and flexible, and for a

politics that can be not only historical, philosophic, and scientific, but when necessary, pragmatic and practical as well.[90]

Wilson grappled perceptively with historical, philosophical, and scientific "experience" in his 1887 essay. Later, in the realm of practical politics, he attempted, not always successfully, to translate this dimension of experience into pragmatic action.

Wilson's scholarly as well as political activities provided benchmarks, theoretically and practically, for the emergence of intergovernmental relations (IGR). The term did not originate until the 1930s, and it has attained broad currency only since the 1950s. The origin, development, and wider usage of the term *IGR* met a need for description on the part of both academicians and practitioners. They needed a phrase that would circumscribe the novel, varied, and complex interactions among public officials. These interactions were inadequately captured by the classic and historic term, *federalism.*

The general and selective usage of *IGR* occurred almost simultaneously with the demise of the politics administration dichotomy in the 1940s and 1950s. A positive spillover of the demise of the dichotomy was that IGR could and did comfortably encompass both the policy-making and administrative dimensions of government action.[91] The scope as well as the originality of the concept made it a useful tool, rather like a new lens or microscope, through which to see and analyze the American political system.

One of the earliest and clearest statements about IGR and the politics/ administration dichotomy appeared in 1940 in an article by G. Homer Durham.[92] Writing under the title, "Politics and Administration in Intergovernmental Relations," Durham speculated about the reasons why IGR was helping to generate an awareness of a new theory of the politics/ administration relationship. He noted that "the growing maze of relationships, legal and extra-legal, within the federal system has radically altered any ancient basis-in-fact for such views as the separation of administration from politics."[93] Durham offered a twofold prescription for the problem, one part conceptual, the other part institutional. The first part of the solution was what Durham termed "administrative politics." The second part was the assertion of party control. Durham's own words best convey the nature of his proposed resolution of the problem of the lost dichotomy:

> So what of politics and administration in intergovernmental relations? Their interlocking indicates the unreality of checks, balances, and divisions into politics *and* administration. As a guide to a "new theory of the division of powers," the idea of *administrative politics,* or the interrelations of public administrators in what appear to be increasingly more permanent offices with tenure, forms a more realistic concept. Too, with the importance of

the Presidency emphasized, the political party emerges as an instrument of policy and consent in a new light. Questions of structure and function in the federal system preclude, under present boundaries and constitutional restrictions, the emergence of a more significant factor than the party in clearly defining the policy-phase of a new "administrative politics."[94]

Both the emphasis and the confidence reflected in this passage represent the period Chester Newland has called the "founding years" and the "golden era" of public administration.[95] Three factors undergird Newland's claim for this era, from the 1930s to the 1960s: (1) the accepted primacy of the executive, especially the President, (2) the "symbiotic relationship between politics and administration as essential in government"[96] and (3) the presence of a cohesive public administration network that produced a strong sense of community. These elements also formed a firm foundation for the emerging consensus on intergovernmental relations.

The term that Durham suggested, "administrative politics," did not endure, but it was clearly indicative of the search for an alternate conceptual framework to capture and characterize the major changes coming about in political, policy, and administrative relationships. The much-discussed separation of administration from politics would soon be demolished. In its place something akin to politics-in-administration would emerge.[97] The rise of big government at the local, state, and national levels from 1930 to 1970 would eventually cast the debate in broader and more ideological terms the politics of the administrative state.

The conceptual and political ferment of the 1930s and 1940s clearly had an impact on what was meant by and included within the concept of IGR. The term subsequently incorporated several distinctive units of analysis. Among them were governmental institutions and officials—especially administrators, the human dimension of management, the persistent patterns and long-term regularities of official interactions, and prominent policy components such as finance and accountability. With these features as focal points for observation, at least four identifiable phases of IGR are discernible from the 1930s through the early 1970s. They have been designated as cooperative, concentrated, creative, and competitive.

The features and phases of IGR allow for a certain descriptive refinement and analytic depth that were unavailable to Woodrow Wilson in addressing and assessing the evolving character of American federalism. Yet it is instructive to observe how perceptive Wilson was in using such phrases as "systems within systems" and "interdependent and cooperative" to designate the IGR phenomenon. Wilson's sensitivity to social and political change and the nuances of his descriptive analysis make many of his century-old statements uncannily contemporary. Several passages from his 1887 essay could be incorporated with ease into a current report of the Advisory Commission on Intergovernmental Relations.

It seems unlikely that Wilson could have accommodated himself to the emergence of the third concept in the trilogy of concepts explored in this essay—Intergovernmental Management (IGM). The seeds of IGM were planted in the 1960s, and they emerged robustly in the 1970s. The movement is largely a product of the scale, scope, depth, and complexity of program implementation activities in the intergovernmental arena over the past two decades.[98] At an academic level, there is an unresolved question: Does IGM constitute a major development that transcends IGR, as IGR transcended, but did not replace, federalism? Or is IGM simply the most recent phase of IGR?

Regardless of how this theoretical question is resolved, it is apparent that several factors ensure the distinctiveness of IGM. Conscious, deliberate, and calculative managerial behavior is one of them. Pressures toward this type of behavior have been accentuated by cutbacks and retrenchment in the public sector generally and in the intergovernmental area in particular. Other distinctive features of IGM include emphasis on coping capabilities, problem-solving skills, and networking/communication strategies among practitioners.

IGM, with its strong emphasis on the word "management," has not only gained extensive usage, it has also generated a significant amount of controversy.[99] This is particularly true when its focus is interpreted to imply or actually attempt to institute a clear hierarchical ordering in the relationships among political jurisdictions.[100]

Stephen Schecter has directly addressed the political danger implicit in the term *intergovernmental management:*

> The popular acceptance of intergovernmental management is not a historically discrete occurrence. The starting premise of this article is that "intergovernmental management" (as that term has developed since 1974) is best understood not as a president's pipe dream but as the completion of the twentieth century revolution in public administration first enunciated by Woodrow Wilson. For its adherents, "intergovernmental management" is more than merely compatible with federalism; it is both the natural extension and resuscitating element of the twin commitment to federalism and managerialism in a time of scarcity—both of resources and leadership.[101]

Schechter's concern is not that IGM is fundamentally incompatible with federalism "but simply that the *constitutional* relationship between the two has been largely ignored."[102] Elsewhere, Schechter sharply contrasts the different orientations of the terms federalism and IGM:

The basic difference between federalism and managerialism, and hence the tension between them, has to do with ends and limits. The end of federalism, in the American system at least, is liberty; the end of managerialism is efficiency. In this sense, the challenge of *public* management consists largely in directing the "gospel of efficiency" to the constitutional ends of limited government.[103]

Sketched on a broader canvas, IGM might be construed as a major manifestation of two prominent and discrete but related tendencies at work in American political and social processes. One of these Sheldon Wolin has termed "the age of organization."[104] Major and massive social/political/administrative organizations, with associated large powers must be managed. These organizations, their subcomponents, and their members must be enticed, herded, or goaded into action toward some explicit goal.

On the contemporary political scene, large administrative organizations, both public and private, have become the primary institutions through which individuals increasingly secure political satisfaction. This satisfaction was once obtained through traditional political participation patterns, such as activity in political parties, clubs, and associations. Wolin says the result has been the sublimination of politics, in which "the problem is not one of apathy, or of the decline of the political, but the absorption of the political into non-political institutions and activities."[105]

A second and associated tendency of IGM is the escalation of regulation. Sometimes called "government by remote control,"[106] this rise in regulation might be traced to a dramatic decline in trust and legitimacy—diminished trust in and among officials and plummeting legitimacy in the relations between citizens and administrative agencies. Increased litigiousness compounds the regulatory aspects of IGM. It produces thousands of problems that can be solved only by courts or newly invented administrative appeals units and processes.[107]

The problem of litigiousness is best exemplified by the explosive growth of what has been called federal grant law.[108] Conflicts over grants-in-aid and entitlements produced by hundreds of legislative authorizations were so pervasive in 1980 that the District of Columbia Bar Association sponsored a conference entitled "Federal Grant Litigation: Suing the Hand That Feeds You."

Studies of regulation from an IGM perspective are readily available.[109] Somewhat surprisingly, however, these studies tend to use the term *federalism* for their most probing analyses of the legal and quasi-legal aspects of national-state-local relationships. Many examples of legal analyses can be cited,[110] but whatever their number and variety, the legal analyses introduce a curious and circular irony. Instead of Wilson anticipating IGM, it may be more accurate to say that IGM is now fostering enough retrospection that we are returning to the spirit of the 1880s, when Wilson defined administration as "the detailed and systematic execution of public law."

The current prominence of the courts in dealing with intergovernmental disputes has prompted James Carroll to elaborate the concept of juridical federalism.[111] Carroll sees the increasing role of the federal courts as a response to: (1) "public distrust of and disenchantment with government," and (2) the mess that is said to exist in the midst of the complexity, confusion, and uncertainty of managing intergovernmental programs.

The litigation emerging from this management morass, Carroll suggests, has prompted the courts to fashion a new interpretation of federalism with three basic components: (1) the body of grant law that has evolved to define the rights and duties of all parties involved in intergovernmental assistance and regulatory programs, (2) personal liability for money damages by state and local officials, and institutional liability by state and local governments for violation of federal constitutional and statutory provisions, and (3) exercise by the federal courts of extensive supervisory control over state and local agencies and institutions whose actions or operating policies are judged to be of questionable constitutional validity.

One of the most arresting points Carroll makes about the components of juridical federalism is court attention to public administrators and public management. Carroll develops a model for understanding this attention, one he calls "the alienation of public policy and administration." "The alienation of public policy and administration derives from the fact that public administration, to the extent that it invokes the exercise of policy making power, is alien to the American constitutional system of government."[112] But in actual practice, administrators do make or signally influence policy. The courts have thus drawn a bead on an appropriate and vulnerable target. As Carroll observes:

> In this model, the courts are directing their orders to the right target when they order changes in administrative policies and processes. The courts are attempting to effect changes in complex mediative, integrative processes by which important aspects of policy are shaped. This may be a more effective strategy in many cases than directing orders to legislators or elected political officials. Elected officials have independent bases of political support, as well as independent powers under the doctrine of the separation of powers.
>
> In this model, the courts are directing orders to what may be the most vulnerable part of the governmental system. Somewhat ironically, the new juridical federalism may strengthen public administration by imposing new requirements which must be met in part by allocation of resources and other actions by legislators and other political officials.[113]

A century ago Woodrow Wilson, in 1885, noted the pivotal role of the American Congress in setting and shaping the direction of public policy in the United States. Wilson argued in 1887 for a capable cadre of career professionals to carry out public policy and for a balanced and healthy set of relationships to exist among the numerous governmental units that constituted the American system. The past century has seen the rise of an administrative state in which unelected officials exert prominent if not dominant influence over the direction of public policy.[114] The same century has recorded changing and variable patterns of relationships among governing organizations, as well as changes and shifts that have been sufficiently revolutionary to require new concepts to describe them.

This essay has been an exposition and interpretation of the concepts of federalism, intergovernmental relations (IGR), and intergovernmental management (IGM). The last of these three ideas, IGM, focuses most directly on the role of administration and management in the policy-making and execution process. IGM has earned the attention of all other constitutional actors, especially the federal courts. In this respect intergovernmental management is also a legacy, albeit an indirect one, of Woodrow Wilson's effort to reconcile administrative practice and constitutional principle.

Endnotes

1. Deil S. Wright, "Managing the Intergovernmental Scene: The Changing Dramas of Federalism, Intergovernmental Relations, and Intergovernmental Management," in William B. Eddy ed., *Handbook of Organization Management* (New York: Marcel Dekker, 1983).
2. Leonard D. White, *The States and the Nation* (Baton Rouge: Louisiana State University Press, 1953).
3. Daniel J. Elazar, *The American Partnership: Intergovernmental Cooperation in the Nineteenth Century* (Chicago: University of Chicago Press, 1962).
4. Woodrow Wilson, "The Study of Administration," *Political Science Quarterly* 2:197–222 (June) 1887; reprinted in 55:481–506 (December) 1941.
5. Arthur Link, *The Higher Realism of Woodrow Wilson and Other Essays* (Nashville: Vanderbilt University Press, 1971); Robert D. Miewald, "The Origins of Wilson's Thought: The German Tradition and the Organic State," in Jack Rabin and James S. Bowman, (eds.), *Politics and Administration: Woodrow Wilson and American Public Administration* (New York: Marcel Dekker, 1984).
6. Arthur Link, "Foreward," in Rabin and Bowman (eds.), op. cit., p. v.
7. For a contrasting view see: Vincent Ostrom, *The Intellectual Crisis in American Public Administration* (University, Alabama: University of Alabama Press, 1973).
8. Wilson, op. cit., p. 494.
9. Robert D. Cuff, "Wilson and Weber: Bourgeois Critics in an Organized

Age," *Public Administration Review* 38:240–244, 1978; Richard J. Stillman, "Woodrow Wilson and the Study of Administration: A New Look at an Old Essay," *American Political Science Review* 62:582–588, 1973.

10. Miewald, op. cit.
11. Wallace Sayre, "The Premises of Public Administration: Past and Emerging," *Public Administration Review* 18:102–105, 1958.
12. Link, op cit., 1971; Henry A. Turner, "Woodrow Wilson as Administrator," *Public Administration Review* 16:249–257, 1956.
13. Robert L. Peabody. "Afterword" to *Congressional Government* by Woodrow Wilson (Baltimore: Johns Hopkins University Press).
14. Link, op. cit., 1971, p. 43.
15. Paul P. Van Riper, "The American Administrative State: Wilson and the Founders—An Unorthodox View," *Public Administration Review* 43:477–490, 1983.
16. Dwight Waldo, *The Administrative State: A Study of the Political Theory of American Public Administration* (New York: Ronald Press, 1948).
17. Wilson, op. cit., p. 486.
18. Woodrow Wilson, *Congressional Government: A Study in American Politics* (Baltimore: Johns Hopkins University Press, 1885).
19. Link, op. cit., 1971, p. 44.
20. Wilson, op. cit., 1941, p. 505.
21. Carl J. Fredrich, "Public Policy and the Nature of Administrative Responsibility," in Carl J. Fredrich and Edward S. Mason (eds.), *Public Policy: 1940* (Cambridge: Harvard University Press, 1940); Herman Finer, "Administrative Responsibility in Democratic Government," *Public Administrative Review* 1:335–350, 1941.
22. Woodrow Wilson, *Constitutional Government in the United States* (New York: Columbia University Press, 1908) at p. 173.
23. Wilson, op. cit., 1941, p. 496.
24. Ibid., p. 503.
25. Wilson, op. cit., 1908, p. 173.
26. Wilson, op. cit., 1941, p. 505.
27. Ibid., p. 485.
28. Idem.
29. Larry B. Walker and Jeremy F. Plant, "Woodrow Wilson and the Federal System," in Jack Rabin and James S. Bowman (eds.), *Politics and Administration: Woodrow Wilson and American Public Administration* (New York: Marcel Dekker, 1984).
30. Wilson, op. cit., 1941, p. 497.
31. Ibid., p. 484.
32. Sheldon S. Wolin, *Politics and Vision: Continuity and Innovation in Western Political Thought* (Boston: Little, Brown, 1960).
33. Wilson, op. cit., 1941, p. 493.
34. Ibid., p. 492.
35. Wilson, op. cit., 1908, p. 173.
36. Jameson W. Doig, "If I See a Murderous Fellow Sharpening a Knife Cleverly . . . The Wilsonian Dichotomy and Public Authority Tradition." *Public Administration Review* 43:292–304, 1983.

37. Wilson, op. cit., 1941, pp. 497–498.
38. Ibid., p. 505.
39. Rochelle L. Stanfield, "Look at the Numbers," *National Journal* (January 9) 1982 at p. 75.
40. Wilson, op. cit., 1941, p. 486.
41. Wilson, op. cit., 1908, pp. 173–174.
42. Alexander Hamilton, James Madison, John Jay, *The Federalist Papers* (New York: New American Library, Mentor, 1961) at p. 247.
43. *The American Heritage Dictionary of the English Language* (Boston: Houghton Mifflin, 1969) at p. 481.
44. Daniel Elazar, ed., "The Federal Polity." *Publius: The Journal of Federalism* 3:1–299, 1973; S. Rufus Davis, *The Federal Principle* (Berkeley, California: University of California Press, 1978); David B. Walker, *Toward a Functioning Federalism* (Cambridge, Mass.: Winthrop Publishers, 1981).
45. William H. Stewart, "Metaphors and Models and the Development of Federal Theory," *Publius: The Journal of Federalism*, 12:5–24, 1982.
46. Davis, op. cit., p. ix.
47. Commission on Intergovernmental Relations, *A Report to the President for Transmittal to the Congress* (Washington, D. C.: GOP, 1955).
48. Deil S. Wright, "Intergovernmental Relations: An Analytical Overview," *The Annals*, 416:1–16, 1974.
49. Arthur W. Bromage, "Federal-State-Local Relations," *American Political Science Review* 37:35, 1943.
50. Joseph E. McLean, *Politics Is What You Make It* (New York: Public Affairs Committee, Public Affairs Pamphlet, 1952); Morton Grodzins, "The Federal System," in *Goals for Americans: The Report of the President's Commission on National Goals* (Englewood Cliffs, N. J.: Prentice-Hall, published for the American Assembly of Columbia University, 1960).
51. Frederick Mosher, *Democracy and the Public Service* (New York: Oxford University Press, 1968).
52. Edmund Muskie, *Congressional Record*, U. S. Senate, 89th Congress, 2nd Session, 1966, p. 6834.
53. Terry Sanford, *Storm Over the States* (New York: McGraw Hill, 1967).
54. James Sundquist with David W. Davis, *Making Federalism Work: A Study of Program Coordination at the Community Level* (Washington, D. C.: Brookings Institution, 1969) at p. 7.
55. Deil S. Wright, *Understanding Intergovernmental Relations* (2nd ed.) (Monterey, California: Brooks/Cole, 1982) at pp. 8–22.
56. William Anderson, *Intergovernmental Relations in Review* (Minneapolis, Minnesota: University of Minnesota Press, 1960) at p. 3.
57. U. S. Bureau of the Census, *Governmental Organization*, Vol. 1, 1982 Census of Governments (Washington, D. C.:GPO, 1983).
58. Anderson, op. cit., p. 4.
59. Jeffrey Pressman, *Federal Programs and City Politics* (Berkeley, California: University of California Press, 1975).
60. Wright, op. cit., 1982.
61. U. S. Bureau of the Census, *Popularly Elected Officials*. Vol. 1, No. 2 of the 1977 Census of Governments (Washington, D. C.: GPO, 1979).

62. U. S. Bureau of the Census, *Public Employment in 1982.* Series GE82, No. 1, (Washington, D. C.: GPO, 1983).

63. Donald Rosenthal, *Sticking-Points and Ploys in Federal-State Relations* (Philadelphia, Pennsylvania: Temple University, Center for the Study of Federalism, 1979).

64. Thomas J. Anton, "Intergovernmental Change in the United States: An Assessment of the Literature." in Trudi C. Miller (ed.), *Public Sector Performance: A Conceptual Turning Point* (Baltimore: Johns Hopkins Press, 1984); Deil S. Wright, "New Federalism: Recent Varieties of an Older Species," *American Review of Public Administration* 16:56–73, 1982.

65. Deil S. Wright, "Intergovernmental Relations and Policy Choice," *Publius: The Journal of Federalism* 5:1–21, 1975.

66. Wright, op. cit., 1983.

67. Executive Office of the President, *Strengthening Public Management in the Intergovernmental System: A Report Prepared for the Office of Management and Budget by the Study Committee on Policy Management Assistance* (Washington, D. C.: GPO, 1975).

68. Advisory Commission on Intergovernmental Relations, *Improving Federal Grants Management* (Washington, D. C.: GPO, 1977).

69. Executive Office of the President, Office of Management and Budget, *Managing Federal Assistance in the 1980's* (Washington, D. C.: GPO, 1980).

70. Ann Macaluso, "Background and History of the Study Committee on Policy Management Assistance," *Public Administration Review,* 35(1975):695–700; Raymond A. Shapek, *Managing Federalism: Evolution and Development of the Grant-in-Aid System* (Charlottesville, VA: Community Collaborators, 1981).

71. Myrna Mandell, "Letters to the Editor: Intergovernmental Management." *Public Administration Times,* 2:2, 6 (December 15) 1979.

72. Wallace Sayre and Herbert Kaufman, *Governing New York City* (New York: Russell Sage Foundation, 1965); Robert A. Caro, *The Power Broker: Robert Moses and the Fall of New York* (New York: Alfred A. Knopf, 1974); Ken Aluetta, *The Streets Were Paved with Gold* (New York: Random House, 1979).

73. Robert Greenblatt, "A Comment on Federal-State Relations," pp. 143–171 in James D. Carroll and Richard W. Campbell, (eds.), *Intergovernmental Administration: 1976—Eleven Academic and Practitioner Perspectives* (Syracuse, New York: Maxwell School of Citizenship and Public Affairs, Syracuse University, 1976).

74. Rochelle L. Stanfield, "Playing Computer Politics with Local Aid Formulas," *National Journal,* (December 9) 1978 pp. 1977–1981.

75. David B. Walker, "Is There Federalism in Our Future?" *Public Management* 61:12, 1979.

76. Executive Office of the President, op. cit., 1980.

77. Catherine H. Lovell and Charles Tobin, "Mandating—A Key Issue for Cities," *The Municipal Yearbook* (Washington, D. C.: International City Management Association, 1980) 47:73–79.

78. Peter J. Petkas, "The U. S. Regulatory System: Partnership or Maze?" *National Civic Review* 70:297–301, 1981.

79. Jerome J. Hanus, ed., *The Nationalization of State Government* (Lexington, Massachusetts: D. C. Heath, 1981).
80. Executive Office of the President, op. cit., 1980, p. 20.
81. Deil S. Wright, "Intergovernmental Games: An Approach to Understanding Intergovernmental Relations" *Southern Review of Public Administration* 3:383–403, 1980.
82. Deil S. Wright and others, *Assessing the Impacts of General Revenue Sharing in the Fifty States: A Survey of State Administrators* (Chapel Hill, North Carolina: Institute for Research in Social Science, University of North Carolina, 1975).
83. Samuel H. Beer, "Political Overload and Federalism," *Polity* 10:5–17, 1977.
84. Beer, op. cit.
85. Mandell, op. cit.
86. Ibid.
87. Ibid.
88. Kenneth Hanf and Fritz W. Scharpf, *Intergovernmental Policy Making: Limits to Coordination and Central Control* (Beverly Hills, California: Sage Publications, 1978); Deil S. Wright and Charles E. Hafter, "A Contact Network Approach to Policy Management Capacity." Paper presented at the annual conference of the American Society for Public Administration, Detroit, Michigan, 1981.
89. Wilson, op. cit., 1941, p. 505.
90. Michael Lienesch, "Interpreting Experience: History, Philosophy, and Science in the American Constitutional Debates," *American Politics Quarterly* 11:381, 1983.
91. Carol S. Weissert, "The Politics-Administration Dichotomy Revisited: An Intergovernmental Perspective," paper presented at the annual meeting of the Midwest Political Science Association, Cincinnati, Ohio, 1981.
92. G. Homer Durham, "Politics and Administration in Intergovernmental Relations," *The Annals* 207:1–6, 1940.
93. Ibid., p. 1.
94. Ibid., p. 6.
95. Chester A. Newland, *Public Administration and Community: Realism in the Practice of Ideals* (McLean, VA: Public Administration Service, 1984).
96. Ibid., p. 36.
97. Paul H. Appleby, *Policy and Administration* (University, Alabama: University of Alabama Press, 1949).
98. David B. Walker, "A New Intergovernmental System in 1977," *Publius: The Journal of Federalism* 8:101–116, 1978; Donald F. Kettl, "The Fourth Face of Federalism," *Public Administration Review* 41:366–371, 1981; Donald F. Kettl, "Regulating the Cities," *Publius: The Journal of Federalism* 11:111–125, 1981.
99. Arnold M. Howitt, *Managing Federalism: Studies in Intergovernmental Relations* (Washington, D. C.: Congressional Quarterly, 1984); Stephen L. Schechter, "On the Compatibility of Federalism and Intergovernmental Management," *Publius: The Journal of Federalism* 11:127–141, 1981.
100. Daniel J. Elazar, "Is Federalism Compatible with Prefectoral Administration?" *Publius: The Journal of Federalism* 11:3–22, 1981.

101. Schechter, op. cit., pp. 127–128.
102. Ibid., p. 129.
103. Ibid., p. 136.
104. Wolin, op. cit.
105. Ibid., p. 353.
106. Hugh Heclo, "Issue Networks and the Executive Establishment," in Anthony King (ed.), *The New American Political System* (Washington, D. C.: American Enterprise Institute, 1978).
107. Advisory Commission on Intergovernmental Relations, *Regulatory Federalism: Policy, Process, Impact and Reform* (Washington, D. C.: GPO, 1984).
108. Advisory Commission on Intergovernmental Relations, *Awakening the Slumbering Giant: Intergovernmental Relations and Federal Grant Law* (Washington, D. C.: GPO, 1980).
109. Donald F. Kettl, *The Regulation of Federalism* (Baton Rouge: Louisiana State University Press, 1983); Donald F. Kettl, "The Uncertain Brides: Regulatory Reform in Reagan's New Federalism," *Publius: Annual Review of American Federalism, 1981* (Philadelphia, PA: Center for the Study of Federalism, Temple University, 1983).
110. George D. Brown, "Federal Funds and Federal Courts—Community Development Litigation as a Testing Ground for the New Law of Standing," *Boston College Law Review* 21:525–556 (March) 1980; George D. Brown, "The Courts and Grant Reform: A Time for Action," *Intergovernmental Perspective* 7:6–14 (Fall) 1981; George D. Brown, "Federalism from the 'Grant Law' Perspective" *The Urban Lawyer* 15:ix–xxi, 1983.
111. James D. Carroll, "The New Juridical Federalism and the Alienation of Public Policy and Administration," *American Review of Public Administration* 16:89–105, 1982.
112. Ibid., p. 100.
113. Ibid., p. 102.
114. Michael J. Malbin, *Unelected Representatives: Congressional Staff and the Future of Representative Government* (New York: Basic Books, 1980).

CHAPTER 8

Congress as Public Administrator

James L. Sundquist
THE BROOKINGS INSTITUTION

JAMES L. SUNDQUIST is Senior Fellow Emeritus at the Brookings Institution. He wrote six books on various aspects of government and politics while at Brookings and is the recipient of the Brownlow Book Prize, the Hardeman Book Award, and the Charles E. Merriam Award of the American Political Science Association. Mr. Sundquist has observed Congressional-administrative relationships from both ends of Pennsylvania Avenue, having served ten years in the Executive Office of the President, principally in the Bureau of the Budget, and two years as Deputy Undersecretary of Agriculture. Between these two tours of duty, he spent six years on Capitol Hill as an administrative assistant in the United States Senate.

James L. Sundquist writes of the Congress as public administrator. Who—which of the separated branches—should administer the miniscule new government was not a matter of concern to the Founders. None raised the issue in their summer-long deliberations of 1787. When the Constitution had been ratified, they did what is normal in such circumstances—they continued existing practices. The Congress established by the Constitution picked up where the one created by the Articles of Confederation left off. Because the earlier Congress had responsibility for executive as well as legislative functions and had made administrative decisions in the form of legislative acts, the new Congress did likewise. It prescribed the organization of the executive branch in complete detail, identifying each

261

job and setting the job's salary by statute. None of the Founders who became officers of the executive branch were offended by this arrangement.

From the outset and for the first hundred years, the division of administrative functions in the American government was heavily weighted in favor of the Congress. With the disputed exception of the President's right to set the nation's diplomatic and military course, the President and his cabinet officers could do nothing in their official capacities except as authorized by law, and laws could go as far as the lawmakers wished in telling the executive not only what to do but precisely how to do it. The President had no inherent administrative powers. He had only such administrative power as might be delegated by the Congress through statutory law. Such delegation has come slowly in American history, and even in the era of the imperial presidency, it has come only partially.

Once the discipline of public administration took form, it began to develop a theory of executive prerogative. Strongly influenced by the awesome figure of the general manager in the new corporate enterprises that were transforming American society, the message of reformers to the legislature was simple and direct: get out of administration. Enact laws that establish the goals of the government and authorize programs, but then stop messing around with the professional administrator. Equip the executive with staff agencies to assist him in his budgeting, personnel management, organizational design, and planning functions. Hidden within such pleadings is the acknowledgement that the decision to delegate or not to delegate is a legislative one.

Over the decades of this century, the President has become the general manager of the government, with the assent and often on the initiative of the Congress. Legislators have yielded to practical necessity, although at no time have they acknowledged any executive prerogative to govern. As the government grew in size and complexity, the Congress had no alternative but to delegate more and more of the myriad administrative decisions that are the daily grist of government.

There are surface contradictions in this arrangement that can mislead the casual observer. One sees in the executive branch a rapid growth in administrative capacity and in the activity of the presidency, centered in powerful specialized agencies reporting to the chief executive. Yet when one looks at the legislative branch, one sees that its power, authority, and responsibility remain essentially undiminished. Presidents may see themselves, as Franklin D. Roosevelt did, as general managers by constitutional intent. But the Congress sees them as agents of the Congress, very much in a corporate board of directors–general manager relationship. Because the statutory delegations of administrative authority are written by the Congress, its view has prevailed.

Whatever the Founders may have intended, the constitutional facts of administrative life are the same in 1987 as they were in 1787. Whatever authority to coordinate and manage the President possesses, it comes not through constitutional right but through the sufferance of the Congress. John F. Kennedy once remarked that a congressman has no idea how much power he has over the executive branch until he sits at the other end of Pennsylvania Avenue.

The Constitution of the United States assigns "all legislative powers" to the Congress and "the executive power" to the President.[1] But it does not define either term. It does not tell us which of the functions in the bundle that today we call public administration are to be assigned to the legislative and which to the executive branch. Perhaps the Founding Fathers thought the boundary line between legislation and execution was self-evident. More likely, they simply did not know where the line should be drawn. The separation of powers was a new idea never before embodied in a written constitution, and no theorist—not even Montesquieu—had offered clarifying definitions. In any case, none of the Founders saw the question as important, for none raised it in their summer-long deliberations of 1787. One basic administrative function did have to be assigned, however, and that responsibility—the selection and appointment of officials—was given to the executive (or, in the case of judicial employees, to the courts if the Congress so determined) but with the Congress authorized to retain the right of senatorial confirmation for as many offices as it might choose. Beyond that, the convention had more weighty issues to resolve than deciding which branch would administer the miniscule new government. Such details did not belong in the Constitution. They could safely be left to the wise and public-spirited men who would assume constitutional responsibilities once the Founders' work had been ratified.

The wise and public-spirited men then did what is normal in such circumstances—they continued existing practices. The Congress established by the Constitution picked up where the one created by the Articles of Confederation left off. And the earlier Congress, having had responsibility for executive as well as legislative functions, had been accustomed to making its administrative decisions in the form of legislative acts. So the new Congress did likewise. It prescribed the organization of the executive branch in complete detail, identifying each job and setting the job's salary by statute. There is no record that any of the Founders who moved on to serve in the executive branch, including George Washington and Alexander Hamilton, were either surprised or offended by this arrangement.

At the outset, then, the division of administrative functions was, by today's standards, heavily weighted in favor of the Congress. The President was the helmsman of the ship of state, but the Congress designed and constructed the ship in every feature. It provided the fuel, and it told the President the direction in which to sail. There was an exception, although a disputed one: Presidents beginning with Washington claimed the right to set the nation's diplomatic course, and later Presidents added the nation's military course as well. But even in these fields, the Congress could legislate, and it could restrict the President through its power of the purse as well as through the Senate's right to reject treaties and confirm cabinet and ambassadorial appointments. Through all these means, the Congress as a practical matter could take effective control of foreign and military affairs whenever and to whatever extent it might choose. And on domestic affairs there was no question. The President and his cabinet officers could do nothing in their official capacities except as authorized by law, and laws could go as far as the lawmakers wished in telling the executives not only what to do but precisely how to do it. The President had no inherent administrative powers; he had only such administrative power as might be delegated by the Congress through statutory law.

Even as the government grew in size and complexity, such delegation came slowly. Indeed, the principal law affecting government-wide administration in the nineteenth century—the Pendleton Act of 1883—was a step in the opposite direction, for it imposed restrictions governing the way the executive branch would exercise its constitutionally derived authority to appoint officials to the lesser jobs that the Congress had excluded from Senate confirmation. By that time, moreover, the Congress had come increasingly to circumscribe the appointment power through extralegal means. Through the custom of senatorial courtesy, the Senate was using its confirmation power to compel the President to nominate individuals of the senators' own choosing, while members of the House were successfully demanding control of local postal service and other appointments as their price for cooperating with the President on legislative matters. Not until the twentieth century would the Congress divest itself of significant administrative burdens by delegating them to the President.

A Theory of Executive Prerogative

Once the discipline of public administration took form, it began to develop a theory of executive prerogative. Public administration reformers, obsessed with inefficiency and corruption in government at all levels, found the root of those evils in the control of patronage by narrow-visioned legislators. They saw the solution in unfettered chief executives—mayors, governors, and presidents—who would be elected on platforms of clean government and who would have the necessary administrative powers to carry out their pledges. The model was readily at hand in the new corporate enterprises that had been transforming American society. The genius of the corporation appeared to the reformers to reside in the principle of hierarchy—the pyramidal structure at the top of which sat the awesome figure of the general manager. Only through hierarchical control could government be made efficient, incorruptible, and businesslike. As Luther Gulick put it in his classic "Notes on the Theory of Organization," an organization must have a "structure of authority" through which orders would be transmitted from "superiors to subordinates, reaching from the top to the bottom of the entire enterprise."[2] At the top must be "a single directing executive authority." Responsibility for efficiency in the public sector would be clearly fixed in elected chief executives who, if they failed, could be defeated at the next election. Better still at the local level, responsibility would be centered in appointed city managers, professionally trained to run cost-effective governments. If they failed they could be replaced even more easily than elected chief executives.

The public administrator's message to the legislature was simple and direct: get out of administration. Enact laws establishing the goals of government and authorizing programs, but at that point stop messing around with professionalism. Approve the budget, but only after it is prepared and presented to you by the executive. Then empower him to control the expenditures it authorizes. Bring directly under the executive the functions of government assigned to boards and commissions and authorize him to group them in hierarchically designed departments, converting the boards to advisory status if they cannot be abolished. Equip the executive with staff agencies to assist him in his budgeting, personnel management, organizational design, and planning functions.

In pleading with legislators to delegate the administrative role, the reformers acknowledged, *ipso facto*, that the decision to delegate or not to delegate was a legislative one. State constitutions and city charters could be, and were, changed to strengthen the control of governors, mayors, and city managers over executive agencies, but they did not significantly curtail the powers of legislatures. The federal Constitution was not altered. Legislatures therefore retained a fundamental role that had to be rationalized and defined in the same body of theory that exalted the chief executive. W. F. Willoughby, who gave the question concentrated attention, saw the relationship between the legislature and the chief executive as analogous to that between the board of directors and the general manager in a corporation. His public administration textbook included a chapter entitled "The Legislature as a Board of Directors," whose function was to delegate administrative functions to the general manager while retaining "direction, supervision, and control."[3] Leonard D. White, in his competing textbook, was less generous to the legislature. He derogated it as only one of the "external relationships of public administration," in a chapter with that title. He did concede to the legislature an oversight function, "to ensure harmony between legislative and administrative policy," to ensure the propriety of expenditures, to satisfy itself with the efficacy of the executive's internal administrative controls, and to inform itself "thoroughly of the conditions of administration" in order to determine whether remedial legislation might be needed. "Further than this it does not need, and is usually unqualified, to go."[4]

Once the principle was established that the general manager's function belonged properly to the chief executive, it was a small step for the public administration fraternity to conclude that in the case of the federal government this was what the Founding Fathers had in mind. After all, they had vested "the executive power" in the President and charged him to "take care that the laws be faithfully executed." Accordingly, when the President's Committee on Administrative Management, headed by Louis Brownlow, carried the developing theories of public administration to Washington, it asserted that "the effectiveness of the Chief Executive is limited and restricted, in spite of the clear intent of the Constitution to the contrary."[5] This was reiterated and embellished in the message Gulick wrote for President Roosevelt transmitting the report to the Congress. "The plain fact is," said the President, "that the present organization and equipment of the executive branch of the government defeats the constitutional intent that there be a single responsible Chief Executive to coordinate and manage the departments and agencies in accordance with the laws enacted by the Congress."[6]

Neither the Committee nor the President attempted to explain why, if the Founders' intent was so clear, they had not expressed it unambiguously in the Constitution. Nor did they explain why the government, from the very beginning, was allowed to operate with severe restrictions on the President's managerial authority. But Roosevelt did not carry this doctrine to its logical conclusion and simply assert a constitutional authority to reorganize the executive branch without reference to the Congress. That would be left to later Presidents, particularly Richard Nixon. Roosevelt merely asked the Congress to affirm his interpretation of the constitutional intent, and when in major respects the Congress failed to give him the powers he sought, he could only accept its decision. Whatever the Founding Fathers may have intended, the constitutional facts of administrative life were the same in 1937 as they were in 1789: Whatever authority to coordinate and manage the President possessed,

it came not through constitutional right but through the sufferance of
the Congress.

An Era of Congressional Delegation

Nevertheless, over the decades of this century, the President did become
the general manager of the government, with the assent and often on
the initiative of the Congress. Although legislators at no time acknowledged any executive prerogative, they did yield to practical necessity.
As the government grew in size and complexity, the Congress had no
alternative but to delegate more and more of the myriad administrative
decisions that were the daily grist of governance.

Yet the power to delegate implies the power to retain ultimate responsibility, with the right to withdraw the delegation or overrule the actions
of the delegatee. It was only with this understanding that the Congress
took the long series of actions that, collectively and ultimately, made
the President the general manager of the executive branch. So the balance
of authority that developed appears on the surface to be somewhat
contradictory. When one looks at the executive branch, one sees a rapid
growth in the administrative capacity and activity of the presidency,
centered in powerful specialized agencies reporting to the chief executive.
Yet when one looks at the legislative branch, one sees that its power,
authority, and responsibility remain essentially undiminished. Presidents
may see themselves, as Roosevelt did, as general managers by constitutional intent. But the Congress sees them as agents of the Congress,
very much in the corporate board of directors–general manager relationship that Willoughby conceptualized. And, because the statutory delegations of administrative authority were written by the Congress, its view
has prevailed.

The constitutional system, however, compelled one important departure from the corporate model. Because a board of directors can replace
its general manager at any time, it can enter into a fixed relationship
of maximum delegation. If the manager does not exercise his delegated
functions to the board's satisfaction, it is free to find someone who will.
But the Congress has no such option. If it does not like the way a
President performs as its agent, it cannot tell him to find another job.
Hence, legislators have been understandably reluctant to delegate authority in permanent legislation. They have, instead, limited their grants
of authority in duration as well as in scope, and they have found ways
to control the use of many of the delegated powers even as they are
being exercised—the most important device for that purpose having
been the now-prohibited legislative veto, discussed later in this chapter.

In deciding what administrative functions to delegate on a contingent basis, the Congress has acknowledged no theory. It has acted, as is its custom, on a case by case basis, responding to pressures and events. So the delegation of administrative authority has been a patchwork. It has varied from function to function, depending on the attitudes and experiences of particular congressional committees. And it has varied from year to year, reflecting the degree of trust legislators have been prepared to place in each particular occupant of the White House.

The Budget and Accounting Act of 1921—the second landmark statute affecting government-wide administration, after the Pendleton Act—illustrates the Congress's conception of the President as agent. As the act sailed through the Congress, virtually unopposed, its sponsors argued that the power of the purse was in no way passing to the executive branch. The Congress would make the same budget decisions it always had. The President, using his new Bureau of the Budget, would simply provide the Congress with better information on which to base its decisions. The estimates of the executive agencies would be better scrutinized, brought into balance, and pared down by the President. All of this would make the job of the Congress easier. Relieved of the need to review and resolve every detailed estimate, the Congress could concentrate on the fundamental policy questions reflected in the budget—and on matters of particular importance to each member's constituents. On any item in disagreement, the Congress could freely substitute its judgment for the President's. While losing none of its responsibility or authority, the Congress in the same act enhanced its own capacity for review and control, by creating a comptroller general to act as an arm of the legislature in auditing transactions and settling the government's accounts.

The Classification Act of 1923, on the other hand, transferred to the executive on a permanent basis the onerous responsibility of assigning salaries to individual jobs within the burgeoning executive branch. The Congress retained the duty of fixing the salaries for each of the grades to which individuals would be allocated, but allocations within grades would become finally an executive responsibility. This did not prevent the Congress, of course, from occasionally fixing or adjusting the compensation of a particular job or group of jobs by statute, but such actions were normally confined to the highest-paid positions, and they usually occurred only at the time a new agency was created.

On the question of who should design the organization of the executive branch, the Congress was unwilling to yield the responsibility permanently as it had done with the classification of positions. Reorganization involved too many constituent interests to let go altogether. Yet, as one leading Congressman said in a 1939 debate: "We now know from long and bitter experience that Congress does not want to do it. We know that Congress is not going to do it, and, furthermore, we know that Congress cannot do it."[7] Out of this dilemma came the invention of the legislative veto, first incorporated in the Economy Act of 1932. That act authorized President Hoover to reorganize the government by executive order, but each order had to be transmitted to the Congress and could be disapproved by either house within sixty days. Over the next half century, the Congress passed a long series of reorganization acts but always with the legislative veto, as well as other carefully crafted restrictions. It always limited the duration of the reorganization authority to not more than a single presidential term. It sometimes specified that certain agencies would be exempt from reorganization, and sometimes it prohibited the creation or dissolution of departments. In some periods it made reorganization easier by making rejection dependent on the adverse vote of both houses of the Congress instead of only one.

The Congress found the legislative veto an increasingly useful means for delegating administrative responsibility yet retaining close control. Initially, the Congress delegated the legislative veto power to committees. In 1944, it required the Secretary of the Navy to "come into agreement" with the two naval affairs committees on the terms of any land disposal or acquisition. In the 1950s, over President Truman's strong objection, it began applying the same procedure to the entire Department of Defense through provisions in the annual military construction authorization acts. This policy reflected an obsession with local land transactions that led one member of the House Armed Services Committee to observe that "military policy is made by the Department of Defense. Our committee is a real estate committee."[8] When the Post Office Department was subjected to the same requirement covering lease-purchase transactions (in this case, two committees in each house were to approve the contracts), President Truman exercised a pocket veto. Legislators had their way in the end by simply withdrawing the general lease-purchase authority and authorizing each transaction individually on the basis of a prospectus presented by the department. The same procedure was followed in authorizing the watershed projects of the Soil Conservation Service.

To give the executive branch greater flexibility in the use of appropriated funds, the appropriations committees gradually consolidated individual line-item appropriations into lump-sum allocations for the broad purposes of an agency or program, but again the Congress retained control. In this case, the means of control is an informal process called "reprogramming." Although appropriations acts may be brief and general, agencies are further bound in practice by the spending plans that they present to the committees initially, as interpreted in committee reports, correspondence, and gentlemen's agreements. These may be modified if reprogramming proposals are reported to and not disapproved by the committees.[9] Between 1956 and 1972, the Defense Department alone undertook annually about a hundred reprogramming actions affecting $2.6 billion.

In the late 1960s, the Congress went even further in expanding the fiscal power of the President. Convinced that spending for the 1969 fiscal year had to be cut below the spending levels projected in President Lyndon Johnson's budget, the Congress directed the President to impound enough of the money contained in the appropriations acts to bring aggregate expenditures $6 billion below the budget total. This was done despite a news conference outburst by Johnson demanding that legislators "stand up like men and answer the roll call" and make the cuts themselves.[10] The next year, the Democratic Congress even granted impoundment power to Republican President Richard Nixon, but only in the amount of $1 billion.

A Period of Congressional Reassertion

The era of easy and trustful delegation of administrative power to the President came to an abrupt end as President Nixon's first term expired. In the stormiest executive-legislative confrontation since the impeachment of President Andrew Johnson a hundred years earlier, Nixon seized administrative power far beyond that of any of his predecessors. He did so in open defiance of the Congress. The angered legislators struck back with a series of measures designed to restrain and control the President in the administration of the laws.

"In this second term," Nixon recalled in his memoirs, "I had thrown down a gauntlet to Congress, the bureaucracy, the media, and the Washington establishment and challenged them to epic battle."[11] The skirmishing had in fact begun earlier, in the final months of Nixon's first term. It was over the issue of impoundment. Having been granted authority to impound enough appropriated funds to reduce the 1969 budget by $6 billion (an authority granted to President Johnson but carried over into the new administration) and the 1970 budget by $1 billion, Nixon proceeded on his own authority to go much further. He announced impoundments totaling $8.2 billion for 1969 and added another $3.5 billion in 1970. He cited only his general "obligation under the Constitution and the laws." He encountered no objection from the Congress. The next year, when the Congress denied him any grant of impoundment authority, he simply seized the power the Congress had withheld. In March 1971 he told the legislators he had withheld $12.7 billion of the spending authorizations they had enacted.[12] This time the lawmakers did protest. Senator Sam J. Ervin, Jr., the North Carolina Democrat who chaired the Separation of Powers Subcommittee, opened hearings on the impoundment issue with a declaration that the Founding Fathers intended that the President "execute all laws passed by the Congress, irrespective of any personal, political, or philosophical views he might have. He has no authority under the Constitution to decide which laws will be executed or to what extent they will be enforced."[13] Several Congressmen introduced bills to compel the President to act, while the intended recipients of the impounded funds filed lawsuits. The President was undeterred, resting his case not only on such anti-inflation statues as the Employment Act of 1946 but also on the executive power vested in him by the Constitution.[14] In October 1972, in the midst of his reelection campaign, when the Congress refused to bring total spending down to the level he demanded—and the level that both houses accepted as reflecting wise fiscal policy—Nixon once more announced his intention to act on his own to make the cuts. "What Congress has refused him, the President has undertaken to seize," cried Speaker Carl Albert.[15] The President was claiming as a constitutional right the item veto power that many Presidents had asked for but none had ever been granted, and in a form that denied the Congress the opportunity to override.

Impoundment was only one of several issues that shaped the constitutional impasse of the time. The President had also put into effect a reorganization plan that the Congress had explicitly rejected. After the legislators had failed to act on his recommendation that seven cabinet departments be consolidated into four, Nixon appointed four cabinet members as presidential assistants to coordinate the seven departments. He was also carrying on warfare in Southeast Asia as an executive prerogative. While the Congress was out of session, and without consulting its leaders, the President had intensified the bombing of North Vietnam and mined the port of Haiphong. He was pressing the doctrine of executive privilege to the ultimate, claiming unlimited power to withhold any information from the Congress.[16]

The "epic battle" that the President precipitated was therefore fought on several fronts. It resulted in historic legislation reasserting control by the Congress over the executive branch, in an intensification of congressional oversight activities, and in a proliferation of statutory provisions authorizing one or both houses of the Congress to veto administrative actions.

The War Powers Resolution of 1973

In matters of war and peace Presidents have traditionally claimed a greater freedom from congressional control than they have asserted in domestic matters. They have rested their claim on some specific language in Article II of the Constitution, which they have interpreted as augmenting the general grant of executive power with which the article begins.

One clause makes the President the commander-in-chief of the army and navy. Others assign him the treaty-making power, subject to senatorial approval, and authorize him to receive ambassadors and other foreign representatives. Interpolating from these provisions, Presidents have usually considered themselves the prime makers of foreign policy, and they have moved troops freely around the globe in support of diplomatic objectives or in response to military initiatives by other powers. In most periods of history, the Congress has been content to acquiesce in presidential leadership in these areas, but at other times it has by law set policy reducing the President in foreign as in domestic matters to the role of administrator of national objectives prescribed by the Congress. In the 1930s, it was the Congress that led the country into a period of isolationism, through a series of neutrality acts that effectively restrained presidential intervention in the conflicts that led to World War II.

During that war, the Congress granted broad powers to President Franklin Roosevelt—including, for example, freedom to create new agencies and reorganize old ones. Legislators typically supported his policies, devoting their energies to looking out for constituent interests and exposing waste and inefficiency in war expenditures. After the war, the Congress continued to follow presidential leadership as the United States took the initiative in creating the United Nations and other global institutions.

Deference to the President depended on trust, however, and during the Lyndon Johnson years trust broke down. Misgivings centered in the Senate Foreign Relations Committee, particularly in the person of its chairman, Democrat J. William Fulbright of Arkansas. Fulbright became convinced that the President had misled the Congress in obtaining the Gulf of Tonkin resolution of 1964 that Johnson said gave him a free hand to make war in Southeast Asia. Fulbright also felt misled in the way Johnson justified the dispatch of troops to the Dominican Republic in 1965. By the time the Congress turned against the Vietnam war in the early 1970s, it not only took control of war policy and forced a termination of the conflict but it also confronted the broader question of how Presidents could, and should, be brought under the control of the Congress in the deployment of military forces outside the United States.

The result was the War Powers Resolution of 1973. Its leading sponsor in the Senate, Republican Jacob K. Javits of New York, sought to codify in law the precise circumstances under which the President could involve the military in hostilities, limiting the purposes essentially to repelling attacks and carrying out commitments to which Congress was a party. But House sponsors contended that no definition could embrace all contingencies, and the President must therefore be granted a flexible authority. Javits had to yield. The final resolution required that the President consult with the Congress before introducing armed forces into hostilities, report when he did so, and, unless the Congress granted authorization within sixty days, withdraw the forces. Moreover, even before the sixty-day period expired, the Congress could exercise a legislative veto through a concurrent resolution of the two houses (which does not require a presidential signature). President Nixon vetoed the resolution both as bad policy and as an usurpation of the President's constitutional prerogatives. The Congress overrode the veto by large majorities.

The question remains unsettled, however, for no President since Nixon has been willing to concede the constitutionality of the War Powers Resolution. Hence each has reserved for future Presidents the right to disregard it. Both Presidents Ford and Carter, however, minimally complied with its terms. Ford made four reports and Carter made one, both Presidents being careful to say they were "taking note" of the resolution or acting "consistent with" it, rather than "pursuant to" it. President Ronald Reagan, when he sent marines into Lebanon in 1983, ignored the resolution and aroused a congressional outcry in doing so. The upshot was a compromise measure in which the Congress invoked the War Powers Resolution and gave the President an eighteen-month authorization to do what he was doing anyway. The President accepted the authorization with a statement disavowing any acknowledgment that such authority was constitutionally required. Shortly afterward, another resolution put a sixty-day limit on the President's use of military forces in Grenada. In each case, the resolution was not tested further because the military was disengaged before the deadline.

While the constitutional dispute continues, the existence of the War Powers Resolution has unquestionably brought the Congress into fuller participation in such national decisions as may lead the country into war. It has compelled itself to take a stand on each individual case, as it did on Lebanon and Grenada, whether or not the President asks it to do so. Otherwise it would yield the constitutional position it took in 1973. Just as no President is likely to concede the constitutionality of the War Powers Resolution, so no Congress is likely to abdicate the claim embodied in that measure: the ultimate control of the armed forces resides not in the President but in the Congress.

The Congressional Budget and Impoundment Control Act of 1974

The historic clash between the Congress and President Nixon over impoundment impelled the Congress to look inward as well as outward.

At the same time that legislators condemned the President for "usurping" the power of the purse, they had to admit he had a point: the Congress was not exercising its fiscal responsibility wisely. That was why, in 1968 and 1969, legislators had found themselves forced to delegate a limited impoundment power to the President, and that was why, when they refused to do so again in 1972, they appointed a joint committee to examine how the Congress should alter its organization and its practices better to control the budget.

"We have lost the capacity to decide our own priorities in this Nation of ours," said Chairman Al Ullman, Democrat of Oregon, of the House Ways and Means committee in presenting the proposed joint committee study to the Congress.[17] The reason was the decentralization of the budgetary process. Revenues were the responsibility of one committee in each house, appropriations of another, and no mechanism existed for weighing the two together. Moreover, appropriations were contained in more than a dozen bills each year, considered separately rather than in the aggregate. And many expenditures were automatic, mandated by law and referred to in budgeteers' jargon as "uncontrollable." The term was not literally true, of course, for laws can be changed, but they were uncontrollable by the Office of Management and Budget where the term originated. They were also beyond the control of the appropriations committees, because the authorizing laws were under the jurisdiction of other committees—committees that had sponsored the spending programs in the first place and usually defended them with paternal passion. The government had no fiscal policy, as one observer put it, only a fiscal result.[18]

Clearly what was needed was a way to consider and adopt each year a fiscal policy that comprehended the entire range of revenues and expenditures. The joint committee's answer was a new budget committee in each house and a new budget process. Each spring, the committees would recommend aggregate revenue and spending levels, with subsidiary limits for the various categories of expenditures. When the two houses had adopted budget resolutions embodying these totals and had resolved their differences through a conference committee, the results would serve as a target to guide the work of all committees. When the committees had completed their work in the fall, the fiscal result derived from the various revenue and spending measures would again be examined and made to conform to sound fiscal policy in a second budget resolution.

Meanwhile, the committees that had been debating how to bring an end to presidential impoundment were in disagreement about how to design an alternative technique. No one wanted to prohibit the President from initiating action to withhold appropriated funds, provided the Congress had the last word. The question was how to give the last word.

The Senate said the Congress should rescind appropriations in the same way it enacted them in the first place: by law. The House contended that was too cumbersome a procedure for the many minor and noncontroversial items for which changed circumstances rendered a planned expenditure unnecessary. The House suggested a legislative veto process whereby a proposed impoundment would take effect unless one or the other house objected. The conference committee crafted an artful compromise: the House approach would be used for simple deferrals, but when the President sought to terminate a program or withhold funds for reasons of fiscal policy, such action would require congressional approval in statutory form.

By 1974, the new procedure was very much in order, for the courts had decided the President had indeed usurped the impoundment power. Of fifty lawsuits challenging impoundment that had been decided by that date, fewer than half a dozen "upheld the President in any way," according to a Congressional Research Service report.[19] With the constitutional question settled, the original impetus for reforming the congressional budget process was removed, and the Congress could have reverted to the status quo ante. But no one suggested that. By exceeding his lawful authority, Richard Nixon had succeeded in forcing the legislative branch to face up to its own inadequacies. It proceeded to establish the new budget process, as well as adopt the impoundment compromise, in the Congressional Budget and Impoundment Control Act of 1974.

The act brought about more profound changes in the legislature's way of doing business than any other single act in modern times. It created two new power centers, backed up by the leadership of both houses, to contest the older and long-powerful authorizing and appropriating committees. It set up a centralizing force to counter the decentralizing tendencies inherent in the committee system. It forced the Congress to look at fiscal policy—which embraces so much of the total realm of public policy—in an integrated rather than a piecemeal fashion. The revolution did not occur all at once. At first, the Congress deliberately chose to liberalize the fiscal policy contained in President Ford's budget, which meant that spending ceilings did not have to be set so low as to put the authorization and appropriations committees under any severe pressure. Nor did the House Ways and Means and Senate Finance Committees have to face demands for new revenues. But soon thereafter conflict between the new budget committees and the older competing committees that had to be brought under the discipline of the new process grew annually more intense. The results were mixed. Sometimes the budget committees as defenders of the approved budget resolutions won, but sometimes they lost and the totals established in the budget resolutions were breached.

By the end of the 1970s, circumstances conspired to give the budget committees the upper hand. Accelerated inflation rates focused public attention more intensely on the budget deficit, and the tax revolt expressed in California's Proposition 13 tax-cutting initiative in 1978, and similar measures that followed in other states, made concern with fiscal policy a political imperative. President Carter and the Democrats who led the Congress agreed that in the election year of 1980 a balanced budget should be enacted. And, to accomplish that end, the authoritative "reconciliation" feature of the new budget process was brought into play for the first time. The authorizing committees were directed to report legislation that would control the "uncontrollable" spending, by reducing the benefits paid to individuals and organizations under a wide range of statutory mandates. The budget was not balanced, but the achievements were "monumental," in the words of the House Budget Committee chairman, Robert N. Giaimo, Democrat of Connecticut.[20] Legislative changes that would have been inconceivable without the discipline of the new budget process were assembled and enacted in a single bill. And the precedent was established for an even more drastic series of cuts in spending when the Congress approved most of the essential features of President Reagan's precedent-shattering slashes in governmental activity in 1981.

All of these decisions were made by the full membership of the House and Senate, of course, but the fiscal goals those bodies set and the directives they imposed on the authorization and appropriations committees were written by the budget committees. A redistribution of power within the Congress that aggrandized upstart groups at the expense of all the other committees was bound to create resistance, and despite a series of successes, the new budget process has appeared repeatedly to be hanging on the edge of failure. Late in 1983, for example, the House voted not to consider some revenue increases that the congressional budget resolution had instructed the House Ways and Means and Senate Finance committees to propose. The final budget resolution for that year—minus the tax boosts—was not passed until April 1984, when the fiscal year was half over. Again in 1985, Congress adjourned with its deficit-reduction final budget resolution still deadlocked in a House-Senate conference committee. But it came up that year with an ingenious substitute procedure named for its sponsors, Senators Phil Gramm, Republican of Texas, Warren B. Rudman, Republican of New Hampshire, and Ernest F. Hollings, Democrat of South Carolina. The procedure would achieve reconciliation through an automatic formula that would distribute spending cuts each year across the various governmental programs to meet designated, and declining, deficit levels. Some programs, such as Social Security payments, would be excluded. The Supreme Court in 1986 invalidated the automatic feature of the act on the ground that it vested the power to apply the reduction formula in an officer of the legislative branch—the comptroller general. The Congress was thus left to meet its deficit-reduction targets through its normal legislature processes. Whether it can muster the resolve to do so is doubtful, but in any case the Congress has retained the ultimate decision-making power in the legislative branch.

Throughout the dozen years of experience under the 1974 act, whenever the new budget process has seemed on the verge of collapse, congressional leaders and enough members of both parties have always rallied to its support. They recognize that for the Congress to retain the power of the purse, it must have a mechanism for making and carrying out a coherent fiscal policy. If the budget process were to be abandoned, the demand to turn that power over to the President could well be irresistible, for annual twelve-figure deficits can hardly be tolerated indefinitely. One branch or the other must be effectively in charge.

As it happens, not every member of the Congress truly wants his branch to be in charge. As John W. Gardner, the former cabinet member, has observed, "There is a deeply unheroic streak in Congress that does not covet responsibility nor welcome tests of courage."[21] Whether because they are simply eager to escape responsibility, or question the capacity of an unwieldy, 535-member bicameral Congress to shape and enforce the country's fiscal policy and set spending priorities within it, more members of Congress than at any time in history have expressed support for giving the president an item veto. That is an obvious and convenient way out for congressmen who would like to be freed to vote generously for spending in their districts, take the political credit, and then let the president make the final, tough decisions as to how much of the money would actually be spent. Yet when the test comes, a majority of the members are sure to rally in defense of the legislature's cherished power of the purse and deny any president the item veto—just as they united to recapture from Richard Nixon the impoundment authority he had seized.

Strengthening Congressional Oversight of Administration

In the climate of suspicion and hostility between the branches that prevailed in the early 1970s, the Congress felt it necessary to go beyond merely reclaiming the power it had allowed to drift away or that had been usurped—the war power and the power of the purse in particular. It moved in whatever ways it could to strengthen its control of the executive branch in the administration of the entire body of federal law.

Constituents were pressing congressmen to assert themselves. It was a time of deep public discontent with everyone in Washington, President and Congress alike. Public opinion polls made this quite clear. The

Congress might try to blame the President—for the failures in Vietnam, for the crimes of Watergate, for inflation, or whatever else made constituents unhappy—but legislators could not wholly extricate themselves. "You're in charge there, aren't you?" constituents seemed to be insisting with a Willoughby-like expectation that over the President as manager sat a Congress with a board-of-directors' ultimate responsibility for what went on. Candidates ran for Congress with a pledge to exercise that responsibility. "I ran for the Senate in part because I am dedicated to bringing the Federal Government under control," said Max Baucus, the new Democratic senator from Montana in 1979. "Citizens in Montana, and throughout the country, are fed up with their Federal Government. They believe that it is too large, that it is insensitive to their regional and individual needs, and that it is not accountable to them or their representatives."[22] Members of Congress are "the human link between the citizen and his Government," said Representative Elliott H. Levitas, Democrat of Georgia. "We are his government. It is making the public cynical to think their government is being run by unelected officials."[23]

In constitutional theory, the President was supposed to take care that the laws were faithfully executed, but clearly in public opinion he was not controlling the bureaucrats. Presumably he could not control them— certainly not in the innumerable and often minor ways in which they were irritating the constituents of congressmen. Further, the independent regulatory commissions were effectively exempt from such control as the President might have. If the bureaucrats had to be controlled, if the President did not and could not supervise them all, and if legislators were expected by the electorate to do what the President could not do, then it was up to the Congress to find the means.

One result was an attempt to increase systematically the attention that the Congress gave to its oversight responsibilities—that is, its duty to review the manner in which the laws were being administered, including an evaluation of effects. In 1974, based on a study of House organization by a bipartisan committee headed by Richard Bolling, Democrat of Missouri, the House instructed all its committees (except Appropriations) either to create an oversight subcommittee separate from its legislative subcommittees or to assign clear oversight responsibilities to the legislative subcommittees. Six committees were given specific responsibility to oversee program areas that overlapped committee jurisdictions. Beyond that, the Government Operations Committee, which already possessed government-wide investigating authority, was made responsible for coordinating the oversight activity of all committees and preparing an annual report setting out plans and priorities. Findings of the oversight groups would be incorporated in the committee reports on recommended legislation.

The quantitative results were impressive. In the first half of 1975,

House committees and subcommittees spent three times as many days in oversight hearings as they did during the same period four years earlier.[24] By 1979, 39 per cent of all House hearings were devoted to oversight, compared to 11 per cent in 1973.[25] The Senate in 1977 clarified the authority of its committees to conduct broad oversight activities, and its reports showed increased attention to this aspect of legislative responsibility. The Congress also augmented the resources of its oversight staff agency, the General Accounting Office. The GAO made twice as many reports on executive branch activities in 1976–80 as it had made in 1966–70, and it testified before committees five times as often.[26] Both houses significantly increased the number of staff members assigned to subcommittees and individual legislators, resulting in an expansion of informal oversight activities that ranged from the casual to the intensive. Finally, the Congress wrote into more than a hundred laws a requirement for advance notification of intended administrative actions, so that committees could intervene through new legislation or otherwise, if they saw fit.

Nevertheless, close observers of and participants in these oversight activities remained far from satisfied. Quantitative gains were not matched by qualitative improvements. The transient, youthful staff members often assigned to the job lacked background and motivation. Hearings and inquiries too often degenerated into publicity seeking or petty intervention.[27] Oversight remained an unpopular part of the legislator's job. Except for instances in which corruption or scandal could be exposed, it was tedious, time-consuming, and unglamorous work. It produced little political reward. Lacking any constituent pressure or other political incentive, members would be bound to carry out the function "in an episodic, erratic manner," as a Senate committee described the process in 1977.[28] An official poll of House members in the same year found that only 4 per cent judged the House oversight activities to be "very effective," while 44 per cent checked the "not very effective" box at the other end of the scale. Only 16 per cent reported spending "a great deal of time" on the oversight part of their job.[29]

In the era of expanding oversight, the Congress effectively asserted its right to oversee the most secret executive branch activities of all— the covert interventions of the Central Intelligence Agency in the internal affairs of countries around the globe. Both houses created intelligence committees to receive regular reports on current and intended operations. Committees with jurisdiction over foreign and military affairs were informed as well. Although the committees respected the secrecy of the information, whenever controversy arose the operations became public enough that the very term *covert* ceased to have much meaning. To stop an operation, of course, the Congress has no recourse except to take open action, as when it prohibited the Ford administration from intervening in Angola in 1975, and when the House voted in 1983 to cut off covert aid to guerrillas seeking to overthrow the Sandinista government of Nicaragua.

The limits of executive privilege remain as undefined as ever. But conflicts over the issue, while often bitter, are still infrequent and usually yield to negotiated settlements. President Nixon's claim to unlimited executive privilege was struck down by the Supreme Court in 1974, but the case involved a demand for information by the Watergate special prosecutor rather than by a congressional body, leaving the rights of congressional investigators unclear. Neither contending branch has been eager for a showdown in the courts. In several cases after the Nixon decision, committees were able to obtain information simply by charging cabinet members with contempt, but in other cases the executive branch held its ground and the committees gave way. One of the sharpest confrontations in recent years arose in 1983 when the Environmental Protection Administrator, under White House orders, refused to yield copies of internal agency communications to the House Public Works and Transportation Committee. The investigation led to the resignation of the administrator and more than a dozen of her top associates. After some—but not all—of the documents were made available, the committee dropped the issue.

The Growth and End of the Legislative Veto

Oversight, by definition, is information gathering. For a Congress that is determined to "bring the Federal government under control" and hold the executive branch "accountable," in Senator Baucus's words, its inquiries are of little use unless it can impose its will on administrators on the basis of the information assembled. Here the separation of powers stands in the way. In a government celebrated for its unique system of checks and balances, the constitutional devices available to the legislature to check the executive branch turn out to be severely limited. They can be exercised only through the collective action of both houses (except for confirmation of appointments and approval of treaties, where the Senate acts alone), which means the matter has somehow to be gotten on the agenda of those overburdened bodies. Even when the Congress is able to act collectively, its controls under the Constitution have to be applied before the administrator acts or afterward—not during the action, which may be the only time congressional control can be effective.

Before the fact, the Congress can attempt to control administration by specifying precisely in each law the circumstances under which the administrator shall act, the action to be taken, and the manner of acting.

The limitations are apparent, an obvious one being the occasional inclination of legislators to evade responsibility by delegating to administrators difficult decisions they prefer not to make themselves. Constitutional purists—including, on occasion, the Supreme Court—have condemned congressional failure to write clear objectives and firm administrative guidance into law. But often such decisions would require a depth of research and a breadth of debate and discussion that the Congress, as a practical matter, simply lacks the time, resources, and cohesion to undertake. If it tried, it would be likely to blunder.[30] More important, the Congress cannot anticipate all of the circumstances that may arise and that may require a prompt response by government. It learned this the hard way when it considered—and abandoned—an attempt to codify the President's power to make war. Regulatory agencies must cope with evolving technology and a changing economic structure. Welfare agencies must adjust to changing caseloads and altered living conditions. Tax collectors must judge an infinite variety of claims. And so on. Even the purists have to concede that an ideal Congress of their own construction, with unlimited resources, would still find it necessary to delegate a great deal of discretion to administrators. Before the fact, also, the Senate has the power to withhold its approval of executives nominated by the President for high office. But divining which of the nominees will prove to be incompetent or corrupt in advance of the events that test them is even more difficult than anticipating the events themselves.

After the fact, the Congress can take corrective action through new legislation, but if the President chooses to uphold his administrators, legislators may find they cannot override the President's veto. Moreover, corrective action may not be possible before irreversible damage has been done.

During the fact, legislators have no authoritative control over the use of delegated power. Through careful and persistent oversight, they may find out what is happening, and extralegally they can advise and harass. These tactics may even prove effective, for administrators know that to ignore a member of Congress—particularly a member of the appropriations committee or a committee with jurisdiction over the agency's legislation—is to risk reprisal in all sorts of unrelated ways. But legislators have no authority to give direction during the fact. Indeed, they have no right under the Constitution even to be consulted.

In these circumstances, an assertive Congress was bound to seize on any means its members could devise to legalize the right of intervention *during* the administrative process. One such means had been invented and lay readily at hand—the legislative veto. That tool, which until the 1970s had been limited to specialized and occasional use—mainly in delegating reorganization power and in requiring committee approval of real estate transactions—came to be routinely applied to a vast range of delegated powers. Two landmark applications were in the War Powers Resolution and the Impoundment Control Act, where the legislative veto proved to be the key compromise that made the legislation possible. Beyond that, the Congress wrote one-house or two-house vetoes into such diverse laws as those dealing with emergency oil supplies, railroads, financial aid to New York City, election finance, the disposition of President Nixon's tapes and papers, the call-up of military reserve units or members, foreign aid to designated countries, arms sales in the Middle East, export controls, public land withdrawals, standby gasoline rationing plans, all regulations of the Federal Trade Commission, and almost all rules of the Department of Education.

By the spring of 1983, the lawbooks carried 207 legislative veto provisions in 126 statutes. But at that point, in the case of *Immigration and Naturalization Service* v. *Chadha* [462 U. S. 919 (1983)] the Supreme Court declared them all invalid. In "one fell swoop," Justice Byron R. White said in his dissenting opinion, the Court struck down more laws passed by the Congress than had been invalidated in all of the country's history. The legislative veto, declared Chief Justice Warren E. Burger, speaking for the Court majority, violated the constitutional principle of separated powers. The Constitution, he reminded legislators, provided for only one way in which the Congress could act—through legislation passed by both houses and presented to the President for his approval or veto. It could not impose its legislative will through the action of one house or even both houses alone. He acknowledged that legislative procedures in which the President was a partner "often seem clumsy, inefficient, even unworkable," and that they made for "cumbersomeness and delays." But these "obvious flaws" were accepted by the Founding Fathers in the interest of a greater objective—to make sure that "arbitrary governmental acts" would not go unchecked. Ironically, that was the very purpose the legislative veto served. What prevents arbitrary acts is not the separation of the branches that Burger was intent on upholding. It is just the opposite—the checks and balances by which an action by one branch is made dependent on approval by another. The legislative veto is an additional check the Founding Fathers did not think of. The Court found that it violated the Constitution's language, but the Chief Justice should have stopped his argument at that point. The veto served to reinforce the very constitutional principle he chose to cite in defending the Court's decision.

Since the *Chadha* verdict, the committees having jurisdiction over the 126 statutes have been groping for alternatives to the veto clauses. No general strategy for the Congress as a whole has evolved or seems likely to. The committees have been deciding on a case by case basis what to do in the absence of the outlawed veto, just as they had originally decided case by case when and how it would be applied.

At one extreme, the Congress has simply withheld delegations of power that in the pre-*Chadha* years it had granted contingent on the right of veto. Predictably, then, reorganization legislation enacted in 1984 simply authorized the President to recommend plans that the Congress would then consider approving as statutes. The only innovation was a "fast-track" provision; to prevent defeat of a presidential proposal through congressional inertia or neglect, each house is required to bring a resolution of approval to the floor within ninety days. This procedure promises to be widely used in instances where the former veto provisions are converted to a requirement for affirmative action by both houses.

At the other extreme, the Congress has agreed to let certain executive actions that were formerly subject to a legislative veto stand unless they are revoked by a joint resolution, which itself would be subject to a presidential veto. This was the procedure adopted by the Congress to replace the provision in the War Powers Resolution of 1973 that required the President to disengage military forces from hostilities if the Congress, by a vote of both houses, so directed. The new provision leaves legislators exactly where they were before 1973, except that it incorporates a fast-track procedure, including a twenty-hour limitation on Senate debate to forestall a filibuster on a motion to override a presidential veto.

Between these extremes is the ever-popular appropriations rider, a means by which a majority of both houses can forbid an executive action without substantial risk of presidential veto. By simply adding to an appropriations bill a sentence beginning "No part of any appropriations under this Act shall be available for . . . ," the Congress can effectively prevent an administrative agency from developing or enforcing a particular rule or taking a specific action. Such limitations on executive discretion have been upheld by the courts as legitimate exercises of the legislature's power of the purse. When Secretary of the Interior James G. Watt announced in 1983 he would ignore a formal instruction from the House Interior Committee to postpone granting leases for coal mining on certain public lands on the ground that the committee veto was unconstitutional, the committee simply got the moratorium included as a rider on the Department's appropriation bill. Other riders in the same bill prohibited the export of timber from the Western states and halted oil leasing on designated sections of the continental shelf.

Finally, the Congress can continue to enact legislative vetoes in the full knowledge that they are unconstitutional but in the full expectation that they will be adhered to anyway. Louis Fisher of the Congressional Research Service counted thirty new legislative veto provisions in laws enacted in the first year after *Chadha*. Nineteen of them required advance approval of various administrative actions by the two appropriations committees, and one called for consent by the authorizing committees as well as the appropriations committees. Two others authorized committees to delay certain types of actions. Six required administrators to report proposed actions to the Congress and allow thirty days for comment, unless designated committees waived the waiting period. One was a two-house veto the Congress chose not to remove from a bill that was reported to the House floor before *Chadha*. The last was a provision allowing either house to prevent the extension of a program.[31]

Particularly in the case of the committee vetoes, administrative agencies may well prefer to follow what they hold to be an unconstitutional procedure rather than risk the displeasure of the congressional authorizing and appropriating committees that can reduce the budgets of the agencies or take reprisal in countless other formal or informal ways. Indeed, even after *Chadha*, one continuing form of de facto legislative veto is the formal resolution by a committee, or a house, or both houses, expressing disapproval of something the executive branch has done or proposes to do. Such a resolution lacks the force of law, but it exerts a powerful influence on responsible administrators. Committees have often controlled administrators by incorporating directives and instructions in committee reports and other communications that the administrators have voluntarily accepted as binding. Secretary Watt's experience with land leasing suggests that they might as well do so. Vetoes have also been attached to authorization bills, to bills raising the debt limit, and to other legislation that the president is forced to sign to enable the government to carry on.

In the *Chadha* decision, the Supreme Court prohibited only the simplest and most convenient device whereby the Congress has been able to delegate administrative power yet retain control. More cumbersome methods such as the appropriations rider have served the purpose in the past and will do so again. One can be sure that on all the issues the Congress cares about, some effective alternative will be found. In the end, the Court will not have freed administration from legislative control as it intended. It will only have added to the complexities of an already complex government and to the strain imposed on those who have to make the system work.

Strengths and Weaknesses of Congress as Administrator

Public administration as a discipline is no less executive-centered today then it was when Leonard White, Luther Gulick, and Louis Brownlow wrote. Not much has appeared in either theory or practice to suggest that public administrators have departed significantly from their model of a structure of authority extending from the top of the executive branch hierarchy to the bottom. Legislatures remain the "external relationship" that White reduced them to a half century ago. Anything bordering on direction from the legislative branch, except as it may be done through law, is seen as subversive to the administrative process. Even legal provisions are sometimes interpreted as controvening the necessary rights of managers.

That may be all right, legislators are apt to respond, if the executive branch actually is directed and controlled from the top. But in the case of the mammoth and sprawling federal government, the bureaucracy appears to those on Capitol Hill to be beyond anyone's control. The President is the only elected official accountable to the people in the entire hierarchy, and he obviously cannot himself supervise his agents scattered throughout the country and the world. If they are supervised at all, it is by unelected subordinates—or "unelected bureaucrats," as congressmen prefer to call them. Because these bureaucrats do not have to face the voters, they do not always respond to the concerns and problems of average men and women with the same alacrity and sensitivity that members of Congress do. In a word, as seen from Capitol Hill, elected representatives are responsive and bureaucrats are not.

Responsiveness is both the strength and the weakness of legislators when they attempt to control or intervene in administration. On the positive side, in a kind of ombudsman role, members of Congress and their staffs maintain constant pressure on administrators to expedite the handling of cases, to treat every individual claimant with sympathy and understanding, and to distribute the benefits of governmental action fairly and widely. In so doing, they right bureaucratic wrongs and prevent other wrongs from happening.

But there is a thin line between asking for prompt, fair, and sympathetic action in a constituent's case and demanding preferential treatment. While every member of Congress or caseworker on the member's staff can cite instance after instance of bureaucratic insensitivity, delay, and bungling that intervention from "the Hill" has corrected, every experienced federal administrator can cite numerous examples of being pressured from the same Hill to bend or break the rules in favor of a particular constituent. When that pressure comes from members of committees having jurisdiction over an agency's authorizing legislation or its appropriations, it can be irresistible. It is no accident that every analysis of the distribution of discretionary federal grants or of the location of federal installations shows a skewing in favor of the states and districts whose representatives sit on the committees and subcommittees that write the legislation and appropriate the funds, particularly the chairpersons of those bodies. In the executive branch, it is an accepted norm that administrators must have good "political judgment" and play "smart politics," while staying within the letter of the law.

On Capitol Hill, each member of Congress draws his own line between proper and unethical forms of pressure. Not all draw it in the same place. The Senate and House ethics committees have laid down no code of conduct nor acted to discipline any member for improper use of influence except when some criminal act, such as bribery, was involved. Attitudes and practices vary widely. Some members, particularly those who rose to influence as antimachine, reformist politicians, take a strict view of what constitutes appropriate intervention. They are likely to rule intervention out altogether in certain kinds of administrative decisions—civil service assignments and promotions, for instance. In other matters they will press for prompt action on a constituent's claim only as they expressly disavow any substantive interest in the outcome. "We try to get an answer out of an agency, but we don't tell them what the answer ought to be," one member told an interviewer conducting a survey of House members' ethics. Another member illustrates a different view: "I start with the attitude that the constituent is always right," he reported, "and then I exhaust every avenue since I don't have any confidence in the bureaucratic system. In nine out of ten cases we get good answers to help our constituents as long as we don't relent." Most members, however, thought that helping an institution get an "undeserved" grant was at least "probably," if not "clearly," unethical.[32] The Watergate scandal heightened congressional sensitivity to moral issues and brought in a wave of new members committed to raising ethical standards in the Congress and shunning the more questionable forms of congressional intervention.

On the questions of administration that are resolved in legislation, the complaint against the Congress is that in its responsiveness to constituency interests it too often sacrifices the broad public interest to the narrow, and the general to the parochial. In matters of government organization, for example, it is liable to pay greater heed to the vociferous protests of interest groups or to a relatively few affected civil servants than to the logic of grouping related functions together for administrative convenience and efficiency. The charge of parochialism applies, of course, to all the policy-making processes in a legislative body that is singularly weak in party cohesion and discipline, as it is in central integrating machinery.

Defenders of the Congress contend that the legislative process needs to blend the general and the particular, balancing the broad public interest the executive is presumed to represent with the narrower interests that members of the Congress are skilled in advocating and explaining.

Thus the zeal to accomplish large objectives will be tempered with concern for the consequences to individual citizens along the way.

At best, the readiness of members of Congress to give every citizen a hearing and to act as ombudsman and intervenor serves to check the inevitable tendency of bureaucracy toward impersonality and rigidity. At worst, in the administration of the laws, congressmen carry responsiveness to the point of irresponsibility by holding national objectives hostage to preferential treatment for favored groups. On balance, most close observers of the Washington scene would probably conclude that in its influence on administration the responsiveness of the Congress leads to more benefits than losses, that legislators are more of the time on good behavior than bad, and that the executive, the courts, the media, and the election process succeed in the long run in curbing and forestalling any gross abuses of the power that legislators have over public administration. Public opinion finally forced an end to McCarthyism, for example. Observers might agree, too, that the trend in recent years has been steadily toward a higher level of congressional responsibility. Although they deplore the mistakes and excesses that will always recur as the Congress performs its administrative role, they would go slow in attempting to lessen that role in any fundamental way. Responsiveness is the essential quality that distinguishes democracy from autocratic rule.

Endnotes

1. Most of the themes in this chapter are more fully developed in my *The Decline and Resurgence of Congress* (Washington, DC: Brookings Institution, 1981).
2. In Luther Gulick and L. Urwick, eds., *Papers on the Science of Administration* (New York: Columbia University Institute of Public Administration, 1937), pp. 6–7.
3. *Principles of Public Administration* (Baltimore: Johns Hopkins Press, 1927). Quotation from pp. 10–11.
4. *Introduction to the Study of Public Administration* (New York: Macmillan, 1926), p. 421. In the 1939 revised edition, White deleted the word "thoroughly" from the legislature's function of informing itself and changed "is usually unqualified" to "is not qualified" in the final sentence. Ibid., revised edition (Macmillan, 1939), p. 567.
5. President's Committee on Administrative Management, *Report of the Committee with Studies of Administrative Management in the Federal Government* (Washington, DC: Government Printing Office, 1937), p. 36.
6. Ibid., p. iv.
7. Representative Lindsay Warren, Democrat of North Carolina, *Congressional Record*, March 6, 1939, p. 2,310.

8. Lewis A. Dexter, "Congressmen and the Making of Military Policy," in *New Perspectives on the House of Representatives*, Robert L. Peabody and Nelson W. Polsby, eds. (Rand McNally, 1963), pp. 311–12.

9. Louis Fisher, *Presidential Spending Power* (Princeton, NJ: Princeton University Press, 1975), pp. 86–87.

10. "The President's News Conference of May 3, 1968," *Public Papers of the Presidents: Lyndon B. Johnson 1968–69* (Washington, DC: Government Printing Office, 1970), Vol. 1, p. 561.

11. *RN: The Memoirs of Richard Nixon* (New York: Grosset and Dunlap, 1978), p. 850.

12. Office of Management and Budget statement, March 23, 1971, in *Executive Impoundment of Appropriated Funds*, Hearings before the Subcommittee on Separation of Powers of the Senate Judiciary Committee, 92nd Cong., 1st sess., pp. 164–65.

13. Op. cit., Hearings, pp. 2–3.

14. "The President's News Conference of January 31, 1973," *Public Papers of the Presidents: Richard Nixon, 1973* (Washington, DC: Government Printing Office, 1975), p. 62.

15. Speech to fiftieth anniversary of Time, Inc., inserted in *Congressional Record*, February 5, 1973, p. 3,239.

16. "Statement About Executive Privilege, March 12, 1973," *Public Papers of the Presidents: Richard Nixon, 1973* (Washington, DC: Government Printing Office, 1975), pp. 184–86. Testimony of Attorney General Richard G. Kleindienst, April 10, 1973, in *Executive Privilege, Secrecy in Government, Freedom of Information*, Hearings before subcommittees of the Senate Government Operations and Judiciary Committees, 93rd Cong., 1st sess., Vol. 1, pp. 18–52, esp. 45–46, 51.

17. *Congressional Record*, October 10, 1972, pp. 34,600–02.

18. Edwin L. Dale, Jr., *New York Times*, June 15, 1975.

19. *Presidential Impoundment of Congressionally Appropriated Funds: An Analysis of Recent Federal Court Decisions*, reported to the House Government Operations Committee, 93rd Cong., 2nd sess. (Washington, DC: Government Printing Office, 1973), p. 3.

20. *Congressional Record*, daily edition, July 21, 1980, p. E3,484.

21. "The Role of the Presidency: What Must Be Done After Watergate," *Current*, No. 153:20 (July-August) 1973.

22. *Congressional Record*, daily edition, June 12, 1979, p. S7,465.

23. *Regulatory Reform and Congressional Review of Agency Rules*, Hearings before a House Rules subcommittee, 96th Cong., 1st sess. (1979), p. 16.

24. Joel D. Aberbach, "Changes in Congressional Oversight," *American Behavioral Scientist* 22:493–515 (May-June) 1979.

25. "Congressional Oversight," *National Journal*, 12:70 (January 12) 1980, quoting a report released by Speaker Thomas P. O'Neill, Jr.

26. U. S. General Accounting Office, *Annual Report, 1980*, pp. 1, 4.

27. See the comments of congressional staff and executive branch officials in Sundquist, *Decline and Resurgence*, pp. 332–40.

28. *Study on Federal Regulation*, S. Doc. 25–26, 95th Cong., 1st sess., Vol. 2, p. 94.

29. Thomas E. Cavanagh, "The Two Arenas of Congress: Electoral and Institutional Incentives for Performance," a paper prepared for the 1978 meeting of the American Political Science Association, reporting on a poll conducted by the House Commission on Administrative Review.

30. See the comments of John Quarles, former Deputy Administrator of the Environmental Protection Administration, on the consequences of rigid specific requirements in environmental regulation. "Federal Regulation of New Industrial Plants" (1979). Unpublished paper.

31. Louis Fisher, "One Year After *INS* v. *Chadha:* Congressional and Judicial Developments," Congressional Research Service, Library of Congress, June 23, 1984.

32. Edmund Beard and Stephen Horn, *Congressional Ethics: The View From the House* (Washington, DC: Brookings Institutions, 1975), pp. 74–76.

CHAPTER 9

⌐∿◊∾⌐

The Public Administration and the Governance Process: Refocusing the American Dialogue

Gary L. Wamsley
Charles T. Goodsell
John A. Rohr
Camilla M. Stivers
Orion F. White
James F. Wolf [1]

THE VIRGINIA POLYTECHNIC INSTITUTE AND STATE UNIVERSITY

GARY L. WAMSLEY is Professor of Public Administration at the Virginia Polytechnic Institute and State University and Director of the university's Center for Public Administration and Policy. He is the author of Selective Service and a Changing America *and, with Mayer Zald,* The Political Economy of Public Organizations. *He has written numerous chapters in volumes, and articles for such journals as the* Public Administration Review, The Western Political Quarterly, *and* The American Journal of Sociology. *Professor Wamsley is the editor of* Administration and Society *and consults extensively with federal, state, and local governments. He holds the doctorate from the Graduate School of Public and International Affairs of the University of Pittsburgh.*

CHARLES T. GOODSELL is Professor of Public Administration at the Virginia Polytechnic Institute and State University. He is the author of Administration of a Revolution, American Corporations and Peruvian Politics, *and* The Case for Bureaucracy: A Public Administration Polemic, *as well as articles in the leading journals of American public administration. Currently Professor Goodsell's interests include comparative administrative behavior and political–cultural interpretations of public architecture. His forthcoming book,* The Social Meaning of Civic Space: Studying Political Authority Through Architecture, *promises to add a new dimension to the study of public institutions and the focus of administrative thought.*

JOHN A. ROHR is Professor of Public Administration at the Virginia Polytechnic Institute and State University. His articles on constitutional themes related to public administration have appeared in the Public Administration Review, *the* Review of Public Personnel Administration, *the* Public Administration Quarterly, *the* American Journal of Public Administration, *and the* International Journal of Public Administration. *He has written three books, the most recent being* To Run a Constitution: The Legitimacy of the Administrative State. *Professor Rohr is Managing Editor of* Administration and Society *and a former member of the Editorial Board of the* Public Administration Review. *He is a leading authority on administrative ethics.*

CAMILLA M. STIVERS is Associate Study Director, Committee on the Future of Public Health, Institute of Medicine, National Academy of Sciences. She holds the B.A. degree from Wellesley College, the M.A. from the Johns Hopkins University, the M.P.A. from the University of Southern California, and is a candidate for the Ph.D. at the Center for Public Administration and Policy, the Virginia Polytechnic Institute and State University. She has worked for a variety of private and nonprofit consortia and community-based health planning and health service agencies. Her research interests include citizenship in the administrative state and the dynamics of health policy-making. She has articles forthcoming in Administration and Society *and* New Directions in Public Administration Research.

ORION F. WHITE is Professor of Public Administration at the Virginia Polytechnic Institute and State University. Previously he served on the faculties on the University of Texas at Austin, the Maxwell School of Syracuse University, and the University of North Carolina at Chapel Hill. Professor White has published numerous journal articles and monographs reporting field studies in federal, state, and local agencies, and he has written extensively on development of the transformational theory of organization and social change, which he helped to originate. He co-authored with Emmette S. Redford a book-length study of policy-making in the National Aeronautics and Space Administration.

JAMES F. WOLF is Associate Professor of Public Administration at the Virginia Polytechnic Institute and State University. Previously he served on the faculties of the School of Public Administration of the University of Southern California and the Institute of Public Service of the University of Connecticut. Professor Wolf's research and writing have focused on the careers of public servants and the career management processes of public agencies. More recently he has concentrated on the changing demographics of the public sector work force, with special attention to the problem of career plateauing. He has been an active consultant to federal, state, and local agencies for over fifteen years.

In this "Blackburg Manifesto," Gary L. Wamsley and his colleagues at Virginia Tech call for a new and refocused dialogue about American public administration. They realize that after a century of the accomplishment of administrative wonders, from digging the Panama Canal to space exploration, public administration has fallen on hard times. It gets harder to run a constitution.

The manifesto's analysis says the reason for the denigration of bureaucracy in the 1980s does not lie simply in a lack of organizational and managerial skills on the part of public administrators—though there is room for improvement—but in public perceptions about the role of government itself. Contradictory pressures are generated as officials of government try to maintain the society's commitment to freedom and justice on the one hand while they also try to make a complex system of capitalism and state intervention work on the other. Equity is continually being balanced against economic and social differentiation, and public administration is the balance wheel. Public administration is in the eye of recurrent political storms and is often the victim of the parochialization of the public interest because it is the counterweight to tendencies toward disintegration.

Wamsley and company wish to reconceptualize bureaucracy as The Public Administration. The latter becomes an institution of government rather than an organizational form. The key talking point in the refocused dialogue becomes the nature and job of government—not *whether* there shall be government, or *how* to reduce whatever role government has, but what form of governmental intervention is most effective in the real world.

The nature and role of the administrative task has never been very far from the center of the American dialogue, but it has often been camouflaged as questions about *government* rather than as questions about public administration. Beginning with the Articles of Confederation and continuing through Shays' Rebellion, the assumption of state debts by the national government, the building of post and national roads, down to the current debate over the sale of government-developed communications satellites to private enterprise, Americans have argued incessantly about the rival claims of order and liberty as questions about government. By shifting the language of the struggle to public administration, where the claims have often been successfully negotiated anyway, we can finally affirm that public administration is a major social asset.

Rather than talk of the disassembly of administrative capacity, we should recognize that the requirement for administrative capacity will only increase in the future, not diminish. We should therefore speak of *which* government intentions should be pursued through the public sector, *which* policies should be part of the administrative agenda, and *which* objectives should be invested with governmental authority and legitimacy while also being subject to the constraints of constitutionalism.

The distinctive character of public administration lies in the fact that it is a part of the process of governance, that administration is accomplished in a political context, that it has an agency perspective, and that it is defined in large part as competence directed toward the public interest. This sets it apart from business management, and it provides the basis for a claim to status too long ignored.

Public administrators are sworn to uphold the Constitution of the United States, not the whims of the powerful. The professionalism of civil servants consists of maintaining the constitutional order as a fundamental duty and searching for ways in which the Constitution can be a living word and symbol for the changing needs of Americans. Public administrators are trustees of the public good. The manifesto insists that if we are to meet the challenges of the future, our political dialogue must shift from *whether* public administration to *the place of* public administration in the third century of the life of the republic.

A century has passed since Woodrow Wilson's essay, "The Study of Public Administration." Some of what he wrote has a disturbingly prophetic quality. For example:

> The weightier debates of constitutional principle are even yet by no means concluded; but they are no longer of more immediate practical moment than questions of administration. It is getting harder to *run* a constitution than to frame one.[2]

If these words command our attention today, it is because they have proven so painfully true for us as the twentieth century draws to a close. We have accomplished administrative wonders since Wilson wrote:

We have dug a canal connecting the world's great oceans; we have organized, equipped, and deployed millions of men and women to win two global wars; we have saved from collapse and altered the nature of the American political economy by massive administrative intervention during the Great Depression; we have organized scientists and workers in a secret and desperate race with Nazi Germany to develop a nuclear weapon; we have built an interstate highway system of unmatched size and capacity; we have put together hundreds of organizations both public and private involving thousands of scientists and engineers and billions of dollars to place American footprints on the moon. The list could and should go on and on. Yet despite these and many other accomplishments it "gets harder to run a constitution." All our administrative accomplishments do not add up to, and some of us wonder if administration even contributes to, the stable and effective functioning of our political system. The authors of this essay believe the essence of what Wilson meant by running a constitution is a public administration that does result in the stable and effective functioning of our political system— in a way that steadily improves the quality of our lives and expands both equity and opportunity.

The problem does not lie simply in a lack of organizational and managerial skills, though we still have plenty of room for improvement. Rather, the problem goes to the task of governing a modern republic that has a commitment to freedom and justice on the one hand, while it maintains a complex mixture of capitalism and state intervention on the other. Several contradictory pressures are generated. The commitment to freedom and justice creates pressures for equity, but the doctrine of state capitalism creates a counterpressure for economic and social differentiation. The requirements of maintaining a vigorous economy in an increasingly dangerous world create the need for a rational and comprehensive policy-making process. Yet our historical and constitutional tradition is based on fractionated power, overlapping jurisdictions, and disjointed incrementalism. The problems of public administration in America result from the difficulties of effectively governing such a political system. These difficulties are not the result of or caused by public administration itself.

Rowland Egger sums up American history in a way that places the problem of governance and bureaucracy in clear perspective. He says the United States has experienced four great social revolutions. The first was the revolution for independence, which set in motion forces of social change only partially crystallized and reflected in the great compromises of the Constitution. The second was the Jacksonian era, which marked our changed conceptions of who was entitled to participate in republican government. The third was the Civil War, which redefined the nature of the federal union and further altered our definition of citizenship. The fourth came with Roosevelt's New Deal, which changed fundamentally and irrevocably the national purpose of the Republic. Egger believes there is yet a fifth social revolution. It began with the Warren Court and was given further impetus by the civil rights movement and now the women's movement. This revolution is redefining our concepts of justice and equity, "slowly and painfully bringing to reality the egalitarianism of which Jefferson dreamed,"[3] and redefining our expectations of government's role in our lives. It involves an effort to find a uniquely American definition for these abstract concepts.

If this is a meaningful synopsis of our history, it is understandable, though no less lamentable, that American public administration is caught in the eye of recurrent political storms. It is reviled by some because it does too much in pursuit of justice and equity and by others because it does too little. Both ends of the political spectrum have seen it as the ominous instrument of their opponent's will. Not only has public administration been forced to bear the opprobrium of being the instrument of the devil but it also has become the scapegoat for the general problems of what Theodore Lowi has labeled "interest group liberalism." The latter is defined as the parochialization of the public interest, the fragmentation and erosion of public purposes, and the franchising of pieces of public authority to policy subsystems. Although American public administration is not without blame for some of these maladies, it has often been victim rather than perpetrator, "compliant with" rather than "cause of" the problems. In fact, it can be argued that it has often served as the strongest available counterweight to tendencies toward disintegration.

Yet political leaders have increasingly used "bureaucracy" as an epithet. Presidents of both parties have made attacks on it the centerpieces of their campaigns for office, only to find that this politically useful tactic becomes a self-inflicted wound in the subsequent struggle to govern. The gap between our system's need for effective governance and the capacity of elected officials to govern is widening at an alarming rate.

Government and the American Dialogue

Much of the denigration of bureaucracy is a natural outgrowth of our politics. Jacksonian democracy was heavily freighted, with negativism toward government because new groups wanted both access to government and control of it. Even though the progressive movement ran counter to this trend, the residual negativism of Jacksonianism has now been amplified by contemporary conservatism. Actors from all parts of the political spectrum are increasingly frustrated by the problems deriving from interest group liberalism. They blame these problems on government or what they erroneously see as its synonym, bureaucracy. Thus our political culture has come to include a pernicious mythology said to describe the public sector and public administrators. A good deal of demythologizing has to take place before the American dialogue can enter a new and meaningful phase. Items:

- Most clients of bureaucracy are not dissatisfied. The vast majority of them are very pleased with the services and treatment they receive.
- The rate of productivity increase in the public sector is not clearly lower than in the private sector. Overall it is probably higher.
- The federal government has not grown in number of employees since the early 1950s.
- The bureaucracy is not a monolith. It is composed of many small and diverse bureaus and offices.
- Public agencies stimulate and implement change. Resistance to change is no more endemic to public organizations than it is to private organizations.
- Studies have shown that the private sector is more top-heavy with administrative personnel than the public sector.
- Waste and inefficiency are no more prevalent in the public sector than in the private sector. In the former it is seen as a waste of taxpayers' money, while in the latter it is often hidden and passed on to consumers in the prices we pay.

The purpose of this essay is neither to bury bureaucracy nor to praise it. Rather, we hope to take a step toward reconceptualizing bureaucracy as The Public Administration. Bureaucracy in its technical sense refers to a form of social organization that is not confined to the public sector, and we carry no brief for any particular organizational form. Our focus is on the *functions* of government agencies rather than their organization. Thus we speak of The Public Administration[4] as an institution of government rather than of bureaucracy as an organizational form.

We see no way of arresting the pathologies of our political system and coming to grips with the sizable problems of our nation's political economy without a new way of thinking about, speaking of, and acting toward The Public Administration. This is not a sufficient condition for the challenges we face, but it is assuredly a necessary one.

There must be a significant change of direction in the American dialogue. The dialogue has traditionally emphasized ideas associated with personel liberty and social equity on the one hand, while it has also stressed public order, fiscal soundness, and the accumulation of capital on the other. The inevitable tension between these two sets of ideas has meant that disagreement about the nature and role of government has always been central to the dialogue, though the disagreement has worn different masks at different times. During the last half century the disagreement has been masked as the "bureaucracy problem" and has become particularly acute as we have sought to redefine liberty and equity while carrying forward our fifth social revolution.

For complex reasons that have to do with the nature of capitalism, we have been socialized to deny that the nature and role of government is the core issue of the dialogue. Nonetheless, the great national debates of our history have more times than not turned on this very question, often framed as the struggle between democracy and order. Today it is imperative that a shift take place in how we talk about the question, for our political rhetoric and symbols have become too far divorced from reality and the conditions we actually face as a nation. We cannot preserve and revitalize American industry and our natural resources in the face of increasing global interdependence, nor improve the quality of our lives, if the public dialogue is focused on *whether* government has any role in these matters, or on how to *reduce* whatever role it has. The reality of our world requires us to grapple with questions of *how* and *what form of* government intervention is most effective.

As Dwight Waldo has reminded us, only in the United States has there been erected a rhetorical and symbolic disjuncture between the concepts of "good government" and "good management." In the rest of the Occident there is a natural and profound linkage between and among all these in legal concepts and institutions rooted in Roman law. Americans sharply attenuated that linkage when we revolted against the British monarchy and a century later reinvented what Waldo calls "self-conscious administration." Administrators strove to be scientific as they employed what were believed to be empirically discoverable and generally applicable principles of management. We believe, however, that both the attenuation and rediscovery have been far more impressive in our rhetoric than in actual fact. We do not say they were less important for being rhetorical. They may be more important for that very reason. Our point is that the nature and role of public administration was never very far from the center of the American dialogue. It was only camouflaged as questions about *government* rather than as questions about public administration.

Beginning with the Articles of Confederation and continuing to this day, Americans have been arguing incessantly about liberty and order and about the nature and role of government in a process that can only be described as the pulling and hauling between polar abstractions. From the suppression of Shays' Revolt and the Whiskey Rebellion, the assumption of the state debts by the national government, the building of post and national roads, the granting of land by the government to railroads and canal companies, the Northwest Ordinance (which dedicated land in each territory to support public schools), through the Interstate Commerce Act, down to current debates over the sale of government-developed communications satellites to private enterprise—in all these decisions we have engaged in a national struggle to define the nature and role of government in the evolution of some kind of ordered liberty. We must now refocus the language of this struggle away from questions about the nature and role of government to questions about the nature and role of public administration. This is a subtle but crucial shift from questions of *whether* there should be a role for public administration to questions of what form that role should take.

As part of our effort to shift the American dialogue, we assert that public administration is a major social asset. Its managerial skills and experience in applying these skills in a political context render it a critical resource of the republic. It is one that should be continually subjected to constructive criticism but not diminished, denigrated, and decapitalized for short-run partisan advantage. There may well be a relationship between the current attacks on public administration and the erosion of civic morality evidenced in dysfunctional behavior ranging from corruption and tax evasion to vandalism and mindless littering. Those who attack public administration for partisan advantage are not friends of the republic. Rather, they inflict considerable harm on the body politic.

Those who wish to disassemble administrative capacity should recognize that subsequent ruling groups and eventually all citizens may have to pay the price of such disassembling. Although public administration needs many alterations and improvements, the requirement for administrative capacity will only increase, not diminish. One of the major questions confronting the American political system, one that·ought to be at the center of a refocused American dialogue is *which* government intentions should be pursued through the public sector, that is, be a part of public administration and therefore be invested with the authority and legitimacy of the state while also being subject to the constraints of constitutionalism.

The Public Administration's Distinctive Character

Public Administration is centered in the executive branch, but it includes parts of all branches of government to the extent that they relate to the constitutional mandate of the executive: that the laws be faithfully executed. The point of view of this essay is decidedly historical and includes not only those events public administrators might claim with pride, such as the Hatch Act, but also the events of which we are ashamed, such as the Teapot Dome scandal.

Public Administration has a distinctive character. It has at its core the generic management technologies that comprise its administrative capacity. These technologies are a vital part of its expertise, and they closely resemble the technologies of management in the private sector. But Wallace S. Sayre put the matter aptly when he said that business and public administration are alike in all unimportant respects. Public administration is more than generic management. It is the administration of public affairs in a political context. As Carl Friedrich noted a half century ago, administration is the core of modern government. It is an application of state power for what we trust are moral and humane ends, yet state power always has the capability of being used otherwise. Because governance involves the state's power to reward and deprive in the name of society as a whole, and because politics is the art of gaining acceptance for those allocations, administration is an inextricable part of both governance and politics. Because of its key role in rewarding, depriving, and distributing, as well as regulating and redistributing, and because it is the only set of institutions that can lawfully coerce to achieve society's ends, the state's administrative machinery is seldom viewed dispassionately. As Murray Edelman has said, it is an object against which people displace fears, hopes, and anxieties.

Public administration's distinctiveness grows out of the displacement against it of intense emotions that leave it with a highly political environment. This political context of public administration means that (1) the public administrator must engage not in a struggle for markets and profits but in a contest with other actors in the political process for jurisdiction, legitimacy, and resources; (2) those persons with whom public administrators interact possess distinctive perceptions and expectations as in the difference between consumers and citizens or suppliers and interest groups; and (3) the requisite skills, foci of attention, and perceived tasks of public administrators differ markedly from those of private sector management. The contrasts are so great, in fact, that a manager who is successful in one sector may not be successful in the other without considerable adaptiveness. To the degree that we lose sight of that distinction, to the same degree do we lose sight of what public administration really is.

Public administration is also self-consciously derived from, and focused upon, what we shall call the agency perspective. By agency we mean those institutions that have grown up in the executive branch of all levels of government and that are the instruments for the pursuit of the public interest. A better understanding of the distinctiveness of the public administration is properly built upon a greater appreciation of the institutional histories of agencies, including their social development and the evolution of their individual political economies.

We feel this appreciation is appropriate and necessary because many agencies are repositories, and their staffs are trustees, of specialized knowledge, historical experience, time-tested wisdom, and a degree of consensus about the public interest as it relates to a particular function of society. Persons staffing agencies have often been charged with executing the popular will in ways that sustain and nurture the public interest. They have generally done so through years of struggle within the larger political system and in careful negotiations in the more limited processes of governance in order to achieve and enact some kind of consensus about the specific requirements of public policy. Surely this unique experience is worth far more than Americans have been willing to acknowledge to date.

That is not to say that agencies have not sometimes been misdirected and misused, or that they have not operated on occasion in self-serving ways. Agencies have at times contributed their own ambitions to the centrifugal forces in American government, and in some respects they may have aided those who aimed to reduce their legitimate sphere, by neglecting substantive relationships with the ultimate source of legitimacy in governance—the citizenry. But the dangers of parochialism are endemic to all social organizations, and to the extent that it is practiced in public administration it is a perversion of the normal agency perspective. Ideally, the agency perspective provides public administrators with a center of gravity or a gyroscope to guide them as they perform their duties. On such a foundation is built a concern for broader public principles and values; in other words, a concern for the more inclusive principles we commonly call the public interest.

Max Weber pointed out that bureaucracies can be used for good or evil. How they are used depends on the human beings who staff and direct them. Fortunately, over the grand sweep of American history and with the notable exception of the period between the election of Andrew Jackson and the passage of the Pendleton Act, agencies have been staffed and directed by people who have taken seriously the task of faithfully executing the laws and pursuing the public interest. Although a few agencies have been concerned with a broader public interest, most have assumed their responsibilities have been met if they have exercised discretion in a way that has satisfied the most powerful of the interests affected. They have assumed that the more inclusive public interest would emerge from the process of governance as a whole. We feel this more limited conception of the public interest and the comfortable assumption that a beneficently invisible hand will result in the broad public interest is no longer adequate. The agency perspective we advocate must go further to the pursuit of the broadest possible definition of the public interest.

Few groups in American society have been given as demanding a set of tasks as those assigned to administrative agencies. The special skills and learning acquired by public administrators as they have performed these tasks over the years are worth far more than our present political dialogue allows and their denigration by political elites has often deprived the nation of their accumulated knowledge. Similarly, the public at large, cut off from the realities of administrative practice, has also denigrated public administrators. For their part, public administrators have been entirely too timid in pressing their rightful claim to legitimacy, for which the agency perspective provides a foundation. They have also been too hesitant about extending the agency perspective in pursuit of a broader definition of the public interest and in building the sense of trust among citizens that would ratify such claims and efforts.

Most recently, we have also allowed public administration to be diminished by the headlong rush to adopt a policy or program perspective excessively focused on output without a balanced concern for the public interest. Output and the public interest are often erroneously assumed to be synonymous, but an agency can generate outputs that are clearly inimicable to the public interest. It can produce short-run results that can have devastating effects upon its own infrastructure and capabilities. A park service, for example, can process a large number of visitors through facilities that it is overloading and allowing to decay through lack of maintenance. It is thus possible for an agency to be responsive to immediate pressures while simultaneously being irresponsible regarding the long-range public interest. One of the characteristics of the agency perspective and of effective public administration is the development of a prudent and reasoned attention to agency performance that gives consideration to both the short- and long-run consequences of policies. Another is the habit of mind that searches for ways of measuring outputs that are qualitative as well as quantitative. A third is an outlook that rejects "the bottom line" as a slogan sometimes antithetical to good public administration.

Although public policy analysis and program evaluation can be valuable in making agency performance accountable, they are not ends in themselves. The simplistic use and clever abuse of these techniques must be constantly guarded against. In executive agencies quantitative measurements make sense only when viewed as part of the larger processes of administration. Policy analysis, program evaluation, and the decision sciences should be subordinated to the agency perspective and to core management processes. Too often the former have been allowed to run the latter, resulting in a process detrimental to imaginative program conception and implementation.

A particularly corrosive influence upon the agency perspective came from humanistic psychology and a variety of cultural dynamics during the 1960s. We refer specifically to the denigration of the role of authority in the administrative process and managerial relationships. The adolescent texture of the cultural upheaval of the 1960s wore heavily on the traditional concepts of hierarchical control in public agencies. Now in cooler perspective it may be time to correct the misconceptions that arose from the debate between the traditionalists and the humanists on the issue of authority.

The traditional point of view was misguided to the extent that it tried to base obedience to authority purely on the principle of deference. It depicted the proper use of authority as a tool by which managers could improve performance in the "shape up or ship out" tradition. It was accurate, however, in depicting the human condition as one requiring authority to check the sometimes capricious tendencies of human beings. It was particularly useful in seeing that encounters with authority are an essential part of the maturation process in people, not only in adolescence but throughout our lives, and for superiors and subordinates alike.

By the same token, the humanists were misguided in carrying their attack on authority to the point of denying that it plays any needed role in institutional life. They erred in maintaining that authority can be replaced completely by processes of participation. The humanists did provide a helpful corrective to the traditional view through their call for more openness in the use of authority and by their advocacy of a greater degree of confidence building in organizations.

The idea can be distilled from this debate that authority is not as useful as feedback and other "humanistic" communication devices for improving performance in administrative settings, but it is essential for dealing effectively with the intractable problem of compliance in cases where reasonable people disagree. It is the issue of compliance that becomes a fulcrum for the personal development of managers, including how they co-opt the people they manage and how effective their agencies are in implementing sometimes controversial public policies. Our opinion is that the vitality of the agency perspective, the health of public administration, and the improved self-concept of the public administrator all hinge upon our return to a fuller appreciation of the positive role of authority in administration. This appreciation, in essence a form of trust, will develop among citizens to the extent that administrators communicate the realities of administrative practice so that citizens can understand them and ultimately acknowledge the legitimacy of administrative authority.

The agency perspective is one that deserves greater legitimacy than it has received in our political culture. The nature of the role the agency plays leads it inevitably to develop a distinctive point of view about the public interest. Public administration that rests upon the agency perspective has an historic, covenantal, organic, and constitutional reason and right of being. Many agencies have been part of the operation of government from the genesis of our nation. Some are mentioned specifically and others suggested in the text of the Constitution.

The distinctive nature of public administration lies in the fact that it is a part of the process of governance, that administration is accomplished in a political context, and that it is defined in large part as competence directed toward the public interest. This sets it apart from business management, and it provides the basis for a truly distinctive claim to status too long ignored. The claim ought to rest, however, on more than competence to manage in a political context. It must also rest upon a claim of competence in the maintenance of (1) the agency perspective; (2) the broadest possible public interest; and (3) the constitutional governance process.

The public interest has long been derided by social scientists as a meaningless concept at best and a mask for arrogant despotism at worst. Setting aside for a moment the difficulties of defining the content of the public interest, it is ironic that many behaviorists profess to be concerned with human behavior but ignore the fact that the public interest has day-to-day, practical consequences for the behavior of hundreds of thousands of public administrators. Caught as they are in a struggle of conflicting interests sometimes as interpreters, sometimes as decision makers, and at other times as victims, they understand intuitively that both the origins of conflict and its resolution must be rooted in some notion of the public interest. This is true even though some administrators may use the concept cynically and self-servingly. It therefore remains a concrete, living, behavioral reality in spite of the problems we have in defining its specific content.[5]

The approach traditionally used in discussing the public interest has led us astray by making a meaningful definition of it virtually impossible. The approach has been to ask about the public interest in terms of the *content* of given policies. Such questions can never be answered. By shifting our perspective from specific content to an ideal and a process, and our emphasis from a search for certainty to recognition of the problematic nature of the public interest, the problem becomes less insoluble. We also restore much of the significance the term has lost. If we think in terms of the public interest as both an ideal and a process, it becomes clear that we must develop certain habits of mind to think through decisions and to choose how to deal with the multiple ramifications of issues. We would thus incorporate into deliberations long-range views rather than an excessive concern for short-term results, and consider the competing demands and requirements of all affected individuals and groups, not just a few. This would lead us to proceed with more knowledge and information rather than less, and to recognize that saying the concept of public interest is problematic is not to say it is meaningless.

Although this type of definition will not satisfy those who have been accustomed to posing this public interest issue in substantive and finite terms, an ideal or process-defined norm that is sought but never quite attained is not that unusual either as practical guidepost or positive symbol. The democrat endorses majoritarianism, the civil libertarian extols due process, lawyers cherish adversarial procedures, and we recommend approaching the public interest in the same spirit. Even the strongest opponent of the concept, the economic conservative, is committed to the process-oriented norm of the competitive market.

Because this definition of the public interest does not provide us with answers that specify the content of policy, it invites the charge that the public administrator who lays claim to pursuing and protecting the public interest is merely insisting on his agency's definition of what is right. Public administrators are not immune to such charges. Like all the other partners in the refocused dialogue, public administrators will need to recognize the subjective elements present in any conclusion reached about which choice is "right." Any posture of certainty about the public interest is a dubious and dangerous one. Should anyone doubt this he or she needs only to be reminded that many of those involved in the Watergate affair were certain the public interest was represented in the President's position. At the same time, it can be said that all decision criteria are alternatively matters of agreement among relevant individuals. The key to the legitimacy of any criterion, including the public interest, is not whether it is subjective but whether all those who have a stake in the matter at hand have had the opportunity to share in defining it and in creating a bit of intersubjective reality.

While we feel that commitment to the public interest as an ideal and a process and manifested as a habit of mind is the best foundation for the concept, we would not preclude other points of view. The search for the specific content of the public interest in the positivist tradition has blinded us to yet another approach to defining its nature: that we have learned a good deal about what the public interest is *not*. Defining something negatively may be unsettling for those of us educated in contemporary social science, but it is a commonplace procedure in our everyday lives and in such diverse fields as theology and developmental psychology. In theology the transcendent is frequently discussed in terms of what it is not. And in what may be a meaningful analogue for the public administrator and the public interest, Rollo May has suggested that the human capacity to say and mean *no* is the most significant first statement of self-discovery. Knowing what we are not must occur before we can know who we are.[6] Although we might continue to define the public interest in terms of an ideal and a process, the pursuit of a positive but ever problematic concept could also proceed by explicating it negatively. We know, for example, that racism is not in the public interest. We may debate what constitutes a manifestation of racism, but even on that issue, we have certain specifications on this point in statutes, administrative regulations, and court interpretation. We probably have more consensus about what constitutes racism than we realize. The consensus is simply not well explicated. Starting with the negative as a means of defining the public interest may yield more insight than the positivist approach has thus far permitted.

In speaking about The Public Administration's distinctive relationship to the public interest, we wish to remain open to the idea that the content, however elusive, might yet be definable to some degree. But more important, we think, is the point that although the content of the public interest remains problematic, when an institutionalized tradition and support system exist to nurture a process and an ideal that emphasize the relatively comprehensive, long-term, deliberative, and informed efforts essential to the search for the public interest, the chances increase that action will follow in accord with these values. Whatever the weaknesses of public administration, it provides more of an institutionalized tradition of this kind than any other part of American society, including the other actors in the political process. Certainly it has a better record in this matter than political parties, interest groups, or mass media. Public administration does not know the content of the public interest, but it is in a relatively good position to nurture the kind of processes essential for its proximate definition; particularly when it takes the enlarged view of the process that encompasses efforts to render faithful interpretations of the interests of all relevant stakeholders, including citizens at large.

The practical and beneficial consequence for public administration of accepting the public interest as being under continuing review is a perspective that fosters (1) tentative steps and experimental action rather than "solutions" for this and "wars" on that, (2) curiosity and dialogue about ends as well as means, (3) individuals who learn as well as respond, (4) humility and skepticism about grand designs; (5) greater awareness of the unique responsibility and potential contribution of each participant in the dialogue about the public interest, and (6) greater attentiveness to the language of public discourse.[7]

Recognition of the distinctive character of public administration can also proceed apace if its academic community can come to a new point of clarity about the venerable question of whether there is a politics administration dichotomy. First, we must acknowledge that public administration theory detoured into an intellectual cul de sac when some of us followed too closely Herbert Simon's attempt to establish a fact value dichotomy. We also erred in taking too seriously the organizational sociologists in their efforts to explain complex organizations. Both movements led us away from the important debate carried on by Wilson, Goodnow, Gaus, Appleby, Waldo, and others. Our temporary obsession with behavioralism and our attempts to stay in step with political science and organizational sociology in the heat of their own behavioral preoccupation delayed progress toward a more sophisticated discussion of the politics administration dichotomy. Organizational sociology, organizational psychology, and business administration were never interested in questions of governance, and political science drifted further and further from the problem of how to govern, pulling public administration with it.

The path to clarity about the dichotomy may lie in conceiving of three levels of understanding about the distinction between politics and administration. First, we should recognize that at the highest level, speaking descriptively and conceptually, there is no dichotomy. Public administration at the highest level of abstraction is an integral part of the political process. Comprehension of this point is the beginning of understanding of public administration's unique role in the political system and the process of governance. But in establishing this point over several decades, realists have lost sight of the fact that at a second level of meaning, still speaking descriptively but at a less abstract level, one encompassing directly observable behavior and action, there is a considerable distinction. When acting in the political process, people at this level of understanding often seek to make and maintain a separation between the roles, behaviors, situations, and phenomena they think of as political and those they conceive of as administrative. Sometimes the distinction is made for purposes of self-interest, but it is made nonetheless. To ignore it is to ignore behavioral and empirical reality and thwart our understanding of the behavioral phenomena we call public administration..

Finally, at a third level of meaning if we speak prescriptively and normatively to persons involved in governing, we should acknowledge, elucidate, and *extend* the distinction between politics and administration. That distinction, at this third level of meaning, is crucial if public administration is to be accepted, not least by the public at large, as a legitimate and valued part of the political process in general and the governance process more particularly.

The emergence of judges and courts as esteemed actors in American government (of, but not in, politics) can serve as an analogue. In the evolution of the English political system, judges began as agents of the king, travelling the realm settling disputes in the king's name. The work of English judges might be looked upon as an early form of nation building. Their reputation for fairness fixed in the public mind wellfounded belief in the superiority of royal justice over the justice administered in the courts of the barons. These royal judges developed the common law, a law that was common throughout the realm and of a higher quality than the particularistic law of the feudal manors. Eventually, however, these officers of the king developed distinctive symbols, rituals, language, way of reasoning, and claim to expertise and legitimacy that gave them a stature and role distinct from that of the king. It led them eventually to use the common law on occasion to stand in loyal opposition to the king. The evolution of such judicial independence was taken a step further on this side of the Atlantic when Chief Justice John Marshall's adroit handling of *Marbury* v. *Madison* established the Supreme Court's authority to review the constitutionality of acts of Congress.

Like the third branch of American government, The Public Administration needs to assert, but also to be granted, its propriety and legitimacy as an institution. It should assert the value of the agency perspective in the effective functioning of the political system and the distinctiveness and worth of the role of The Public Administrator in the governance process. It is a role of competence directed to pursuit of the broadest possible definition of the public interest and to the maintenance of the constitutional governance process. If this assertion of legitimacy is done successfully, it is conceivable that public administrators, like judges and military officers, could question a directive of their political superiors and have the question regarded as a sober second thought rather than an act of bureaucratic sabotage. When this happens, the Public Administration, the Public Administrator, and our political system will have come of age. It may be, however, that just as the judicial agents of the king developed their reputation by going out among the people and visibly demonstrating the superiority of their practice, public administration's assertion of legitimacy will need to be founded on more direct linkages with the people in order to win their trust.

Public Administration and Capitalism

In *The Administrative State*, Dwight Waldo questioned whether the rationalistic mentality reflected in the literature of public administration could sufficiently comprehend what he called the "imponderable emotional substructure" of society. His point was that the emotional aspect of social life had to be adequately understood if general social health is to be ensured. We wish to address this question in its current applicability in the United States, though we hope our suggestions will have implications beyond our own political system.

In our view, social health depends critically upon the existence of a reflexive relationship between an individual's emotional substructure or unconscious and the conscious processes engaged in by all human beings. This reflexive relationship requires on the one hand a relative openness to the designs of the unconscious that emerge in ambition, the pursuit of personal agendas, risk, and adventure. On the other hand it requires that these designs of the unconscious be juxtaposed to collective needs and concerns and with needs for introspection, judgment, and moral reasoning applied to matters affecting others, beyond the gratification of the selfish impulse. In the case of the United States, capitalism as an institution has well provided for that half of the reflexivity equation containing things like personal agendas. The genius of the market is that it can easily and quickly give expression to the emergent needs and tastes that are constantly forming in the personal conscious. It is this aspect of capitalism that correctly leads advocates of laissez faire to equate it with individual freedom. Suppression of the emotional substructure is hardly a problem in capitalist society. The growth and development, whether economic, social, or psychological, which stem from unconscious impulses proceed unimpeded for most Americans. The exception, of course, is the disturbingly large and persistent underclass.

Unfortunately, capitalism has been notably less successful in serving the other half of the reflexivity equation. The marketplace can so facilitate the expression of the personal unconscious and emotional substructure that it sometimes overwhelms the conscious and reasoned side of society. As wants are expressed and satisfied with increasing speed and facility, a point is reached where new wants are created by the process itself. Gratification, divorced from content and substance, then becomes the motivating orientation of individual citizens and eventually of society itself. Society loses its bearings, its moral and practical points of reference are obscured, and the public standards that are essential for the exercise of collective human discretion and judgment fail. The market is necessary, but it is not in itself sufficient for maintaining social well-being. Public authority expressed through the stable institutions of The Public Administration can serve as a cooling, containing, and directing foil to the capitalist economic system. Public institutions represent the collective consciousness of American society and serve as a vehicle for mature efforts to bring to bear knowledge, reason, and moral judgment on our problems and the design of our future. Historically, capitalism has released the energy required to move the American ship great distances, but it alone is not an adequate navigator through the shoals of no-growth or scarcity. We would suggest that The Public Administration should play a major role in navigating the American ship of state, but we also believe that we must continue to look to American political institutions for the role of captaincy.

Public Administration and the Constitution

American political rhetoric and symbols are badly out of synchronization with our enacted Constitution, or at least with the Federalists' interpretation of it. The Federalists' position encouraged and anticipated public administration as an institution of American government. Unfortunately, public administration theory is distressingly weak in recognizing this point, and members of the public administration community have themselves frequently failed to grasp such theory as does exist. Instead we have sought simply to emphasize the nonpartisan instrumentalism of public administration and emulate the management practices of business. Valuable though a claim of nonpartisan instrumentalism was in the emergence of self-conscious public administration at the turn of the century, it is neither well grounded in the Constitution nor adequate for the administrative role demands of the late twentieth century. The Constitution implicitly, explicitly, and through historic practice has assigned a demanding and significant role to public administration. We know from our first civics class that the Constitution is designed to preserve freedom by dividing power. But we have not always connected that profound truth to our circumstances as public administrators. In the never-ending, constitutionally induced battle between the chief executive, the legislature, and the courts, public administration is a free-fire zone. Public administrators often serve as targets of opportunity for the combatants.

When we assert that the Constitution, or at least a Federalist interpretation of it, anticipated the public administration, do we mean that the framers foresaw the size and scope of contemporary public administration or thought of it in the bleak metaphors of war used above? Assuredly not. With the possible exception of Alexander Hamilton at his most prescient, they did not foresee the complex administrative institutions of today any more than they could have foreseen the myriad changes in other facets of American life. Nonetheless, the history of the earliest days of the republic and the actions of the framers themselves show that as soon as constitutional government began, public servants were caught in a no-man's-land of ambiguity and discretionary choice. The responsibilities they shouldered were viewed as a threat to republicanism on the one hand and a challenging opportunity for virtuous public service on the other. The immediate task was to keep the constitutional process from becoming a stalemate in which the public interest would be the ultimate casualty.

In dealing with constitutionally derived ambiguity and discretion, public administration must always act within the constraints imposed by its origins in the idea of covenant as manifested in the Constitution, the civil service reform tradition, and historic experience. The word *covenant* has sacral overtones not altogether inappropriate for our purposes. Its secular usage preserves a fundamental sense of solemn agreement about obligations between parties. Public administration was, is, and always ought to be conceived of as being based on a solemn agreement between the public administrator and the citizens he or she serves. It is a professed obligation to serve the public with competence directed toward the public interest and toward maintaining the democratic processes of governance. Competence is informed and constrained by the American Constitution, statutory law, and our common history. The Public Administration we advocate would look to the past as prologue to the public discourse that continually inspires a free society. It views the Constitution not as the Word but as the Living Word.

The Public Administration is neither monolithic nor homogeneous. It assumes a rich diversity of perspectives born of differentiation and specialization. It welcomes constructive criticism from within and outside its ranks. Differing perspectives should not be judged as *ipso facto* self-serving but as part of a constitutional heritage of robust dialogue. In this respect public administration is an analogue to the pluralism of the political process, with all the attendant assets and liabilities. It differs, however, in accepting as a conscious goal of its activities the pursuit of what might be called the "public good." This is something that theories of pluralism trust to an invisible hand. The conflict among the differing perspectives of public administration is a valuable part of the creative tension essential to the continuing exploration of what constitutes the public good.

If the public administration can assert and accept its moral authority and rightful claim to be a legitimate participant in the process of governance, it can contribute a great deal to the correction of a major defect in the Constitution. This is the Constitution's unsatisfactory resolution of the problem of representation. The problem was the centerpiece of George Mason's brilliant argument against the Constitution's ratification, and it was a source of embarrassment to such staunch Federalists as George Washington and Alexander Hamilton. Both friends and foes of the Constitution wondered how the sixty-five members of the original House of Representatives could represent over 3 million people. Today we wonder how 435 members can represent over 220 million people. Pluralist theory suggests that the competition of interest groups is the best assurance of representation of all the people. It says the public interest emerges as the vector sum of interest group pressures. Although such a claim is not without merit, it has never been convincingly demonstrated, and in fact it has been subjected to devastating criticism. It is painfully clear that not all citizens and interests are represented by interest groups.

In light of this constitutional defect, The Public Administration as an institution of government has as valid a claim to being representative of the people in both a sociological and functional sense as a federal judge appointed for life, a freshman congressman elected by a small percentage of the citizens of southeast Nebraska, or a senator from Rhode Island. Public administration may be as representative of the people as a whole as is a president elected by a coalition of voting blocs and interest groups claiming victory based on less than 51 per cent of the popular vote and 29.9 per cent of the eligible voters, which in turn translates to about 19 per cent of the total populace. Political commentators err in looking for representation from elected officials alone.

We advance the proposition that the popular will does not reside solely in elected officials but in a constitutional order that provides a variety of legitimate titles under which others participate in the process of governance. Created by statutes based on the constitutional order, public administration holds one of these titles. It is not appropriate, therefore, for public administration to cower before a sovereign legislative assembly or a sovereign elected executive. Our tradition and our Constitution know no such sovereign. The task of The Publc Administration is to share in governing wisely the constitutional order that the framers intended as an expression of the will of the people. Only the people are sovereign.

Public Administration and The Public Administrator

We have spoken at length of The Public Administration. Now we wish to speak more specifically of public administrators.

First, we remind ourselves that the public administrator takes an oath to uphold the Constitution of the United States, not the whims of the powerful. This oath brings administrators into a community created by the Constitution and obliges them to know and support the constitutional principles that affect their official spheres of responsibility. When law empowers rather than commands, that is, when it confers discretion upon administrators instead of issuing specific orders to them, the oath obliges administrators to exercise their discretion in a manner that is informed and guided by constitutional values as well as by immediate political requirements.

Much has been said in recent years about the development of professionalism in public administration and what it means to be a professional. What is important from our point of view is not whether the public administrator has accumulated enough experience, training, and credentials to claim professional status but whether he or she has an expressed concern for the development of competence and standards, for orienting work toward service to society, and for establishing a set of values that regards the broadest possible definition of the public interest as a public trust. For us, professionalism entails the public administrator holding the maintenance of the constitutional order as a fundamental duty.

Our perspective on professionalism sees The Public Administrator as a trustee of the public good and a legitimate participant in the process of governance. As a trustee, The Public Administrator will look beyond the political pressures of the day and the degrading image of the civil servant as instrumentalist. He or she will develop a role that is critically conscious and purposive in pursuit of the public good. The role will facilitate the democratic process, but it will be disciplined by the rule of law and the constitutional tradition of limited government. It will be conscious of the need at times to prudently accommodate powerful forces that may represent a temporary retreat from, or pause in, the pursuit of the public good. Progress toward the broader public interest will not always be steady, and it will not always move forward in a straight line.

The Public Administrator must, however, be steadfast and persistent, heeding Hamlet's advice to play to the judicious few rather than the powerful few or the vociferous many. He or she will play to the long-term public interest rather than to short-term pressures. The judicious few need not be a small and closed elite group. There are no limits to its size. It is an article of democratic faith—at least it is an object of democratic hope—that the judicious few might become the judicious many. It is the duty of The Public Administrator to work to expand the ranks of the judicious few by stimulating reasoned debate about the meaning of the public interest, and by taking advantage of opportunities to facilitate substantive involvement by citizens in the governance process. The judicious few will become the judicious many only when more of the people develop the practical wisdom that is the essence of politics. This wisdom is best learned in the course of public sphere activity itself. As the success of numerous publicly funded programs run by citizens attests, the administrative state is neither too big nor too complex for meaningful citizen involvement.

In large measure, it is the administrator's unwarranted faith in technical expertise and in the possibility of comprehensive solutions that makes him or her hesitant to turn to citizens. But the uncertainty and complexity of modern-day governance demand not comprehensiveness but tentative strategies, social interaction, and frequent feedback and adjustment.

From this perspective, not only is the postindustrial administrative state compatible with involvement by citizens but it positively requires it.

Much has been written about making bureaucrats more responsive and responsible. The Public Administrator must indeed act responsibly, and for the most part this means being responsive to constitutionally and legally valid orders. It also means being attuned to the clientele being served and the elected officials who make policy. It does not, however, mean just being seismographic and a hired lackey. Neither does it mean being merely a faithful servant. Nor does responsiveness refer to the footwork of an artful dodger working between and among interest groups. It refers to being a trustee of what we have been referring to above as the public good, something more broadly defined than the pluralists' notion of the public interest. Indeed, we feel responsiveness and responsibility on the part of The Public Administrator ought to refer to being a trustee of what people of earlier ages called the common good. The role of trustee of the public (or common) good is a role shaped by the agency perspective, the broadest possible definition of the public interest, and fidelity to the living word of the Constitution. Fidelity to the living word of the Constitution means to serve the constitutional order and the democratic processes of governance.

In their role as trustees of the public good, Public Administrators may have to incline their agencies' responsiveness toward the President at one point and Congress at another. At other times an agency may lean toward the courts or the interest groups that are likely to serve the long-term public interest or public good as the agency sees it. Less often, Public Administrators will have to act on behalf of a public interest defined even more broadly than their agency perspective. On rare occasions, they may have to act on behalf of the constitutional order itself. Public administrators are often called upon now to play the role of balance wheel, using their statutory powers and professional expertise to favor whichever participant in the process needs their help at a given time to preserve the intent of the Constitution. We need to make this role explicit and win acceptance of it as a legitimate one in our constitutional order.

Inevitably, some participants will view public administration merely as a means to status and power, and some administrators will pervert their duty into a sinecure. In spite of the inevitable human frailties of a few and the fragmenting pressures of careerism and specialization, The Public Administration must strive to remain and continue to become a vocation that is given meaning in the service of a cause. The cause is characterized by such terms as *civil servant, career executive,* and *public employee.* With a self-conscious shift in the American dialogue, we feel a sense of a calling can be added to these phrases in a way that will encourage public administration to grow and flourish as never before. Most people will live *for* it as a cause, and fewer will live off it for less noble impulses.

Certainly the founders of the republic viewed public service as both a calling and a trusteeship. So did the reformers who came later in our history: the Populists, the Progressives, and the New Dealers. If the vision of the founders and the reformers is not already lost, it is at least in grave peril.

Much of our loss of transcendent vision has been brought about by our concern for professional status. We have paid a heavy price for adopting too slavishly the scientific trappings believed essential to claims of expertise. A focus on the *means* of governance, as in management science, systems analysis, planning/programming/budgeting systems, and program evaluation is indeed important to professionalism. But when we advocate these means to the exclusion of transcendent purposes and a moral commitment to community building, and when we allow ourselves to be deflected from the enhancement of freedom and dignity as well as the improvement of the quality of citizens' lives by preoccupation with management techniques, we erode the legitimacy of public administration and reduce the public administrator to the role of technician. Too narrow a focus on the application of value neutral instrumentalities costs public administration and the nation dearly.

The role of the public administrator must be broadened to include approaches to practice that will support this transcendent commitment. First, as we have said, administrators must seek to expand opportunities for direct citizen involvement in governance, so that citizens develop the practical wisdom that is the ultimate basis of trust in administrative good faith. Also, administrators must develop personal reflexivity, that is, consciousness of their own values and assumptions, and how they affect daily decision making. Such consciousness will enable them to become critical of established institutional practices that inhibit the expansion of freedom and justice, and lead them to work toward change where it is possible. Finally, public administrators must be able to give reasons for what they do. Though established practices may frequently preclude direct dialogue with relevant stakeholders, it is The Public Administrator's responsibility to consider who all these stakeholders may be, what their concerns are, and what reasons he or she would give for a decisive action if dialogue were possible.

The Public Administrator assumes that the human condition can be improved though never perfected. He or she must work for the amelioration of societal problems without expecting quick, cheap or permanent solutions. The Public Administrator must work with the knowledge that some problems can best be alleviated and some goals achieved by outcomes of the market or by the use of marketlike devices, while others can be better addressed by forms of state intervention. Although Public Administrators must be responsive to the ideological or party-based views of elected officials on social problems, they must also provide these officials with sound, prudent, and feasible options based on agency competence. The Public Administrator therefore should be both an analyst and an educator but not a philosopher-king or a mandarin. He and she must work for the long-term education of elected officials and other actors in the process of governance, as well as citizens at large, knowning that this will often be an arduous and thankless task.

The Public Administrator should be committed to (1) praxis, critically conscious action and the pursuit of goals, and (2) reflection, thoughtful assessment of action taken, and self-conscious learning from experience. Both praxis and reflection are essential to a vocation that directs its competence toward the kind of transcendent purposes we have outlined. They are also essential to the day-to-day goals of serving the public with grace and dignity, respecting those we serve while not fogetting to respect our peers and ourselves as well.

Conclusion

Whether or not The Public Administrator and The Public Administration are living up to the prescriptive ideals we have outlined is a question that should be asked repeatedly and answered as honestly as possible. There are inherent problems and pathologies among us that we deny or ignore at our peril. Those of us associated with public administration in the academic community have a special task that goes beyond teaching skills and techniques to new members of the profession and even beyond trying to instill transcendent values in them. It is the special task of caring enough to offer constructive and friendly criticism.

We believe all of us have a special responsibility to help refocus the American dialogue. We hope this essay will serve in some way to initiate the discussion and precipitate the changes essential for Egger's fifth revolution to be successful. Seeking to redefine equity and justice in a system that has considerable socioeconomic differentiation as both a consequence and a catalyst of its capitalist commitment is as great a challenge as any democratic society has ever faced. If we are to have any chance of meeting that challenge, our political dialogue must shift from *whether* public administration to *the place of* public administration and the public administrator in the governance of the republic as it enters the third, and perhaps most perilous, century.

Endnotes

1. The co-authors of this paper bear equal responsibility for the ideas it contains and with one exception are listed alphabetically. Wamsley's name appears first simply because he was assigned the role of faithful scribe.

   Camilla Stivers was not one of the authors of the original manuscript which received considerable circulation. As one of our students she criticized the original manuscript because we failed to consider the crucial role citizens should play in public administration and in the shift of the American political dialogue. We decided the best way to deal with the criticism was to include her as co-author and become her students in this matter.

   We wish to thank our many colleagues who provided criticism and encouragement. Particularly helpful were the comments of Phillip Cooper, Bayard Catron, Linda Wolf, Fred Thayer, Philip Schorr, and Eugene Lewis. The faults that remain belong to us; they did all they could to save us. Obviously we are drawing on the thoughts of many other persons in the intellectual community associated with public administration. Except in the case of the direct quotes noted below, however, we have chosen not to use footnotes. The list of persons whose ideas we have drawn from would be insufferably long, but surely it would begin and end with the name of Norton Long. We do not intend this to be an academic paper but a statement, perhaps a manifesto, that we hope will encourage dialogue.

2. Woodrow Wilson, "The Study of Administration," *Political Science Quarterly* 2:197–222, 1887.

3. Rowland Egger, "The Period of Crisis: 1933 to 1945," in *American Public Administration: Past, Present and Future,* ed. Frederick C. Mosher (University, AL: The University of Alabama Press, 1975).

4. We will use The Public Administration and The Public Administrator to connote our prescriptive ideals of what public administration and the public administrator should and can become.

5. We are especially indebted to Professor Bayard Catron for this point. Indeed most of the words of the foregoing three sentences are his. We could do little to improve on them. Correspondence with the authors.

6. Our thanks to Linda Wolf for this point. Correspondence with the authors.

7. Ibid.

PART IV

Public Administration in Practice

CHAPTER 10

Managing Human Resources

N. Joseph Cayer
ARIZONA STATE UNIVERSITY

N. JOSEPH CAYER is Professor of Public Affairs at Arizona State University. He has also taught at Lamar University, the University of Maine, and Texas Tech University. He is the author of Public Personnel Administration in the United States *and* Managing Human Resources *and co-author of* American Public Policy *and* Labor Relations in the Public Sector: An Annotated Bibliography. *He has written numerous articles in public affairs journals and several book chapters on his areas of expertise: public personnel administration and labor relations in the public sector. Professor Cayer holds B.A. and M.P.A. degrees from the University of Colorado and the Ph.D. from the University of Massachusetts.*

N. Joseph Cayer focuses our attention on the development of public sector human resources management over the 100 years since the publication of Woodrow Wilson's "The Study of Administration." He lays the groundwork by first reviewing pre-Wilsonian personnel management philosophy and practices, the major themes of which are the relationship of personnel and politics and the responsiveness of public servants to public pressures. The spoils system that characterized the Jacksonian era was supposed to make government more responsive and accountable but resulted in making it less respectable. The Tenure of Office Act of 1867, in which Congress attempted to place some limits on the President's patronage powers, signaled the end of the worst of the spoils system for the federal government.

Between 1867 and 1883, Congress experimented with several limited merit bases for public personnel management, and finally in 1883 passed the Pendleton Civil Service Act. The Pendleton Act became the basis for the national civil service system and a model for state and local governments. The system it created remained in place with little change for almost 100 years. Although the Pendleton Act originally applied to only about 10 per cent of federal government employees at the lowest levels of administration, subsequent legislation and executive orders extended civil service coverage to almost 95 per cent of the civilian federal work force.

The autonomy and insulation achieved by the civil service system was described by Wallace S. Sayre as the triumph of technique over purpose. Personnel managers became enforcers of rules and regulations designed to assure that other managers did not violate what personnel systems defined as merit-based principles. Many public managers came to view public personnel administration as an obstacle to effective management rather than as a supporting mechanism.

The personnel reform and scientific management movements were married in 1914 after a long and polite courtship. It was averred by some that they had actually slept together before the council-manager system of government was established in 1914, but no one could be sure. Now the separation of politics and administration had a form of government in which its worth could be demonstrated, and professional managers could find the one best person to match the one best way of accomplishing goals set by elected officials. Because both movements strove for efficiency in public service, personnel reformers identified objective procedures for carrying out personnel functions. Job analysis, position classification, equal pay for equal work, and selection through examination are examples of the standard tools that came to be employed by public personnel managers.

Cayer makes use of Muriel Morse's seven commandments of civil service, utilizing an analogy to George Orwell's *Animal Farm*. The commandments are:

1. Whatever is best for the public is good.
2. Whatever is political in nature is bad.
3. No one shall tamper with the selection process—least of all, management.
4. No one shall make employees feel less secure.
5. The law and rule shall be memorized.
6. Civil Service shall serve operating management. (Obviously, the sixth commandment is inconsistent with the third commandment, but some statement is needed to rationalize the existence of the personnel function.)
7. Equality for all.

Uncritical obedience to these commandments so separated public personnel administration from the rest of the management process that eventually it was transformed into modern-day human resources management. The prescriptions of the reformers have endured amazingly well, however.

Since the 1960s public personnel managers have recognized that they cannot escape policy issues, that psychology and human behavior are crucial factors in managing organizations, and that equal employment opportunity must be a major factor in making public personnel management truly professional in systems design. Collective bargaining, citizen participation, and techniques of retrenchment management also have to be accommodated as closed personnel systems necessarily become open ones.

Today public personnel administration is intimately involved in politics. Among the major purposes of the Civil Service Reform Act of 1978 is the reintegration of personnel management and general public management. The Reform Act attempts to make personnel management an instrument for responding to the policy preferences of the administration in power. Although the law decentralizes many functions and gives operating managers greater flexibility in their personnel activities, it continues to specify merit principles. It makes provision for monitoring them, and it sanctions those who violate them.

The original reform ideas were advanced with an intensity that left little room for rational discourse about their practical effects. They cloaked questionable practices and policies in the sanctity of merit to the extent that objective observers could not always examine and validate the personnel tools involved. These ideas have now yielded to a better balance of political neutrality and managerial responsiveness. It is true the holy of holies of merit has been violated, but only after Richard M. Nixon desecrated the rest of the temple with the Malek Manuel. The evidence so far is that the new system has been abused less than the old one.

No aspect of public administration better exemplifies the purposes and impact of Woodrow Wilson than public personnel or human resources management. The attempt to purge public personnel of partisan politics became the overriding concern of personnel reformers. Their success in 1883 with the passage of the Pendleton Act established a model for development of public personnel management at all levels. The imprimatur of Wilson, indicating that politics and administration were and should be separate entities, provided major legitimacy to the reform effort. Even the notion that merit and politics are incompatible draws heavily upon the Wilsonian model separating administration from politics. Although Wilson's essay, "The Study of Administration,"[1] was not published until 1887, it was the major intellectual justification for much of the personnel reform movement then under way. That tradition remains an important foundation for current thinking about the practice of human resource management in the public sector.

The Wilsonian view of politics is a very limited one, especially as it has been interpreted by the personnel literature. The tendency in personnel literature has been to view politics only in terms of political party politics. As Frank Thompson notes, such a view ignores a politics of personnel management that has little to do with what we know as partisan politics.[2] Personnel decision makers have discretion to choose among alternative options. In so doing, they are influenced by competing value systems and preferences. They marshal the resources at their command to obtain the results they wish to achieve. Thus, the exercise of power involved in choosing among preferences makes personnel decision a political process.

The focus of this essay is the development of public sector human resources management over the 100 years since Wilson wrote his essay. To provide the context in which to understand the connection between Wilson's ideas and the tradition of public personnel management, it is also necessary to provide a brief review of pre-Wilsonian personnel developments. The major themes of this treatment of public personnel are the relationship of personnel and politics and the responsiveness of public personnel to the public. Both of these are major themes of Wilson's article.

Pre-Wilsonian Personnel Developments

Government service in the first few administrations of the independent United States of America was very small and uncomplicated compared to what we now know as the public service bureaucracy. Positions in government were filled by those who held political power, notably the landholding aristocracy. Because no one else had the right to vote, there was little concern for staffing the public service on a basis representative of the population as a whole. Partly because of the aristocratic background of public servants and partly because of the European tradition's influence, public service was prestigious in early American government.[3]

Although explicit partisan political considerations seemed to be absent from early government personnel decisions, there were, in fact, many political factors involved. Presidents George Washington and John Adams had to appease numerous political interests although they tended to resist placing pressure on lower-level government servants to become actively involved in partisan political activities. Nonetheless, their choices for government positions had to meet some political tests. Among those tests were support for the federal republic and geographic representation to foster integration of the new nation. Similarly, attention was paid to congressional influences, and limited preference was extended to Revolutionary Army officers. These factors were considered along with a requirement of competence; thus, the staffing of the new national government began on a political note and with consideration for staff's responsiveness to politically influential interests. It is interesting to note that both Washington and Adams commented on the necessity of political considerations and lamented the limits the President had in influencing subordinates because of general political forces and, specifically, political party pressures. Adams found it necessary, for example, to remove the customs collector at Portsmouth, New Hampshire, because of political pressure by New Hampshire politicos.[4]

Political qualifications and concerns about responsiveness to the electorate became more pronounced with the election of Thomas Jefferson. His Republican party turned the Federalists out of office in the election, but the new president felt constrained in implementing the policies his party supported in coming to power. After the long Federalist rule, the public bureaucracy was staffed by Federalist sympathizers. Jefferson began the process of removing and replacing public servants on the basis of political party affiliation. In that sense, he, not Andrew Jackson, is the real initiator of the spoils system.[5]

Although party affiliation was a major consideration in staffing the public service for Jefferson and his successors, ability was equally important. Similarly, the economic and social elite maintained a monopoly on public service. This trend continued through the administration of John Quincy Adams. As Mosher notes, despite these political criteria for public employment, early administrations maintained a public service "remarkably free of corruption, nepotism, and even patronage."[6]

The administration of Andrew Jackson represents a major break with preceding administrations in the sense that the aristocracy gave way to the common people in public employment. The broadening of suffrage and admission of new states to the union led to the election of Jackson. Like Jefferson before him, he felt the need to reward his political supporters with appointment to office. Major themes of his administration were making government more responsive to the citizenry as a whole and loosening the tight hold the aristocracy had on the political system.[7] Even though Jackson proudly used the spoils approach in selecting personnel, he was no less concerned about the ability of public servants to perform the jobs for which they were chosen than any of his predecessors. He would probably be as uncomfortable as any of them to see what developed with the use of spoils.

Jackson's approach was important because it was based on the idea that government should be responsive to all citizens, not just those who have economic power. One way of making it responsive is to include people from the broad spectrum of society in government jobs. Jackson used that idea, although his expanded vision extended only to the common white man. Modern-day reformers recognized the wisdom of the approach in championing equal employment opportunity and affirmative action as ways of including women and minorities.

Jackson's successors embraced the spoils concept wholeheartedly, and public servants changed with each new administration. Oftentimes, re-election of a president ensured no security for appointees. Instead, political supporters of the re-elected president were likely to press for changes in personnel to reward new groups active in the campaign. As a result, the status and prestige of the public service plummeted. Working for government became equated with partisan political activity. Because of the smoke-filled rooms and rampant corruption, politics also became synonymous with corruption. One hundred years after the establishment of the United States government, public service careers had definitely lost their luster. Ironically, spoils was supposed to make government more responsive and accountable but resulted in making it less respectable.[8] In order to re-establish its prestige and make government trustworthy to the citizens once again, reformers made serious efforts to develop an alternative to spoils. The Tenure of Office Act of 1867, in which Congress attempted to place some limits on the President's patronage powers, signaled the end of the worst of the spoils system for the federal government. Between 1867 and 1883, Congress and presidents experimented with several limited merit bases for public personnel management. Finally, in 1883, Congress passed the Pendleton Civil Service Act, which became the basis for the national civil service system and a model for state and local governments. That system remained in place with very little change for almost 100 years.

Reform and Its Effects

The unsavory reputation of public service under the spoils system caused reformers to champion insulation of public service employment from partisan politics. To many observers, the merit system represented the triumph of good over the evil of spoils. There was a moralistic fervor to the reform movement that made it difficult to question any practice or policy justified in the name of merit.[9] Besides removing the public service from direct partisan politics, the reformers also strove to insulate it from direct congressional and presidential control. Although it was a very gradual process, the public personnel system achieved a great deal of autonomy and seemed not to be very well integrated into the rest of management. The Pendleton Act of 1883 originally applied to about 10 per cent of federal government employees at the lowest levels of the administration. Through subsequent legislation and by executive orders, the civil service system gradually covered approximately 95 per cent of civilian federal employees.

State and local governments followed the national model and began passing reform acts of their own.[10] Although many reform efforts had been mounted earlier at the state and local levels, none were actually successful until 1883, when New York adopted the first state civil service law. Massachusetts was the only other state to do so before the turn of the century. Albany, New York, was the first city to adopt civil service, in 1884, and other jurisdictions followed slowly. As at the national level, coverage was very limited in the early reform legislation. Nonetheless, the interests of reformers were every bit as moralistic and intense as at the national level.[11] Reform spread widely among state and local level governments during the early twentieth century, and the theme of separating politics and administration, which was so important at the national level, permeated state and local personnel policy changes.

The appearance of Wilson's essay, "The Study of Administration," in 1887 provided strong intellectual support for the reform effort and gave it even greater visibility and political legitimacy. Wilson's strong defense of separating politics and administration helped place the concept among the sacred tenets of the developing field of public administration. There was no better place to implement the concept than in personnel management, where legislation could conveniently make the separation. A major part of the reform effort called for the political neutrality of public employees. President Grover Cleveland established a precedent for the civil service in issuing an executive order in 1886 that forbade political activity by federal civil service employees.[12] Although earlier attempts to stem partisan political activity were made, Cleveland's order was the first to have much legal force. Eventually, the Civil Service Commission developed a set of rules implementing an executive order issued in 1907 by President Theodore Roosevelt that expanded upon the earlier order of Cleveland.[13] The Civil Service Commission rules served as the basis for the Hatch Act of 1939, which legislatively prohibits many partisan political activities for federal service employees. Amendments in 1940 and state statutes adopted later restrict political activity of state and local government personnel.

Political neutrality was a major concern of the reformers, although their positive theme was the establishment of merit as the basis for public employment. Although there was a positive aspect to reform, much of the effort seemed to emphasize the negative. Rather than focusing on how to serve management in achieving its goals, public personnel management seemed to concern itself with telling management what it could not do.[14] Personnel managers became policers of rules and regulations developed to assure that managers did not violate what personnel systems defined as merit-based principles. Little evaluation of the validity of these "merit practices" took place. As a result, many public managers viewed public personnel management as an obstacle to effective management rather than as a support function. As Wallace Sayre noted, public personnel management became a "triumph of technique over purpose."[15] So much attention was paid to making sure that managers followed the rules that it became difficult to know that merit was, in fact, being practiced, and managers often found it difficult to make personnel decisions that would facilitate accomplishing the purposes for which their organizations were created in the first place.

At the same time that public personnel management was purging itself of partisan politics, Scientific Management became the dominant paradigm in public administration. In the beginning of the twentieth century and especially in the 1920s and 1930s, Scientific Management dominated management in the public sector. Its emphasis on applying the lessons of business to government enterprise underscored the separation of politics and administration. The management process devolved to a search for the one best way to accomplish any given task. Because it was assumed that one best way could be found for every action, political choices were irrelevant. Thus, the personnel reform movement and Scientific Management were eminently compatible.[16] The approach was epitomized by the council-manager system of government first adopted in 1914. The plan assumes a separation of policy and administration. Political leaders make policy and hire professional, nonpolitical administrators to execute these politically based policy decisions.

The marriage of personnel reform and Scientific Management had effects other than increasing the separation of politics and administration. Both movements strove for efficiency in public service and to find the most objective fashion by which work could be accomplished. Personnel reformers accepted the challenge of identifying objective procedures for carrying out personnel functions. Job analysis, position classification, equal pay for equal work, selection through examination, and the like became the standard tools of public personnel managers. With these tools, managers could theoretically find the one best person to fit into the one best way of accomplishing any of their goals.

Of course, the Scientific Management movement also fostered greater specialization of the work as a means of achieving greater efficiency. With specialization, workers often became further insulated from management because their depth of expertise made it difficult for generalist supervisors to understand their work. Consequently, supervisors and their superiors confronted a situation in which they had little basis for evaluating or directing the specialized work of their subordinates.

In a provocative article, Muriel Morse captures the tone of civil service reformers and the tenacious way in which the public personnel profession clung to the principles emanating from reform.[17] Utilizing an analogy to George Orwell's *Animal Farm*, she discusses the "seven commandments of civil service" as they evolved from the reformers' ideas. The first commandment is "whatever is best for the public is good," and the second is "whatever is political in nature is bad." These commandments represent the moralistic underpinnings of the reform effort. Civil service and neutrality represent the triumph of good over the evil represented by spoils and patronage. Often there is little concern about the real nature of the civil service system; if it is called "civil service" or "merit," it is equated with good. The depiction of politics as bad has already been discussed extensively.

Morse's third commandment is "no one shall tamper with the selection process—least of all, management." The fervor with which public personnel managers adhere to this idea has been the source of much of management's frustration with personnel people. Lack of concern with the real needs of management is often suggested as the culprit in selection procedures. Closely related is the fourth commandment, "No one shall make employees feel less secure." A career service presents protection for the employee, and often that protection becomes "protectionism" in the sense of insulating the employee from accountability and control. As Morse notes, all of these commandments are interpreted and explained in detail through rules and regulations, and a fifth commandment requires that "the law and rule shall be memorized." The adherence to and quotation of the rules is legendary. Of course, the rules also become excuses for not taking responsibility for acting.

Morse suggests two other commandments followed by Civil Service in order to gain legitimacy with management, the public, and elected officials. First, "Civil Service shall serve operating management." This commandment seems inconsistent with commandment three, involving selection, and in fact, Morse suggests that it exists to rationalize the existence of the personnel function. It is a way of currying favor with management and suggesting a positive role for personnel management. Unfortunately, personnel professionals have had the reputation for claiming to serve operating management while actually placing obstacles in the way of achieving management's objectives. The slavish devotion to rules and regulations without concern for their consequences belies the noble intent of personnel professionals.

"Equality for all" is yet another commandment accepted by professionals in public personnel. Equality often had more meaning for efficiently processing people or carrying out the objective practices of personnel management than for creating a system of equality based on human differences. The challenges of equality of opportunity and affirmative action, requiring a complex definition of equality, exposed this commandment for what it was—another catch-all phrase to lend legitimacy to the personnel effort.

In her usual infectious, upbeat fashion, Muriel Morse views each of these commandments and the public personnel profession's implementation of them as opportunities for growth. Rather than decrying the negative consequences of their implementation, she suggests that questions raised by management, the public, and political leaders gave public personnel administrators the opportunity to examine their approaches. From that examination evolved professional approaches to personnel management.[18]

The message in Morse's article is a very important and instructive one. In a precise manner, the piece captures the criticisms that have been leveled against the personnel function since the adoption of civil service systems in the United States. At the same time, it presents a view of how public personnel professionals have now developed a more positive and creative approach to managing the human resources of governments. It would seem that modern personnel management has learned some lessons from the long obedience to commandments that separated them from the rest of the management process. The transformation of public personnel management into modern-day human resource management provides the focus for the rest of this essay.

The prescriptions of the reformers have been amazingly enduring. Very little serious challenge to their ideas regarding public personnel management seemed apparent until long after World War II. While public administration began to recognize that human beings are not easily placed as cogs in a machine and human relations became the hallmark of the public service, public personnel management was able to continue as though nothing had changed. If anything, after World War II the professionalization of public personnel management led to greater sophistication in developing presumably objective tools to better perform personnel functions. As Sayre notes, the objectivity of these tools was only in appearance.[19] Selection procedures and qualification requirements became more sophisticated, but they were not validated to ensure their appropriateness to the purposes for which they were used. Thus, subjective decisions were masked by the trappings of objective procedures. The reformers and Scientific Management had a strong and long hold on public personnel managers.

It was not until the 1960s that any successful challenge to the accepted principles of public personnel management occurred.[20] Frederick Mosher's *Democracy in the Public Service* was the first among many intellectual challenges to the idea that politics and public personnel management are separable. From the middle sixties onward, most analyses of the personnel function paid attention to the inescapable link between public personnel and politics. Clearly, personnel professionals were not suddenly deciding that the public service should become active in partisan politics. What was and still is happening is that public personnel managers are recognizing that they cannot escape policy issues and are evaluating their relationship to management in general. Recognizing that being perceived as a negative force for management is not the most effective way to have impact, the public personnel field has made dramatic strides in finding positive ways to contribute to and serve management in the public sector.

At the same time the politics/administration dichotomy was being debunked in personnel management, the human element was being recognized as an important factor and not a nonthinking tool. Taking lessons from the Hawthorne Studies of the late 1920s, public administration took note of psychology and human behavior as factors in managing organizations. Chester Barnard utilized the findings of the Hawthorne Studies as the foundation for his influential *The Functions of the Executive*, published in 1938 and republished in 1968.[21] The Hawthorne Studies became the foundation for the Human Relations School, which greatly influenced post–World War II public management. Once again, however, the public personnel field seemed to resist the trends of the rest of public administration. Nonetheless, findings relative to motivation, productivity, and performance could not be ignored. Public personnel managers were confronted with more challenge to their universal, "objective" tools for doing their work.

The post–World War II recognition of more humanistic concerns by public managers forced public personnel professionals to recognize that they had to deal with people as unique human beings while trying to develop standards that apply to all employees. These challenges opened the door to more flexible and open personnel policies.

The 1950s and early 1960s were relatively tranquil periods for government administrators, including personnel managers. Despite that tranquillity, employees and society in general began to question the reasonableness and equity of many of the rules of civil service. The image of the public service as protected, secure, and not particularly competent or industrious forced personnel professionals to begin to refine their practices and experiment with new and different ways of handling issues. The result was the beginning of a new and positive approach to public personnel management. While most of the old trappings remained, public personnel professionals and organizations such as the Public Personnel Association (later to become the International Personnel Management Association) fostered a new concern for being supportive to both management and employees. Instead of concentrating on what management could not do, progressive personnel professionals sought alternatives for operating management to deal with the personnel problems they encountered. Personnel became part of the management team.

If the 1950s and early 1960s were periods of tranquillity, the mid-1960s through the mid-1970s were periods of unrest. Society was undergoing many changes brought about by challenges to the old ways of doing things. Among the most important challenges for public personnel were the civil rights movement and the growing strength of labor organizations. The civil rights movement dominated the public policy agenda of the mid-1960s and raised equity questions about virtually all social institutions. The employment arena was a major target for change, and Congress worked with the Kennedy and Johnson administrations in developing major nondiscrimination protections for employees in all aspects of personnel processes.

Nondiscrimination policies applied primarily to the private sector, although the Civil Service Commission acted to require federal departments and agencies to eliminate discriminatory personnel practices. Some state and local jurisdictions did the same, but it was not until 1972 that federal legislation extended civil rights provisions to state and local levels. The Equal Employment Opportunity Act of 1972 requires nondiscrimination in personnel policies and practices among those employers.

Equal employment opportunity requirements challenged many of the practices of public personnel managers and continue to serve as stimuli for change. Virtually every personnel tool now has to be analyzed to determine whether it serves its purpose without illegally discriminating on the basis of race, color, sex, religion, or national origin. Later legislation and administrative rules and regulations proscribed discrimination against the handicapped and on the basis of age or, in some cases, sexual preference. Some state and local government legislation also extended protections on these or similar bases for their employees. In order to enforce these kinds of provisions, personnel managers were forced to find ways of validating their personnel instruments. These efforts actually caused the personnel profession to question and evaluate its activities, often for the first time. The assumptions carried over from the reform movement and Scientific Management tradition now were being tested. A major implication of these tests is that personnel professionals now are developing the evidence to support the processes and decisions they utilize.

Among the many instruments and procedures challenged by equal employment opportunity concerns are exams, qualification requirements, compensation plans, evaluation systems, promotion policies, and disciplinary and grievance processes. Nothing in the personnel system is immune from scrutiny relative to equal employment opportunity concerns. The important factor is that methods are being found to ensure that each of these processes and tools is appropriate (valid) for the decisions for which it is used. Thus, equal employment opportunity has been a major force in making public personnel management truly professional in design of its systems.

At the same time the civil rights movement made its mark on the public service, public employees began looking to collective bargaining as a means of exerting influence on their work situations. New York City granted bargaining rights to its employees in 1954, and Wisconsin was the first state to do so, in 1959. President Kennedy's Executive Order 10988 in 1962 granted bargaining rights to federal government employees and served as a legitimation of the efforts of public employees to gain such rights at all levels of government. Collective bargaining for public employees grew rapidly during the 1960s and 1970s.

The challenges of collective bargaining to personnel managers were many. First of all, the authority to make personnel policy, assumed to be the exclusive province of management, became a shared authority. Representatives of employees placed much pressure on decision makers to consider the needs and desires of the employee in every element of the process. No longer would it be possible to develop new rules, regulations, or instruments without consulting the employees affected by them. These challenges once again helped make public personnel management more professional and more human resources–oriented. In order to justify its policy recommendations to employee groups, management had to do solid groundwork on the need for and implications of the policy.

Collective bargaining also challenged assumptions about employee perquisites and rights. Like equal employment opportunity, collective bargaining focused on procedural protections for employees, thus making public personnel management much more legalistic in its practice. In order to assure employee rights, rules and regulations were developed on what could and could not be done. In part, personnel management was returning to its traditional focus on rules and regulations to ensure that they served legitimate personnel purposes.

Perhaps the most significant effect of collective bargaining has been in developing benefits packages for public employees. While the federal benefits package generally has been a good one, state and local employees, by and large, have not been so fortunate. Employee bargaining changed that situation as unions and other representatives pressed for improved benefits. Public personnel managers found themselves working in whole new fields of endeavor such as insurance, pension fund management, and counseling.

General challenges to the authority of government and its accepted way of doing things went hand in hand with the civil rights and collective bargaining movements. Citizen and clientele groups demanded and were granted rights to participate in program and policy development. The expertise of managers was often challenged by community input and control. Additionally, citizens and clientele often demanded and received some voice in the selection of administrators of many programs.

Just as the personnel profession became comfortable with accommodating these many forces, and prospects looked good for positive personnel developments, a new challenge arose. The taxpayer revolts of the 1970s meant personnel managers had to find methods for retrenching rather than expanding. Skills in dealing with the human element faced strong tests. Personnel managers had to reduce their costs and assist operating managers in reducing the size of their staffs. Personnel managers became employment counselors in the sense of finding alternative placements for employees of their organizations. They also had to become experts on improving productivity and individual performance, all the time facing the pressure of those still seeking equal employment opportunity and employee bargaining rights.

The Current Context

The growth in the size and complexity of public bureaucracy helped make the public service relatively independent of political authority.[22] In part, the vision of the nineteenth-century reformers was served well by the autonomy civil service systems achieved. Although reformers did justify the reform in part on the basis of protecting employees from political pressures, that was not their major issue. Instead, the reformers of the 1880s seemed most interested in neutrality—that was the basis of the politics/administration dichotomy. As Theodore Lowi argues, "Bureaucratic agencies are not neutral: they are only independent."[23] Lowi's contention is that bureaucracies are the new machines, replacing political machines in shaping public policies and distributing services without being responsible or accountable to political authorities. The insulation from political authority makes it possible for public bureaucracies to determine the content and implementation of many public policies. Woodrow Wilson and the reformers would hardly have expected or favored such an outcome.

In implementing personnel reforms, managers adopted theoretically neutral instruments and processes. It is ironic that many of them have been invalidated on the basis that they are not neutral. The challenges arising from equal employment opportunity cases, for example, resulted in the invalidation of many exams and selection devices presumed to be neutral. In fact, these instruments often have biases built into them.

Again, in their zeal for reform, civil service managers often adopted practices that appeared neutral on very superficial grounds.

As noted at the very beginning of this essay, the notion that politics represents only partisan political activity ignores the fact that politics involves the competition of various values and forces over the distribution of resources in society. Modern personnel managers recognize that their activities have a great impact on the way the competition for resources is shaped and on what values dominate in decision making. As such, public personnel is integrally involved in politics. The reformers of the 1970s and the 1980s recognize just how linked personnel and politics are. The Civil Service Reform Act of 1978 had as major purposes the reintegration of personnel management and general public management, and making it an instrument for responding to the policy preferences of the administration in power. While many safeguards still exist to protect against political coercion, the fact that the Office of Personnel Management is responsible to the President is a significant shift. Additionally, the reintroduction of the Senior Executive Service permits the administration to utilize personnel in more political ways. Some personnel experts, including a former executive director of the U. S. Civil Service Commission, fear that the integrity of the federal civil service is being jeopardized.[24] Clearly, the reforms of 1978 represent some reversal of the reform of ninety-five years earlier that focused on neutrality. The 1978 reform attempted to strengthen the responsiveness rather than the insulation of the federal service. The Civil Service Reform Act of 1978 stimulated similar reforms in state and local governments throughout the nation.

In suggesting that personnel management is political, it is necessary to consider how it is so. Thus, it is necessary to examine how it is political in process, in terms of values, and in terms of participants in the process.

The Process

Frank Thompson suggests three basic ways in which personnel management is political.[25] First, office politics is an ever-present feature of the personnel function. In that process, participants attempt to exert power over personnel decisions. The operating manager who tries to find every way around specified selection procedures in order to select a favored candidate plays politics. So does the personnel officer who uses every device available to reverse a decision deemed not appropriate. Conflicts between personnel offices and operating management are the source of many organizational problems, and the resolution of those conflicts may depend upon the power each enjoys in the organization.

Secondly, Thompson notes that the personnel function allocates scarce

goods and symbols such as jobs, pay, status, prestige, and the like. Classification and reclassification decisions may seem to be rather mundane
and boring to many observers. However, those decisions often represent
major conflicts and affect the status and prestige of the employee in
the position as well as superiors. The status of a supervisor or department
manager usually depends in great part upon the number and classification levels of subordinates. Thus, the decision on classification or reclassification affects the pay and status not only of the employee in the position
but of those who supervise or manage the unit as well. Is it any surprise,
then, that supervisors often exaggerate job descriptions in order to
achieve a higher classification of subordinates? The personnel analyst
reviewing the request receives pressure in making the decision and must
make the decision on allocation of these resources.

The selection process itself allocates a good: the job. The challenges
to selection procedures on grounds that they are discriminatory clearly
indicate the importance of the allocation process. If patronage is used,
we tend to consider the process political. Merit, however, is just as important in establishing criteria for allocating jobs. If discriminatory criteria
are employed, one group has advantages over another in the process.
Equal employment opportunity and affirmative action represent attempts
by other groups to obtain their fair share of jobs.

Finally, Thompson notes that personnel management shapes the general level of efficiency and effectiveness of government. The quality of
the personnel function certainly affects the quality and productivity of
employees. As such, the level and quality of services is affected. Selection
procedures that permit the use of irrelevant criteria may lead to the
selection of employees who do not have the ability to perform the job.
If so, the public is not getting the service it pays for.

Values

It should be no surprise to anyone that public personnel management
involves conflicts over differing values. The reformers of the nineteenth
century and their followers expressed very strong values in supporting
the civil service system. They favored merit as a basis for making personnel decisions and held political neutrality to be an important value in
designing civil service systems. These values, among many others, permeated personnel management throughout government.[26] While their
values were being fostered in the service, the personnel profession had
a strong tendency to argue it was being objective in its practice. But
some of the tools adopted actually fostered some values over others
without recognition or acknowledgement that such was so.

It would be difficult to catalog all the possible values represented by
personnel decisions. However, it is possible to examine some examples

of value conflict and illustrate the importance of that conflict to personnel management. David Rosenbloom does an excellent analysis of the conflicts between administrative values of the personnel system and basic democratic values deriving from the United States Constitution.[27] He suggests that as public personnel management attempted to depoliticize and dehumanize the public service, it imposed numerous forms of uniformity upon public employees. These limitations placed upon employees clash with basic values of democracy, such as individuality and diversity. Political neutrality and ideological, social, and moral uniformity, as well as uniformity in appearance, are some of the demands made upon public employees. Rosenbloom acknowledges that the courts have generally acquiesced to government's wishes in these areas of control over public servants but that challenges arise and changes occur.

Political neutrality is a theme discussed at length in this essay, so it will not be examined any further here. Uniformity, in an ideological sense, was and is required of public employees through loyalty and security programs. Although less intense today, the concern with loyalty and security is still important, especially in jobs involving information sensitive to national security.

Social and moral uniformity are more elusive values but, either by law or practice, have had their impacts. As Rosenbloom notes, women and minorities were not represented in public service because personnel decisions and practices kept them out. These practices kept government service socially uniform. Moral uniformity is a very sensitive issue and is reflected in policies that deny public employment to homosexuals or others who do not meet the behavior standards of society. Of course, demonstrating that these values are the values of only part of society, advocates of alternative values have been successful in bringing about changes in personnel policies. Affirmative action and equal employment opportunity certainly challenge social uniformity. Similarly, some jurisdictions have changed their policies to prohibit discrimination on the basis of sexual preference.

Uniformity in appearance has also been challenged. Personnel rules and regulations on dress, length of hair, and the like have been very common in public sector employment (as well as in private organizations). Legal challenges and pressures by employee groups and others have resulted in changes in these provisions as well, but many jurisdictions still impose them.

As Rosenbloom indicates, these basic values of uniformity sometimes facilitate management of the organization. At the same time, they conflict with some more basic political values we hold dear as a democracy. The politics of the process is manifested in the way these competing values are weighed and made part of the personnel system. In politics, nothing is ever permanent. Thus, depending upon the influence of

the advocates of competing value sets, the personnel system varies in
the extent to which different values dominate.

The Political Actors

The potential actors in personnel politics are those who have stakes in
the outcomes of policy decisions. It is difficult to imagine any participant
in public affairs who is not affected in some way by public personnel
management decisions. Of course, the executive, legislative, and judicial
branches of government make the decisions resolving policy conflicts.
Each may have a different interest in the outcome. The legislative and
executive branches are usually the most active participants. The city
council, for example, may wish to limit the number of positions in city
government that are exempt from the civil service. The mayor, on the
other hand, may wish to have more discretion in appointing loyal partisans to key positions. Political decisions resolve the differences.

The bureaucracy itself is also an issue. Technically part of the executive
branch, the bureaucracy and people in it fight hard for personnel policies
with which they can work. When a state legislature, for example, considers
legislation to ban public employee strikes, operating agencies and personnel offices often lobby hard against such an act. They know that the
morale of public employees and their willingness to do their jobs depends
in part on good will. If no-strike legislation is used as a vehicle to curry
public favor and make an example of public employees, public servants
may be more grudging in the way they perform their duties.

Although the courts are less active in their political participation, they
often have to be the arbiters in disputes over alternative policies. Their
decisions on the constitutionality of laws prohibiting political activity
or discrimination present policy statements on the issues. Although
parties may still argue over whether changes should be made, the
courts' decisions give legitimacy to what they say is the current law.

Political parties and interest groups also concern themselves with public
personnel policy issues. Of course, political parties are interested in
being able to implement their policy preferences through control over
the public service selection process. Patronage is a fact of life in most
jurisdictions, although it is relatively limited in most. Nonetheless, restrictions on partisan political activity and the like directly affect political
parties.

Interest groups vary from those generally concerned with fair and
effective service for their members (welfare rights organizations) to those
which have specific personnel concerns in mind. Veteran's groups, for
instance, are very protective of preference given veterans while minority
and womens' groups work to overturn such policies.

Public employee groups are particularly interested in public personnel policy decisions. Employee unions, associations, and professional associations take sustained and active part in personnel deliberations. They often make those deliberations a political issue. Highlighting city council candidates' views on labor issues is one effective way to do so. Often they will put an issue such as arbitration for public employee labor impasses on the ballot through intiative petitions.

Finally, the media and general public help shape personnel policy. They often frame the debate on personnel issues. A television news story following the work patterns of public works employees can have significant implications for personnel management. If the workers are found to be sleeping on the job or running personal errands, the reports may lead to new policies for assigning and monitoring employees. Of course, if the employees are found to be doing a good job, the story is not newsworthy and unlikely to be aired.

Public response to a news story is one way in which the general public participates in political discourse on personnel policy. In recent years, however, the general public has spoken more directly in elections on tax reductions (and increases), bans on discrimination based on sexual preference, public employee bargaining rights, and pay for public employees, among many other personnel-related issues. Through initiative petitions or referenda, they participate directly in the decision and are treated to electioneering and lobbying by all the other participants in the process.

This brief review of the political nature of public personnel management illustrates that politics, in a very general sense, is part of our system of governance. As such, it is not reasonable to suggest that the public bureaucracy that has the greatest burden in governing us on a daily basis could ever be divorced entirely from politics. If it were, the public service would become unresponsive to the public it serves. Modern public personnel professionals recognize the need to balance the political nature of government work with the technical tools and skills available to them for conducting their work. As such, they manage human resources in a political environment.

Conclusion

In examining the political nature of public personnel management and the politics/administration dichotomy, it is easy to rail against the naivete of the reformers and advocates of the separation. It is unfair, however, to suggest that Woodrow Wilson and the civil service advocates were so naive. They recognized that politics and administration could work together and abuse the system. They advocated a system in which the public service was depoliticized as much as possible as a way of curbing abuse. It must also be remembered that their primary concern was with prohibiting partisan political activity. But the public personnel profession took reform ideas and refined them and implemented them with an intensity that left little room for rational discourse. Cloaking their practices and policies in the sanctity of merit, they were able to avoid examination and validation of their personnel tools.

Even though civil service was embraced with a moral fervor, suggestions for changes have been heard. Critics of the unresponsive nature of most civil service systems achieved at least a symbolic victory with the passage of the Civil Service Reform Act of 1978. Various task forces on the public service had made suggestions for improving the federal civil service since the 1930s, and many of those suggestions helped shape the report on the *Personnel Management Project* used as the basis for the 1978 reforms.[28] Perhaps most important in the 1978 reform effort was that supporters of the act recognized that a technically efficient personnel system is not very effective if it is not used to support the efforts of those providing government services. In other words, advocates of reform recognized a need to balance political neutrality and political and managerial responsiveness.[29]

The 1978 reform decentralizes many functions, thus giving operating managers greater flexibility in their personnel activities. At the same time, the law specifies merit principles and provides for monitoring of their implementation and sanctions against those who violate them. For more explicit political responsiveness, the Senior Executive Service (SES) permits political executives to reassign career servants. Although the idea behind SES is to allow greater flexibility and responsiveness in the use of career personnel, there are critics who worry that the service might become too politicized.[30] To this point, there is not much evidence to suggest the system has been abused. Of course, an administration bent on abusing the system can find ways of accomplishing its objectives. Under the old civil service system, the Nixon administration developed an elaborate guidebook for assuring selection of politically supportive personnel.[31] The national civil service reform is being used as a model for state and local levels as they adapt to changing times as well. The lessons learned from a very narrow adherence to the recommendations of the nineteenth-century reformers are being used to develop modern personnel systems.

Trying to predict the future in human resources management is hazardous. A review of the public personnel literature at the beginning of the 1970s suggests just how difficult predictions can be. Virtually all experts at that time predicted a continuing growth in the size of the public service and explosive growth in public sector collective bargaining. The taxpayer revolt and election of an administration committed to reversing these trends was not foreseen. Thus, the current situation in public human resources management was not predicted.

Although stargazing may not be particularly helpful, it is possible to note some problems and challenges the personnel profession must face. Perhaps no concern should be greater than the image of the public service. Public opinion polls consistently show that government is not held in very high esteem in our society. Candidates for election often run against the bureaucracy, thus contributing to the negative perceptions of the general public.[32] In this environment, human resource professionals face the difficult task of attracting and keeping highly talented and dedicated people. There is also the challenge of maintaining good morale and motivating people to perform. It is difficult to do so when the system seems constantly under attack.

The attack on the public service is also reflected in the efforts at cost cutting at all levels of government. Public employees often feel tax cuts very directly as pay increases and benefits take a heavy toll. At the same time, jurisdictions at all levels are engaging in retrieval bargaining in which they try to reverse many of the gains public employees received in the past through bargaining. With high unemployment and a political environment that seems increasingly hostile to collective bargaining, public employees, once again, feel under attack. Personnel managers confront the task of dealing with labor organizations and employees increasingly frustrated by the attacks upon them. In the long run, it is likely that a balance will be struck and labor organizations will see the tide turn in their favor. Personnel professionals realize this likelihood and must work in such a way as to serve the political interests of public officials while maintaining a good working relationship with the employees. Again, the personnel system faces strong challenges.

It is also likely that we will see greater diversity and experimentation in human resources management. The thrust of the Reagan administration is decentralization of the administrative process and the return of many activities to state and local levels. These trends should result in experimentation with differing approaches to management and already appear to be leading to greater privatization of public services. Joint public/private ventures create new demands on personnel professionals. They must now learn the complexities of contracting for services and monitoring contracts, among other activities.

One hundred years after adoption of the civil service system at the national level, public personnel management still draws heavily upon the ideas of the reformers. At the same time, personnel professionals recognize that as times change so do the demands on the personnel function. The human resource management systems in government demonstrate great stability and durability. They would not be durable if they could not adapt to deal with the challenges presented by societal change. The next 100 years are certainly going to bring as many challenges as the last century. Human resources managers have demonstrated they can meet the challenges.

Endnotes

1. Woodrow Wilson, "The Study of Administration," *Political Quarterly* 2:197–222 (June) 1887.
2. Frank J. Thompson, *Personnel Policy in the City: The Politics of Jobs in Oakland.* (Berkeley, CA: University of California Press, 1975), pp. 6–10. Thompson's analysis is a classic in demonstrating the political nature of public personnel management.
3. Frederick C. Mosher, *Democracy and the Public Service* (New York: Oxford University Press, 1968), pp. 58–64, presents an excellent analysis of the early experience. Also see Paul P. Van Riper, *History of the United States Civil Service* (New York: Harper and Row, 1958).
4. H. Eliot Kaplan, "Political Neutrality of the Civil Service," *Public Personnel Review* 1:10–23, 1940. Pages 10–12 detail the pressure felt by Washington and Adams.
5. Leonard D. White, *The Jeffersonians: A Study in Administrative History 1801–1829* (New York: Macmillan, 1961), examines Jefferson's approach to public personnel management in detail.
6. Mosher, op. cit., p. 58.
7. See Mosher, op. cit., pp. 63–64, and Leonard D. White, *The Jacksonians: A Study in Administrative History* (New York: Macmillan, 1954).
8. See Mosher, op. cit., pp. 63–65, and Carl Russell Fish, *The Civil Service and the Patronage* (New York: Russell and Russell, 1963), originally published in 1904.
9. Mosher, op. cit., p. 65, and Wallace S. Sayre, "The Triumph of Technique Over Purpose," *Public Administration Review* 8:134–137 (Spring) 1948.
10. Albert H. Aronson, "State and Local Personnel Administration," in *Classics of Personnel Policy*, Frank J. Thompson, ed. (Oak Park, IL: Moore, 1979), pp. 102–111, based on material from U. S. Civil Service Commission, *Biography of An Ideal* (Washington, D C: Government Printing Office, 1974, pp. 127–135 and 138–144), presents a good review of state and local developments.
11. For example, see Wilbur C. Rich's account of New York City in *The Politics of Urban Personnel Policy: Reformers, Politicians, and Bureaucrats* (Port Washington: NY: Kennikat, 1982).
12. Kaplan, op. cit., p. 13.
13. See Otto Kirchheimer, "The Historical and Comparative Background of the Hatch Act," *Public Policy* 2:341–373, 1941.
14. Benton G. Moeller, "What Ever Happened to the Federal Personnel System?" *Public Personnel Management* 11:1–8 (Spring) 1982. At pages 3–5, the author evaluates negative themes in the reform effort.

15. Sayre, op. cit., 1948.
16. See William H. Smits, Jr., "Personnel Administration—A Viable Function in Government?" *Public Personnel Management* 11:91–103 (Summer) 1982. See pages 92–94 for a discussion of the relationship.
17. Muriel M. Morse, "We've Come a Long Way," *Public Personnel Management* 5:218–224 (July-August) 1976.
18. Ibid., p. 220.
19. Sayre, op. cit., p. 137.
20. Frank J. Thompson, "The Politics of Public Personnel Administration," in *Public Personnel Administration: Problems and Prospects,* Steven W. Hays and Richard C. Kearney, eds. (Englewood Cliffs, NJ: Prentice-Hall, 1983), pp. 3–16.
21. Chester I. Barnard, *The Functions of the Executive* (Cambridge, MA: Harvard University Press, 1968, originally published in 1938).
22. Mosher, op. cit., pp. 76–78.
23. Theodore J. Lowi, "Machine Politics—Old and New," *The Public Interest* 9:83–92 (Fall) 1967.
24. Bernard Rosen, "Effective Continuity of U. S. Government Operations in Jeopardy," *Public Administration Review* 43:383–392 (September/October) 1983.
25. Thompson, op. cit., pp. 1–3.
26. David Rosenbloom, *Federal Service and the Constitution* (Ithaca, NY: Cornell University Press, 1971) provides an outstanding analysis of the durability of these values.
27. David H. Rosenbloom, "The Sources of Continuing Conflict Between the Constitution and Public Personnel Management," *Review of Public Personnel Administration* 2:3–18 (Fall) 1981.
28. President's Reorganization Project, *Personnel Management Project,* Vols. I & II (Washington, DC: Executive Office of the President/Office of Management and Budget, 1977).
29. See Naomi B. Lynn, "The Civil Service Reform Act of 1978," in *Public Personnel Administration: Problems and Prospects,* Steven W. Hays and Richard C. Kearney, eds. (Englewood Cliffs, NJ: Prentice-Hall, 1983), pp. 346–357, for an excellent discussion of the 1978 reform.
30. See Rosen, op. cit., for example and Fred C. Thayer, "Civil Service Reform and Performance Appraisal: A Policy Disaster," *Public Personnel Management* 10:20–28 (Special Issue) 1981.
31. A copy of the manual appears in U. S. Senate, Select Committee on Presidential Campaign Activities, Executive Session Hearing, *Watergate and Related Activities: Use of Incumbency Responsiveness Program,* Book 19, 93rd Cong., 2nd Sess., pp. 8903–9017, and in "Federal Political Personnel Manual: 'The Malek Manual'" *The Bureaucrat* 4:429–508 (January) 1976.
32. For an insightful discussion of this issue, see Alan K. Campbell, "The Institution and Its Problems," in Eugene McGregor, Jr., "Symposium: The Public Service as Institution," *Public Administration Review* 42:305–308 (July/August) 1982.

CHAPTER 11

~⟨0⟩~

The Development of Public Budgeting in the United States

Jerry L. McCaffery
THE NAVAL POSTGRADUATE SCHOOL

JERRY L. McCAFFERY is Professor of Public Budgeting at the Naval Postgraduate School. He has held several fiscal management and analysis positions with the Wisconsin Department of Revenue, and holds the B.S., M.A., and Ph.D. degrees from the University of Wisconsin, Madison. Professor McCaffery has published a number of articles and book chapters on budgeting and financial management topics, notably in Public Budgeting and Finance *and the* Public Administration Review, *on whose editorial board he has also served. He taught on the faculties of the School of Public and Environmental Affairs, Indiana University, and the Department of Political Science, the University of Georgia, before assuming his present position.*

Jerry L. McCaffery takes us on an historical tour of the development of public budgeting in the United States. The recurrent themes he identifies revolve around how budgetary power shall be divided between Congress and the President and how the budget power can be used as a tool both to manage and to govern.

The budgetary pattern in Revolutionary America was to create fiscal systems from which the executive was excluded. Just as the colonies had turned the power of the purse against the royal governors of George III in a replication of the struggle between Parliament and the Crown, so on gaining independence their representatives argued about whether the executive branch was legally empowered to frame budget estimates and

345

whether the Secretary of the Treasury should submit a budget to Congress. The Revolutionary War had been fought largely over the question of the extent of the executive's budget power, specifically the prerogative of the Crown simply to impose duties and excises intended to regulate trade and navigation without the approval of the colonists. Hence the cry "taxation without representation."

It has been a long journey from the early American practice of the 1780s to vest budgetary power in legislative committees to the accumulated budgetary power of the executive branch in the late 1960s. Along the way the influence of the Bureau of the Budget and the presidential use of impoundment gave the executive overwhelming leverage in the budgetary process.

But as nature abhors a vacuum, the American federal system abhors an imbalance of power. The Congressional Budget and Impoundment Control Act of 1974 re-established the role of Congress in the budgetary process. In both 1980 and 1982 Congress used the provisions of this act eventually to rewrite the President's budget. Over the past decade there has been a startling reversal in form of most of the twentieth-century practices that had relegated Congress to the role of making only marginal and incremental changes in the President's budget.

The developmental nature of American public budgeting has been largely determined by forms of budget technology. For the first century, simple forms were sufficient for simple functions. As the functions and responsibilities of government expanded, changes had to be made in budget technique, with the eventual result that more reforms have been attempted in the last 25 years than in the first 175 years of the American experience.

The most far-reaching of the early reforms was the Budget and Accounting Act of 1921. It is the watershed in the pursuit of executive budgetary efficiency. By the end of the first decade of the twentieth century it had become apparent that current government resources were insufficient for the task of achieving the nation's manifest destiny. The federal budget was in a deficit position for eleven of the seventeen years from 1894 to 1911, including five of the seven years from 1904 through 1910. The old revenue system was inadequate to fund America's expanding world role. A nation cannot fight a Spanish American War and build a Panama Canal on revenues derived from customs and excise taxes. The result was ratification of the Sixteenth Amendment in 1913 permitting a personal income tax.

In the years from 1919 through 1921 the income tax provided over 57 per cent of the federal government's revenues. With this direct taxation came earnest queries from taxpayers about where their money was being spent. Thus the income tax law can be seen as part of the pressure for budget reform and a stronger executive budget presence. The year 1921 marks not only the passage of the Budget and Accounting Act, but the established dominance of a major new revenue source.

McCaffery pays close attention to historic figures in the development of formal budgeting: (1) that it began with the reforms of William Pitt the Younger, Chancellor of the Exchequer in England from 1783 to 1801, (2) that as Secretary of the Treasury from 1789 to 1794, Alexander Hamilton was the founder of the American budgetary system because of his role in debt management, securing the currency, and providing a stable revenue base for the new nation, and (3) that as the first Director of the Bureau of the Budget Charles G. Dawes instituted significant technical innovations, such as the concepts of reserves and allotments.

The author says the history of American public budgeting can be divided into three phases: (1) Making the System Work, 1800–1921, (2) Neutral Competence, 1920–1970, and (3) Substantive Budget Reforms, 1949–1974. Since the Congressional Budget and Impoundment Control Act of 1974, Congress has assumed full partnership in budgeting for the modern welfare state. The nation has now embarked on a new course of shared executive and legislative responsibility for managing the economy. In the reconciliation instruction of 1981, Congress for the first time in the history of the United States set budget targets for taxing, spending, and debt management, and thereby established a sense of what the national budget should be before it started enacting budget bills. At no other time since 1789 had this been done. After almost 200 years Congress organized itself to pursue a budget prospectively instead of adding up the total appropriations and expenditures and calling that result a budget.

Budgeting began in the United States as a legislative enterprise. In periods of extreme crisis, the legislature has tended to cede the power of the purse to the executive and then reclaim it after the crisis has passed. Although there is a good deal of conflict in such give-and-take, there is also a good deal of reconciliation and adaptation. All sides agree that the most important function of the federal budget at this juncture in American history is the pursuit of economic stability. The long sweep of history teaches us that techniques of budgeting are not as important as the purposes for which public money is spent.

The history of budgeting in the United States reflects recurrent themes over how budgetary power shall be divided between Congress and the President, and developmental themes focused on improving the use of the budget power as a tool to both manage and govern. Although the budget power has changed markedly over the last two centuries, these recurrent and developmental themes may still be used to form a discussion of the American budget powers. This essay examines these themes.

The recurrent theme describes the division of power between the executive and legislative branches. Shortly after the Revolutionary War, Congress appeared to have taken the initiative in debate over the current role of the executive branch by debating whether the executive branch was legally empowered to frame estimates or whether the Secretary of Treasury should or could submit a budget framework to Congress. Many were averse to having the Secretary of Treasury even submit plans for the next fiscal year. By contrast, the steady accretion of power in the executive branch and within it in the Bureau of the Budget appeared to give the Chief Executive overwhelming leverage in the budget process by the late 1960s. Presidential use of impoundment power and politicization of the Bureau of the Budget essentially consolidated these gains for the Presidency vis-à-vis both Congress and the executive branch.

However, just as nature abhors a vacuum, the American federal system abhors an imbalance of power.

The Congressional Budget Reform Act of 1974 re-established Congress's role in the budget process. In 1980, Congress used the provisions of this act eventually to rewrite the President's budget. While President Ronald Reagan used the reconciliation instruction to seize a great victory in Congress in 1981, Congress again rewrote the President's budget in 1982. The few years from 1974 to 1980 concluded in a startling reversal in form of most of the twentieth-century practices that had seen Congress primarily relegated to the role of making marginal and incremental changes in the President's budget.

In 1789, arguments centered on the extent to which the President should prepare a budget; and although this is no longer debatable, the limits to the advantage that preparation gives the executive branch are still debatable. This theme is still as current and as obvious as it was in 1789. Within this recurrent theme is an idea central to American democracy: Power is balanced at the national level between the executive and legislative branches. When a serious imbalance occurs, corrective action ensues to restore and ensure the balance so that when one side is a leader the other remains a powerful modifier.

The developmental nature of American budgeting evolves with the uses of the budget power and the forms of budget technology. Typically, the developmental context of budgeting is associated with budget reform. However, reform presumes form, and early debates focused on the form of the budget process. For the first century, simple forms seemed sufficient for simple functions, a premise that held true through the opening decades of the twentieth century. Then, as the functions and responsibilities of government expanded, changes were made in budget technology and technique. This seems to be a linear and expanding process, with more reforms attempted in the last 25 years than in the first 175 of the American experience. Nonetheless, those in charge of the earliest stages of budgeting in this country recognized the need for different budget forms. As early as 1800, civilian agency budgets were presented as carefully detailed object-of-expenditure sums, while military expenditures tended to be appropriated as sums not unlike specific program categories.

Early debates on budget development focused on flexibility and program accomplishments rather than on strict agency accountability.

Discussion about reform accelerated as a result of local government reform measures at the beginning of the twentieth century and culminated in the Budget and Accounting Act of 1921. This marked the end of the beginning of the reform movement. The function of the federal government expanded under the impress of the Great Depression of the 1930s and the social service revolution of the 1960s. Simpleminded parallelisms of state and local to federal functions became less and less tenable. Local government reform is generally credited with stimulating federal government budget reform during the early decades of this century; however, with the development of the modern post-industrial welfare state and its concomitant assumption of duties and obligations, the need for better budget mechanisms became both more important and more difficult. Moreover, reforms enjoying success at subnational levels of government no longer become automatic candidates for success at the national level. The swift passage of zero-based budgets is a case in point. The developmental context of budget form and reform is a crucial chapter in modern budgetary history, and made even more poignant by the sense that once begun, there is no turning back. For example, decisions about the Social Security program in the 1930s, and social service programs in the 1960s, will shape tax needs and benefit payouts in the 2030s. Budget reforms help predict, justify, describe, and illuminate these budget decisions. This is the developmental context of budget reform.

Early American Patterns

Early American budgetary patterns were both part of and separate from their English colonial heritage. They were part of that heritage in that the American colonies inherited the full line of English historical experience with a limited monarchy and expanding legislative powers. The historical legacy may be dated to 1215, when a group of dissident nobles forced the King of England to accede to the Magna Carta. Of this document's sixty-one articles, the most important was that which said "No scutage or revenue shall be imposed in the kingdom unless by the Common Council of the Realm. . . ."[1] The Common Council preceded Parliament, and the statement that revenue may be raised only with the consent of a legislative assembly remained constant. It is often hailed as a beginning of popular government, but it is useful to note that this was basically a sharing of power between the king and the most powerful nobles in the realm, the two top tiers in an elite-dominated society where status was conferred mainly by birth. Nonetheless, by the end of the thirteenth century the principle was established that the Crown had available only those sources of revenue previously authorized by Parliament.[2]

In England, the Magna Carta was only the beginning of a long process toward popular government, a process completed in this century when the House of Lords lost the power to reject money bills. By the middle of the fourteenth century, the House of Commons had been established and quickly realized that a further check upon the power of the king would be control over appropriations. At first, revenue acts were phrased broadly, and once the money authorized was available the king could spend it as he wished. However, Parliament began to insert appropriation language in the Acts of Supply and other similar legislation, stating that the money be used for a particular purpose. Moreover, rules were made for the proper disposal of the money and penalties imposed for noncompliance.[3] Consequently, by the middle of the fourteenth century fiscal practices included a check on the Crown's right to tax, spending bills that carried notice of intent designating what the money was to be used for, rules for disbursement of money, and penalties when those rules were not followed.

The refinement of this system would take centuries, and its progress was not linear. Some kings were more skillful, personable, or powerful than others, and Parliament's role manifested steady evolution only in the most general terms. Aaron Wildavsky suggests that if a benchmark is needed, formal budgeting can be dated from the reforms of William Pitt the Younger.[4] As chancellor of the English Exchecquer from 1783 to 1801, Pitt, faced with a heavy debt load as a result of the American Revolution, consolidated a maze of customs and excise duties into one general fund from which all creditors would be paid, reduced fraud in revenue collection by introducing new auditing measures, and instituted double-entry bookkeeping procedures. Moreover, Pitt established a sinking fund schedule for the amortization of debt, requiring that all new loans made by government impose an additional 1 per cent levy as a term of repayment.[5] Pitt raised some taxes and lowered others to reduce the allure of smuggling. Because his actions were made in response to the debt load occasioned by the Revolutionary War, however, the model Americans had to follow was, at best, incomplete. This model encompassed a royal executive with varying degrees of strength and a legislative body attempting to exert financial control over the Crown by requiring parliamentary approval of sources of revenue and expenditure through appropriations legislation. The model ultimately demanded accountability of administrative officials to Parliament.[6]

The history of the American colonies has been described as a replication of the struggle between Parliament and the Crown, with the colonies, like Parliament, gradually winning a more and more independent position.[7] The colonies turned the power of the purse against the royal governors. Colonial legislatures voted the salaries of governors and their agents, appropriating them in annual authorizations rather than for longer periods. Indeed, one colonial governor's salary was set semiannually. In theory, the royal governors had extensive fiscal powers, but in fact these powers were often exercised by colonial legislative assemblies. These included raising taxes, appropriating revenues, and granting salaries to the royal governors and their officers. Generally, neither expenditures nor taxes were heavy, and England did not extract much revenue from the colonies except in periods of war.[8] What was troublesome to the colonists was that the Crown could and did impose duties and excises intended to regulate trade and navigation, *without the colonist's approval;* hence the cry "taxation without representation." Before the Revolutionary War, then, the colonies followed the British pattern of a gradually developing budget power. The decision about taxation was the paramount one, and the exercise of the budget power was basically sought as a check upon royal power. Taxation, appropriations, and accounting were all evidenced in this pattern, but it was not a budget system.

The colonies departed from the English tradition after the Revolutionary War. They created fiscal systems from which the executive was excluded. Power was vested in various legislative arrangements lodged in the newly independent colonies. As the result of a fear of central government, congressional powers under the Articles of Confederation were very weak. The fear was evident in the manner in which powers were delegated to both the executive and legislative branches. The colonists were also averse to a system of national taxation. Taxation imposed a special hardship on the colonies because hard coinage were scarce and bills or letters of credit used irregularly. Consequently, the colonies were chronically short of cash and coinage schemes abounded. During the Revolution borrowing and promising to pay either with bills of credit or by coining paper money became endemic as the colonists pursued the war and made expenditures without tax revenues. Washington's continuing struggle to adequately equip his armies is well known, with the winter at Valley Forge standing for all time as a symbol of heroic efforts to contend with a new nation's ineffectual and rudimentary governmental systems. As Vincent J. Browne observes:

> Until the framing of the Constitution, the future of the States was almost as much imperiled by financial indiscretions as it had been previously jeopardized by the forces of George III.[9]

The costs of war were great. Thomas Jefferson estimated those costs at $140 million from 1775 to 1783. By contrast, the operating budget in 1784 was $457,000. Bills of credit were issued both by the states and by Congress from 1775 to 1779. Bills of credit rapidly depreciated. In 1790 Congress was forced to admit that a dollar of paper money was worth less than two cents and passed a resolution to redeem bills of credit at one fortieth their face value.[10] Paper currency did not become legal tender again until after the Civil War.

Operating Budgets		*Expenditures*[11] *1775–1783*	*Bills of Credit*
1784	457,000	$140,000,000	1775–1779
1785	404,000	(Jefferson, 1786)	Federal 241,000,000
1786	446,000	$134,645,000	State 209,000,000
1787	417,000	(Hamilton, 1790)	
1788	326,000		

The Articles of Confederation provided that revenues were to be raised from a direct tax on property in proportion to the value of all land within each state, according to a method stipulated by Congress. These limitations upon Congressional taxing power left it dependent upon the states. Congress was not disposed to provide effective fiscal leadership, at least in part because Congress was debating the question of its own leverage regarding fiscal power. Congress was attempting to be both executive and legislative in a system where the preponderance of power was held by the individual states. Not only was this a departure from the English tradition but it was a model of government that would be short-lived in this country.

Constitutional government began, then, with a long history of British practices further shaped by both the inefficiencies of the Confederation and the cost of the Revolutionary War. If American institutions were shaped by an antiexecutive trend, they were also shaped by the chaotic nature of legislative government under the Articles of Confederation. This period was marked by extraordinary negligence, wastefulness, disorder, and corruption, as Congress or its committees prepared all revenue and appropriation estimates, legislated them, and then attempted to exercise exacting control of the accounts.[12]

Nonetheless, there was an indication of things to come when, in this period of rule by legislative committee, Congress created the post of Superintendent of Finance in early 1781. This was a new approach to the budget process, intended to overcome the suspicions of a single executive. Robert Morris, the first Superintendent of Finance, was charged with oversight of the public debt, expenditures, revenues, and accounts to the end that he would "report plans for improving and regulating the finances, and for establishing order and economy in the expenditure of the public money . . . ,"[13] as well as oversight of budget execution, purchasing and processing, and collecting delinquent accounts owed the United States.

The legislation itself has been called "a bit radical for the times," because of the vast authority it delegated to one man.[14] Morris's pressure for revenue collection seemed to have angered some members of Congress; consequently, in 1784, a Treasury Board or committee was established. However, the benefits derived from a single able, executive head equipped with broad powers had been seen, and the pattern would reappear later. As a practical matter, the whole period of Confederation was a time of experimentation designed within a context of antimonarchical rule. If the events of this period seem somewhat confusing in direction, let it be remembered that there existed no model financial system to lead or follow. If William Pitt the Younger's approach was the model, let it be remembered that he was the contemporary of Morris and the Founding Fathers and did not take office until after Morris, and that Pitt's power would be exercised in a system where tradition still lent the balance of power to the Crown. Pitt was the king's minister. The Americans were busy negotiating the mechanics of representative government.

Constitutional Government

The Constitution sets forth four qualifications on spending power:

1. No money shall be drawn from the Treasury but in consequence of appropriation.
2. A regular statement and account of all receipts and expenditures must be rendered from time to time.
3. No appropriations to support the army shall run for longer than two years.
4. All expenditures shall be made for the general welfare.[15]

The first two points contained in Article I, Section 8 of the Constitution are the cornerstones of the budget process. On the revenue side, all money bills were directed to originate in the House because of its proportional and direct representation of the people. The role of the Senate was debated, with the compromise that the Senate could concur with or propose amendments to revenue bills. Fiscal power would be shaped within an environment where the legislature was expected to be supreme and the states were expected to be jealous guardians of their powers.

Under the impact of the Revolution, planning had been nonexistent, management had been a legislative responsibility, and control for propriety was honored more in its absence than in its presence. The period from 1789 to 1800 marked the movement toward executive management and perhaps could be called the first stage in budget reform. The talents of Alexander Hamilton did much to shape this period.

Hamilton was a man of no mean achievement. He learned applied finance at the age of 11 while a clerk in a countinghouse on the island of St. Croix in the Danish West Indies. He learned quickly and was promoted to bookkeeper and then to manager. Before Hamilton was of age, he had impressed friends with his abilities to the extent that they sponsored him in a course of studies, first at a preparatory school and then at the predecessor to Columbia University in New York. Here he quickly gained a reputation as an adroit protagonist for the cause of the American colonies.[16]

In 1776 he won George Washington's eye with his conspicious bravery as a provincial artillery captain at the Battle of Trenton. Washington used him as a staff officer until 1781 when Hamilton, chafing under the limitations of staff routines, seized upon a trivial quarrel to break with Washington and leave his staff position. Washington seems to have understood his impetuous subordinate well. He gave Hamilton command of a battalion that attacked a British stronghold at the seige of Yorktown in October of 1781, a seige that ultimately became the decisive battle of the Revolutionary War.

During the 1780s, Hamilton practiced law in New York City and was active in Congressional politics and arguments for a strong central government. Hamilton believed that English government as then constituted under George III should be the American model. Hamilton proposed a president elected for life, who would exercise an absolute veto over the legislature. The central government would appoint the state governors, who would have an absolute power over state legislation. The judiciary would be composed of a supreme court whose justices would have life tenure. The legislature would consist of a Senate, elected for life, and a lower house, elected for three years. In this system the states would have virtually no power.

Hamilton's ideas seem to have had little influence upon the Constitutional Convention. However, when opponents attacked the document brought forth by the convention, Hamilton, with James Madison and John Jay, authored *The Federalist,* a collection of eighty-five essays that were widely read, helped shape contemporary opinion, and have become one of the classics in American political literature. This, then, was the man Washington appointed Secretary of the Treasury in September of 1789.

Hamilton fused his own goals for a strong central government with the new nation's fiscal needs. His first efforts were directed toward establishing the credit of the new government. His first two reports[17] on public credit urged funding the national debt at full value, the assumption by the federal government of all debts incurred by the states during the Revolution, and a system of taxation to pay for the debts assumed. Strong opposition arose to these proposals, but Hamilton's position prevailed after he made a bargain with Thomas Jefferson, who delivered southern votes in return for Hamilton's support for locating the future capital on the banks of the Potomac.

Hamilton's third report to Congress proposed a national bank, modeled after the Bank of England. Through this proposal, Hamilton saw a chance to knit the concerns of the wealthy and mercantilist classes to the business of the central government. Washington signed the bill into law, establishing the National Bank based, in part, on Hamilton's argument that the Constitution was a source of both enumerated and implied powers, an interpretation used to expand the powers of the Constitution in later years. Hamilton's fourth report to Congress was perhaps the most philosophic and visionary. Influenced by Adam Smith's *The Wealth of Nations 1776,* Hamilton broke new ground by arguing that it was in the interest of the federal government to aid the growth of infant industries through various protective laws and that, in order to aid the general welfare, the federal government was obliged to encourage manufacturing through tax and tariff policy. Hamilton's contemporaries seem to have rejected the latter view; Congress, at least, would have nothing to do with it. Nonetheless, in a little more than two years Hamilton had submitted to Congress four major reports, gaining acceptance of three that funded the national debt at full value, established the nation's credit at home and abroad, created a banking system and a stable currency, and developed a stable tax system, based on excise taxes, to fund steady recovery of the debt and future appropriations. Indeed, Hamilton was to oppose the popular view of engaging in war with England in the mid-1790s, when France and England were at war and England was seizing American ships in the Caribbean. He believed that commerce with England and the import duties it provided were crucial to his program. Hamilton's essays, published in New York newspapers in 1795, helped avoid war with England and at the same time saved Hamilton's revenue system.

These were bitterly contested issues, and groups began to coalesce around them. Hamilton became the leader of one faction, the Federalists, and because Washington supported most of Hamilton's program, he in effect became a Federalist. The two most prominent individuals of the opposition were James Madison in the House of Representatives and Thomas Jefferson in the Cabinet. Madison and Jefferson were the Republican leaders. Hamilton and Jefferson feuded constantly for several years beginning in 1791, as each tried to drive the other from the Cabinet. Finally, tired, stung by criticism of his operation of the Treasury Department, and needing to repair his personal fortunes, Hamilton announced his intentions to resign his post as Secretary of the Treasury at the end of 1794. Hamilton did not, however, retreat to obscurity. He still held presidential ambitions, which were narrowly frustrated, was appointed to high military command, and remained within the inner circle of the political elite before departing center stage, killed in a duel with Aaron Burr in 1804. He made both great accomplishments and bitter enemies.

Hamilton's role in debt management, securing the currency, and providing and defending a stable revenue base mark him as a founding father of the American budgeting system. Without faith in the currency, a credit system, and a revenue base, it is difficult indeed to make any budget system work. The federal taxing power alone was a dramatic change from the system envisioned under the Articles of Confederation, which approximated a contributory position by the separate states hectored by the central government. Only a sure and certain revenue base, providing predictable revenue collections, allows for the creation and maintenance of the modern nation-state. It was Hamilton's genius to direct the United States onto that pathway.

To Congress, Hamilton represented a transitional figure. Before his appointment, the House, in the summer of 1789, had a committee on Ways and Means. But this committee fell into disuse when a Secretary of the Treasury was appointed. At this juncture in history Congress viewed the Treasury Department as a legislative agency and the Secretary of Treasury as its officer.[18] The first appropriations bill for an operating budget came about because the House ordered the Secretary of Treasury to "report to this House an estimate of the sums requisite to be appropriated during the present year; and for satisfying such warrants as have been drawn by the late Board of the Treasury and which may not heretofore have been paid."[19]

When the articles of the Constitution were being debated, Hamilton himself wrote:

> The House of Representatives cannot only refuse, but they alone can propose, the supplies requisite for the support of the government. They, in a word, hold the purse. . . . This power over the purse may, in fact, be regarded as the most complete and effectual weapon with which any constitution can arm the immediate representatives of the people for obtaining a redress for every grievance and for carrying into effect every just and salutary measure.[20]

Whatever the flaws of the act creating a Department of the Treasury, it seems clear that its intent was to make the legislature alone responsible for the budget process. That there was little room for executive leadership is demonstrated in the fact that the act mentions the President only in connection with the appointment and removal of officers. Furthermore, while the act was being debated, opinion was divided over the wording of the duties of the Secretary of the Treasury in respect to whether he was to digest and *report* plans or whether he was to digest and *prepare* plans. Those Congressmen hostile to a strong executive power felt that giving the Secretary the power to digest and report plans would result in taking the initiative away from the House. The Secretary would report only what he had already done; this would deprive the House of its ability to exercise a prior restraint on the actions of the Secretary. The word *report* was deleted and *prepare* inserted and carried by the majority.[21]

Later observers have mistaken Hamilton's approach to appropriation bills as an executive budget system. The traditional model of an executive budget system would encompass a presidential review of departmental documents, revision of estimates, and a unified submission by the President or his agent of those estimates to Congress for approval. Hamilton, as Secretary of the Treasury, did not function in this manner; he acted as an agent of Congress. The development of an executive budget system was a gradual process with a steady line of development toward an executive budget system in 1921.

The first appropriation act was brief and general:

> That there be appropriated for the service of the present year, to be paid out of the monies which arise, either from the requisitions heretofore made upon the several states, or from the duties on impost and tonnage, the following sums, viz. A sum not exceeding two hundred and sixteen thousand dollars for defraying the expenses of the civil list, under the late and present government; a sum not exceeding one hundred and thirty-seven thousand dollars for defraying the expenses of the department of war; a sum not exceeding one hundred and ninety-six thousand dollars for discharging the warrants issued by the late board of Treasury and remaining unsatisfied; and a sum not exceeding ninety-six thousand dollars for paying pensions to invalids.[22]

Although salaries are the largest item in this list, mandated expenditures—bills and pensions—comprise 45 per cent of the budget, defense 21 per cent, and entitlements 14.8 per cent. De facto uncontrollability was high. Again, true to modern practice, this appropriation bill was not the only money bill passed by Congress. Between the summer of 1789 and May of 1792, numerous bills were passed to provide for a variety of expenses, including defense, Indian treaties, debt reduction, and establishment of the federal mint.[23]

The first three general appropriation bills were written in terms of general appropriations, for example, the civil list, the department of war, invalid pensions, the expenses of Congress, and contingent charges upon government. Appropriating by lump sum seemed to cause some resentment among Congressmen. One wrote in his diary of the appropriations bill of 1790:

> The appropriations were all in gross, and to the amount upward of half a million. I could not get a copy of it. I wished to have seen the particulars specified, but such a hurry I never saw before. . . . Here is a general appropriation of above half a million dollars—the particulars not mentioned—the estimates on which it is founded may be mislaid or changed; in fact it is giving the Secretary the money for him to account for as he pleases.[24]

Notwithstanding their general nature, appropriation bills were linked to estimates of expense as specified in other bills. Expenditures for salaries were generally governed by laws enumerating the salary and number of the officers stipulated; for example, five associate supreme court justices at a salary no more than $3,500 per year. Estimates for the military were assumed to control the appropriations voted for the military. Therefore, even though the appropriations were voted in gross, the calculations adding up to the total were assumed to control the total. By 1792 Congress was appropriating money in gross but stipulating what the money was to be used for with "that is to say" clauses; for example, $329,653.56 for the civil list, with a "that is to say" clause followed by specific sums attached to an enumeration of the corresponding general items.[25]

By 1792, Congress was planning in detail and the executive branch accepted that detail, although knowing full well that the dictates of administering might make it imperative to depart from the detailed plans expressed in the appropriation acts. Budgeting by lump sum was not a characteristic of the routine of American government except in case of emergency appropriations.

By 1792, Congress increasingly specified the itemization of appropriation bills, in part as a strategy to control Secretary of the Treasury Hamilton, who was increasingly seen as a member of the executive branch. In 1790, the House had sixty-five members, and most of its business could be carried out as a committee of the whole, but by 1795 it was clear that the Treasury Department could not serve the needs of Congress as well as it could serve the needs of the executive. Therefore, Congress reinstituted the Committee on Ways and Means, initially as a select or special committee, and by 1802 as a standing committee. During this period, Woolcott, Hamilton's successor at Treasury, was embroiled in an increasingly bitter argument with Congress over the transfer of appropriations. Although Congress could appropriate in very specific terms, it could not stop the administration from transferring from one account to another when the situation seemed to warrant such transfer.

The War and Navy Departments seemed particularly prone to transfer funds, thereby dissolving the discipline of detailed itemization.

In 1801, when the Federalists were defeated and the Republicans took office, Thomas Jefferson spoke to the need for increased itemization of expenditure in appropriations. Nonetheless, the transfer of appropriations was an accepted practice in the administration, albeit an illegal one.[26] Jefferson himself made the Louisiana Purchase after a liberal interpretation of executive authority to issue stock when government revenues were insufficient to cover necessary expenditures. Congress's insistence on itemization led to deficiencies in accounts. By 1800, however, the initial pattern had been set. The debt was honored, national credit established, a currency and national banking system had been created, a revenue system set up with appropriation bills passed linked to specific estimates for specific purposes, some flexibility made between military and civil expenditures, and a recognition established that transfer of funds between categories was technically illegal but necessary to meet contingencies unforeseen at the time of appropriations.

The House held major control of the purse. By 1802, it had developed a standing committee to deal with revenues and appropriations, while on the executive side, the Secretary of Treasury would become more and more the President's agent in shaping appropriations bills, collecting revenues, and seeing to debt management. Both the legislature and the executive were elected by and responsible to the people. Rudimentary and disconnected as it seems from modern perspectives, no other country had such a budget system, nor would this country again repeat this process of change and adaptation.

Making the System Work: 1800–1921

The transfer of power to Jefferson and the Republicans marked the end of the creation of the Republic, the end of the process of separating from England and the setting up of a new government. Much remained to be done, but many of the basic mechanisms were now in place. In fiscal affairs the federal government had established its powers to tax and to budget, as well as to issue notes of credit when revenues did not match expenditures. Budgeting was in the main a legislative power. The Department of the Treasury was originally conceived as the legislature's assistant. Budgeting power in the legislature was basically held in the House, which was small enough so that it could operate as a committee of the whole. As the Treasury more and more served the President, Treasury's power in Congress declined, and Congress chose its own internal review body, the Committee on Ways and Means. This committee would gain great power. During the course of the nineteenth century, appropriation bills would be sent to other committees as the Ways and Means Committee work load became heavier or as political factors dictated. After the Civil War, a committee on appropriations would be created. When it used retrenchment powers to reach into substantive legislation under the jurisdiction of other committees, appropriation bills were factored out to several committees, thereby diminishing the power of the appropriations committees. Thus legislative forms changed, but budgeting maintained eminence as a vital legislative process.[27]

The issues changed with the times during the nineteenth century. Early debates seemed to focus on the necessity of budget flexibility in administering the War and Navy Departments. Without these powers the new nation could not long survive. Andrew Jackson's presidency changed the focus to internal improvements. Jackson, a conservative, was against extravagance and averred that many of the internal improvement bills were passed to rectify specific situations but did not necessarily secure the general welfare. He tried to veto these bills while Congress sought ways to pass them as riders on other legislation. The War Between the States caused great fiscal strain on the Union, and the decades after the war were marked by fierce battles over pensions and veterans' benefits. It is instructive to note that the last Revolutionary War benefit was paid out 123 years after that war was over.[27]

Although tariffs, customs, and excises were good sources of revenue, they were not large enough to underwrite the costs of wars, were sometimes changed for political reasons that had nothing to do with balancing expenditure needs, and did not constitute a stable revenue base. Generally, throughout the nineteenth century revenue and expenditures were not coordinated. In addition to the general appropriations bills, there were numerous other bills legislating appropriations in each session of Congress. Indeed, it can be argued that an imperative to balance expenditures against revenues did not exist on the legislative level until after the passage of the Congressional Budget and Impoundment Act of 1974.

Congress also struggled with other problems, including deficiency appropriations, surpluses that departments carried forward into the next fiscal year, transfers from one service to another, and expenditures made without the authority of law. Although Congress legislated against these various budgetary sins, it also recognized that it had to leave the Treasury Department some flexibility or it would have to appropriate sums for additional items or expenditures in order to provide for unforeseen contingencies. Congressional budgeting was effective but not necessarily efficient.

The Budget and Accounting Act of 1921 is frequently observed to be the watershed in the pursuit of executive budgetary efficiency. The period from 1789 to 1921 is sometimes dismissed as being unimportant. The functions of government were few, revenues small, and debates focused on what should be itemized. Because taxes were drawn from tariffs intended to protect infant industries, and expenditures spent on pensions or internal improvements, legislators could appease all by both increasing spending and tariffs. Agencies became expert in the art of the coercive deficiency, spending the money on a "good" project and then going to Congress for the remainder, confident that their own particular committee would recommend additional appropriations. The crucial variable in this picture emerged as the relationship between the committee chairman and the agency head. Although this is an arguable interpretation of events, it is a cavalier treatment of the effort that both Congress and the executive expended on budget preparation and control.

Louis Fisher says:

> We are led to understand that, prior to 1921, Presidents had little to do in framing the financial program of the federal government. Individual spending agencies transmitted their budget requests to Congress in what was called a "book of estimates." The Secretary of the Treasury could have played a coordinating role, but studies conclude that his handling of budget estimates was routine and perfunctory. According to this point of view, Presidents and their Secretaries of the Treasury were passive bystanders during those years, mechanically forwarding budget estimates to Congress without revision or comment.[28]

Fisher suggests that during the nineteenth century a number of Presidents revised departmental estimates before they were sent to Congress, including John Quincy Adams, Martin Van Buren, John Tyler, James K. Polk, James Buchanan, Ulysses S. Grant, and Grover Cleveland, and were assisted in this task by a number of Secretaries of the Treasury. As has been observed earlier, although the budget system was basically a legislative budget system, the executive branch did play a role in its execution.

The first decade of the twentieth century was pivotal for the exercise of budgetary power. Government revenues based on customs and excise taxes were insufficient for the task of achieving manifest destiny. Although the budget had been in a surplus position from the conclusion of the Civil War to 1893, some policymakers worried that the economy had become penurious and prevented the assumption of new needs. The Spanish American War and the expenses of the creation of the Panama Canal created budget deficits. Moreover, customs revenues began to decline. The federal budget was in a deficit position for eleven of the seventeen years from 1894 to 1911, including five of the seven years from 1904 through 1910. The point to be made is that the old revenue system was inadequate to the task of funding America's new expanding world role. The passage of the sixteenth Amendment permitting an income tax alleviated some of the difficulty.

However, it created another problem. Now, with direct taxation, policymakers came to fear that taxpayers would be even more concerned about where their money was being spent. Thus, the income tax law must also be seen as part of the pressure for budget reform and a stronger executive budget presence. In the years from 1919 through 1921, the income tax provided over 57 per cent of the federal government's revenues. The year 1921 marked not only for the passage of the Budget Act but the dominance of a major new revenue source.

The debate over strengthening the presidential spending power was essentially complete by 1912, with the report of the Taft Commission on Economy and Efficiency. The Commission's position was succinctly stated: "[. . . the budget was the only] effective means whereby the Executive may be made responsible for getting before the country definite, well-considered, comprehensive programs with respect to which the legislature must also assume responsibility either for action or inaction."[29] In 1912, Taft submitted to Congress the report, along with a plan for a national budget system, but his party did not control the House during that session of Congress, and the two branches of government could not agree on a new budget process.

Budget reform was further delayed at the national level by the First World War, but reform continued apace at the local and state levels. Indeed, some observers have suggested that budget reform during this period in the American context began at the local level. Reform efforts resulted from indignation over corruption, graft, and mismanagement prevalent in local governments, which was exposed by journalists and good government movements, and supported by the Progressive party. Budget reform complemented such other innovations as city manager and commission government forms, and initiative, referendum, recall, and short-ballot electoral procedures. Budget reform may be considered a local affair that carried the federal government with it.[30]

The fiscal stress of American commitments to World War I and Woodrow Wilson's own interest in budget reform precipitated the adoption of the executive budget process. In his 1917 annual message to Congress, Wilson stressed his party's platform on budget reform. Although reform seems to have been possible in any of these years, Wilson chose to wait until the end of World War I. After the peace treaty had been signed, he opined that he would now have a better grasp of the continuing level of defense spending, the effect of the disposal of surplus military property, and the impact of demobilization upon the economy.[31] In 1918 and 1919 a series of bills intended to reform the budget power were passed, and by 1921 Congress had created and passed the Budget and Accounting Act.

This bill created the Bureau of the Budget (BOB), to be located in the Department of the Treasury with a Director appointed by and responsible to the President. The Bureau was given the authority to "assemble, correlate, revise, reduce, or increase" departmental budget estimates.[33] In view of the Bureau's later move from Treasury to the Executive Office, history often judges this first placement harshly. However, the intention of the proponents of the Act was to avoid unnecessary friction between the President and his cabinet officers over conflicts within the BOB in order to avoid setting the Bureau against the more powerful cabinet officers, and by placing the Bureau in the Department of the Treasury to facilitate the coordination of expenditures and revenues.[34]

The initial accomplishments of the Bureau of the Budget were not insignificant. Its first Director, General Dawes, instituted significant technical innovations, including the concept of reserves and an allotments system. He also engendered a climate of economy and efficiency. Dawes also adopted a technical and nonpartisan profile, describing employees of the BOB as akin to stokers in a ship's engine room, not steering the ship but simply feeding the fires that drove the engines of government. Dawes' stance defused some potential political problems, but the true usefulness and meaning of the Bureau of the Budget would not be seen until the stress of the Depression captured the attention of the nation. In a sense, the turmoil of the first two decades of the twentieth century was followed by a period of relative fiscal calm by the 1920s. The innovations that the deficits of the period of 1903 to 1920 created would not be tested and used until the mid-1930s.

Neutral Competence: 1920–1970

One way to look at budget power is to envision it as a tool that operationalizes fiscal values. These fiscal values are basically economizing values. As stated by Paul Appleby, they include fiscal sense and fiscal coordination: "Fiscal sense and fiscal coordination are certainly values. The budgeting organization is designed to give representation in institutional interaction and decision-making to this set of values."[35]

Appleby argues that the budget function is inherently and preponderantly negative because it is against program expenditure and expansion. He goes on to argue that this is proper because the program agencies and pressure groups are so extensive that there is no danger the values they represent will be overlooked or smothered by budgeteers.

Appleby concedes that a budget bureau cannot always be negative, for there are ways to save money by spending money, and the bureau has to be on the lookout for those occasions. In the main, however, the agencies will be the aggressors, pushed by their clienteles and tempering their requests by their judgment of what is wise and practical. The budget bureau is at the center of this struggle, and yet it is removed from direct contact with many of the political pressures. Consequently, the budget bureau should act as a counterweight to ensure that economizing fiscal values are entered into the decision-making calculus.

Two problems have haunted the Bureau of the Budget from its inception. First, if the whole structure is dedicated to economizing, then the role of a budget bureau is preempted. With its role preempted, the usefulness of a budget bureau diminishes. This relationship was true of the period from 1921 until the 1930s, and again during the Eisenhower years, from 1952 to 1960. Secondly, when a budget bureau is very good at what it does, it tends to get drawn into the role of general staff advisor, or even roles that would seem to be more political and belonging to, for example, the White House political staff. This was probably true of the BOB during the Johnson and Nixon years from 1964 through 1972. When a budget bureau serves as political advisor, representation of fiscal values may tend to get suppressed by the necessity of offering political alternatives. In 1967 a BOB self-study described the Bureau's nonpolitical professionalism as an Achilles' heel. It acknowledged that although examiners were generally knowledgeable about their program, they did not have a political point of view. This had been seen as the height of professional behavior. The administrator merely presented the alternatives, and the politicians would make the right decision, a view dating back into public administration history, at least as far as the Prussian general staff model was concerned, and typified by the folklore the Bureau perpetuated about itself.

"BOB officials often told the story that if a martian army marched on the Capitol, everyone in Washington would flee to the hills, except the Budget bureau staff, which would stay behind and prepare for an orderly transition in government."[36]

Neutral competence was the keystone of the philosophy of the BOB. The Bureau stood ready to serve the master with fidelity and expertise. However, in the late 1960s this was not enough. The Bureau was reorganized in 1970 to add political acumen by layering political appointees over the career staff.[37] After 1970, the Bureau's representation of fiscal values would be filtered through nets of political values before they reached the President, a change that may have improved the advice the Bureau could give the President but probably changed the character of neutral competence. Gone was the pure technician.

This may well have been a necessary change. Allen Schick observes that the Bureau as a simple representative of fiscal values could serve every President with "fidelity, but it could effectively serve only a caretaker President. It could not be quick or responsive enough for an activist President who wants to keep tight hold over program initiatives."[38] As the functions and responsibilities of the Presidency changed, so did the role of the budget bureau.

Jesse Burkhead has called the institution of budgetary systems in the United States a revolutionary change. Burkhead argues: "The installation of a budget system is implicit recognition that a government has positive responsibilities to perform and that it intends to perform them."[39]

To do this would mean reorganizing administrative authority in the executive branch, says Burkhead, and an increase in publicly organized economic power relative to privately organized economic power. Thus, the institution of budgetary systems in the United States clashed with customary doctrine about public versus private economic responsibility, but more importantly it was fundamentally at odds with the basic organizing precepts of the founding fathers. The budget system was an integrating system that allowed positive movement toward goals by relatively small groups of participants within the political system. It had to, or it could not be an efficient system. But this kind of organizational efficiency ran counter to the great Constitutional doctrines of separation of powers and checks and balances. Consequently, Burkhead suggests that not only would the practices of government have to be altered before budget systems could be installed and operated but their development and installation alone were "revolutionary" in the context of American society. Burkhead concludes that although budget systems need not be synonymous with an increase in governmental activities (budget systems can be used for retrenchment), their installation is synonymous with a clarification of responsibility in government. It is this framework of goal accomplishment that makes the installation of a budget system so important. The Bureau of the Budget was to be the key to this system.

What then happened to the Bureau in its early years? For almost a decade after Dawes, the Bureau had no great mission. It spent its time in trivial gestures toward economy in an era when the great impulse toward economy was generated elsewhere, either as a result of the winding down of expenses of World War I or because of the philosophies represented by conservative Presidents. For example, the Bureau's mandate included authority to conduct government-wide studies to secure greater economy and efficiency, but it ignored that aspect of its role. Instead, it proudly announced that it had taken its "own medicine," spending little more than half of its appropriation in 1921 and indulging in such activities as checking employees' desks for excessive use of official stationery, paper clips, and other supplies, and directing federal employees to use the Army radio network instead of making long-distance telephone calls and to take the upper berth in Pullman train cars when traveling because they were cheaper.[40]

Faced with the depression in the 1930s, Franklin D. Roosevelt could have strengthened the BOB, but he chose as his first director a conservative with whom he could not work. In 1934, the BOB remained a small, rigid, and inactive agency attached to the Treasury Department. It, however, became the logical candidate for expansion.

As a result of the reorganization initiatives contained in the 1937 report of the Brownlow Committee, the Bureau of the Budget was transferred into the newly created Executive Office of the President.[41] This was done under reorganization Plan No. 1 of 1939, which marked the beginning of a truly effective budget bureau in the United States. Under Roosevelt's administration, the BOB employed various fiscal management tools, including practical control over allotments, central legislative clearance, and bill analysis. It was, however, in 1939 a small agency with about forty staff. By the end of World War II, the staff would increase to 600, representing an expansion unmatched before or since.

The halcyon days of the Bureau of the Budget existed from 1939 through the end of the 1940s. During this time, the Bureau built and held a reputation for unsurpassed excellence as a neutral, analytic power operating as a staff instrument for the executive. The reputation for excellence gained during these years of depression and war would mantle the Bureau into the late 1960s. By then it would become tainted with the politics of Watergate, accused of exerting too much power and failing as an intergovernmental program manager for the multiplicity of programs resulting from Johnson's quest for the Great Society.[42] During this time, however, for better or worse, it was the executive budget-making power, and if it were at its height during the 1940s, it still functioned as such in 1921, just as it does today.

The search for substantive reforms of the budget must also be seen as part of the process shaping a positive executive budget system.

Substantive Budget Reforms: 1949–1974

Historical American budgeting systems have represented object-of-expenditure classifications, with each classification given a budget line; hence the name *line item*. Typical line-item objects include such expenditure items as personnel, travel, rent, office supplies, and the other supporting expenses necessary to support personnel, which was the single largest item in most government budgets until well into the twentieth century. Line-item budgets focus on the inputs bought to perform the functions of government. Line-item budgeting is easy to adapt to different situations, and easily understood. It is appropriate for governments faced with simple, stable tasks. It does not, however, lend itself easily to analysis of what government is doing. It does not coordinate the costs of objects purchased with the services performed or the outputs accomplished.

As government became more complex and its responsibilities for providing a better quality of life increased, the need for budget systems that measured government's impact became more and more apparent. Moreover, as the study of administration, both in the private and public sector, progressed, the budget function fell under increased scrutiny as a managerial tool to help the executive manage government or a large corporation. The trend accelerated in the 1930s and the 1940s with the theories promulgated by the scientific management movement in the private sector and the recognition that public administration was a career field for practitioners as well as an academic discipline with its own theory base for the public sector. During World War II, many of the leading academics moved to Washington to assist the administrative process and took their experiences back to their universities.

The budget power was expanding and defining its responsibilities. The taxing power got used during World War II to prevent inflation through extremely high marginal rates, a signal that the federal government was committed to maintaining stability in the economy and not just in purchasing inputs. This trend was accelerated with the passage of the Full Employment Act of 1946, which in essence made the President manager of the economy. This legislation entrusted the President with the responsibility to maintain full employment levels. Later, in the 1960s, the President was routinely held responsible for managing supply and demand, using macroeconomic tools to keep the economy on a stable course with neither too much inflation nor too much unemployment. In 1964, on the advice of macroeconomic advisors, the President asked for and received a tax cut that actually resulted in increased revenues.[43] This may have marked the high-water mark of macroeconomic management, inasmuch as the economy has since then become increasingly less tractable and more open to external shocks like oil price increases.

Currently, perhaps the major budgetary responsibility incumbent upon a President is managing the economy, irrespective of the extent of his power to actually affect the economy. On the expenditure side, the passage of the Social Security Act in 1935 and its subsequent expansion has led to commitments for future spending both to its beneficiaries and to other programs developed to transfer income directly to those whose standard of living is below an acceptable minimum level. These programs commit the government to future expenditures that are not controllable without changing benefits in a separate legislative process. A majority of the annual budget has become uncontrollable.[44]

More importantly, with macroeconomic management and social welfare spending growing in importance, the budget power has been subject to a revolutionary refocus of responsibility. This process began with the New Deal programs, was intensified with World War II, and was confirmed by the period of the Great Society. Defense, one of the standard categories of the American budget, gained impetus with the dawning of the atomic age. No longer was defense spending a matter of protecting borders or projecting forces to battlegrounds thousands of miles from the United States. When Russia became an atomic power in the 1950s and then succeeded in beating the United States into space in the same decade, the defense establishment was confronted with defending America from atomic war. Budgeting for this mission required an adjustment so vast as to be revolutionary. Moreover, the problem of defense budgeting was exacerbated by the traditional separations between the armed services, where rivalries sometimes produced duplication and waste. The budgeting apparatus was also used to maintain and improve military services.[45] What budget system could embrace these enhanced roles for government and cope with these developing strains?

The most current sequence of budget reform starts with performance budgeting and concludes with zero-based budgeting. Performance budgeting[46] connects inputs to outputs. It is typified by indicators of cost per unit of work accomplished and focuses on the activities of government. Its history reaches back to the Taft Commission of 1912, its implementation in the Department of Agriculture in 1934 and the Tennessee Valley Authority in the later 1930s, as well as its being strongly recommended by the Hoover Commission in 1949. In 1949, Congress required that the budget estimates of the Department of Defense be presented in performance categories. Performance budgeting was a manager's budget tool.

Program budgeting[47] is a variation of performance budgeting in which information is collected by program categories without the details of the performance-budget construction. Activities are grouped by agency, and then by mission, purpose, or function. This was a transitional type of system used in the Department of Defense and other places.

Programming, Planning, Budgeting[48] is a thorough planning system that incorporates many sets of plans and documentation and draws upon various disciplines, including economics, planning, cybernetics, and administration, in order to set goals and then derive benefit/cost ratios that indicate which goal to choose. Budgeting becomes a simple matter of costing out the goal chosen. This system reached its epogee under Robert McNamara in the Department of Defense in the early 1960s. The complexity of this system made it difficult to implement in other departments of the federal government, and thus it was a short-lived experiment in budgeting.

Management by Objectives (MBO) is a work-planning system, equivalent in some respects to performance budgeting. It was used by the Nixon administration to bring business principles to government. It featured setting program objectives and stressed evaluation of program accomplishments in contractual process between supervisor and subordinate. Its failure was in large part due to the stigma of the excesses occasioned by Nixon administration.

Zero-based budgeting[50] features zero-based analysis, decision packages, and funding at various levels of effort, including levels below the accepted budget base. It is a retrenchment-oriented system used in many states and local jurisdictions. Many consider ZBB too small a system to encompass the problems of the modern welfare state, the Social Security system, or even the major elements of economic management. In 1977, Jimmy Carter mandated its use by all federal departments and agencies.

Currently, the federal budget apparatus uses an amalgamation of many of these techniques. Line-item budgeting is an underlying theme, with elements from other budget systems adopted to suit individual agency preferences. One of the clear trends seems to be toward multiyear budgets directed by both the President and Congress. Some requests for authorization are moving toward annual review in an effort to reduce the number of uncontrollable accounts, while planning appears to be moving toward multiyear consideration.

Moreover, recent federal budgets have been dominated by the macro problems of inflation and unemployment, and by huge deficits. These factors have forced the budgetary system to adopt a crisis posture at the top, while the more mundane agency-level routines of budgeting are carried out by using managerial budgeting systems with no guiding theory. What we learn from this experience is that theories are sometimes replaced by events and that no one system is appropriate for all events, but consideration must be given to the use of some elements of several systems. It is also useful to reflect that the modern welfare state provides a vast array of services and is held responsible for societal welfare. Some budget systems simply do not lend themselves to these responsibilities. From this perspective, zero-based budgeting and management by objectives would seem to be less useful as national budgeting systems.

Congressional Budgeting Revisited: 1974

Perhaps the reason why no other grand budget system has sprung forth on the executive side is that Congress reasserted its power with the Congressional Budget and Impoundment Control Act of 1974. This Act sought to correct certain abuses of presidential impoundment powers, but more importantly, it also sought to reorganize the Congressional budget power to give Congress a better chance at full partnership in budgeting for the modern welfare state. If the Full Employment Act of 1946 gave the presidency responsibility for managing the economy, it was the Congressional Budget and Impoundment Act of 1974 that extended the same opportunity to Congress. In addition, Congress equipped itself with more analytic power by creating the Congressional Budget Office, comprised of a neutral staff imbued with a sense of high calling and professionalism similar to that found in the Bureau of the Budget of the 1940s but in a somewhat more complex fiscal world.

The Congressional Budget Act centralized the budget power in the House and Senate Budget committees. These two committees have the responsibility to develop a target resolution in June of each year containing detailed appropriations to guide the work of the appropriations committees. The target resolution shows the overall situation, including the level of spending by area, taxing projections, and the level of debt forecasted. Then, in September, the budget committees were to shepherd a second resolution through Congress that matched the early planning target to the final appropriation bills. Through the reconciliation process, these committees may also ask Congress to tell its appropriation and taxing committees what and where reductions are appropriate in order to reconcile the final bills against the target resolution. In June of 1981, Congress attached reconciliation instructions to the first resolution and in effect dictated what would be done in later appropriations committee work.

The reconciliation instruction of June 1981 marked a turning point in the American budgetary process. For the first time in the history of the United States, the legislature set budget targets for taxing, spending, and debt, and thereby had a sense of what the national budget ought to be before it started enacting budget bills. At no other time since 1789 was this done. After 190 years of titular vesting of the power of the purse in Congress, Congress organized itself to pursue a budget prospectively, rather than adding up the total appropriations and expenditures and calling it a budget.

The 1981 budget was basically an executive budget, but it was endorsed in Congress only after a bitter struggle. However, Congress used its newly developed budget power to develop Congressional budgets basically different from the proposed executive budgets of 1980, the final Carter budget, and again in 1982, the second Reagan budget.[52] Congress has exercised its budget power both with and against the executive. Although the power to prepare and submit budgets remains with the executive, as formidable a power it is, Congress has evolved into a powerful and systematic modifier of budgets.

Congressional modifications have not been piecemeal modifications.

From 1945 to 1970, Congressional scrutiny of budgets was characterized by students of budgeting as one of incremental review and marginal adjustments by budget committees to whom the other members of Congress deferred. Incremental behavior was rational, according to Aaron Wildavsky, because in reviewing that in which he or she was most interested, members allowed individual self-interest to protect the public good. Richard Fenno documented the success of final adoption of appropriations committees' recommendations as being 87 per cent. Ira Sharkansky observed that congressional behaviors could be summarized as the concept of contained specialization-elite status, specialized expertise, deference to the acknowledged experts, and conflict management.[53]

During this era of stability of review, enormous changes were taking place within society, and the composition of the budget reflected it. Social service expenditures increased dramatically. Although each bill was intensely scrutinized, no one knew what all the appropriations bills would be until the end of the fiscal year. As macroeconomic management became more important to the nation, Congress had no apparent forum of its own to make and enforce economic policy through the budget. Thus, the budget process became less and less useful to the realities of managing a modern welfare state. Scizing on the Nixon abuses of the impoundment power to reorganize the budget process and making itself a full partner in the process once more was an outcome not totally anticipated by Congress. Some thought that Congress had merely changed the fiscal year in an attempt to give itself more time to look at budget bills to offset its difficulty in passing them on time. Others saw it as a weighting of the budget power in favor of Congress at the expense of the executive. Although the act does improve congressional potential, it need not be said that it usurps executive prerogatives. There is more than enough budget power for both branches to share. Congress does become a powerful critic, however. It has the power to redevelop an executive budget when the President's original submission does not match congressional interpretations of the needs of a particular year.

Concluding Observations

Many dysfunctions still exist within the budgetary process.[54] From 1962 to 1981, 85 per cent of the appropriations bills for federal agencies were passed after the beginning of the fiscal year. Passage of the Congressional Budget Act has reduced this percentage to 65[55] but has not eliminated the problem. It still disrupts agency work-load planning cycles, especially those involving new programs. Critics have suggested that the budget is made on an installment plan, emphasizing continuing resolutions in Congress and deferrals and rescissions from the Oval Office.

The Gramm-Rudman-Hollings Act of 1985 further complicated budget choice even as it simplified choices. By linking deficit reduction to across-the-board cuts, it struck at the heart of the budget decision: selective choice.

Other dysfunctions include the growth of off-budget spending, the growth of tax expenditures, and the impact of interest expenditures caused by the burgeoning national debt. While there is constant traffic in supplemental appropriations for various purposes, the Department of Defense carries over huge sums in unobligated balances. About 60 per cent of the budget is available without annual appropriation because of social service spending and entitlement programs. These programs, in addition to defense, interest payments, and civil service salaries, make the budget uncontrollable about 90 per cent of the time. The same factors indicate that for each annual increment a high percentage of the increase will be uncontrollable. Congress's choice of alternatives is limited or guided by its previous choices.

So long as social welfare spending and defense appropriations comprise so large a portion of the budget, it will remain relatively intractable. In defense, expenditures escalate as systems become more complex and more expensive than originally calculated. In social welfare, expenditures have to be made when people qualify. Definitions of the point at which people may fend for themselves may shift somewhat, but the basic policy is unlikely to be changed. The basic commitment to a Social Security system that provides for a dignified retirement should remain intact. All of these factors only compound the budget problem. The struggle over defense and social welfare programs may seem grim and repetitious, but the stakes are high and worth the struggle.

What else is there to observe in 200 years of budget history? Budgeting began in this country as a legislative enterprise. The people exercised the power of the purse through elected representatives. Effective representation of demands was emphasized over the needs of executive efficiency. Our experience with a prominent executive budget power is relatively limited. In periods of extreme crisis, the legislature has tended to cede power to the executive and reclaim it after the crisis has passed. Although there is a good deal of conflict in the budget process, there is also a good deal of reconciliation and adaptation.

Of the men and eras we have surveyed, Alexander Hamilton seems to have been uniquely placed. History has tended to give more prominence to Charles Dawes, the first Director of the Bureau of the Budget. It is clear that at some time during the midtwentieth century the budget power assumed burdens that made it different in kind from anything that had gone before. The coming together of responsibilities for social welfare, macroeconomic management, and defense strategies precipitated the modification. No convenient date appears to mark this change, but it probably occurred somewhere between 1946 and 1964.

Ironically, the most important function the federal budget has at this juncture in history is the pursuit of economic stability, what this chapter has called macroeconomic management. It is a goal that the federal government attempts to achieve by making miniscule shifts in the federal budget to stimulate contraction or expansion of the economy. Such a goal may be outside the ability of a single nation to achieve.

The long sweep of history teaches us that techniques of budgeting are not as important as the purposes for which the money is spent. The process itself is a resilient and flexible procedure able to accommodate changing conditions. Part of the genius of the American character resides in its impulse to find a better way but not to depart radically from tried and tested methods. Social engineers, rationalists, and autocrats might have done better, but experience with the budget process leaves us with a demonstration that representative government works. Government of the people, by the people, and for the people is a strong and durable form of government.

Endnotes

1. Jesse Burkhead, *Government Budgeting* (New York: John Wiley, 1959), p. 3.
2. Vincent J. Browne, *The Control of the Public Budget* (Washington, D C: Public Affairs Press, 1949), p. 12.
3. Mark A. Thomson, *A Constitutional History of England* (London: Methuen & Co., 1938), Volume IV, p. 206.
4. Aaron Wildavsky, *Budgeting: A Comparative Theory of Budgetary Processes* (Boston: Little, Brown, 1975), p. 272.
5. The standard biography on Pitt has been that of J. Holland Rose, *William Pitt and National Revival* (1911), *William Pitt and the Great War* (1911), and *Pitt and Napoleon* (1912) (London: G. Bell and Sons).
6. Browne, p. 15.
7. See Leonard W. Labaree, *Royal Government in America: A Study of the British Colonial System before 1783* (New Haven, CT: Yale University Press, 1930, 1958), p. 35.
8. Browne, p. 16.
9. Browne, p. 17.
10. Davis R. Dewey, *Financial History of the United States* (New York: Longmans, Green, 1931, 1968), p. 36.
11. Browne, pp. 18–19.
12. Albert S. Bolles, *The Financial History of the United States from 1774 to 1789* (New York: D. Appleton, 1896, 1969), p. 358.

13. Fred W. Powell, "Control of Federal Expenditures" (Washington, D C: The Brookings Institution, 1939), p. 33.
14. Browne, pp. 21–22.
15. Daniel T. Selko, *The Federal Financial System* (Washington, D C: The Brookings Institution, 1940), p. 45.
16. For an excellent biography of Hamilton, see John C. Miller, *Alexander Hamilton: Portrait in Paradox* (1959). For an excellent summary of Hamilton's thought on executive leadership, see L. K. Caldwell, "Alexander Hamilton: Advocate of Executive Leadership," *Public Administration Review* 4 (Spring) 1944; reprinted in James W. Fesler, *American Public Administration: Patterns of the Past* (Washington, D C: ASPA, 1982), pp. 71–89.
17. Hamilton's program was outlined in four reports: *Reports on the Public Credit* of January 14, 1790 and December 13, 1790; *The Report on a National Bank,* December 14, 1790; *The Report on Manufactures,* submitted to Congress on December 5, 1791.
18. Browne, p. 34.
19. 1 Annals of Congress 929.
20. Alexander Hamilton, *The Federalist Papers,* No. 58.
21. Browne, p. 31.
22. 1 Statutes at Large U. S. Congress, p. 95, Ch. XXIII, Sept. 29, 1789.
23. There were fifteen appropriations bills passed between the founding of the Federal government and May 8, 1792. A listing of these may be found at 3 Annals 1258–1259. From 1789 to 1792 the United States had a surplus of $21,762 on revenues of $11,017,460. (p. 1,259) During this period general appropriations grew steadily, from $639,000 in 1789 to $1,059,222 in 1792, ranging from a high of $2,849,194 for payment of interest on the national debt in 1790 for 1792 to a low of $548 for sundry objects in 1790. Protection of the frontier was a growing expense: $643,500 in 1792, not included in the general appropriation. In 1791, Congress appropriated $10,000 for a lighthouse; in 1792, $2,553 was appropriated for a grammar school. Of the $11 million raised to the end of 1792, over $6.3 million was applied to the debt, either interest or principal. It's clear that these are still transitional years.
24. Lucius Wilmerding, Jr., *The Spending Power: A History of the Efforts of Congress to Control Expenditures* (New Haven, CT: Yale University Press, 1943), p. 21.
25. Wilmerding, p. 23. See also Louis Fisher, *Presidential Spending Power* (Princeton, NJ: Princeton University Press, 1975). See especially Chapter III, "Lump Sum Appropriations." Fisher suggests lump-sum appropriations are especially noticeable during periods of war and national depression, when the crisis is great and requirements uncertain; then the legislature tends to delegate power (p. 61).
26. Wilmerding, p. 48.
27. The description in this section is summarized from Browne, op. cit. and Wilmerding, op. cit.
28. Fisher, p. 9. This position was supported by both academics and administratives. Notable among the former were Arthur Smithies, *The Budgetary Process*

in the United States (1955), p. 53, and Leonard D. White in his four-volume history of the federal government, notably *The Jeffersonians* (1951), pp. 68–69; *The Jacksonians* (1954), pp. 77–78; and *The Republican Era* (1958), p. 97. The bureaucrats who argued this included two budget bureau directors, Maurice Stans and Percival Brundage. See Fisher, pp. 269–270. Fisher describes the executive budget power as a steady accretion of power through numerous statutes, financial panics, ward, "a splintering of congressional controls," and demands from the private sector for economy and efficiency.

29. The *Need for a National Budget*, H. Doc. 854, 62–2 (1912) 138. This commission report was submitted to Congress on June 27, 1912. See also Faft's message on *Economy and Efficiency in the Government* Service, H. Doc 458 62–2, January 27, 1912.

30. Burkhead suggests that the interest of the business community in reform was the crucial element in this mixture. Business men expected lower taxes. Burkhead, op. cit., p. 15. See also Allen Schick, "The Road to PPB: The Stages of Budget Reform," *Public Administration Review* 26 (December) 1966, pp. 243–258.

31. Fisher, p. 33.

32. Burkhead, pp. 26–28. Burkhead suggests Congress's main motive in passing the budget was to reduce taxes, not to improve executive leadership.

33. 42 STAT. 20 (1921)

34. Fisher, p. 34.

35. Paul Appleby, "The Role of the Budget Division," reprinted in *Perspectives on Budgeting*, Allen Schick, ed. (Washington, D. C.: ASPA, 1980), p. 134. See the discussion pp. 134–137.

36. Larry Berman, *The Office of Management and the Budget and the Presidency, 1921–1979* (Princeton, NJ: Princeton University Press, 1979), p. x.

37. Reorganization Plan No. 2 of 1970.

38. Allen Schick, "The Budget Bureau that was: Thoughts on the Rise, Decline and Future of a Presidential Agency," *Law and Contemporary Problems* 35 (Summer) 1970, pp. 519–539 (p. 532).

39. Burkhead, pp. 28–29.

40. Berman, pp. 7–8.

41. 53 STAT 1423, Executive Order 8248: 4 Fed. Reg. 3864. See Norman M. Pearson, "The Budget Bureau: From Routine Business to General Staff," *Public Administration Review* 3:126, 1943, and Herald D. Smith, "The Bureau of the Budget," *Public Administration Review* 1:106, 1941, for descriptions of the Budget Bureau in this era. Smith was Director of the Bureau in this period. For a later look at neutral competence, see Hugh Heclo, "OMB and the Presidency: The Problem of Neutral Competence," *Public Interest* 38 (Winter) 1975.

42. Fisher concludes that what the OMB lacked in the mid-1960s was political judgment that would allow it to operate in the policy process. Rather, it became a "captive" of "abstract theories of organization, doctrinaire views of management and impractical claims of constitutional power." Fisher, p. 58. For a description of OMB at work, see James W. Davis and Randall B. Ripley, "The Bureau of the Budget and Executive Branch Agencies: Notes

on their Interaction," *Journal of Politics* 29:749–769 (November) 1967. Perhaps it was the bureau leaders who failed at political shifts; or it may have been the problems were intractable.

43. Lawrence C. Pierce, *The Politics of Fiscal Policy Formation* (Pacific Palisades, CA: Goodyear, 1971).

44. See, for example, *The Budget of the United States Government, 1976*, p. 49. See also Blechman, Gramlick, and Hartman, *Setting National Priorities: The 1976 Budget* (Washington, D C: The Brookings Institute, 1975), pp. 197–207 and the tables on pp. 193, 202, 206. See also John Gist, "Increment and Base in the Congressional Appropriation Process," *American Journal of Political Science* XXI:342, (May) 1977.

45. Bertram Gross, "The New Systems Budgeting," *Public Administration Review* 29:113–137, 1969.

46. The literature on these budget reforms is voluminous. The citations listed below are intended for entry in the subject. For performance budgeting, see Burkhead, *Government Budgeting*, Chapters 6–7, "Performance Budgeting," and "Applications of Performance Concepts," pp. 133–181.

47. For program budgeting see Frederick C. Mosher, *Program Budgeting: Theory and Practice* (New York: Public Administration Service, 1954). See also *Program Budgeting*, David Novick, ed. (New York: Holt, 1969).

48. For Planning-Programming-Budgeting, see Robert D. Lee and Ronald Johnson, *Public Budgeting Systems* (Baltimore: University Park Press, 1983), Chapter Five. See also Harley Hinricks and Graeme Taylor, eds., *Program Budgeting and Benefit-Cost Analysis* (Pacific Palisades, CA: Goodyear, 1969); see also Leonard Merewitz and Stephen H. Sosnick, *The Budget's New Clothes* (Chicago: Markham, 1972). For the first and last words on PPB, see Allen Schick, "The Road to PPB: The Stages of Budget Reform," *Public Administration Review* 26:243–258, 1966, and Schick "A Death in the Bureaucracy: The Demise of Federal PPB," *Public Administration Review* 33:146–156, 1973.

49. See the symposium edited by Jong S. Jun, "Management by Objectives in the Public Sector," *Public Administration Review* 36:1–45, 1976; Richard Rose, "Implementation and Evaporation: The Record of MBO," *Public Administration Review* 37:64–71, 1977.

50. See Peter A. Phyrr, "The Zero-Base Approach to Government Budgeting," *Public Administration Review* 37:1–8, 1977; Allen Schick, "The Road from ZBB," *Public Administration Review* 30:177–180, 1978; U. S. Senate, Subcommittee on Intergovernmental Relations, *Compendium of Materials on Zero-Base Budgeting in the States* (Washington, D C: U. S. Government Printing Office, 1977).

51. Perhaps the most comprehensive coverage of the Congressional Budget and Impoundment Act is Allen Schick, *Congress and Money: Budgeting, Spending and Taxing* (Washington, D C: Urban Institute, 1980). For a description of reconciliation, see Schick's *Reconciliation and the Congressional Budget Process* (Washington, D C: American Enterprise Institute, 1982).

52. See *Setting National Priorities: The 1984 Budget*, Joseph A. Peckman, ed. (Washington, D C: The Brookings Institution, 1983), p. 19.

53. For three classic summarizations of legislative budgetary politics, see Aaron Wildavsky, *The Politics of the Budgetary Process* (Boston: Little, Brown, 1979);

Richard Fenno, *The Power of the Purse* (Boston: Little, Brown, 1966); Ira Sharkansky, *The Politics of Taxing and Spending* (New York: Bobbs Merril, 1969).

54. For an excellent summary, see Naomi Caiden, "The Myth of the Annual Budget," *Public Administration Review* 42, (November/December) 1982, pp. 516–523.

55. Comptroller General of the United States, *Funding Gaps Jeopardize Federal Government Operations* (Washington, DC: General Accounting Office, 1981), PAD-81-31, March 3.

CHAPTER 12

On the Balance of Budgetary Cultures

Aaron Wildavsky

THE UNIVERSITY OF CALIFORNIA
(BERKELEY)

AARON WILDAVSKY is Professor of Political Science and Public Policy at the University of California, Berkeley. He is the author of the most widely cited book in American public administration, The Politics of the Budgetary Process, *and many other pacesetting works as well, such as his two most recent books,* The Nursing Father: Moses as a Political Leader *and* A History of Taxation and Expenditure in the Western World *(with Carolyn Webber). Professor Wildavsky is a Fellow of the Association of Public Policy Analysis and Management, of the American Academy of Arts and Science, and of the National Academy of Public Administration. He was President of the American Political Science Association in 1985– 1986.*

Aaron Wildavsky analyzes the budgetary process in America from the middle of the seventeenth century to the second decade of the twentieth century. He is struck by the differences between American national budgets and their European analogues. They have been consistently more balanced, the per capita revenue and expenditure ratio has been markedly lower, and the American budgetary process has stressed the budgetary power of the legislature to a far greater degree than is the case in the European cabinet system. Where European budgets have been unitary, with expenditures and revenues considered as one, American budgets have been fragmentary, with each agency submitting its own spending proposals and considering revenue sources separately. A unitary mechanism came to exist with the establishment of the Ways and Means Committee in the

379

House of Representatives, but it has been subjected to frequent fragmentation since 1865. Wildavsky wonders why America has been so different.

An obvious explanation, of course, is that the United States of America
was born in a revolution against a sovereign executive. Distrust of executive
power tells us part of the story of American exceptionalism, but it does
not tell us how the difference was translated into budgetary behavior.
Wildavsky hypothesizes that American differences are a product of almost
equal competition among three main cultures, namely, collectivism, individualism, and voluntarism. Their corresponding political regimes are, respectively, hierarchies, markets, and sects.

The winning side of the American Revolution was composed of three
social orders: a weak social hierarchy that wanted to replace the English
king with a native variety better suited to colonial conditions; emerging
market men who wanted to control their own commerce; and the heirs
of a continental republican tradition that stressed small, egalitarian, and
voluntary associations.

The balanced budget at low levels, except in wartime, was the crucial
compromise that allowed these three social orders to coexist. Unlike the
signing of the Declaration of Independence, the compromise was not made
in a single day, nor was there a formal declaration. The informal understanding lasted for a century and a half, however. A new understanding
was forged during the 1960s, and whether our generation can fashion a
new consensus that will do as well in our time and last as long as the old
one is being decided now.

What was this understanding? How was it verified and enforced? And
what was in it for all concerned?

The Revolution was fought against the power of the English king. Even
the Federalists, who joined social hierarchy and market forces to form
the first independent American establishment, had their qualms about
how strong the executive should be. They wanted political unity and economic order but on a minimal, not a maximal, basis. Republicans, first
the social order and then the political party, originally known as Anti-
Federalists, knew best what they were against: established churches, standing armies, and powerful executives. They were *for* life on a smaller scale,
and limitations on status and economic differences so as to permit people
to manage their own affairs.

Left to their own devices, social hierarchs would have desired relatively
high revenues and expenditures to support a stronger and more splendid
central government. Because the market men would have to pay, they
preferred a smaller central apparatus, except where spending and taxing
provided direct aid. Together this establishment supported what were
called "internal improvements," namely subsidies for canals, harbors, and
railroads.

But the establishment had to contend with the Republican belief in
small, egalitarian collectives who threatened to withdraw consent to union
unless the size and scope of the central government were severely limited.
These egalitarians did not believe that government spending was good
for the common man, the small farmer, and the artisan of their day.

Government took from the people to support the establishment. Limiting, not expanding, central government was the hallmark of republicanism.

Governments that ran deficits might have been acceptable to the hierarchical social order as a necessary accompaniment to domestic grandeur. The "public interest" was their phrase. But continuous deficits were unacceptable to market forces, who feared financial instability, debasement of currency, and inflation. So market men would compromise to balance the budget. It was the egalitarian Republicans who insisted on lower levels of taxing and spending.

In the compromise that emerged, market men, the adherents of competitive individualism, won the opportunity to seek economic growth with government subsidy and internal improvement, and gained the stability that comes from knowing that spending will be limited by a willingness to increase revenues. Egalitarian republicans were able to place limits on central government. And the supporters of social hierarchy obtained a larger role for collective concerns, provided they were able to gather sufficient revenue. No order of society received all it sought, but all got assurances that they would not be subject to severe disadvantages in the compromise. The belief, widely espoused in the Jacksonian era, that equality of opportunity would lead to equality of result and that pure market relations would achieve sectarian objectives helped cement this cultural union.

Thus the doctrine of the balanced budget, a doctine that became powerful over time because of the attendant negative impact should it be violated, was more than an economic theory. It meant, and, to some extent, still means, that things are all right. The "balance" referred to was not only between revenue and expenditure but between social orders. If the competing cultures that make up American life are in balance, meaning that they still accept the legitimacy of their uneasy alliance, all is indeed well in the New World.

A successful financial system will conform to the political ideas which for the time being control society, and adjust itself to the political structure of the particular society to which it applies. (Henry Carter Adams, *The Science of Finance: An Investigation of Public Expenditures and Public Revenues.* New York: Henry Holt, 1899, p. 8)

I wish it were possible to obtain a single amendment to our constitution. I would be willing to depend on that alone for the reduction of the adminis-

This paper is a revised version of a chapter in Carolyn Webber and Aaron Wildavsky, *A History of Taxation and Expenditure in the Western World* (New York: Simon and Schuster, 1986).

tration of our government to the genuine principles of it's [sic] constitution; I mean an additional article, taking from the federal government the power of borrowing. I now deny their power of making paper money or anything else a legal tender. I know that to pay all proper expences within the year, would, in case of war, be hard on us. But not so hard as ten wars instead of one. For wars would be reduced in that proportion; besides that the State governments would be free to lend *their credit* in borrowing quotas. . . . It is a singular phenomenon, that while our State governments are the very *best in the world,* without exception or comparison, our general government has, in the rapid course of 9. or 10. years, become more arbitrary, and has swallowed more of the public liberty than even that of England [Jefferson's emphasis].

(Jefferson to John Taylor, November 26, 1798. Paul Leicester Lord, ed., *The Works of Thomas Jefferson, Vol. VIII.* New York: G. P. Putnam's Sons, The Knickerbocker Press, 1904, p. 481.)

The habits of private life are continued in public; and we ought carefully to distinguish that economy which depends upon their institutions from that which is a natural result of their manners and customs. (Alexis de Tocqueville, *Democracy in America,* V. I, p. 222)

From the middle of the seventeenth century to the second decade of the twentieth century, the period covered by this essay, America's difference from rather than its similarity to Europe's approach to a budgetary process is striking. The per capita revenue and expenditure ratio has been markedly lower in the United States. The process in America has historically stressed the budgetary power of the legislature. Europe has relied on the influence of the executive, in the form of a legislative committee called the cabinet. Where European budgets have been unitary, with expenditures and revenues considered as one, American budgets have been fragmentary, with each agency submitting its own spending proposals and considering revenue sources separately. A unitary mechanism existed with the establishment of the Congressional Ways and Means Committee. However, since 1865 it has been subjected to frequent fragmentation. Still, when viewed as an historic whole, American national budgets have been consistently more balanced than have European analogues. This most unideological of peoples practices more than it preaches. Why has America been so different?

Obvious explanations should not be ignored merely because they are familiar. The United States of America was born in a revolution against a sovereign executive. Therefore, no one should be surprised by the

American distrust of executive authority. However, the threat of Indian and foreign attack and the need for the adoption of social and economic order necessitated the institution of a central government. The "Second American Revolution," the replacement of the Articles of Confederation with the Constitution, was devised to counter disorder by establishing a stronger central authority. Its radicalism consisted in a design for self-government rather than for economic and social equality, or "leveling," as they called it. Facilitating competition among elites instead of advocating their abolition, the constitutional debates and the Federalist papers reflected a distrust of the people being governed by mob rule as well as a paradoxical dependence upon the consent of those governed. The problem was to negotiate a balance between the suspicions inherent in big government and the specter of government by "mobocracy." Distrust of executive power tells us part of the story of American exceptionalism but not how that difference was translated into its budgetary behavior.

The framers of the Constitution feared that elected officials would compete for the support of the electorate by adopting measures to limit property rights. They had in mind the debasement of currency, they favored debtors over creditors, and they feared a repetition of the days of Roman bread and circuses. Politicians did compete for popular favor, but why, for the longest time, did they reject large spending and heavy taxation?

Writing near the end of the nineteenth century, Lord James Bryce was one among many to say that Americans had been saved from their financial follies, presumably their failure to imitate Europeans, by the endowment of natural resources.[1] But how would Bryce explain today's suddenly oil-rich nations managing to raise their spending to empty a cornucopia of wealth? Thus, natural abundance alone does not explain why American governments raised only a fraction of the public funds that the wealth of their people might otherwise have dictated.

Perhaps it is not so much what America possessed but what it fortunately lacked. Louis Hartz has maintained that the absence of a hereditary hierarchy and feudal tradition has made America different.[2] But the question of the correlation between a weak hierarchy and a different pattern of budgeting remains. In *Democracy in America,* the magisterial interpretation of American politics, Alexis de Tocqueville saw a relationship between the availability of land and the general equality of condition promoting a proclivity to voluntary association.[3] Presumably, the more Americans devoted themselves to private groups, the less they would want government, especially central government, to do things for them. Though this argument could not explain the continuing controversy over the role of government in regard to what were called "internal improvements," it suggested that there was a rival social order to challenge the prevailing hierarchies. How does a desire for equality interact with a desire for order, voluntary with involuntary organization?

If one asks the related contemporary question of why the United States has "lagged behind" European social democracies in expanding welfare provisions, the best answer comes from Anthony King: American values are opposed to large government.[4] American government does less because its people are opposed to doing more.

The same sort of question underlies the perennial debate over why the United States, alone among Western industrial nations, does not have a strong socialist party.[5] Apparently, America has imbibed the values of a commercial nation, opposing free enterprise to governmental intervention, and has done well enough for business to stem protest. In the end, values seem to explain everything.

That could be the problem. These explanations resolve into new questions: Why are American values structured the way they are? If these values follow in a single, cohesive, and consistent direction, how can one explain the ubiquity of political conflict? The answer could perhaps rest in disagreements over values.

It would be a mistake, therefore, to assume that there is one dominant culture in one country at one time. Presuppositions concerning cultural uniformity lead to tortuous efforts to account for diverse behavior through a single set of values thought to be operative at the time. By abandoning uniformity and postulating diversity in cultures, and the shared values and the social orders they support, this essay hopefully will explain the discrepancies between European and American budgetary behavior in the mobilization and allocation of resources.

American exceptionalism is a product of a more equal competition among three main cultures, namely, collectivism, individualism, and voluntarism, whose corresponding political regimes are, respectively, hierarchy, markets, and, sects. The special circumstances of American life have created conditions in which people pursuing these various cultures have been more evenly balanced than elsewhere. Americanism consists in the ability to pursue not the same vision but separate visions. What outcomes would result from conflict and cooperation among hierarchic social orders, decentralized market anarchies, and voluntary egalitarian sects? An answer to this question overwhelms the imagination. But if one can pinpoint the manifestation of the political regimes representing these cultures in the budgetary arena, one can come closer to understanding American differences.

Collectivism has been weaker in America than elsewhere, partly because its elites compete for popular favor. Competitive individualism has always been strongly encouraged. Voluntarism has waxed and waned in strength. In the budgeting sphere, to recall the basics, hierarchies prefer to follow forms, punctual tax collection, and spending to shore up the regime. Sects, by contrast, prefer no executive discretion, little spending on the regime, and revenues, when possible, collected from the more prosperous. Markets are indifferent to forms or discretion but insist on getting a return for their money, including that part which government collects. They prefer lower taxes and spending, except for supporting projects from which they benefit. Assuming that these three political regimes are relatively equal in strength and appeal, on what budgeting issues do they agree, and on which do they disagree?

In regard to the choice of budgeting style, sects prefer detail as a means of controlling extravagance and virtually demand a person-by-person, object-by-object description. Hierarchies favor funding by organizational level; they essentially mimic their own niches. Competitive individualists choose lump-sum budgeting because they care only about outcomes. The result, if collectivists and individualists are in the majority, is likely to be a compromise between extreme and minute detail, for example, the use of line-item budgeting with lump sums reserved for emergencies when results matter. The unity of the budget is another issue, however, because voluntarists and collectivists oppose the external control a unified budget signifies, especially if it limits market transactions or individual liberty.

Because markets and sects prefer to keep government on a short and parsimonious leash, spending levels are low. Spending to enhance equality attracts sects, however, and markets favor spending to aid business. Hierarchies tend to prefer spending for its own sake inasmuch as each level seeks to spend to maintain its own position. Bargaining can result when the hierarchy offers to aid business or "the people" in return for support of governmental establishments.

What about revenues? All regimes would like someone else to pay for their privileges. Because no regime commands a majority at any given time, compromises are made in an attempt to keep taxes low. When circumstances permit—for example, when there is a surplus—government, business, and the populace share the proceeds. On the other hand, when circumstances dictate—during war, for example—taxes are raised to satisfy sects, debt is incurred to satisfy markets, and the government grows to satisfy hierarchies.

Why did the need for a balanced budget become almost a religion? Consider the answer to be that it is the one thing about which all three cultural tendencies could agree. Start with the voluntarists in a sectarian regime. Their humble posture, coupled with low spending, is their chosen style. Perennial outsiders, they are not likely to enjoy the largesse of government spending. Nor, believing as they do in equality, would they easily justify the imposition of taxes that distinguish among individuals. Tying spending directly to the pain of raising revenues, they insist on balanced budgets as a means to curtail establishment spending.

Adherents of markets emphasize credit and currency because without stable financial values their endless transactions cannot be carried out.

Inflation is anathema to market adherents because it gives debtors advantages over creditors. Market people do not object to deficits in principle so long as they benefit from the borrowing and, therefore, must be concerned about its inflationary effects. They temper the desire to redistribute losses with the need for stability by agreeing that revenues should, as often as possible, cover expenditures. This practice limits the efforts of sects to please the populace (common in the state legislatures) and of hierarchies to dress up government in finery inappropriate for a commercial people. Left to their own devices, hierarchies would run deficits as each level spent to maintain its distinctive niche.

During the era of the Continental Congress, in which revenues were more often promised than paid, hierarchies agreed to limit spending in exchange for raising revenues. Because hierarchies agreed to raise sufficient revenue, markets and sects limited their need for government spending. Thus, the inability of any one regime to dominate the others led to a common-denominator consensus: the balanced budget. And, as follows from any boundary formation, violations became subject to penalties: unemployment, inflation, public immorality, private vice, and collective ruin.

So much for large-scale speculation. Let us see how the hypothesis of cultural diversity characterizes American budgetary behavior.

The Colonial Period

In the fifty to one hundred years after the first settlers arrived during the latter 1600s and early 1700s, there was no money. The first colonists were poor; gold and silver had not yet been discovered. The only currency in circulation was a motley mixture of Dutch, English, and later, Spanish coins. Prices, particularly in New England, might be specified in guilders, pistoles, pieces of eight, doubloons, rit-dollars, as well as pounds and shillings. Each colony valued the separate sets of coins differently, running the metal back and forth, as it were, so one kind of coin disappeared in one place to be succeeded for a time in another.[6] Understandably, the shortage of ready cash was a constant theme of financial complaints.

When coins did not suffice, which was most of the time, trade was conducted in barter. Various staple commodities were declared legal currency. Rice and tobacco in the South, and cattle, corn, and furs in New England, were used to pay bills. A college student might pay tuition with a cow or a goat. Lacking a better method, Dutch settlers began to use Indian shell beads, or "Wampampeake" currency, composed of white beads taken from conch shells and the more rare, and hence more valuable, black beads from mussel or clam shells. Taxes, labor, and, court judgments were payable in wampum.[7] Inevitably, the ratio of two white to one black shell varied as much as the value of the currency and depreciated even more given charges levied by settlers or Indians that one or the other had dyed white shells black.[8]

In the absence of commercial banks (before the American Revolution there were none), credit was extended and commerce carried on by merchants. Merchants minted silver "pine-tree shillings," deliberately made twenty-two and a half times lighter than the English variety so they would be retained in the colonies rather than shipped abroad.[9] Other merchants acted as agents of exchange or issued letters of credit to Americans traveling abroad. It was a hit-or-miss business. Debt was undesirable because it was considered by many to be a form of immorality; indeed, the debtor laws were so severe that a hapless soul might find himself in prison without the ability to raise ready money for his release. The desire to experiment with various issues of paper money may well have sprung from the understandable need to facilitate trade and to mitigate the sanctions imposed on debtors.[10]

Another form of currency, treasury bills, were issued by colonies in anticipation of tax notes created to pay for wars or for general administration. These notes passed through so many hands and were of such uncertain value that the practice was finally halted in favor of floating loans in advance of tax collections.[11] Dependent as the colonists were on whatever credit they could internally muster, it is understandable that the English Bubble Act of 1719, forbidding bills of credit to be issued first in England and then in America, led by 1751 to considerable opposition.[12]

Shortage of specie was exacerbated by the wars against the French that occurred intermittently between 1730 and 1760. Taxes rose by as much as ten to twenty times their prewar rates,[13] and under the lash of necessity, several colonial legislatures issued "paper money" in the form of bills of credit that bore interest and required repayment in specie. So long as these bills were only a small portion of available currency, they held up, but eventually they depreciated from half to a tenth of their former value.[14]

Under massive popular pressure, many colonies began to issue paper money, much of which not only fluctuated but rapidly depreciated in value as the printing presses ran overtime. In response, moralistic tracts were written that stressed the desirability of limiting the amount of money in circulation as a bar to inflation. One of Benjamin Franklin's earliest papers was on this subject, though the warning was generally not as necessary in pacifist Pennsylvania, where Quakers steadfastly refused to issue paper money to pay for war.[15] Nonetheless, Franklin's support of British restrictions on paper money led to his only electoral defeat.[16]

Though government in colonial times was simple, frugal, and rudimentary, its start-up costs were considerable in relation to income, especially in regard to specie, or hard cash. Forts had to be constructed, courts established and supplied with personnel, roads built, and prisons established. And to these local needs for revenue were added those of the mother country, which occasionally tried to rule in fact as well as name.

Mercantilism held sway in England. The major purpose of the trade and navigation laws, and the customs and revenue services, was to provide an outlet for British manufacturers. At the end of the Seven Years War, the English navy was freed to form a "colonial squadron" in an effort to cut off unauthorized trade. Perhaps natural advantage would have won the trade for England anyway, but the prevailing economic doctrine was against such a trial.[17] Competition outside the mother country was not considered a virtue. The revenue realized was small and was designed to support the custom service rather than to raise funds.[18]

Within the colonies, types of taxes varied according to circumstances. The property tax dominated in New England. It included taxes on personal property, such as cattle and slaves, as well as on houses and land, assessed at current value multiplied by six. Rates were a penny to the pound of assessed valuation and varied from a high of sixteen times during King Phillip's war of 1676 to a low of half a rate. This tax weighed most heavily on farmers whose barns, cattle, and houses were difficult to hide. In an effort to shift the burden of taxation from farmers, a poll tax was instituted in which an individual was considered to be worth twenty pounds and was assessed at a rate of one penny per pound. The poll tax fluctuated according to the property tax. Because it placed particular hardship on the poor, the poll tax was later abandoned. There were exemptions to payment, of course, including the governor of the colony, schoolteachers, ministers, invalids, and students at Harvard College. Because the property and poll taxes were not directly related to income, there was also a "faculty" (or income or ability to earn) tax imposed on those who earned more than a given sum. This tax presumed, often with little evidence, that certain occupations could earn an anticipated salary.[19]

In the South one would not expect taxes on property, including land and slaves, or on income to be popular among the landholders. They preferred indirect taxes on exports and imports. Poll taxes were levied and usually were paid in pounds of tobacco or some other commodity.

The middle colonies, New York, New Jersey, and Maryland, used a combination of direct and indirect taxes. They added refinements of their own, including a graduated poll tax that levied the heaviest rates on apparently unpopular segments of the community, such as wig wearers, rich bachelors, and lawyers. Despite Quaker opposition, all of the colonies, at one time or another, indulged in lotteries to finance education: Dartmouth, Princeton, Harvard, and Yale all gained financial assistance from lotteries. Instead of forced labor on public projects, several colonies required that contributions in kind, such as tobacco, be paid for building a fort or as a fine in case one failed to attend church.[20]

Viewed outside of the contemporary context, colonial expenditures were as simple and bland as colonial taxation. Care of the poor, insane, sick, or otherwise indigent was a local responsibility. Public works were few and sparse. Highways were short and rough, and courthouses, though sometimes gilded with a handsome facade, were small. Judges were few and did not require much assistance. No colonial navy existed, and the army, except in the period of the great Indian wars and during the war with France for control of the North American continent, was composed of local militia. Legislatures met only for short periods of time and, if received, payments for service and attendance were in minimal amounts. The colonial executive departments were tiny, and officials were often paid by fees for services rather than from general revenues. The royal governors alone received substantial salaries.

Yet it was not the actual expenditures that mattered but the power relationships they signified. Why should the colonists be taxed to support governors who might flaunt their will and whom they did not appoint? Why should the home country pay for distant wars? Even the remnants of feudal dues, known as quit-rents and paid to government in return for land use, went to colonial treasuries. By 1762, the King refused to supply garrisons to those colonies who would not maintain them.[21]

The extraordinary effort of colonial legislatures to control executives by limiting their expenditures, the duration for which they could be paid, and the objects for which the money could be spent, gives this era its peculiar stamp. If the colonies belonged to England, and if the colonists were English subjects, then it was their duty to support royal governors. Because the colonists wanted British protection but not British rule, however, they freely used the English tradition of denying supply in order to force compliance with the legislative will. The commonplace view, so assiduously peddled by the colonists in the prerevolutionary period, that if the English king were only reasonable they would love him, is not supported by monetary or fiscal fact.

To say that royal governors were kept amenable to colonists' will does not do justice to their "Yankee" ingenuity in devising financial restraints.[22] Connecticut may have been extreme in making the salary of the governor and other important executives dependent upon semiannual appropriations, but it was a common practice to vote salaries annually. It might be thought that indirect taxes, excises, and import duties would be perpetual until changed, but these were often reenacted yearly. Royal governors were not permitted permanent sources of revenue.[23] Appropriations were specified by object and amount. Extremely long appropriation clauses prescribed exactly what could and could not be done. The requirement that all unexpended balances revert back to the treasury added insult to injury. It might be thought that once an appropriation was voted, the executive could proceed to spend the money for the purpose stipulated. Several colonies, however, elected treasurers independent of the colonial governors, which precluded management of his own finances. Other colonial legislatures insisted that no payment might be made except with their specific consent, a requirement which gave them control over the disbursement of public funds. And when an emergency arose that appeared to all to justify a special appropriation, colonial assemblies might well appoint a special commission accountable to them rather than to the governor. Colonial legislatures often segregated revenues by voting taxes for specific purposes, for example, the building of a fort, or of a lighthouse, or the salary of a governor. A clause would often be added stipulating that once these purposes had been accomplished the money could be spent for "no other use or purpose whatsoever."[24] Colonial assemblies frequently reduced the salary of royal officials. The assemblies stipulated the name of the person who was to do the work, making these officials legally accountable for all funds expended. Often these actions were accomplished without a specific legislative act. If the character of a government is known by its monetary policies, America was already "independent" in many respects.[25]

During the colonial period, the dimensions were understood: Royal governors and their supporters wanted a civil list of appointments and perquisites independent of the funds appropriated by legislatures, and the colonists wanted to create uncertainty, parsimony, and narrowness to keep royal governors amenable to the will of the colonies. To the English, it seemed only reasonable that the colonists should pay for the support of the royal government. The Stamp Act, duties on tea, and other tax impositions on the colonies were royal efforts to provide independent sources of income for their officials in America. Power, not money, was the issue. The American Revolution was fought over a revolutionary issue, the issue of who should rule in America. A contemporary of the period on the colonial government of New York commented:

> It will be seen that the democratick branch of the colonial government had placed the governor, and almost every other office, in a state of dependence upon its votes and measures. Not a single shilling could be withdrawn from the treasury but by legislative consent. This was particularly galling to the lieutenant governor. It had stripped him of that executive patronage and influence which was deemed by him so essential to the support of his administration. In truth, it was a great step towards that independence which was afterward obtained.[26]

This brief background should help the modern reader to appreciate the colonists' insistence on legislative direction of fiscal policy. Their strategy for financing the Revolutionary War would not have been chosen by any contemporary European country, nor would it be recommended today. However, for the colonists it was entirely natural. A war for independence from a distant authority would be perverse, especially if it only replaced an English king with a new American hierarchy.

The First and Second American Revolutions

The Continental Congress was a temporary association of colonial assemblies gathered to fight a "temporary" war. Executive bodies, in addition to symbolizing the wrong kind of authority, suggested a future permanence that could not be envisioned by the colonial assembly. It could imagine what colonial governments had been, and it proceeded to behave in its new congressional form just as it had in the colonies. The Congress copied colonial assemblies by setting up committees, called boards, to direct foreign affairs and other essential activities, including finance. The fiscal committees named the Board of Treasury and the Treasury Office of Accounts were to act not directly but through colonial entities. The story is well known, a patchwork narrative of endless difficulties, embarrassments, ineptitudes, and contradictions, with only the final victory lending contour to its plot. If we rehearse this well-worn tradition, it would be not only to outline the weaknesses that the Constitutional Convention attempted to overcome but also to see in its methods a different and more decentralized mode of operation.

Fiscal policy during the Revolutionary War was inadequate and chaotic. The colonies in rebellion against the king differed in their devotion to the war, in their capabilities and suffering, and in their ability to figure out what they were expected to do. It is true that colonial militia, paid and supplied by colonial assemblies, conducted part of the fighting, but they did not assist the major army under the command of General George Washington.[27] As the Continental Congress began to demand larger contributions, colonial payments lagged further behind. Because neither payments in kind nor in coinage were adequate, the Continental Congress began to print paper. In a short time, the currency depreciated to almost nothing, leaving as its legacy only a phrase that survives as the epitome of worthlessness: "not worth a Continental."[28] In the doggerel of the time:

> A refugee captain lost two of his men;
> And ardently wishing to have them again,
> To the Major applied, on an exchange to fix,
> And requested to know if for two he'd tax six?
> Major Adams agreed, nor said a word more,

> And Paddy was order'd to fetch them ashore;
> Who cried out in surprise: 'By Ja—s, my honey,
> Our men now depreciate as fast as our money.'[29]

Soldiers were paid little and were often not paid on time. Officers were paid even less, on the supposition that they were independently wealthy. After several years of confusing policy, Robert Morris, a signer of the Declaration of Independence, was called in to restore financial order. A full-time executive rather than a part-time legislator was given the challenge. But even with his legendary ingenuity, Morris could not create something from nothing. At the end of a lengthy correspondence to Morris, General George Washington wrote:

> I must entreat you, if possible, to procure one month's pay in specie for the detachment which I have under my command. Part of the troops have not been paid anything for a long time past, and have upon several occasions shown marks of great discontent. The service they are going upon is disagreeable to the northern regiments; but I make no doubt that a douceur of a little hard money would put them in proper temper. If the whole sum cannot be obtained, a part of it will be better than none, as it may be distributed in proportion to the respective wants and claims of the men.[30]

Robert Morris replied:

> I have already advised Your Excellency of the unhappy situation of money matters, and very much doubt if it will be possible to pay the detachment a month's pay, as you wish. Therefore it will be best not to raise in them any expectation of that kind. Should it come unexpectedly, so much the better.[31]

Pressed from all sides, and sometimes subject to the anger of creditors and soldiers, Morris took the view that if he could not pay everyone he would pay no one at all.[32] As William Graham Sumner comments: "This reasoning shows that he had high qualifications for the Financier of the Revolution."[33] Under such circumstances, it was Morris's policy to get money from whatever sources he could and worry later about making payment. One of his tactics involved making a draft on Benjamin Franklin in Paris; he then cashed it and sent the paper for collection through Cuba and thence to Madrid, knowing that his private communications would reach Franklin weeks before the paper did. It was then "Poor Richard's" task to find an expedient way to raise money for payment of the bill when it did arrive. Of course, Morris was not thoughtful of Franklin's feelings, but then again, anyone with scruples would not have been suitable for the task. No doubt, as Grayson put it, Morris "told some grand lies," but that, in another writer's opinion, did not justify criticism by little men "none of whom would have been able to save a country when it was flat broke."[34] Morris later received his reward, however. Because of unfortunate speculation in a land transaction, he ended his days in a debtors' prison in Philadelphia. His one recorded solace was given by George Washington, who, upon hearing of the debacle, brought Morris supper and spent the night with him in prison.[35]

The Continental Congress lasted from 1775 to 1781, when it was replaced by the Articles of Confederation. The Articles spoke of a common treasury but left the taxing power in the hands of the individual states. Financial difficulty continued to plague the revolutionary forces. As debts multiplied, both during the war and in the years following, it became necessary for the states to print money to pay the debts incurred. Nonetheless, the debts incurred during the war remained unsatisfied. This situation was compounded by certain financial measures that made it difficult for states to trade abroad and with each other. Currency depreciated from state to state. The revolutionary elite wondered whether sufficient order could be maintained to keep the republic together.

That view may have been expressed by some, but it was not the only view. William Schultz and M. R. Caine have described an alternative view:

> The Colonials accepted the situation philosophically. Paper money they would and must have. If these were the evils of paper money, they would take the evil along with the good. As a Mr. Wise of Massachusetts wrote, in a pamphlet entitled *A Word of Comfort*, "Gentlemen! You must do by your Bills, as all Wise Men do by their Wives; Make the best of them."[36]

Far from condemning inflation, a writer in the *Pennsylvania Packet* gave his opinion that

> the natural unavoidable tax of depreciation is the most certain, expeditious, and equal tax that could be devised. Upon the scale which has lately existed, every possessor of money has paid a tax for it, in proportion to the time he held it. Like a hackney coach it must be paid for by the hour.[37]

Given time, a common market of currency and credit might have been created. No one will ever know, however, because the Constitutional Convention, without legal warrant under the Articles of Confederation, ended the experiment.

Then came a central government sufficiently strong to levy taxes on its own, giving it the potential to restore economic order.[38] Yet in 1789, the Constitution was still only a document with which the people had yet to have a practical experience. They had had over 200 years of experience being governed by England and of self-government under colonial assemblies. It is not surprising, therefore, that the practices and habits of mind gained in two centuries of day-to-day operations manifested themselves under the new rubric that was created as their chosen instrument of self-government. The framers realized that they had undertaken an experiment in self-rule that had little precedent. It was a then-prevailing tenet that governments evolved by practice of the common law rather than as a result of a willful act of self-creation. Yet it was, if we wish to explain American exceptionality, not all new; it had a new structure, but it was composed of old practices. Nowhere was this interaction more evident than in the development of budgeting. Taxing and spending focused direct attention on how the general structure established by the Constitution was to be actually practiced. The import of the American story has been missed. The lack of a hierarchical European structure has been taken to mean no structure at all because the uniformity of practice indicated the lack of an operating ideology when it should have suggested the opposite. The significance of the commitment to budget balance is great, as is that of the rejection of a centralized executive, with its concomitant preference for decentralized, legislative forms of budgeting. There was an extraordinary combination of the absence of anything that could be called a central budget with a powerful, though informal, coordination of expenditure and revenue. This phenomenon needs neither criticism nor praise but understanding. The rise, at the beginning of the twentieth century, of a budgetary reform movement that was hostile toward past practices and structures (including the separation of powers in the Constitution) and monolithic by favoring executive domination has obscured a different way of budgetary life.

Understanding the present requires resurrecting the discarded ghost of budgets past. Therefore, in the following sections, we depart from a strict historical chronology to trace key questions of budgeting through time. The next section takes up the balance between expenditure and revenue.

Public Debt and Balanced Budgets

The history of American attitudes toward public debt may be translated into formulas for relating revenues to expenditures that are no less powerful for being simple. The first of these budgetary equations[39] is simplicity itself: revenues minus interest on the public debt equal allowable national government spending. The new Constitution provided ample taxing authority, including direct levies on individuals and internal excise taxes. In the debate over ratification, however, the proponents of the Constitution frequently insisted that the bulk of taxes be raised by custom duties and sale of public lands, with income and excise taxes reserved for emergencies. Despite Hamilton's major effort both to exert executive authority and simultaneously to give the government a sounder financial basis by invoking internal taxes,[40] the Jeffersonians soon reverted to their preferred version, in which tariffs predominated. Given the widespread agreement on balanced budgets and parsimony in government, as well as the desire to pay off the public debt, the first equation had appeal.

Life soon provided the circumstances that lawyers say alter cases. During war the second equation prevailed: revenues, this time including internal taxes, equal ordinary civilian expenditures minus wartime debt. When surpluses appeared or the attractiveness of internal improvements proved irresistible, or both, a third equation operated: revenues in surplus minus interest on debt, minus ordinary spending, minus internal improvements, equal central government spending. It was only with the revolution in fiscal thought following the Great Depression of the 1930s that the fourth equation, sometimes called a full-employment surplus, took center stage. The idea was to balance not the budget but the economy at full employment. The fourth equation stipulates that revenues plus a deficit sufficient to secure full employment equals spending. The formulation of a fifth equation is under discussion today.

The first American Constitution reacted against the Articles of Confederation. A major motivation behind the new governmental structure was to provide the national government with sufficient powers to levy taxes (without the direct concurrence of the states) so that national credit might be placed on a firm foundation. In the first month after President George Washington took office and before a treasury department existed, laws were enacted establishing customs duties and providing for their collection.[41] In his magisterial reports on public credit of 1790 and 1795, Alexander Hamilton argued the importance of consolidating state debts by adding them to the national debt and arranging to fund them with revenues provided for that specific purpose. This was hard for his agrarian, small-farmer Jeffersonian opponents to accept. Much of the debt had been severely discounted and was owned by speculators who stood to gain far more than the original holders. Additionally, there was no way to effect even rough equanimity of burden in states who, had they done more during the revolutionary period, would be owed less. Yet the idea of public faith and sound credit proved as difficult to resist as the related idea that funding the debt would help balance the budget each year. Each generation was, therefore, encouraged to pay its own costs.[42] The problems Hamilton's argument created for his agrarian opponents were well placed and succinctly stated by John Taylor of Carolina:

> We moderns; we enlightened Americans; we who have abolished hierarchy and title; and we who are submitting to be taxed . . . without being deluded or terrified by the promise of heaven, the denunciation of hell . . . or superstition. A spell is put on our understandings by the words "public faith and national credit.". . .[43]

Yet there was more to the argument than a magic charm. In a classic case of bargaining, Hamilton arranged the transfer of the nation's capital from New York to Washington, D.C., which was nearer Virginia and the South, in exchange for votes to pass the bill concerning assumption of debt.[44] Critical discussion of the subject usually ends here, but such an ending is inappropriate. Without a general value congruence on the virtue of a balanced budget, this political exchange would not have been feasible. Moreover, the attack by the Republican party on the powers of the executive branch has not been considered. The agrarian, egalitarian Republicans did agree to assume state debts. Using the same skill as those who sought to incorporate institutional safeguards through the Constitution, however, the Republicans filled in the Constitutional interstices with articles designed to limit the executive branch's use of whatever spending powers it gained through an assumption of debt. The Republicans relied on their own financial formulas more than they did on those promulgated by the federalist position.

President Thomas Jefferson (1801–1808) promoted a budgetary belief corresponding with his conviction that the soil of liberty had to be nurtured in every generation with the blood of martyrs. Thinking it wrong for one generation to bind the next by its debts, Jefferson believed that, when incurred, debts should be paid within twenty years. For Jefferson, economy meant frugality and parsimony. Favoring the lowly style and the lingua humis popular at the time, Jefferson viewed economy and debt payment as necessities for a moral life. "I place economy among the first and most important of republican virtues," he wrote, "and public debt as the greatest of the dangers to be feared."[45] Though he believed that "the earth belongs always to the living generation," and therefore favored rapid retirement of the public debt, Jefferson would rather cut spending than raise taxes. "I am for government rigorously frugal and simple," Jefferson wrote, "applying all the possible savings of the public revenue to the discharge of the national debt."[46]

Jefferson, however, gave enough importance to a balanced budget to propose enshrining the concept in the Constitution. For him, as for other anti-Federalists, it was the Republican form of government that was at stake. Looking back to political philosopher James Harrington and to the Whig "party of the country" in England, Jefferson viewed debt and its holders as the equivalent of the place in Parliament of the King, who corrupted government by financial interests and hence exerted executive control.[47]

Observe that Jefferson's rejection of debt was not merely abstract but depended on a certain historical context: a central government led by its executive power trying to introduce new inequalities or maintain old ones. State governments, thought to be free from this corrupting influence, could presumably assume as much debt as desired.

Life was good in early America. Despite the repeal of internal taxes in the first year of Jefferson's administration and the $11 million spent to acquire the Louisiana Territory, the increase in American commerce enabled both substantial repayments on the debt and an increase in Treasury reserves. Part of the impetus that drove Jefferson and Gallatin to retire the debt was surely the reduction of this "moral cankor," but they also believed that erasing the debt would free the remaining revenues for public purposes. The conflicts between those favoring economy for its own sake and those wishing better education or other internal improvements could be mitigated by including expenditures under the mantle of the balanced budget.[48]

The War of 1812 upset budgetary expectations for two reasons: It was expensive, and it disrupted commerce and thereby reduced income. Initially, the war was to be strictly financed by debt, but by 1813 millions of dollars in internal taxes were voted, as were rate increases on tariffs. The net result was a substantial increase in debt. Taxes were willingly paid in view of the urgency and proximity of war, but there were substantial misgivings about the debt incurred.[49] Following Jefferson's lead, President James Madison (1809–1817) wanted his administration "to liberate the public resources by an honorable discharge of the public debt." Similarly, James Monroe (1817–1824) and John Quincy Adams (1825–1829) wanted to reduce debt to free customs revenues.[50] The ideal of a balanced budget took on increasingly moralistic overtones. John Quincy Adams considered its achievement "among the maxims of political economy," and his Secretary of the Treasury called debt reduction "amongst the highest duties of a nation" because it showed that a government is a prompt payer.[51] Debt reduction was a good thing either in and of itself or as a prelude to incurring still more debt. Debt reduction could mean both less and more spending.

By the time of President Andrew Jackson (1829–1836), debt reduction had become a patriotic duty. Realizing that the remaining debt might be retired during his administration, Jackson waxed lyric: "We shall then exhibit the rare example of a great nation, abounding in all the means of happiness and security, altogether free from debt." American exceptionality was publicly proclaimed when Secretary of the Treasury Levi Woodbury heralded the extinction of the debt as an "unprecedented spectacle . . . presented to the world."[52]

Then, from within the wellsprings of abundance, the specter of a corresponding evil surfaced: "the unnecessary accumulation of public revenue," as Andrew Jackson called it, or more simply, a surplus. Why should this cornucopia be an embarrassment? Because, as President Martin Van Buren (1837–1841) remarked, governments would be "constantly exposed to great deficiencies or excesses, with all their attended embarrassments." In his last annual message, Van Buren argued that the surplus "would foster national extravagance" and would thus encourage rapid accumulation of a larger and more onerous debt. His theory was that if a government does not have revenues, it cannot spend them. Once a surplus existed, it would be too tempting to resist spending, and a vicious cycle of increasing expenditures would begin.[53] As depression brought debt, President John Tyler (1841–1845) railed against owing money, maintaining, as did his successor James K. Polk (1845–1849), that debt reduction was a source of strength among the nations of the world. Warning against the errors occasioned by the War of 1812, in particular the excessive and unnecessary expenses, Polk argued that war was an additional reason for economy in all ordinary expenditure.[54]

These presidents did not believe government spending would encourage redistribution of wealth from the rich to the poor. "Melancholy is the condition of that people," President Polk wrote, "whose government can be sustained only by a system which periodically transfers large amounts from the labors of the many to the coffers of the few."[55] For these men, as for the citizens they governed, debt was equated with privilege. Between 1849 and 1861, when the Civil War began, every national government had pledged itself both to apply surpluses to extinction of the debt and to reduce revenues to the level of spending. Beyond this minimum, President James Buchanan (1857–1861) would only allow expenditures clearly warranted by the Constitution, such as increases in naval and coastal defenses.[56]

Faith in the balanced budget ideal was strengthened by an economic theory that negatively tied wages to debt. As Secretary of the Treasury Robert J. Walker claimed in 1838: "Wages can only be increased in any nation, in the aggregate, by augmenting capital, the fund out of which wages are paid. . . . The destruction or diminution of capital, by destroying or reducing the fund from which labor is paid must reduce wages." This wage/fund argument had the added value of suggesting that the wage earner would be hurt by any effort to go into debt to improve his lot.[57] During the recession of 1837 and 1838, when efforts were made to increase federal spending in order to alleviate suffering, President Van Buren invoked the sagacity of the Founding Fathers, who "wisely judged that the less government interferes with private pursuits the better for the general prosperity."[58] The economy would improve by reducing the deficit, not by building railroads or canals. President Buchanan blamed the financial panic and recession of 1857 and 1858 on "the habit of extravagant spending."[59]

The Civil War of 1861 to 1865 marked the first break in consensus on debt reduction. The necessity for balanced budgets remained the norm, but the growth of presidential discretion and the rise of industrial expansion left the role of debt open to argument. Abraham Lincoln (1861–1865) thought that citizens "cannot be much oppressed by a debt which they owe to themselves." His theory, followed by President Rutherford B. Hayes a decade later (1877–1881), was to effect a wider distribution of the debt among citizens. Postulating that the debt might be paid over time, President Ulysses S. Grant (1869–1877) asserted that the capacity to pay grew with the wealth of the nation. Rather than raising taxes to pay the debt over a shorter period, he suggested a cut in taxes to increase wealth and thereby provide greater subsequent revenues.[60] During a time of expansion the desire for internal improvements seemed compatible with fiscal prudence.

Expressing the prevailing sentiment, Grant's Secretary to the Treasury, George S. Boutwell, claimed in 1870 that "a public debt is a public evil, especially injurious to working people." Having inherited a debt of some two and a half billion dollars, President Andrew Johnson (1865–1869) considered debt a burden on the economy that should be paid off within twenty years. Despite the considerable increase in population and wealth, Johnson was startled to learn that expenditures during his term would be around $1.6 billion, only slightly less than the entire amount for the period from 1789 to 1861. He feared that per capita expenditure would reach nearly $10. The expenditure before the war had been held to $2 per person. He responded by urging retrenchment.[61] These were days during which spending, and the revenues supporting it, could not be too low.

President Grover Cleveland (1885–1889) believed that withdrawing capital from the people and transferring it to government imperiled prosperity. His words were a last stand against the spending boom that followed:

> When we consider that the theory of our institutions guarantees to every citizen the full enjoyment of all the fruits of his industry and enterprise, with only such deduction as may be his share toward the careful and economical maintenance of the Government which protects him, it is plain that the exaction of more than this is indefensible extortion and a culpable betrayal of American fairness and justice. This wrong inflicted upon those who bear the burden of national taxation, like other wrongs, multiplies a brood of evil consequences. The public Treasury, which should only exist as a conduit conveying the people's tribute to its legitimate objects of

expenditure, becomes a hoarding place for money needlessly withdrawn
from trade and the people's use, thus crippling our national energies. . . .[62]

Viewing debt as something a people owes itself, to be judged not as
an inherent evil but relative to a country's ability to pay, is not far
from the idea that the size of the deficit matters less than the government's, and through it the people's, return on monies expended. The
presidents from 1898 to 1920 were all opposed to unbalanced budgets.
But their twentieth-century successors, imbued with the progressive gospel of efficiency, were more inclined to stress the quality of spending.
For this new breed of president, efficient organization, and "value for
money," as the English say today, mattered more than parsimony.[63]
The American people, Woodrow Wilson said, "are not jealous of the
amount their Government costs if they are sure that they get what they
need and desire for the outlay, that the money is being spent for objects
of which they approve, and that it is being applied with good business
sense and management."[64]

Supporting this development of professional interest in efficiency and
the new civil service movement's concomitant stress on neutral competence and expertise was a homiletic literature urging thrift. Mr. Micaw-
ber's advice to David Copperfield in King's Bench prison that spending
just below income is happiness while spending just above it is misery
was endlessly repeated. Thriftiness was synonymous with morality and
success.

These vague rumblings of fiscal prudence, both against the growing
debt and for a balanced budget, reasserted themselves with a vengeance
in the 1920s. World War I had been largely fought on borrowed money.
From 1914 to 1918, the government's role in directing economic activity
expanded enormously. There was a sudden public concern that the
profligate habits of wartime would carry over into peacetime civilian
life. The Victory Liberty Loan Act of 1919 established a sinking fund
to reduce the debt, which was cut by a third—from $24 to $16 billion—
by the end of the 1920's. Wilson's Secretary of the Treasury, Carter
Glass, pointed out the "grave danger that the extraordinary success of
the Treasury in financing the stupendous war expenditures may lead
to a riot of public expenditures after the war, the consequences of which
could only be disastrous." His successor under President Harding (1921–
1923), David F. Huston, similarly observed that "we have demobilized
many groups, but we have not demobilized those whose gaze is concentrated on the Treasury."[65]

The idea that government should function like a business, that "our
public household," like a successful private enterprise, should be operated
under a "rigid and yet sane economy" was a leitmotif of the 1920s.
Whereas in past decades decrease of the public debt was said to reduce
the influence of its foreign holders, President Calvin Coolidge (1923–

1928) argued that low taxes and spending would give the American people "that contentment and peace of mind which will go far to render them immune from any envious inclination toward other countries." Competition over markets would subside if Americans were prosperous at home.[66] Coolidge contended that "economy reaches everywhere. It carries a blessing to everybody." Whereas "the result of economic dissipation to a nation is always moral decay," Coolidge believed that "economy is idealism in its most practical form."[67] The substance of this practical idealism was probably less important than the spirit it conveyed.

This economic mood could and did get more mawkish. Speaking at the tenth regular meeting of the Business Organization of the Government, the second head of the Bureau of the Budget, Director Lord, exclaimed, "We still follow you, Mr. President, singing the old and tried battle song, economy with efficiency, one and inseparable. May we continue to sing it until in a noble paean of praise it heralds the day when taxes cease to be burdensome and serve what is a grateful expression of our appreciation of the numberless privileges and boundless blessings we enjoy in this most favored Nation of the earth."[68] Director Lord accordingly founded various clubs to hold expenditures down, such as the Two-percent Personnel Club in order to cut personnel spending in that amount per year and a Correspondence Club to save money on messages. He also established the Loyal Order of Woodpeckers, "whose persistent tapping away at waste will make cheerful music in government offices and workshops during the coming year."[69]

Then came the market crash of 1929, followed by the Depression of the 1930s. The Depression marked both an end to the primacy of the balanced budget and a beginning of the variable expenditure as an instrument of economic stabilization. The great budgetary equation had been fundamentally reoriented. The emphasis shifted from matching spending and revenue at the lowest possible level to manipulation of the difference between them. The Employment Act of 1946 signaled a new equation focusing federal policy on the goal of full employment, with deficits and surpluses left to vary in its wake. Spending and owing, instead of being the great enemies of economy, had become its greatest friends. There was also the tradition of internal improvements to which supporters of higher spending could turn for historical justification of their position.

Internal Improvements

The subject of internal improvements may be taken broadly to include any sort of governmental subsidy for any purpose whatsoever, and not just those subsidies for roads and canals that gave the controversy its historical name. Advocates of markets might generally wish lower taxes and spending, but they always stood ready to accept subsidies that would diffuse the costs of sustaining commerce over a range of taxpayers. Adherents of hierarchy are generally willing to undertake expenditures that will add to national unity and help maintain order throughout the nation. Egalitarians would be opposed to internal improvements, seeing in them unjustified advantages for those in government who would occupy places of profit and those in society who already had more than their share of wealth and privilege. Americans who straddled the line between equity and hierarchy, and who viewed internal improvement as a means of assisting small farmers scattered throughout the vast extent of the nation, would be conflicted. They would resolve this conflict by adhering first and foremost to the doctrine of a balanced budget, believing that when that was achieved they might spend the surplus to benefit the general lot of citizens. Given this rough division of forces, it could be expected that over time there would be more rather than less subsidy. And, as the nation industrialized, giving market adherents greater prominence, internal improvements would turn out to be even a better thing.

With 30 per cent of the federal budget devoted to interest payments on the national debt and 55 per cent given over to the army and navy, and with the nation still recovering from the war, the administrations of George Washington and John Adams resorted to long-term loans to cover current deficits. In that situation no room for internal improvements existed. The Republicans under Jefferson engaged in a policy of retrenchment, practically eliminated the navy, slimmed down the army, and reduced the rest. The Republicans also cut internal taxes but left tariffs intact to create a surplus.[70] By 1805, with commerce improved and the end of the public debt in sight, Jefferson hoped that "the revenue thereby liberated may . . . be applied, *in time of peace,* to rivers, canals, roads, arts, manufacturers, education and the other great objects within each State." Undecided on the constitutional validity of such spending, Jefferson recommended that there be a constitutional amendment to remove doubt on the subject. Gallatin, his Secretary of the Treasury, had already made room for building the Cumberland Road and National Pike. The funds came from the sale of public lands in Ohio, which was then still a territory.[71] At the end of Jefferson's administration, Gallatin prepared a major report on public works calling for a $20 million program of canal and highway construction.[72]

Except for tariffs, which were already firmly ensconced because industry in America called for protection against Europe, Jefferson's administration did not otherwise attempt to act on the economy. Though its abandonment of old Republican principles concerning internal improvements caused considerable conflict within the party, these departures were made good by a strict constitutionalism, concern for states' rights, and meticulous circumscription of the role of executive officials. Older Republicans, such as John Randolph and John Taylor, were absolutely opposed to these new federal commitments to internal improvements. But new Republicans, such as John Calhoun, John Quincy Adams, and later, Henry Clay, were in favor of liberal spending for canals and roads. Whatever the decline of partisanship in the "era of good feelings," extending from the presidencies of Monroe and John Quincy Adams (1817–1828), the consensus did not extend to internal improvements.

Criticized for adopting Monroe's proposed plan for internal improvements, President John Quincy Adams avidly sought appropriations for rivers, harbors, lighthouses, beacons, piers, and most of all, roads. Adams' major effort had been to use the surplus to provide "a permanent and regular system . . . of . . . internal improvements" so that "the surface of the whole Union would have been checkered with railroads and canals. . . ."[73] During his presidency there were set up a House Committee on Roads and Canals, a Civil Engineer Corps inside the Army Engineers; grants of public lands were routinely made to new states to encourage them to build roads and canals, and "Rivers and Harbors" appropriations were made. The (in)famous "Pork Barrel" legislation had its beginning in which it was alleged, with good reason, that congressmen dipped their hands to get goodies for their districts, much as the boys at the country store did around a barrel of real pork.[74]

What was to stop this bucolic movement for internal improvements from continuing? This answer rested in President Andrew Jackson (1828–1836), whose forces had fought internal improvements in Congress. "Old Hickory" stopped them in their tracks. Jackson maintained himself in office by dethroning "King Caucus," the method of presidential nomination by senatorial caucus, in favor of a more egalitarian and popular national nominating convention. I mention this only to show that the same voluntaristic impulses that led to the one—opposition to federal support or subsidy of internal improvement—also led to the other—the replacement of an oligarchical by a more egalitarian mode of presidential nomination. Because Jacksonians believed that interest payment on the national debt meant a redistribution of income from the poor to rich, the fund from which wages were drawn was depressed by such payments, and the capital released from government spending into private hands would increase productivity and therefore wages, their disapproval of internal improvements was to them part of their public policy in favor of the ordinary citizen. Favoring the common man, in those days, meant favoring individual and not governmental enterprise.[75]

The same strictures that applied to federal debt did not apply with equal force to the states. On the contrary, if egalitarians viewed state governments as enhancing equality by virtue of popular control, then they might also be encouraged to help the citizenry by all manner of activities. Louis Hartz has shown that laissez-faire was hardly the prevailing practice in Pennsylvania before the Civil War.[76] When the states warmed up to their task after the demise of the Second Bank of the United States, they borrowed more from 1835 to 1838 than the total federal deficit from 1789 to 1838. The debt was devoted to canal and railroad construction and to capital for chartering state banks.[77]

Support for and opposition to internal improvements waxed and waned for the thirty years before the Civil War. Congressional advocates like Henry Clay produced one bill after another. What would stop "a disreputable scramble for public money," President Polk asked while vetoing a rivers and harbors bill, if all that were left were congressional discretion as to the fitness of things? Why, internal improvements were "capable of indefinite enlargement and sufficient to swallow up as many millions annually as could be extracted from the foreign commerce of the country." Allied with a protective tariff that brought in ever-larger sums, Polk believed that "the operation and necessary effect of the whole system would encourage large and extravagant expenditures, and thereby . . . increase the public patronage, and maintain a rich and splendid government at the expense of a taxed and impoverished people."[78] Acquiring Texas or another large expanse of territory was another matter, properly a part of the nation's "manifest destiny." Even so, many of the promises made to get Texas into the Union, promises in the way of Federal largesse, remained unfulfilled.[79]

If it was money that mattered to Polk, it was public morality about which Presidents Pierce and Buchanan cared. They rejected internal improvements on the grounds that these were unconstitutional because they usurped state functions. They saw internal improvement as a means by which the general government would aggrandize itself at the expense of states.[80] For other leading men of the day, however, from Daniel Webster to John Calhoun and President Millard Fillmore, the great issue was, as it had been to Jefferson, the growth of the nation. They believed that although the work might be done locally, it had a larger general or national importance. Although no one would ever say that they wanted to encroach on the right of any single state, it was a case of a big brother helping a smaller one so as, as Fillmore put it, to "strengthen the ties which bind us together as a people."[81]

Needless to say, in that day as today, the learned scribes were on both sides of the situation. It was not Adam Smith's *Wealth of Nations* or Ricardo's *Principles of Political Economy* but, rather, Jean-Baptiste Say's *A Treatise on Political Economy*, which appeared in 1803, that became popular in the United States. Louis Kimmel, whose brilliant book on federal debt I have often cited, believes that "a factor in Say's favor was that he avoided Smith's distinction between 'productive' and 'unproductive' employment. Neither professors of moral philosophy nor the clergy had been quite willing to accept an exposition into the moral science of political economy that classified them as unproductive." Say did agree with Adam Smith, however, on the crucial consideration that consumption of wealth by government, although it might be necessary, was justified only to the extent that it brought in returns of equivalent value. The doctrine of opportunity costs, the value of the object is what has to be given up to acquire it, here finds an early statement. And so does a notion of cost-benefit analysis: "The whole skill of government," Say says, ". . . consists in a continual and judicious comparison of the sacrifice about to be incurred, with the expected benefits to the community."[82] A native book, Henry Vethake's *The Principles of Political Economy*, objected to debt financing because it led to less care in the spending of public money. But so long as government funds were used for productive purposes, he thought such spending was as good as if the money had been left in private hands.[83] All in all, it does not appear that the writings of learned men exerted much influence one way or the other on the debate about internal improvements.

Compared to European countries, spending in the United States stood practically still, barely keeping up with the increase in population. Nevertheless, the federal government did do some things outside of its limited sphere. As early as 1796, collectors of revenue assisted in the enforcement of state quarantine laws. Medical care for disabled and sick seamen was instituted in 1798, eventually leading to the establishment of the United States Public Health Service. Small numbers of agricultural statistics were collected and free seeds distributed. Statistics on commerce and lifesaving stations on the Atlantic coast were established. Moving onto larger matters, there were subsidies to carriers of ocean mail and railroads.[84] The mail subsidies were justified by a parallel policy adopted in Great Britain for the purpose of encouraging steamships that could be readily converted to naval use.[85] From the 1830s through the 1850s, despite presidential opposition, substantial subsidies were made available to a variety of railroads, either by way of subscription to their stock or by deeding over to them large amounts of public land. States' rights were preserved. The money was given to states which then passed it on to finance the construction of railroads. The justification was that a nation was being built.[86] Yet by European standards or even by absolute standards, the amounts were small. Support for agriculture hardly amounted to $5,000 by 1860.[87]

There was regulation. *Nile's Register* reported in 1830 that 1,500 people had died from steamboat explosions. Boilers blew up with such regularity that it eventually caused scandal and led to the establishment of federal inspection. The same was also true of mass importation of foreign drugs; questions as to the prevalence of impurities led to investigation and then regulation.[88]

Major developments were occurring in the states, where combinations of private and public funding led to the development of canals and railroads. The first and most famous was the New York Erie Canal, which, despite all prognostications to the contrary, returned handsome profits on its multimillion dollar investment. The boom in canal building was on, and many states followed suit. In the 1820s and 1830s the State of Virginia floated bonds to build a number of canals and railroads, and though only one railroad survived the Civil War, Virginia kept paying the debt, which was finally paid off in 1966.[89] A typical example was the Central Ohio Railroad, chartered in 1847, whose management found it difficult to get people to subscribe. The vendors made stump speeches throughout the territory, indulged in newspaper and pamphlet publications, went door to door with only indifferent success. The deficit was eventually made up by subscriptions from counties and towns, with some state money contributed. A more enterprising company went to London and borrowed on State of Maryland bonds. Less savory, though equally enterprising, were the railroads that issued paper script worth so little that workers sometimes rioted. Unfulfilled subscriptions might be used as collateral for still new loans.[90] By the early 1840s, things were so bad that seven states defaulted in failing to pay the interest on their debt. This was called "repudiation," though within a few years all states had made good on their defaults. The specter of repudiation led English bards to remonstrate in the manner of the Reverend Sidney Smith:

> Yankee Doodle borrows cash,
> Yankee Doodle spends it,
> And then he snaps his fingers at
> The jolly flat who lends it.
> Ask him when he means to pay,
> He shows no hesitation,
> But says he'll take the shortest way
> And that's Repudiation!
>
> Yankee vows that every State
> Is free and independent:
> And if they paid each other's debts,
> There'd never be an end on't.
>
> They keep distinct till "settling" comes,
> And then throughout the nation
> They all become "United States"
> To preach Repudication! . . .

And what does freedom mean, if not
To whip our slaves at pleasure
And borrow money when you can,
To pay it at your leisure?[91]

For the federal government, however, the era before the Civil War remained a time of tiny government. Between 1800 and 1860, as Table 12.1 shows, federal expenditures rose from near $11 to $63 million. More than half were military expenditures. The general category of "Civil and miscellaneous" included a substantial amount for the postal deficit, thus covering everything except defense, pensions, Indians, and interest on the debt. Kimmel is correct in his conclusion "that federal expenditures made little or no contribution to the level of living. Only a minor portion of Civil and miscellaneous expenditures were for developmental purposes. . . ."[93]

The Civil War changed all that. The government grew from tiny to small. It promoted the interests of businessmen and farmers, sometimes aiding railroads and at other times intervening to regulate railroads in the interests of farmers. Beginning with the Morrill Act of 1862, which gave huge land grants to states for the purpose of establishing agricultural and mechanical universities, a variety of measures were adopted to aid education. Not unlike Thomas Jefferson, post–Civil War presidents generally regarded education as an exception to whatever strictures they laid upon unnecessary expenditures. And as the nation was settled and the frontier neared its end, the beginnings of a movement to set aside land for conservation purposes appeared. But it is not in these modest departures from the strict doctrine of minimum states' rights that one can find the sources of budgetary conflict or the seeds of future spending.

Money may or may not be the root of all evil. But the availability of

TABLE 12.1   Federal Expenditures, Fiscal Years 1800, 1825, 1850, and 1860[a]
(*In millions of dollars*)

	1800	1825	1850	1860
Civil and miscellaneous	1.3	2.7	14.9	28.0[b]
War Department	2.6	3.7	9.4	16.4
Navy Department	3.4	3.1	7.9	11.5
Indians	—	0.7	1.6	2.9
Pensions	0.1	1.3	1.9	1.1
Interest	3.4	4.4	3.8	3.2
	$10.8	$15.9	$39.5	$63.1[b]

[a] *Annual Report of the Secretary of the Treasury on the State of the Finances for the Fiscal Year Ended June 30, 1934*, pp. 302–303.
[b] Includes postal deficit of $9.9 million.[92]

substantial surpluses in the post–Civil War period proved a greater temptation than most private interests and public officials were able to withstand. No one can say whether it was the change in national opinion attendant to the swift pace of the industrial revolution, the change in public morality signified by the term "robber barons" applied to the new industrialists whose business scruples and public behavior were less than exemplary, or the huge revenues generated by the growing protective tariff or the attendant changes in the process of budgeting that mattered most. Suffice it to say that soon enough even the $3 billion Civil War debt became readily manageable and that higher tariffs still produced substantial surpluses.

It would be difficult to overemphasize the part played by high tariffs in the public policy of the Republican Party. The tariff, and the surpluses it generated, enabled Republican governments to do several things simultaneously: It allowed subsidized domestic manufacturing, provided "infrastructure" for industry, paid off a substantial part of the Civil War debt, used debt payments to strengthen central banking, discouraged efforts to introduce progressive income taxation, and generally cemented an alliance between a stronger central government and business enterprise. But I cannot follow that path here.

Repeating the litanies of past presidents, Grover Cleveland (1885–1889) voiced the fears that growing surpluses would "tempt extravagance" and that public extravagance "begets extravagance among the people."[94] Cleveland's predecessor, President Chester A. Arthur (1881–1884), who, in 1882, experienced a Congressional override of his veto of the Rivers and Harbors Act, also condemned surpluses on the grounds that they corrupted public morality and inexorably contributed to rising expenditures.[95] Whether as cause or reflection of the temptations provided by having money to spend without having to raise taxes, changes in the Congressional appropriations process facilitated the spread and extent of internal improvements.

The issue of internal improvements experienced a change of perspective as a result of the Depression of the 1930s, when they were seen as a positive aid to increasing employment. The soup line was added to the pork barrel. The earlier notion of internal improvements as a means of increasing national harmony by extending communications was replaced by a belief in social cohesion as a result of putting people back to work. The era of entitlements that bound people to government by giving them rights to its revenues was yet to come.

In the budgetary sphere, hierarchies prefer to follow forms, punctual tax collection, and spending to shore up the regime. Sects, by contrast, prefer no executive discretion, little spending on the regime, and revenues collected from the more prosperous. Markets are indifferent to forms or discretion but insist on getting a return for their money, including the part that government collects. They prefer lower taxes and spending, except for supporting projects from which they benefit. The special circumstances of American life have created conditions in which people pursuing these various cultures have been more evenly balanced than elsewhere.

In regard to the choice of budgeting style, collectivists favor funding by organizational level, individualists typically choose lump sums (because they care only about outcomes), and voluntarists prefer detail as a means of controlling extravagance. Voluntarists demand a person-by-person, object-by-object description. If collectivists and individualists are in the majority, the result is likely to be a line-item budget with lump sums reserved for emergencies when results matter. The unity of the budget is another matter, however, inasmuch as collectivists and voluntarists oppose the external control a unified budget signifies.

In regard to spending levels, both individualists and voluntarists want to keep the levels low because they prefer to keep government on a short and parsimonious leash. Spending to enhance equality does attract voluntarists, however, and individualists favor spending to aid business. Collectivists tend to prefer spending for its own sake because each level of the hierarchy seeks to spend to maintain its own position. Bargaining results when the hierarchy offers to aid business or "the people" in return for support of governmental establishments.

In regard to revenues, all regimes would like someone else to pay for their privileges. Since no regime commands a majority at any given time, compromises are made in an attempt to keep taxes low. When there is a surplus, government, business, and the populace share the proceeds. When circumstances are trying—during war, for example—taxes are raised to satisfy sects, debt is incurred to satisfy markets, and the government grows to satisfy hierarchies.

The need for a balanced budget became almost a religion in American society because it is the one thing about which all three cultures can agree. Because voluntarists in a sectarian regime are perennial outsiders, they are not likely to enjoy the largesse of government spending. A humble posture with low spending is their chosen style. Believing as they do in equality, they could not easily justify the imposition of taxes that distinguish among individuals. Tying spending directly to the pain of raising revenues, they insist on balanced budgets as a means to curtail establishment spending.

Individualist adherents of markets emphasize credit and currency because without stable financial values their endless transactions cannot be carried out. Inflation is anathema to them because it gives debtors advantages over creditors. Market people do not object to deficits in principle as long as they benefit from the borrowing. They must therefore be concerned about inflationary effects. They temper the desire to redistribute losses with the need for stability by agreeing that revenues should cover expenditures. This practice limits the efforts of sects to please the populace (common in state legislatures) and of hierarchies to dress up government in finery inappropriate for a commercial people.

Left to their own devices, hierarchies would run deficits as each level of the hierarchy spent to maintain its distinctive niche. But since markets and sects limit their need for government spending, hierarchies typically seek to limit spending also, in exchange for agreement on raising sufficient revenue. The inability of any one regime to dominate the others led to a common-denominator consensus: the balanced budget. As follows from any boundary formation, violations became subject to penalties—unemployment, inflation, public immorality, private vice, and collective ruin.

Endnotes

1. James "Lord" Bryce, *The American Commonwealth* (London: Macmillan, 1891), p. 188.
2. Louis Hartz, *The Liberal Tradition in America* (New York: Harcourt, Brace, 1955).
3. Alexis de Tocqueville, *Democracy in America* (New York: Knopf, Vintage Books, 1945).
4. Anthony King, "Ideas, Institutions and the Policies of Governments: A Comparative Analysis: Part III," *The British Journal of Political Science*, 3:409–423 (October) 1973.
5. Seymour Martin Lipset, "Why No Socialism in the United States?", in *Sources of Contemporary Radicalism*, Seweryn Bialer and Sophia Sluzar, eds., (Boulder, CO: Westview Press, 1977).
6. William J. Shultz and M. R. Caine, *Financial Development of the United States* (New York: Prentice-Hall, 1937), pp. 7–9. There was ingenuity. Lacking small change, the colonists cut Spanish dollars into quarters, eighths, and sixteenths, a phenomenon known as "sharp" change or cut money.
7. Ibid., p. 10.
8. Margaret G. Myers, *A Financial History of the United States* (New York & London: Columbia University Press, 1970), p. 3; and Davis R. Dewey, *Financial History of the United States* (New York: Longmans, Green, 1939), pp. 18–19.
9. Shultz and Caine, p. 9.
10. Dewey, op.cit., p. 8.
11. Charles Bullock, "The Finances of the United States from 1775–1789 with Special Reference to the Budget," *Bulletin of the University of Wisconsin*, Vol. 1 (1894–1896) (Madison, WI: University of Wisconsin Press, 1897), p. 225.
12. Myers, op.cit., p. 11.

13. Gary B. Nash, *The Urban Crucible: Social Change, Political Consciousness and the Origins of the American Revolution* (Cambridge: Yale University Press, 1979), pp. 60–70.
14. Ibid., pp. 225–253.
15. Franklin's argument was so effective his printing company got the contract for putting out the paper money. The money Franklin left in his will to aid industrious and honest mechanics was due in large part to his recognition of the difficulty ordinary people faced in amassing any amount of capital in the absence of a plentiful sound currency (Myers, op.cit., p. 10).
16. Dewey, op.cit., pp. 23–30.
17. Shultz and Caine, op.cit., p. 23.
18. Dewey, op.cit., pp. 9–10.
19. Myers, op.cit., pp. 15–16; and Dewey, op.cit., pp. 11–12.
20. Myers, in Ibid., pp. 17–18; and Dewey, in Ibid., p. 17.
21. Shultz and Caine, op.cit., p. 15.
22. See Robert C. Tucker and David C. Hendrickson, *The Fall of the First British Empire: Origins of the War of American Independence* (Baltimore: Johns Hopkins University Press, 1982), pp. 152–159, 174–175, 406–410.
23. Bullock, pp. 217, 225.
24. Ibid., pp. 216–219.
25. Ibid., pp. 219–221.
26. Ibid., p. 218.
27. Shultz and Caine, op.cit., pp. 60–61.
28. Myers, op.cit., pp. 30–31; and Bullock, op.cit., pp. 214–215, 257.
29. Shultz and Caine, op.cit., p. 69.
30. William Graham Sumner, *The Financier and the Finances of the American Revolution* (New York: Dodd, Mead, 1891), pp. 301–302.
31. Ibid., pp. 302–303.
32. Theodore J. Grayson, *Leaders and Periods of American Finance* (New York: John Wiley, 1932), pp. 36–37.
33. Sumner, op.cit., p. 301.
34. Grayson, op.cit., p. 34.
35. Ibid., pp. 44–45.
36. Shultz and Caine, op.cit., pp. 37–38.
37. Albert S. Bolles, *The Financial History of the United States 1774–1789* (New York: D. Appleton, 1979), p. 201.
38. Bullock, op.cit., pp. 115–120.
39. See Samuel P. Huntington, *The Common Defense* (New York: Columbia University Press, 1969); and Patrick Crecine et al., "Presidential Management of Budgetary and Fiscal Policymaking," *Political Science Quarterly*, 95:395–425 (Fall) 1980, for contemporary versions during the administrations of Harry S. Truman and Dwight D. Eisenhower.
40. Dall W. Forsythe, *Taxation and Political Change in the Young Nation 1781–1833* (New York: Columbia University Press, 1977), p. 38.
41. Lewis Kimmel, *Federal Budget and Fiscal Policy 1789–1958* (Washington, DC: Brookings Institution, 1959), p. 8.
42. Ibid., p. 9.
43. Forsythe, op.cit., p. 31.

44. Ibid., pp. 28–29.
45. Kimmel, op.cit., p. 14.
46. Ibid.
47. I am indebted to James Savage's dissertation ("Balanced Budgets and American Politics") on the balanced budget idea for elaboration of this point. All serious students of the subject should read his forthcoming book from Cornell University Press.
48. Kimmel, op.cit., pp. 14–16.
49. Ibid., pp. 27–28; and Forsythe, op.cit., p. 60.
50. Kimmel, pp. 16–17.
51. Ibid., pp. 17–18.
52. Ibid., pp. 19–21.
53. Ibid., pp. 21–22.
54. Ibid., p. 28.
55. Ibid., p. 23.
56. Ibid., p. 24.
57. Ibid., pp. 24–25.
58. Ibid., pp. 25–26.
59. Ibid., pp. 26–27.
60. Ibid., pp. 65–69.
61. Ibid., pp. 71–73.
62. Ibid., pp. 71–73.
63. Ibid., pp. 84–85.
64. Ibid., pp. 87–88.
65. Ibid., p. 88.
66. Ibid., p. 96.
67. Ibid., pp. 95–96.
68. Ibid., p. 96.
69. Ibid., p. 97.
70. Shultz and Caine, op.cit., pp. 134–135.
71. Myers, op.cit., pp. 106–108.
72. Shultz and Caine, op.cit., pp. 137–140.
73. Leonard D. White, *The Jeffersonians: A Study in Administrative History 1801–1829* (New York: Macmillan, 1951), p. 483.
74. Myers, op.cit., pp. 108–109.
75. Kimmel, op.cit., p. 19; and White, *Jeffersonians*, p. 483.
76. Louis Hartz, *Economic Policy and Democratic Thought: Pennsylvania 1776–1860* (Chicago: Quadrangle Books, 1968).
77. See Henry C. Adams, *Public Debts: An Essay in the Science of Finance* (New York: D. Appleton, 1887), p. 321; and B. U. Ratchford, *American State Debts* (Durham, North Carolina: Duke University Press, 1941), pp. 77–83. Chapter 3, "Colonial America to the Civil War," of James Savage's dissertation is an indispensible guide to the intricacies of this subject.
78. Kimmel, op.cit., pp. 31–32.
79. Ibid., p. 33.
80. Ibid., pp. 34–35.
81. Ibid., p. 34.
82. Ibid., p. 41.

83. Ibid., p. 52.
84. Leonard D. White, *The Jacksonians: A Study in Administrative History 1829–1861* (New York: Macmillan, 1954), p. 438.
85. Ibid., pp. 450–451.
86. Ibid., p. 451.
87. Ibid., p. 442.
88. Ibid., pp. 450–451.
89. Myers, op.cit., p. 116.
90. Ibid., pp. 115–116.
91. Shultz and Caine, pp. 235–236; see also Myers, p. 109.
92. Kimmel, op.cit., p. 57.
93. Ibid.
94. Ibid., pp. 71–72.
95. Ibid., pp. 70–71.

PART V

Public Administration in Theory

CHAPTER 13

Changing Public Bureaucracy: Values and Organization-Management Theories

Fred A. Kramer
THE UNIVERSITY OF MASSACHUSETTS

FRED A. KRAMER is Professor of Political Science at the University of Massachusetts, Amherst. He is the author of Dynamics of Public Bureaucracy *and has edited* Perspectives on Public Bureaucracy *and* Contemporary Approaches to Public Budgeting. *He has contributed articles to the* American Political Science Review, *the* Public Administration Review, *and* Public Personnel Management, *as well as other scholarly and professional journals. Professor Kramer has also been involved in designing and implementing management training programs for local, state, and foreign governments. He holds the Ph.D. in political science from the Maxwell School of Syracuse University.*

Fred A. Kramer examines various currents of thought about the allocation of values and the utilization of power in American public bureaucracies by clarifying two related questions: *who* decides what should be done, and *how* can government do what should be done? He addresses Herbert Kaufman's contention that the pandemic fear of bureaucracy being out of control might be confusion arising from the conflicting views of critics about what constitutes control and what constitutes power.

The who and how questions are simplifications of more abstract questions about control and power evident in public administrative thought since the time of Woodrow Wilson. One cannot consider the *how* question of organization and management apart from the *who* question of decision making. William G. Scott suggests three groups of organization theories that have affected public bureaucracy in these areas: classical, neoclassical, and organizational humanist.

1. Classical organization theories have been strongly influenced by the intellectual work of Max Weber and the practical legacy of Luther Gulick through his work as a member of the Brownlow Committee in the late 1930s. Gulick's "Notes on the Theory of Organization" has provided the basis for most major governmental reorganizations since 1939. His principal concerns were how an organization might be structured when each position was characterized by the *purpose* served, the *process* used, the *persons* or *things* dealt with, and the *place* where the work was done. The organizational hierarchy would appear quite different depending on the values an executive wished to promote or was willing to sacrifice, and according to the precedence given certain organizational factors. The acronym POSDCORB, the use of which Gulick popularized, serves as a summary statement of the activities an executive must engage in to attain even a minimal degree of organization effectiveness. *P*lanning, *o*rganizing, *s*taffing, *d*irecting, *co*ordinating, *r*eporting, and *b*udgeting do not by themselves ensure power within the hierarchy, however.

2. Neoclassical organization theories stem from studies conducted by Elton Mayo and Fritz Roethlisberger at the Hawthorne Works of the Western Electric Company in Chicago in the late 1920s and early 1930s. Neoclassical theories imply a human-relational aspect of power that is different from the hierarchically based concept of power inherent in top-down organizations. Neoclassicists do not abandon hierarchy as an organizational base, but they redirect the emphasis of hierarchy to encompass the human dimension of organizational life. Chester Barnard offered an explanation of relational power within a hierarchy by describing the zone of indifference, wherein a subordinate is willing to accept certain demands made by the boss as legitimate demands that he or she will carry out. Neoclassical theories assume that social interaction throughout the organization affects how things get done and who decides what is to be done. In public bureaucracies informal organization interaction takes place both within the agency and in exchanges with its immediate environment. Neoclassical organization theories recognize legislative subcommittee relationships as well as the clientele of an agency as legitimate sources of power, for example.

3. The intellectual sire of organizational humanism is Abraham Maslow. Other proponents have added such values as a focus on the personal growth and development of individuals within an organization, an apolitical basis for decision making where truth rather than power is the guide, and the resolution of conflict in an integrative manner as opposed to an authoritarian one. Organizational humanism suggests that decision makers in public bureaucracies should be open to a wider range of participation from the external environment

than either classical or neoclassical organizations would allow. The policy networks characterizing such participation would be dissimilar in size and strength but linked together by interest. They would have the potential to meet any expressed need when policy making demands knowledge-based competence.

It is not practical to assume that any single theory would always be appropriate. Values change, people change, and the environment is never completely stable. Public managers can make qualified choices affecting the *who* and *how* questions only when they are sensitive to the people in their organizations and the range of theories available to accomplish their goals.

Academics, bureaucrats, and citizens have tried to describe and understand the sources of power within public bureaucracies, how it is used, and the role it plays in American society. Thinking about power in public bureaucracy has not been a linear progression. Instead, different eddies of thought have intermingled over the years, emerging as identifiable currents at various times. The acceptance of these thoughts at any time depends on the predominant values of those academics, bureaucrats, and citizens at that particular time.

The search for a single description or explanation of power and public bureaucracy is fruitless and will not be undertaken here. Instead, this essay attempts to identify the main currents in American thought regarding public bureaucracy and the values associated with those currents.

The predominant values of the 1980s have led Herbert Kaufman to note that "antibureaucratic sentiment has taken hold like an epidemic. More and more people are apparently convinced that bureaucracy is whirling out of control."[1] But when Kaufman begins to peel away the layers of the onion of fear of public bureaucracy, he finds conflicting views of what is meant when various observers assert that public bureaucracy is out of control. Some critics, he notes, claim that bureaucracy is out of control because it is out of *their* control. Others are concerned because the hierarchy does not seem to exercise what they deem to be proper control. Others believe the legislature has lost control. Still others believe the people have been dealt out by capitalistic controls on bureaucrats who are supposed to serve the disadvantaged but do not. Because of the conflicting views of what constitutes control and power, Kaufman concludes that the expressed fears of bureaucratic power are more rhetoric than reality.[2]

The questions of control and power have appeared in American public administrative thought since Woodrow Wilson's time. Essentially, these are two related questions that can be restated as follows: *Who* decides what should be done? And *how* can government do what should be done? Observers of public bureaucracy over the past 100 years have tended to emphasize the second question, but because the two are so intertwined no satisfactory solution to the how question—one of organization and management—can surface without concern for the who question. If we accept politics to mean "the process by which power is employed to affect whether and how government will act on any given matter,"[3] both questions become ones of politics and values.

To explore the who and how questions in a systematic fashion, we will look briefly at the changing organization theories that have influenced public bureaucracy in the United States. Following the suggestion of William G. Scott, we will designate three groups of organization theories: (1) classical, (2) neoclassical, and (3) organizational humanist. Each of these theories corresponds in a rough way to various political theories. Classical organization theory shares a common intellectual tradition with the more autocratic political theories, espoused by Thomas Hobbes. Neoclassical organization theories bear a rough similarity to liberal political thought and may be traced back to John Locke's view of power. Organizational-humanist theories have some common features with the theories of John Dewey.[4]

Although classical organization theories owe their largest intellectual debt to Max Weber, Luther Gulick's work as a member of the Brownlow Committee in the late 1930s represents a stream of influence that has been strongly felt in American public bureaucracy at all levels. Building from the essential classical bureaucratic notions of division of labor, the hierarchy, and rules to govern behavior, Gulick tried to turn "principles" of administrative theory into administrative practice. Despite criticism from academics, Gulick left a remarkable imprint on American public bureaucracy. Every major federal governmental reorganization since 1939 has been based, to a large degree, on ideas that were pulled together in Gulick's "Notes on the Theory of Organization," which was the lead article in a volume he edited for the Brownlow Committee.[5] Whereas Weber represented one branch of the classical tradition that dealt with bureaucracy at a cosmic level, Gulick's principal concerns were how organizations might be structured and what the roles were of the executives within them.

Gulick's presentation of four ways of organizing work has provided useful rules of thumb and the rationale for virtually all governmental reorganizations. Gulick suggested that each position in an organization could be characterized by the *purpose* served, the *process* used, the *persons* or *things* dealt with, and the *place* where the work was done. If people were doing the same work in the same way for the same people at the same place, there would be little difficulty in designing an organizational unit for supervision and control purposes. The unit could be organized on the basis of any of the four categories, and the result would be the same from the point of view of the hierarchy. If, however, there were not a perfect correlation between the type of work being done, the way that work was being done, the people or things that were to be benefited by that work, and the place in which the work was being done, then the choice of an organizational structure would not be so simple. The hierarchy would look quite different, depending upon which basis of organization was given precedence in determining how the organizational unit should be established.

Gulick sought to guide executives in deciding upon which basis to restructure public bureaucracy. He tried to spell out which values would be enhanced and which would be sacrificed by organizing administration primarily along one dimension or another. For example, if one organized by purpose or function—what later became the basis for program budgeting and project management—Gulick saw several advantages accruing: (1) a single-purpose agency would be more certain of attaining its objectives because a whole job would be under a single director, (2) the purpose would be easily understood and recognized by the public, and (3) the central purpose would be useful in motivating the personnel. But these alleged advantages would have to be balanced against several alleged defects of organization by purpose. Among the problems were (1) the impossibility of cleanly dividing government work into clear purposes that do not overlap extensively, (2) the strong internal cohesion under a single director might lead to serious external conflict and confusion, and (3) several other problems, such as the possible failure to make use of modern technology, the danger of overcentralization, and the corresponding lack of democratic control.

As part of his concern for structure, Gulick stressed such problems as unity of command, span of control, and line-staff relationships, which are dear to the hearts of all classical organization theorists. Gulick is best remembered, however, for his interest in the roles of executives and the need for staff support. Gulick popularized the acronym POSDCORB to describe the activities of executives. POSDCORB stands for *p*lanning, *o*rganizing, *s*taffing, *d*irecting, *co*ordinating, *r*eporting, and *b*udgeting. He thought these seven elements were the basis of organization for staff activities to the executive. Generally, the concept of staff refers to support activities done by organizational units that are not directly involved in the production of the product or service for which the agency is organized. Staff is usually contrasted with the line—those units that are directly engaged in producing the organization's products or services.

Clearly, not all staff or executive functions are included under the POSDCORB umbrella. Data processing could be considered a staff activity in a governmental agency. So could evaluation. Certainly, leadership is a key executive role. Criticism of POSDCORB has revolved around this lack of comprehensiveness, but the acronym has proven to be a useful summary of what executives must do to maintain even a minimal degree of organizational effectiveness.

Proposals for governmental reorganization to achieve greater effectiveness and efficiency are often offered as if they were developed according to value-free principles. The standard prescriptions call for limiting the number of line subordinates who must report to an executive, organizing by purpose or function, providing executives with staff assistance, and allowing executives to take responsibility for reorganizations.[6] All of these recommendations assume the scientific purity of classical organization theory. But rather than providing scientific principles for organizing, the classical solutions are, as Herbert Simon pointed out, proverbs.[7] "Look before you leap" and "He who hesitates is lost" are two proverbs that purport to guide choice under similar circumstances. Which does one follow? Similarly, Simon viewed most of the principles of classical public administration as offering contradictory advice.

Although attempts to implement reorganization based on contradictions inherent in classical organization theory might have caused problems for academics, there were some clear implications of most attempts to restructure public bureaucracy according to the dictates of classical theories. Classical theories hold the hierarchy to be the primary source of power within an agency. Power that has its source in the division of labor or in legal and technical rules takes a secondary position to power through the hierarchy. Power that comes from personality and informal organization has virtually no place in the classical schema. Instead, the classical organizational view of bureaucracy is that power comes from the top down. Classical organizational theory assumes that power should be centralized. The Brownlow Committee, the Hoover Commissions, the Ash Council, and the waves of reorganizations of state governments in the 1960s and 1970s, as well as efforts to develop program structures to support program budgeting, all accepted the classical view of power in an organization.

Implicit in this view of top-down power is an answer to the who and how questions raised at the outset. According to the classical view, line officers, with staff support, have the right to determine what will be done, and they have the power to see that subordinates carry out the orders or face the consequences. Often in the name of accountability, classical organization theory sanctifies the centralization of power.

Although classical organization theory has been the basis for virtually all efforts to restructure public bureaucracy, it serves only a limited number of values and reflects a limited view of political and organizational reality. Classical organizational theory assumes the legitimacy of the politics administration dichotomy. Policy is assumed to be made through legislative and executive interaction. It is then grafted onto the hierarchy at some point. Policy is assumed to be implemented below that level through the chain of command. In theory, democratic accountability is served and things get done. In addition, classical organization theories assume that people in the hierarchy respond to the demands of the hierarchy as if they were cogs in a machine. Unfortunately, the theory is at variance with reality.

Neoclassical organization theories offer a more realistic picture of the dynamics of public bureaucracy. Neoclassical theories accept the basic pillars of classical theory—hierarchy, division of labor, and rules— but add the human dimension and the role of informal organization. This recognition of the role of people in the organization gives neoclassical organization theory a management, rather than a structural, emphasis and implies a different notion of power in the organization.

The intellectual roots of neoclassical organization theories are in the landmark studies conducted by Elton Mayo and Fritz Roethlisberger of the Harvard Business School at the Hawthorne (Chicago) Works of the Western Electric Company in the late 1920s and early 1930s. In a series of experiments, the Hawthorne researchers discovered informal organization flourishing within and sometimes creating situations contrary to the needs of the formal organization.[8] Implicit in the findings of the neoclassical school was a different concept of power in organizations. Whereas classical organization theorists saw power and authority as a unidirectional relationship going through the hierarchy from the top down, the neoclassicists, while keeping the hierarchy as the major way for coordinating individual efforts in large-scale organizations, saw power as a relational concept. The bosses might give orders, but the informal organization had real power in determining the extent to which those orders were obeyed.

This concept of relational power in the hierarchy is best shown by Chester Barnard, who was a president of the New Jersey Bell System and a major influence on administrative thought since the 1930s. Barnard described the power relationship in any hierarchy as involving a zone of indifference. To Barnard, each subordinate was willing to accept certain demands made by the boss. Each employee had a perceptual zone in which he or she would accept the boss's orders as legitimate and carry them out. If an order fell within this perceptual zone, the subordinate would be indifferent to the order; he or she would not give it a second thought.[9] If a secretary were given a letter to type, he or she would not question the demand. A boss, however, could give orders that were clearly outside that secretary's zone of indifference. A request to "entertain" an influential legislator might fall outside the zone. The subordinate might not accept such an order as being legitimate and therefore could refuse to carry it out.

An interesting feature of the zone of indifference, or as Herbert Simon called it, the zone of acceptance,[10] is that the zone is flexible. The zone of acceptance can be broadened by offering incentives. Barnard saw a range of incentives available for management to expand an employee's zone of acceptance. Money could be used to encourage that secretary to treat that influential legislator in ways that he or she might ordinarily not see as part of the job. Barnard, however, was more concerned with other incentives. To Barnard, the attractiveness of the informal social group and opportunity to show distinction in one's work were more effective incentives to broaden the zone of acceptance than more money or improved working conditions.

To Barnard, one of the key management tasks was to develop a package of incentives that would keep subordinates contributing to the organization at a high level. He developed the concept of a contribution satisfaction equilibrium in which individuals contributed their talents to an organization in return for a range of satisfactions that they received from the organization. Unless management could continue to provide satisfactions in the form of incentives, employees would not contribute as much as they might.

The notions of the zone of indifference or acceptance and the contribution satisfaction equilibrium depict vastly different power relationships than those of the classical theories. Neoclassical theories assume that social interaction throughout the hierarchy greatly affects how things get done and who decides what is to be done. It takes into consideration a much broader environment than does the structural emphasis of classical theories. Neoclassical theories give legitimacy to the power of people in organizations and imply that the policy administration dichotomy does not hold because at all points in the hierarchy informal organization can influence policy choices and outcomes.

One of the clearest early statements concerning politics and administration stemming from the power relations implicit in neoclassical organization theory was by Norton Long in the late 1940s:

> It is clear that the American system of politics does not generate enough power at any focal point of leadership to provide the conditions for an even partially successful divorce of politics from administration. Subordinates cannot depend on the formal chain of command to deliver enough political power to permit them to do their jobs. Accordingly they must

supplement the resources available through the hierarchy with those they can muster on their own. . . . Administrative rationality demands that objectives be determined and sights set in conformity with a realistic appraisal of power position and potential.[11]

If the formal hierarchy cannot provide the power to carry out policy mandated through the formal legal channels, successful administration in public bureaucracy depends upon informal organization both within the agency and in the immediate organizational environment. Among the potential power sources from the immediate environment are higher political and career executives, the legislature, other governmental agencies, the clientele, and the general public.

Of the potential power sources, the ones most easily developed by an agency are those having an intense interest in its work. Not many actors in an agency's environment have that intense interest. Higher-level political and career executives are worried about a range of issues in addition to the work of any particular agency. They will not routinely invest their time in an agency that is not giving them problems. Other government agencies may have some peripheral interest in the work of the agency; certainly the central budget and personnel offices could either help or hinder the work of any agency. But generally, except when they are protecting their turf, the other agencies are not intensely concerned. The general public, whether unorganized or loosely organized, has such diffuse interests that it would be difficult for most agencies to mobilize the public at large for political support of agency goals.

There are, however, two groups of actors in an agency's environment that have a great deal of interest in the agency's work. These are members of legislative committees and subcommittees dealing with the agency, and the agency's clientele. Although the legislature is interested in a wide range of issues, individual legislators in committees or subcommittees specialize in policy areas. Usually, legislators get committee assignments because they already have an interest in a particular policy area or agency. Is it so strange that members of Congress from agricultural states like to get on agricultural committees? The choice of committee assignment enables legislators to serve the constituents from their districts better. These people have a strong interest in an agency's work. They are sources of political power that public managers must understand and cultivate according to neoclassical organization theories.

The symbiotic relationships between agency, legislative subcommittee, and clientele have been widely reported. Whether called the iron triangle, policy subsystems, bureaucratic clientelism, or interest group liberalism,[12] they define an important part of an agency's environment. But they should not be assumed to have a determining policy role at every turn.

Neoclassical organization theory opens the agency to a relational view of power. No longer is power seen as a monopoly of the hierarchy. Instead, neoclassical organization theory legitimizes many power sources. In the political realm, it accepts the informal links of an agency to its policy subsystem, which is outside the agency. This affects the who question. In the management realm, it accepts the informal power of individuals and social organization, which bears upon the how question.

The recognition of the human factor in management of public bureaucracy has not always meant that managers could successfully cope with human problems within an organization. Developing a basket of satisfactions capable of motivating a work force as diverse as that of the public agencies in the United States is more of a challenge than perhaps any management theory could handle. The need to have a motivated work force varies with the conditions under which particular agencies operate. Under conditions of stability, neoclassical management practices seem to work quite well. Routinized work at moderate workloads of a Division of Motor Vehicles might be adequately handled by an unsatisfied work force.

Under conditions of rapid change, however, neoclassical management practices based on a balance of power between the hierarchy and individuals and formal versus informal organization might not be capable of responding to the challenges raised by change. Change might come about from a wide range of demands coming through the political system. These could be demands for more service, more effective service, more efficient service, or service to different clients. Whatever the demands, the cozy informal relations that might have developed through neoclassical political and managerial practices may inhibit the ability of the agency to respond to change.

Organizational-humanist theories seek to enable agencies to cope with changes from the environment by creating a problem-solving work climate that is more able to deal with change. Organizational survival under conditions of rapid change demands that individuals within the organization share their skills for the good of the organizational mission rather than for power games. Instead of power coming from the top down, as in the classical organization theories, or the recognition of essentially two competing power sources of the neoclassical theories, organizational humanism posits a shared-power concept.

The intellectual father of organizational humanism is Abraham Maslow,[13] but Warren G. Bennis, an outspoken advocate, may be considered a typical representative of these kinds of theories. Bennis looked to organizational humanism to support the democratic values that he saw as necessary to permit organizations to deal with chronic change. Organizational humanism would encourage the following values, according to Bennis and Philip Slater:

- Full and free communication, regardless of rank and power;
- A reliance on consensus, rather than the more customary forms of coercion or compromise, to manage conflict;
- The idea that influence is based on technical competence and knowledge rather than on the vagaries of personal whims or prerogatives of power;
- An atmosphere that permits and even encourages emotional expression as well as task-oriented acts;
- A basically human bias, one that accepts the inevitability of conflict between the organization and the individual but that is willing to cope with and mediate this conflict on rational grounds.[14]

Organizational humanism attempts to deal with conflicts caused by changes in the environment through a variety of organizational arrangements designed to enhance the commitment of individuals to the organization. Organizational humanism maintains that such commitment is possible only if individuals can grow and develop personally as they work toward achieving agency goals. In many cases, the hierarchy inhibits this growth, so organizational humanists often see project and matrix organizational forms as being more compatible with individual goal attainment. Because organizational values often need to be changed to accommodate this full and free communication, organizational humanists advocate organization development techniques. Because jobs are often structured in such a way as to inhibit personal growth, organizational humanists support job-enrichment efforts.

Mary Parker Follett anticipated the major ways in which power in organizational humanism differs from power in classical and neoclassical organization. Follett saw three basic ways of resolving conflict: (1) domination, (2) balance of power, and (3) integration.[15] More recently, John Kenneth Galbraith has suggested a tripartite taxonomy of power, too. To Galbraith, "condign" power is the ability to inflict punishment in the case of noncompliance. "Compensatory" power is based on promises of rewards or incentives, and "conditioned" power is based on persuasion and education.[16] These strikingly similar views of power seem to correspond with the various organization theories that we have discussed.

In the classical organizations, the boss would seek to end conflict by domination. He or she would use the power of the hierarchy to force subordinates to act in accordance with his or her wishes. This would lead to a lack of cooperation and repressed behavior. In a neoclassical organization, conflict would generally be treated as a balance of power relationship. In an organizational setting, the boss may have the formal power to make a decision, but the subordinate, who has specialized knowledge of the problem under consideration, has de facto power. Under the ensuing balance of power situation, bargaining and compromise would be the main ways of resolving the conflict. Follett maintained, however, that the bargaining would leave a residue of resentment. These resentments would eventually have negative effects on the organization.

Instead of domination or balance of power, Follet preferred the third way of resolving conflict—integration. If people could be honest with each other and not have to worry about taking positions to enhance their bargaining strength, conflicts could be resolved more successfully. The technique for this kind of integration for conflict resolution is to be based not on the relative power positions of people within the organization or even on their personalities but on the problem situation at hand—the "law of the situation." Organizational humanism also sees this as the way to resolve conflicts in a way that enables the organization and the individuals who are a part of it to grow and develop.

Organizational humanism assumes that the individuals in organizations have high needs for growth. Furthermore, it assumes that such people are going to seek to develop and grow within the context of the organization. Perhaps most important for our purposes, however, is that organizational humanism assumes that people within the organization have the technical competence to deal with the problem at hand, and other participants in the decision-making process recognize this. The claim that decisions should be made through shared power on rational, technical grounds can hold only if participants share the same values or the same view of what is the truth.

In essence, organizational humanism advocates an apolitical decision-making process within organizations. "Henceforth, decisions are to be made on the basis of truth rather than power" seems to be the dictum. Surely, decision making in public bureaucracies should reflect reality rather than what Galbraith called "bureaucratic truth,"[17] but in many cases, information is lacking. There may be no clear view of what is the truth. Experts can disagree. Experts can be wrong. Who is to be responsible for decisions?

Still, the aim of organizational humanism to devalue hierarchy in favor of a free exchange of information within an organization has promise and has been used extensively in the public sector. Project management and task forces abound, although one could not make a judgment as to their objective versus political decision-making processes except on an individual basis. Controlling for such variables as the kinds of individuals in an agency and the kinds of problems the agency faces, researchers might find that organizational humanism has the capacity to affect positively the how question.

Organizational-humanism theory suggests that decision makers in public bureaucracy would be open to a wider range of participation from the environment than either classical or neoclassical organizations. Rather than limit access to those participants in the policy subsystem as in neoclassical theory, organizational humanism would encourage all who might be interested in a particular policy area. Instead of policy subsystems, we would have what Brinton Milward and Gary Wamsley call "policy networks." According to Milward and Wamsley, in part, policy networks

> are composed of institutions, organizations, groups, and individuals linked on the basis of shared and salient interests in a particular policy. In the American polity these might include bureaucratic agencies from all levels of government, interest groups, legislative committees and subcommittees, powerful individuals, or relevant others.[18]

A policy network can have powerful and weak participants, strong or weak linkages, but generally it will not represent a planned, centrally coordinated entity. Virtually any interested party could join a policy network by merely showing up where a particular policy is being debated. Organizational humanism would suggest that these interested parties would get a fair hearing independent of their power position. Instead of power influencing the acceptance of their views, clear argument would lead all the participants to recognize innovative solutions. Although the decision-making process might be protracted, policies coming out of such a process might by more effective and, therefore, more efficient in the long run.

Given the three broad organization theories of public bureaucracy that have been discussed here, and their value bases, one should not expect a single theory to illuminate behavior of all public agencies through time. Both internal and external environmental demands mitigate against rigidly programmed policy and management decisions and decision-making styles. When the polity demands strong executive control, classical organizational practices may appear to dominate. When the polity demands decentralization, neoclassical modes may appear to provide answers. When the polity demands knowledge-based competence, organizational-humanist practices may appear to fill the bill. But whatever the prevailing mood of the polity, one can be certain that that mood is not shared by all aspects of the policy. Even within the attentive publics concerned with a particular agency, there is likely to be significant value conflict.

Because of this value conflict, decision makers within agencies can choose to develop an organizational style that will enable them to better attain whatever their vision of their agency's role is. Agency decision makers can encourage individual growth of employees if it fits their goals for the agency. They can encourage wider participation of potentially interested people if it fits their goals for the agency. Organizational-humanism techniques suggest how this can be done. Similarly, neoclassical techniques can be employed to keep employees relatively happy and working closely with established clientele. In certain kinds of government work, classical practices can efficiently deliver services even if the transaction is not a memorable event for either the provider or the consumer.

Within any currently dominant management or political style within large agencies, especially, there is always room for alternative styles, provided such style gets the called-for results. One who chooses to operate with a style different from the dominant one in the agency might not receive the praise of peers and superiors, but if the style allows for the continued productive work of the unit, individual managers and decision makers in agencies can feel that they are being effective. Furthermore, the existence of alternative management styles within an agency can serve as model if environmental demands on the agency as a whole change. Knowledge of various organization theories and their value bases allows public managers to choose among them. The consequences of their choices affect the who and how questions.

Endnotes

1. Herbert Kaufman, "Fear of Bureaucracy: A Raging Pandemic," *Public Administration Review* 41:1 (January–February 1981).
2. Ibid., pp. 1–9.
3. Kenneth M. Dolbeare and Murray J. Edelman, *American Politics: Policies, Power and Change.* 3rd ed., rev. (Lexington, MA: D.C. Heath, 1979), p. 14.
4. See William G. Scott, "Organizational Government: The Prospects for a Truly Participative System," *Public Administration Review* 29, 43–53 (January–February) 1969. William G. Scott and David K. Hart, "Administrative Crisis: The Neglect of Metaphysical Speculation," *Public Administration Review* 33, 415–422. (September–October) 1973.
5. Luther H. Gulick, "Notes on the Theory of Organization," in *Papers on the Science of Administration*, Luther H. Gulick and Lyndell Urwick, eds. (New York: Institute of Public Administration, 1937), pp. 3–44.
6. Herbert Kaufman, "Reflections on Administrative Reorganization," in *Setting National Priorities: The 1978 Budget,* Joseph A. Pechman, ed. (Washington, D C: Brookings Institution, 1977).
7. Herbert Simon, *Administrative Behavior.* 3rd ed. (New York: Macmillan, 1976), Chapter 2.
8. See Fritz J. Roethlisberger, *Management and Morale* (Cambridge, MA: Harvard University Press, 1941).
9. Chester I. Barnard, *Functions of the Executive* (Cambridge, MA: Harvard University Press, 1938), especially Chapters 10 and 11.
10. Simon, *op. cit.,* p. 12.
11. Norton E. Long, "Power and Administration," *Public Administration Review* 9:257 (Autumn) 1949.

12. Among others, see Grant McConnell, *Private Power and American Democracy* (New York: Knopf, 1966); Theodore J. Lowi, *The End of Liberalism.* 2nd ed. (New York: W. W. Norton, 1979); Randall B. Ripley and Grace A. Franklin, *Congress, the Bureaucracy, and Public Policy* (Homewood, IL: Dorsey, 1983). For a slightly different view of this phenomenon, see Eugene Lewis, *American Politics in a Bureaucratic Age: Citizens, Constituents, Clients and Victims* (Cambridge, MA: Winthrop, 1977).

13. Douglas McGregor developed the Theory Y cosmology from Maslow's hierarchy of needs, which first appeared in "A Theory of Human Motivation," *Psychological Review* 50 (July) 1943.

14. Warren G. Bennis and Philip E. Slater, *The Temporary Society* (New York: Harper & Row, 1968), p. 4. Bennis has stepped back from his advocacy of complete full and free communication. See his "The Cult of Candor," *Atlantic* 246, 89–91 (September) 1980.

15. Mary Parker Follett, *Dynamic Administration: The Collected Papers of Mary Parker Follett,* Henry Metcalf and Lyndell Urwick, eds. (New York: Harper & Row, 1940).

16. John Kenneth Galbraith, *The Anatomy of Power* (Boston: Houghton-Mifflin, 1983).

17. John Kenneth Galbraith, *How to Control the Military* (New York: Signet Books, 1969), p. 17.

18. H. Brinton Milward and Gary L. Wamsley, "Policy Networks and the Tools of Public Management: Units of Analysis for a Mixed Economy." Paper presented at the national meeting of American Society of Public Administration, New York, April 1983, p. 9.

CHAPTER 14

Public Sector Organization: Why Theory and Practice Should Emphasize Purpose, and How to Do So

Robert T. Golembiewski
THE UNIVERSITY OF GEORGIA

ROBERT T. GOLEMBIEWSKI is Research Professor at the University of Georgia and Distinguished Visiting Professor on the Faculty of Management at the University of Calgary, Canada. His latest book, Stress in Organizations, *is the forty-seventh he has written or edited. He has also published over 250 scholarly articles and contributions in a variety of professional journals. Professor Golembiewski's research has been signally acknowledged throughout his career: early, when he won the Hamilton Book of the Year Award for his* Man, Management, and Morality *in 1967, and later, in 1984, when he was awarded the Research Medal of the University of Georgia. He is an active consultant for both governmental and business enterprises.*

Robert T. Golembiewski laments the fact that organization theory is stuck. Woodrow Wilson's prediction in 1887 that organizations would receive explicit attention immediately after the moral tone of public management was raised by personnel reforms has not yet come true. Although incredible effort and ingenuity have gone into personnel reforms for over a century, the basic model for organizing public work in the administrative state has remained largely unchanged over the same period. The standard line/

433

staff model outlined by the President's Committee on Administrative Management in 1937 is still in place, for example. Even though major attention has been given to new techniques of budgeting, and such intended palliatives as planning/programming/budgeting systems (PPBS) have been offered, there has been only limited realization that budgeting problems may be structurally induced. Some organizational structures provide easy targets for PPBS applications even as their characteristic processes and dynamics minimize the need for the information PPBS can provide. Traditional bureaucratic structures present the ironic contrast that even the most powerful modern tools of administrative reform—several generations of computers and their assorted software—can be rendered ineffective by the structural subversion of organizational purposes.

Why the stuckness? Golembiewski says the reasons are weighty. They can be summarized under two headings: (1) safeguarding sovereignty in simplistic ways, and (2) neglecting phases in public sector development. Under the predisposition of organizations to safeguard sovereignty is classified the concept that provides the central linkage in democratic political philosophy, i.e., unity of command. Applied to the office of President, for example, unity of command suggests a direct-line democracy. The electors choose a President who serves as the head of a plural executive whose officials are the bodily appendages of his directing will. This primitive ideation still provides the major linkage between those doing the public work and the publics who constitute the republic. It is a vexacious problem in political philosophy. It has caused stuckness because most of the time the focus is on *who* exercises power rather than *how* the public work is to be organized for accomplishment. The disability is most apparent in Jacksonian views of administration and administration surviving under a protected civil service.

Under neglected phases in public sector development Golembiewski lists factors of environmental pace that no single organizational model can comprehend. The traditional bureaucratic model has dominant mechanistic features illustrated by a smoothly running watch or well-meshed gears. Such metaphors imply a bias toward placid environments typically defined in terms of simple and slowly changing products or services. The history of organizational theory in the public sector has not reflected sensitivity to differing environmental paces in which turbulence pertains and all of one's constants become galloping variables.

Unlike other analysts who believe that stuckness may be unavoidable, Golembiewski is more optimistic. The purpose of his writing in fact is to offer constructive thinking about how to move beyond the present condition. One characteristic of an alternative model for organizing the public work is that it needs to give increasing attention to the general theme of personal and psychological liberation. This view has basic normative foundations, of course, but urgent practical need also supports the search for greater congruence between organizational requirements and pervasive social and political trends. Golembiewski says powerful evidence exists for two propositions: (1) Reduced discrepancy between organizational requirements and greater personal freedom has a major impact not only on how much work gets produced but also on levels of personal satisfaction. (2) A tolerably efficient technology-with-values for such discrepancy reduction not only exists but closely fits American political ideals.

Golembiewski concludes that basic progress in public sector organization theory and practice involves a shift from emphasizing function toward emphasizing purpose. He offers empirical and normative reasons for doing so, as well as five modes for reorientation. His eight exhibits thoroughly illustrate the points he makes. His summary view of Wilson on the occasion of this commemorative volume is that Wilson's view of responsibility was too individualistic to be of full service in the present administrative era.

Thought and theory about public sector organization have not only failed to experience their own reformation but, far worse, the consciousness of the need seems but little developed and seldom gets expressed in ways that motivate effective remedial efforts. Overstated somewhat, but not much, the matter of organization has historically been treated either as a residual category of other dominating concerns, most often broadly political, or as a given that may be awkward or even unpalatable, but nonetheless inescapable.

Brief chapter-and-verse make the present point. Incredible effort and ingenuity over a century have gone into the reform of public personnel systems: (1) the bare idea of a protected service; (2) classification systems of diverse sorts; and (3) the use of financial incentives for performance.[1] In contrast, the basic model for organizing public work appeared early and has remained dominant until today,[2] with the major efforts at reform being restricted to fine-tuning the basic model. For example, the President's Committee on Administrative Management adapted standard line/ staff notions to the presidency,[3] a significant but quite limited effort with a growing constellation of costs over benefits.[4] Relatedly, major attention has been accorded to budgeting concerns and to such intended palliatives as PPBS, but with little explicit realization of the basic fact that many phenomema of concern are structurally induced.[5] Briefly, for example, some organization structures provide easy targets for PPBS applications even as their characteristic processes and dynamics are such as to minimize the need for the information PPBS can provide. The traditional bureaucratic structure presents an ironic contrast: its characteristic dynamics and processes require PPBS but also make successful application unlikely.[6] The irony has become appreciated at great costs of time and fortune. In addition, the present burgeoning emphasis on "policy" and "policy evaluation" accords little attention to the specific structuring of organizations,[7] beyond the traditional caveats that "politics" can be a mischievous and arbitrary master that generates mishmashes of policy directives and inconstant oversight from multiple sources. Finally, for present purposes only, even that most powerful modern tool—the several generations of computers and their associated software—has been widely relied on, with precious little attention to how traditional concepts for organizing can subvert major organization purposes.[8]

In sum, matters remain more or less where Woodrow Wilson left them in 1887 when he noted that civil service reform would come first "but [only as] a prelude to fuller administrative reform." In his charming but oversimple terms:

> We are now rectifying methods of appointment; we must go on to adjust executive functions more fitly and to prescribe better methods of executive organization and action. Civil-service reform is thus but clearing the moral atmosphere of official life by establishing the sanctity of public office as a public trust, and, by making the service un-partisan, it is opening the way for making it businesslike. By sweetening its motives it is rendering it capable of improving its methods of work.[9]

Why the Stuckness?

Woodrow Wilson predicted in his seminal 1887 paper that organization would get explicit attention immediately after the moral tone of public management was raised by personnel reforms, but that has not yet occurred. And the stuckness exists for many weighty, if unfortunate, reasons. Two of these basic reasons get summary attention here. They involve a disingenuous approach to safeguarding popular sovereignty and, in turn, a failure to take explicit account of phases in the organization of the public sector.

SAFEGUARDING SOVEREIGNTY IN SIMPLISTIC WAYS.   Inadequate wit and will may have determined the outcomes, but several related historical and conceptual forays[10] highlight a curious imbalance in the remarkable history of the bureaucratic model that came to dominate, mercurially and almost ubiquitously, prescription and practice related to the organization of all work. Exhibit 1 sketches the major properties of that model. The bureaucratic model can be faulted easily enough on logical,[11] normative,[12] and empirical[13] grounds. Grave faults notwithstanding, the model

EXHIBIT 1   The Conventional Bureaucratic Model for Organizing Work

- A well-defined and integral chain of command that has each subordinate reporting to one superior, with the number of subordinates being kept to a small number so as to enhance "unity of command"
- Departmentation below the chief executive by separate "functions" at the highest levels, and by "processes" or "tasks" at lower levels, which commonly fragment a flow of work so as to preclude any agent or agency from handling a "complete transaction"
- A system of procedures and rules for dealing with all contingencies, which reinforces the insularity of each component unit or person, and thus supports the unity of command
- Impersonality in relations between organization members and between them and their clients
- With even modest growth and complexity, "staff" resources must augment the personal qualities of the chief executive in controlling the total system, and such staff is considered as advisory only and outside the chain of command so as to preserve the sense of unity of command

remains essentially in place in the public sector, despite fundamental revisionism in major areas of business.[14]

What accounts for this curious imbalance of relinquishing the bureaucratic model in many areas and yet clinging to it in the public sector? Consider the notion of "unity of command" central in the bureaucratic model. At the broadest level, the concept provides perhaps *the* central linkage in democratic political philosophy, albeit simplistically. Unity of command in the office of the presidency suggests a kind of "direct-line democracy," with the electors/people choosing a president who serves as the "head" of the plural executive, whose officials are in turn the bodily appendages serving his directing will.[15] This primitive ideation still provides the major linkage between those doing the public work and the publics constituting the republic, a vexacious problem in political philosophy.

Thompson[16] put it more directly than most. Conceptually, unity of command is the critical ideological tether that keeps the technocrats from stealing sovereignty that rightly is popularly owned.

If simple, this conceptual linkage has proved long-lasting and flexible. Thus "direct-line democracy" provided the conceptual umbilical at two critical points in the development of the American nation-state and its administrative apparatus.[17] The bureaucratic model served Jacksonians well through the "spoils politics" that was so important in giving local interests clear and immediate stakes in the young republic.[18] Later, the model served when the focus was on developing a public service protected from spoils politics and yet responsive to political direction. *The* goals then had a national focus, especially in connection with what might well be called the professionalization and nationalization-in-scope of the economy and the military.[19]

At two critical periods in American administrative institution building, the focus became *who* would exercise power. The *how* of the exercise of that power and the basic structural arrangements for organizing the public work got attention only in the sense of establishing the superficial linkage of the conventional model to the basic choices—partisan politics in Jacksonian times, and later a protected civil service.

Alas, however, the two solutions soon became *the* problem. As Skowronek writes: "The plight of Presidents severely constrained in their leadership by the normal routines of the party state has been replaced by the plight of Presidents constrained by the normal routines of the bureaucratic state."[20]

NEGLECTING PHASES IN PUBLIC SECTOR DEVELOPMENT. Saving sovereignty simplistically was made more attractive by the general failure to respect phases or stages in administrative development. These phases imply different requirements and demands, which any single model for organizing might not serve uniformly well. Hence the crucial character of the general neglect.

Let us rely on Wilson to gain perspective on this central point. He distinguished three phases of development:

1. the period of absolute rulers, in which administrative systems evolved consistent with the priorities, if not vagaries, of the absolute ruler;
2. the period of constitution making, in which the prerogatives of absolute rulers were variously hedged but only by absorbing such great energies that administration tended to be neglected; and
3. the period of the increasingly sovereign people, in which administration developed under the aegis of popular mandates expressed within the constraints of the new constitutions.[21]

Wilson illustrates well the differential impact of these phases in administrative institution building. For example, the absolute rulers had by far the easiest time of it. The personality and energies of a determined ruler could become reflected in an administrative structure and style, quite directly. In popular governments, the problems became greatly magnified. Wilson suggests the point in several ways that permit this forceful contrast:

It is harder for democracy to organize administration than for monarchy. . . . The very completeness of our most cherished political successes in the past embarrasses us. We have enthroned public opinion [and this makes] the task of organizing that rule just so much more difficult. . . .

An individual sovereign will adopt a simple plan and carry it out directly: he will have but one opinion, and he will embody that one opinion in one command. But this other sovereign, the people, will have a score of differing opinions.[22]

These points are telling, but they understate the challenge of organizing. To illustrate, at least three other interacting sets of considerations influence phases of development. They are labeled as "levels," "pace," and "basic outcomes." Note that the labeling owes more to convenience than to rigor.

Levels of Organizing

The question of who is sovereign should impact on administrative institution building, to be sure, but that effect interacts in significant ways with at least three levels of organizing. Suggestively rather than exhaustively, one can distinguish:

1. initially structuring a territory into viable subnational units;
2. later structuring at a national level, especially in connection with a growing economy and a more sophisticated military;
3. structuring the full-service state.

Of course, these three "levels" were not casually chosen. The first two relate quite directly to the two earlier critical periods in American institution building already referred to. The final level corresponds to our present critical period, which began with Roosevelt's New Deal but gained urgency only with Johnson's New Society.

Only a highly technical analysis could develop the full catalog of differing structural demands encountered at these several "levels," but parsimonious illustration will suffice here. Three progressive strategies for growth can be considered beyond the elemental one of increasing volume at a central site where the traditional model applies most directly: developing field units; adding functions or activities; and diversifying products or services.[23] Even developing field units stresses the bureaucratic model, raising questions about headquarters/field relationships and the "multiple supervision" that often characterizes them. That is, field operatives often face simultaneous and conflicting demands from headquarters' specialists and field managers. Such tensions grow exponentially under more advanced strategies for growth. Adding functions and, especially, diversifying products or services exacerbates problems with the traditional model, at once challenging the comprehension of any one central elite and creating major and often conflicting identifications with the multiple professions and programs necessary for the two most advanced strategies for growth.

The basic conclusion merely requires stating. In effect, the two most advanced strategies at once challenge any simple notion of "unity of command" and create complex patterns of socialization that undercut it. And, of course, the full-service state relies heavily on these two most advanced strategies for growth.

Environmental Pace

As has been widely recognized by organization theorists, at least since Thompson,[24] what may be called "environmental pace" has major implications for appropriate structure. Theorists often distinguish two kinds of environment: "placid" and "turbulent." In numerous particulars, the traditional bureaucratic model is more attuned to the former than to the latter. To suggest the point, the metaphors underlying that model have dominant mechanistic features: a smoothly running watch or well-meshing gears. These metaphors clearly imply a bias toward placid environments, which typically get defined in terms of a simple and stable technology producing a small number of simple and slowly changing products or services.

The history of organization theory in the public sector has not reflected sensitivity to differing environmental paces. Quite the opposite, in fact. The same organization model was retained in basic service at two earlier critical phases: (1) when the prime focus was on an intial structuring of the territory via a reliance on spoils politics that had a local bias; and (2) later, when the focus had shifted dramatically to a national structuring with prime concerns about the economy and the military. The transition was radical, from relatively placid to turbulent. Skowronek characterizes this transition as a deliberate movement "away from a state organization that presumed the absence of extensive institutional controls at the national levels toward a state organized around national administrative capacities."[25] The same basic model for organizing did double duty, this radical shift in pace notwithstanding, and a direct contrast seems fair:

> In early days of the republic, the conventional model supported a reigning-in of the size and scope of basically-local government consistent with a Jacksonian theme that "the world is governed too much," a scaling-down facilitated by a felicitous "rotation in office." Later, the conventional model was put in the service of burgeoning national mandates, via a restricted entry into a public service of the technically competent with guarantees of indefinite employment intended to subvert party politics of the spoils sort.[26]

Three Basic Outcomes

Thought about organization in the public sector also suffers a partial myopia with regard to what will be called "basic outcomes." Three get distinguished here, and almost all early commentary focuses on only the first two. Again, this bias stultified the development of thought and theory about organization and contributed to stuckness.

Western opinion is curiously schizoid concerning the conscious manipulation of our environment and its resources, by management as well as more broadly by science. On the one hand, bright visions dwell on a well-articulated tomorrow featuring the efficient provision of public goods and services, in businesslike ways by the application of management principles and scientific discovery. A kind of Frankenstein myth provides historic counterbalance to this idyllic view. Here the mad scientist or power-crazed manager can use that same mastery over nature to create the efficient but repressive state, a view powerfully described in negative utopias such as *1984* and forcefully expressed in the antitechnocratic strain that has been so dominant in much social commentary over the last century or so, perhaps most prominently in Marxist thought.

These two well-emphasized "basic outcomes" may be described in terms of different levels of associated repression, both of which curiously accept the bureaucratic model. The idyllic view posits some *minimum level of personal and social repression* associated with living the good life in the efficient state. Here the bureaucratic model either constitutes the "principles" that map the smooth road to managerial efficiency, or that model is considered somewhat awkward but unavoidably so, as in the view that, "Autocracy during hours of work is the price we pay for democracy after hours."[27] In contrast, the Frankenstein view worries about the extensive *surplus repression* in the same bureaucratic model, with a stark opposition between its worldview and that reflected in popular government: (1) an informed and active electorate versus a docile, highly specialized, and perhaps leisure-oriented work force; and (2) a political system prescribing multiple sources of influence contrasting with a worksite model oriented toward a monopoly by elites over planning, direction, or control.

These two "basic outcomes" do not exhaust all major possibilities, of course, and much recent attention has been given to what may be called *positive organization for responsible personal freedom*. Expressions of the general point of view are diverse. Observers like Toffler see a "third wave" coming with "a far more varied, colorful, open, and diverse society than we have ever known," far more decentralized and participatory.[28] These romantic visions get some support from more disciplined and data-based efforts, even as the co-romanticists can have a falling-out as to scope and method.[29] At the individual level, such work is typified by Tough's[30] efforts to get people to take greater charge of their personal lives and to take back power and control that have been vested in various professional and specialized functionaries in such areas as medicine and government. At the macrolevel, such efforts get expressed in burgeoning areas of interest such as Organization Development, which seeks to create collective enterprises with a higher potential for "responsible freedom" for their participants.[31]

We might consider only one variant of the general theme of personal and psychological liberation, which has received political expression in the efforts of Californian John Vasconcellos. He observes broadly: "Today the political issue that is emerging is for liberation at a psychological level: owning one's own body, mind, and feelings, and being one's self. This includes not passively surrendering ourselves and our power to some authority figure or institution who thinks that they know better than we do who we ought to be." Somewhat more specifically, Vasconcellos isolates five major steps in this radical perspective that he has seen emerging over the past several decades:

1. moving away from personal and organizational models that imply that others have all (or most of) the authority and power
2. shifting toward "horizontal sharing" of power, influence and responsibility, in contrast with "vertical" models of superiority/inferiority
3. moving toward "organizing institutions whose function is to fit individuals," rather than adapting individuals to fit organizations
4. focusing attention on the "whole person" in policy-making, which proposes a kind of "personal impact statement" to complement environmental variants
5. moving toward empowerment of people—"to evoke, encourage, and support . . . human beings to be healthy, whole, self-aware persons . . ."[32]

Patently, the bureaucratic model poorly suits this third "basic outcome"—positive organization for greater responsible personal freedom. Hence also the neglect of this third basic outcome both contributes to, and reflects, the stuckness of organization thought and theory.

SUMMARIZING THIS PRIMER ON STUCKNESS.   These sketches serve a trinity of purposes, in effect. They suggest a description of *why* our basic notions about public sector organization are stuck. They also suggest *what* basic challenges have already emerged or may yet gain greater prominence. Fortunately, these brief descriptions even suggest some firm elementals of *how* to move beyond the present condition. Hence this analysis differs radically from that of careful observers such as Mohr.[33] Although we both agree on the stuckness of organization theory, he argues in detailed ways that stuckness not only exists but may be fundamentally unavoidable.

This analysis proposes some ways around or even out of stuckness. Basically, the considerations reviewed imply that we need to develop an alternative model for organizing the public work where sovereignty is safeguarded, to be sure, but in less simplistic ways than the bureaucratic model. This alternative model serves other purposes as well.

This effort rests on several main elements in a consciousness about what needs doing. First, we seem to be in a third critical period of our public institution building, each of which is associated with a different kind of effort. In short, how is the full-service state to be organized? The bureaucratic model provided tolerable guidance for a first critical period that sought to build a local base for organizing the territory. That model was less serviceable for the national institution building that followed, and it holds far less promise for this third critical period, which the present analysis emphasizes.

Second, this new model must substantially shift attention to turbulent versus placid environments. As one observer noted in the 1960s: "All my constants have become galloping variables." The end of that has yet to come, if it ever will.

Third, the evolving model needs to give increasing attention to greater responsible personal freedom. This view has basic normative foundations, of course. But urgent practicalities also support the search for a greater congruence between organizational requirements and pervasive social and political trends. At one level, substantial and growing discrepancy might well create powerful tensions that would endanger social as well as organizational life. In addition, increasingly powerful support exists for two propositions: (1) reduced discrepancy between organizational requirements and greater personal freedom has major impact not only on how much gets produced, but also on levels of personal satisfaction;[34] and (2) a tolerably efficient technology-cum-values for such discrepancy reduction not only now exists but it also closely fits our broad political ideals,[35] at least at initial levels of approximation.

Fundamentals for Decreasing Stuckness

Substantial specificity is possible regarding moving beyond these trinitarian elementals for facing a third critical period in our administrative institution building. Three major thrusts preoccupy this effort. They deal, in turn, with: (1) the probably growing costs of the bureaucratic model that focuses on specialized processes or functions; (2) some assumptions concerning major aspects of future public sector management; and (3) the relative advantages-minus-disadvantages as well as other major properties of several purpose-oriented models.

PROBABLY GROWING COSTS OF BUREAUCRATIC MODEL.   When early efforts are made to organize some territory or collectivity, and the environment is relatively placid, the burcaucratic model has substantial attractions, perhaps even major advantages. Thus the emphasis on organizing around processes or functions promotes the specialization of skills, exposes specialists to their peers, which may stimulate performance and advance standards, and also provides clear pathways for personal and professional advancement in large departments of specialists. The emphasis on vertical relationships, such as the "unity of command" and "one person, one boss" linkages, also may be useful in substituting some system or order for the kind of chaotic localism that often characterizes the early histories of evolving collectivities. That is, the bureaucratic model encourages high degrees of centralization and formalization that may be helpful in reducing wasteful diversity of practices, if not arbitrariness or outright lining of pockets by officials in parts of the system or territory.[36]

The biases of the bureaucratic model are perhaps most clearly reflected in a monumental irresolution—the model's simultaneous prescription of unity of command and specialization. These core notions do not have complementary thrusts, and may even sharply undercut one another.[37] Witness the great energies devoted to differentiating "line" from "staff." Line is "on top" and staff is "on tap." Line has the power to command, although staff can have superior knowledge and technical competence, and so on. Even organizational cartography has created ways to express the intended resolution of opposed tendencies. Consider the functions or processes A, B, C, of which the last is "staff," but all of which contribute to some total flow of work. The conventional organization chart takes the form illustrated in Figure 14-1.

The broken line indicates "advisory lines," which are subordinate to the command structure indicated by the solid lines. Given this priority of unity of command through simple hierarchy, the skeletal structure also reveals the coprominence accorded to differentiation and specialization in that the basic departmentation builds around separate functions or processes.

The basic point may be put in generalized terms. Exhibit 2 distinguishes four perspectives that can be applied to models for structuring work and four kinds of rationality against which structure can be tested. The bureaucratic model essentially relates to technical and organizational rationality. Even there forces in substantial opposition are involved. Spe-

Figure 14-1

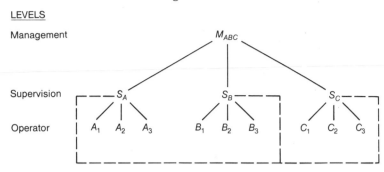

cialization and integration/control can be antagonistic in practice even as they ideally should be complements and supplements.

Two general points highlight the negative consequences of this fundamental tension in the bureaucratic model between hierarchy and specialty. First, the features of that model will be exacerbated in the full-service state, with its attendant turbulent environment and complex lines of changing products or services. Convincing evidence[38] supports this view of the probably growing awkward effects under contemporary conditions. Although the full catalog of advantages and disadvantages of the emphasis on functions and processes is well beyond present ambitions,

EXHIBIT 2   Varieties of Rationality Served by Models for Structuring Work*

Perspectives on Structure	Basic Objectives	Emphases
Technical Rationality	Efficiency of Individual Functions/Processes	Specialization and Associated Reward/Motivation
Organizational Rationality	Coordination of Total Flows of Work	Integration and Control
Political Rationality	Justice	Substantive and Procedural Due Process
Human Rationality	Ennoblement and Empowerment of Individuals	Personal Growth and Productivity via Satisfaction of Human Needs

* Based in part on William G. Scott, Terence R. Mitchell, and Newman S. Peery, *Handbook of Organizational Design,* Paul C. Nystrom and William Starbuck, eds. (New York: Oxford University Press, 1981), p. 142

Exhibit 3 summarizes some central consequences of the traditional approach to organizing.

Second, the bureaucratic model does not deal directly or satisfactorily with the last two structurally relevant perspectives in Exhibit 2—political and human rationality. Indeed, one might well say that this model neglects or even rejects them. Whatever that judgment, even brief comment can suggest the major senses in which the bureaucratic model poorly suits both political and human rationality.

Many observers have long appreciated the problems with political rationality posed by the bureaucratic model. The list includes Wilson, for example, who was vaguely optimistic that the "foreign gases" and kingly overtones of that model's concept of authority would somehow be "vaporized" by the heat of our republican institutions. Others were less sanguine, and especially concerning employees at lower hierarchical levels. They emphasized the conflicts between attitudes and skills relevant in republican political systems—a sense of efficacy, or participation in decision making, and the consequences that might credibly be associated with the bureaucratic model. Exhibit 4 provides one view of this clash of normative political expectations with the consequences of the traditional model. Growing evidence suggests these concerns have merit. Rather than our basic political consciousness impacting on worksite structure and practices, the causal arrow seems pointed the other way around, in important if not necessarily exclusive senses.[42]

Viewed another way, by far the dominant expressions of political rationality in organizations have been gained in adversarial modes—as by the wearing processes of protracted court battles, unions combatting militantly antagonistic managements, and so on.[43] This history implies that what is here called political rationality had low priority in common approaches to organizing. Paradoxically, moreover, even "victories" here would often be expressed in legalisms and procedural hurdles that would burden technical performance and complicate relationships at work.

As for human rationality, the traditional model focuses on the systemic or technical, and human needs or features tend to be treated as residual categories. This bias gets reflected dramatically, as in the historic tendency to consider "human relations" as some tentative overlay tacked onto the formal structure for work, or as a kind of pacifier to encourage acceptance of the technical demands of work, viewed as somehow immutable and monolithic. This halting respect for human rationality in organization theory also helps explain the historic fascination with such concepts as Maslow's pyramid, Theory X versus Y, and Herzberg's motivators versus satisfiers.[44] Despite problems with their formulations, these views contrast starkly with the conventional neglect and hence attract attention, perhaps even yearning.

These broad perspectives on the conventional model suggest useful

EXHIBIT 3 Advantages and Disadvantages of Functional/Processual Bias in Organizing

Advantages	Disadvantages
• appropriate for simple and stable technologies, product lines, and markets	• focuses on parts rather than integrated wholes
• long-standing and direct concepts provide convenient guides for structure and behavior	• as the numbers of employees, functions, and programs increase, organizations quickly become tall, with an escalating distance between "action level" and "decision level" while problems rise to the level of some integrative manager like M_{ABC} in Figure 14–1
• builds around and enhances specialties: exposes functional and processual specialists to each other, with implications for consistent standards and performance; provides clear career ladders for specialists; etc.	• as layers of authority increase, time lags probably will grow, and responsiveness to local needs will decrease
• performance appraisal of specialists by fellow specialists	• numerous externalities between subunits often result in executive overload and the specification of ever more elaborate rules and procedures
• reduces duplication of resources, as in lower "fractional loss"[39]	• complicates measuring performance—a paradoxical consequence of the effort to limit individual or unit control over some complete transaction that makes it difficult to assign reward or punishment for meaningful effects—and obscures accountability for overall purposes
• facilitates centralization and formalization, which are valuable at several stages of organizational growth, and perhaps especially at early stages of institutionalization	• subunits often develop local identifications and loyalties and variously reinforce/undercut executive thrusts
• seems supported by deeply rooted patterns of socialization[40]	• attempts to preserve unity of command by the common line/staff distinction can help fragment the flow of work[41]
	• communication and cooperation between subunits become more and more difficult and less likely even as the need for them increases
	• lower-level managers tend to have specialized views and perspectives, which not only complicate communication and cooperation between subunits but also can limit developing a pool of future executives
	• can cause morale problems at lower levels, due to routinization of work

EXHIBIT 4   A Self-Heightening Cycle Induced by Traditional Notions for Organizing work

Ideology and technology emphasize centralized and hierarchical control	Jobs are simplified and repetitive; employees are "hands"
"Democratic elitism" evolves, because few employees have necessary resources to participate effectively	The "mind functions"—planning, supervision, and so on—are reserved to higher hierarchical levels
Employees develop few politically relevant resources: they are socialized into passivity, learn powerlessness, accept low political efficacy, and may resort to "compensatory leisure"	Employees reflect low "educational potential": they are discouraged from seeking higher-level skills as well as exerting control over their worksite

Source: Based on Max Eldon, "Political Efficacy at Work," p. 3. Paper presented at Seminar Social Change and Organization Development, Inter-University Center for Graduate Studies, Dubrovnik, Yugoslavia, February 1972.

directions for subsequent analysis. Although the specifics of their application will differ, depending on the locus and level, two points seem generally appropriate concerning the bureaucratic model. Thus its emphasis on "parts" rather than "integrative wholes" dominates most thought and practice about organizing. For various reasons, moreover, the need for change will be far greater in the full-serivce administrative state than in the private sector where, for various reasons, the domination of the conventional model has been more successfully challenged in both thought and practice.

This paradoxical, if not perverse, situation can be approached in two general ways that provide perspective on Fesler's prescient characterization of the federal administrative state: "Everything seems to be connected with everything else. Yet centrigual forces create narrowly oriented, substantially autonomous policy communities in the governmental system."[45] Reality is unkind, in short: integration is especially lacking where it is most needed. The next two sections deal with generic contributors to the disadvantages of the conventional model and, in turn, with those contributors more specific to the public sector.

Generic Contributors to Disadvantages

General agreement exists that the conventional structure will generate an increasingly unfavorable balance of advantages and/or disadvantages under specific conditions. For example, the bureaucratic model will tend to generate an increasingly awkward balance as (1) organizations grow larger;[46] (2) organizations age and tend toward greater formalization;[47] (3) technologies become less stable and more complex; (4) product lines or services become diversified and have short half-lives; and (5) environments are turbulent and unpredictable. The tendencies are not inevitable. But the evidence implies that only basic structural change can directly cope with them.[48]

Site-Specific Contributors to Disadvantages

The full-service administrative state seems an obvious candidate for an unfavorable balance of effects of the bureaucratic model, given even the short list of conditions above. And brief illustrations show how those generic contributors to an unfavorable balance are significantly heightened by contributors more site-specific to the American public sector.[49] For example, numerous observers have drawn telling attention to the problems of managerial integration involving political and career executives, whose tenures are shockingly low[50] and whose tendency is to "marry the natives," which may have legal as well as practical motivators.[51] Another feature that leads to this common complaint is that "the institutional structure did not respond to the political directives."[52] Such a factor patently reinforces the bureaucratic model's focus on the "parts," on fragmentation of the several contributions to the purposes of governance. Relatedly, "normal tendencies" toward fragmentation are powerfully reinforced by the "little groups of policy neighbors" endemic at operating levels in the public service—single-interest constituencies that "can accede only in the narrow interest and are incapable of adjudicating in the national interest."[53]

A similar picture results from considering a few of the palliatives suggested for remedying public sector managerial problems. Consider the basic line/staff distinction consistent with the conventional model, as reflected in the Rooseveltian innovations involving the presidency. For a time, when the focus was on a handful of competent and discrete staff, this prescription was not particularly mischievous. Fesler concludes that day has come and gone: the effort "to strengthen the president by furnishing him with a staff of several hundred," he concludes, "creates more problems than it solves."[54] The view of staff as advisory well suits the conventional model, of course, but reality is another matter. Traditional concepts notwithstanding, power tends to come to reside in such presidential staff aides, in part because interdepartmental coordinating arrangements "can all too easily end in deadlock." This at once invites reliance on presidential staff,[55] who in turn might be led to encourage or at least appreciate deadlock because it supports staff power.[56] This conclusion seems to obtain even when major initiatives are taken to encourage "policy coordination," as by Reagan's Cabinet Councils. Indeed, one might argue that the crosscutting effects are greater *when* such initiatives are taken. For the very existence of the Councils may either encourage deadlocks or urge very gentle coordination, both of which will tend to increase the centrality of presidential staff. Other issues complicate the inadequate resolution of hierarchy and specialty reflected in the traditional line/staff distinction. For example, presidential staff are often younger and less experienced than either the political or career executives, which helps widen the gaps often found between them.[57]

Similar arguments can be developed for other palliatives to overcome the basic structural emphasis on "parts." Perhaps the most conventional proposal has been to heighten the responsiveness of the bureaucracy by increasing the number of political appointments, for example. In the context of the traditional model, however, this solution may cause other and even greater problems. Thus a large cadre of political appointees could have many awkward effects, on balance. It may only encourage more formalization and attempted centralization; it may pose greater problems for presidential direction and influence as the appointees "marry the natives." The general point has not escaped attention. Witness the influential, and often unexpected, voices who have urged the virtues of *fewer* political appointees at the federal level.[58]

Site-specific contributors to the bureaucratic model's disadvantages in the public sector could be amplified in additional ways, but five summary points seem safe enough.

1. Observers typically use similar terms to characterize public sector management, and particularly at the federal level: "piecemeal," "balkanized," "fragmented," "substantially autonomous policy communities," "partitioned," and so on.
2. The complex problems alluded to by such terms have burgeoned in the last decade or so and are growing progressively more severe. As Shultz and Dam observe: "The trend of events is toward greater fragmentation."[59]
3. Problems do not derive entirely from the conventional structure, but they get powerful reinforcement from it. Consider the American failure to implement a regional population policy, a record that stands in quite marked contrast with that of European countries. Sundquist isolates several contributors to the puny American record, among which he includes the "gulf between the career bureaucracy which was familiar with the data and had some degree of competence to analyze it, and the [White House] staff advisers who had responsibility for developing policy recommendations."[60]

In part, this gulf derives from American practices associated with drawing sharp distinctions between policymakers and implementers as "political" and "career" employees, and with excluding the latter from policy councils. In America, Sundquist concludes:

> many of the most competent and ambitious of the career officials—the kind that rise to the top in European civil services—find themselves excluded from the inner policy-making circles, or subordinated to younger, less experienced political appointees, and so depart. The capability of the career service is reduced, which leads to pressures for further politicization in a vicious circle.[61]

In Europe, in contrast, the typical "respected policy advisor" also is a "long-time career civil servant."[62] Hence the firmer overseas policy-implementation linkage.

In part, also, the gulf between political appointees and the career bureaucracy derives from the conventional model. Growing demands on the presidency, within the context of the bureaucratic model, get translated "inexorably [into] the enlargement of staff functions."[63] And the simplicity of that model, in its linking hierarchy to staff specialty as command is related to advice, cannot contain the practical dynamics unleashed by the "inexorable enlargement" of staff.

4. Ameliorative attempts often will be attenuated if not gutted by the general persistence of the bureaucratic model. For example, witness the recent vicissitudes of the integrative effort embodied in the Senior Executive Service that constituted the centerpiece of the Civil Service Reform Act of 1978. The SES had to swim against very powerful currents generated by the particularistic organization structure characteristic of the federal service. As Ring and Perry conclude:

> The newly designed personnel system was created to increase the flexibility of political executives by placing greater emphasis on generalist skills. The realities of federal programs are such, however, that specialization provides greater promise for advancement than does the generalist role. . . . effective dealings with relevant congressional committees and client groups put a premium on staying with one agency and developing an area of functional expertise within it. Moreover, this pattern of careers was deeply embedded in the federal service, and expectations of a sharp, immediate reversal may have been unrealistic from the beginning.[64]

5. Consequently, a reasonable stragegy for change emphasizes multiple attempts to bore from within, whenever and at whatever levels

targets of opportunity present themselves. This approach seeks to increase reliance on purposive or integrative structures, so as to chip away at the dominance of the fragmented and particularistic bureaucratic model, as well as to reduce the drag of associated policies and practices that have developed over the years.

This strategy guides the analysis below, which has two basic thrusts. Several assumptions concerning the future will be sketched, by way of circumscribing the operating constraints on what follows. Subsequently, five purpose-oriented approaches to organizing will be outlined, so as to provide some realistic sense of available integrative alternatives to the particularisms of the bureaucratic model.

SOME ASSUMPTIONS ABOUT THE FUTURE. Much recent handwringing has been devoted to our ability to govern ourselves, of course, and common simplistic analyses emphasize that *the* problems inhere in the size of the public enterprise and/or in the "unresponsive" protected service. The derivative prescriptions also have an appealing directness and simplicity: "Reduce the size of government" and do various things to limit the scope and coverage of the protected service. The prescriptions are not mere words, as illustrated by the few jurisdictions that have gone as far as the government of British Columbia in 1983. Some years ago, British Columbia zigged dramatically toward a drastic welfare statism, with a corresponding burgeoning of the public sector. In recent days, it has zagged in even more radical ways: cutbacks of 25 to 50 per cent in some public services, and a momentous enlargement of the circumstances under which public employees can be released without cause.

This analysis draws little inspiration or comfort from such efforts, basically because it disagrees that we are experiencing a "crisis of competence," despite the temptation to short-circuit both analysis and prescription in such dramatic terms. As this author noted elsewhere: "Rather, we are experiencing ever-clearer *limits on the competence possible within our basic organization structure.*"[65]

The present perspective implies that common analysis/prescription is gravely myopic and probably will fail. Several assumptions add depth and dimension to this central posture:

- Whether smaller or larger, and with whatever degree of deinstitutionalization or politicization, a *big* executive apparatus at the national level will remain, and it will challenge popular control.
- Power does need to be checked, but the conventional model in large organizations does not do so effectively. It complicates management problems, trivializes and often misdirects legislative oversight, pre-

cludes power-checking, and exacerbates the problems of popular control.

- Technical skills and merit should constitute the dominant standards for staffing public jobs, and if anything, standards should be progressively raised over time.

- Emphasis on technical skills and merit does not necessarily require a protected service, but changes should be evolutionary.

- Greater emphasis on performance evaluation is necessary at all levels, perhaps coupled with time-limited appointments (e.g., five years) that provide opportunities for review and renewal.

- Political parties require reinvigoration, especially via specific and compelling incentives to become more programmatic.

- Legislators must be motivated to increasingly focus on the national and departmental levels rather than on subdepartmental levels or bureaus.

- Reorganizing Congress to "be compatible" with the present organization of the executive branch—to create parallel structures of legislative committees with agencies—on balance will further complicate popular control of administration and probably would enhance "iron triangle" influences.

- Efforts to meet problems within the *current administrative structure* will be of limited usefulness; for example, centralization faces enormous centrifugal tendencies, led by the separation of powers; and decentralization tends to create a power vacuum that reinforces "iron triangles" influences.

TOWARD PURPOSE IN ORGANIZING. Such assumptions imply that only fundamental changes in our organization theory will meet our near-future needs, despite the admitted allure of simple and sovereign approaches that are so much with us in numerous political arenas. Those fundamental changes can be broadly viewed as requiring a reorientation away from the "parts" of organizations to "wholes," from fragmentation to integration. As a shorthand, this analysis will speak of "purpose organization," as contrasted with the bias on functions or processes in the conventional model. No rigorous definition of "purpose" will be attempted here, but the text will focus on major illustrations that should provide sufficient content for present purposes.

How then can purpose be approached more closely in organizing, in contrast to particularistic function or process? Substantial guidance is available, in fact, that derives from the author's work and from related efforts such as two contributions in a recent encyclopedic compendium—by Child and Kieser, and McCann and Galbraith[66]—as well as from the efforts of others too numerous to single out. The converging character and quality of this guidance permits a major analytical convenience in

Figure 14-2

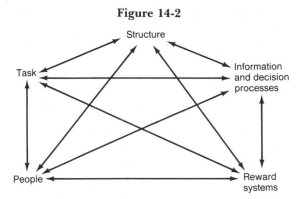

the use of four large summary tables that focus on typical features, advantages, and disadvantages of alternative ways of reflecting an emphasis on purpose in organizing.

More specifically, the analysis that follows proposes that purpose can be emphasized in organizing in two basic ways: by "value overlays" on traditional structures that seek to normatively moderate awkward features of function or process structures like the bureaucratic model; and by basic structural innovation, four types of which get explicit attention below. These types are: (1) collateral or parallel; (2) project management; (3) flow of work structures; and (4) the mature matrix.

Note that the descriptions are deliberately kept general, which has both advantages as well as disadvantages. Hence the several models have to be adapted to different settings, such as levels of administration, policy loci, and so on. Moreover, the view of organization design here has a deliberate myopia. A more complete view would follow an approach such as that of Galbraith,[67] which extends far beyond the present limits (see Figure 14-2).

Value Overlays on Conventional Structures

The sense of "value overlays" may perhaps best be approached in terms of the current emphasis on the conscious creation of appropriate cultures at work,[68] which has diverse roots. Thus various practical reasons motivate concern with cultures at work and the values that characterize them.[69] For example, values guide decision making and action taking; clarity in such particulars can powerfully facilitate work. At another level, numerous observers worry about the human tendency to develop "an administrative, rather than moral, outlook" as members of organizations.[70] Such practical or moral concerns encourage a focus on the specific values that characterize specific organizations, of course. Finally, if only for present purposes, the quality of an organization's values is seen as crucial in managerial legitimacy: by what warrant do managers presume to manage? Donald A. Schön answers this central question in terms that highlight the values that managers respect themselves and model for others. Schön explains:

> The power of social systems over individuals becomes understandable, I think, only if we see that social systems provide for their members not only sources of livelihood, protection against outside threat, and the promise of economic security, but a framework of theory, values, and related technology which enables individuals to make sense of their lives.[71]

The emphasis on cultural overlays on conventional structures basically proposes that all organizations become infused with value. Consequently, organization planners can either seek to induce an appropriate culture, or one will develop, willy-nilly and perhaps with awkward features. Building organization cultures is something we all do, not unlike the way in which we speak prose. We differ only in the consciousness and quality of the effort, which has significant consequences for both the character and quality of specific workplaces and their products. The point is currently receiving massive reinforcement in the managerial best-seller *In Search of Excellence*.[72] The authors propose that organizations with reputations and records for high performance are quite explicitly and consciously value-driven. Standing in contrast are those organizations that avoid, or seek to finesse, conscious concern with the value-infused cultures that characterize them. Most organizations are rule- and role-bound, an ethos that is likely to develop in organizations unreflectively adopting the conventional model. At best, procedural due process prevails in such organizations, whose extremes are red tape and perversion of substantive issues.

Good models exist for developing value overlays in conventional structures. The focus in Exhibit 5 is on one such model, reflected in the "self-forcing, self-enforcing" efforts at the 1970s NASA.[77] These characteristics are consistent with somewhat similar efforts on the POLARIS program.[78] Other examples include the long-run program in the Metropolitan Atlanta Rapid Transit Authority, or MARTA.[79]

Typically, organizations with such value overlays have at least five common features. They face a critical and complex task, to begin, with great time pressures. For this reason, the awkward features of the functional model cannot be dealt with effectively by such time-honored methods as slowly and carefully developing complete roles and rules. Success in that approach, in fact, would imply a failure of the mission.

In addition, frequently because of applicable legislation, the basic functional model is a given. Its awkward consequences are recognized, however, and efforts taken to moderate those consequences.

EXHIBIT 5 Value Overlays of Conventional Structures: Features, Advantages, and Disadvantages

A. Typical Features[73]	B. Advantages

Value overlays seek to *increase*:

1. The use of multiple ways of generating valid and reliable knowledge of the several worlds of actual and potential organizational collaborators

2. A sense of an organization that seeks excellence in being "problem-solving" in contrast with being hierarchy-serving or role-bound

3. The sense and reality of "creative redundancy," as in alternative centers of initiative and responsibility that complement or on occasion supplement functional responsibilities

4. The degree to which progress and problems gain visibility among numerous publics

5. The senses in which hiding an error is viewed as the major organizational transgression

6. The development of norms and rewards that promote interdependence

Value overlays seek to *decrease*:

1. The reliance on formal authority—indeed, to look on the need to rely on formal authority as signaling a managerial failure, as in formal termination unexpected by the individual

2. "Throwing of dead cats in backyards of others," as in avoiding or seeking to relocate responsibility

3. The fragmentation or balkanization of organization units, line from staff, and so on

4. "Tunnel vision," both individual and organizational, as by encouraging actors to "take the role of the other"

B. Advantages

- Seeks to normatively reinforce the integration of structurally segregated activities
- Some well-known examples exist
- Preserves the functional model while seeking to moderate its awkward features
- May be reasonable "next step," an intermediate phase in a later movement to basic structural change
- May be perceived as less threatening than basic structural change
- Does not directly challenge policies and procedures commonly in place—e.g., traditional position classification, specialist career ladders, and so on
- Law or tradition often mandate functional structures, which are thus givens, perhaps especially but not solely in the public sector[74]

C. Disadvantages

- Specialties remain structurally reinforced even as exhortation supports integration
- The value-loaded culture may be vulnerable during crises or managerial successions
- The value-infusing process often depends on a charismatic leader, whose success at one site may lead to quick promotion which, ironically, may threaten that process in direct proportion to its success[75]
- Values may inhibit convenient actions, reducing the flexibility of key actors and their motivation to support the values
- Value-driven organizations may not satisfy personal needs of key actors—for style or even flair, dominance, arbitrariness, and so on
- Stress on participants may be high[76]

Moreover, convenient overlays may just occur, but they often result from conscious planning. It is far from clear what completely characterizes successful efforts at developing overlays, but records of failures do exist,[80] and they reinforce the common wisdom that comprehensive cultural shifts are difficult even as they have been achieved.

Further, organizations with the features of the value overlay illustrated in Exhibit 5 have reputations for managerial excellence and high-level performance. Hence, these organizations provide useful role models.

Finally, limited evidence[81] suggests that such value overlays may exact a substantial human toll, one suspects in part because of the cross-pressures induced between the normative overlay and the tendencies inherent in the functional model. Some ways of moderating these strong cross-pressures seem clear enough,[82] but the issues are far from being understood, let alone resolved.

Collaterals as Structural Adjuncts

In part because of the issues just sketched, attention has been directed at what might be called "temporary value systems" in the form of collateral or parallel structures. Here the conventional formal structure is retained, and a temporary or episodically activated structure is constituted for specific purposes or a defined period. In one form, parallel structures may deal with a needed change while the permanent structure remains for implementing day-to-day activities. As Stein and Kanter observe, parallel organizations represent "an attempt to institutionalize a set of externally and internally responsive, participatory, problem-solving structures alongside the conventional line organization that carries out such routine tasks."[83] Typically, the temporary structures rest on norms or values that may be starkly at odds with those common in conventional structures:[84] participation, rank-in-ideas, creativity, quick-reacting, temporariness, and so on.

Most experience with collateral or parallel structures comes from business settings, but public sector applications can draw encouragement from two sources. Thus, the reported experiences with collaterals seem decidedly positive.[85] Moreover, such temporary complements may be particularly useful in the public sector, as Stewart and Garson reflect in these revealing terms:

> Particularly in public sector organization, clear lines of authority and responsibility drawn by conventional hierarchy facilitate achieving the important objective of official accountability. Parallel structures do not displace bureaucratic structures which continue to do what they do best, define job titles, pay grades, fixed reporting relationships, and related formal tasks. Rather this is an attempt simultaneously to introduce environmental

EXHIBIT 6   Project Management: Features, Advantages, and Disadvantages

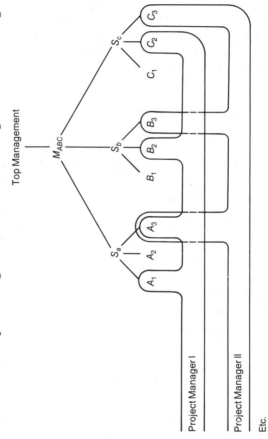

A. Typical Features	B. Advantages
	• Widely applicable, especially for complex and changing technologies, product lines, and markets
1. Scalar principle: one person, one boss	• Maintained in regular functional departments, but balanced by project managers who integrate functional contributions
	• Flexible, and emphasizes interdependence between functions and projects
2. Unity of direction	• From balance of functions and projects
3. Basis of departmentation	• Dual: functions and projects
4. Degree of permanence	• Focuses on overall outcomes and specific clients
	• Functional departments are relatively permanent; projects can come and go
	• Highlights integration of specialties for specific purposes, which can heighten cohesion, collaboration, and involvement of contributors
5. Flexiblity of application	• Widely applicable
6. Line/staff distinction	• Facilitates organization change, as by birth/death of project units
	• Conventional concept may exist within functional departments, but is overridden by integrative demands in project departments
	• Builds on functional model, but transcends it
7. Basic loyalties	• Provides early opportunities for integrative managerial development for S and even A, B, or C
	• Multiple and even conflicting for those in projects, especially employees with 2 or more project memberships
	• Facilitates decentralization, which can be useful in complex activities
8. Locus of basic conflict resolution	• Between individual projects and functions
	• Focuses responsibility for performance at mid and lower levels
9. Loci of high stress	• Project managers, especially when budgetary control is in functional departments; and those with multiple-project memberships

C. Disadvantages

- Can induce high stress, especially in project managers and those with multiple-project memberships
- Can induce win/lose competition between functions and projects
- Complicates performance appraisal, especially that of specialists by generalist project managers
- Limits specialists' exposure to fellow specialists, and may limit their career advancement[87]
- May reduce useful influence of functional departments

responsiveness and thus change capability into bureaucratic organizations through alternative formal structures.[86]

Given the modest experience with parallels or collaterals, no formal set of advantages or disadvantages will be presented here. Patently, however, the collateral promises some of the best of both worlds: stability and continuity, as well as flexibility and innovation. The basic concern inheres in the possibility that the values associated with the collateral cannot be induced and maintained in the face of contrary pressures from the permanent conventional structure.

Project Management as Structural Innovation

We now shift attention to three generic kinds of structural innovation that reflect a bias toward purpose in organizing, beginning with the project management model dealt with in Exhibit 6. In common with the two following innovations, Exhibit 6 reflects four emphases. Thus, the basic structural form gets simplified illustration; the model's typical features receive some elaboration; and separate attention goes to both major advantages and disadvantages of each model.

Note also that certain simple conventions have been adopted in all three cases of structural innovation. Thus, all three illustrative structures each have four basic organization levels: top management, middle management (indicated by an M), direct supervision (indicated by an S), and operators designated, for example, as A_1, B_1, and C_1. Three functions or processes, indicated as A, B, or C, are assumed sufficient to generate some product or service in the rough form $A + B + C$.

Basically, project management retains the functional model but adds major structural counterbalance to it in the role of the project manager or director. The functional departments may be seen as having a vertical bias, in the abstract, and as constituting a "home base" for many employees. The specific balance of power between function and project may shift substantially, not only in different phases of projects but also in terms of such critical conditions as the degree of budgetary control that remains in the functional departments.

In retaining a strong and permanent "home base" for organization members, typically excepting the project manager, and by adding to it a set of changing and often multiple project memberships, the model may be seen as usefully transitional. In point of fact, it tends to appear in those situations, as in construction and defense,[88] where quite strong functional and/or professional subunits antedated the project management mode.

Project management has received substantial and growing use in the public sector. Perhaps the most dramatic applications occurred in Lockheed's "Skunkworks," which generated a number of high-technology systems for military and intelligence uses. In federally funded urban mass transit construction programs, the mode has received much procedural and even legislative legitimation, with bid guidelines often requiring project management structures and personnel. More recently, project management has appeared in a broader array of administrative contexts.[89]

The advantages and/or disadvantages in Exhibit 6 imply that project teams do not constitute an integrative cure-all for the particularisms of the bureaucratic model. Patently, project structures seek to structurally frame the issues of organization power and balance between hierarchy and specialization in a direct way, in effect providing formal pathways for integration in addition to differentiation by functions or processes. Efforts to achieve this subtle balance could careen to extremes, of course, even as the structure seeks to generate a framework for resolution of competing claims. Thus, project managers could report to a project or program office, and long trails of paper might characterize relationships up and down that vertical chain, as well as up across and down the several other functional chains of command. Note also that many project team successes might reflect factors in addition to design. These reinforcing factors include forceful leadership pushing major urgencies and high priorities, also having access to substantial pools of resources.

Flow of Work as Structural Innovation

A second generic mode drastically reorients structure toward purpose. While project management can be said to add a counterbalance to the vertical tendencies of the functional mode, the contrasting horizontal flow of work becomes *the* basis for departmentation in this structural innovation. Flows of work can be distinguished at high levels of organization, as in the divisionalization by products common in business organizations.[90] At lower levels, "discrete subassemblies" can provide the foci for departmentation, as may be done by charting the incidence and significance of interactions between specific people, skills, or whatever, and departmentalizing around the densest clusters of interaction.[91] Commonly, at whatever level, the flow-of-work mode acknowledges that all or most activities in a complex organization are related. But the mode also proposes that some clusters are more persistently and significantly related than others. These clusters become *the* basic units of organization, whereas other more distal activities may be reserved as staff supports for M_{ABC} or otherwise located.

Exhibit 7 provides a summary of the features, advantages, and disadvantages of the mode. A horizontal or integrative thrust characterizes this model. This feature relates to significant aspects of human and

EXHIBIT 7   Flow of Work Structures: Features, Advantages, and Disadvantages

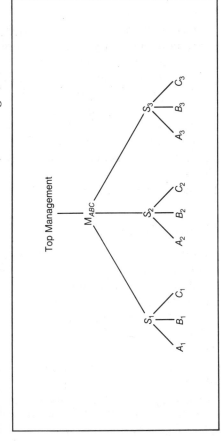

A. Typical Features		B. Advantages
1. Scalar principle: one person, one boss	• Essentially maintained	• Focuses on overall outcomes via integration at lower levels of functions or processes
2. Unity of direction	• Through S in decentralized mode	• Relatively permanent
3. Basic departmentation	• Total flows of work	• Organizations can grow very large in total size, while remaining "flat"
4. Degree of permanence	• Relatively permanent, with the caveat that various measures of comparative performance provide constant stimuli and a basis for change or termination of individual S-units	• Encourages innovation in S-units
		• Provides motivationally rich structural opportunities at lower levels—e.g., job enrichment, poly-specialization, and autonomous teams[94]
5. Flexibility of application	• Requires several similar flows of work and/or measures of comparable performance (e.g., return on investment)	• Provides early opportunities for integrative managerial development for A, B, and C.
		• Facilitates decentralization
6. Line/staff distinction	• Strong loyalties within S-units moderate the distinction and encourage integration;[92] some conventional staff may report to M_{ABC}	• Fixes responsibility for performance at lower levels
		C. Disadvantages
7. Basic loyalties	• Sharply focused within S-units	• Applicability is limited to situations where comparable measurement of S-unit performance is possible and convenient, most commonly at top levels or in more routine processing of things or people[95]
8. Locus of basic conflict	• Within S-units, but some between-unit externalities can exist	• May result in duplication, as in greater "fractional loss"
9. Loci of high stress	• Ss, but moderated by strong loyalties of S-unit members "to pull together"[93]	• May encapsulate experience in an S-unit re useful innovations and complicate their diffusion
		• Complicates performance appraisals of specialists by generalist S
		• Limits specialists' exposure to fellow specialists, and shortens specialist ladders for advancement

political rationality. To illustrate, the model raises the probability that socioemotional attachments between S-unit members will reinforce the technical contributions necessary for the flow of work. Moreover, the basic structural reorientation has significant implications for power dynamics. The comparative measurement of S-unit performance will inhibit such socioemotional attachments from resulting in the kind of high cohesiveness that is sometimes reflected in low productivity among mono-specialized work units,[96] for example. In addition, the S-units can compete in terms of more efficient performance on comparable flows of work, which encourages a useful discipline unlike the win/lose dynamics associated with the separate functions or processes of the bureaucratic model.

Business reliance on the flow-of-work mode has been mixed. Its earliest appearance was in the 1920s,[97] when it provided at top levels the basic structure for the divisionalization around product lines that constituted a major breakthrough at Du Pont and elsewhere. The mode has been less common at low levels of organization in business and industry, despite its patent compatibility with the burgeoning recent attention given to job enrichment and autonomous teams. All too often, such interventions are grafted onto organizations structured functionally at midmanagement levels. This has often caused more enduring problems, especially where the interventions "worked" and were positively received at lower levels.[98]

Public sector reliance on the flow-of-work mode has not been strong. Early conceptual exhortations supporting the mode do exist,[99] but the functional model for diverse and weighty reasons is well entrenched in the public sector. A few public sector applications have been made, however, perhaps most notably in the attempted restructuring of police departments,[100] and in the successful application at the Rehabilitation Services, Division of Youth, the State of New York.[101]

Mature Matrix as Structural Innovation

The mature matrix may be viewed as an amalgam of various prominent features of the functional model, as well as of the three other structural innovations summarized previously. Yet the model has a definite uniqueness.

Uniqueness may be established directly and economically. The mature matrix "will almost certainly be an unnecessary complexity," its most prominent exponents explain, except in the "overwhelming" presence of three necessary and sufficient conditions:

- two or more critical organization sectors—functions, products, services, markets, areas—that require a balancing of power, multiple command, and simultaneous decision making

- the performance of uncertain, complex, and interdependent tasks, which requires an enriched capacity to process vast amounts of information
- economies of scale that are motivated by stiff competitive pressures and only can be achieved by the rapid deployment of resources to various products, services, clients, or markets.[102]

Few organizations are seen as meeting these requirements, although their number may well be increasing.

Exhibit 8 describes this amalgam-cum-uniqueness, but brief attention may be drawn to four prominent aspects of the mature matrix that justify its present characterization. First, the mode distinguishes between those "in the matrix" and others. The managers of the two or more interdependent organization "sectors"—functions, products, area, and so on, depending upon the specific locus—join the supervisors or directors immediately below them "in the matrix." For them, especially, subtle attention must be given to all aspects of the "matrix organization," which Davis and Lawrence define suggestively:[103]

$$\frac{\text{Matrix}}{\text{Structure}} + \frac{\text{Matrix}}{\text{Systems}} + \frac{\text{Matrix}}{\text{Culture}} + \frac{\text{Matrix}}{\text{Behavior}}$$

These four interacting perspectives imply complex requirements that distinguish the mature matrix but that can be given only perfunctory attention below.

Second, the traditional notions of command tend to dominate at several points. Generally, they may characterize those relationships not in the matrix—between top management and the sector managers, between overhead resources reporting to specific Ms, and perhaps between the Ss and those resources assigned to them (e.g., A_1, and B_1). This preserves an essential element of the functional model in major parts of the mature matrix.

Third, the several sector Ms in effect constitute bosses for each S. Put another way, each S is a multibossed manager. This departs radically from the functional model and makes more explicit some of the essential flavor of project management. As in project management, also, the sector managers do not "control" specialized resources (A_1, B_1, etc.) as they would in the conventional model. They subtly share that "control" with the several S's below them and, in that sense, M's may see a mature matrix as reducing their authority and influence.

Fourth, each S who can be called an "enterprise manager" essentially heads the kind of an integrative unit prescribed by the flow-of-work model. One aspect of the mature matrix is the creation of "little enterprises" whose performances can be variously compared. To each S are

EXHIBIT 8 Mature Matrix: Features, Advantages, Disadvantages

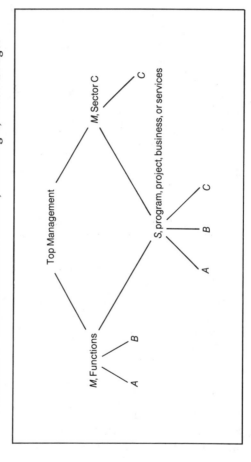

A. Typical Features	B. Advantages

B. Advantages

- Highlights interdependence of two or more sectors—functions, products, area, etc.
- Legitimates flexible responses to environmental changes and to differences between programs or projects
- Focuses on overall outcomes, while providing specialized resources for each program and thus reducing duplication
- May be temporary projects or permanent enterprises
- Focuses accountability for integration on S, while acknowledging coprimacy of multiple sectors
- Appropriate for very complex and changing technologies, product lines, and markets

C. Disadvantages

- Applicability is sharply limited by costs and necessary supports, e.g., an appropriate culture and reward system
- High stress for those "in the matrix"
- Low clarity about appropriate attitudes, behaviors, and values
- May disproportionately reward political vs. technical skills[106]
- Requires delicate balances: between individual programs and sectors; and between sectors
- Call for high-order interpersonal skills, especially in raising and resolving issues constructively

A. Typical Features

1. Scalar principle: one person, one boss
   - Maintained for most participants, but multiple supervision characterizes those "in the matrix"—Ms and Ss

2. Unity of direction
   - Through multiple supervision of each project by two or more critical sectors, e.g., functions, products, services, markets, or areas; and by bargaining with S

3. Basis of departmentation
   - Variegated for those "in the matrix," likely to be functional for others

4. Degree of permanence
   - Highly variable: projects "in the matrix" may be short-lived, but units organized as businesses and functional groups may be relatively permanent

5. Flexibility of application
   - Costs and complexities imply stringent and limited conditions under which model is reasonable[104]

6. Line/staff distinction
   - For those "in the matrix," power is balanced in subtle and complex ways that transcend the conventional distinction[105]

7. Basic loyalties
   - Can be multiple and conflictual for those "in the matrix"

8. Locus of basic conflict resolution
   - Between Ms and S

9. Loci of high stress
   - Ms and often especially Ss

delegated substantial powers, as well as responsibilities for innovation, "learning to learn," and more or less continually "making a market."

Despite the central role in the literature of NASA's "program office" and its famous "diamond" structure,[107] the public sector through the 1970s infrequently relied on the mature matrix.[108] Davis and Lawrence speculate in a 1977 publication that the record in federal agencies may derive in part from the fact that they seldom face "stiff competitive pressures."[109] That may be true in part, but more of the explanation may lay in the deep public sector commitment to the conventional model for organizing work. This basically inheres in a simple concept of "direct-line democracy" between the voters and the President acting on legislative mandates through the executive, as suggested earlier. The conventional model, directly if simplistically, suits direct-line democracy. The mature matrix less easily fits with direct-line democracy.

This summary of the mature matrix is included here for dual and related reasons. Lately, "stiff competitive pressures" seem to have grown significantly in the public sector. The motivation may well be accumulating to more aggressively challenge the central notion of direct-line democracy. Perhaps relatedly, resorting to the mature matrix in the public sector seems to be increasing.[110] Applications have been reported recently at both federal[111] and state levels,[112] and some observers even propose that the mature matrix may be *the* design of choice for certain purposes such as headquarters/field relationships.[113] Of course, such relationships often have been central and sore points in public management.

Conclusion

Basic progress in public sector organization is seen as involving the shift from an emphasis on function toward purpose, for various empirical and normative reasons. Five modes consistent with this reorientation are considered, their properties having been distinguished, with attention to their several advantages and disadvantages.

Essentially, the analysis confirms Wilson's most basic early notion even as it requires its modification in one particular. Thus Wilson concluded in 1883 that "large powers and unhampered discretion seem to me the indispensable conditions of responsibility," and that power need not be dangerous "if only it be not irresponsible."[114] The present orientation toward purpose echoes the same themes. The focus on specialties served well enough in an earlier day when general competence levels were rightly questioned and ethical or professional sensibilities were quite undeveloped. Now, however, the focus on organizational parts often has the effect of compromising the performance of the whole by fragmenting loyalties and effort, and by dispersing responsibility for managerial integration—for making some product or delivering a service, or for performing some bundle of activities associated with governance.

But Wilson's view of responsibility was too individualistic to be of full service in the present administrative era. His focus was singular and, understandably for his times, masculine: "Public attention must be easily directed, in each case of good or bad administration, to just the [one] man deserving of praise or blame."[115] This analysis shows that such singular attribution for integrative performance is poorly served by the traditional model. Moreover, approaches to focusing on purpose in organizing imply that often it is not meaningful, if it ever was, to focus responsibility on an individual. Indeed, "large powers and unhampered discretion" in Wilson's sense commonly will require an expanded and expanding sense of: Who is responsible?

Endnotes

1. For example, see Peter Smith Ring and James L. Perry, "Reforming the Upper Levels of the Bureaucracy," *Administration and Society* 15:119–144 (May) 1983.
2. Robert T. Golembiewski, "Organizing Public Work, Round Three: Toward A New Balance Between Political Agendas and Management Perspectives," in *The Costs of Federalism*, Golembiewski and Aaron Wildavsky, eds. (New Brunswick, NJ: Transaction, 1984).
3. President's Committee on Administrative Management, *Report* (Washington, DC: Government Printing Office, 1939).
4. For example, see Laurence E. Lynn, Jr., *Managing the Public's Business* (New York: Basic Books, 1981), especially pp. 52–72; and Joseph A. Califano, *A Presidential Nation* (New York: W. W. Norton, 1975), especially p. 49.
5. Robert T. Golembiewski, "Accountancy as A Function of Organization Theory," *The Accounting Review* 39 (April) 1964, pp. 333–341.
6. Consider the central role of "cross-walks" in PPBS, which testify to the fragmenting features of the conventional model for organizing that could profit from PPBS but also complicate its application.
7. Consult, for example, the lack of a structural emphasis in such sources as: Thomas R. Dye, *Understanding Public Policy* (Englewood Cliffs, NJ: Prentice-Hall, 1978); and J. L. Pressman and Aaron Wildavsky, *Implementation* (Berkeley, CA: University of California Press, 1973). Notice also the breathless quality of the discovery of a structural emphasis in Ervin C. Hargrove, *The Missing Link: The Study of the Implementation of Public Policy* (Washington, DC: Urban Institute, 1975).

8. The point gets useful emphasis from William E. Reig, *Computer Technology and Management Organization* (Iowa City, IA: Bureau of Business and Economic Research, University of Iowa, 1968); and Thomas L. Whisler, *The Impact of Computers on Organization* (New York: Praeger, 1970).

9. Woodrow Wilson, "The Study of Administration," *Political Science Quarterly* 2:210 (June) 1887.

10. Robert T. Golembiewski, "The Ideational Poverty of Two Modes of Coupling Democracy and Administration," *International Journal of Public Administration* 4:25–49, 1982; and Golembiewski, "A Third Mode of Coupling Democracy and Administration," *International Journal of Public Administration* 3:423–454, 1981.

11. Herbert A. Simon, "The Proverbs of Administration," *Public Administration Review* 6:53–67 (Winter) 1947.

12. E.g., Robert T. Golembiewski, *Men, Management, and Morality* (New York: McGraw-Hill, 1965).

13. See the discussion around Exhibit 5, later in Chapter.

14. For the early history of this revisionism in the United States, see Alfred D. Chandler, *Strategy and Structure* (Cambridge, MA: MIT Press, 1962).

15. See Emmette S. Redford, *Democracy in the Administrative State* (New York: Oxford University Press, 1969), especially pp. 70–72.

16. Victor Thompson, *Without Compassion or Sympathy* (University, AL: University of Alabama Press, 1975).

17. For extended analysis, see Golembiewski, "Organizing Public Work, Round Three."

18. Matthew A. Crenson, *The Federal Machine: Beginnings of Bureaucracy in Jacksonian America* (Baltimore, MD: Johns Hopkins University Press, 1975).

19. Stephen Skowronek, *Building A New American State* (New York: Cambridge University Press, 1982).

20. Op. cit., pp. 290–291.

21. Wilson, op. cit., p. 204.

22. Ibid., pp. 207.

23. Chandler, op. cit.

24. James D. Thompson, *Organizations in Action* (New York: McGraw-Hill, 1967).

25. Skowronek, op. cit., p. 4

26. Golembiewski, "Organizing Public Work, Round Three," in press.

27. Quoted in Dwight Waldo, *The Enterprise of Administration* (Novato, CA: Chandler and Sharp, 1980), p. 90.

28. Alvin Toffler, *A Third Wave* (New York: Morrow, 1980), p. 420.

29. Robert T. Golembiewski, "Two Kinds of Romantics in Planned Organization Change," *Dialogue* 5:1–5 (Summer) 1983.

30. Allen Tough, *Intentional Changes: A Fresh Approach to Helping People Change* (Chicago, IL: Follett, 1982).

31. Robert T. Golembiewski, *Approaches to Planned Change* (New York: Marcel Dekker, 1979), Volumes 1 & 2.

32. John Vasconcellos, "Humanizing Politics," *New Age* 4, 1978, pp. 37–38.

33. Lawrence B. Mohr, *Explaining Organizational Behavior* (San Francisco: Jossey-Bass, 1982), especially pp. 182–186.

34. For one overview, see Paul Bernstein, *Workplace Democratization* (New Brunswick, NJ: New Transaction Press, 1980).
35. See John M. Nicholas, *Academy of Management Review* 7 (October 1982), pp. 531–542; and Robert T. Golembiewski, Carl W. Proehl, Jr., and David Sink, "Success of OD Applications in the Public Sector," *Public Administration Review* 41:679–682 (November) 1982.
36. This certainly was a powerful attraction of the bureaucratic model in Jacksonian days. Amos Kendall, *Organization of the Post Office Department* (Washington, DC: 1835).
37. Robert T. Golembiewski, *Organizing Men and Power* (Chicago: Rand McNally, 1967).
38. See, for example, Chandler, op. cit.
39. "Fractional loss" refers to direct personnel savings when (for example) some functional or processual activity requires only 2 person-days. If the resources were located in three separate units, 3 persons might have to be employed. Unit workloads might be .7, .6, and .7 days, and departmentation by functions or processes might save the "fractional loss," which in the present case would be .3, .4, and .3, or 1.0 person-day.
40. Herbert G. Wilcox, "The Culture Trait of Hierarchy in Middle Class Children," *Public Administration Review* 28:222–235 (May) 1968.
41. Golembiewski, *Organizing Men and Power.*
42. As Peter Drucker observes: "Increasingly it is in his work that the citizen of a modern industrial society looks for the satisfaction of his creative drive and instinct, for those satisfactions which go beyond the economic, for his pride, his self-respect, his self-esteem." *The Practice of Management* (New York: Harper and Bros., 1954), p. 183.
43. David H. Rosenbloom, *Public Administration and Law* (New York: Marcel Dekker, Inc., 1983).
44. See the discussion in Robert T. Golembiewski, "Structuring the Public Organization," *Handbook of Organization Management,* William B. Eddy, ed. (New York: Marcel Dekker, Inc., 1982), pp. 202–203.
45. James W. Fesler, "Politics, Policy, and Bureaucracy at the Top," *Annals of the American Academy of Political and Social Sciences* 466:26 (March) 1982.
46. As the number of organization members increases, the conventional model prescribes a narrow span of control. Hence, numerical growth under that model induces "tall" organizations, with many levels of supervision.
47. John Child and Alfred Kieser, "Development of Organizations Over Time," *Handbook of Organizational Design,* Volume 1, Paul C. Nystrom and William Starbuck, eds. (New York: Oxford University Press, 1981), pp. 44–46.
48. See the argument in Malcolm Warner, "Organizational Experiments and Social Innovations," in Nystrom and Starbuck, op. cit., Volume 1, pp. 171–172.
49. The anomalies in American practice have been noted often and can be highlighted by comparing the sketch immediately following with the description in Albert M. Craig, "Functional and Dysfunctional Aspects of Government Bureaucracy," *Modern Japanese Organization and Decision Making,* Azra F. Vogel, ed. (Berkeley, CA: University of California Press, 1975), pp. 3–32.

50. Fesler, op. cit., pp. 29–30.
51. As Fesler usefully notes. Ibid., p. 28.
52. James L. Sundquist, "A Comparison of Policy-Making Capacity in the United States and Five European Countries," *Population Policy Analysis,* Michael E. Kraft and Mark Schneider, eds. (Lexington, MA: D. C. Heath, 1978), p. 71.
53. Joseph Califano, *Governing America* (New York: Simon and Schuster, 1981), p. 452.
54. Fesler, op. cit., p. 26.
55. Elliot Richardson, *The Creative Balance* (New York: Holt, Rinehart, and Winston, 1976), p. 73.
56. For example, see Joseph W. Bartlett and Douglas N. Jones, "Managing A Cabinet Agency," *Public Administration Review* 35:63 (January) 1974.
57. Fesler, op. cit., pp. 25–26.
58. Frederick Malek, *Washington's Hidden Tragedy* (New York: Macmillan, 1978), pp. 102–103.
59. George P. Shultz and Kenneth W. Dam, *Economic Policy Beyond the Headlines* (New York: W. W. Norton, 1977), p. 173.
60. Sundquist, op. cit., p. 73.
61. Ibid.
62. Ibid.
63. Richardson, op. cit., p. 80.
64. Ring and Perry, op. cit., pp. 137–138.
65. Golembiewski, "Organizing Public Work, Round Three."
66. Child and Kieser, op. cit.; and Joseph McCann and Jay R. Galbraith, "Interdepartmental Relations," in Nystrom and Starbuck, op. cit., Volume 2, pp. 60–84.
67. Jay R. Galbraith, *Organization Design* (Reading, MA: Addison-Wesley, 1977), p. 31.
68. See such current sources as Ralph H. Kilmann and Mary J. Saxton, *Organization Cultures* (San Francisco: Jossey-Bass, 1983).
69. See the summary in Debra W. Stewart and G. David Garson, *Organizational Behavior and Public Management* (New York: Marcel Dekker, Inc., 1983), pp. 181 ff.
70. Stanley Milgram, *Obedience to Authority* (New York: Harper & Row, 1974), p. 186.
71. Quoted in Robert B. Denhart, *In the Shadow of Organization* (Lawrence, KS: The Regents Press of Kansas, 1981), p. 15.
72. Thomas P. Peters and Robert H. Waterman, *In Search of Excellence: Lessons from America's Best-Run Companies* (New York: Harper & Row, 1982).
73. These features are elaborated in Golembiewski, *Approaches to Planned Change,* Volume 2, pp. 65–69. See also, especially, Leonard R. Sayles and Margaret Chandler, *Managing Large Systems* (New York: Harper and Row, 1971).
74. In a change program in Alcan, for example, extraordinary efforts were sanctioned by top management to "improve communication" between plant-level officials. But management support evaporated when a change-agent directed attention to the structural causes of communication problems.

Structural change was considered out-of-bounds, in part because the existing structure permitted convenient overhead control, or at least the comfortable allusion of control.

75. The phenomenon has been widely observed, as in quality circles that "work" and soon find their principals transferred and promoted because of their successes. See also Paul S. Goodman and Associates, *Change in Organizations* (San Francisco: Jossey-Bass, 1982).

76. See Robert T. Golembiewski and Alan Kiepper, "Organizational Transition in a Fast-Paced Public Project," *Public Administration Review* 43:246–254 (June) 1983.

77. Sayles and Chandler, op. cit.

78. Harvey Sapolsky, *The POLARIS System Development* (Cambridge, MA: Harvard University Press, 1972).

79. Robert T. Golembiewski and Alan Kiepper, "MARTA: Toward An Effective, Open Giant," *Public Administration Review* 36:46–60 (January) 1976.

80. Donald P. Warwick, *A Theory of Public Bureaucracy* (Cambridge, MA: Harvard University Press, 1975).

81. Robert T. Golembiewski and Alan Kiepper, "Organizational Transition in A Fast-Paced Public Project."

82. Robert T. Golembiewski and Alan Kiepper, "Lessons From A Fast-Paced Public Project," *Public Administration Review* 43:547–556 (November) 1983.

83. Barry A. Stein and Rosabeth Moss Kanter, "Building the Parallel Organization," *Journal of Applied Behavioral Science* 16:371–388 (July) 1980.

84. Dale E. Zand, "Collateral Organization," *Journal of Applied Behavioral Science* 10:63–90 (January) 1974, especially pp. 63–71. See also Zand, Matthew B. Miles, and William O. Lytle, Jr., *Enlarging Organization Choice Through Use of A Temporary Problem-Solving System* (mimeo., no date).

85. Ibid. See also Stein and Kanter, op. cit.

86. Stewart and Garson, op. cit., p. 191.

87. McCann and Galbraith, op. cit., p. 61.

88. Adolph Vleck, Jr., "Minimizing Line-Staff Friction at Martin-Baltimore," pp. 29–53, in *Line-Staff Relations in Production* (New York: American Management Association, 1957).

89. See Walter F. Baber, *Organizing the Future* (University, AL: University of Alabama Press, 1983), and Peter Jennergren, "Decentralization in Organizations," in Nystrom and Starbuck, op. cit., Volume 1, especially pp. 44–55.

90. Chandler, op. cit.

91. Eliot D. Chapple and Leonard R. Sayles, *The Measure of Management* (New York: Macmillan, 1961).

92. Golembiewski, *Organizing Men and Power*.

93. For an early emphasis on this key point, see Robert T. Golembiewski, "Small Groups and Large Organizations," *Handbook of Organizations*, James G. March, ed. (Chicago: Rand McNally, 1965), especially pp. 88–94 and 101–106.

94. Golembiewski, "Structuring the Public Organization," especially pp. 216–227.

95. In business organizations, such devices as "return on investment" calcula-

tions reinforce flow-of-work structures at top levels. Public sector analogues have not yet appeared, despite some early ideation about their possible character. See Golembiewski, "Organizing Public Work, Round Three."

96. The phenomenon seems particularly likely in the last operation in a long sequential link, for obvious political reasons that may be reinforced by technical issues such as product deterioration or in-process inventory costs.

97. Chandler, op. cit.

98. Consult Richard Walton, "Work Innovations at Topeka," *Journal of Applied Behavioral Science* 13:422–433 (July) 1977.

99. Robert T. Golembiewski, "Civil Service and Managing Work," *American Political Science Review* 56:961–973 (December) 1962.

100. See John P. Kenney, *Police Administration* (Springfield IL: Thomas, 1972).

101. Donald K. Carew, et al., "New York State Division for Youth: A Collaborative Approach to the Implementation of Structural Change in a Bureaucracy," *Journal of Applied Behavioral Science* 13:327–339 (July) 1977.

102. Stanley M. Davis and Paul R. Lawrence, *Matrix* (Reading, MA: Addison-Wesley, 1977), pp. 20–21.

103. Ibid., p. 18.

104. Davis and Lawrence, op. cit., pp. 18–24.

105. Ibid., pp. 46–48.

106. McCann and Galbraith, op. cit., p. 62.

107. Andre Delbecq and Alan Filley, *Program and Project Management in a Matrix Organization* (Madison, WI: Bureau of Business Research, University of Wisconsin-Madison).

108. For a few early public sector examples, see Davis and Lawrence, op. cit., pp. 170–181.

109. Davis and Lawrence, op. cit., p. 174.

110. For a recent overview of applications, see Baber, op. cit.

111. Mary Ellen Simon, "Matrix Management at the U. S. Consumer Product Safety Commission," *Public Administration Review* 43:352–356 (July) 1983.

112. C. E. Teasley III and R. K. Ready, "Human Service Matrix: Managerial Problems and Prospects," *Public Administration Review* 41:261–267 (March) 1981.

113. Mark Lincoln Chadwin, "Managing Program Headquarter Units," *Public Administration Review* 43:305–314 (July) 1983.

114. Wilson, op. cit., pp. 213–214.

115. Ibid.

PART VI

Comparative Public Administration

CHAPTER 15

Comparative Public Administration in the United States

Ferrel Heady

THE UNIVERSITY OF NEW MEXICO

FERREL HEADY is Professor Emeritus of Public Administration and Political Science at the University of New Mexico, Albuquerque, where he served as Academic Vice President (1967–68) and President (1968–75) prior to returning to a full-time faculty position from 1976 through 1981. He received the University of New Mexico Outstanding Graduate Teacher Award in 1982. Previously, Professor Heady was at the University of Michigan, Ann Arbor, from 1946 through 1966. There he directed the Institute of Public Administration and in 1961 received the University of Michigan Faculty Distinguished Achievement Award. Professor Heady is the leading authority on comparative and development administration in the United States. His Public Administration: A Comparative Perspective *sets the standard for the field.*

Ferrel Heady surveys the comparative dimension of American public administration. His chronological review demonstrates that there has been a recurrent tendency among major contributors to American public administration to show knowledge of and interest in the administrative experiences of other countries. This tendency antedates the publication of Woodrow Wilson's 1887 essay. Wilson himself stressed the importance of foreign attainments to the conduct of public administration in the United States. Some of his successors continued to recognize the significance of comparative information, even during the decades when American public administration was most inner-directed. They kept alive an interest that was renewed and expanded at midcentury, culminating in the emergence of comparative public administration as a major field of concentration.

Two of the three primary sources of early American thought about political and administrative institutions are comparative. Lynton K. Caldwell identifies the three sources as English laws and history, colonial experience, and "the general body of political thought and . . . theories pertaining to the republics of classical antiquity."* The authors of *The Federalist* frequently referred to foreign examples in explaining their own views on domestic issues. Commentators from abroad such as Alexis de Tocqueville brought their knowledge of other governmental institutions to bear on their analysis of American institutions. The contributions of such people are sufficient to justify the assertion of Fred W. Riggs that the American tradition in comparative administration extends back over 200 years and is not confined to recent decades or even the last century.

Leonard D. White and other administrative historians have identified numerous instances of American administrative changes based on comparative knowledge prior to the 1880s. These include methods for managing public money, regulations for steam navigation safety, customs warehousing systems, lighthouse construction and maintenance, the construction and equipping of naval vessels, the operation of postal systems, and the management of public printing. White said these borrowings indicate that "executive officers were not only anxious to improve the operations of their respective departments but were ready to borrow from the politically despised monarchies of Europe."† The most dramatic adaptation of all was the civil service reform movement based on the Northcote-Trevelyan reforms in England during the 1850s. Paul Van Riper calls the Pendleton Act of 1883 the last stage of the Americanizing of a foreign invention.

Heady describes Woodrow Wilson as a comparativist. Two years before the publication of his famous essay, Wilson referred in a personal letter to his "work upon comparative systems of administration," and there is ample evidence in the text of the essay that Wilson regarded comparative knowledge as indispensable for systematic progress in the study and practice of public administration. Even a cursory reading of "The Study of Administration" forces one to conclude that one of its main purposes was to urge Americans to catch up with other nations—notably France and Germany—in the application of administrative techniques.

From the time of Wilson's contributions until the decade of the 1940s, American public administration was identified with what Riggs has called a "counter-tradition" to the earlier tendency to examine foreign administrative experience for the benefit of American administrative practice. Exceptions to such parochialism are numerous, however, and include the notable work of Frank J. Goodnow, Ernst Freund, Leonard D. White, and W. F. Willoughby. These authors varied in the extent of their treatment

---

* Lynton K. Caldwell, "Novus Ordo Seclorum: The Heritage of American Public Administration," *Public Administration Review* 36:476–488 (September–October) 1976, at p. 477.

† Leonard D. White, *The Jacksonians* (New York: Macmillan, 1956), pp. 532–533.

of comparative material, but each in his way kept the comparative dimension of public administration alive. Even the scientific management movement admitted that the principles of management were universally applicable across time, cultures, and countries, and that the validity of the principles could be tested in a variety of settings.

The 1940s brought a reshaping of American public administration. Thinkers such as Herbert A. Simon, Paul H. Appleby, John M. Gaus, and Dwight Waldo were responsible for establishing new foundations for the discipline. New textbooks such as *Elements of Public Administration*, edited by Fritz Morstein Marx, included more substantial comparative information than had existed in prewar texts. The single most influential statement that stimulated new research in comparative public administration was made by Robert A. Dahl in 1947. He said, "The comparative aspects of public administration have largely been ignored; and as long as the study of public administration is not comparative, claims for a 'science of public administration' sound rather hollow."*

The surge of interest in cross-national analysis of systems of public administration that emerged from both academic opinion and the exposure of Americans to foreign countries during and after World War II led to a comparative administration "movement" during the 1950s and 1960s. It had personnel, organizational, and financial underpinnings that together accounted for its progress. Financial support was provided by major grants from the Ford Foundation for a decade beginning in 1962. Heady says the major shared characteristics during the heyday of the movement were an optimistic outlook and a tolerance for diversity. The optimism arose from the prevailing mood of hope and anticipation that followed the end of World War II, combined with a conviction that administrative technology could be exported from the more advanced to the less developed countries through bilateral and multinational technical assistance programs. Disappointing results gradually increased skepticism about such possibilities and led to more realistic expectations.

Subsequent evaluations of the comparative administration movement have emphasized such problems as a general lack of agreement about what is and is not within the scope of comparative studies. Discussions continue about what critics admit was an impressive accumulation of knowledge through the 1970s. Charles T. Goodsell now suggests a "new" comparative public administration enlarged to include comparisons at supranational and subnational levels of analysis, as well as cross-national levels. Peter Savage, on the other hand, argues that a separate identity for comparative administration as a field of study is no longer needed because its concerns and perspectives have been absorbed and are now a part of the broader disciplines of public administration and political science. They parallel the earlier effect of the behavioral movement in the social sciences generally.

Heady agrees with Jong S. Jun and Fred W. Riggs that public administra-

---

* Robert A. Dahl, "The Science of Public Administration: Three Problems," *Public Administration Review* 7:1–11, 1947, at p. 8.

tion can no longer be treated, either in study or in practice, as exclusively concerned with the system of government in a single nation-state. The comparative theme in American public administration, present from the beginning and persisting even when it was muted, is now strong enough to compel recognition that understanding American public administration, or any other national system of administration, is possible only when it is placed in a cross-cultural setting.

Both in theory and practice, American public administration has historically exhibited an orientation that is primarily national, concentrating on the past experience and future needs of the United States and only incidentally concerned with cross-national comparison.

This tendency is reflected in the commonly accepted view that parochialism is a persistent dominant feature of American public administration, evidenced in the curricula of institutions of higher education preparing young people for public service careers and in the conduct of public administration by practicing professionals.

Such an overall assessment is probably correct, but it must be qualified to a considerable extent by recognition of significant trends during the last three or four decades. The period since World War II has brought about shifts of emphasis in both the operating and academic aspects of public administration. The most obvious indicators are the massive programs of exportation, through technical assistance projects, of our presumably advanced administrative technology to Third World countries, and the academic impact of the "comparative administration movement" on study and research in public administration.

As a result, comparative public administration has now gained recognition as a major focus of interest among American public administrators, but this is usually looked at as a phenomenon of the last third of the century of the American administrative state, taking 1887 as the starting date.

Our objective is to survey the comparative dimension in American public administration. Developments during recent decades will deservedly receive the greatest attention, but for fuller understanding a longer-range view must be taken.

Available evidence demonstrates that there has been a recurrent tendency by major contributors to American public administration to show knowledge of and interest in the administrative experiences of other countries. This antedates the publication of Woodrow Wilson's 1887 essay, which opened up the era of sustained study of public administration. Wilson himself stressed the importance to this country of foreign attainments in the conduct of public administration. Some of his successors continued to recognize the importance of comparative information, even during the decades when American public administration was most inner-directed, keeping alive an interest that was renewed and expanded at midcentury, culminating in the emergence of comparative public administration as a major point of concentration. These variations on the comparative theme in American public administration can best be examined chronologically.

Pre-Wilsonian Pioneers

American political and administrative institutions and practices inevitably have a comparative dimension, because they are basically derivative as to their origins. Lynton K. Caldwell identifies three pre-independence sources: English laws and history, colonial experience, and "the general body of political thought and . . . theories pertaining to the republics of classical antiquity."[1] Two of these sources are comparative, in the sense that they were external forces at work during the formative period when the American system was taking shape. This comparative input is undoubtedly of great significance but was usually not the result of a suggestion that some external model should be followed and a deliberate decision to do so. We are primarily interested in instances where a comparative approach was consciously and explicitly used.

Those who pioneered as comparativists in this way were primarily active American statesmen who referred to foreign examples in explaining their own views on domestic issues, or commentators from abroad who brought their knowledge of other governmental systems to bear as they analyzed American institutions. The authors of *The Federalist*—Alexander Hamilton, John Jay, and James Madison—are leading representatives of the first group, and the Frenchman Alexis de Tocqueville, author of *Democracy in America,* is undoubtedly the most knowledgeable and influential of the foreign observers. Although often peripheral to their main concerns, the comparative contributions of such individuals are sufficient to justify the assertion by Fred W. Riggs that the American tradition in comparative administration extends back over 200 years and is not confined to recent decades or even the last century.[2]

The collection of papers in *The Federalist* had the purpose of advocating ratification of the proposed constitution for the newly independent coun-

try. In doing this, the authors repeatedly referred to experiences elsewhere, ranging from the Greek city-states of classical times to the contemporary nations of eighteenth-century Europe. Their primary thrust was
to demonstrate the weaknesses of confederations and the necessity for
the proposed federal system. Ancient confederacies were scrutinized,
their relative successes and failures evaluated, and their overall inadequacies reviewed, with observations on the conduct of administration included in the analysis.[3] Two papers in the series were devoted to more
recent experiences with confederations in Germany, Poland, Switzerland,
and the Netherlands, and to comparisons among them.[4] In justifying
the attention given to these precedents, the author of No. 20 states:
"Experience is the oracle of truth; and where its responses are unequivocal, they ought to be conclusive and sacred."[5]

At this early stage of American history, comparative knowledge and
comparative analysis were effectively brought to bear by authors who
were both students and practitioners, collaborating in an effort that
helped to assure adoption of constitutional federalism in the United
States. During the remainder of the eighteenth century, Hamilton became the leading spokesman on administrative matters during the Federalist presidencies of George Washington and John Adams, formulating
what Leonard D. White has described as the "most consistent and most
precise body of administrative doctrine" of the first century after independence, emphasizing energy in the executive branch, executive responsibility and power, and "a fully organized federal administrative system independent of the states."[6]

During the Jeffersonian period beginning in 1801, however, White
discerns no equivalent clear-cut enunciation of administrative doctrine.
The Jeffersonian Republicans, he asserts,

> did not enrich the literature of public administration. There were no writ-
> ings of the nature of the *Federalist Papers,* either by officials or citizens.
> . . . The writings of Thomas Jefferson are singularly barren of views or
> comments on the art of conducting public business. . . . The attention
> of most executive, administrative, and middle management officers was
> confined to the particular duties that were assigned to them, and to the
> disposition of the business that automatically came to their attention, in-
> structed by law, regulation, and common sense. The art of public adminis-
> tration continued to be practiced, but not to be written about.[7]

The task of writing about public administration during the first half
of the nineteenth century was taken up by Alexis de Tocqueville. I
will comment on only one noticeable feature of his monumental study
of American democracy. Almost every topic treated by de Tocqueville
includes historical and contemporary comparisons between American
and foreign experience, with special attention to European nations. Of

course, most of these comparisons do not directly concern public administration, but many of them are of tangential interest, including his discussions of corruption, civil associations, patterns of centralization and decentralization of power, freedom of the press, individual rights, judicial power, the role of the military profession, attitudes toward property, and distribution of wealth among social classes, to mention a few examples. One of his most explicit comments on administration presages a central point made by Woodrow Wilson several decades later, although it has received much less attention:

> "All European governments have in our time introduced immense improvements in the science of administration. They both do more and do each thing more systematically, quickly, and cheaply. . . . European princes daily bring their agents under ever stricter control and invent new ways of keeping a closer hold on them and supervising them more easily. They are not satisfied just to have agents to conduct all business, but try to control the conduct of their agents in all matters. As a result, public administration not only depends on one sole power but also is more and more controlled from one spot and concentrated in ever fewer hands. The government centralizes its activity at the same time that it increases its prerogatives. . . ."[8]

De Tocqueville, although not an American himself, through his writings and their widespread dissemination made a significant early contribution to the comparative tradition in American public administration.

White and other administrative historians, nevertheless, have identified for us numerous instances of administrative changes based on comparative knowledge during the decades of relative sparcity in American contributions to the literature of public administration prior to the 1880s.

The public service, White reports, was

> affected by borrowing from European experience in ways and means of carrying on the King's business. English forms and procedures had always been significant, and the system set up by the Federalists was based heavily on English precedents, notably in the customs service. Now both Congress and the executive branch began to make specific investigations of foreign experience as a guide to administrative and technical improvement.[9]

He gives numerous illustrations, including methods for managing public money, regulations for steam navigation safety, customs warehousing systems, lighthouse construction and maintenance, the construction and equipping of naval vessels, operation of postal systems, and management of public printing. These borrowings indicate, White concludes, that

> executive officers were not only anxious to improve the operations of their respective departments but were ready to borrow from the politically

despised monarchies of Europe. The administrative process began to appear, almost intuitively, as something in part at least independent of constitutional structure and adaptable from an undemocratic to a democratic environment.[10]

The mid–nineteenth-century movement for civil service reform, culminating in adopting of the Pendleton Act in 1883, is an especially dramatic instance of American adaptation of foreign experience, primarily British in this case. In his *History of the United States Civil Service*,[11] Paul P. Van Riper chronicles how post–Civil War reform efforts in this country were inspired and guided by the Northcote-Trevelyan reforms of the previous decade in Great Britain, but he points out that interest was also shown in the civil service systems of other countries. American reform leaders such as George William Curtis corresponded with Northcote, Trevelyan, and others for detailed information about the British accomplishments. An official report on the United States civil service sponsored by Congressman Thomas A. Jenckes in 1868 contained eighty-two pages of information on Chinese, Prussian, French, and English civil service procedures.[12]

In 1871 Congress authorized President Grant to establish a Civil Service Commission that, although short-lived,

> succeeded in drawing up a group of civil service rules acceptable to the President. These rules were comprehensive and detailed. Patterned roughly after the British experience, they laid down procedures and devised terminology in use to this day.[13]

After a decade of setbacks, passage of the Pendleton Act in 1883 completed what Van Riper calls "Americanizing a foreign invention." He considers this act to be "essentially a modification of a British political invention in terms of the constitutional and administrative inclinations of this country," and "even more intriguing as a case study in cross-cultural adaptation."[14] This revamping of the British pattern of civil service reform to American environmental circumstances is the most significant and conspicuous instance of the application of comparative knowledge to public administration in the United States prior to the Wilsonian era.

Wilson as a Comparativist

Woodrow Wilson's essay on "The Study of Administration"[15] has become so famous that its publication in 1887 not only marks that year as the usually accepted starting point for public administration as an academic field of specialization in the United States but is also the main reason for considering 1987 as the end of the first century of the American administrative state.

Like the Bible and other venerable texts, Wilson's essay has different meanings for different readers and has been cited in support of incompatible points of view, reflecting probably both ambiguities in Wilson's presentation and the understandable urges of later writers to invoke him as a confirming authority. For example, Richard Stillman notes that even as to the most essential point of Wilson's presentation, conclusions vary. Frederick C. Mosher interprets Wilson as stressing the dichotomy between politics and administration; Fred W. Riggs sees him as emphasizing that politics and administration are intertwined and inseparable; John C. Buechner says that his basic premise is that the affairs of public administration are synonymous with those of private administration.[16] Each is able to cite passages from the essay to back up his understanding of Wilson's intent. Stillman's explanation is that Wilson was indeed ambivalent on many points, raising more questions than he resolved. He recommends that we accept Leonard White's moderate assessment that Wilson merely "introduced the country to the idea of administration," and that to argue that he did more "would exaggerate the influence of his essay."[17]

Keeping in mind this caution and recognizing that I am presenting yet another individual and partial interpretation, my comments will focus on Wilson as a comparativist in his contributions to public administration. As Stillman and others have pointed out, Wilson's writings on administration were limited after publication of his 1887 essay; his subsequent work as a scholar was mostly devoted to political rather than administrative topics. During the last two decades of his active career, of course, he was a prominent participant in public administration, but as a practitioner rather than as a scholar—first as a university president, then as a state governor, and finally as President of the United States. Even in his administrative writings, comparative aspects were subsidiary rather than central to his concerns, but his views seem to me less ambiguous on this than on other topics which he addressed.

In 1885, when he was just beginning his college teaching career at the age of twenty-nine, and two years before publication of his essay, Wilson referred in a personal letter to his "work upon comparative systems of administration," and there are fragments in his collected papers indicating how his thinking was evolving during this period before completion of the published version.[18] This background evidence and the text of the essay itself are persuasive that Wilson regarded comparative knowledge to be indispensible for systematic progress in the study and practice of public administration.

In his essay, Wilson's attention is first directed to the history of "the science of administration," which he regarded as "the latest fruit of that study of the science of politics which was begun some twenty-two hundred years ago."[19] Wilson regarded systematic study of administration, however, as distinct from constitutional aspects of government, as a recent phenomenon, which did not emerge until earlier in the century in which he was writing. The reason was to him clear. Government functions, which historically had been simple, had become complex. He put it neatly in this often quoted sentence: "It is getting to be harder to *run* a constitution than to frame one."[20]

Wilson considered that credit for advancement of the science of administration up to the time he wrote had to be given to Europeans, mainly French and German professors, and that Americans had contributed very little. It was a "foreign science" employing only "foreign tongues," and it was "adapted to the needs of a compact state, and made to fit highly centralized forms of government."[21] Governments that had taken the lead in administrative practice had rulers who were still absolute but also enlightened. Prussia under Frederick the Great and his successors was the prime example where administration had been "most studied and most nearly perfected." French administration after it had been recast by Napoleon was Wilson's second example of "the perfecting of civil machinery by the single will of an absolute ruler."[22]

In contrast, England and the United States had concentrated on constitution making and popular reform rather than administrative development. "The English race," according to Wilson, "has long and successfully studied the art of curbing executive power to the neglect of perfecting executive methods. It has exercised itself much more in controlling than in energizing government."[23] The time had now come, in Wilson's judgment, to catch up with nations ahead in administrative organization and administrative skill.

The obvious question that Wilson had to address was how a democratic country could safely utilize the administrative science developed by absolutist regimes without running the risk of becoming like them politically as well. Wilson's response was surprisingly unequivocal. He conceded that the United States would not want to have had "Prussia's history for the sake of having Prussia's administrative skill," but he saw no risk or danger in striving to have one without the other, and he urged no delay in "naturalizing this much-to-be-desired science of administration."[24]

In the latter part of his essay, after he had elaborated on his views concerning the separability of administration from politics and the similarities between public and private administration, Wilson returned to the argument that comparative studies could help get rid of "the misconception that administration stands upon an essentially different basis in a democratic state from that on which it stands in a non-democratic state." Instead, he asserted that monarchies and democracies, "radically different as they are in other respects, have in reality much the same business to look to," and that through comparative studies would be found "but one rule of good administration for all governments alike." He insisted that "nowhere else in the whole field of politics . . . can we make use of the historical, comparative method more safely than in this province of administration."[25]

Why is the comparative method so safe? It is because of the distinction between administration and politics that he had presented. This distinction, whatever its exact meaning might be, is the essential basis for Wilson's assurances that foreign administrative systems could be studied and borrowed from selectively without danger of political contamination. Without it, he could not have written the statement that is probably most often quoted from his essay:

> If I see a murderous fellow sharpening a knife cleverly, I can borrow his way of sharpening the knife without borrowing his probable intention to commit murder with it; and so, if I see a monarchist dyed in the wool managing a public bureau well, I can learn his business methods without changing one of my republican spots. He may serve his king; I will continue to serve the people; but I should like to serve my sovereign as well as he serves his.[26]

Despite his insistence on the importance of comparative knowledge and the absence of risk in using it, Wilson did not actually give a single specific example of foreign practices that should be imported, and he cautioned that preference should be given to arrangements "not only sanctioned by conclusive experience elsewhere but also congenial to American habit."[27] He was much more enthusiastic about the idea of benefiting from foreign experience than he was precise in saying how this should be accomplished. In its comparative dimension as well as in other respects, the essay raises more questions than it supplies answers.

Whatever faults of ambiguity and generality may be detected, however, there is no doubt that as America's first notable scholar of public administration, Wilson was intent on stressing the comparative approach and the global applicability of a science of administration. This became even more evident during the decade following publication of his essay while he was lecturing on administration at Johns Hopkins University. His surviving lecture notes show that he placed increasing emphasis on the political foundations of public administration and on the universality of administrative problems, as these excerpts indicate:

> Administration cannot be divorced from its intimate connections with the other branches of Public Law without being distorted and robbed of its true significance. Its foundations are those deep and permanent principles

of politics which have been quarried from history and built into constitutions. . . . The problems of administration are . . . in a very real sense
universal, international. A wide examination of governmental organs will
discover, not only the differences which may exist between government
and government, but likewise the general likenesses between them.[28]

Wilson's initial imprint on the study of public administration in the
United States, blurred though it was in some details, was clear in its
delineation of how important comparative knowledge was to advancement on either scholarly or practical fronts. The century of the American
administrative state did not begin with a posture that rejected the relevance of foreign experience and concentrated exclusively on national
self-study and self-improvement. In his emphasis on the inevitable interdependence between politics and administration even when drawing a
distinction between them, in his search for external sources of information for internal administrative progress, and in his recognition that a
science of administration must have universal applicability, Woodrow
Wilson showed a closer affinity to comparativists of the mid-twentieth
century than to most of the spokesmen for American public administration during the intervening decades.

Exceptions to the Countertradition

From the time of Wilson's contributions until the decade of the 1940s,
American public administration was mainly identified with what Riggs
called a "counter-tradition" to the earlier tendency to examine foreign
administrative experience for the benefit of American administrative
practice. This post-Wilsonian trend he regarded as a "new and non-
traditional viewpoint," which "was initially parochial and subsequently
became arrogantly ethnocentric,"[29] and he examined some of the conceptual roots of this "counter-tradition."

Although this parochial characterization must be accepted as essentially
accurate in describing central tendencies during these decades, interest
in comparative analysis and recognition of its value and importance
did not disappear. Exceptions to the "counter-tradition" are in fact numerous, even during the era of mainline parochialism, and those deserving credit for keeping the comparative thread unbroken include some
of the best-known figures in American public administration, although
they used comparative data for a variety of purposes in different subject
matter specializations.

The most conspicuous early examples are Frank J. Goodnow and
Ernst Freund, whose primary subject was administrative law but who

had wide-ranging interests related to problems of public administration and the impact of government operations on the citizenry. They had overlapping careers, but Goodnow was older and more of a ground-breaker, with Freund building upon and adding to Goodnow's work.

Goodnow was a professor of administrative law and municipal science at Columbia University. In his view, administrative law could be properly understood only in the context of politics and its relationship to public administration. As Arthur T. Vanderbilt says, "Goodnow viewed administrative law from the standpoint of the State."[30] He is best known to present-day students of public administration for his twofold division of governmental functions into expression of the will of the state and execution of the will of the state—the familiar dichotomy between politics and administration. The nuances of this distinction as expressed by Goodnow, and the accuracy of subsequent interpretations of what he meant, need not be explored for our purposes in considering him as a comparativist.[31]

Goodnow's magnum opus was a two-volume treatise, *Comparative Administrative Law*, published in 1893. In the Preface to this work, he made the following statement:

> The great problems of modern public law are almost exclusively administrative in character. While the age that has passed was one of constitutional, the present age is one of administrative reform. Our modern complex social conditions are making enormous demands of the administrative side of government, demands which will not be satisfied at all or which will be inadequately met, unless a greater knowledge of administrative law and science is possessed by our legislators and moulders of opinion. This knowledge can be obtained only by study, and by comparison of our own with foreign administrative methods.[32]

The subtitle of Goodnow's work was *An Analysis of the Administrative Systems National and Local, of the United States, England, France and Germany*. His approach was indeed both comprehensive and comparative. It was comprehensive in the sense that he was concerned with administrative law not narrowly as a subfield of public law but broadly as the study of administration, "not taken up exclusively with a consideration of the rules of administrative action" but devoted also "to the subject of administrative organization."[33] His first volume dealt with these organizational matters, including the theory of separation of powers and relations among the executive, legislative, and judicial branches; territorial distribution of administrative functions; and exhaustive discussion of both central administration and local administration. The second volume was more directly concerned with legal relations, but it contained a thorough review of methods of control over administration.

Goodnow was comparative in his consideration of these topics not just incidentally but fully. He devoted essentially equal attention to the experience in each of the countries included in his limited range of comparison—England, France, and Germany, in addition to the United States. To accomplish this, he found it necessary to be familiar with European theories and practices, and to bring this knowledge to bear in dealing with American problems. His perspective was definitely not a parochial one.

Ernst Freund, as a disciple and younger colleague of Goodnow, shared his comparative interest and pursued it well into the early decades of this century. His most influential publication was *Administrative Powers Over Persons and Property*, published in 1928.[34] As the title implies, Freund focused particularly on the impact of the exercise of administrative powers on private rights, and thus his work had a somewhat more restricted coverage than Goodnow's. In another sense, however, Freund's approach was even more comprehensive. As Oscar Kraines observes, his viewpoint was that

> the increasingly growing industrial and technological revolutions were so greatly and rapidly transforming our society that government inevitably had to respond to these huge, profound pressures both by discouraging and preventing their evil results.[35]

Even as early as 1894, Freund had described "how to combine bureaucracy and self-government" as "one of the most important political problems of the present day."[36] This range of concern led him also to cover a wide variety of topics in treating the system of administrative powers, including how administrative authorities should be organized, operated, and controlled.

Freund likewise explored his interests on a comparative basis and subtitled his book *A Comparative Survey*. Although born in New York City while his German parents were visiting there, he grew up and was educated in Germany before returning to the United States for advanced study at Columbia University and a career as a member of the political science faculty at the University of Chicago. With this background, he was able to invoke comparative data from other countries, particularly from Great Britain and Germany, and to a lesser extent from France. This cosmopolitan point of view is in the tradition of Wilson and Goodnow.

Another pair of writers with a noticeable but less conspicuous comparative dimension consists of the authors of the first two textbooks on American public administration—Leonard D. White and W. F. Willoughby. White's book, first published in 1926, with later editions in 1939 and 1948, was the standard for several generations of college students. Its coverage was essentially confined to public administration in the United

States and thus conformed to the "counter-tradition" image, but it did contain occasional references to other countries. For example, White acknowledged that "much of substance and ceremonial" in American administration "can be traced back to eighteenth-century precedents." He described the American system of administration as "English in its general form and underlying spirit," despite "traces of French institutions in Louisiana and of Spanish in the Southwest,"[37] but he did not elaborate. At another point, he listed distinguishing features of the American administrative system "differentiating it from the French or the Swedish, the Mexican, the Russian, or the Chinese, and broadly classifying it with the Anglo-Saxon."[38] He did not, however, detail points of comparison or contrast among these national systems.

White's main contribution as a comparativist was his role as primary author of *The Civil Service in the Modern State,* published in 1930.[39] This volume is basically a collection of documents on national civil service systems, with introductory background comments, produced by White and a dozen collaborators. White himself contributed the sections on the United States and Great Britain; others dealt with Canada, Australia, France, Belgium, Italy, Roumania, Switzerland, Germany and Prussia, Austria, Sweden, Norway, and Japan. Despite its limitations, including failure to obtain coverage from other important countries, this is a landmark effort in comparative public administration prior to World War II.

Willoughby's textbook appeared in 1927.[40] It was not as influential and popular as White's, and there was no subsequent edition. Also concentrating on American public administration, Willoughby nevertheless had many more references (though incidental and usually brief) to public administration in other countries than did White. A sampling includes these comparative items: the contrasting preference to fix the number of departments and independent establishments by statute in the United States and by executive decree in France and other European countries;[41] the advantage of the British parliamentary system over the American system in formulating and executing administrative programs;[42] the non-political character of administration in Switzerland;[43] citation of the British Treasury as an outstanding example of an organ of general administration;[44] characterization of personnel systems by type as bureaucratic (Prussian and German), aristocratic (British), and democratic (American);[45] government service as a permanent vocation in Great Britain and an intermittent one in the United States;[46] and a series of comparisons as to particulars in budgetary and fiscal control practices between the United States and countries such as Great Britain, France, and Canada.[47] As these illustrations show, the comparative examples provided by Willoughby dealt mostly with specifics and did not attempt to offer comparisons on a systemic basis.

Another cluster of those working in comparative public administration includes spokesmen for the "scientific management" movement stemming from the time-and-motion studies of Frederick W. Taylor around the turn of the century and culminating in one of the classics of pre–World War II public administration, *Papers on the Science of Administration*, edited by Luther Gulick and Lyndall Urwick, which was published in 1937.[48] In considering administration a science, these writers shared a view that was also accepted by W. F. Willoughby, who stated that

> in administration, there are certain fundamental principles of general application analogous to those characterizing any science which must be observed if the end of administration, efficiency in operations, is to be secured, and . . . these principles are to be determined and their significance made known only by the rigid application of the scientific method to their investigation.[49]

The principles themselves dealt with such familiar issues as span of control, unity of command, bases for work specialization, and line and staff relationships.

Advocates of such a science of administration were not outspoken in emphasizing a comparative approach, but their work was indeed comparative in some respects. In the first place, the implication of their faith in the claims as to a science of administration was that the scientific principles discovered would be universally applicable across time, cultures, and countries, and that the validity of the principles could be tested in a variety of settings. Second, their writings did in fact contain illustrations drawn from a number of different national sources. The *Papers on the Science of Administration* volume, for example, included references to mechanisms for coordination in British government administration; the command structure of a British infantry division; a reorganization plan for the French Department of Posts, Telegraphs and Telephones; organizational arrangements in the General Motors Export Company; and the effects of social environment in the Hawthorne Plant of the Western Electric Company. Third, the scientific management community was indeed an international community. The individual contributors of papers for this same collection included two Britishers and two Frenchmen, as well as several Americans.

Identification of these instances of comparativeness, plus others that might be added, does not alter the generalization that for a period of several decades, from late in the nineteenth century through the 1930s, American public administration was introspective rather than outward-looking in its search for knowledge and in its efforts to improve administrative practices. The shift to major emphasis on comparative aspects of public administration did not come until midcentury, and it was dependent on events that occurred during the decade of the 1940s.

1940 Decade Initiatives

A multifaceted reshaping of American public administration, affecting both study and practice, took place during World War II and the immediate postwar years. Several academic contributors questioned earlier orthodoxies and mapped new paths for advance. These seminal thinkers varied in the extent of their emphasis on non-American administration. For some, historical or cross-national comparison was of minor importance. These included Herbert A. Simon, who characterized existing principles of administrative science as no more than proverbs and urged efforts to achieve a value-free science of administration, and Paul H. Appleby, who challenged the earlier acceptance of a strict dichotomy between politics and administration, stressing instead the interrelationships between the making and execution of policy.

John M. Gaus advocated an ecological approach to the study of public administration, drawing upon the work of botanists and zoologists concerned with the adaptations of plant and animal organisms to their environments, and of sociologists concerned with the interdependence of humans and their environments. He used such an approach to identify key ecological factors and utilize them for an understanding of contemporary American public administration.[50] Although Gaus himself did not direct his attention to other national systems of public administration, his stress on ecological factors was influential later when pioneers in comparative administration realized that such considerations would be even more important in comparative studies than they were in analyzing a single national system of public administration.

Dwight Waldo examined deficiencies in the theoretical underpinnings of public administration[51] and identified emerging trends in administrative studies.[52] He pointed more explicitly toward the importance of comparative data by stressing the concept of culture as a tool for dealing with variety in administration:

> The feeling or intuition that administration is administration wherever it is comes very quickly to the student of administration; and this theme is heavily emphasized in the American literature dealing with administration. Yet the student will also become aware, as he advances, that there are important differences between administrative systems, depending upon the location, the tasks, the environment and the inhabitants of the system. . . . The concept of culture—plus knowledge about the actual culture— enables us to see administration in any particular society in relation to all factors which surround and condition it. . . . And enabling us to see administration in terms of its environment, it enables us to understand differences in administration between different societies which would be

inexplicable if we were limited to viewing administration analytically in terms of the universals of administration itself.[53]

Recognizing that administrative history remained for the most part unwritten, with historians customarily using some other perspective than that of the student of administration,[54] Waldo also advocated more sustained interest in the historical roots of administration. He thus gave early encouragement to consideration of cultural and historical factors that later were central to comparative public administration studies.

Some of the newer textual materials appearing in the late 1940s also included more substantial comparative information than had been in prewar texts. A leading example was *Elements of Public Administration*, a collaborative effort by fourteen contributors, which was first published in 1946 and revised in 1959.[55] The editor was Fritz Morstein Marx, who was himself a comparativist both in background and approach, having been educated in Germany and having established himself as a member of the German higher civil service before emigrating during the Nazi regime to the United States. There he continued a distinguished career combining bureaucratic and academic obligations. The other contributors were Americans, most of them young academics who had been exposed to administration in action during World War II and who later became well known as teachers, researchers, and practicing administrators.

It would be misleading to describe *Elements of Public Administration* as basically comparative, either in its original or revised versions. The 1946 edition did, nevertheless, have scattered through its text numerous references to the European background of American administrative institutions or to contemporary European practices in such varied areas as training for administrative careers, civil service reform, delegated legislation, political participation of civil servants, departmentalization, field organization, use of public corporations, administrative management improvement, legislative controls over administration, regulatory procedures, administrative law tribunals, and measures to provide fiscal accountability. The 1959 revision stressed the importance of research into foreign administrative experience and noted that "comparative study, long largely ignored, is currently moving forward with new vitality."[56] These developments were not detailed, however, and neither edition made more than the most incidental reference to administration in countries outside of Western Europe.

Another source of attention to non-American administrative experience was a book of readings on general public administration compiled by Albert Lepawsky and published in 1949 under the title *Administration: The Art and Science of Organization and Management*.[57] It included chapters on both administrative history and comparative administration.

These publications, and others to a lesser extent, exposed public administration students after World War II to at least some information about national systems of administration elsewhere considered relevant to American public administration. Such relevance was the touchstone for inclusion, however, and the coverage did not extend to administrative experience in the newly independent countries that were emerging on the world scene.

The single most influential statement that stimulated interest in comparative public administration was what has become a frequently quoted excerpt from an essay by Robert A. Dahl that appeared in 1947 in *Public Administration Review*. Writing on "The Science of Public Administration: Three Problems," Dahl cited as one of these problems the absence of valid scientific principles transcending national boundaries:

> The comparative aspects of public administration have largely been ignored; and as long as the study of public administration is not comparative, claims for a "science of public administration" sound rather hollow. Conceivably there might be a science of American public administration and a science of British public administration and a science of French public administration; but can there be a "science of public administration" in the sense of a body of generalized principles independent of their peculiar national setting?[58]

Contemporaneously with these developments on the academic scene, equally significant changes occurred in how and where American public administration was being practiced. During World War II, trends begun during the New Deal years toward greater centralization, professionalization, forward planning, and governmental intervention in economic and social affairs were continued and accentuated. Military campaigns required manpower, material resources, and organizational capability to be applied on multiple fronts. Victory in the war led to extensive occupation operations in the territories of the defeated powers, and to massive material aid and technical assistance programs widely spread around the world. All of these events had the dual effects of stimulating administrative innovation and testing, and of exposing young Americans to novel and stimulating experiences, often in a foreign setting.

The Comparative Administration Movement

The surge of interest in cross-national analysis of systems of public administration that emerged from these background factors during the 1950s and peaked during the 1960s has most commonly been known as the comparative administration "movement."[59]

This movement had personnel, organizational, and financial underpinnings that accounted for its progress. The people involved were numerous and varied in their backgrounds and interests, but they tended to be young political scientists or other social scientists who had combined academic and administrative work experience and who had become acquainted with one or more foreign countries through military or technical assistance assignments. Fred W. Riggs soon became the best known and most influential single individual connected with the movement, and he has remained a central figure, but the leadership group has been fluid and diverse in membership.

Professional associations have provided an organizational base for the movement. As early as 1953, the American Political Science Association appointed a temporary ad hoc committee on comparative administration. Since 1960, the sponsoring organization has been the American Society for Public Administration, first through an affiliate called the Comparative Administration Group (CAG), and since 1973 through the Section on International and Comparative Administration (SICA). An important cooperating entity in recent years has been the International Association of Schools and Institutes of Administration (IASIA), which is an affiliate of the International Institute of Administrative Sciences, headquartered in Brussels. From 1969 to 1974 a specialized *Journal of Comparative Administration* was published, before it was merged with *Administration and Society,* a new journal of somewhat broader scope that is still being published.

Financial support for the Comparative Administration Group during its period of greatest activity (which included an elaborate committee structure, special seminars and conferences, experimental teaching projects, and a publications program) was provided by major grants from the Ford Foundation for a decade beginning in 1962, supplemented by other minor revenue sources. After 1971, reduced resources led to program curtailment by both CAG and SICA, its successor. The resulting pattern is a modified bell-shaped curve of organized activities, with the righthand part of the curve plateauing at a relatively low level in recent years.

Characterization in brief compass of the comparative administration movement over three decades is difficult, but some distinguishing traits can be identified and some major tendencies can be described.

The major shared characteristics during the heyday of the movement were an optimistic outlook and a tolerance for diversity. The optimism arose from the prevailing general mood of hope and anticipation that followed the end of World War II, combined with a conviction that administrative technology could be exported from the more advanced to the less developed countries through bilateral and multilateral techni-

cal assistance programs. As Garth N. Jones recalls, the decade of the
1950s

> was a wonderful period. The "American Dream" was the "World Dream"—
> and the best and quickest way to bring that dream into reality was through
> the mechanism of public administration. . . . The net result of all this
> enthusiastic action was that in the 1950s public administration was a magic
> term and public administration experts were magicians.[60]

William J. Siffin takes 1955 as the baseline year, describing it as

> a vintage year in a time of faith—faith in the developmental power of
> administrative tools devised in the West. It was a sanguine year in a time
> of hope—hope that public administration could lead countries toward
> modernization.[61]

Over time, disappointing results gradually increased skepticism about
such extreme optimism and led to more realistic expectations but did
not displace general acceptance of the desirability of positive intervention
as a means of bringing about change.

Diversity in approach has been a hallmark of the comparative administration movement from the beginning, recognized as characteristic of
the field and generally accepted as a sign of vitality, but also often criticized as a sign of immaturity and lack of focus. The most common
assessment is that expressed by Fred Riggs, who acknowledged that
"dissensus prevails," with no agreement on "approach, methodology,
concept, theory, or doctrine," but considered this "a virtue, a cause for
excitement," normal in a preparadigmatic field.[62]

Considering the complexities of comparative studies of political and
administrative systems, this lack of consensus as to how to proceed is
understandable. It has been evident in the related field of comparative
politics (the study of whole political systems), as well as in comparative
public administration (concerned primarily with the administrative subsystems of these polities). A basic dilemma is the necessity since World
War II of including in the comparison the newly independent developing
nations of Africa, Asia, and Latin America and the countries in the
Communist bloc, as well as the nations of Western Europe and their
former colonies (such as the United States and members of the British
Commonwealth), which had been the earlier focus of interest. Such
extended coverage raised doubts as to the adequacy of earlier institutional
or structural approaches to comparison because of the frequent absence
or atrophy of many familiar Western political institutions in these polities,
and led to substitution of a functional approach to comparison that
emphasized political functions assumed to be essential in all contempo-

rary nation-states. Comparative public administration, while sharing the problems of comparative politics and benefiting from advances made in that field, has had to face the additional necessity of finding a way to single out the administrative segment of the political system for more specialized comparison.

Within the comparative administration movement as a whole, three preferred ways of doing this have been mapped out and followed during the last three decades. These tendencies or schools can be labeled the *development administration* approach, the *general systems* approach, and the *middle-range* or *bureaucratic theory* approach.

Development administration is a much-used term that is clear as to its basic intended meaning but has never been specifically defined in a generally accepted way. Coined and popularized in the 1950s, it was designed to concentrate attention on the administrative requisites for achieving public policy goals, particularly in the developing countries of the Third World. This purpose was linked to an assumption that the more developed countries could help in this effort through a process of diffusion or transfer of administrative capabilities by means of programs of technical assistance. The development administration approach thus was appealing to those who were primarily interested in the developing countries, who wanted to enhance their administrative capabilities by emulation of what were considered more developed nations, and who had only a subsidiary concern with relationships between the administrative subsystem and its surrounding political and social systems. It offered several advantages to furtherance of the comparative administration movement. It suited the faith in positive results from purposive intervention to improve administration. It was attractive to leaders in the developing countries because it highlighted an intent to assist them in reaching domestic goals. Potential supporters of CAG activities preferred such an emphasis on developmental objectives; this explains the willingness of the Ford Foundation to become the CAG's principal financial benefactor. The net result was that during the 1960s the terms *development administration* and *comparative administration* were used almost as synonyms, and most of the publications sponsored by the CAG included the words *development* or *developmental* in their titles.

Although this approach continues to be used, it no longer enjoys such popularity, for several reasons. The problem of precise definition has never been resolved. George Gant, who is generally credited with coining the term when he was on the staff of the Ford Foundation, has suggested that it donates "the complex of agencies, management systems, and processes a government establishes to achieve its development goals," and that it is centered in what he calls "nation-building departments or ministries," in fields such as agriculture, industry, education, and health, rather than "law and order" agencies such as justice or defense.[63] This would indicate that although every country is concerned with development administration problems, these concerns are most acute in developing countries, and it implies that they can continue to benefit from the accumulated experience of more developed countries, but it does not sharply differentiate "development" from "nondevelopment" administration.

Another complication has to do with the performance record of programs of technical assistance. For a variety of reasons, including negative or unanticipated results and declining support from both bilateral and multilateral donor agencies, earlier confidence in the efficacy of technical assistance in public administration has been shaken, and a major reassessment and reorientation of technical assistance goals and strategies has been undertaken in recent years, with results that are still uncertain.

Finally, the development administration approach has the disadvantage that, however defined, development administration is more restricted in its coverage than either public administration or comparative public administration, and is not synonymous with either. Comparative studies that are confined to issues of development administration automatically exclude many topics that can legitimately be considered within the scope of comparative public administration.

The general systems approach clearly avoids this problem of exclusion, while encountering the opposite criticism that it is overcomprehensive. Fred W. Riggs is most closely identified with this approach and has been its most persuasive and influential advocate. In essence, the position taken is that national systems of public administration, particularly in the so-called developing countries, can be adequately understood only if they are examined in the context of the societies in which they function. Hence, comparison must begin with the analysis of whole societies before it can proceed to segments of the society such as the political system and its administrative subsystem. Over a period of three decades, Riggs has formulated and reformulated a theoretical framework of ideal-types for societies and their component parts designed to facilitate such a general systems approach.[64]

Generally referred to as the "prismatic-sala" set of models, because of its focus on the characteristics of developing countries, the revised presentation by Riggs in fact offers a two-dimensional framework for characterization of any sort of society. The two dimensions are degree of integration and degree of differentiation. Integration refers to the ability of the society to achieve harmonious coordination among its constituent structures, with societies being ranked on a malintegrated–integrated scale. Differentiation refers to the extent to which these constituent structures are subdivided and the specificity of their functions, with societies being ranked on this dimension from a hypothetically undifferentiated "fused" society to one that is as highly differentiated as is possible.

The terminology used by Riggs is complex, and over time he has changed the connotations given to key terms. In his current usage, societies that are well integrated and significantly differentiated are designated as "diffracted." Societies that are malintegrated and significantly differentiated are labeled as "prismatic." Both diffracted and prismatic societies are further subdivided according to their placement on the scale of differentiation.

Although this framework permits placement of any historical, contemporary, or potential future society, it has been of interest to students of comparative administration mainly because of its applicability to societies that are moderately differentiated and seriously malintegrated. These are what Riggs now calls "orthoprismatic" societies, with characteristics corresponding closely to those typical of many developing countries of the Third World.

Such a model, dealing with the full range of social phenomena, outlines the ecology of public administration in a type of society, subsuming political and administrative aspects. Riggs also examines public administration in orthoprismatic society more specifically and evolves the sala model for the administrative subsystem. He regards public bureaucracies in such societies as inefficient and wasteful in operation, with a wide gap between formal expectations and actual behavior, and as contributing to malintegration by not meshing well with other institutions in the political system.

The prismatic-sala model has received much attention and has been praised for stimulating interest in the characteristics of public administration in developing countries, but the Riggsian framework has not actually been used much for systematic classification and comparison of groups of nation-states. Riggs himself has published a valuable study of Thailand as a "bureaucratic polity" with typical orthoprismatic features,[65] and he has written extensively about other individual countries, but he has not attempted precise location of large numbers of contemporary nations within his framework of models.

The middle-range or bureaucratic theory approach, which has by now become the most common one, is claimed to avoid both the limitations in coverage of the development administration approach and the difficulties in application of the general systems approach. As early as 1959, Robert V. Presthus stressed the need for middle-range theory because of the gap between what he termed theory of "cosmic dimension" and the available empirical data.[66] In 1964, Dwight Waldo observed that the central problem of model construction in the study of comparative public administration is "to select a model that is 'large' enough to embrace all the phenomena that should be embraced without being, by virtue of its large dimensions, too coarse-textured and clumsy to grasp and manipulate administration."[67]

Among middle-range models for comparative studies, the concept of bureaucracy drawn from the work of German social scientist Max Weber and others has provided the preferred theoretical base, making it what Ramesh K. Arora has identified as "the single most dominant conceptual framework in the study of comparative administration."[68] The choice of national public bureaucracies as the primary focus for cross-national comparison is due to the existence in every contemporary nation-state of a public bureaucracy conforming to Weberian specifications with regard to bureaucracy as a form of organization. The institution of public bureaucracy thus can be used as the point of concentration for analysis of particular national systems of public administration, and for comparisons among them.[69]

The prevalent but of course not unanimous view is expressed by Lee Sigelman, who has stated as his assessment that comparative public administration should concentrate on studies of bureaucracies, examining "the backgrounds, attitudes, and behaviors of bureaucrats and those with whom they interact." He has also identified some of the deficiencies of such efforts. The volume of research has been limited, partly because of inadequate resources, and the literature reporting results has been scattered and diffuse. It has been cross-national in scope only occasionally, and generally it has been noncumulative. "Different scholars with different research perspectives use different instruments to interview different types of bureaucrats in examinations of different problems in different nations."[70]

Despite these shortcomings, the gradual accumulation of work based on this approach has now become impressive, with a considerable number of studies examining bureaucracies in Third World countries, many of them done by Third World scholars. The range of coverage is wide, but topics most commonly emphasized include the following: historical roots of contemporary nation-state bureaucracies; recruitment processes and career paths of bureaucrats; hierarchical arrangements and patterns of specialization within the bureaucracy; attitudinal viewpoints and behavioral tendencies among bureaucrats; participation in the making of public policy decisions by higher-ranking bureaucrats; sources of external controls over the bureaucracy and effectiveness of these controls; and patterns of bureaucratic relationships in different types of political regimes.[71]

Centennial Dilemmas and Prospects

As the century since Woodrow Wilson's essay was published comes to a close, the comparative public administration movement has been the

subject of extensive scrutiny and appraisal, and the future of the comparative dimension in American public administration has become a topic
of speculation and prediction.

Beginning about 1970, individuals long identified with the Comparative Administration Group as well as younger scholars have evaluated
the movement in a series of critiques, emphasizing disappointments
and shortcomings.[72] The understandable assumption has been that the
comparative administration movement, after an existence of two decades
or more and with rather lavish support for a number of years, should
be evaluated as to results. The usual judgment has been that potential
accomplishments have not been realized, but the evaluators have not
agreed with one another as to what was wrong or what ought to be
done about it. Some of these criticisms, and the responses so far to
them, can be examined briefly.

The most common complaint has been that the field suffers from
what Keith Henderson called an "identity crisis,"[73] demonstrating lack
of agreement as to what is and what is not within the scope of comparative
public administration. This impression was bolstered by Lee Sigelman,
who made a content analysis of the *Journal of Comparative Administration*
as the primary vehicle for scholarly output in the field and found that
"no single topic or set of questions came close to dominating."[74] Disenchantment with the lack of consensus as to a focus or paradigm has
not led, however, to much success in finding one, beyond emergence
of the preference for the bureaucratic theory middle-range approach
for comparison already discussed.

Another theme has been the relevance of the comparative administration movement to development administration, combined with concerns
about problems arising from ambiguities in meaning and disagreements
as to results of development administration. The usual judgment has
been that although leaders of the Comparative Administration Group
intended that CAG output should be useful for practitioners in technical
assistance programs, this did not actually happen. A dissenting view,
expressed mainly by opponents of the outcomes of these programs in
recipient countries, has been that the CAG was all too relevant in providing intellectual grounds for misguided policy.[75] As already noted, the
result has been that use of the development administration approach
in comparative studies has diminished, and development administration
concepts and strategies are being thoroughly reexamined.

A third alleged fault is that students of comparative administration
have not kept pace with progress in closely related fields and that this
has been a hindrance. Sigelman made an unfavorable contrast between
research in comparative administration and in comparative politics as
to the use of quantitative techniques. Several critics have suggested that
revitalization of comparative studies would have to incorporate recent
developments in the broader parent field of public administration, partic-

ularly with regard to organization theory and analysis of the process of public policy-making. As a consequence, a modest number of comparative studies have been carried out in a cross-cultural context on problems of organizational change and development. Much more progress has occurred in comparative public policy as a field of specialization.[76] Since the mid-1970s, the proliferation of studies centering on cross-national public policy comparisons has reflected this trend, bringing with it many of the same challenges and frustrations faced earlier by the original comparative public administration movement.

In these reappraisals, even the most severe critics of the CAG and its record acknowledge that productivity during the 1960s was impressive and resulted in a vast accumulation of knowledge in comparative public administration, considering the obstacles of data base inadequacy and unreliability, methodological diversity, and limited personnel and financial resources. There is no dissent from the overall conclusion that the comparative public administration movement has made an impact on American public administration that will prove to be significant and durable. There are several differing perceptions, however, as to the long-range consequences for the future of this enhanced comparative dimension.

Charles T. Goodsell has been most expansive in his proposal for a "new" comparative public administration. His suggestion is that the scope of the term *comparative administration* should be enlarged to include comparisons at supranational and subnational levels of analysis, as well as cross-national comparisons, thus embracing "all studies of administrative phenomena where the comparative method—in some guise—is explicitly employed."[77] This would encompass a very large proportion of all public administration research, as was illustrated by a panel convened by Goodsell at the 1980 annual conference of the American Society for Public Administration, which featured studies of delivery of police services in two American cities. This proposed extension of scope by redefinition departs from past usage and seems to me more confusing than helpful. If adopted, it would require some other designation for the cross-national comparative dimension that I have been discussing.

At the other end of the scale of perceptions is the view of Peter Savage that separate identity for comparative public administration as a field of study is no longer needed because its concerns and perspectives have been absorbed and become a part of the broader disciplines of public administration and political science, paralleling the effect earlier of the behavioral movement on political science. He regards the influence of the comparative administration movement as supplementary rather than revolutionary, having a "rounding out" rather than a transformational effect. As he put it in 1976: "The movement's ten years are up and it passes."[78]

Jong S. Jun and Fred W. Riggs share somewhat similar views that the impact of the comparative administration movement has been consequential enough to convert American public administration into only a subfield of a master field that is global in scope. Jun's position is that comparative administration as an isolated and separately identified field has served its purpose and that it should become an integral part of the larger field of public administration, which can be enriched by placing it in a world context.[79] Riggs has stated the point more explicitly and forcefully:

> The new paradigm for "public administration" must be "comparative,"
> i.e., global, since the solution of the problem to which it addresses itself
> will require increasing communication between scholars and practitioners
> in all countries. The American dimension of these problems will surely
> come to be seen as a "subfield" or a parochial aspect of the broader subject.[80]
> . . . No one can claim to understand "public administration" when all
> she or he knows is the administrative experience of one country. As a
> result what was once thought of as "public administration" in the United
> States must now be re-categorized as merely *"American* public administra-
> tion." What we used to think of as "comparative public administration"
> must now be viewed . . . as nothing more than ordinary *"public administra-
> tion."* In short, public administration today, in a global sense, is essentially
> and necessarily comparative.[81]

Whatever the preferred terminology, I agree with the cardinal point made by Jun and Riggs that public administration can no longer be treated, either in study or practice, as exclusively concerned with the system of public administration in a single nation-state. The comparative public administration movement must be credited with converting the parochialism of American public administration from what was generally regarded as one of its points of strength, during most of the century of the American administrative state, into an acknowledged point of weakness as that century ends. The comparative theme in American public administration, present from the beginning and persisting even when it was muted, is now strong enough to bring recognition that understanding of American public administration or any other national system of administration is possible only when it is placed in a cross-cultural setting.[82]

Endnotes

1. Lynton K. Caldwell, "Novus Ordo Seclorum: The Heritage of American Public Administration," *Public Administration Review* 36:476–488 (September-October) 1976, at p. 477.

2. Fred W. Riggs, "The American Tradition in Comparative Administration," prepared for the 1976 National Conference of the American Society for Public Administration, 28 pp. mimeographed.

3. Alexander Hamilton, John Jay, and James Madison, *The Federalist* (New York: Macmillan, 1948), No. 18.

4. Ibid., Nos. 19 and 20.

5. Ibid., No. 20, p. 97.

6. Leonard D. White, *The Jacksonians* (New York: Macmillan, 1956), p. 561.

7. Leonard D. White, *The Jeffersonians* (New York: Macmillan, 1951), p. 556.

8. J. P. Mayer, ed. *Democracy in America* (Garden City, NY: Anchor Books, Doubleday, 1969), p. 683.

9. White, *The Jacksonians*, p. 531.

10. Ibid., pp. 532–533.

11. Paul P. Van Riper, *History of the United States Civil Service (Evanston, IL and White Plains, NY: Row, Peterson, 1958).*

12. Ibid., p. 64.

13. Ibid., p. 69.

14. Ibid., p. 96.

15. *Political Science Quarterly* 2:197–222 (June) 1887. The essay has been reprinted frequently, once in the same journal, 55:481–506 (December) 1941. A readily available source is Richard J. Stillman II, *Public Administration: Concepts and Cases* (Boston: Houghton-Mifflin, 1976), pp. 269–281.

16. Richard Stillman, "Woodrow Wilson and the Study of Administration: A New Look at an Old Essay," *American Political Science Review* 67:582–588 (June) 1973, at p. 582.

17. Ibid., p. 588.

18. Ibid., p. 585.

19. Stillman, op cit., p. 269.

20. Ibid., p. 270.

21. Ibid., p. 271.

22. Ibid., pp. 272–273.

23. Ibid., pp. 273.

24. Ibid., p. 274.

25. Ibid., pp. 279–280.

26. Ibid., p. 280.

27. Ibid., p. 281.

28. Quoted in Stillman, "Woodrow Wilson and the Study of Administration," at p. 587.

29. Riggs, op. cit., p. 5.

30. Arthur T. Vanderbilt, "One Hundred Years of Administrative Law," in *Law: A Century of Progress*, Volume I (New York: New York University Press, 1937), pp. 117–144, at p. 121.

31. The fullest exposition is in Frank J. Goodnow, *Politics and Administration* (New York: Macmillan, 1900).

32. Frank J. Goodnow, *Comparative Administrative Law*, Student's Edition, Two Volumes in One (New York and London: G. P. Putnam's Sons, The Knickerbocker Press, 1893), Preface, p. iv.

33. Ibid., Volume One, p. 5.

34. Ernst Freund, *Administrative Powers Over Persons and Property* (Chicago: The University of Chicago Press, 1928).
35. Oscar Kraines, *The World and Ideas of Ernst Freund* (University, AL: The University of Alabama Press, 1974), p. 13.
36. Ernst Freund, "The Law of the Administration in America," *Political Science Quarterly* 9:403–425 (September) 1894, at p. 405.
37. Leonard D. White, *Introduction to the Study of Public Administration*, 3rd ed. (New York: Macmillan, 1948), p. 120.
38. Ibid., p. 20.
39. Leonard D. White, *The Civil Service in the Modern State: A Collection of Documents*, published under the auspices of the International Congress of the Administrative Sciences (Chicago: The University of Chicago Press, 1930).
40. W. F. Willoughby, *Principles of Public Administration* (Baltimore, MD: The Johns Hopkins Press, 1927).
41. Ibid., pp. 19, 20.
42. Ibid., p. 35.
43. Ibid., pp. 50, 51.
44. Ibid., pp. 58–60.
45. Ibid., pp. 213–219.
46. Ibid., pp. 286, 287.
47. Ibid., pp. 439, 479–486, 500, 501, 541–544, 549–553, 621–624, 651, 652.
48. Luther Gulick and L. Urwick, eds., *Papers on the Science of Administration* (New York: Institute of Public Administration, 1937).
49. Willoughby, op. cit., Preface, p. ix.
50. John M. Gaus, *Reflections on Public Administration* (University, AL: The University of Alabama Press, 1947).
51. Dwight Waldo, *The Administrative State: A Study of the Political Theory of American Public Administration* (New York: Ronald Press, 1948).
52. Dwight Waldo, *The Study of Public Administration* (Garden City, NY: Doubleday, 1955).
53. Ibid., pp. 10, 11.
54. Ibid., pp. 15, 16.
55. Fritz Morstein Marx, ed., *Elements of Public Administration* (Englewood Cliffs, NJ: Prentice-Hall, 1946; 2nd ed., 1959).
56. Ibid., 2nd ed., p. 46.
57. Albert Lepawsky, *Administration: The Art and Science of Organization and Management* (New York: Knopf, 1949).
58. Robert A. Dahl, "The Science of Public Administration: Three Problems," *Public Administration Review* 7:1–11, 1947, at p. 8.
59. The most recent bibliographical resource for the literature in comparative administration, with emphasis on the years 1961 to 1981, is Mark W. Huddleston, *Comparative Public Administration: An Annotated Bibliography* (New York: Garland, 1983). The most comprehensive general survey of the field is my *Public Administration: A Comparative Perspective*, 3rd ed. rev. (New York: Marcel Dekker, Inc., 1984). For a valuable collection of case studies of public administration in selected countries, refer to Krishna K. Tummala, ed., *Administrative Systems Abroad*, revised edition (Washington, DC: University Press of America,

1982). Each of these publications contains much information on additional sources.

60. Garth N. Jones, "Frontiersmen in Search for the 'Lost Horizon': The State of Development Administration in the 1960s," *Public Administration Review* 36:99–110, 1976, at pp. 99, 100.

61. William J. Siffin, "Two Decades of Public Administration in Developing Countries," *Public Administration Review* 36:61–71, 1976, at p. 61.

62. Fred W. Riggs, *Frontiers of Development Administration* (Durham, NC: Duke University Press, 1970), p. 7.

63. George Gant, *Development Administration: Concepts, Goals, Methods* (Madison, WI: The University of Wisconsin Press, 1979), pp. 19–21.

64. Refer to Fred W. Riggs, *Administration in Developing Countries: The Theory of Prismatic Society* (Boston: Houghton-Mifflin, 1964); and *Prismatic Society Revisited* (Morristown, NJ: General Learning Press, 1973).

65. Fred W. Riggs, *Thailand: The Modernization of a Bureaucratic Policy* (Honolulu: East-West Center Press, 1966).

66. Robert V. Presthus, "Behavior and Bureaucracy in Many Cultures," *Public Administration Review* 19:25–35, 1959.

67. Dwight Waldo, *Comparative Public Administration: Prologue, Problems, and Promise* (Chicago: Comparative Administration Group, American Society for Public Administration, 1964), p. 22.

68. Ramesh K. Arora, *Comparative Public Administration* (New Delhi: Associated Publishing House, 1972), p. 37.

69. For a fuller discussion of bureaucracy as a focus of comparison, see Heady, *Public Administration: A Comparative Perspective*, Chapter 2.

70. Lee Sigelman, "In Search of Comparative Administration," *Public Administration Review* 36:621–625, 1976, at pp. 623 and 624.

71. For a suggested political regime classification system for developing countries designed to place special emphasis on the relationship between regime political characteristics and the policy role of the bureaucracy in the system, refer to Heady, *Public Administration: A Comparative Perspective*, Chapter 7, pp. 274–280. Another recent classification proposal is by Fred W. Riggs in "Bureaucratic Politics and Political Domination," 32 pp. mimeo., prepared for the Conference on Comparative Research on National Political Systems, Berlin, Wissenschaftszentrum, 9–12 July, 1984.

72. Refer to a symposium edited by Dwight Waldo in *Public Administration Review* 36:615–654, 1976; and my article, "Comparative Administration: A Sojourner's Outlook," *Public Administration Review* 38:358–365, 1978.

73. Keith Henderson, "Comparative Public Administration: The Identity Crisis," *Journal of Comparative Administration* 1:64–84, 1969.

74. Sigelman, "In Search of Comparative Administration," at p. 622.

75. Brian Loveman, "The Comparative Administration Group, Development Administration, and Antidevelopment," *Public Administration Review* 36:616–621, 1976.

76. For surveys of these changes, see Keith M. Henderson, "From Comparative Public Administration to Comparative Public Policy," *International Review of Administrative Sciences* 47:356–364, 1981; and M. Donald Hancock, "Com-

parative Public Policy: An Assessment," in *Political Science: The State of the Discipline*, Ada W. Finifter, ed. (Washington, DC: The American Political Science Association, 1983), pp. 283–308.

77. Charles T. Goodsell, "The New Comparative Administration: A Proposal," *International Journal of Public Administration* 3:145–155, 1981.

78. Peter Savage, "Optimism and Pessimism in Comparative Administration," *Public Administration Review* 36:415–423, 1976, at p. 422.

79. Jong S. Jun, "Renewing the Study of Comparative Administration: Some Reflections on the Current Possibilities," *Public Administration Review* 36:641–647, 1976, at p. 647.

80. Fred W. Riggs, "The Group and the Movement: Notes on Comparative and Development Administration," *Public Administration Review* 36:648–654, 1976, at p. 652.

81. Fred W. Riggs in Tummala, ed., op. cit., p. 407.

82. Gerald E. Caiden and Naomi J. Caiden have projected a revitalization of comparative administration in "Towards the Future of Comparative Administration," 56 pp. mimeo., prepared for a forthcoming volume, *Comparative Public Administration*, edited by O. P. Dwivedi and Keith Henderson.

CHAPTER 16

The Higher Public Service in Western Europe

James W. Fesler
YALE UNIVERSITY

JAMES W. FESLER is the Alfred Cowles Professor Emeritus of Government at Yale University. He served on the staffs of the President's Committee on Administrative Management and the War Production Board, was Vice President of the American Political Science Association, Editor-in-Chief of the Public Administration Review *and Associate Editor of the* American Political Science Review, *and is a member of the National Academy of Public Administration. Professor Fesler chaired the Europe Committee of the American Society for Public Administration's Comparative Administration Group and directed the Yale research project on comparative field administration. He has written, co-authored, or edited six landmark books, including* Public Administration: Theory and Practice *and* American Public Administration: Patterns of the Past.

James W. Fesler provides the kind of comparative perspective on the higher public service systems of the major Western European nations—Britain, France, and West Germany—that rarely informs discussions of the American system.

At the highest political level—what Americans call "the Administration" and Europeans call "the Government"—differences among these countries are more prominent than similarities. Britain's government is drawn from Parliament, France requires that its ministers not be members of the National Assembly, and West Germany permits a mixture of legislative members and nonmembers.

Britain's prime minister is first among equals under the principle of cabinet government and collective responsibility, a committee pattern that is weakening under presidentialist tendencies in the evolution of the prime minister's role. The Fifth Republic of France is intendedly in the presidential mode, with the elected president and normally his chosen prime minister dominant. Similarly, the chancellor of the German Federal Republic has a strong position, though each of his ministers bears individual responsibility for his department and operates it with considerable autonomy. From 1945 forward Britain alternated Conservative and Labor governments with some frequency while France and West Germany experienced long incumbencies by parties and coalitions of the right (and in West Germany of the left).

The policy-formulating band of positions in these countries mixes higher civil servants and temporarily serving outsiders in a complex way that nonetheless has a pattern. First, civil servants predominate in each country's mix near the top. Second, the Continental countries' party governments and individual ministers choose the civil servants who serve as their principal aides and administrators. Third, the opportunity for such choice does not entail a wholesale changing of the guard that served the prior government or minister. Rather, it involves judgments about the policy orientations of civil servants, their competence, and their sensitivity to the political effects of policy initiatives. Partisanship plays a lesser role, though its relevance peaks when a party or coalition long in power is succeeded by one with a strikingly different constituency.

From an American perspective the notable European features are (1) the close relations of higher civil servants with heads of governments and ministers in policy formulation and departmental management; (2) the substantial degree of continuity of civil service membership in the policy-administration band, whether of individual civil servants or, as in France with its tradition of mobility, of colleagues within the same corps; and (3) the ease of retreat by civil servants from the band. British civil servants are not likely to be displaced at all; French civil servants are assured of other, often higher, posts; and German civil servants are guaranteed retirement pensions or new employment in the private sector.

Fesler identifies two seemingly contradictory themes. One is the distinctness of each country's system, a feature that is lodged in historical traditions and that triumphs over rarely exploited opportunities for borrowing from one another. The other is the degree to which the Western European countries share important characteristics. Among the details of the distinctness theme are these prominant features;

1. Britain's heavier reliance on a closed, presumptively neutral, permanent civil service, with little place for outsiders and none for "political civil servants" in the Continental sense.
2. The key position of the British Permanent Secretary, the hierarchy-heading deputy to the Minister, a model attractive to American reformers and once approximated by each department's chief clerk.

3. France's ministerial cabinets, enviously regarded by Britons and Germans critical of their own classically hierarchical systems.
4. The dominance of jurists among Germany's administrative elite, a feature unenviously viewed from abroad and much criticized at home.

The second theme, that of shared characteristics, is best illustrated by comparing European systems to the United States. Europe deliberately recruits and trains generalists and accords them key roles in policy-making and top-level management. Except in West Germany, careers feature remarkable mobility among positions, departments, and supradepartmental offices, including that of the chief executive. Those achieving successful careers are handsomely rewarded. In both France and West Germany, civil servants may engage in partisan politics and serve in legislative bodies, later resuming, if they choose, their civil service careers. In these countries one also finds "political civil servants," careerists raised for a time by ministers and governments to key staff and managerial roles. As to a lesser degree in Britain, civil servants at these levels work in concert with a minority of temporary appointees on the formulation of policies. This is a task calling less for partisanship than for competence allied with political sensitivity. The recognition of higher civil servants as critical resources at the policy-making level stands as the major contrast to American practice.

The major Western European nations—Britain, France, and Germany—fixed the character of their higher public service systems in the nineteenth century. Then and later they developed administrative concepts and institutions that, despite differences, appear broadly congruent when contrasted with the aberrant shaping of the American higher public service.[1] What the European systems have in common and what is distinctive to each should provide a comparative perspective that rarely informs discussions of the American system.[2]

At the highest political level (what Americans call "the Administration" and Europeans call "the Government"), differences among countries are more prominent than similarities. Britain's government is drawn from Parliament, France requires that its ministers not be members of the National Assembly,[3] and West Germany permits a mixture of members and nonmembers. Britain's prime minister is first among equals under the principle of cabinet government and collective responsibility, a committee pattern that is weakening under "presidentialist" tendencies in the evolution of the prime minister's role. The Fifth Republic of France is intendedly in the presidential mode, with the elected president and normally his chosen prime minister dominant. Similarly, the German Federal Republic's chancellor has a strong position, though each minister bears individual responsibility for his department and operates it with considerable autonomy. From 1945 forward Britain alternated Conservative and Labor governments with some frequency, while France and Germany experienced long incumbencies by parties and coalitions of the right (and in Germany of the left).

The three countries differ in the role of the central government vis-à-vis provincial and local governments. The federal structure of the German Federal Republic is the most distinctive. The central government's ministries, with few exceptions, engage primarily in policy development. Execution of the bulk of the Republic's domestic legislation is by the *Länder,* the constituent states of the federation. This system is constitutionally well protected by the *Bundesrat,* the federation's upper legislative house, which consists of representatives of the Länder governments and whose concurrence is necessary for legislative measures affecting the Länder.[4] In France, the national administration long operated directly through its prefects and the ministries' field services, and the communes were subjected to prefectoral tutelage. In England, the national inspectorates, much expanded since their initiation by Sir Edwin Chadwick in the nineteenth century,[5] so weightily carry legislation and regulations to localities that some plausibly argue that England is more centralized than France.[6] The case is summarized by Theodore Zeldin:

> French government may once have been more centralized than that in Britain, but that is no longer true. . . . Whitehall . . . controls nearly two-thirds of the income spent locally, and insists that the money be spent according to central directives. . . . By contrast, central subsidies are distributed in France . . . through a large variety of sources, so that there is more room for bargaining. . . . Only one-third of British members of parliament have experience in local government; few remain local councillors when they get into parliament, but four-fifths of French deputies and 93% of French senators also hold local elective office. The consequence is that local grievances get much more attention in Paris, and the French central government has a lot of difficulty in applying its policies at the local level; it is considerably nearer than the officials of Whitehall, who have no links with and no personal experience in local government.[7]

Radically decentralizing reforms in French government, set in train by a 1982 law "relating to the rights and liberties of the communes, departments, and regions of the State" promise to sharpen the contrast between Britain and France."[8]

A final distinction is a historical one. Britain developed a professional, merit-based public service after Parliament had well established its dominance and had placed a parliamentary committee, the Cabinet, in effective charge of the executive branch. In France and Germany (and Prussia before Germany was unified), the bureaucracy was early in place, serving a king or emperor. The State acquired a mystical meaning, unmatched by that of the Crown in Britain, and laid claim to a transcendant knowledge of the general interest, a claim readily translated by bureaucrats to their own advantage. Only considerably later did a national parliament come into existence and achieve a significant role vis-à-vis the chief executive and his bureaucracy. These differences in historical development continue to inform higher civil servants' ideologies and their attitudes toward political ministers and members of the national parliament, though more so in Britain and France than in Germany.

These differences granted, there remain common features. In contrast to the President of the United States, the European executive authority, alone or with assured support of a parliamentary majority, can create, abolish, merge, and split departments. So, too, with the appointment (and changing) of ministers, though factional and coalition politics imposes constraints. The number of departments falls within a fairly narrow range of fifteen to twenty.[9] As in the United States, there are additional agencies—in Europe nationalized industries, the postal service, the social security and health service administrations most prominently—some of which are essentially autonomous and others lightly overseen by relevant departments. In each country government departments vary in prestige and therefore in ability to attract the ablest members of the administrative elite. The pattern tends to be self-perpetuating, for the quality of top staff affects the prestige ranking of departments.

The central administrations are all hierarchically organized, and at the level below the British Permanent Secretaries and comparable levels elsewhere the number of key officials and their units varies little. Britain has 180 Deputy Secretaries, France 140 Directors heading "directions," and Germany about 100 Ministerial Directors heading divisions.[10]

The membership of the political echelon, composed of non–civil service officials who change with a change of party or sometimes with a change of individual ministers, is modest. In Britain about 120 members of Parliament serve in the government as Cabinet ministers, ministers outside the Cabinet, junior ministers, and government whips.[11] The political echelons in France and Germany are less clearly distinguishable from the higher civil service. In the French Fifth Republic until 1981 all presidents and prime ministers and from 43 to 66 per cent of ministers were civil servants.[12] But, putting that curiosity aside, in the pre-1981 period the French political echelon had 100 members: about 40 full and junior ministers and 60 "outsiders" serving alongside civil servants on the staffs of ministers. The total probably reached 150 after the 1981 elections, as more outsiders were introduced.[13] In West Germany, the strictly political echelon is thin: about 40 members, including ministers and parliamentary secretaries.[14]

The European political bands, then, range from 40 to 150 members, one thirty-fifth to one ninth of the 1,400 top political appointees in the United States. One consequence is that European higher civil servants have a greater role in the policy-formation process than do their American counterparts. On the Continent this role is facilitated by incumbent governments' and ministers' discretionary power to choose the civil servants who will serve as collaborators at the highest levels.

Our main concern will be the higher civil service. The dimensions of that sector of the whole civil service are disputable in all three countries.[15] An initial confusion for Americans is the existence of a special category of European officials whose differences in age, experience, and salary are irrelevant to their being regarded as members of the administrative elite. Britain's Administrative Class (formally abolished but effectively persisting), the *grands corps* in France, and the "higher" general-administration career group in West Germany embrace junior as well as senior members of the category. The nearest American analogies may be Foreign Service Officers[16] and the commissioned officers of the armed services. But the analogies are imperfect, for European juniors are often engaged in minor and major tasks of policy formation, and the best of them serve on staffs at top hierarchical levels where they may be effectively in directive or monitoring roles over much older civil servants.

In the European countries, the higher public service has generally commanded such prestige that ambitious, well-educated, and talented candidates have eagerly sought to join it. In France a multigenerational feature has been "civil service families," with, for example, middle-grade and higher civil servants successfully urging sons and daughters to qualify for membership in the administrative elite. In Germany and Britain, too, the high respect accorded their civil service elites gave them recruitment advantages over private sector alternatives.[17]

Three features largely define the character of higher public services: recruitment, career patterns, and the interplay of policy, politics, and administration. We shall examine each in turn.

Recruitment

Recruitment for the European higher civil services is designed to attract and select talented young persons of substantial educational attainment, who are equipped to serve in a variety of posts rather than as subject matter specialists. In this sense, all are generalists, though the term has a different content in each country. Britain is devoted to "the cult of the generalist," France to the "polyvalent" official, Germany to the wide usefulness of lawyers. The countries differ in how young generalists are educated and recruited and in how their subsequent careers are shaped. All governments need and recruit specialists, but in contrast to the United States, none of our European countries assumes that recruited specialists will be the future top administrators. Instead, such high officials come from a group recruited at early ages for generalist roles.

Without doing great violence to differentiating features, one can find a quite remarkable set of shared characteristics in the initial recruitment, the advanced-education and internship period, and the early career stage of generalist administrators:

1. Admission to civil service preparatory status (with pay) is on the basis of competitive examinations. In two countries, Britain and France, candidates from outside the government have been no more than twenty-seven or twenty-eight years old. (However, some German candidates and in the 1980s some French candidates are older and have started in other careers.)

2. A two-to-five year period of in-service training, combining practical, supervised internships with further coursework, immediately follows the competitive admission process. (The British use of this period sharply differs from the Continental pattern.)

3. At the end of this preparatory period occurs an assessment (including written examinations in France and Germany), which affects sharply the locus and character of each person's initial service and which may substantially shape lifetime careers.

4. Within two to five apprenticeship years thereafter the careers of Britons identified as "high flyers" and members of France's most prestigious grands corps take off, typically by vaulting to the staffs of high political officials. (German recruits follow more conventional lines of advancement.)

More broadly, all three systems' emphasis on selection by merit, exhibited both in examinations and in early performance, yields a higher civil service that is unrepresentative of the class and occupational backgrounds of the general population. The administrative elite is a social elite, whose roots reach back to successive selection points in the educational system. Despite efforts to broaden recruitment, the European administrative elite remains socially unrepresentative to a degree unmatched in the United States.

Britain

In Britain the generalist concept was explicit in the Northcote-Trevelyan Report of 1855, and in the Order in Council of 1870 (which mandated competitive, in place of pass, examinations for the Home Civil Service). Periodic challenges, including that by the Fulton Committee in 1968, have failed to dislodge the concept.[18] The generalist concept is an elitist version of Andrew Jackson's assertion of the ease with which ordinary persons can master the tasks of administration. The traditional British version ran: Select the brightest graduates of the best universities, no matter what their major subjects, and, without further pre-entry training, plunge them into a variety of assignments that together amount to internship training. This meant drawing on Oxford and Cambridge, where most of the bright students went, and it meant adaptation of administrative recruitment needs to the ancient universities' curricula, rather than the other way around.

In a pattern invariant for much of the twentieth century, Oxford and Cambridge accounted for four fifths of the successful candidates for the administrative elite. And two thirds or more of the open-competition entrants had concentrated on literary subjects—classics, modern languages, or literature.[19]

Now, as earlier, a high proportion of entrants to Oxford and Cambridge rank among the brightest persons of their generation.[20] When they complete their studies the civil service is only one of the callings competing for their talents, and so it gets a mix of first-class and second-class honors graduates.[21] Efforts to broaden Oxbridge's recruitment of students (particularly through grants to applicants otherwise financially unable to attend) have helped to broaden the social configuration of Britain's administrative elite. Similarly, shifts in the universities' offerings and student preferences have increased the proportion of graduates in the social sciences, and this is reflected in recent recruits to the administrative elite. The change does not indicate a new taste for relevance by government recruiters, an option favored by the Fulton Committee but explicitly rejected by Prime Minister Wilson.[22]

Though officially the Administrative Class is no more, having been absorbed in the large Administration Group (40 per cent of all nonindustrial civil servants), it remains identifiable in practice as the corps of general administrators directly involved in policy-making. Entrants to this Class, numbering annually between 170 and 240 in the 1970s, are dubbed Administrative Trainees (ATs).[23] They achieve entrance by a series of written examinations, performance in group exercises, and interviews. Appraisal of candidates in the latter two stages is thought by some to introduce a bias favoring reproduction of the examiners' own kind.[24] Some entrants to the AT grade, between 11 and 29 per cent in most of the 1970s, are persons already in the civil service (most with university degrees), and no older than thirty-one, whereas direct entrants' age must be twenty-seven or less. However, few such entrants rise high in their careers.

Persons appointed as ATs hold this status for two to four years, during which they move among a variety of assignments in their departments and in each of the first two years spend a ten-week period taking courses at the Civil Service College, which was established in 1970. Its courses in public administration, economics, staff and financial management, and policy areas might be expected to compensate for the irrelevance of many trainees' prior educational interests. Indeed, the parallel to France's postgraduate training of her administrative elite is superficially striking. But ten or twenty weeks are short periods, the departments are unsupportive of such "academic" work, and many trainees are unhappy with such work, wishing they could remain in their on-the-job internships in departments. At the end of their internship period, some ATs are chosen for "fast-streaming," which identifies them as "high flyers" to be moved along rapidly in their career development; oddly, though, about 80 per cent, instead of the originally intended one third of ATs have been fast-streamed.[25]

France

France, as Britain, recruits and trains young administrators who have qualified earlier by outstanding academic accomplishment, but the French system is far more elaborate. French universities figure only modestly in the formation of administrators. Napoleon and regimes following his lavished energies and resources on secondary schools—*lycées*—and on a group of postsecondary schools of preparation for the public service—*grandes écoles*. The universities were neglected. Even today, with their policy of open admission to any graduate of a *lycée*, and too crowded for accommodation of more than a fraction of students in lecture halls and libraries, they lack prestige comparable to that of the *grandes écoles*. Sadly, as Theodore Zeldin says, "no one is clear what these universities are supposed to do apart from harbouring nearly a million restless adolescents."[26]

Historically, law was the universities' most relevant subject for prospective civil servants. In France, as in Germany, law is an "undergraduate" curriculum competing with the liberal arts and the sciences. It attracted the most university students, for it "had long been looked upon as a kind of finishing school for gentlemen, as well as providing professional training for many lucrative professions, including the civil service."[27] The law faculties were traditionally possessive, insisting that such social sciences as were taught should be theirs. If this to some degree made law training broader in scope than that in most American law schools, it reciprocally cast a juridical pall on the approach to social studies. The French Political Science Association was not established until 1949.

Access to posts in the administrative elite is through the *grandes écoles*. Two at the postlycée or a later stage are the principal filters: the *Ecole Polytechnique* and, since 1945, the *Ecole Nationale d'Administration* (ENA).[28] In contrast to the universities, both are highly selective: they admit few students, and those on the basis of stiff examinations (the *concours*). The Polytechnique admits only about 300 students a year and the ENA generally admits about 140.[29] The entrants of both immediately become salaried civil servants. However, some Polytechnique students intend to pursue careers in the private sector, and some ENA students look forward to political careers. The Polytechnique specializes in science, mathematics, and engineering, the ENA in more general matters of policy and administration.

The routes to the Polytechnique and the ENA differ. Admission to the Polytechnique is generally from *lycées*, but after an additional two years of intensive preparation for the admission examinations. Until the early 1980s, about two thirds of ENA students were direct entrants less than twenty-five years old, and one third were civil servants less than thirty years old aspiring to the administrative elite (with each group having a separate examination). As in Britain, the students with civil service experience usually achieve only modest success in their careers. At graduation they rank lower than most direct entrants, and this clouds their prospects.

The Socialist government launched a short-lived experiment in 1983. It increased the proportion of entrants from the civil service. It also reserved ten entry posts for people up to age 40 who passed a third kind of examination, after nomination by provincial and municipal councils, trade unions, and voluntary associations. The reformers sought to assure a student body less dominantly upper-middle-class and Parisian. In the event, entrants through the "third way" examinations were fewer than ten. The Chirac conservative government ended the experiment in 1986. At the same time it initiated its own reform, which will halve the number of entrants to ENA. The effect will be to make ENA graduates even more prestigious and to accelerate their rise to top positions.[30]

Of ENA's direct entrants, some come from university law programs and a diminishing proportion, but three fourths over the postwar years, from the elite *Institut d'Etudes Politiques* at Paris. In 1945 this government institution succeeded the private *Ecole Libre des Sciences Politiques*, which dated from France's defeat in the Franco-Prussian War. Before the Ecole Libre's nationalization (and the simultaneous creation of ENA), the high-prestige grands corps directly recruited most of their members from it.[31] As does the Institute, the School offered broad training in administration, diplomacy, economics, finance, and social affairs. It was "unique in its international outlook and its interest in foreign politics and institutions, particularly those of England and the United States."[32]

The two principal *grandes écoles* feed their graduates into different sectors of the administrative elite, and it is tempting to think of ENA as training generalists and the Polytechnique as training specialists. But both prepare generalist administrators. ENA clearly trains generalists. In their twenty-four to thirty month program, ENA students "major" in either general administration or economic administration and, after brief orientation, spend their first year as interns, typically as aides to prefects, themselves general administrators for their provincial *départements*.[33]

The Polytechnique case is the more problematic because of terminology. Its graduates are "engineers," but a French engineering degree or diploma marks the successful completion of virtually all higher scientific and technical training given outside the universities. F. F. Ridley succinctly corrects misconceptions:

> The engineers are not narrow specialists. They will have studied literature and classics, as well as mathematics, at school [i.e., at the lycée]. At the *Polytechnique*, their studies are almost entirely theoretical (general science). . . . There are thus two points to note about the members of the elite engineering corps. First, they are men of "general culture" (in the sense that the term is applied in Britain to the administrative class). Indeed, there are those who maintain that they are men of greater culture than the graduates of ENA. Second, they are trained from the start to become "polyvalent" (i.e., "all purpose" or "generalist") administrators after a period of field service.[34]

Graduates of ENA and the Polytechnique are ranked by performance on final examinations, and those near the top (the top 20 per cent at ENA and the top 25 per cent at the Polytechnique) are appointed to the most prestigious grands corps: from ENA to the Finance Inspectorate, Council of State, and Court of Accounts; from the Polytechnique to the Mines Corps and the Roads and Bridges Corps. Appointees have not been trained specifically for the corps, high-prestige or not, that they join. Polytechnique graduates, though, spend about three years in "schools of application" operated by the corps they have joined, but two of the three years are devoted to on-the-job internships. Both those finishing such schools and ENA graduates have an initial period of service in a "home base" ministry of their corps. After this brief apprenticeship, a matter of two to four years, the careers of the most talented accelerate, typically demonstrating a remarkable mobility among ministries and a consistency in high levels of responsibility.

Though interpretations of French administration tend to focus on the elite of the elite, the sizable proportion of graduates who fail to enter the most prestigious corps are still members of grands corps and, so, of the administrative elite. Those from ENA join the diplomatic corps, the prefectoral corps, and the large civil administrator corps,[35] those from the Polytechnique join a variety of technical corps. Some who join such corps, like their higher-ranked classmates, will enjoy interdepartmental assignments at high levels; this was more common under the Mitterand Socialist government than under pre-1981 governments.

The German Federal Republic

In Germany, training for the higher public service centers in the universities' law faculties. This reflects a shift in the nineteenth century from Cameralism, which had emphasized economics and public administration.[36] The displacement had lasting consequences, irrespective of regime. As Dahrendorf reported, "more than two thirds of all top administrative positions . . . were held by lawyers in the Weimar Republic, the Third Reich, and the Federal Republic."[37] Law is the preferred subject for university students who have not settled on a specialization, and so, Dahrendorf writes:

> Precisely because the student of law is not committed to any specific subject, he can become an expert on general matters, a man at the top. . . . In principle, the law faculties of German universities accomplish for German society what the exclusive Public Schools do for the English, and the *grandes écoles* for the French. In them an elite receives its training.[38]

Yet, as Herbert Jacob observed in 1963, there were costs to the training and recruitment pattern:

> It sensitized German officials only to legal problems, for it meant that almost all literature on administration was restricted to its legal aspects. For instance, there are dozens of German books and countless articles on financial law, the civil service code, and administrative courts, but scarcely one on the budgetary process, on personnel management, or on the politics of administrative regulation.[39]

University graduates hoping to enter a general-administration career must pass a state examination, after which they undertake a preparatory program of about two and a half years. This, as is the case with university education, is provided by the individual Länder. The program embraces graduates preparing for judicial careers as well as candidates for administrative careers. The training, therefore, continues the legal emphasis, while providing practical experience through administrative internships, typically served under field administrators. At its conclusion, passage of a second state examination enables a candidate to apply to any federal or Land department or agency for appointment in the higher administrative service. As Renate Mayntz and Fritz Scharpf note, "Civil servants in general are recruited for a career, that is, for entry into a category and not . . . for specific positions. Their training accordingly is to enable them to fill a variety of positions. This 'generalist' orientation holds especially for the functional category of general administration," which is where the administrative elite is located.[40]

In contrast to French practice, German appointees tend to settle into a particular ministry, whether it be the locus of their first appointment or of a preferred second one that was initially inaccessible.

Differences and similarities in the three countries' recruitment and training of general administrators compete for emphasis. To those attentive only to the European scene the differences will seem to dominate. Those familiar with the United States' stress on recruitment of specialists and minimal preparation of talented young civil servants for future responsibilities will be struck by the convergent tendencies of the European systems. The career patterns of the European administrative elites present the same dilemmas of likeness and unlikeness, depending on the perspective chosen.

Career Patterns

Mobility—vertically, horizontally, and diagonally—is the principal feature of the careers of members of the European administrative elites. This is certainly so in Britain and France, less so in Germany.

Many factors contribute to mobility. First is the closed character of the administrative elite. Those recruited, by definition junior in age, will later face little or no competition for higher posts from lateral entrants. Though all countries admit some older outsiders, the number is small and their roles substantially distinct from those of higher civil servants, who are protected in their careers by both law and custom. Second, the number of entrants to the administrative elite is restricted, which facilitates horizontal and vertical movement. Third, early retirement (at sixty in Britain and sixty-two to sixty-five in Germany) and shifts to private and nationalized industries (in France) open the path of ascent for junior and midcareer colleagues.

Britain

In Britain, the rate of mobility attracts considerable criticism. Most of the mobility occurs among posts within a single department. The average tenure in midlevel positions (Assistant Secretaries and Under Secretaries) is between one and a half and two and a half years.[41] This occasions great discontinuity in the handling of policy issues on the agenda of a position. Issues initiated by a predecessor need to be mastered before one can proceed. Issues initiated during one's own tenure cannot be seen through to completion. The hallowed argument is that variety of experience, rather than depth of subject matter competence, is essential to development of a cadre of generalist administrators.

For young "high flyers," a different pattern of mobility is followed. They are seconded for about two years as private secretaries to Ministers and Permanent Secretaries, as staff members of the Treasury, and as members of the Cabinet Office's secretariats and its Management and Personnel Office. This experience at the very top is typical of most juniors who eventually become Permanent Secretaries. Before reaching that pinnacle some will have been private secretaries in the Prime Minister's Office and have experienced interministerial mobility as Deputy Secretaries and Under Secretaries.

France

In France, much the same pattern is followed. For example, all ENA graduates, after completing their two to four year apprenticeship in a ministry dominated by their corps, must be shifted to another ministry for a broadening experience before resuming normal careers.

The high flyers, whether from ENA or the Polytechnique, and including some only thirty years old, enjoy a heady, brief experience as members of high staffs. These staffs are the secretariat of the Presidency and the *cabinets* (i.e., staffs) of the Prime Minister and the departmental Ministers. Before 1981, about twenty-four civil servants were in the President's secretariat, about twenty to thirty in the Prime Minister's cabinet, and over two hundred in ministerial cabinets. The proportions of staff members belonging to the grands corps and, more particularly, to the most prestigious corps, have varied with successive governments.[42] The greatest change came with the Socialists. Their Mauroy government reduced the grand corps share of high civil servant membership in ministerial cabinets from the 61 per cent in the preceding government to 34 per cent.[43]

The career importance of service in cabinets is of an order with that of the staff service rendered by British high flyers. But the resultant career acceleration is more marked. In some French cabinets the young members get experience in actually directing groups of divisions (much resented by division directors), as distinguished from the purely staff roles of British apprentices. More significant is the career-launching potential of their usually brief cabinet membership. They have been chosen by the minister, who may later reward their service by advancement to posts superior to those held before service in the cabinet.[44]

Careers, however, are closely associated with grands corps membership. This is determined, we have seen, by one's ranking in examinations at the time of graduation from ENA or the Polytechnique. Ever after, the high civil servant is marked and his or her career opportunities are distinctively tied to his or her corps. Each grand corps has historic claims to staff the upper reaches of certain ministries, parts of ministries, and a share of a minister's cabinet. These claims are sturdily defended, and the corps compete, often aggressively, to extend their sway.[45] A minister's choice of directors and his cabinet is, therefore, considerably restricted. Senior members of a corps or, often, a "pope" or grand master, oversee the careers of younger members. This, as well as *esprit de corps*, is facilitated by the small size of the most prestigious corps. Except for the rather large Roads and Bridges Corps, each has about 200 to 400 members.

Many corps members become "detached" from their corps for career-advancing opportunities (high posts in ministries remote from their corps' established terrain, membership in the National Assembly, membership in the government as ministers, or directorships or subdirectorships of industrial enterprises). Movement from the specifically administrative sector of the government to highly paid posts in the over 500 public enterprises or, via *pantouflage*, to similar posts in private enterprises, is one of the most valued prospects of grands corps careerists. Though ministerial patronage is a factor in such appointments, particular corps have strong claims to certain fields of activity. Most conspicuously, the Finance Inspectorate dominates the directorships of nationalized banks, and the members of the Corps of Mines are in charge of a number of manufacturing companies, irrelevant though they may be to mining.

In sum, careers of members of the prestigious grands corps, and of some members of other grands corps, are marked by remarkable mobility.[46] And, in contrast to the pattern in Britain, from an early age the mobility is interdepartmental, the exercise of power near top political executives extensive, and the prospect of reward a strong incentive to loyal and effective performance. Virtually knighted on emergence from the grandes ecoles, Enarchs and polytechnicians alike have a self-confidence that, critics say, is little short of arrogance.

The German Federal Republic

Members of the German administrative elite usually pursue their careers in individual ministries, moving ahead in considerable part by age and experience, which is to say by seniority tempered by competence. Though prepared as generalists by law school and their subsequent internship training, they develop specialized knowledge on the job because of the narrow confinement of their careers. To the degree that they become specialists the pattern is not unlike that of the United States. A key difference, though, is that their work is focused on policy formation from an early stage, a natural consequence of the federal government's dependence on the Länder for implementation of federal laws.

The executive branch's structure strongly encourages specialization. There are about 1,600 subject matter sections or bureaus (*Referate*), an average of 100 per ministry. Each is tiny, most typically four members, two of them higher civil servants and two intermediate-level civil servants.[47] Despite the fine distinctions in subject matter that such a multiplicity of sections imposes, it is the sections that initiate policy proposals and to which must be referred policy issues raised at higher levels of their ministries or communicated by interest groups and parliamentarians.

Career advancement in the normal course appears rather sluggish. But several features modify this view. First, the multiplicity of section headships opens opportunities for advancement elsewhere in the department by assistant section heads currently blocked by the durability of their superiors. Second, most higher positions in a ministry are reserved for higher civil servants. Above the sections are division directorships and subdirectorships, and above them State Secretaryships. Third, as in Britain and France, the head of government, the German Chancellor, has an office whose staffing opens an opportunity for some civil servants to have an overview of a set of ministries or policy areas. About a hundred higher civil servants have this opportunity at any one time, and they are rotated in and out of the Chancellor's Office.

What, then, do the European career patterns have in common, at least when viewed with an American perspective? First, careerists serve at high levels. Rare in the White House, civil servants are important participants in the British Prime Minister's Office and Cabinet Office, the French President's secretariat and Prime Minster's staff cabinet, and the Office of the German Chancellor. They also count almost exclusively as the staff of British Ministers, as heads of French directions and significantly but not exclusively in French Ministers' cabinets, and as German Ministries' State Secretaries and division directors. Second, in Britain and France (though not in Germany), young high flyers experience a high rate of mobility. Third, careerists in all three countries find themselves involved from the start in policy formation.

From a European perspective, the career systems show great contrasts. Members of the French elite corps experience a variety of assignments, both in different departments and in semipublic and private enterprises.

Their career courses receive close attention from senior members of their respective corps and by ministers impressed by their performance. In Britain and Germany, however, most of a career is pursued in a single department. Interdepartmental mobility occurs, if at all, when one is young and, in Britain, at full maturity when one approaches candidacy for a Permanent Secretaryship. The two countries differ, however, in the management of careers. The British Management and Personnel Office (in the Cabinet Office) selects Administrative Trainees, oversees the initial stage of Administrative Class careers, and, with a committee of Permanent Secretaries, manages the climactic stages, recommending the promotion and placement of the topmost careerists. Germany, without a strong central personnel agency, leaves initial appointments and subsequent promotions to departmental officials, subject only to their observance of rules and regulations. Career lines promote loyalty to one's grand corps in France, to one's department in Germany, and to the civil service as a whole in Britain.

Policy, Politics, and Administration

All countries have a broad band of posts where administration and politics mix. Who belong to this band and how they interact varies by country. Three patterns, often overlapping, can be discerned. First, the band may be populated preponderantly by "outsiders," temporary appointees assisting the government currently in power. Second, the band may be largely filled by civil service careerists having partisan, policy, or personal compatibility with the current government and department head. And, third, it may consist mostly of civil servants who are expected to be neutral, to outlast governments and department heads, and yet to give loyal service to whatever party government is in power and to successive incumbents of the department headship.

The United States has gone furthest in use of layers of political appointees. France and Germany fit the second category, where each key member of the government (head of state, of government, and of each department) chooses the civil servants to serve on his or her immediate staff and as the principal administrators. Britain is preeminently in the third pattern. The Prime Minister and department heads rely heavily on permanent civil servants; assignments to such high levels are normally determined by senior civil servants following standard career-advancement criteria.[48] The Minister heading a department deals primarily with his careerist Permanent Secretary, whose adaptability to the Minister's initiatives may be attenuated by devotion to the long-established "department position."[49] As we shall see, the second and third patterns do not exclude the appointment of outsiders alongside high-level civil servants, but they are a minority of the whole.

Political Activity of Civil Servants

A distinction exists regarding careerists' political activity. In the United States and Britain, though civil servants may belong to political parties and vote, they cannot be candidates in partisan elections nor, it follows, members of legislative bodies. In France and Germany, not only do many careerists belong to political parties but their memberships are common knowledge. They can and do run for political office, and some sit in the national parliament. In 1981, 56 per cent of the members of the French Chamber of Deputies had civil service backgrounds (but three fifths of these were lycée professors and lesser-ranked teachers). More relevant to our concerns, 22 per cent were from the higher civil service and over half of these from the administrative elite corps.[50] In 1980, about 40 per cent of the German Bundestag's members were tenured civil servants or contractual public employees, but this is a global figure; higher civil servants were only about 10 per cent of Bundestag membership, a proportion that, in contrast to that of France, has been decreasing.[51]

In Britain and the United States, careerists must resign if they seek political candidacy and legislative service. Not so on the Continent. A French civil servant retains status and salary while running for office. If elected to the National Assembly or appointed as a Minister, a leave of absence suffices and return to one's corps is assured. A civil servant's political career is thus both subsidized and risk-free, an occupational advantage that Ezra Suleiman finds astonishing.[52] In Germany, too, civil servants who become legislators take leave of absence from their posts and if defeated for re-election can return to the civil service.[53] One unintended effect in both countries is to attract to the civil service some recruits whose real goal is a political career.

The political orientations of British, French, and German higher civil servants are centrist. More precisely, in the early 1970s they were supportive of the existing balance between free enterprise and state intervention in their own countries. This bell-shaped distribution pattern contrasts with the dumbbell-shaped pattern of left and right orientations of their own countries' legislators. It contrasts, too, with American senior civil servants' rather even distribution across the spectrum.[54] Centrist, of course, is not rightist. But even so obvious a statement inadequately registers the fact that an administrative elite recruited from the middle and upper-middle classes and with an education most accessible to the privileged is further leftward than its background predicts. In the early

1970s, over one third of ENA alumni supported parties of the left,[55] and in the early 1980s the Enarchs were "almost exactly divided in their politics, between left and right."[56]

"Outsiders" Near the Top

In no country, whatever the politician/careerist band may be, is the policy/administration dichotomy operative near the top. Ministers need help in policy formulation and top careerists are their major in-house resource. This is least realized in the United States, where careerists have the least contact with their department heads.[57] Careerists predominate in European top staffs. The question is not whether this should be the case. Rather, two questions need to be explored: How large is the minority of "outsiders" appointed near the top? And how much freedom exists and is used to lift to those levels civil servants likely to be congenial collaborators with the government in power and with the minister heading a department?

"Outsiders"—businesspersons, members of labor union and political party staffs, journalists, and scholars—are appointed to give counsel on broad policy initiatives and to contribute to the political survival and advancement of the in-office government or minister. Expansion of non-civil service staffing is most likely when an incoming party perceives the higher civil service as inadequate or hostile because of its social origins, its bureaucratic resistance to change, its lack of expertise in high-priority policy fields, or a preceding, long-lived government's colonization of top career staffs with its own adherents.

Although the use of outsiders is modest, the scope of the practice tends to be exaggerated. In Britain, for example, the Central Policy Review Staff in the Cabinet Office was established by Prime Minister Edward Heath to assure "an amalgam of individuals aware of the art of the possible in Whitehall and those with fresh ideas about the problems faced by the cabinet."[58] Half were to be careerists and half outsiders, a ratio that in fact was sometimes two thirds and one third. Yet the staff comprised only eighteen officials, of whom, therefore, only six to nine were outsiders. Similarly, Prime Minister Thatcher's halving of the number of ministers' special (outside) advisers might suggest a major depoliticization. Not so. Her predecessor had allowed a total of only twenty special advisers, distributed among thirteen departments, so in either government a minister had to work closely with that paragon of careerism, the Permanent Secretary.[59]

In France, a long-time pattern was broken with the coming to power of the Socialist government in 1981. The twenty-five-member presidential secretariat of Valery Giscard d'Estaing had had one non-civil servant (4 per cent), while that of François Mitterand, with thirty-seven members, included fourteen non-civil servants (38 per cent). Exactly the same change of percentages occurred in the Prime Minister's cabinet, though, with the total membership shifting from twenty-six to fifty, the number of civil servants actually increased from twenty-five to thirty-one. Finally, outsiders' share of posts in ministerial cabinets changed from 14 per cent to over 31 per cent.[60] All this noted, entrants from outside the civil service filled only about one hundred thirty-five out of the over four hundred high-level staff roles under the Socialist government. And that is a highly unusual proportion. During the Fifth Republic's first twenty years, outsiders never constituted more than 25 per cent of the ministerial cabinets' membership and in most governments were between 11 and 15 per cent.

In Germany, a minority of the staff of the Chancellor's Office is drawn from outside the civil service. Sixty per cent of the staff are permanent officials and an additional but indeterminate number are long-term but untenured high-level "employees."[61] About 25 per cent of officials serving Ministers at the highest two departmental levels may normally be outsiders, lateral entrants to the bureaucracy who receive civil service status. In principle, they are expected to meet the educational criteria for the higher administrative service.[62]

Though the numbers and proportions of outsiders brought into higher European administrations may still be modest, concern exists that a trend toward greater politicization is under way. Party militants expect to be rewarded when their party achieves victory. Further, a new government that seeks to reverse its predecessor's policies will need loyalists in those posts that have strategic leverage in the bureaucracy. One consequence may be greater displacement of civil servants by outsiders. Another may be that higher civil servants, defensively resisting that threat, may more conspicuously identify themselves with parties in power or likely to attain power.

Political Civil Servants

Although in all our countries the majority of top-level aides and deputies are civil servants, the key question is to what degree the selection of careerists to serve at these levels is political. A difference between the continental languages and English handicaps the search for answers. In English, "politics" and "policy" are distinct terms. In French, *politique*, and in German, *Politik*, embrace both meanings—or either one alone.[63] To read, then, that aides and deputies belonging to a continental higher civil service are political or are chosen with political criteria in mind can mislead one unless the ambiguity of terms is resolved by the context of such statements. Such resolution is often lacking.[64]

Another contrast between Britain and the Continent lies in patterns of party control since World War II. Such variations affect the role conceptions imposed on or chosen by higher civil servants. Consider the British case, where Labor and Conservative governments have alternated at fairly frequent intervals, with an equal total incumbency between 1945 and 1979. This helps to explain, as Richard Rose notes, that "while higher civil servants are extremely concerned with politics, they are also anxious to maintain their bipartisan status," serving readily whichever party is in power. Administrative-class civil servants, during careers of nearly forty years, are likely "to see the party in power change six to ten times, and the particular minister they serve change fifteen to twenty times." Constrained by the Official Secrets Act of 1911 as well as by their long-established role conceptions, the civil servants pursue their functions privately "to an extent perhaps unique in the Western World."[65] Outside Whitehall they keep themselves to themselves. And as senior civil servants, not politicians, generally manage the careers of members of the Administrative Class, partisanship is not a factor. In the party-commitment sense, "political civil servants" is an oxymoron in Britain. Even Prime Minister Thatcher's unusually active role in selection of Permanent and Deputy Secretaries turned on criteria of managerial competence and policy support, not partisan affiliation.[66]

In France and Germany, most careerists in the policy/administration band are termed "political civil servants." Ministers may determine which careerists to retain and which to replace by other careerists in top staff and administrative positions.[67] Some of those chosen are members of the party in power. Others are competent civil servants without strong party indentification, some of them serving under a succession of governments and ministers. And members of opposition parties are also found at this high level. All are expected to give loyal service to the government and the minister, whether by reason of partisan, policy, or neutral civil service motivations. And all are expected to be politically sensitive, obligated "to measure the political and electoral incidences of a matter and to appreciate its repercussions in public opinion and in Parliament."[68]

Two general propositions seem sound. One is that the greatest test of politicization of high civil service posts occurs when party control of the government shifts dramatically from right to left or vice versa. The previously out-of-power party distrusts the high "political" civil servants it inherits, and campaign rhetoric is likely to have promised a purge. The second is that neither in France nor in Germany have such shifts entailed the number of replacements of careerists that could be called a purge. Instead, relatively few partisan replacements, in absolute numbers, concentrated in strategic posts (such as State Secretaryships in Germany) suffice to bring coherence to the formulation and implementation of the governing party's program.

The normal German pattern since 1945 (and the French from 1959 to 1981) is long incumbency by a party or coalition in power. So a large-scale purge has rarely figured in rhetoric, let alone in practice. However, even with such governmental stability, ministers change. As most of the political civil service positions are in the ministries, and compatibility of their incumbents with the minister is important, substantial politically motivated turnover might be expected. But partisan politics does not play a large part.

"Discretionary appointments" in French ministries include directors of the major programmatic units and members of the ministerial cabinets. In the extraordinary transfer of power when the Socialists took command of the government in 1981, about half the directors of the central administration were replaced and half retained.[69] The proportions are comparable to those attending the earlier, less dramatic shift in 1974 from Pompidou's to Giscard d'Estaing's presidency (each of the right) and are not regarded as a purge, though devoted Giscardists were no doubt among those found replaceable.[70] By December 1984, when the Socialist government was almost four years old, 86 per cent of the directors had been changed. But directors' tenure normally averages four years, so "the situation undoubtedly would not have been very different" if the right had remained in power.[71]

Turnover of careerists in French ministerial cabinets cannot readily be measured in political or personal terms. Calculations fail for several reasons. First, by definition, as we have seen, compatibility with the current minister is a major criterion for membership. Second, a retiring minister often arranges for his favored cabinet members to move to career-advancing posts elsewhere; some new members, therefore, fill vacancies rather than displace incumbents. Third, in France, as in Germany, the authority to replace political civil servants with a change of ministers gracefully legitimates the nonpartisan displacement of top careerists whose performance lacks distinction. Fourth, and most important, is the understanding that cabinet membership, certainly for young careerists, is a short-term apprenticeship, often lasting only one to three years.

One clear change under the Socialists in France was reduction of the grands corps' representation in ministerial cabinets. It fell from 61 per cent to 34 per cent of civil service members. And, though the three most prestigious corps of ENA graduates maintained their share (about a fourth) of the grands corps' cabinet membership, their proportion of *all* civil service members in cabinets fell by 40 per cent. Only the lower-ranked corps of civil administrators increased its share of grands corps representation (by over 50 per cent). The balance of civil servants in Socialist cabinets were teachers and other nonmembers of the grand corps.[72]

To gain perspective on the proportions cited, one should recall that less than 230 civil servants were members of the ministerial cabinets under the Socialist government. A 10 per cent share or shift, therefore, would involve only about twenty-three positions throughout the departments of the government, or an average of about one position per department.

In Germany the policy/administration band includes a category known as "political civil servants," composed of all State Secretaries and Ministerial Directors and numbering between 135 and 155.[73] A Minister can place any political civil servant on "provisional" or "temporary" retirement, a status that carries a pension, 75 per cent of the former salary. The Minister himself is minimally staffed. He has nothing comparable to a French ministerial cabinet, and the political civil servants serve in the regular departmental hierarchy.

German governments make only moderate use of the authority to place political civil servants on temporary retirement. The most extensive use has been in the Ministry of Foreign Affairs (where some officials below Ministerial Directors are political civil servants). Excluding that Ministry except for parenthetical note, only thirty-four temporary retirements (plus sixteen in Foreign Affairs) occurred between 1953 and 1969, a sixteen-year period without significant change in the political makeup of the government. The Social Democrats' coming to power in 1969 led to eighty-eight temporary retirements (plus sixty-two in Foreign Affairs). Yet after 1969 only 27 per cent of the higher civil servants were members or sympathizers of the Social Democrats, while 43 per cent identified themselves with the opposition Christian Democrats and 30 per cent were neutral.[74] After their thirteen years in office, another sea change of government occurred with the Christian Democrats' victory. The new Kohl government effected forty-four temporary retirements.[75] Though this figure suggests high politicization, two thirds of the high officials exposed to the possibility of retirement actually remained in their posts.[76]

The French Socialists and the British Conservatives, without apparently conscious borrowing from Germany, accelerated retirements of senior civil servants by legislative measures and informal persuasion.[77]

The European countries' policy-formulating band of positions mixes higher civil servants and temporarily serving outsiders in a complex way, which nonetheless has a pattern. First, civil servants predominate near the top in each country's mix. Second, the Continental countries' party governments and individual ministers choose the civil servants who serve as their principal aides and administrators. Third, the opportunity for such choice does not entail a wholesale changing of the guard that served the prior government or minister. Rather, it involves judgments of civil servants' policy orientations, competence, and sensitivity to political effects of policy initiatives. Partisanship plays a lesser role, though its relevance peaks when a party or coalition long in power is succeeded by one with a strikingly different constituency.

From an American perspective the notable European features are the close relations of higher civil servants with heads of governments and ministers in policy formulation and departmental management; the substantial degree of continuity of civil service membership in the policy/administration band (whether of individual civil servants or, as in France, with its tradition of mobility, of colleagues within the same corps); and the ease of civil servants' retreat from the band (British ones not even likely to be displaced, the French assured of other high posts, and the Germans guaranteed retirement pensions—and often welcomed by private sector employers).

Conclusion

Two seemingly contradictory themes have recurred. One is the distinctiveness of each country's system, a feature that is lodged in historical traditions and that triumphs over the often perceived but rarely exploited opportunities for borrowing from one another. The other is the degree to which the Western European systems share important characteristics.

The details of the first theme, the distinctiveness of each nation's system, have been set forth earlier. Among the prominent features are the following:

1. Britain's heavier reliance on a closed, presumptively neutral, permanent civil service, with little place for outsiders and none for "political civil servants" in the Continental sense;
2. The British Permanent Secretary, the hierarchy-heading deputy to the Minister, a model attractive to American reformers and once approximated by each department's "chief clerk";[78]
3. France's ministerial cabinets, which are enviously regarded by Britons and Germans critical of their own classically hierarchical systems; and
4. Jurists' dominance in Germany's administrative elite, a feature unenviously viewed from abroad and much criticized at home.

The second theme, that of shared characteristics, is clearest when European systems are compared to that of the United States. Europe deliberately recruits and trains generalists and accords them key roles in policy-making and top-level management. Careers, except in Germany, feature remarkable mobility among positions, departments, and supradepartmental offices, including that of the chief executive. Those achieving successful careers are handsomely rewarded.[79] In both Continental countries, civil servants may engage in partisan politics and serve in legislative bodies, later resuming, if they choose, their civil service careers. There, too, is found the phenomenon of "political civil servants," careerists raised for a time by ministers and governments to key staff and managerial roles. Civil servants at those levels, as to a lesser degree in Britain, work in concert with a minority of temporary appointees on the formulation of policies, a task calling less for partisanship than for competence allied with political sensitivity. The recognition of higher civil servants as critical resources at the policy-making level stands as the major contrast with American practice.

Endnotes

For helpful comments on a preliminary draft I am indebted to Alfred Diamant, Joseph LaPalombara, Renate Mayntz, Richard Rose, and Ezra Suleiman.

1. See Joel D. Aberbach, Robert D. Putnam, and Bert A. Rockman, *Bureaucrats and Politicans in Western Democracies* (Cambridge, MA: Harvard University Press, 1981) for frequent noting of "American exceptionalism."
2. This essay does not deal with the American system, save for occasional side glances, See Hugh Heclo, *A Government of Strangers* (Washington, DC: The Brookings Institution, 1977); Frederick C. Mosher, *Democracy and the Public Service*, 2nd ed. (New York: Oxford University Press, 1982); James W. Fesler, "Politics, Policy, and Bureaucracy at the Top," in *Annals of the American Academy of Political and Social Science* 466:23–41 (March) 1983; and Hugh Heclo, "In Search of a Role: America's Higher Civil Service," in *Bureaucrats and Policymaking: A Comparative Overview*, Ezra N. Suleiman, ed. (New York: Holmes and Meier, 1984), pp. 8–34.
3. French Ministers may come from the National Assembly and some nonmember Ministers seek and win election to it, but none may retain a legislative seat.
4. In practice, the protective role is conditioned by whether the *Bundesrat*'s party control is congruent or at odds with that of the *Bundestag* and government.
5. See S. E. Finer, *The Life and Times of Sir Edwin Chadwick* (London: Methuen, 1952).
6. Douglas E. Ashford, *British Dogmatism and French Pragmatism: Central-Local Policymaking in the Welfare State* (London: George Allen & Unwin, 1982), and Jerry A. Webman, *Reviving the Industrial City: The Politics of Urban Renewal in Lyon and Birmingham* (New Brunswick, NJ: Rutgers University Press, 1982).
7. Theodore Zeldin, *The French* (London: William Collins, Sons, 1983), pp. 171–172.

8. Law No. 82–213 of March 2, 1982, *Journal Officiel,* March 3, 1982, p. 730. See Alfred Diamant, "French Field Administration Revisited: The Beginnings of the Mitterand Reforms," in *The Costs of Federalism,* Robert T. Golembiewski and Aaron Wildavsky, eds. (New Brunswick, NJ, and London: Transaction Books, 1984), pp. 143–164. The complexities of implementation are chronicled in *Revue française d'Administration publique* and *La Revue Administrative.*

9. France's first Mauroy government had forty-four members, heading thirty-five ministries and nine secretariats. The second Mauroy government, formed in March 1983, had a fifteen-member Cabinet.

10. D. R. Steel, "Britain," in *Government and Administration in Western Europe,* F. F. Ridley, ed. (New York: St. Martin's Press, 1979), p. 23; Ezra N. Suleiman, "From Right to Left: Bureaucracy and Politics in France," in Suleiman, *Bureaucrats and Policymaking,* p. 112; and Renate Mayntz, "The Political Role of the Higher Civil Service in the German Federal Government," in *The Higher Civil Service in Europe and Canada: Lessons for the United States,* Bruce L. R. Smith, ed. (Washington, DC: The Brookings Institution, 1984), p. 63.

11. "Outsiders" in the Cabinet Office and some ministries are so few as not to affect the general dimension.

12. Francis de Baecque, "L'Interpénétration des Personnels Administratifs et Politiques," in *Administration et Politique sous la Cinquième République,* 2nd ed., rev. and expanded, Francis de Baecque and Jean-Louis Quermonne, eds. (Paris: Presses de la Fondation Nationale des Sciences Politiques, 1982), p. 28 (Tableau 1).

13. Pre-1981 data from Jean-Luc Bodiguel and Jean-Louis Quermonne, *La Haute Fonction Publique sous la Ve République* (Paris: Presses Universitaires de France, 1983), pp. 24, 55. The post-1981 estimate is calculated from data in Baecque and Quermonne, op. cit., pp. 372–377.

14. The count of French and West German members of the political echelon excludes "political civil servants," those members of the higher civil service subject to "discretionary appointment" to particular posts in France and subject to "temporary retirement" in West Germany. Because of this exclusion, the count of forty for West Germany differs from the eighty "top political appointments" that I elsewhere have said "a new group in power in Germany makes." James W. Fesler, "The Higher Civil Service in Europe and the United States," in Smith, op. cit., p. 88. The larger figure included those "political civil servants" who were actually retired and replaced following the Kohl government's coming to power. See below, p. 531.

15. For a valiant but indeterminate wrestling with this problem in France, see Bodiguel and Quermonne, op. cit., pp. 11–70.

16. See William I. Bacchus, *Staffing for Foreign Affairs: Personnel Systems for the 1980's and 1990's* (Princeton, NJ: Princeton University Press, 1983).

17. Public esteem, however, has been declining. In 1968 such decline was noted for Britain, while some German problems were attributed to the "too high standing" of the civil service. By 1983 the prestige of German civil servants had declined. Bruce Headey, "The Civil Service as an Elite in Britain and German," *International Review of Administrative Sciences* 38:41–48, 1972, at

p. 44; Nevil Johnson, *State and Government in the Federal Republic of Germany: The Executive at Work* 2nd ed., (Oxford: Pergamon Press, 1983), pp. 187–188. Public prestige is not a good index of competence, incorruptibility, and devotion to the public interest. Informed judgments credit these qualities as characteristic of each of the three countries' higher public service.

18. Peter Kellner and Lord Crowther-Hunt, *The Civil Servants* (London: Sedgwick and Jackson, 1980).

19. John D. Armstrong, *The European Administrative Elite* (Princeton, NJ: Princeton University Press, 1973), pp. 155, 160.

20. Under the rigid examination system, "in 1980 83 percent of the new undergraduates in Cambridge, and 72 percent in Oxford, had gained A-levels consisting of at least two Bs and an A; compared to an average of 27 percent in other universities." Anthony Sampson, *The Changing Anatomy of Britain* (New York: Random House, 1982), p. 144.

21. Richard Rose, "The Political Status of Higher Civil Servants in Britain," in Suleiman, op. cit., p. 145.

22. Steel, op. cit., p. 43.

23. In 1982 only forty-four AT vacancies were "on offer" and not all were filled. William Plowden, "The Higher Civil Service in Britain," in Smith, op. cit., p. 34.

24. See Colin Campbell, *Governments Under Stress: Political Executives and Key Bureaucrats in Washington, London and Ottawa* (Toronto: University of Toronto Press, 1983), pp. 244–245.

25. R. G. S. Brown and D. R. Steel, *The Administrative Process in Britain* (London: Methuen & Co., 1979), p. 89.

26. Zeldin, *The French*, p. 389.

27. Theodore Zeldin, *France 1848–1945*, Volume II: *Intellect, Taste and Anxiety* (Oxford: Oxford University Press, 1973), p. 327.

28. A third school is of the same elite ranking, the *Ecole Normale Supérieure*, which trains teachers. Though they are counted as civil servants, they are outside our principal concern.

29. Ezra N. Suleiman, *Elites in French Society: The Politics of Survival* (Princeton, NJ: Princeton University Press, 1978), pp. 70–71. In the forty years since 1945 the ENA has graduated only 3,808 students. Robert Chelle, "Les étapes de l'Ecole Nationale d'Administration," *La Revue Administrative* 38, No. 227 (Septembre–Octobre) 1985, pp. 431–434, at p. 432.

30. Eric Rhode, "L'ENA a-t-elle échoué?" *Le Monde de l'Education* (Avril) 1982, pp. 55 f; Charles Vallée, ENA's Director of Studies, remarks at the Brookings Institution's Conference on the Higher Civil Service in Europe and Canada, June 24, 1983; letter of October 24, 1983, from the scientific attaché for social sciences, French Embassy, Washington, D. C.; and Richard Bernstein, "Where France's Ruling Classes Take Their Classes," *New York Times* (August 24) 1986, Section 4.

31. Between 1901 and 1935, 93 per cent of the four high-prestige grands corps' recruits were from the Ecole Libre. Ezra N. Suleiman, *Politics, Power, and Bureaucracy in France: The Administrative Elite* (Princeton, NJ: Princeton University Press, 1974), p. 48. We have drawn other data from pp. 54–63.

32. Zeldin, *France, 1948–1945*, Vol. II, p. 343.

33. "Décret No. 71–787 du 21 Septembre 1971 relatif aux conditions d'accès à l'école nationale d'administration et au régime de la scolarité" [as modified of decrees of 29 May 1973 and 11 May 1976], printed as *Ecole Nationale d'Administration: Conditions d'accès et régime de la Scolarité* (Paris: Journaux Officiels, c. 1980).

34. F. F. Ridley, "French Technocracy and Comparative Government," *Political Studies* 14:34–52 (February) 1966, at p. 38.

35. Choices open correspond approximately in this sequence to graduates' ranking at ENA. This is detailed in Bodiguel and Quermonne, *La Haute Fonction Publique*, p. 47.

36. The Cameral School, its fading with the shift to juridical training, and its relations to France's ENA are treated in Fritz Morstein Marx, "German Administration and the Speyer Academy," in *American Public Administration: Patterns of the Past*, James W. Fesler, ed. (Washington, DC: American Society for Public Administration, 1982), pp. 57–68.

37. Ralf Dahrendorf, *Society and Democracy in Germany* (Garden City, NY: Doubleday, 1967), p. 234. The same proportion held in the early 1980s. Johnson, op. cit., p. 183.

38. Dahrendorf, op. cit., p. 236.

39. Herbert Jacob, *German Administration Since Bismarck: Central Authority versus Local Autonomy* (New Haven, CT: Yale University Press, 1963), p. 205. For more encouraging developments since 1963, see Heinrich Siedentopf, "Administrative Science in the Federal Republic of Germany: B. Present Position," *International Review of Administrative Sciences* 49:158–163, 1983. Nonetheless, "the dogmatism of administrative law is experiencing a significant revival" (p. 159).

40. Renate Mayntz and Fritz W. Scharpf, *Policy-Making in the German Federal Bureaucracy* (Amsterdam: Elsevier, 1975), p. 52.

41. Brown and Steel, op. cit., p. 90.

42. Francis de Baecque, in Baecque and Quermonne, op. cit., p. 372–379. See also, in the same source, Marie-Christine Kessler, "Le cabinet du Premier ministre et le Secrétariat général du gouvernement," pp. 69–103, and Samy Cohen, "Le Secrétariat général de la présidence de la République," pp. 104–127.

43. Baecque, in ibid., p. 376. Percentile declines can be deceiving. Similarly precipitate declines for the President's secretariat and the Prime Minister's cabinet reflect expansion of total membership, whereas the number of grands corps members changed only slightly.

44. "One-third of all *directeurs* in the central administration are ex-*cabinet* members who owe their positions to grateful ministers—although this is usually largely because of their administrative experience rather than political loyalty." Ella Searls, "Ministerial *cabinets* and elite theory," in, *Elites in France: Origins, Reproduction and Power*, Jolyon Howorth and Philip G. Cerny, eds. (New York: St. Martin's Press, 1981), p. 164.

45. The Roads and Bridges Corps' capture of the city-planning function is the most striking recent example. In prospect is the possibility of that Corps' dominating the expanded ministry charged with protecting the environment. Philip Le Prestre, "France's Administration of the Environment," *International Review of Administrative Sciences* 47:42–50, 1981.

46. For striking examples, see Bernard Gournay, "The Higher Civil Service in France," in Smith, op. cit., pp. 77–78.

47. Mayntz and Scharpf, op. cit., pp. 64, 68. Since the book's publication in the mid-1970s, Mayntz advised (in 1984) that the average staffing has increased, partly reflecting a tendency to group sections.

48. However, Prime Minister Thatcher used her formal authority over appointment of Permanent Secretaries to an unusual degree. See Yvonne Fortin, "Madame Thatcher et la politisation des échelons supérieurs de l'Administration centrale en Grande-Bretagne 1979–1984, mythe ou réalité?" *International Review of Administrative Sciences* 50:337–354, 1984.

49. For vivid portrayal of this relationship, see Richard Crossman, *The Diaries of a Cabinet Minister*, Volume I, *1964–1966* (New York: Holt, Rinehart and Winston, 1975), pp. 23–26, 272–273, and passim.

50. Henry W. Ehrmann, *Politics in France*, 4th ed. (Boston: Little, Brown, 1983), pp. 158, 161. The 22 per cent figure is six times that under the Fourth Republic of 1945–1958.

51. Jacques Ziller, "Hauts fonctionnaires et politique en République fédérale d'Allemagne," *International Review of Administrative Sciences* 47:31–41, 1981, at pp. 39–40 f; Renate Mayntz, "German Federal Bureaucrats: A Functional Elite Between Politics and Administration," in Suleiman, op. cit., p. 189.

52. Suleiman, "From Right to Left," in Suleiman, *Bureaucrats and Policy-making*, pp. 189–190.

53. David Southern, "Germany," in Ridley, *Government and Administration*, p. 145. Until 1975 such members of Parliament received both parliamentary salaries and 60 per cent of their former civil service salaries, and qualified for pensions in both capacities!

54. Aberbach, Putnam, and Rockman, op. cit., pp. 119–132.

55. Anne Stevens, "The contribution of the Ecole Nationale d'Administration to French political life," in Howarth and Cerny, op. cit., p. 140.

56. Zeldin, *The French*, p. 163.

57. Aberbach, Putnam, and Rockman, op. cit., p. 234.

58. Campbell, op. cit., p. 66.

59. For a full account, see Yvonne Fortin, "Un aspect do l'evolution des super-structures du gouvernement central en Grande Bretagne (1970–1980): Conseillers particuliers des ministres, conseillers politiques personnels et 'cellule politique' du Premier ministre," *International Review of Administrative Sciences* 47:332–348, 1981, and her "Madame Thatcher et la politisation des échelons supérieurs . . . 1979–1984, in ibid., 50:337–354, 1984.

60. Baecque and Quermonne, op. cit. pp. 375–378.

61. Nevil Johnson reports that about 40 per cent of the Office's staff are non-tenured employees serving under private-law contracts, and the balance permanent officials. He notes elsewhere that "in reality the distinction between officials and employees has become extremely blurred." Johnson, op. cit., pp. 64, 176. However, some of the contractual employees in the Chancellor's Office are outsiders, "in-and outers," serving only temporarily.

62. Mayntz, "The Higher Civil Service of the Federal Republic of Germany," in Smith, op. cit., pp. 62, 65.

63. For the origins and consequences of the linguistic differences, see Arnold J. Heidenheimer, "*Politics, Policy,* and *Police* as Concepts in the Western

Languages or: Why Are the 'Kontis' [Continentals] Deprived?", a paper for the 1983 Annual Meeting, American Political Science Association.

64. For an excellent clarification, in the German setting, see Mayntz, "German Federal Bureaucrats," in Suleiman, op. cit., pp. 189 and 201.

65. Richard Rose, "The Political Status of Higher Civil Servants in Britain," in Suleiman, ibid., pp. 168, 136. However, with the renaming and expansion of parliamentary committees, civil servants down to the Assistant Secretary level find themselves testifying at Westminster. Between 1970 and 1974 over 300 civil servants, but only 14 ministers, gave evidence. Brown and Steel, op. cit., pp. 145, 148.

66. Yvonne Fortin, "Madame Thatcher et la politisation," in *International Review of Administrative Sciences* 50:337–354; and her "Mme Thatcher et l'administration centrale: amorce d'une revolution culturelle," in *Notes et etudes documentaire,* No. 4765 (1984), pp. 81–99.

67. One formal constraint on a minister, though rarely of practical effect, is the requirement that most such appointments be formally made or approved by the chief executive or Cabinet.

68. Bodiguel and Quermonne, op. cit., p. 61.

69. Those retained include six transferred to other directorships.

70. Suleiman, "From Right to Left," in Suleiman, op. cit., p. 112.

71. Herbert Maisl and Celine Wiener, "Politique et administration," *Revue politique et parlementaire* 87:68–78 (Septembre-Octobre) 1985, at p. 77; Jean-Luc Bodiguel, "A French-Style 'Spoils System'?" *Public Administration* (London) 61:295–300 (Autumn) 1983, at pp. 296–297.

72. Calculated from data in Baecque, in Baecque and Quermonne, op. cit., pp. 372–377.

73. Sources vary in inclusiveness of the category. See Mayntz, "The Political Role of the Higher Civil Service," in Smith, op. cit., p. 63; and Johnson, op. cit., p. 190 n. Johnson, taking account of some posts just below Ministerial Director, says that an "estimate of 200 posts subject to political appointment may be on the low side."

74. Jacques Ziller, op. cit., pp. 34–35, 38.

75. Mayntz, "The Political Role of the Higher Civil Service," in Smith, op. cit., p. 63.

76. However, half the State Secretaries were replaced, and about forty top officials, though below the political-official category, were transferred, Most of the latter were members or known sympathizers with the Social Democratic Party. Idem.

77. Guy Druot, "La limite d'âge dans la fonction publique, le secteur public et pour les magistrats hors hiérarchie de la cour de cassation," *La revue administrative* 38:7–16 (Janvier-Février) 1985.

78. See the brief discussion of chief clerks in Heclo, "In Search of a Role," in Suleiman, op. cit., pp. 17 f. As late as the mid-1930s a long-tenured chief clerk had a powerful role in the Interior Department.

79. In Britain, "41 officials are paid a higher salary than the Prime Minister, and another 157 are paid higher salaries than leading Cabinet Ministers." Rose, "The Political Status of Higher Civil Servants," in Suleiman, op. cit., p. 152. [For "Salary Tables" see Great Britain, Management and Personnel

Office, *Civil Service Year Book 1982* (London: HMSC, 1982), pp. xii–xiv.]
French rewards are generous but incalculable because of varying side benefits
(such as residence in government buildings). German "top civil service salaries
. . . permit, if managed well, a middle/upper-middle-class style of life."
Mayntz, "German Federal Bureaucrats," in ibid., p. 181.

PART VII

Administration in Fiction

CHAPTER 17

How Novelists View
Public Administration

Howard E. McCurdy
THE AMERICAN UNIVERSITY

*HOWARD E. MCCURDY is Professor of Government and Public Adminis-
tration in the College of Public and International Affairs at the American
University. He is Director of the university's doctoral programs in political
science and public administration. In addition to his work on the relationship
of fiction to public administration, Professor McCurdy has published books
and articles on public management, Congressional politics, science policy,
and the operation of the White House staff. His titles include the highly
respected* Public Administration: A Bibliographic Guide to the Literature *and* Public Administration: A Synthesis. *Professor McCurdy received
the doctorate from the Johnson School of Management at Cornell University.*

Howard E. McCurdy reflects on the ways in which novelists have viewed
public administration from *Huckleberry Finn* to modern times, how that
view has changed, how novelists have simultaneously helped to create
and disparage the rise of the administrative state, and which type of administrative arrangements they favor.

McCurdy contends that a novel need not describe public administration
per se in order to transmit a message about it. Appearing in 1884, just
three years before Woodrow Wilson's landmark essay, *Huckleberry Finn*
lays down a message about public administration without ever saying anything explicitly on the subject. In Mark Twain's view, institutions do not
serve us well. People are a conglomerate of good and evil, and institutions
provide the opportunity to elevate the wrong tendencies. Like Twain,

543

Ernest Hemingway believed that only by escaping from institutions, as the old man escaped to the sea, could an individual hope to develop a satisfactory moral code.

A year after the publication of *Huckleberry Finn,* the French writer Emile Zola published one of the first modern administrative novels, *Germinal.* The novel is based on a strike that actually occurred in the coalfields of France in 1884. Zola recognized how events and circumstances beyond anyone's personal control could cause power to shift from the owners and workers to the technical managers of the mines. By virtue of their expertise and administrative skills, the engineers were simply better suited to take charge of the situation.

From *Huckleberry Finn* and *Germinal,* McCurdy moves through an impressive list of novels in his analysis of administration in fiction. He gives special attention to (1) Upton Sinclair's *The Jungle,* (2) Harper Lee's *To Kill a Mockingbird,* (3) Franz Kafka's *The Castle,* (4) George Orwell's *1984,* (5) Joseph Heller's *Catch-22,* (6) Ken Kesey's *One Flew Over the Cuckoo's Nest,* (7) John Hersey's *A Bell for Adano,* (8) Michael Crichton's *The Andromeda Strain,* and (9) Mario Puzo's *The Godfather.*

The debate over whether such a study constitutes a valid view of administration has been going on for over forty years. Scholars accustomed to empirical proofs remain skeptical about conclusions drawn from works of fiction, even works where novelists labor to produce realistic pictures of life or express scientific theories in their world view. No matter how realistic the writer seeks to be, the facts in any work of fiction will always be distorted to some degree to fit the purpose of the story.

Facts also suffer some measure of distortion simply by passing through the minds of individuals, as they inevitably must. Novelists understand this. Rather than minimize the distortion, which is the approach of the scientist, the novelist explores it. Relative to empirical research, fiction makes its most significant contribution to administrative understanding in the areas where individual perceptions matter most: the realm of private motives and personal character. Here fiction does more than simply reflect public attitudes toward government and public administration. It provides insights into administrative issues that are difficult to approach with other tools. The validity of works of fiction in areas such as these must ultimately be judged on the basis of the credibility of the ideas the author seeks to express and whether the experiences shared with the reader seem reasonable, given the purpose of the story.

In the decade when scholars first read Woodrow Wilson's essay on "The Study of Administration," they also had the opportunity to purchase a first edition of *Huckleberry Finn*. Mark Twain's masterpiece of American fiction appeared in 1884, three years before the publication of Wilson's landmark.

Huckleberry Finn, of course, has utterly nothing to do with public administration. It describes the adventures of a young man floating on a raft through nineteenth-century America. The same could be said for the interests of political science at that time. Wilson complained in his essay that the "science of government" gave scant attention to public administration and called upon scholars to show more concern. As he wrote, novelists began to investigate. In 1885, between the publication of Twain's novel and Wilson's essay, the French writer Emile Zola published one of the first modern administrative novels.

Since that decade of transition, both scholars and novelists have significantly expanded the attention they give to the workings of the administrative state. Administrative novels like *1984* and *Catch-22* have become part of the public consciousness, and it would not be too much of an exaggeration to suggest that educated people are more familiar with the details of George Orwell's *1984* than with Wilson's essay. At least, more copies of Orwell's work have been sold. After twenty-five years in print, *1984* passed the 8 million book mark, an impressive number even in an age of paperbacks.

This chapter will explore the ways in which novelists have viewed public administration from *Huckleberry Finn* to the modern time, how that view has changed, how novelists have simultaneously helped to create and disparage the rise of the administrative state, and which type of administrative arrangements they favor.

Who Needs Institutions?

A novel need not describe public administration in order to transmit a message about it. Novelists can leave civil servants out of their stories and still make important statements about the nature of governmental bureaus. *Huckleberry Finn* lays down a message on administration without ever saying anything on the subject. That, and the fact that it bridges traditional and modern literary attitudes, makes it an important starting point for the study of administration in fiction.

Huckleberry Finn takes place on a raft on the Mississippi River and in the small farm towns that float by. Scarcely any government exists, and certainly no administration. No cities appear. Twain presents a few judges and colonels, but only as local color, not as officials in an administrative society.

In one small place, "pretty well down the state of Arkansaw," Huckleberry Finn watches one Colonel Sherburn shoot the town drunk.[1] The inebriate staggers up and down the single street, accusing the colonel of swindling him, much to the amusement of the loafers under the awnings of the dry-goods store who know what Boggs, the old drunk, is all bluster. Sherburn steps out of the store and announces to the source of the noise.

> "I'm tired of this, but I'll endure it till one o'clock. Till one o'clock, mind— no longer."[2]

Boggs keeps it up till one o'clock, when his friends try to hurry him down the road. The colonel appears, "a pistol raised in his right hand," and kills Boggs with two shots.[3]

The incident excites the loafers, someone suggests a lynching, "so away they went, mad and yelling, and snatching down every clothesline they come to."[4]

The mob meets Sherburn on his front porch, the colonel calm and deliberate with a double-barrel in one hand. He addresses the crowd:

> "The pitifulest thing out is a mob; that's what an army is—a mob; they don't fight with courage that's born in them, but with courage that's borrowed from their mass, and from their officers."[5]

The crowd breaks up. Huck goes to the circus, leaving town with the Duke, the Dauphin, and the slave Jim two days later. There is no arrest, no trial. As the Colonel himself tells the mob, your juries don't hang murderers. "They always acquit . . . because they're afraid the man's friends will shoot them in the back, in the dark—and it's just what they *would* do."[6]

Huckleberry Finn can be viewed as a relic, a picture of a preadministrative America in the period before the Civil War. In part, the novel belongs to the genre literary critics classify under the heading of "local color." Such stories portray the geography and panorama of a particular region, the whimsical characters that inhabit it, and the different dialects of its inhabitants. Local-color fiction was enormously popular in the 1880s. It lost its preeminent position in American literature after 1900, but not before launching the most romantic of all American novel types— the western.

Huckleberry Finn connects the local-color movement of the nineteenth century with the modern American novel of the twentieth. Ernest Hemingway once wrote that "all modern American literature comes from one book by Mark Twain called *Huckleberry Finn*."[7] Twain earned this accolade by discarding the romantic plots that typically guided local-color fiction, as in Owen Wister's archetypal western novel, *The Virginian*. Instead, Twain sought to portray people and places as faithfully as possible, not romantically or with extensive commentary, letting the pictures that emerged from that portrayal carry the story. In so doing he helped to launch the movement that became known as literary realism.

The rejection of institutions through literary realism establishes the moral tone of *Huckleberry Finn*. The most famous episode concerns Huck's decision to help his friend Jim escape from slavery. During one of their forays into town, the Duke sells Jim back into captivity for forty dollars. Huck remembers the lessons from Sunday School, that anyone who helps a slave escape "goes to everlasting fire."[8] On the other hand, Huck gets to remembering all the good times he had with his friend Jim. "All right, then, I'll go to hell," Huck resolves, and begins to plot Jim's getaway.[9]

By the time that Twain wrote *Huckleberry Finn,* slavery as an institution had been abolished. Descriptions of it no longer shocked the public as much as *Uncle Tom's Cabin* had. Critics generally agree that Twain uses slavery, along with incidents like the shooting of old Boggs, as a metaphor for institutions in general. In Twain's view, institutions do not serve us well. They become vehicles for bondage and injustice. Only when someone like Huck can be as free from institutions as possible can he or she hope to act morally. Even then, the redemption is likely to be short-lived. At the end of the story, Twain has Huck and the newly freed Jim light out for Indian territory:

> I reckon I got to light out for the territory ahead of the rest, because Aunt Sally she's going to adopt me and sivilize me, and I can't stand it[10]

Skepticism about the civilizing influence of institutions continues throughout modern literature. Twain was not being cynical, he was merely trying to be realistic. People are a bundle of good and evil, and institutions provide an opportunity to elevate the wrong tendencies.

Like Twain, Hemingway believed that only by escaping from institutions, as the old man did to the sea, could an individual hope to develop a satisfactory moral code.

Administrative Power

The sour view of institutions dominates much of American literature. It often leads novelists to an ill-informed view of administration, to write about administration in metaphors, or to ignore it altogether. Writers like Twain and Hemingway apparently preferred to master boats and fishing rather than spend much time studying administration.

In his essay on administration, Woodrow Wilson observed this same tendency among Americans in general. Americans, Wilson said, pay little attention to the "burdens of administration." He blamed this on our penchant for self-government. "Government is so near us," he said, "that we can with difficulty see the need of any philosophical study of it."[11] To gain perspective on the importance of administration, he urged Americans to examine "such systems as those of France and Germany."[12]

At the time of Wilson's essay, creative literature was more advanced in Europe than it was in America. While American novelists formulated local-color fiction, European writers experimented with a new type of writing called naturalism. In 1885, two years before the appearance of Wilson's essay, the French novelist Emile Zola published *Germinal*. Not only did the novel help to launch the movement toward naturalism, it became one of the first novels to deal directly with modern problems of administration.

The world of naturalism draws on the world of social and natural science. The naturalistic writer takes findings from the world of science and incorporates them in a human story. Naturalistic writers like Zola would throw their characters into a particular situation and see how they would behave according to scientific theory. The result was generally deterministic. No longer did the hero of the story control the plot; the hero was pushed around by hereditary, social, economic, and later psychological forces beyond his or her control. Committed to portraying events as realistically as possible, the author could not alter reality for the purpose of creating a happy ending. Accuracy became the standard by which these novels were judged. Novelists, in effect, created fictional experiments and reported on their findings. Zola, who coined the term, said that his naturalistic novels were like "lab reports."

Zola wrote between 1865 and 1902. At that time, the scientific theories of Charles Darwin and Karl Marx were widely discussed in literary circles—especially in Europe—and emerged in works of fiction. Sigmund Freud's theories, which began to appear in 1900, had a similar though later impact. *Germinal*, published twenty-six years after the appearance of Darwin's theories, relies heavily upon biological theory.[13] Zola describes his characters in animal-like terms. He stresses their genetically inherited characteristics and shows how their social environment determines their chances for survival.

Out of this biological determinism rises the administrative question that underlies the story. The novel is based on a strike that actually occurred in the coalfields of France in 1884. By virtue of their heredity and environment, Zola asks, which group will emerge with the power to run the mines—the workers, the owners, or the managers?

Zola's sympathies are clearly with the miners. If this were a romantic novel, Zola might let the miners triumph. Nevertheless, he remains realistic. The miners simply do not have the organizational skill or resources necessary to sustain a long strike through the winter. Their strike fund is too small, their leadership too variable. Not even outside agitators from the French socialist movement can organize the workers into an effective force. All the miners seem to be good at is rioting, starving, getting killed, and enduring misery.

The owners are no better prepared. Zola portrays them as foolish aristocrats, poorly situated to deal with the technical problems of operating the mines. They precipitate the strike by miscalculating the reaction of the miners to an incentive pay system, based on piece-rate work, which effectively lowers the wages of the workers. The owners try to crush the embryonic union movement with strikebreakers and fail. They miss the opportunity for a negotiated settlement by misinterpreting the position of the workers. They try to end the strike by reopening the mines, but only a few workers return.

The strike ends, but is not resolved, through the efforts of an engineer who is directly in charge of mine operations. Sensing that the owners may try to reopen the mines, one of the leaders of the strike sneaks down a shaft and creates enough damage so that the mines cannot be put back in operation. Typically, he fails to tell anyone about this, so that when a few workers return, they are trapped in a subterranean sea.

The rescue is a technical administrative problem. It requires decision making, planning, the organization of work teams, and expert supervision as the miners on the surface dig a rescue tunnel toward the spot within the earth where the miners trapped by the flood should be. All the strikers rush to help. The mining engineer channels their enthusiasm, organizes them, and directs them toward the cavern where they rescue the surviving worker. The strike is forgotten.

Zola wrote *Germinal* fifty-seven years before James Burnham wrote *The Managerial Revolution*. In *Germinal* Zola recognized how events and circumstances beyond anyone's personal control would cause power to shift from the owners and workers to the technical managers of the mines. By virtue of their background and administrative skills, the engineers were simply better suited to the environment of the operation. Burnham said much the same thing in developing the thesis that managers were in the process of seizing control of the means of production and the state.

Naturalistic fiction induces a sort of pessimism, not only because naturalistic writers deal with the darker side of human existence but because they let their characters be victimized by forces over which they have so little control. The horror of an individual soldier blown on the winds of circumstance in war made Stephen Crane into America's first premier naturalist with *Red Badge of Courage*. Jack London let his characters in *Call of the Wild* and *White Fang* be pushed around by natural selection and the determinism of Friedrich Nietzsche. Theodore Dreiser and Eugene O'Neill incorporated Freud's belief in psychological determinism into their works.

Some writers, like Dreiser and Crane, were "hard" naturalists in the sense that their stories held little hope for the ability of individuals to gain control over the forces that controlled them. Others, like Zola and London, were "soft" naturalists and less pessimistic. The lives of their characters might be directed by social conditions, but those social conditions were not beyond the reach of reform. To individuals, life might be deterministic, realistic, pessimistic, and grim. At the same time, these authors possessed an underlying optimism about the chances of altering the underlying causes.

A Role for Government

"Social protest" fiction from the turn of the century contains this double view. On the one hand, the doctrines of naturalism and realism encouraged novelists to take a grim view of life and a sour view of institutions. On the other hand, the "soft" naturalists could not resist the temptation to ally themselves with the advocates of reform.

Governmental reform required a radical alteration in public attitudes toward the state. For centuries, human hardship had been viewed as more or less inevitable, and government was not thought to have the power to modify hunger, poverty, disease, or mercantile avarice. The idea that government agencies could be managed by professionally trained public administrators was no less radical. Scholars like Woodrow Wilson and Frank Goodnow, as well as journalists like Lincoln Steffens, strained to promote the idea that government could be run differently. In their efforts to raise the public consciousness on issues such as these, the reformers were joined by novelists. Authors like John De Forest, Henry Adams, Frank Norris, Hamlin Garland, Upton Sinclair, and even Mark Twain made social evil the subject of their novels and held out the possibility of reform. Even in France, Zola's novels were widely cited by champions of social legislation. In this way, social protest writers helped to lay the groundwork for the modern administrative state.

No book or article had as much impact on the public desire for reform as Upton Sinclair's *The Jungle*. The novel, which appeared for sale in early 1906, contained graphic descriptions of the preparation of meat and sausage in the packinghouses of Chicago. Immediately following publication of the novel, Sinclair was invited to the White House by Theodore Roosevelt, who dispatched a secret commission to investigate charges made in the book. President Roosevelt was already familiar with meat industry practices, having testified earlier before Congress that he would have eaten his hat during the Spanish-American War rather than the canned meat sent to his troops under government contract.[14] Up to that point, Congress had sided with meat industry lobbyists. The public response to Sinclair's novel overwhelmed them, however, and before the year was up Congress had passed legislation establishing what would become the U. S. Food and Drug Administration.

The meat industry wanted the public to believe that traditional inspection techniques guaranteed wholesome meat. Not only did Sinclair expose those techniques, showing, for example, how foremen would sneak diseased carcasses past government inspectors. He also explained that a carcass rejected by federal inspectors would simply be sold *within* the state. The federal inspectors "had no authority beyond that; for the inspection of meat to be sold in the city and state the whole force of Packingtown consisted of three henchmen of the local political machine."[15] When one of the three state inspectors, a physician, ordered that some poisoned carcasses at least be treated before sale, the packers had him dismissed:

> So indignant were the packers that they went farther, and compelled the mayor to abolish the whole bureau of inspection. . . . There was said to be two thousand dollars a week hush money from the tubercular steers alone, and as much again from the hogs which had died of cholera on the trains.[16]

The terminal blow was Sinclair's allegation that workers in the rendering plants had been known to slip from high-level walking planks and fall into the melting vats. They emerged later in a somewhat different form, neatly wrapped as packages marked "Durham's Pure Leaf Lard."[17]

Sinclair intended the novel to be an exposé of wage slavery. "I aimed at the public's heart and by accident I hit it in the stomach."[18] The public, he hoped, would be moved by the crippling effect of industrialism on a Lithuanian immigrant and his family. In the beginning Jurgis Rudkus praises "the American way," astonishing himself with the knowledge that he can earn "more than a dollar and a half in a single day."[19] He believes in his strength. "Do you want me to believe," he asks, "that with these arms (and he would clench his fists and hold them up in the air so that you might see the rolling muscles) that with these arms people will ever let me starve?"[20]

Assembly-line bosses quickly pick Jurgis out of the crowd for work. When told that other men have been waiting for a month for work, Jurgis simply points out that they are "broken down."[21] His enthusiasm for Social Darwinism diminishes, however, as industry saps his strength and poverty buries his family. He is cheated by real estate developers, injured on the job, left to recover without pay, blacklisted by the company, and jailed for assaulting his foreman. Family members must cure themselves of horrible diseases, his wife dies at the hands of an ignorant midwife, the women become prostitutes, and his son drowns in a cesspool. Enough darkness flows through this novel to motivate a half century of social legislation.

Sinclair ends the story optimistically, announcing that the liberal labor vote is growing at the polls. He yearned for socialistic reform and government ownership of the packing yards, although the general public contented itself with regulatory agencies and the welfare state. Either way, the resulting growth in governmental responsibility led inevitably to growth in the public administration of meat inspection, public housing, workmen's compensation, unemployment insurance, labor legislation, health care, and environmental protection.

Sinclair's hopes for reform lay with government, for only government was big enough and sufficiently removed from the corrupting influence of commerce to gain control of the deterministic forces that shaped the lives of people like Jurgis Rudkus. Social protest novelists in general have been friendly toward the expansion of government power. Even when government provided the complaint, as in De Forest's treatment of corruption in the army, the solution remained a stronger and better government.

Though friendly toward government, novelists have at the same time been very suspicious of public administration. Public agencies are institutions, and novelists have been taking a skeptical view of institutions since well before the publication of *Huckleberry Finn*. These two points of view appear inconsistent. Reformers agitate for food and drug regulation and then proceed to loathe the administrative agency they have helped to create. Whatever one may think of the apparent contradiction (and later novelists resolve it somewhat), the point must clearly be made that some of the most widely read works in American fiction take a pro-government, anti-administration view.

To Kill a Mockingbird was the third-best-selling novel of its time (the period between 1950 and 1975).[22] Over 12 million copies passed across the sales counter. An academic work on public administration, by contrast, is considered successful if it sells forty thousand copies. Even a novel like *The Jungle*, published before the era of paperbacks, has sold nearly 3 million copies.

Novels, as well as movies made from them, reach a mass audience. They shape public attitudes toward government and public administration. In *Mockingbird*, government remains a saving grace. The story creates serious doubts, however, about the saving powers of local institutions, including public administration.

On the surface, *Mockingbird* is a marvel of local color, a study of southern blacks and whites in the tradition of *Huckleberry Finn.* The story is set in Maycomb, Alabama, told by a precocious girl who is six years old when the novel begins. As she grows older, she is allowed to join the ladies of Maycomb at tea. The ladies assemble to build support for the work of the Reverend J. Grimes Everett, who has removed himself to some distant jungle to sacrifice his health helping the poor Mrunas.

> "Oh child, these poor Mrunas. Living in that jungle with nobody but J. Grimes Everett. Not a white person'll go near 'em but that saintly J. Grimes Everett. The poverty . . . the darkness . . . the immorality—nobody but J. Grimes Everett knows."[23]

The author, Harper Lee, uses the plight of the Mrunas to introduce the position of blacks in this rural southern county seat. Toward the salvation of their own Mrunas, the leading ladies possess a somewhat different attitude.

> "We can educate 'em till we're blue in the face," [explains Mrs. Farrow, the second most devout lady in Maycomb]. "We can try till we drop to make Christians out of 'em, but there's no lady safe in her bed these nights."[24]

A black man in Maycomb has been brought to trial on the charge of assaulting a white woman. Judge Taylor knows that the charges are fabricated. During the trial he stares at the father of the assaulted woman, who has brought the complaint, "as if he were a three-legged chicken or a square egg."[25] The judge asks Atticus Finch, the father of the girl who is narrating the story, to defend the accused. Although Atticus is the town attorney, the representative to the state legislature, and a descendant of the county's founders, his defense of a black man so accused turns nearly all of Maycomb against him. Along with the judge, Atticus is one of the few people in Maycomb who demonstrates any moral courage. The only other characters so endowed are the narrator, too young to have suffered the ill effects of civilization, and Boo Radley, who might as well be a child owing to the fact that in twenty-five years he has never emerged from his house next door.

Atticus expresses his view toward institutions in general with these words to his daughter on the likely fate of Tom Robinson, the accused black man.

> "A court is only as sound as its jury, and a jury is only as sound as the men who make it up."[26]

Institutions have no innate power to improve the quality of the people who file into them. Institutions by themselves are not a civilizing influence; their quality is merely a reflection of the substance of the people who make them up. This personal interpretation of institutional life stands as one of the great themes of administrative fiction.

Based on what the reader knows about the distribution of moral character in Maycomb County, there is not much hope for the falsely accused. One member of the jury holds out for a while, but gives in to peer pressure and the innocent man goes to jail.

If change is to come to Maycomb County, Alabama, as it did a few years after the publication of the book in the presence of the civil rights movement, it will have to come from people outside the area who have the force of a much stronger government behind them. And it must come from the government. The author, Harper Lee, says as much. The virtuous adults in Maycomb are government officials who have seen a bit of the outside world, like Atticus and the judge, not the local folk who are trapped by their social code and local institutions.

Town management remains one of those local institutions. On the way to the trial the narrator describes the public administrators who manage the affairs of Maycomb County:

> To reach the courtroom, on the second floor, one passed sundry sunless county cubbyholes; the tax assessor, the tax collector, the county clerk, the county solicitor, the circuit clerk, the judge of probate lived in cool dim hutches that smelled of decaying record books mingled with old damp cement and stale urine. It was necessary to turn on the lights in the daytime; there was always a film of dust on the rough floorboards. The inhabitants of these offices were creatures of their environment; little grey-faced men, they seemed untouched by wind or sun.[27]

Public administrators are "creatures of their environment," a certain reference to the doctrines of naturalism. When that environment becomes the institutionalized operations of a routine bureaucracy, the people in it, from the novelists' point of view, become "little grey-faced men." In the hands of Atticus, who is untainted by institutions, governmental power is an instrument of reform. But when government transforms its advocates into institutionalized bureaucrats, government becomes the enemy of reform. As a "shaping environment," bureaucratic government elevates the meaner side of humanity.

No Room for Bureaucracy

As the regulatory and social functions of the modern state expanded, so did the bureaucracy. Although novelists viewed government as a great salvation, they viewed bureaucracy with great distress. In the eyes of most novelists, bureaucratic government had the potential to take back the social gains that the progressive reform movement had installed in the modern state. By the middle of the twentieth century, the antibureaucratic novel came to replace novels like *The Jungle* as the premier type of social protest fiction.

Once again, Europeans helped to define the movement. During the time that Max Weber was exploring the inevitability of bureaucratic society, the novelist Franz Kafka was analyzing its effect upon the individuals who would have to work within it. Kafka himself was a public administrator. He worked for the state insurance company of Bohemia in western Czechoslovakia from shortly after his graduation from college until a few years before his death. In contrast to the characters in his stories, Kafka apparently proved to be a competent manager. One of his colleagues described him as reliable, pleasant, and "an excellent member of the staff."[28]

As Weber finished his essay on bureaucracy, across the border in Czechoslovakia Kafka began to write one of his strangest works of fiction. In "The Metamorphosis," Kafka describes in a most extraordinary way how people who work for bureaucracies become "creatures of their environment." The short story describes the transformation of one Gregor Samsa, who has a minor position with a firm. The job requires him to rise at 4:00 A.M. each day. Through the early morning darkness of his bedroom window he can tell that the day will be overcast and rainy.

> Oh, God, he thought, what an exhausting job I've picked on! Traveling about day in, day out. It's much more irritating work than doing the actual business in the office.[29]

Gregor would quit tomorrow, but he needs to pay the debts of his parents and dreams of sending his sister to music school. In bed, he thinks of calling in sick. His position is quite insecure, however, and his boss could fire him for missing the train, "since during his five years' employment he had not been ill once."[30]

> The chief himself would be sure to come with the sick-insurance doctor, he would reproach his parents with their son's laziness and would cut all excuses short by referring to the insurance doctor, who of course regarded all mankind as perfectly healthy malingerers.[31]

Gregor's anxieties have led, during the night, to his transformation. Kafka reports in the first line of the story that when Samsa awoke "from uneasy dreams he found himself transformed in his bed into a gigantic insect."[32] The transformation is not metaphorical; he really is a bug. In fact, he has become a cockroach.

The chief clerk soon shows up at the house to berate Samsa for "neglecting your business duties in an incredible fashion."

> "Your position in the firm is not so unassailable. I came with the intention of telling you all this in private, but since you are wasting my time so needlessly I don't see why your parents shouldn't hear it too.[33]

Gregor has spent the morning trying to figure how to get off his armorplated back and onto the floor. With great effort, he struggles toward the door, unlocks it, and apologizes. His words, however, are heard only as the hisses of an oversized insect. His mother faints, the chief clerk flees down the stairs, and his father beats Gregor back into his room with a rolled-up newspaper, where he remains until he dies.

Gregor's remaining days are less complicated than his life with the firm. His sister brings him food, although his father throws apples at him in disgust. The family becomes productive, taking jobs and taking in boarders.

The idea of a person turning into a cockroach is not strikingly realistic. Yet Gregor's work life is equally dreamlike—disjointed, incomplete, impossible to accept, defying rational interpretation.

Kafka presents a more complete interpretation of the dreamlike quality of modern life in the posthumously published novel, *The Castle*.[34] Released in 1926, *The Castle* is the first major bureaucratic novel. The story, to the extent that one exists, is uncommonly simple. A man comes to a small town at the request of the county to take a position with the government as the local land surveyor. The device seems so simple that a reader could expect the story to be over in a few pages. The person should arrive, take the job, and begin his duties.

It never happens. This simple conclusion turns out to be unattainable. The castle bureaucracy is not capable of recognizing that the surveyor, named K, has arrived in the town, much less of hiring him. K is never able to enter the castle. He starts out for it one day, but it seems to get farther away as he walks toward it. He receives a letter from one of the castle bureaucrats ordering him to report to the superintendent of the town. The superintendent tells him that his arrival has been the result of confusion.

The story has been likened to *Pilgrim's Progress*.[35] In that seventeenth-century novel, a pilgrim sets out to reach heaven and receive the grace of God. Difficulties and temptations are placed in the pilgrim's path. Strengthening his spirit, the pilgrim progresses, and at the end of the story finds himself at the foot of a hill on top of which he sees the gates of heaven. Many odysseys, from *Huckleberry Finn* to *The Castle*, can be likened to this early novel.

K makes his odyssey through the confusion that permeates the bureaucratic world. Unlike Huckleberry Finn, the barriers that K confronts are not giant concerns like slavery. K's frustrations are petty and unnecessary. The castle bureaucracy is not some awesome power exercising total control over the village. Kafka paints the castle bureaucracy as relatively ineffective in its management of what turns out to be a poor, dirty little town. It dominates the life of the town, but the castle bureaucracy is so technically ineffective that it cannot even tell K whether to start his job or go away.

The Castle contains one of the earliest catalogs of bureaucratic sin, some fourteen years before Robert Merton popularized the term *bureaucratic dysfunction*.[36] The novel is difficult to read. Like life in the village, it lacks structure and direction. In 1949, George Orwell published what would become the most widely read statement about life in the bureaucratic state. Orwell set the story in 1984. In fact, he believed that such things were already happening. Orwell's *1984* is a prime example of a novel that is based on a scholarly tome. It is based on the theories of James Burnham, whose *Managerial Revolution* appeared in 1942.[37]

In *The Managerial Revolution,* Burnham attempts to explain the rise of the modern totalitarian state. Burnham observed that power was passing from entrepreneurs, or owners of capital, to managers. The managers, he said, would create a planned, centralized society. Government would control the means of production, and managers would solidify their position as the dominant social class. The working class, Burnham predicted, would disappear. In its place the managers would organize a docile class of clerks, or bureaucrats, to operate the state apparatus and secure the political and economic privileges of the new elite.

Thus *1984* is a novel about Burnham's thesis come true. Like *The Jungle,* the novel is often remembered more for its backdrop than for its plot. There is, for example, the official language of the state, known as Newspeak.

> A great many [words] were euphemisms. Such words, for instance, as joycamp (forced-labor camp) or Minipax (Ministry of Peace, i.e., Ministry of War). The intention was to make speech . . . as nearly as possible independent of consciousness.[38]

Today, in the real world, a nuclear bomb is known as a "nuclear device," the President calls a tax increase "revenue enhancement," and Congress announces a "district work period" when it decides to go on vacation.

The central character in *1984*, one Winston Smith, works for the Ministry of Truth, in the Records Department. It is known as *Recdep*, a collapsing of terms familiar to anyone who has spent much time in Washington, D. C., where the Office of the U. S. Secretary of Defense is known as *SecDef*. The collapsing, said Orwell, not only saves space

on government stationery but, more important, it eliminates moral connotations that cling to whole words like *defense*.

Winston's job in Recdep is to rewrite history. During the previous
year the government had forecast the production of consumer goods
for the current quarter. "Today's issue [of the *Times*] contained a statement of the actual output, from which it appeared that the forecasts
were in every instance grossly wrong. Winston's job was to rectify the
original figures by making them agree with the later ones."[39] In *1984,*
truth is what the bureaucracy says it is. It bears no resemblance to the
actual facts but serves the need of the state to preserve its image of
infallibility and strength.

That image needs maintaining. The striking feature of Orwell's bureaucratic state is its ineffectiveness in running the country. Housing is poor.
"The hallway smelt of boiled cabbage and old rag mats." The gin is
bad, the tobacco falls out of cigarettes, and Smith's face is "roughened
by coarse soap and blunt razor blades."[40] Food is rationed and the rations
are growing smaller, although the state daily announces that they are
growing larger. Winston Smith wonders if life was better before the
"glorious Revolution."

> How could you tell how much of it was lies? It *might* be true that the
> average human being was better off now than he had been before the
> Revolution. The only evidence to the contrary was the mute protest in
> your own bones, the instinctive feeling that the conditions you lived in
> were intolerable and that at some other time they must have been
> different.[41]

The state remains effective at one thing: preserving the power of its
managers. Preserving power is, in fact, the sole purpose of the state.
The government does not, in Orwell's view, exist to improve the lot of
its citizens. When Winston is finally arrested by the Ministry of Love
(i.e., the Ministry of Torture), O'Brien explains the reality behind the
revolution:

> "The Party seeks power entirely for its own sake. We are not interested
> in the good of others; we are interested solely in power. . . . One does
> not establish a dictatorship in order to safeguard a revolution; one makes
> the revolution in order to establish the dictatorship."[42]

Organizational scientists recognize this as the tendency toward goal
displacement. Administrative agencies may be set up with a noble purpose
in mind; at least, the public can be led to believe so. But once the
organization is in place and staffed by average, corruptible people, the
original objectives can get lost as people struggle for power and force
obedience to the rules. Organizational control and personal advancement
may be emphasized so much that they become the actual goals of the

enterprise, the official goals notwithstanding. Michel Crozier, the French sociologist, places power struggles at the center of this theory of bureaucratic pathology.[43]

A few years before Crozier published his theory, the novelist Joseph Heller described this bureaucratic phenomenon in painful detail. Heller's novel dissects the bureaucratic struggles for power and their effect on the operations of a bomber squadron of the U. S. Army Air Force stationed on the Mediterranean island of Pianosa during World War II. The novel, *Catch-22*, remains one of the most distinguished clinical studies of an administrative operation in fictional form.

Here is an ostensibly noble objective—to defeat the invading fascist armies—that can be accomplished only through large-scale governmental administration. Yet when large institutions and average people get involved, operations are damaged beyond all recognition as members of the organization use the war to fulfill their personal ambitions.

In *Catch-22*, Colonel Cathcart orders his pilots to fly in tight formations, even though that is dangerous, because he wants "a good clean aerial photograph he won't be ashamed to send through channels."[44] General Peckem recommends that the men wear full dress uniforms on combat missions "so they'll make a good impression on the enemy when they're shot down."[45]

The officers promise the men that they will be rotated out of combat after flying twenty-five missions. But Colonel Cathcart, determined that his unit will have "averaged more combat missions per person than any other," continues to raise the number to better his chances for promotion.[46] Only by feigning insanity can the flyers escape, because the rules require the colonel to ground any flyer who is mentally unfit to fly. But there is a catch. The rules require the man to ask. If he asks, that constitutes prima facie evidence that he comprehends the perils of combat, has a rational mind, and must keep flying.

> "That's some catch, that Catch-22," [Yossarian] observed. "It's the best there is," Doc Daneeka agreed.[47]

The mess officer, Milo Minderbender, parlays a talent for swapping scarce supplies into an international airborne supply syndicate. In a piercing forecast of the multinational conglomerate, Heller shows Milo buying and selling from the Germans. One day four German aircraft land at the U. S. airbase, delivering yams, collards, mustard greens, and black-eyed peas. Milo chases off the guards when they try to arrest the enemy pilots. The planes are on business for M & M Enterprises. All the troops on the island of Pianosa own shares in the syndicate and participate in the profits. Milo eventually wins a contract to conduct bombing missions for the enemy, at "cost plus six per cent."[48]

"Frankly," says Milo, "I'd like to see the government get out of war altogether and leave the whole field to private industry."[49]

Colonel Cathcart desperately wants to be promoted, whereas General Peckham wants to consolidate Cathcart's operations under his command. Peckham is outmaneuvered by General Scheisskopf, whose specialty is parades, so Milo promises Cathcart a vice-presidency in M & M Enterprises. The object of the war, to defeat the Germans, is never mentioned. "The Germans," Milo retorts, "pay their bills a lot more promptly than some allies of ours I could name."[50] At the end of the story, Yossarian decides to follow the example of Orr, who ditched his plane and escaped from "civilization" by rowing away to Sweden in a yellow rubber raft.

Like *The Castle,* parts of *Catch-22* seem dreamlike and unreal. This device, one of the most important techniques available to writers of fiction, allows the reader to view the organization as it appears to someone who does not accept its premises. By describing organizational life as it appears to outsiders, authors enhance their message about the nature of authority in a bureaucratic world.

In the modern bureaucratic novel, that message often draws on the doctrines of existentialism. As a philosophic doctrine, existentialism holds that life has always been absurd, fundamentally disordered, and lacking in purpose. People may want to believe in a "higher authority," such as the need to respect duly constituted authority, but in the eyes of the existentialist all such beliefs are strictly the result of personal decisions.

In bureaucratic terms, this means that organizational authority exists not as a result of rules of law, but strictly as a result of the willingness of the members of the community to believe that it exists. If a person wants to believe that higher law creates an obligation to obey bureaucratic authority, then bureaucratic authority will appear sanctified, but only because the individual has made a personal decision.

When officials of the organization begin to abuse that authority, to convert it to personal gain, then the exercise of authority will appear disorderly to someone standing outside of the system. The dreamlike quality of organizational life in a bureaucratic novel like *Catch-22* is exactly what the author expects the hero to see. To Yossarian, it is realistic. The officers try to convert Yossarian to their version of reality, forcing him to accept the system as it is, but Yossarian refuses to give in. So long as he stands outside of an alien system, reality will seem disorderly. When the official perception of reality differs significantly from that of the individual viewing it, the system may even come to treat the individual as if he or she were insane.

To emphasize this point, writers of bureaucratic fiction often choose to tell their stories through the eyes of characters who are far removed from the mainstream of society. In *One Flew Over the Cuckoo's Nest,* Ken

Kesey relates events at the state mental hospital in Salem, Oregon, as they appear to one of the inmates. Chief Bromden, the narrator, is driven mad after the federal government seizes his tribal fishing grounds to build a dam. Bromden views the establishment as a machine, which he calls the "combine," that appears and disappears through the fog of his psychosis.

Into this fog struts Randall Patrick McMurphy, an outlaw of sorts who has chosen what he believes will be light duty in the state mental hospital rather than serve time at the Pendleton work farm. The novel deals with the struggle between McMurphy and the chief authority figure in the ward, Big Nurse. The purpose of the hospital, Bromden dimly observes, is to "fix up mistakes made in the neighborhoods and in the schools and in the churches" and send the "completed product . . . back out into society."[51]

Big Nurse seeks to do this through repetitive procedures, adjustment to rules, an inflexible daily routine, and when that fails, electroshock therapy. As she explains to the therapy group she leads:

> "A good many of you are in here because you could not adjust to the rules of society in the Outside World. . . . Perhaps in your childhood you may have been allowed to get away with flouting the rules of society . . . You wanted to be dealt with, needed it, but the punishment did not come. That foolish lenience on the part of your parents may have been the germ that grew into your present illness."[52]

McMurphy brings excitement to the ward, challenging the rules and organizing poker games, a basketball team, and, finally, an insane fishing expedition to the Oregon coast with one of his girlfriends from Portland. The inmates, dulled by years of institutionalization, begin to improve. McMurphy gives them a sense of their own power and ability to live in the outside world. By the end of the story, most of them check out of the ward.

Big Nurse recognizes this not as an achievement of the objective but as a challenge to her authority. Determined to maintain her rigid procedures, she sets a trap for McMurphy, threatening him with shock therapy and, in her final victory, condemning him to a radical lobotomy.

The orderlies wheel McMurphy back to the ward in a vegetative state, a lasting example "of what can happen when you buck the system."[53] That is too much for Chief Bromden, who has regained his strength and sanity. He is a huge man, and before he throws the control panel through the tub-room window and escapes, he uses a pillow to give McMurphy a peaceful death.

As a social protest novel of the realistic school, *Cuckoo's Nest* played an influential role in the movement to deinstitutionalize state mental facilities. As an administrative novel, it is a powerful indictment of bureaucracy and its potential for the abuse of power.

In theory, bureaucracies are designed to reduce the opportunity for misused authority. They are supposed to eliminate particularism, favoritism, nepotism, and any other types of behavior that are irrelevant to the official objectives of the organization.[54] Novelists such as Orwell and Kesey clearly do not buy this argument. As they see it, bureaucratic government increases the opportunity for organizational pathology.

Bureaucracies vest enormous power in the hands of individuals under the pretense that the vesting is done rationally. But individuals, whether a Colonel Sherburn or a Colonel Cathcart, remain imperfect beings. In the eyes of the novelist, large institutions hand over to individuals a form of technology that vastly expands their tendencies to practice mischief, while the impersonality of the bureaucracy shields them from personal responsibility for their acts. Novelists place little faith in the power of formal organizations to restrain such individuals. Given their tendency to emphasize the personal side of life, novelists have come to believe that mischievous officials will outfox whatever such restraints the formal organization tries to place on their desire for power.

The Best Sort of Administration

The most popular bureaucratic novels land on the side of grim pessimism or "hard" determinism. Winston Smith is brainwashed. Randall Patrick McMurphy gets a lobotomy. Meursault, the hero in *The Stranger,* is executed. Alex, of *A Clockwork Orange,* commits suicide. Billy Pilgrim returns to earth and is assassinated in *Slaughterhouse Five.* Ivan Denisovich remains in jail. Even when an author like Jerzy Kosinski musters the courage to let his hero live, it is only because the confusion and inflexibility of the state aid in his escape.[55]

There is little question but that twentieth-century novelists have let centralized bureaucratic authority overwhelm the lives of their characters. Novelists have not, however, held *organization* to be a constant force of darkness. Nor has government been transformed into a disappointment. Quite the contrary. Even if the state bureaucracy is a source of evil, novelists still view governmental action as a saving power, provided that the government is properly organized.

In *A Bell for Adano,* John Hersey reveals one method by which government can become an instrument for reform while avoiding the entanglements of bureaucracy. *Adano* is one of a small but impressive group of novels that outlines a successful public administration. It is probably the finest administrative novel in print. Rowland Egger said of it:

In 269 pages of simple, beautiful, vivid fiction, Hersey has said more
that is valid for all sincere and humble men everywhere who are honestly
attempting to discharge their administrative mandates than is contained
in all the pompous tomes which have so far appeared on the subject of
public administration.[56]

Adano is a small town on the southern coast of Italy. The story takes
place during the liberation of Italy by the allied armies in World War
II. The Americans liberate the town, the fascist mayor flees to the hills,
and troops disappear up the coast. Adano comes under the command
of the Allied Military Government. Its administrator, until an indigenous
government can be established, is Major Victor Joppolo, U. S. Army,
an Italian-American from the Bronx. His governmental experience is
limited to a short tour of duty with the New York City Departments of
Sanitation, Taxation, and Finance.

Lacking administrative experience, Joppolo's first act as "mayor" of
Adano consists of tearing up the standard operating procedures manual
for military government officials. Reading it seems such a waste of time;
it is so voluminous, and so much work waits to be done. The town
needs bread, food, and fish. There is no water, no sanitation, no transport,
no commerce, and no bell. Only a month earlier, the fascists took the
town bell and melted it down for munitions. Most of all, the townspeople
tell Joppolo, they need a bell.

Joppolo walks through Adano to the docks to speak with Tomasino,
the fisherman. Tomasino believes that Joppolo has come to arrest him
for not paying protection money to the Supervisor of the Fisheries.
Joppolo wants him to go back to fishing. Under the Americans, Joppolo
tells him, Tomasino will not have to report to a bureaucrat.

> "There will no longer be a [supervisor] over the fishermen. I want a fisher-
> man to be in charge of the fishermen."[57]

Joppolo asks Tomasino to organize the fishing. Tomasino hates authority, having been its victim for so many years, and does not want to be
its instrument. Joppolo labors to convince him.

> "It is possible to make your authority seem to spring from the very people
> over whom you have authority. And after a while, Tomasino, it actually
> does spring from them, and you are only the instrument of their will."[58]

The boats cannot return to their fishing grounds without a navy escort
because the waters around Adano have not been cleared of mines. The
navy lieutenant in charge of the harbor claims that he does not have
the authority to permit Tomasino to leave.

"We'd have to get permission from ComNavIt and he'd have to refer it to ComNavNaw, and they're both Admirals. Not a chance."[59]

Joppolo chides the lieutenant for hiding behind the admirals. "Don't they give you any responsibility at all?"[60] After a short discussion, Lieutenant Livingston issues the order for an escort. He then helps the town raise the fascist motor ship Anzio, sunk in the waters off Adano, which contains 10,000 tons of crude sulphur that the townspeople can sell at a great profit. He even arranges—after Joppolo gives him the idea—for the U.S.S. Corelli to donate its ship's bell to the town.

Joppolo is a master of organization. He gets things done by getting other people to do them, by convincing them that they have the responsibility for seeing things through. In a short time, the town is functioning, running itself, and Joppolo is not really needed.

This is just as well, because the second plot that runs through the book is the effort of Captain Purvis, who is one of Joppolo's assistants and a very uptight military type, to get Joppolo removed. The "by the numbers" system of military discipline lurks alongside Joppolo's efforts to delegate responsibility and eventually does him in. Joppolo is shipped off to Algeria, having countermanded an order from the commanding general regarding mule carts. Higher-ups would have never noticed the countermand except that Purvis snuck it through to the General's desk.

Joppolo knew from the beginning that he would not be mayor of Adano forever. Eventually, the town would be turned back to the Italians. He knew he had a short period of time—shorter than he thought, in fact—to prepare the town for self-government. He wanted to make sure that when that time came the town would be ready for self-government and not go back to the old authoritarian, fascist system.

"Now that the Americans have come," Joppolo tells the town leaders, "we are going to run the town as a democracy." His view of government is not one of a businesslike institution, providing permanent services, but of a self-help mechanism based in the community. This is Joppolo's gift to the land from which his parents came. "You are servants of the people of Adano," he continues. "And watch: this thing will make you happier than you have ever been in your lives."[61]

Through *Adano* and other works like it, novelists suggest strategies for transforming government into an agent of reform without producing the difficulties that arise from the struggles for power within large, permanent bureaucracies. It is a very Jeffersonian view of administration.[62] When administration works, or at least starts to work, the hero possesses a clear sense of the social purpose of the enterprise. Joppolo realizes that the people of Adano must learn how to exercise authority over themselves or someone else will exercise it over them. Randall Patrick

McMurphy believes, much more than Nurse Ratched, that the purpose of the state asylum is to return people to the outside world. McMurphy plots to help them escape while Big Nurse plans to make them more dependent upon her and the institution.

Such a hero's stay in the community is typically temporary. A theme first expressed in the gospels, the idea of an emissary who appears for a short period of time and galvanizes the community has proved to be an enormously popular vehicle in the world of creative literature. In one of the best Depression-era administrative novels, *In Dubious Battle,* John Steinbeck describes how labor organizers from San Francisco transform passive farm workers into an effective strike force.[63] The organizers know that they will be run out of the Torgas Valley by the farm owners. Before this happens, the workers must be taught how to organize themselves. If the leaders succeed, then their confidence will be passed on to the workers and institutionalized.

Where the hero works for a large institution, as in the case of Joppolo and an endless number of spy novels, the institution typically gives the hero the opportunity to exercise the maximum degree of personal responsibility. The hero rarely relies upon his or her formal authority. The reliance upon this sense of personal responsibility means that the hero typically works with a very small cast of supporting characters. Although Joppolo serves in the U. S. Army, a gargantuan institution, he arrives in Adano with less than half a dozen men. The success or failure of Joppolo's mission depends upon the grit of a very small number of people. To novelists, who have long held that people count for more than institutions, this is a perfectly natural strategy.

It is startling to realize the degree to which writers of fiction pass on their personalized view of organizational life to the general public through novels that ostensibly have nothing to do with administration. Technically speaking, an administrative novel should be one in which the principal character is a public servant, conflicts arise from organizational issues, and administrative operations are described in some detail.[64] Using such criteria, *The Exorcist,* the second-best-selling novel of its time, falls outside of the administrative category.[65] Yet it transmits a subtle but powerful message about administration, one that plays to popular suspicions about the curative powers of large institutions.

In *The Exorcist,* three of the principle characters are on the payroll of large institutions. Two are Catholic priests. The other is a detective with the District of Columbia police department.

These characters operate well apart from their institutional systems. The detective and the priest who performs the exorcism are "loners" rather than "organization men." The possessed girl, Regan, is treated at home. The one attempt to seek institutional help, when physicians try to diagnose Regan's disorder, ends in frustration.

In *Adano,* institutional authority remains a source of evil. In *The Exorcist,* a second case of individual success, institutions simply stay out of the way. In a few cases, institutional authority actually backs up the curative powers of heroes in the stories. Such administrative novels are fairly rare. It is hard to find a work of fiction that removes the residue of evil from institutions while sticking to the idea that the quality of administrative leadership will affect the outcome of the story.

One such novel is *The Andromeda Strain.* The author, Michael Crichton, deals with the awful possibility that a biological experiment might get loose and start killing people. In this case, the death germ is not manufactured by genetic engineers but scooped up in outer space by an experimental satellite. As the microorganism races to wipe us out, scientists and public officials race to isolate the microorganism, identify it, and find an antidote. In Crichton's view, this is a job for a special type of organization.

The team of physicians and bacteriologists who must solve the puzzle work for top flight hospitals and universities. They are on call, should the federal government need them in an emergency such as this. Having never worked together as a team, they have less than four days to identify and neutralize the microorganism, or it will neutralize them. This is obviously a temporary assignment, in the best meaning of "the coming adhocracy."

The members of the team are introduced, as it were, into a supporting government institution constructed ahead of time for this contingency. The institution, known as the Wildfire facility, is located in an uninhabited section of Nevada. The government has disguised it as a U. S. Department of Agriculture facility, even offering tours for farmers interested in the problem of growing corn in low-moisture, high-alkalinity soil. The team members open a door marked "Storage."

> They found themselves staring at a narrow cubicle lined with rakes and hose and watering hoses.
>
> "Step in," Leavitt said.
>
> Hall did. Leavitt followed and closed the door behind him. Hall felt the floor sink and they began to descend, rakes and hoses and all.[66]

The actual Wildfire facility consists of five levels, all underground. The levels are organized hierarchically, but it is not a hierarchy of authority. The administrator does not work on the top floor, the typing pool in the basement. It is instead a hierarchy that corresponds to the stages that the team must go through to isolate and neutralize the microorganism. Sterilization and decontamination of the team begins on level I.

This continues, in increasing degrees, through level IV. The Scoop satellite, along with the only two survivors from the landing site, rests on level V. It is as if the facility was physically designed by turning a PERT chart on end and slicing it up into five floors.

The total resources of the facility are at the disposal of the five-member team for the duration of their stay. The team is temporary; the facility permanent. It is as graphic a description of matrix management as one can find in creative literature.

The Wildfire facility is designed to maximize the creativity of the five-member team, not only in the biochemical process of isolating the andromeda strain but also in deciding what to do if the killer strain eats its way out of the protective seals of level V. Here at last is a novel in which the heroes are not frustrated by an unresponsive bureaucracy or by the stupidity of their superiors.

The Wildfire facility contains the most sophisticated computer-assisted detection devices, described in detail. There is even a nuclear bomb, preset to vaporize the facility and its personnel if the microorganism should get loose. At no time do these high-tech devices, nor the chain of command, defeat the work of the team. The technology and organization of Wildfire is designed to leave the five-member team in charge.

The Andromeda Strain, along with other futuristic novels such as *Congo* and *2001: A Space Odyssey,* take a step beyond traditional administrative novels like *A Bell for Adano.*[67] In Adano, Joppolo is a wise administrator, but he is eventually done in by the system. The system is represented by General Marvin, who is a thinly disguised version of George S. Patton. A mule cart on a country road slows the General's progress. He orders his men to throw the cart off the road and "shoot that goddam mule," then storms into Adano and issues an order banning all cart traffic into and out of the town.[68]

> "Keep the goddam carts out of this town, you hear me?"
>
> "Yes sir, I'll take care of that right away."
>
> The General shouted: "Right away? That's not good enough for me."[69]

Mule carts are the principle means of transport in Adano. To enforce the order, Joppolo would have to shut down the town. The order, which must seem sensible enough to General Marvin, would prove disastrous if actually implemented at the local level. In a fully deterministic novel, like *1984* or *The Castle,* the author might let some local cog actually execute the order. *Adano,* however, is half optimistic. Joppolo countermands the order, although he is eventually removed for doing so.

In *Andromeda Strain,* organization disappears entirely as a source of evil or stupidity. Evil, ever a constant element in the fictional formula, is still present, but in the *Andromeda Strain* it is the evil of nuclear and biological chemistry escaped from its cage, not administration. Because administration plays a supporting role to the ability of people to carry out their responsibilities, it is cast in a favorable light. Novelists are capable of taking a friendly view of administration when people are left in charge.

The Third Dimension

Novelists have been sensitive to the importance of administrative power ever since the 1880s. In *Germinal,* which appeared in that decade, the workers fail because they lack rudimentary administrative skills. By the time that John Steinbeck wrote *In Dubious Battle,* he was ready to let workers persevere by adopting paramilitary organizational tactics and a few human relations techniques. Wartime novels like *Adano* and *Mister Roberts* showed how individuals operating apart from the orthodox organizational system could command greater loyalty and better results than their superiors operating within it.[70] In the era of the space program, novelists experimented with nonbureaucratic forms of organization.

In these views of administration, the optimism of the author varies with the degree to which individual responsibility can triumph over institutional authority. In novels like *Cuckoo's Nest,* where institutional authority appears to win out, the administrative system remains a source of evil. In novels like *Andromeda Strain,* where authority takes a back seat to individual responsibility, the author feels more comfortable painting a picture of an assisting public administration.

The emphasis upon individual responsibility arises in large measure because of the way that writers of fiction tell their stories. A work of fiction will not succeed unless it is personified and told through the mind of some individual. To do otherwise would render the story dull and scholarly. The scholar, it must be noted, faces no similar compulsion. In fact, it would be quite out of form for a scholar studying administration to personify in any way a research report.

By showing us what organizations look like to individuals who are affected by them, writers of creative literature bring to administration a perspective that scholars are in many ways compelled to avoid. Mort Kroll has called this perspective the "third dimension" of public administration.[71] Kroll suggests that scholars deal with administration on basically one of two levels. The first dimension is that of the formal organization and its official objectives. Through the second dimension scholars explore aspects of the informal organization, sometimes in terms of the whole organization but practically never below the level of the informal group. Very few scholars, Kroll observes, have been able to successfully treat the organization from the private, individual dimension.

Because they deal from this "third dimension," novelists can stress certain aspects of administration that tend to be de-emphasized in scholarly literature. First of all, novelists emphasize the quality of people as a factor in administration much more than scholars typically do. The quality of people cannot be quantified easily, and scholars tend to avoid it as a variable or simply presume that the organization is made up of average people. The novelist, on the other hand, is much more inclined to tie the success of administration to the goodness or intelligence of the people who staff the organization. As Hersey says in the introduction to *Adano:*

> Theories about administering occupied territories all turned out to be just theories, and in fact the thing which determined whether we Americans would be successful in that toughest of all jobs was nothing more or less than the quality of the [people] who did the administering.[72]

Because they deal from the third dimension, novelists are much more likely to believe that personalities and private motives play an important role in administrative decisions. Officially, a decision such as the promotion or approval of a new program should be made strictly on the basis of organizational objectives. This ideal, as any practitioner knows, can be compromised in practice. As Kroll points out, scholars have difficulty dealing with private motives in administrative decisions. Private motives are difficult to identify with any degree of confidence. The tools of the administrative scientist are not suited to the task of making private motives explicit, even though everyone suspects that they exist.

The tools of the novelist, on the other hand, are ideally suited for displaying this dimension of decision making. Operating from the world of fiction, the novelist is free to describe private motives and ask the reader whether they are reasonable given the direction of the story. In *The Godfather,* the best-selling novel of its time, Mario Puzo assigns a great deal of importance to the role of private motives in building up organizations.

Puzo does not ignore the official side of administration. He describes, for example, the formal organization of the Corleone family. These "links of the chain," as Puzo calls them, are a major source of strength for the family enterprise.[73] The family relies upon the formal organization, however, only for routine business and the maintenance of loyalty. When it comes to really important decisions, Puzo retreats into the realm of personalities. When the singer Johnny Fontane asks the Godfather how in the world he can get a producer to place Fontane in a movie that he wants so badly, Corleone replies:

"He's a businessman," the Don said blandly. "I'll make him an offer he can't refuse."[74]

To those who have not read the book, be assured that the offer that Don Corleone makes to the producer of the picture has nothing to do with the formal financial objectives of the movie industry.

The emphasis upon private motives works to shape the fictional view of the "ideal" organization. Hostility to centralized, bureaucratic administration is no accident of art. In the eyes of the novelist, organizations are no better than the people who make them up. The people who make them up, by and large, are imperfect. That is a theme that stretches from Colonel Sherbern in *Huckleberry Finn* to Colonel Cathcart in *Catch-22*. Institutions and technology may have improved over the last century, but people have not. They are still capable of exhibiting stupidity, cruelty, and blind ambition. Even Joppolo, says the author of *A Bell for Adano*, has his faults, although Hersey is quick to point out that they are "attractive, human" weaknesses.[75]

Because human imperfections form so much of their subject matter, novelists are naturally suspicious of efforts to concentrate authority in the hands of officeholders like Colonel Cathcart, Big Nurse, or General Marvin. The idea that authority can be devolved upon "the office, not the man" runs contrary to the novelist's instincts about human nature. Distribute authority to offices, the novelist would say, without accounting for variations in the individuals who would occupy them, and you are letting yourself in for a lot of trouble.

In addressing his ally, Joppolo challenges Lieutenant Livingston to exercise the *responsibility* that has been delegated to him. The choice of words is revealing. Joppolo does not ask Livingston to exercise his authority. "Why do you have to go running to the Admirals?" Joppolo asks. "Don't they give you any responsibility at all?"[76]

Both Henri Fayol and Woodrow Wilson understood the need to invest a sense of responsibility among officials in order to guard against the abuse of authority. "Generally speaking," said Fayol, "responsibility is feared as much as authority is sought after."[77] Fayol understood that executives would face little resistance in delegating authority. Bureaucrats seek authority. The harder problem is how to make responsibility equal authority, not the reverse. Bureaucrats turned that phrase around and insisted on the priority of authority. Wilson, who is too often credited with trying to take policy-making out of administration, actually believed that "large powers and unhampered discretion" create the "indispensible conditions of responsibility" that protect against the abuse of power. "There is no danger in power," he said, "if only it be not irresponsible."[78]

The debate over whether or not this constitutes a "valid" view of administration has been going on for at least forty years. Scholars accustomed to empirical proofs remain skeptical about conclusions drawn from works of fiction, even ones where novelists labor to produce realistic pictures of life or express scientific theories in their work. No matter how realistic the writer seeks to be, the facts in any work of fiction will always be distorted to some degree to fit the purpose of the story.

All facts, of course, suffer some degree of distortion when they pass through the minds of individuals, as they inevitably must. Novelists understand this. Rather than minimize this distortion, which is the approach of the scientist, the novelist explores it. Relative to empirical research, fiction makes its most significant contribution to administrative understanding in those areas where individual perceptions matter most. This is the realm of private motives and personal character. Here fiction does more than simply reflect public attitudes toward government and public administration. It provides insights into administrative issues that are difficult to approach with other tools. The validity of works of fiction in areas such as these must ultimately be judged on the basis of the credibility of the ideas that the author seeks to express and whether the experiences shared with the reader seem reasonable given the purpose of the story.[79]

Endnotes

1. Mark Twain, *The Adventures of Huckleberry Finn.* (New York: Harper and Row Perennial Classics, 1884), p. 121. In all cases, the original date of publication is shown, even though that may not be the date of the cited edition.
2. Twain, op. cit., p. 125.
3. Twain, op. cit., p. 216.
4. Twain, op. cit., p. 127.
5. Twain, op. cit., p. 129.
6. Twain, op. cit., p. 128.
7. Ernest Hemingway, *Green Hills of Africa* (New York: Charles Scribner's Sons, 1936), p. 22.
8. Twain, op. cit., p. 186.
9. Twain, op. cit., p. 187.
10. Twain, op. cit., p. 254.
11. Woodrow Wilson, "The Study of Administration," *Political Science Quarterly* 2:217 (June) 1887.
12. Wilson, op. cit., p. 219.
13. Emile Zola, *Germinal* (Middlesex, United Kingdom: Penguin Classics, 1885).
14. Upton Sinclair, *The Jungle* (New York: New American Library, 1906). For this statement as well as reactions to the novel, see the "Afterword" in this edition prepared by Robert B. Downs, p. 344.
15. Sinclair, op. cit., p. 98.

16. Sinclair, op. cit., pp. 98–99.
17. Sinclair, op. cit., p. 102.
18. Sinclair, op. cit., p. 349.
19. Sinclair, op. cit., p. 46.
20. Sinclair, op. cit., p. 26.
21. Sinclair, op. cit., p. 26.
22. The sales figures are taken from Alice P. Mackett and James H. Burke, *Eighty Years of Best Sellers, 1895–1975* (New York: Bowker Company, 1977).
23. Harper Lee, *To Kill a Mockingbird* (New York: Warner Books, 1960), p. 233.
24. Lee, op. cit., p. 235.
25. Lee, op. cit., p. 253.
26. Lee, op. cit., p. 208.
27. Lee, op. cit,, p. 164.
28. Ronald Hayman, *K: A Biography of Kafka* (London: Weidenfelf and Nicholson, 1981), p. 73.
29. Franz Kafka, "The Metamorphosis," from *The Penal Colony: Stories and Short Pieces* (New York: Schocken Books, 1913), p. 68.
30. Kafka, "Metamorphosis," op. cit., pp. 69–70.
31. Kafka, "Metamorphosis," op. cit., p. 70.
32. Kafka, "Metamorphosis," op. cit., p. 67.
33. Kafka, "Metamorphosis," op. cit., p. 77.
34. Franz Kafka, *The Castle* (New York: Schocken Books, 1926).
35. John Bunyan, *The Pilgrim's Progress* (New York: New American Library, 1687).
36. Robert Merton, "Bureaucratic Structure and Personality," in Robert Merton et. al., *Reader in Bureaucracy* (New York: The Free Press, 1952).
37. James Burnham, *The Managerial Revolution* (New York: John Day, 1942).
38. George Orwell, *Nineteen Eighty-Four*, from Irving Howe, ed., *Nineteen Eighty-Four: Text, Sources, Criticism* (New York: Harcourt, Brace & World, 1963), p. 135.
39. Orwell, op. cit., p. 18.
40. Orwell, op. cit., p. 2.
41. Orwell, op. cit., p. 33.
42. Orwell, op. cit., p. 116.
43. Michel Crozier, *The Bureaucratic Phenomenon* (Chicago: University of Chicago Press, 1964).
44. Joseph Heller, *Catch-22* (New York: Dell Publishing Company, 1955), p. 337. For an administrative interpretation of the novel, see Peter Sederberg, "Bureaucratic Pathology: A Diagnostic Vision of Catch-22," *The Bureaucrat* 2:316–324 (Fall) 1973.
45. Heller, op. cit., p. 224.
46. Heller, op. cit., p. 435.
47. Heller, op. cit., p. 47.
48. Heller, op. cit., p. 261.
49. Heller, op. cit., p. 266.
50. Heller, op. cit., p. 263.

51. Ken Kesey, *One Flew Over the Cuckoo's Nest* (New York: New American Library, 1962), p. 40.
52. Kesey, op. cit., p. 171.
53. Kesey, op. cit., p. 270.
54. For a presentation of this argument see, for example, Charles Perrow, *Complex Organizations* (Glenview, Illinois: Scott, Foresman and Company, 1972).
55. Albert Camus, *The Stranger* (New York: Vintage Books, 1942). Anthony Burgess, *A Clockwork Orange* (New York: W. W. Norton & Company, 1962). Kurt Vonnegut, *Slaughterhouse Five* (New York: Delta Books, 1969). Alexander Solzhenitsyn, *One Day in the Life of Ivan Densovich* (New York: Praeger Publishers, 1963). For additional bureaucratic fiction, including the Kosinski short story, see Marc Holzer, Kenneth Morris and William Ludwin, eds., *Literature in Bureaucracy: Readings in Administrative Fiction* (Wayne, New Jersey: Avery Publishing Group, 1979).
56. Rowland Egger, "Fable for Wise Men," *Public Administration Review* 4:371–376 (Autumn) 1944.
57. John Hersey, *A Bell for Adano* (New York: Bantam Books, 1944), p. 71.
58. Hersey, op. cit., p. 71.
59. Hersey, op. cit., p. 73.
60. Hersey, op. cit., p. 73.
61. Hersey, op. cit., pp. 41–42.
62. For a definition of the Jeffersonian view of administration, see Lynton Caldwell, *The Administrative Theories of Hamilton and Jefferson* (Chicago: University of Chicago Press, 1944).
63. John Steinbeck, *In Dubious Battle* (New York: Bantam Books, 1936).
64. Dwight Waldo, *The Novelist on Organization and Administration: An Inquiry into the Relationship Between Two Worlds* (Berkeley: Institute of Governmental Studies, 1968).
65. William Peter Blatty, *The Exorcist* (New York: Bantam Books, 1971).
66. Michael Crichton, *The Andromeda Strain* (New York: Dell Publishing Company, 1969), pp. 98–99.
67. Michael Crichton, *Congo* (New York: Avon Books, 1980). Arthur C. Clarke, *2001: A Space Odyssey* (New York: New American Library, 1968).
68. Hersey, op. cit., p. 47.
69. Hersey, op. cit., p. 49.
70. Thomas Heggen, *Mister Roberts* (Boston: Houghton Mifflin, 1946).
71. Morton Kroll, "The Third Dimension: The Uses of Fiction in Public Administration," *Dialogue: The Public Administration Theory Network* 3:9–12 (March/April) 1981.
72. Hersey, op. cit., p. v.
73. Mario Puzo, *The Godfather* (New York: G. P. Putnam's Sons, 1969, p. 49.
74. Puzo, op. cit., p. 39.
75. Hersey, op. cit., p. v.
76. Hersey, op. cit., p. 73.
77. Henri Fayol, *General and Industrial Management* (New York: Pitman Publishing Company, 1916), p. 22.
78. Wilson, op. cit., p. 213.

79. Morton Kroll discusses the validity of fiction in these terms in "Administrative Fiction and Credibility," *Public Administration Review* 25:80–84 (March) 1965. For other discussions of administrative fiction not cited above see Rowland Egger, "The Administrative Novel," *American Political Science Review* 53:448–455 (June) 1959. Howard E. McCurdy, "Fiction, Phenomenology and Public Administration," *Public Administration Review* 33:52–60 (January/February) 1973. Thomas R. McDaniel, "The Search for the 'Administrative Novel,' " *Public Administration Review* 38:545–549 (November/December) 1978.

Epilogue

Ralph Clark Chandler
WESTERN MICHIGAN UNIVERSITY

RALPH CLARK CHANDLER is Professor of Political Science at Western Michigan University. He has written or co-authored seven books in public administration, constitutional law, and theology. They include, with Richard A. Enslen and Peter G. Renstrom, The Constitutional Law Dictionary: Individual Rights, *which received the American Library Association's Outstanding Academic Reference Book Award for 1985. He has also published some twenty-three articles in a variety of professional and scholarly journals. Professor Chandler consults extensively with governmental organizations and is a frequent speaker at workshops and special events across the nation. He holds the doctorate in Public Law and Government from Columbia University and graduate degrees in ethics from Union and Princeton Theological Seminaries.*

I

The classic psychological defense of the legitimacy of American administrative institutions is that advanced by Gary L. Wamsley and his colleagues in Chapter 9, the so-called Blacksburg Manifesto. The manifesto argues that there is a reflexive relationship between an individual's emotional substructure or unconscious and the conscious processes monitored by government. The unconscious designs projects of personal aggrandizement that must be compared by government to collective needs and social concerns. The administrative institutions that have the responsibility of defining the public interest against legitimate private interests are called upon to employ processes of moral reasoning, judgment, and, finally, lawful coercion that render them a free-fire zone for the displacement of the fears, hopes, and anxieties of people they may have regulated. Institutions that presume to apply state power for humane ends and that reward, deprive, distribute, and redistribute in the name of society as a whole cannot expect to have their administrative machinery viewed dispassionately. Thus *bureaucracy* has become an epithet in modern political discourse.

Capitalism is largely responsible for this unhappy development. It is singularly well suited to provide for the gratification of the self. The genius of the market is that it can easily and quickly give expression to the emergent needs and tastes that are constantly forming in the personal unconscious. It is this aspect of capitalism that correctly leads advocates of laissez-faire to equate it with individual freedom. Suppression of the emotional substructure has never been much of a problem in capitalist America, which is one reason Americans experience more than their share of expressed violence.[1] For most Americans the ambition that stems from unconscious economic, social, and psychological impulses can proceed unimpeded. The exception, of course, is our disturbingly large and persistent underclass.

The marketplace can so facilitate the working out of the personal unconscious and emotional substructure that it sometimes overwhelms the conscious and collective side of society. As wants are expressed and satisfied with increasing speed and facility, a point is reached where new wants are created by the process itself. Society loses its bearings, its moral and practical points of reference are obscured, and the public standards that are essential for the exercise of collective human discretion and judgment fail. Wamsley and company see administrative institutions as a cooling, containing, and directing foil to the capitalist economic system. They are the other half of the personal-social reflexivity equation. Public administration represents the collective consciousness of American society. It serves as a vehicle for mature efforts to bring to bear on our common problems and the planning of our uncertain future the knowledge, reason, and moral judgment that are the heritage of our enacted Constitution.

The Federalists would recognize this noble vision. One might even hope they would now admit the extent to which they overestimated the capacity of interest to play the role of virtue in the commercial republic they founded.

II

The psychological dimension of administrative legitimacy in modern America is infinitely more complex than the reflexivity equation allows. First, it is more complex at the level of economic analysis. As Dwight Waldo points out in Chapter 3, liberalism and economics developed in the same historical matrix. Each supports the other in ways the names of John Locke, Adam Smith, and David Ricardo bring to mind. The names of Jeremy Bentham, John Stuart Mill, and John Maynard Keynes also signify that the relationship is highly controversial.

Liberalism is subject to qualifying and differentiating adjectives. One brand is distinguished from another and is held antagonistic thereto. And these are not just academic debates. They are the verbalization of contests in the real world in which one person's right to liberty may be viewed as another person's condemnation to penury and servitude. Recently, liberalism has moved from its moorings in civility, compromise, pragmatism, and commitment to democratic norms and drifted toward ideological rigidity, intolerance, and increasing disrespect for American institutions and traditions. Liberalism today is dealing with the totalitarian temptation.

The emergence of economics as a field of specialization and a preeminent social science runs parallel with both the rise of capitalism and the development of classical liberalism. Economics and capitalism together enunciate the widely accepted idea that society exists apart from government and indeed is prior to and greater than government. The vast increase in productivity achieved by the dynamics and organization of capitalism—organization that put science and technology in capitalism's service—fostered the idea that life finds its central meaning in the consumption of goods and services. A large and varied literature justifies the economization of the world.

The stakes in the economization process are higher than those envisioned in the reflexivity equation. Government in the economization model is not just an obstacle to the pursuit of private interests. It is a source of enrichment and a general utility-maximizing mechanism. Thus in the Spring/Summer 1985 issue of the *Cato Journal*, a self-described libertarian or "free market-orientated" publication, the current Director of the Office of Management and Budget (then chairman of the Federal Trade Commission), James C. Miller III, argued that the Postal Service's 140-year monopoly on first-class mail should be abolished and private enterprise allowed to deliver letters "just as it did in the Old West."[2]

Miller's article is a polemic against public administration, an open invitation to companies to enter profit-making arrangements with high-volume business mailers such as banks and utilities *under the sponsorship of the United States government.*

Miller's argument is more than a restatement of the public-choice economic theory of a generation ago. Under that theory public agencies should compete to provide citizens with goods and services instead of acting as monopolies under the influence of organized pressure groups. Because the citizen is a *consumer* of government goods and services, the theory goes, administrative responsiveness to individual citizen demands would be increased by creating a market system for governmental activities based on microeconomic theory. In this market system the citizen-consumer would be given a choice, as in free-enterprise economics, between competing services.

The new public-choice economics is as much politics as economics.[3] It is also a fundamental challenge to the validity of the assumptions on which American government is based. The Founders assumed, for example, that groups are good. Federalist theory assumed that groups of individuals with common interests would act on behalf of their common interests much as single individuals would act on behalf of their personal interests. John Locke assumed that individuals join groups to further their common interests. The social contract is a common interest, an unspoken agreement, that brings civilized people together to draft constitutions and form governments. Paul Appleby assumed the public interest to be a product of the activity of organized groups. Chester Barnard used the assumption of common interest focused in group cooperation to help formulate the foundations of modern organization theory.

Against these doctrines of pluralist faith the new public-choice economics asserts that people will *not* act to advance their common or group objectives unless they are coerced to do so, or unless some separate incentive distinct from the achievement of the group interest is offered to the members individually. Social contract theory is rejected, and the elemental forces of personal aggrandizement without any necessary regard for others are reengaged. President Reagan's remark that "I am not my brother's keeper; I am my brother's brother," epitomizes the position. Theorists might analyze the possible ramifications of this position along a spectrum ranging from how mail will be delivered to citizens in rural and ghetto areas, where it is not cost-effective for companies to go, to theological reflections about the reasons for the fall of man in Genesis 3 and God's negotiations with the Archangel Lucifer in Job 1.

This is really not so grand a fight as that between good and evil, however. Neither is it fundamentally a fight about economic theory. The Reagan administration does not emphasize market-based means of implementing public policy, and it does not popularize such phrases as "free the forces of the market" just because of the neoclassical economic principle that markets generate an optimal allocation of goods and services. The Reagan administration simply does not trust public administrators or administrative institutions. It perceives the public bureaucracy to be a generalized failure and threat. The fight is about the role of government in modern society. The administration subverts public administration through such ideas as urban enterprise zones and voucher systems to help low-income families purchase housing in the private market because it believes government to be too inefficient adequately to meet the needs of the American people. Underneath the fight about the role of government is the problem of efficiency.

III

Waldo said he had puzzled over the concept of efficiency in Chapter 10 of *The Administrative State*. He observed in 1948 that efficiency was used in the literature of public administration as premise and value in arguments that could only be construed as arguments in political theory. But unlike the other concepts Waldo studied, efficiency had no place in the history of political ideas.

The reason is that efficiency is not a word from the public realm. It is a word from economics. Waldo mused that it seems to be a denotative and hard principle, but on examination it becomes a rather vaporous and protean one. Nevertheless, in the last century efficiency has become a sacred concept in the American political and administrative cultures. Its esteemed place in the liturgy of public discourse is a fact of the centennial this volume commemorates. But in what way is efficiency a value, Waldo wondered. How valuable is it, and in relation to what? Is it possible to turn efficiency on itself and subject it to a cost-benefit analysis?

Efficiency is most frequently understood as a public word in terms of its analogy to business. When presidential candidates campaign against the inefficient bureaucracy, for example, they are assuming that government and business are run in the same way. The knowledge, skills, and tools of the private sector manager are interchangeable with those of the public sector manager. Despite Wallace S. Sayre's celebrated critique of the generic model of management—that government and business are alike in all unimportant respects—the fact remains that there are notable similarities.[4] All complex organizations, for example, face problems of allocating resources, defining their domain, securing legitimacy, maintaining political support, and managing succession. Both government and business have a wide range of jobs; both have jobs that greatly affect the general citizenry; and both have intrinsically dull jobs. Industry has the assembly line and government has paperwork. Both business and government have units that range from small to large. There are mom and pop stores, and there are mom and pop local governments. There is General Motors, General Dynamics, and General Electric, and there is Detroit, Los Angeles, and New York.

What presidents discover when they try to govern, of course, is that Sayre was more right than wrong, and that the efficiency model from business and the scientific management period of public administration simply does not adequately describe the real requirements of managing in the public sector. Perhaps educators and ethicists will eventually make the same discovery. To design public administration curricula on the assumption that competence consists of mastering certain administrative techniques, and to define ethical behavior as scrupulously following the established procedures of a value-neutral public service, is to invite into the professional tent a rather grotesque perversion of both the civic culture and imperial traditions of public administration.

Because efficiency remains the standard by which public administration is often judged and found wanting, a careful examination of the efficiency model as it applies to public administration is long overdue. The concept of efficiency does *not* apply to public administration in at least the following ways:

(1) *The private sector is profit-oriented, whereas the public sector is not.* Because profits result from selling goods and services at prices that are higher than costs, costs are minimized in the private sector in order to maximize profits. Industry has an incentive to hire only those people who are needed. Not only does industry avoid overhiring, it hires only those people who will be productive. Private sector employees whose productivity declines tend to be demoted or dismissed.

Government, on the other hand, is concerned with providing quality services with as few resources as possible. But government lacks the profit incentive that encourages an effort to keep personnel costs down. Government is considered by the public, and sometimes by legislation, to be a proper employer of people who may not otherwise be employable or a place where social equity can be more legitimately pursued than in the marketplace. The use of seniority as an automatic basis for promotion in many civil service systems breeds mediocrity, limiting employee motivation to innovate or excel. With no clear standards for defining competence, and no linkage between revenues and results, there is little incentive to improve performance.

The civil service, masquerading under the guise of professionalism, actually promotes unprofessional practices by protecting government personnel against demands for accountability. It has created independent, insider-dominated power groups of long-term career officials who often defy the authority of politically appointed administrators who only serve for short terms. The system protects the upward mobility opportunities of those who already have access to agency jobs and who control examination procedures.

Thus the civil service insider machine that has evolved in government bureaucracies has much more political staying power than the oldline patronage machine it replaced. It perpetuates the image of professionalism while it blocks outside review of employee performance. It does not follow, however, that the insider machines in government are less efficient than the insider machines in industry.

(2) *The private sector is competitive, whereas government in most instances operates as a monopoly.* A corporation attempts to keep prices and production costs low in order to have competitive advantage over other firms. If personnel costs push prices upward, the firm's sales will fall and so will profits. But a city fire department, for example, has a monopoly on its service. Consumers do not have a choice about quality and cost. Consumers cannot decide which fire department to call, or which water department to use. Similarly, government has the option of raising tax rates and borrowing extensively to offset higher operating costs. A corporation might be forced out of business if personnel costs rise excessively, but government is not under such a constraint. Rapidly rising expenditures coupled with tax increases can result in taxpayer revolts and can lead to bankruptcy, as in the close call New York City had in the late 1970s, but governments are not threatened with extinction.

(3) *The public sector is labor-intensive, while the private sector is not.* Industry uses raw materials and machines that turn materials into finished goods. Government, however, typically provides services rather than products, and in most instances these services must be provided by people rather than machines. Industry frequently has a choice between people and machines. If the cost of labor increases, industry can replace expensive workers with less expensive machines. The profit incentive encourages such shifts in personnel utilization.

Much of what government does defies mechanization. Mail-sorting machines, for example, may be able to replace some workers, but people are still required to deliver the mail. Yet it is inefficient from a management point of view to deliver mail to rural areas. Such areas, as well as inner-city areas, would suffer if mail delivery were a profit-making enterprise. It is a general proposition of the liberal democracies, however, that government has a responsibility to promote the common good at the price of comparative efficiency by private sector standards.

(4) *Society expects more of government workers than it does of private workers.* High ethical standards are expected of public employees, whereas some private sector practices may be shrugged off as "just business." Different standards of quality control are used, and different levels of visibility pertain. Automobile manufacturers may have hundreds of thousands of callbacks to correct deficiencies in specific models of a car—a clear and expensive example of poor management— but one horror story from the public sector tends to cancel out the callback story in the daily newspaper. In fact, such mistakes are human problems that have little to do with whether the person or persons responsible work in the private or public sector.

Bureaucratic horror stories go a long way toward perpetuating the myth of private sector superiority in terms of management efficiency. Charles T. Goodsell gives five examples of these stories in *The Case for Bureaucracy:*[5]

a. A Chicago woman undergoing chemotherapy for cancer of the breast applied for Medicare. She received a computer-produced letter saying she was ineligible because she had died the previous April.

b. A chronic alcoholic was arrested and mistaken for another man. When he protested, his claims of misidentification were diagnosed as paranoia and schizophrenia, and he was committed to a mental hospital.

c. A woman on welfare ran up astronomical medical bills because of her terminal illness. She was denied Medicaid on grounds that her welfare payments created a personal monthly income of $10.80 above the eligibility maximum.

d. The Department of Energy set out to declassify millions of documents inherited from the Atomic Energy Commission. Eight of the released documents contained the basic design principle of the hydrogen bomb.

e. A unit of what is now the Department of Health and Human Services sent fifteen chimpanzees to a Texas laboratory for the purpose of launching a chimp-breeding program. All were males.

It is generally supposed that errors such as these never happen in a private corporation. They do, of course, but the details of them are not as easy to obtain. The details are important, however, and myth-destroying ones are frequently left out of newspaper accounts of public sector mismanagement. Goodsell points out that in case (a), for example, a new computer-based information system was being installed at the time the letter was sent, and the bugs had not yet been worked out of it. In case (b), another man with exactly the same name, a similar physique, and an almost identical birth date was indeed in the police records. In case (c), personal income maximums are not set by local welfare departments, and, if exceeded by them in any amount, the result is an adverse state audit that has its own effect on public confidence. And so on. But explanations do not make good copy.

(5) *Managers in the private sector typically have greater freedom in personnel matters than public sector managers.* A corporation has considerable flexibility in how it hires and fires people. Public personnel administrators, on the other hand, have many more rules and regulations to follow in personnel actions. This distinction should not be overdrawn, however. Both federal and state laws affect most private sector personnel policies. Occupational safety, pension systems, unemployment compensation, equal employment opportunity, and labor relations are all regulated by government.

For some time public servants had no protection in their jobs. Constitutional provisions of due process did not apply to public employment because the Supreme Court said a person did not have a right to a public job.[6] But over a period of twenty years the presumption of due process was gradually built into administrative procedures applicable to public employment. A liberty interest was found in 1972,[7] and a property interest was found in 1974.[8] Due process must now be shown before such interests may be terminated in public sector employment.

With regard to protections afforded employees in the private sector, traditionally these employees had no more job rights than those set forth in their written employment contracts.[9] Again, courts and legislatures have in recent years accorded more and more protections to private sector workers. They cannot now be terminated for reasons specified in both the National Labor Relations Act and the Civil Rights Act, and they cannot be fired for taking actions in compliance with statutory obligations. Courts have also implied reasonable contracts of employment based on custom, and they have said that employer actions motivated by bad faith, malice, or in retaliation for an employee exercising his or her constitutional rights may be overturned as being contrary to public policy.

The fact that public personnel administrators have more rules and regulations to administer than their private sector counterparts is often overlooked by proponents of the myth of private sector superiority. Public employees' political activities are limited by the Hatch Act and implementing regulations, for example.[10] Public employees are subject to codes of ethics, residency requirements, proscriptions against certain associations and ownership of certain interests, and in some cases they are subject to dress codes more restrictive than those in the private sector. The part of the myth of private sector superiority that says public sector employees are less accountable for their actions is clearly not supported by the facts.

(6) *Authority is more structured in the private sector than in the public sector.* In a corporation an employee is rarely uncertain about who the boss is. Authority in government is much more dispersed. Not only are there conflicting lines of authority within the executive branch, but there are also continuing uncertainties about the relative powers of the executive and legislative branches vis-à-vis public employees. Workers are expected to be responsive both to their administrative superiors and to legislators. Public employees may find themselves in positions where they are responsible for implementing a statute having strong legislative support, but which is basically opposed by the political leadership within the executive branch.

The management model of a private company is constructed like a pyramid. At the top of the pyramid senior managers play two roles. Part of the time they work with each other formulating policy, and part of the time they implement policy by managing a segment of the organization under them. This arrangement results in a number of organizational characteristics:

a. There is a relatively small group of policymakers.

b. The policymakers bring the expertise of their segment of the organization to the policy-making process.

c. The policymakers carry the decisions of the policy-making group back to their segment of the organization and try to implement them.

d. The policymakers bring further insights gained from attempting to implement policy back to the policy-making group and decide whether and how the policy should be modified.

Thus the corporate decision-making model has the characteristics of a self-correcting system: input, throughput, output, and the crucial dynamic feedback loop. Like a biological organism, the system exchanges with its environment and mechanically and homeostatically restores equilibrium to elements out of synchronization.

The doctrine of separation of powers creates a number of problems for this kind of systems theory in public administration. For one thing, the policymakers, the legislature, comprise a very large group of people. They represent diverse backgrounds, and they do not gain feedback experience from implementing their decisions. They must make policy based on indirect experience—from the testimony of witnesses before various legislative committees, for example. The result is the opposite of the private sector model, in which a small and tightly knit group of senior executives make policy and help carry it out in the organization.

A second problem for public policymakers is that well-intentioned politicians may vote contrary to their better judgment. They may need to gain another, presumably higher, legislative objective; or they may need to represent the views of their constituency in cases where the constituency's views differ from their own.

Third, all authoritative policy decisions in the public sector are made through written law in the legislative branch. It could not be otherwise if another branch of government is to implement policy it did not make. The private sector rarely attempts to document a policy decision to the extent necessary to produce a law. It has learned the value of ambiguity. If there is a dispute about what public law means, it is the courts—yet another separated power not part of the original policy-making process—that interpret legislative intent and/or constitutional principle.

Fourth, the senior executives who implement legislative policies may be from the political party that opposed the policy in the legislative branch. Professing the neutrality of the civil service, they may find ways to dilute or defeat policies with which they disagree.

The public sector executive, whether elected, appointed, or a career civil servant, is trapped in an organizational structure that is deliberately designed to be weak. Given these built-in constraints on public management efficiency in the United States, it is remarkable that public administrators act as efficiently as they do.[11]

(7) *The executive branch of government is led by amateurs and politicians with short tenure, while the private sector tends to have more experienced executives at the top.* A departmental secretary is appointed by and serves at the pleasure of the chief executive. Continuity of leadership in departments and major agencies is rare in any large government. Politically appointed executives obtain positions in part because of their roles in partisan politics, whereas private sector executives are more likely to be chosen because of their technical and managerial efficiency. This does not mean that politically appointed managers are incompetent or that private sector managers are always capable. It means that different sets of criteria are frequently applied in selecting executives in the two sectors.

Because top public sector executives have limited tenure, they have little time to develop a power base from which they can effectively deal with insiders and engage in the long-term planning necessary to get significant innovations under way. In fact, the new political appointee often enters an agency run by long-term career bureaucrats who have seen his or her kind come and go since Harry Truman or even Franklin Roosevelt. The new administrator who is supposed to have some political power cannot match the oldtimer in real political power, the kind that knows the files and the personal idiosyncrasies of the work force and has the institutional memory Max Weber said was a key to administrative effectiveness.

(8) *Personnel in the private sector tend to have a single purpose to serve, whereas public sector employees typically serve multiple purposes.* Industry uses people to make products and deliver services. Government does that, too, but it uses people for other purposes as well. Government jobs have been used to reward the politically faithful, patronage being a common characteristic of all governments. Government employment is used to aid veterans. It is used to stimulate the economy. Unemployed people are hired by government as a device for increasing consumer spending. Public employment is sometimes a disguised form of welfare. Government jobs have been handed out as part of a regional quota system. Until 1978, the federal government set quotas on the mix of its workers in the Washington, D.C., area, for example. By setting limits on the number of people hired from each state, it was thought the bureaucracy would be more representative of all the people.[12]

Given all these purposes of government employment which have little to do with management efficiency and which even militate against it, the criterion of efficiency appears to be misplaced in the extent to which it is used to evaluate the effectiveness of American public administration.

IV

Why does efficiency persist as sacred doctrine and ethical norm for professional education and administrative practice? The economization model does not quite tell all. It is true that policy analysis, program evaluation, and the decision sciences are all output oriented, and that output, like efficiency, is a word from economics. But efficiency is also an historical artifact from the lore of public administration itself. It characterized public administration in its golden age, and it is difficult for modern administrative thought to admit that the golden age has passed.

Let us conclude by reiterating Louis C. Gawthrop's trenchant analysis in Chapter 6. There have been two other periods in which public confidence in government has been at the same low ebb as exists in the 1980s: (1) in the 1880s, when the excesses of political cronyism had functionally disenfranchised millions of American citizens, and (2) in the 1930s, when citizens became almost comatose as public policy stagnated, the machinery of government broke down, and economic collapse resulted.

Faith in democratic government was restored in the first instance by the emergence of a professional career service, and in the second by an inventive public administration that combined ideas of administrative efficiency with political effectiveness. Public confidence in government was epitomized by the elite status of the Bureau of the Budget in the early 1950s. Efficient and politically sagacious public administration was largely responsible for overcoming the turbulence of a global depression and a global war, and the nation was grateful. Not an eyebrow was raised when Norton Long wrote in 1952: "Accustomed as we are to the identification of elections with both representation and democracy, it seems strange at first to consider that the non-elected civil service may be both more representative of the country and more democratic in its composition than the Congress."[13]

Gawthrop says those halcyon days of the early 1950s also triggered policy decisions that gradually encircled the federal administrative cadre in a constrictive grip. The long-term result is that today a once proud profession stands immobile and virtually mute in the face of an accelerating dynamic of systems change. Now the methods of administrative efficiency and political efficacy that served us well for forty years have become value-drained techniques of expediency. By 1983, even Luther Gulick feared that these techniques had "doomed the human species to extinction in the near future."[14] He said the problem of scale or what he calls "the significance of size" has much to do with bringing about the crisis of public confidence in the ability of administrative institutions to prevent catastrophe.

> I have the feeling that the sheer size of the government and the complex interrelations of the national and world economies are crucial factors demanding recognition in any consideration of the future of democracy and public administration.[15]

Among the factors contributing to the steady deterioration of administrative competency since about 1953 are these, according to Gawthrop:

1. the insidious psychological destructiveness of McCarthyism, with questions of disloyalty, distrust, and disdain reviewed intermittently from year to year;
2. the opening up of congressional committee oligarchies as a result of television's influence on political campaigning, a major effect

being the decline of the bureau chief component of the iron triangle
of policy-making;

3. the establishment of the supergrades, drawing a distinction between
policy careerists at the GS-16, 17, and 18 levels and proceduralists
at the GS-15 level, thus fragmenting political and administrative
power;

4. the venture of the Eisenhower Administration into global responsibility for the civil service in implementing the containment policy,
a policy that extended the competency of the American administrative system beyond its capacity; and

5. the fragmentation of the bureaucracy into a multiplicity of suzerainties, with centrifugal forces occasioned by single-issue politics, the
new politics of litigation, and a system of intergovernmental relations that defies administrative control.

In Gawthrop's analysis, the federal bureaucracy is stretched and balkanized virtually beyond recognition. It has been politicized in a manner
far more insidious than that envisioned by the most blatant spoilsman.
Yet the career service endures. It endures despite the indignity, distrust,
suspicion, and injury visited upon it for over three decades. It persists
in a manner that suggests that if democracy and civic virtue are to
have any meaning in the twenty-first century, these values will have to
be realized through the machinery of public management and mediated
by public administrators.

The traditions of public service that have intermittently inspired the
impulses of American democracy in the past can do so again if a new
way of thinking about public service can be developed. Gawthrop believes
that innovative thought will have at least these characteristics:

1. The politics of being will no longer be repressed by the politics
of having and doing.

2. Public administration will no longer be paralyzed by a trained incapacity to discuss the difference between means and ends, facts and
values, and the processes and purposes of policy.

3. The individual citizen will no longer be defined almost solely in
terms of his or her aggregate characteristics.

4. The qualitative aspects of democracy will no longer be understood
primarily in terms of quantitative measurements.

5. In carrying out its transfer function in an exemplary way, the career
service will take the time to consider the qualitative consequences
of its actions.

In short, public administration will develop an antiefficiency model.
It will understand how Gresham's law applies to its current difficulties:

concern for the mechanics of having and doing drives out concern for being. And if all other efforts at understanding itself fail, it will resort to Howard E. McCurdy's opinion in Chapter 17 that the reality of any period of history can be captured in the leading fictional characters of its literature.

For Gawthrop, that fictional character in the 1980s is undoubtedly George Smiley, the career civil servant in the best-selling spy novels of John le Carre. Smiley is a generic model of the modern public administrator. Proceeding without sympathy or enthusiasm but with absolute dedication to his profession, he combines the best vocational training of Max Weber and the unchastized Luther Gulick. In a manner that would have warmed the heart of Louis Brownlow, he is totally driven by a passion for anonymity. He is a parade example of the kind of public administrator who emerged in the 1930s, combining professional expertise with political astuteness and prudent pragmatism. Smiley makes the science of muddling through a pure art form.

If Smiley represents the best of public administration as it developed from the 1930s through the early 1950s, he also represents the worst of the profession as it has emerged in the 1980s. The legacy of Smiley has frozen the civil service in its current inert, unimaginative, nonresponsive, and ethically vacuous position. He could easily subscribe to the Code of Ethics of the American Society for Public Administration because the code says so little and says that so badly.

Smiley has no difficulty with the operating maxim that means and ends are indistinguishable. In fact, means become ends. Process becomes purpose. Any effort to raise higher-order and more fundamental questions about purpose is dismissed as either theological, philosophical, literary, or naive. This is particularly true with the Byzantine model of American pluralist and incremental decision making. In the struggle between the forces of good and evil that has gone on since the 1950s, public administration has been forced to operate somewhere on the other side of midnight, feeling its way through the murky gray of whatever works. Whatever works becomes the good. The lowest common denominator of agreement becomes the ethical. This in fact describes the process by which the ASPA's Code of Ethics was adopted in the early 1980s. By refusing to take the moral basis of leadership seriously, the Professional Standards and Ethics Committee of the Society confused and trivialized ethics to the extent that it probably innoculated the profession against the real thing. An earlier version of the code produced by a drafting subcommittee of the Professional Standards and Ethics Committee dealt straightforwardly with the problem of moral reasoning, but the draft fell victim to a co-optation process that produced a child of procedural, instrumental, and political necessity. The drafting subcommittee felt that any discourse on ethics requires some elegance of thought and language, some demonstrated knowledge of moral philosophy and constitutionalism, and some subtlety of understanding of the public administrator as trustee of public good.[16]

Both Smiley and his Soviet counterpart, Karla, kill without compunction. Gawthrop says both men see the world as a world of reverse negatives, distorted perspectives, and blurred images. In the universe of the permanent career service, seemingly incongruous criteria are often imposed on administrative behavior as accepted measures of worth. Scholastic aptitude tests become the measure of the quality of one's education. Crime statistics, caseloads, urban renewal grants, and body counts are used as surfeits of performance.

The treatment accorded professional colleagues who cannot or will not conform to the rules of the game is unequivocally unambiguous in the world of Smiley and Karla. The nonconformists are branded traitors. In domestic agencies they are whistle-blowers, or, at the day-to-day operating level, they are simply troublemakers. Very little tolerance is accorded such discordant behavior even if it is characterized by hope.

It is increasingly clear that as efficient as Smiley and Karla are, they must not be the heirs of the future. They are detached pragmatic purists who know love only in terms of the specialized and silent service of the self. They are narcissists who have lost their souls.[17]

V

John le Carre argues through the character of George Smiley that public servants should no longer make a virtue of disinterest by suspending judgment on the normative consequences of their actions. Neither should they continue to avoid moral responsibility by maximizing their interest in the problems of aggregate policy clusters and projecting that concern to higher and higher levels of analytical abstraction. Graded ranks of aggregation cannot replace graded ranks of authority and responsibility in ethical practice.

There is a rich psychological literature dealing with the fragmentation of conscience characteristic of aggregate thinking. In such a process, moral blame can easily be transferred from the individual to the bureaucracy or to the process itself. By abnegating personal responsibility for organizational decisions, one also neglects his or her moral obligation to recognize, face, and examine personal failure. Psychiatrist M. Scott Peck says that evil is exemplified by an individual's consistent use of scapegoating in order to avoid the anguish of self-examination. He describes people who habitually involve themselves in group escape as "people of the lie."[18]

The professional consciousness advocated by Gawthrop is motivated by the willingness of individual administrators to render critical judgments at the most basic level of policy output: the existence and quality of life of individual citizens. Administrators will think larger and act smaller as they try to translate values on a scale more directly related to people who have names. Democratic theory and administrative politics will converge at the point of professional ethics. Public policies and programs will be converted into ethical encounters between public administrators and unnumbered persons. Reciprocal relationships will forge linkages of trust and loyalty between public servants and citizens, and these linkages will provide a dynamic new source of energy for the revitalization of American democracy.

Looking to the methods of public administration's golden age will not do anymore. Surely that is obvious to all concerned. Privatization is the answer from economics, made more creditable by its kinship to the archetypal idea of efficiency. Public administration's answer, as otherworldly as the notion may sound, has to do with the soul and ontological ethics, the ethics of being. The soul of the state and the souls of the servants of the state must be rediscovered.

Gawthrop notes that over forty years ago David M. Levitan concluded his essay on "Political Ends and Administrative Means" with these words:

> An outstanding government administrator once remarked that "administration must have a soul." That, in a way, magnificently summarizes the thesis I have been developing. It needs to be added, however, that administration should contribute to the fuller development of the soul of the state.[19]

How can public administration today hope to carry out such an exalted mandate as the fuller development of the soul of the state? Gawthrop believes the answer is deceptively simple. Public administration can re-unite citizens to the state by enhancing the essential integrity of each individual citizen. It can do that by assuming the responsibility for delineating the distinction between the unauthentic politics of having and doing and the authentic politics of being. The former breeds personal isolation, narcissism, and self-aggrandizement. The latter breeds the capacity for innovation, renewal, and hope.

Talk of the soul-building function of public administration will be perceived as ludicrous by many. Gawthrop rightly observes that the political dyslexia that threatens our capacity as individual citizens to adapt effectively to systemic complexity is seen by them as being *caused* by public administration. To assign the virtues of the future to people who are viewed as being responsible for a host of villainies in the past is a gamble that many of us would describe as foolhardy and dangerous.

Yet the historical fact is that public administration has had dramatic successes in the past in destroying the sense of anomie that has separated citizens from government.

Public administration has been too modest in pointing out its accomplishments and too passive in response to the political abuse it has received. Inversely related to public administration's tendency to understate its role and responsibility is the predisposition of individual administrators to define their role and responsibility too broadly. The attacks on such definitions by political mountebanks invariably are qualified to exclude truly dedicated and conscientious career civil servants. Nevertheless, in the absence of a positive, cohesive, and professional voice responding to political ploys, the strategy of choice for most individual public administrators is to save themselves.

Such a strategy means that individual administrators must be prepared to conform to whatever bell-shaped curve of behavior happens to prevail within any given political regime at any given time. Prudence precedes principle when there is no unified profession to insist on the reverse. It should not be surprising, therefore, that individual administrators frequently attempt to minimize risk and maximize certainty in their efforts to preserve personal reputations. Nor should it be surprising that individual administrators try to disassociate themselves from the popularly perceived negative image of their profession, and that in carrying out their duties they tend to make a virtue of disinterest by suspending judgment on the normative consequences of their actions.

It is precisely at this point that the requirements of professional ethics intervene. The ambiance of anxiety provides the context for personal and social ethical choices, not the ethical choices of proceduralism but those of ontological responsibility, not the ethics of having and doing but the ethics of being. H. Richard Niebuhr said the only practical utility of ethics is its capacity for clarifying a pattern of meaning in the crucible of risk and obedience.[20]

To the historical artifact of efficiency, then, modern administrative thought compares the idea of critical realism. The basic ethical question "What should I do?" is no longer just an empirical question of performance by technique or code. It is an existential and relational question based on the anticipated response of another self in a transaction and rooted in the ancient idea of covenant.

The exclusive function and responsibility of public administration is to create a network that turns the amorphous body politic into an organic matrix of authentic human relationships. Somewhere in the organic compounds of public service there may be diamonds more valuable than the gold of efficiency. In the third century of the administrative state they can provide the cutting edge of a new birth of American democracy.

Endnotes

1. According to Handgun Control, Inc., in 1980 handguns killed 4 people in Australia, 8 in Canada, 8 in Great Britain, 23 in Israel, 77 in Japan, 18 in Sweden, 24 in Switzerland, and 11,522 in the United States.

2. James C. Miller III, "End the Postal Monopoly," *Cato Journal,* 5:149–155 (Spring/Summer) 1985. See also in the same issue Stuart Butler, "Privatization: A Strategy to Cut the Budget," pp. 325–335.

3. See Mancur Olson's description of the new public choice economics in Ralph C. Chandler and Jack C. Plano, *The Public Administration Dictionary* (New York: John Wiley, 1982), p. 96.

4. David Rogers, "Managing in the Public and Private Sectors: Similarities and Differences," *Management Review,* May 1981, pp. 49–54. One of the opening salvos of the discussion of the question of whether there are generic principles of management that have universal application was fired by Michael A. Murray in "Comparing Public and Private Management: An Exploratory Essay," *Public Administration Review* 5:364–371 (July/August) 1975. Following the next year was Hal G. Rainey, Robert W. Backoff, and Charles H. Levine, "Comparing Public and Private Organizations," *Public Administration Review* 6:233–244 (March/April) 1976. Although Murray suggested that public and private organizations were converging and faced similar constraints and challenges, and that management in all types of organizations should be viewed as a generic process, Rainey, Backoff, and Levine said their inquiry into the comparative question pointed to the conclusion that "it is premature to discount the significance of public-private differences and their implications for management training and practice" (p. 233).

5. Charles T. Goodsell, *The Case for Bureaucracy, A Public Administration Polemic* (Chatham, NJ: Chatham House Publishers, Inc., 1983), p. 3. Goodsell argues persuasively that the myth of private sector superiority is persistent because it is useful. It serves the twin functions of validation and justification. It validates people whose constructions of reality do not square with the empirical world, people who fail to achieve personal goals in interaction with public agencies, and people who wish to mask interest group activity as their sacred duty to save the republic. It justifies ideological politics. It enables conservatives to rationalize the decimation of welfare programs and liberals to associate efficient management with endangering civil liberties. In both validation and justification, bureaucracy serves as an effective enemy. It justifies righteousness, intensifies feelings, focuses enmity, diverts attention, and silences critics. It is abstract enough to fit anyone's value system.

6. *Bailey* v. *Richardson,* 341 U.S. 918 (1951).

7. *Board of Regents* v. *Roth,* 408 U.S. 564 (1972).

8. *Arnett* v. *Kennedy,* 416 U.S. 134 (1974).

9. This is the rule of employment at will. See *Corbin on Contracts,* Section 684. Arthur L. Corbin, *A Comprehensive Treatise on the Rules of Contract Law,* Vol. 3A (St. Paul, MN: West Publishing Company, 1960), pp. 224–231.

10. The Supreme Court has consistently upheld Hatch Act restrictions, finding

a compelling governmental interest reasonably calculated to achieve a legitimate purpose and not overly broad in scope. See *United Mine Workers* v. *Mitchell*, 330 U.S. 75 (1947) and progeny requiring a showing of nexus.

11. Donald A. Curtis, "Management in the Public Sector: It Really Is Harder," *Management Review*, October, 1980, pp. 70–74.

12. Subcommittee on Civil Service and General Services, Senate Committee on Governmental Affairs, *Repeal of Apportionment Requirement: Hearings*, 95th Congress, First Session (Washington, DC: Government Printing Office, 1977).

13. Norton Long, "Bureaucracy and Constitutionalism," *The American Political Science Review* 46: 812 (September) 1952.

14. Luther Gulick, "The Dynamics of Public Administration Today as Guidelines for the Future," *Public Administration Review* 43:195, 1983.

15. Luther Gulick, "Response" to Terry L. Cooper, "Citizenship and Professionalism in Public Administration," *Public Administration Review* 44:150 Special Issue/(March) 1984.

16. Ralph Clark Chandler, "The Problem of Moral Reasoning in American Public Administration: The Case for a Code of Ethics," *Public Administration Review* 43, 1983.

17. William F. Buckley is not comfortable with the fact that le Carre finds little difference between Smiley and Karla. "I have in the past been discomfited by trendy ventures in ideological egalitarianism," he writes, "such that the reader ends by finding the Communist spy and the Western spy equally heroic." William F. Buckley, Jr., "Terror and a Woman," *The New York Times Book Review*, March 13, 1983, p. 23.

Five years earlier Denis Donoghue took Graham Greene to task for taking a position similar to that of Buckley: "A reflective person cannot avoid the limp conclusion that we are all innocent, a conclusion not much more convincing than that we are all guilty. It is certainly possible to go through life by withholding judgment, keeping every moral act in suspension until we have known the worst and transcended it. Disinterested virtue is possible in practice as in theory. The passing of sentence can be postponed indefinitely, but meanwhile the gangsters have taken over the world." Denis Donoghue, "A Novel of Thought, Action, and Pity." (A critique of Graham Greene's *The Human Factor*) *The New York Times Book Review*, February 26, 1978, p. 1.

It is helpful for the reader to bear in mind that le Carre is assuming the moral responsibility of passing judgment on the immorality of Smiley and Karla so the gangsters will not take over the world.

18. M. Scott Peck, *People of the Lie* (New York: Simon and Schuster, 1983). See especially Chapter 6, "Mylai: An Examination of Group Evil," pp. 212–253.

19. David M. Levitan, "Political Ends and Administrative Means," *Public Administration Review* 3:359 (Winter) 1943.

20. H. Richard Niebuhr, *The Kingdom of God in America* (New York: Harper and Brothers, Torchbooks, 1959), p. 1.

INDEX

Adams, Henry, 23
Adams, John, 129–131
Adams, John Quincy, 397, 403
Administration: The Art and Science of Orga-
nization and Management (Lepawsky),
494
Administration
and federalism, Wilson's view, 228–229
Roman nature of, 97–98
Administration and Society, 496
Administrative authority, delegation by
Congress, 268–269
Administrative Behavior (Simon), 45, 46, 47
Administrative law, second administrative
state, 21–22
Administrative management, school of, 43
Administrative Office of the United States
Courts, 22
Administrative politics, 250–251
Administrative Powers Over Persons and
Property (Freund), 490
Administrative principles, 42–45
academic activity, 43–44
administrative management theorists,
43
challenges to, 46–47, 48
early phase, related works, 42, 43
focus versus locus, 44
POSDCORB, 45, 48, 418, 421–422
Administrative Procedure Act (1946), 26
Administrative Science Quarterly, 56, 60
Administrative state, 5–33
versus bureaucratic state, 5–6, 25–29
characteristics of, 6
constitutional principle, 116–149
Anti-Federalists and, 123–125, 126
constitution, examination of, 117,
121, 123
House of Representatives and, 143–
148
Senate and, 125, 133–142

separation of powers, 126–133
Wilson's work, 118–119
definitions of, 5–6
first administrative state, 6–7, 9–12
characteristics of, 9–11
Federalist contributions, 10–12
Jacksonian reforms, 13–14
founders, 5, 8–9
politics and, 32
retrenchment (1980's), 29–32
second administrative state, 14–25
administrative law, 21–22
classical management theory, 15
corruption, attack on, 23–24
decline of, 27–28
Federalist tradition and, 15
Federal Register, 22
government corporations, 18
grant-in-aid programs, 22
intellectual activity, 15, 19–20
major achievements, 24
management analysis, 17
personnel management, 19
Presidential leadership and, 24–25
procedural analysis, 22
public administration education, 15,
19–20
public employment, 18–19
rational decision making, 20–21
regulatory agencies, 17–18
selection by merit, 18–19
staff concept, 15–16
Taft Commission, 17, 20
technological advances, 22–23
Administrative State: A Study of the Political
Theory of American Public Administration
(*Waldo*), 5, 47, 308
Administrative Trainees (ATs), 516–517
Administrators, *See* Public administrators.
Advisory Commission on Intergovernmental Relations, 231, 236, 243, 252

Agencies
administrative agencies, tasks of, 302
impact of 1960's, 303
performance analysis, 302
staff, impact of, 301
Agency perspective, public administration,
300–304
Aiken, Howard, 23
Akerman, A.T., 14
American politics, pluralist tradition in,
164–167
American Society for Public Administration (ASPA), 496
founding of, 41, 44
Anderson, William, 238, 239
Andromeda Strain (Crichton), as bureau-
cratic fiction, 566–568
Anti-Federalists, 120, 124
and House of Representatives, 143–145,
146–148
influence of, 124–125
and Senate, 135–137, 138–139, 141,
142
Appleby, Paul H., 50, 363, 493, 578
Appointments, role of Senate, 138–140
Appropriations bills, post-Revolutionary
period, 356–359
Appropriations rider, 283
Arendt, Hannah, 121, 122, 123
Arora, Ramesh K., 501
"Art of Governing, The" (Wilson), 224
Arthur, Chester A., 408
Articles of Confederation, fiscal issues,
352, 393
Ashby's Law of Requisite Variety, 4, 31
Ash Council, 422
Association for Public Policy Analysis and
Management, 64

Barnard, Chester I., 45, 331, 423–424
Baucus, Max, 278, 280
Beard, Charles A., 20
Beer, Stafford, 31
Behavioral approach
impact of, 94
and public administration, 47, 49, 52,
62
Behavioral Theory of the Firm, A, (Cyert and
March), 56
A Bell for Adano (Hersey), as bureaucratic
fiction, 562–565, 568
Bennis, Warren G., 426
Bicameralism, 132–133

Blacksburg Manifesto, 575–576
Bok, Derek C., 27
Boling, Richard, 278
Boutwell, George S., 399
British influences, budget system, 354–
358, 395–396
on American government, 98–99
Browne, Vincent J., 351
Brownlow, Louis, 20, 266
Brownlow Committee (1937), 19, 22, 366,
420, 422
Broyard, Anatole, 207, 209
Bryce, Lord James, 24, 383
Bubble Act (1719), 387
Buchanan, James, 398, 404
Budget, 273–277
recent legislation
Budget and Impoundment Control
Act (1974), 26, 275–277, 282,
360, 369–370
Gramm-Rudman-Hollings Act, 276–
277
Budget and Accounting Act (1921), 17,
268, 349, 360–361, 363
Budget and Impoundment Control Act
(1974), 26, 275–277, 282, 360, 369–
370
Budgeting (historical view), 345–373
balanced budget, ideal, 385–386, 397–
399, 402
Civil War period, 399
Colonial period, post-Revolutionary
changes, 354, 351–353
internal improvements, 402–409
nineteenth century
activities of period, 361
Jacksonian era, 360, 397–398
Ways and Means Committee, 359–
360, 382
post-Revolution, 351–359
appropriations bills, 356–359
Constitution, on spending power, 353
Department of the Treasury, beginning of, 356–357, 359
Hamilton's contributions, 354–358,
395–396
Jefferson's contributions, 359, 396–
397, 402–403
Secretary of Treasury, beginning of,
354, 357, 358, 359
Treasury Board, 353
Ways and Means Committee, 356,
358

recurrent theme, 348
twentieth century
  Budget and Accounting Act (1921),
    349, 360–361, 363
  Budget and Impoundment Control
    Act (1974), 360, 369–370
  Bureau of the Budget, 348, 363, 364–
    366
  Colonial period, 349–353, 386–391
    British influence, 349–350
  Congressional Budget Office, creation
    of, 370
  Congressional Budget Reform Act
    (1974), 348
  Dawes contributions, 363
  Depression and, 402
  developmental nature of, 346, 348–
    349
  dysfunctions within system, 371–372
  executive budget process, origin of,
    362
  Executive Office of the President, cre-
    ation of, 366
  first decade activities, 361–362
  Full Employment Act (1946), 367,
    370, 401
  Gramm-Rudman-Hollings Act (1985),
    372
  line item budgeting, 366–367, 369
  Management by Objectives (MBO),
    368–369
  1981 budget, as turning point, 370
  performance budgeting, 368
  Presidential Management, 367
  program budgeting, 368
  programming, planning, budgeting,
    368
  quality of spending concept, 400
  Taft Commission (1912), 362, 368
  Victory Liberty Loan Act (1919), 400
  zero-based-budgeting, 369
Bureau of the Budget, 17, 348, 363, 364–
  366
  change to Executive Office of the Presi-
    dent, 366
  creation of, 363
  problems of, early years, 365–366
Bureaucracy
  alliances of, 162
  historical role, 162
  Jacksonian era and, 162
  myths about, 297

and pluralism, 162
representativeness of, 167
  executive leadership, 172–176
  neutrality, 169–172
spoils system, 162
Bureaucratic clientelism, 425
Bureaucratic Experience, The (Hummel), 6
Bureaucratic model, *See* Public sector or-
  ganization.
Bureaucratic state, 25–29
  versus administrative state, 5–6
  as scapegoat, 28
Bureau of Efficiency, 17, 22
Bureau of Labor Statistics, 23
Bureaus, 179–180
  importance of, 179
  salience of, 179–180
Burkhead, Jesse, 365
Burnham, James, 549, 557
Burr, Aaron, 356

Caine, M. R., 393
Calculative phase, intergovernmental
  management, 243–247
Caldwell, Lynton K., 12, 49, 481
Calhoun, John C., 12, 161
Call of the Wild (London), 549
Campbell, Alan, 203
Canal building, 406
Capitalism
  and public administration, 308–310
  reflexive relationship, 309
Carroll, Charles, 11
Carroll, James D., 221, 254
Case for Bureaucracy, The (Goodsell),
  582
Case study method, 51–53
  beginning of, 51
  significance of, 52
  university programs, 51–52
Castle, The (Kafka), as bureaucratic fiction,
  556–557
Catch-22 (Heller), as bureaucratic fiction,
  559–560
Cato Journal, 577
Cayer, N. Joseph, 321
Central Ohio Railroad, 406
Chandler, Ralph Clark, 575
Chase, Samuel, 144
Civil service, seven commandments of,
  322, 329–330
Civil Service Act (1883), 194

Civil service classification system, 201–202
  Classification Act (1949), 201
  supergrade positions, increasing, 201–202
Civil Service Commission, 16, 171
  Division of Efficiency (1912), 17
  first (1871), 14, 484
  first head, 8
Civil Service in Great Britain (Easton), 8
Civil Service in the Modern State, The (White), 491
Civil Service Reform Act (1978), 31, 93, 185, 204, 335, 340, 451
Civil War period
  budget, 399
  and internal improvements, 407–408
Clark, Jane Perry, 22
Classical democracy, 163–164
  pluralism and, 164, 165
Classical organization theories, 418, 420–423
  Gulick's contribution, 420–422
    bureaucratic structure, 421
    POSDCORB, 418, 421–422
    top-down power structure, 422
Classification Act (1923), 268
Classification Act (1949), 201
Classical management theory, second administrative state, 15
Clay, Henry, 404
Cleveland, Frederick A., 20
Cleveland, Grover, 15, 23, 29, 195, 327, 399, 408
Clientism, 173–174
  rise of, 173
Code of Ethics of the American Society for Public Administration, 589
Collective bargaining, 333
  effects of, 333
  personnel management, 333
Collectivism, American, 384, 385
Colonial period, budgeting, historical view, 349–353
Committee on Department Methods, Keep Committee, 22
Commission on Economy and Efficiency, 22
Commission on Intergovernmental Relations, 235
Committee on Governmental and Legal Processes of the Social Science Research Council, 64

Committee on Instruction in Government of the American Political Science Association, 41
Committee on Political Science as a Discipline of the American Political Science Association, 51
Committee on Practical Training for Public Service, 41, 43
Committee on Public Administration Cases, 51
Communitarianism, 170
Comparative Administration Group (CAG), 53–55, 496, 498, 502–503
Comparative Administrative Law (Goodnow), 21, 489
Comparative public administration, 53–55, 477–504
  characteristics of, 496–498
    diversity, 497
    optimism, 496–497
  Comparative Administration Group (CAG), 53–55
  compared to public administration, 54
  criticisms of, 502–503
  development administration approach, 498–499
  early American contributions, 481–484
  Ford Foundation support, 53–54, 55, 498
  Freund's contribution, 488, 490
  future of, 55
  general systems approach, 499–500
  Goodnow's contribution, 488–490
  issues addressed in, 53–54
  middle range/bureaucratic theory approach, 500–501
  movement in, 495–501
  1940's, major contributions of era, 493–495
  "parochialism of," 54
  professional organizations related to, 53–55, 496
  science of administration movement, 492
  suggestions for enlargement of, 503–504
  White's contribution, 490–491
  Willoughby's contribution, 491
  Wilson's contribution, 484–488
  See also Higher public service (Western Europe).
Comparative public policy, 65
Compensatory power, 427

Competency, deterioration of, basic factors, 587–588
Competitive phase, 237
Complete Anti-Federalist, The, (Storing), 124
Concentrated phase, intergovernmental relations (IGR), 235–236
Condign power, 427
Conditioned power, 427
Congress
  administrative authority, delegation of, 268–269
  as administrator, strengths/weaknesses of, 284–287
  appropriations rider, 283
  Congressional Budget and Impoundment Control Act (1974), 275–277, 282
  congressional delegation, era of, 267–270
  legislative veto
    alternatives to, 283–284
    end of, 282–283
    use of, 269
    Nixon's actions, 270–271, 273–274
  oversight of administration, expansion of, 277–280
  reprogramming, 269–270
  War Powers Resolution (1973), 272–273, 282
Congressional Budget and Impoundment Control Act (1974), 26, 275–277, 282, 360, 369–370
  preceding events, 274–275
  results of, 275–277
Congressional Budget Office, creation of, 370
Congressional Budget Reform Act (1974), 348
Congressional Government (Wilson), 225
Constitution
  and federalism, 233
  fragmentation of power, 177–179
  historical overview, 120–121, 123, 124–125
  House of Representatives, 143–147
  legitimacy of administration state, 117, 119–121, 123
  and public administration, 310–312
    ambiguity of, 310–311
  public interest in, 120
  Senate, 126, 135–137
  separation of powers, 126–133
  on spending power, 353
Constitutional Government in the United States (Wilson), 227, 230
Contribution satisfaction equilibrium concept, 424
Cooley, Thomas M., 19
Coolidge, Calvin, 21, 401
Cooperative phase, intergovernmental relations (IGR), 235
Corporation Control Act (1945), 26
Corruption, attack on, Progressive era, 23–24
Council-manager, municipal government, 171–172, 173
Crane, Stephen, 549
Creative Experiences (Parker), 43
Creative federalism, 236
Creative phase, intergovernmental relations (IGR), 236–237
Crichton, Michael, 566–568
Cross-cultural public administration, *See* Comparative public administration.
Crosscutting requirements, assistance programs, 245–246
Currency, development of system, 386–388
Curtis, George William, 14, 484
Cyclopedia of Political Science (Lalor), 3, 9
Cyert, Richard, 56

Dahl, Robert A., 46, 53, 495
Dana, Richard Henry, 19
Darwin, Charles, 548
Data management, technological advances (1870's–1940's), 22–234
Dawes, Charles, 17, 196, 363, 372
Defense of the Constitutions of Government of the United States of America (Adams), 129
Delegation, Congressional era of, 267–270
Democracy, pluralism and, 164, 165
Democracy in America (de Tocqueville), 383, 481
Democracy in the Public Service (Mosher), 330
Department of the Treasury, beginning of, 356–357, 359
Depression
  budget, 401
  and internal improvements, 408

de Tocqueville, 161, 170, 180, 383, 481, 482–483
Development administration approach, problems of, 498–499
Dewey, Melvil, 23
Direct-line democracy, 437
Dissention in field, 45–48
  alternative to traditional school, 48–50
  beginning of, 45–46
  behavioral tone of, 47
  works related to, 45–47
Division of Efficiency (1912), Civil Service Commission, 17
Doig, Jameson, 230
Drucker, Peter, 25, 27
Dual federalism, 229, 234
Dulles, John Foster, 202
Durham, G. Homer, 250

Easton, David, 49
Eaton, Dorman B., 3, 8, 14, 18, 25
Ecole Nationale d'Administration (ENA), 518–520, 522, 523
Ecole Polytechnique, 518, 522, 523
Economization of world, and politics/administration dichotomy, 102–103
Economy Act (1932), 269
Edelman, Murray, 300
Education for Public Service Clearinghouse Project, 51
Efficiency
  maximization goals, 185
  private sector versus public sector, 580–586
  as public term, 579–580
Egger, Rowland, 295–296
Eisenhower, Dwight D., 28, 201–203
Elements of Public Administration (Morstein Marx), 45, 494
Elitism, pluralism and, 166
Ely, Richard T., 3, 9
Emerson, Harrington, 15
Employment Act (1946), 271
Equal Employment Opportunity Act (1972), 332
Erie Canal, 11, 406
Ervin, Sam J., Jr., 270
"Estimate of the situation" format, 20
European civil service, *See* Higher public service (Western Europe).
Exceptionalism, American, 384
Executive budget process, origin of, 362

Executive Office of the President, creation of, 366
Executive prerogative, 264–267
  chief executive as general manager, 266
Executive privilege, limits issue, 280
Exorcist, The (Blatty), as bureaucratic fiction, 565–566

Fairchild, Charles S., 196
Fayol, Henri, 15, 43, 570
Federal grant law, 253
Federalism
  creative federalism, 236
  dual federalism, 229, 234
  as fragmentation of power, 178
  fused federalism, 237
  as political slogan, 233–234
  uses of term, 233–234
  Wilson's view, 226–233, 249
    administration, 228–229
    historical change, 229–230, 232
    large powers for public officials, 230–231
    legalism of, 227
    local government, 228
    state-national relations, 227
    systems within systems, 231–232
Federalist, The (Jay, Hamilton and Madison), 16, 20, 27, 39, 48, 51, 58, 62, 63, 66, 71, 77, 116, 117, 120, 124, 139, 140, 145, 146, 180, 233, 354, 482
  Federalist 27, 116, 117
  Federalist 48, 129
  Federalist 51, 130
  Federalist 58, 146
  Federalist 62, 137
  Federalist 63, 140
  Federalist 66, 128
  Federalist 71, 126
  Federalist 77, 139
Federalists
  compared to Anti-Federalists, 124–125
  first administrative State, contributions of, 11–12
  and rational decision making, 10
  and second administrative state, tradition continued, 15
Federal Register, second administrative state, 22
Federal Reserve Board, 18
Federal Trade Commission, 18
Feldman, Elliot J., 66

Fesler, James W., 509
Fiction and public administration, 543–571
  Andromeda Strain (Crichton), 566–568
  A Bell for Adano (Hersey), 562–565, 568
  The Castle (Kafka), 556–557
  Catch-22 (Heller), 559–560
  The Exorcist (Blatty), 565–566
  Germinal (Zola), 548–549, 568
  The Godfather (Puzo), 569–570
  Huckleberry Finn (Twain), 545–547
  The Jungle (Sinclair), 550–552
  "The Metamorphosis" (Kafka), 555–556
  naturalistic fiction, 548–550
  1984 (Orwell), 557–559
  novels as "third dimension" of public administration, 568–571
  One Flew Over the Cuckoo's Nest (Kesey), 560–562, 568
  social protest fiction, 550–554
  To Kill a Mockingbird (Lee), 552–554
Fillmore, Millard, 404
Finer, Herman, 226
First administrative state
  historical view, 6–7, 9–12
  turning point in, 222
First Civil Service Commission (1871), 14, 484
First United States Bank, 11
Fiscal policy (historical view)
  Colonial period, 386–391
    colonial expenditures, 388–389
    currency, forms of, 386–388
    during Revolutionary War, 391–393
    power issues, 389–390
    simplicity of, 389
    taxation, types of, 388–389
  Revolutionary period
    Articles of Confederation, 352, 393
    inadequacy of, 391–393
  See also Budgeting (historical view).
Fisher, Louis, 283, 361
Flemming, Arthur S., 19
Focus, of public administration, 39
Follett, Mary Parker, 15, 43, 427, 428
Ford Foundation, and comparative administration, 53–54, 55, 498
Foreign aid program, Eisenhower era, 203
Formula grant, 245
France, civil service
  career patterns, 522–523
  political civil servants, 527–528, 529, 530
  recruitment, 517–520
Frankfurter, Felix, 20
Franklin, Benjamin, 387–388, 392–393
Fredrich, Carl, 226
Freeman, J. Leiper, 200
Freud, Sigmund, 548
Freund, Ernst, 488, 490
Friedman, Milton, 26
Friedrich, Carl, 300
Fulbright, J. William, 272
Full Employment Act (1946), 367, 370, 401
Fulton Committee (1968), 516
Functions of the Executive, The (Barnard), 45, 331
Fused federalism, 237

Galbraith, John Kenneth, 427, 428
Gallatin, Albert, 12
Gant, George, 498
Gaus, John Merriman, 50, 493
Gawthrop, Louis C., 189, 586–590
General Accounting Office (GAO), 17, 279
General Services Administration, 16
General systems approach
  prismatic-sala model, 499–500
  Riggs' contribution, 499–500
Generic weaknesses, in bureaucratic model, 448–449
Germany, civil service
  career patterns, 523–525
  political civil servants, 528, 529–530, 531
  recruitment, 520–521
Germinal (Zola), as bureaucratic fiction, 548–549, 568
Gestetner, David, 23
Giaimo, Robert N., 276
Gilbreth, Frank, 43
Gilbreth, Lillian, 43
Glass, Carter, 400
Godfather, The (Puzo), as bureaucratic fiction, 569–570
Godkin, E.L., 19
Golembiewski, Robert T., 39, 44, 48, 55, 66, 433–435
Goodnow, Frank, 20, 21, 40, 41, 488–490
Goodsell, Charles T., 291–292, 503, 582
Gorham, Nathaniel, 145–146

Governmental units, intergovernmental relations, 238
Government corporations, 18
Government Operations Committee, 278
Gramm, Phil, 276
Gramm-Rudman-Hollings Act (1985), 276–277, 372
Grant, Ulysses S., 14, 399, 484
Grant-in-aid programs
  intergovernmental relations, 235
  second administrative state, 22
Grants
  federal grant law, 253
  project grants, 236
Grayson, William, 135
·Great Britain, civil service
  career patterns, 521–525
  political civil servants, 526, 527, 528–529
  recruitment, 516–517
Great Society, 236
Greeks
  influences on politics, 96–97, 98, 101, 204
  public order, view of, 121
Grodzin, Morton, 22
Gulf of Tonkin resolution, 272
Gulick, Luther, 15, 20, 44–45, 265, 420–421, 492

Hamilton, Alexander, 4, 10, 12, 395–396
  background information, 354
  budget system, contributions to, 354–358, 395–396
Hansen, Susan B., 65
Harding, Warren, 24
Hartz, Louis, 383, 404
Hatch Act of 1939, 18, 327, 583
Hawthorn studies, influence of, 331, 423, 492
Hayes, Rutherford, B., 8, 399
Heady, Ferrel, 53, 477–479
Heller, Joseph, 559–560
Henderson, Keith M., 56
Hersey, John, 562–565
Higher public service (Western Europe), 509–533
  career patterns, 521–525
    Britain, 521–522
    France, 522–523
    German Federal Republic, 523–525
  governmental systems, comparison, 511–513

policy/administration, 531–532
political civil servants, 526–531
  Britain, 526, 527, 528–529
  France, 527–528, 529, 530
  German Federal Republic, 528, 529–530, 531
  "outsiders" near top, 527–528
political echelon, 513–514
recruitment, 514–521
  Britain, 516–517
  common characteristics, 515
  France, 517–520
  German Federal Republic, 520–521
History of the United States Civil Service (Van Riper), 484
Hobbes, Thomas, 420
Hollerith, Herman, 22
Hollings, Ernest F., 276
Holmes, Oliver Wendell, 19
Hoover, Herbert, 269
Hoover Commission (1949), 26, 175, 368, 422
House, Colonel, 20
House of Representatives
  historical view, 143–148
    Anti-Federalists and, 143–145, 146–148
    and Constitution, 143–147
    Madison and, 145, 146–147, 148
    major concerns about, 144–148
    size issue, 145–146
Huckleberry Finn (Twain), as bureaucratic fiction, 545–547
Human resources management, 321–342
  Jacksonian era, 325–326
  pre-Wilsonian developments, 324–326
  reform era, 326–334
Hummel, Ralph P., 6
Hunter, Robert M. T., 13
Huntington, Samuel, 99
Huston, David F., 400

Immigration and Naturalization Service v. Chadha, 282
Impeachment, historical view, 127
Impoundment, 274–275
  Budget and Impoundment Control Act (1974), 26, 275–277, 282, 360, 369–370
Income tax, beginning of, 22
Individualist, and marketplace ideology, 180

Industrial and General Management (Fayol), 43

Industrialism, types of, 30

Inquiry Scholars, 20

Institute of Public Administration, 20

Intellectual activity, second administrative state, 15, 19–20

Intercollegiate Case Clearinghouse, 52

Interest groups, 311
  in American politics, 164, 166, 178–179
  "big seven" public interest groups, 237, 238
  interest group liberalism, 296, 425

Intergovernmental management (IGM), 242–248
  calculative phase, 243–247
    fungible aspect, 247
    gamesmanship in, 246–247
    overload dimension, 247
  as coping approach, 248
  distinctive nature of, 252
  litigation emerging from, 253–254
  networking, 248
  as new era, 247–248
  origin of, 243
  political danger and, 252
  problem-solving focus, 247–248
  publications related to, 243
  regulation, escalation of, 253

Intergovernmental relations (IGR), 234–242
  difficulties in, 241–242
  features of, 238–241, 251
    all governmental units, 238
    decision-making and public officials, 240
    human dimension, 239
    interactions among officials, 239–240
    policy component, 241
  grant-in-aid programs, 235
  origins of term, 234–235
  phases of, 235–238
    competitive phase, 237
    concentrated phase, 235–236
    cooperative phase, 235
    creative phase, 236–237
  politics/administration dichotomy, 250–251
  project grant funds, 236

Internal improvements
  compared to European countries, 405
  historical view, 402–409
    canal building, 406
    Depression era, 408
    Jacksonian era, 403–404
    post-Revolutionary period, 402–403
    pre-Civil War period, 404–407

International Association of Schools and Institutes of Administration (IASIA), 496

International Personnel Management Association, 331

Interstate Commerce Commission Act (1887), effect on administration, 222, 228

Interstate Commerce Commission (ICC), 18, 19
  creation of, 171, 172

Inter-University Case Program, 51

Introduction to the Study of Public Administration (White), 41, 42

Iron-triangle, 162, 200, 423

Jackson, Andrew, 167, 360, 397–398, 403

Jacksonian era, 295
  budgeting, historical view, 360, 397–398
  bureaucracy in, 162
  and first administrative state, 13–14
  and internal improvements, 403–404
  personnel management, 325–326
  spoils system, 325–326
  pluralism, 167–169

Jacob, Herbert, 520

Javits, Jacob K., 272–273

Jay, John, 354

Jefferson, Thomas, 10, 324, 355, 359, 396–397, 402–403

Jenckes, Thomas A., 13, 484

Johnson, Andrew, 399

Johnson, Lyndon B., 26, 31, 233, 236, 270, 272

Jones, Garth N., 497

Journal of Comparative Administration, 55, 496, 502

Jun, Jong S., 503–504

Jungle, The (Sinclair), as bureaucratic fiction, 550–552

Kafka, Franz, 555–557

Kaufman, Herbert, 184, 419

Keep Committee, 22

Kennedy, John F., 26

Kesey, Ken, 560–561

Kimmel, Louis, 405, 407

King, Rufus, 128

Kraines, Oscar, 490
Kramer, Fred A., 417
Kroll, Mort, 568–569

La Follette, 20
Lalor, J.J. 3, 9
Landau, Martin, 50
Larvi, Theodore F., 181
Le Carre, John, 207, 589–590
Lee, Harper, 553
Lee, Richard Henry, 136
Legislative veto
  alternatives to, 283–284
  end of, 282–283
  use of, 269
Lepawsky, Albert, 494
Levitan, David M., 205, 591
Levitas, Elliott H., 278
Liberalism
  and politics/administration dichotomy,
    103–104
  types of, 577
Lienesch, Michael, 249
Lincoln, Abraham, 30, 399
Line-item budgeting, 366–367, 369
Line and staff management, 16
Lloyd-La Follette Act (1912), 19
Local government, and federalism, Wil-
    son's view, 228
Locke, John, 180, 420
Locus, of public administration, 39, 40
London, Jack, 549
Long, Norman, 177, 197, 424
Lord, Director, 401
Louisiana Purchase, 359, 397
Lowi, Theodore, 334

McCaffery, Jerry L., 345–347
McCarthy, Joseph R., 198
McCarthyism, impact on civil servants,
    198–199
McCurdy, Howard E., 543–544
McLean, John, 12
McNamara, Robert, 368
Madison, James, 125, 126, 128, 134, 140,
    145–148, 161, 355, 397
Magna Carta, 348–350
Majority rule, 161
  doctrine of the concurrent majority, 165
  pluralism and, 165–166
Management
  and public administration, 55–61, 68–
    72

business education, influence of, 71–72
  methodological impact, 70
  positive impact of, 68–69
  public versus private administration,
    58–60, 69
  quantitative methods and, 70
Management analysis, second administra-
    tive state, 17
Management by Objectives (MBO), 185,
    368–369
Managerial Revolution, The (Burnham),
    549, 557
March, James G., 56
Marini, Frank, 71
Market place ideology, bazaar concept,
    180–181
Marshall, John, 308
Martin, Luther, 136, 138
Martin, Roscoe, 49
Marx, Karl, 548
Maslow, Abraham, 426
Mason, George, 136, 138, 145, 311
Master of Public Administration, 55, 57,
    67, 75–76
Matrix organization, mature matrix, 464–
    468
Mature matrix, in bureaucratic model,
    464–468
Maxwell School, 20
Mayntz, Renate, 521
Mayo, Elton, 423
Meigs, Montgomery C., 13
Merit system, early, 10, 18
Merriam, Charles, 20
"Metamorphosis, The" (Kafka), 555–556
Meyers, Marvin, 118
Middle range (bureaucratic theory) ap-
    proach, 500–501
  bureaucracy in, 501
  shortcomings of, 501
Miles, Rufus F., Jr., 27
Military-industrial complex, 162
Miller, James C., III, 577–578
Milwar, Brinton, 429
Minnowbrook Conference (1968), 38
Minority rule, pluralism, 166, 169–170
Mobilization of bias, 175–176
Monroe, James, 136, 397, 403
Mooney, James D., 43
Morality movement, in government/public
    administration, 170–171
Morrill Act (1862), 407

Morris, Gouverneur, 134, 138
Morris, Robert, 352–352, 392–393
Morrow, William L., 161
Morse, Muriel, 328–329
Morstein Marx, Fritz, 5, 45, 494
Mosher, Frederick, 28, 50, 236, 330
Muskie, Edmund, 237

National Association of Schools of Public
    Affairs and Administration
    (NASPAA), 71–75
  curriculum requirements and, 72–73
  origins of, 72
  political science departments and, 75
National Bank, establishment of, 11, 355
National Bureau of Standards, 23
National Civil Service Reform League, 8
National Federation of Federal Employ-
    ees, 21
National Resources Planning Board, 17
Naturalistic fiction, as bureaucratic fiction,
    548–550
Nelson, William E., 169
Neoclassical organization theories
  agency/legislative subcommittee/clientele
    relationship, 425–426
  Barnard's contribution, 423–424
  contribution satisfaction equilibrium
    concept, 424
  Hawthorn studies and, 423
  power sources, 424–426
  roots of, 423
  zone of acceptance/indifference in, 424
Networking, intergovernmental manage-
    ment (IGM), 248
Neutrality movement, 169–172
  administrative reforms, 175
  chief executives and, 172
  clientism, 173–174
  major effect of, 172
  morality in government movement,
    170–171
  reform/regulation, 171–172
  Taft Commission, 174
"New Federalism," Reagan, 232, 233
"New Freedom," Wilson, 231
Newland, Chester, 251
New public administration, 38, 62
New York Bureau of Municiple Research,
    20
Niebuhr, H. Richard, 213–214, 592
1984 (Orwell), 557–559

Nixon, Richard, 26, 31, 273, 280
  and Congress, 270–271, 273–274
Noncompliance, cost of, 246
Northcote-Trevelyan Report (1855), 516
"Notes on the Theory of Organization,"
    (Gulick), 265, 418, 420
Novels
  as "third dimension" of public adminis-
    tration, 568–571
  See also Fiction and public administra-
    tion.

Office of Management and Budget, 17,
    192
Official Secrets Act (1911), 529
O'Lessker, Karl, 207, 208
One Flew Over the Cuckoo's Nest (Kesey), as
    bureaucratic fiction, 560–562, 568
Operating management, 335
Order in Council (1870), 516
Organizational-humanist theories, 418–
    419, 426–429
  Bennis' contribution, 426–427
  conflict, treatment of, 427–428
  decision-making, 428
  policy networks in, 429
  shared-power concept, 426, 427
  tripartite taxonomy of power, 427
Organizations in Action (Thompson), 56
Organizations (Simon), 56
Organization theories, 416–430
  choice of, for decision-makers, 429–430
  classical organization theories, 418,
    420–423
  "environmental pace" in, 440
  neoclassical organization theories, 418,
    423–426
  organizational-humanist theories, 418–
    419, 426–429
  See also specific theories.
Orwell, George, 545, 557–559
Ostrom, Vincent, 116
Oversight, Congressional, expansion of,
    277–280

Panama Canal, 23
Panama Railroad Company, 18
Papers on the Science of Administration
    (Gulick and Urwick), 15, 44–45, 492
Peck, M. Scott, 590
Pendleton Act (1883), 8, 14, 16, 19, 171,
    264, 326, 484
  revision of, 21

Performance budgeting, 368
Personnel management
 civil service, seven commandments, 322,
  329–330
 collective bargaining, 333
 decentralization, 19
 historical view
  Civil Service Reform Act (1978), 335,
   340
  collective bargaining, 333
  equal employment opportunity, 332
  Hawthorn studies, 331
  humanistic concerns, 331
  Jacksonian era, 325–326
  politics/administration dichotomy,
   330–331, 334
  pre-Wilson developments, 324–326
  reform era, 326–334
  scientific management, 328, 330
 political nature of, 335–339
  participants and, 338–339
  selection process, 335–336
  values, 336–338
 reform era, activities of, 326–334
 second administrative state, 19
Personnel Management Project, 340
Pfiffner, John, 9
Phillips, Wendell, 170
Pinchot, Gifford, 20
Pitt, William, the Younger, 350, 353
Planning-programming-budgeting (PB),
 185, 368
Planning/programming/budgeting systems
 (PPBS), 434, 435
Pluralism, 161–187
 administration and, 176–182
  bureau, dominance of, 179–180
  confederal political parties and, 181–
   182
  constitutional fragmentation of power
   and, 177–179
  federalism and, 178
  forces of American society and, 176–
   177
  marketplace ideology and, 180–181
 administrators and, 162–163
  political style needed, 163
 American politics and, 164–167
  balanced rule by minorities in, 166
  efforts on political system, 165
  elitism, 166
  interest groups in, 164, 166, 311
  majority rule and, 165–166

 bureaucracy's role and, 162, 167–176
  executive leadership, 172–176
  neutrality movement, 169–172
  representativeness, 167
 classical democracy and, 164, 165
 consequences of, 185–186
 expression of self-interest and, 162
 ideal form of, 166
 Jacksonian era, 167–169
 public management and, 183–185
  policy management, 183–184
  politics of, 184–185
  productive management, 183
 public policy as casualty, 163
Policy, intergovernmental relations, 241
Policy management, 183–184
Policy networks, organizational humanism, 429
Policy Studies Journal, 64
Policy Studies Organization, 64, 65
Policy Studies Review, 64
Political civil servants
 Britain, 526, 527, 528–529
 France, 527–528, 529, 530
 Germany, 528, 529–530, 531
"Political Ends and Administrative Means"
 (Levitan), 205, 591
Political experience, use of term, 249–250
Political parties, confederal nature, 181–
 182
Political Process, The (Freeman), 200
Political science
 public administration and, 41, 49, 50–
  55, 62–68
  case study method, 51–53
  comparative public administration,
   53–55
  decline in interest, 51
  public policy, 63–67
  separation of fields, 67–68, 75
 scientific status, 94
Political System, The (Easton), 49
Politics
 Greek nature of, 96–97, 98
 political context of public administration, 300, 304
Politics/administration dichotomy, 40–42,
 89–108, 306–308, 330–331, 334
 challenges to, 46, 47
 complexity of, 106–107
 criticism, rejection of, 93
 decision versus execution in, 92, 106

government bureaucracy and, 40–41
historical view, 96–102
   American governmental system, 99–
      100, 103–105
   civic-culture-imperial-tradition thesis,
      98–102
   econimization of world and, 102–
      103
   English tradition in, 98–99
   Greek influences, 96–97, 98, 101
   intergovernmental relations (IGR),
      250–251
   liberalism and, 103–104
   Roman influences, 97–98, 102
   levels of understanding, 307
   locus-centered concept, 41, 42
   politics versus public administration,
      41–42
   value/fact dichotomy, 42
Politics and Administration (Goodnow), 40
Polk, James K., 398, 404
POSDCORB, 45, 48, 418, 421–422
   criticism of, 422
Power sources
   classical organization theories, 422
   newclassical organization theories, 424–
      426
   organizational-humanist theories, 426–
      427
Presidency, American, historical view, 9–
   10
President, as general manager, 266
Presidents Committee on Administrative
   Management, 15, 20, 266, 435
President's Committee on Administrative
   Science, 44
Presthus, Robert V., 500
Princeton report, 43–44
Principles of administration, *See* Adminis-
   trative principles.
Principles of Organization (Mooney and Rei-
   ley), 43
Principles of Political Economy (Vethake),
   405
Principles of Public Administration (Wil-
   loughby), 42
Principles of Scientific Management (Taylor),
   43
Prismatic-sala model, general systems ap-
   proach, 499–500
Private sector versus public sector
   basic assumptions, 580–586
   management and, 58–60, 69

Problem-solving focus, intergovernmental
   management (IGM), 247–248
Procedural analysis, second administrative
   state, 22
Productive management, 183
Professional Standards and Ethics Com-
   mittee, 589
Program budgeting, 368
Progressive movement, 224
Project grants, 236
Project management, in bureaucratic
   model, 458–459
Proposition 13, 276
"Proverbs of Administration, The" (Si-
   mon), 46
Public administration
   as academic field, 2, 39–78
      administrative principles, 42–45
      beginning of, 41
      behavioral revolution and, 47, 49, 52,
         62
      case study method, 51–53
      comparative public administration,
         53–55
      dissention in field, 45–48
      focus in, 39
      future of, 77
      locus in, 39
      management, relationship to, 55–61,
         68–72
      new public administration, 38, 62
      political science, relationship to, 41,
         49, 50–55, 62–68
      politics/administration dichotomy, 40–
         42
      public administration programs, 72–
         77
      "pure science" approach, 48
      "science and society" curricula, 61, 62
      textbooks in field, 41, 42
      Wilson's contribution, 39–40
   as academic study, major developments,
      95
   agency perspective, 300–304
   capitalism and, 308–310
   Constitution and, 310–312
   distinctiveness of, 299–308
   enduring quality of, 192–193
   executive prerogative, theory of, 264–
      267
   founders of, 3–4

(continued)

(continued)
  historical view, 192–196
    Budget Director, first appointment,
      196
    Civil Service Act (1883), 194
    civil service classification system, 201–
      202
    first administrative state, 193–194
    McCarthyism and, 198
    Senior Executive Service (SES), 202,
      203
    television, impact of, 199–200
    Wilson's impact, 195–196
  political context of, 300, 304
  politics/administration dichotomy, 306–
    308
  public interest and, 302, 304–306, 311
  Smiley character and, 207–209
Public administration education, 15, 19–
  20
  programs in
    curriculum requirements and, 72–73
    faculty, qualifications and, 73, 77
    NASPAA, 72–75
    organizational patterns, 73–75
    quantitative approach, 70, 76
    student profiles, 75–76
Public Administration Review, 44
Public administrators, 312–316
  commitment, areas of, 316
  professionalism and, 312–313
  role definition, 212–213
  role of, 313–316
  terms related to, 314
  as trustee of public good, 314
Public Choice Society, 64
Public employee groups, 338–339
Public employment, second administrative
  state, 18–19
Public interest
  definitional issues, 304–305
  and public administration, 302, 304–
    306, 311
Public interest groups, "big seven," 237,
  238
Public management
  pluralism and, 183–185
    policy management, 183–184
    politics of, 184–185
    productive management, 183
Public officials, intergovernmental relations, 239–240

Public opinion, Wilson's view, 229–230
Public Personnel Association, 331
Public policy, 63–67
  comparative public policy, 65
  generic management schools, 57–58
  organization development, 56
  popularity of field, 64
  programs, offered, variations of, 57–58
  recognition of value, 64
  scope of discipline, 56–57
  substantive branch, 65, 66
  theoretical branch, 65
Public Policy and Management Programs
  for Case/Curriculum Development, 52
Public sector organization, 433
  basic outcomes, 441–442
    liberation as, 442
  bureaucratic model
    faults of, 436–437
    hierarchy versus specialization, 444–
      445
    rationality and, 445, 446
  collateral/parallel structures, 457–458
  diversification and, 439
  "environmental pace" and, 440
  field units, developing, 439
  future assumptions, 452–453
  organizing
    levels of, 439
    purpose in, 453–454
  phases of development, 438–439
  public personnel systems, reform, 435
  structural innovation
    flow of work as, 459, 464
    mature matrix as, 464–468
    project management, 458–459
  traditional approach, 466–452
    generic weaknesses, 448–449
    site-specific weaknesses, 449–452
    value overlays, 454–457
  unity of command and, 437, 444
Public sector versus private sector
  basic assumptions, 580–586
  management and, 58–60, 69
Public service movement, 41
Puzo, Mario, 569

Quantitative approach
  forecasting and, 244
  and public administration, 70, 76

Ramspect Act (1940), 19
Randolph, John, 403

Ranney, Austin, 63
Rational decision making
    Federalists, 10
    second administrative state, 20, 20–21
Reagan, Ronald, 232, 233, 273, 578
    retrenchment, 29–32
Red Badge of Courage, The (Crane), 549
Reductions-in-force (RIF), 201
Reform, alteration of management styles,
    185
Reform era, events of, 326–334
Regulatory agencies, 211, 228
    rise of, 171–172
    second administrative state, 17–18
Reiley, Alan C., 43
Reorganization Act of 1939, 15
Reprogramming, 269–270
Repudiation, states' default on debts, 406
Retrenchment (1980's), 29–32
Revolutionary War
    costs of, 352
    fiscal policy during, 391–393
Ridley, F. F., 519
Riggs, Fred W., 54, 481, 488, 497, 499,
    503–504
Rise of a New Federalism (Clark), 22
Rivers and Harbors Act, 408
Robber barons, 408
Roethlisberger, Fritz, 423
Rohr, John A., 113–115, 292
Roman Catholic Church, and govern-
    ment, 97, 102
Romans
    concept of authority, 121–123
    founding of cities, 122
    influence on administration, 97–98,
        102, 204
Roosevelt, Franklin D., 44, 366
Roosevelt, Theodore, 4, 14–15, 16, 19, 30
    contributions of, 20–22, 23, 24–25
Root, Elihu, 16, 20
Rose, Richard, 529
Rudman, Warren B., 276

Sanford, Terry, 237
Savage, Peter, 503
Say, Jean-Baptiste, 405
Sayre, Wallace, S., 179, 300
Scharpf, Fritz, 521
Schecter, Stephen, 252
Schick, Allen, 46, 364
Schon, Donald A., 455
Schultz, William, 393

Schurz, Carl, 19
Science of administration movement, 492
"Science of Public Administration: Three
    Problems, The" (Dahl), 46, 495
"Science and society" curricula, 61, 62
Scientific management, 173, 209, 492
    personnel reform movement, 328, 330
Scott, William G., 420
Second administrative state
    historical view, 14–25
    See also Administrative state, second ad-
        ministrative state.
Secretary of Treasury, beginnings of, 354,
    357, 358, 359
Section on International and Comparative
    Administration (SICA), 496
Sedition Act, 10
Seidman, Harold, 185
Selection process, political nature of, 335–
    336
Self-interest, pluralism and, 162
Senate
    Anti-Federalists and, 135–137, 138–139,
        141, 142
    basic characteristics of, 141–142
    historical view, 125, 133–142
        as continuing body, 138
        and "due sense of national character,"
            140–141
        executive character of, 134–137
        role in appointments, 138–140
        term of office, 137–138
    modern Senate, 142
    role of senators, 141
Senior Executive Service (SES), 142, 340,
    451
Separation of powers, 263
    historical view, 127
        Adams and, 129–131
        Anti-Federalists, 131–132
        bicameralism, 132–133
        Hamilton and, 128–129
        Madison and, 126, 128
    and problems for public policymakers,
        585
Sherman, Roger, 134
Siffin, William J., 497
Sigelman, Lee, 501, 502
Simon, Herbert A., 38, 45, 46, 47, 48, 56,
    65, 306, 422, 424, 493
Sinclair, Upton, 550–552
Site-specific weaknesses, in bureaucratic
    model, 449–452

Slater, Philip, 426
Smiley, George, 589–590
  character of civil servant, 207–209
Smith, Adam, 405
Smith, Melanchthon, 137, 147
Social protest fiction, as bureaucratic fiction, 550–554
Social revolutions, in U.S. history, 295–296
Social Security Act (1935), 367
Society for the Promotion of Training for the Public Service, 41
Specialization, rise of, 328
Spoils system, 13, 162–168, 175, 325–326, 437
Staff concept
  General Staff Act (1903), 16
  second administrative state, 15–16
Stanfield, Rochelle, 232
State-national relations, and federalism, Wilson's view, 227
Steinbeck, John, 568
Stimson, Henry L., 20
Stivers, Camilla, 292
Stockberger, W.W., 16
Stone, Donald C., 44
Storey, Moorfield, 19
Storing, Herbert J., 124–125
"Study of Administration, The" (Wilson), 5, 39, 195, 323, 327
  analysis of, 223–233
  and comparative administration, 485–488
  federalism, 226–233
  prophetic quality of, 294–295
Substantive branch, public policy, 65, 66
Sub-systems, 162, 200
Sumner, William Graham, 392
Sundquist, James L., 261
Supergrade positions, increasing, 201–202
Superintendent of Finance position, 352–353

Taft Commission on Economy and Efficiency in Government (1912–13), 362, 368
  performance budgeting, 368
  purposes of, 174
  second administrative state, 17, 20
Taft-Hartley Act (1947), 21
Taxes, types of, Colonial era, 388–389
Taylor, Frederick W., 15, 43, 492
Taylor, John, 403

Teapot Dome, 24
Technological advances
  first administrative state, 11
  second administrative state, 22–23
Television, impact on politics, 199–200
Tenure of Office Act (1867), 326
Textbooks, first, public administration, 41, 42, 490–491
Theoretical branch, public policy, 65
Thompson, Frank, 335
Thompson, James D., 56
Time-and-motion studies, 15, 492
To Kill a Mockingbird (Lee), as bureaucratic fiction, 552–54
Toward a New Public Administration: The Minnowbrook Prespective (Waldo), 62
Toward a New Public Administration (Marini), 71
Training School for Public Service, 20
"Trauma of Politics, The" (Schick), 46
Treasury Board, 353
Treasury Department, establishment of, 11
Treatise on Political Economy (Say), 405
Truman, Harry S., 32
Trumball, Lyman, 14
Turner, Frederick Jackson, 180
Twain, Mark, 545–547
Tyler, John, 398

Ullman, Al, 274
United States Court of Claims, 21
United States Veterans Bureau, 16
Unity of command, in bureaucratic model, 437, 444
Urwick, Lyndall, 15, 44–45, 492

Value overlays, in bureaucratic model, 454–457
Values
  personnel management, 336–338
  uniformity of, 337
Van Buren, Martin, 14, 398, 399
Vanderbilt, Arthur T., 489
Van Hise, 20
Van Riper, Paul P., 3, 225, 484
Vasconcellos, John, 442
Veterans Administration, 16
Vethake, Henry, 405
Victory Liberty Loan Act (1919), 400
Voluntarism, American, 384

Waldo, Dwight, 5, 8, 15, 32, 204, 298,
      308, 493–494, 500, 579
Walker, Harvey, 9
Walker, Robert J., 398
Walso, Dwight, 39, 47, 51, 53, 62
Wamsley, Gary, 429
War Powers Resolution (1973), 272–273,
      282
   preceding events, 272
Washington, George, 10, 146, 324, 354,
      392
Watt, James G., 283, 284
Ways and Means Committee
   origin of, 359–360
   post-revolution, 356, 358
Weber, Max, 5, 7, 209, 301, 420, 501, 555
Weeks Act (1911), 22
White, Andrew D., 19
White, Byron R., 282
White, Leonard D., 9, 11, 12, 40, 41, 42,
      53, 223, 228, 266, 482, 483, 490–491
White, Orion F., 292
White, William Allen, 20
White Fang (London), 549

Wildavsky, Aaron, 379–381
Willoughby, W. F., 9, 20, 42, 265, 491,
      492
Wilson, James, 9
Wilson, Woodrow, 15, 19, 30, 39–40, 114,
      115, 118, 170, 193, 195, 209, 223–
      233, 323, 327, 362, 400, 436, 438
   analysis of essay, 223–233
   as founder, 3–4, 5, 8–9
   See also "Study of Administration, The"
      (Wilson).
Wirt, William, 12
Wisconsin Plan, 20
Wolcott, Oliver, 11
Wolf, James F., 292–293
Wolin, Sheldon, 229, 253
Woodbury, Levi, 398
Wright, Carroll B., 23
Wright, Deil S., 219–220

Zeldin, Theodore, 512, 517
Zero-Base Budgeting (ZBB), 185, 369
Zola, Emile, 545, 548–549
Zone of acceptance, 424